THE IMPUDENT SNOBS

Agnew vs. the Intellectual Establishment

THE IMPUDENT SNOBS

Agnew vs. the
Intellectual
Establishment

by

JOHN R. COYNE, JR

Arlington House   New Rochelle, N.Y.

Library of Congress Catalog Card Number 72–183676

ISBN 0–87000–154–x

MANUFACTURED IN THE UNITED STATES OF AMERICA

THE IMPUDENT SNOBS

Agnew vs. the
Intellectual
Establishment

1

THE BEST TV show of 1969 didn't win an Emmy. It originated in Des Moines, Iowa, on November 13. The subject: the liberal bias of the national media. The star: Vice President Spiro T. Agnew. And the country has never been the same since.

Reaction among the media men was almost uniformly hysterical. Dr. Frank Stanton of CBS accused Agnew of practicing censorship through intimidation. Walter Cronkite heard "an implied threat to freedom of speech in this country." Julian Goodman of NBC claimed that Agnew advocated a national media "subservient to whatever political group was in authority at the time." Frank Mankiewicz and Tom Braden heard Nazilike echoes, implying that somewhere in Agnew's statements ran the ". . . theme that America's press and television is controlled and dominated by a small group of Jews in New York and Washington [although, of course, there was no reference in the speech, implicit or explicit, intended or unintended, to Jews]. . . ." In New York, John Lindsay's commissar of culture, Thomas Hoving, said: "Agnew's disgraceful attack against network television officially leads us as a nation into an ugly era of the most fearsome suppression and intimidation — the beginning of the end for us as a nation. His terrible and fraudulent evaluation is the most shocking use ever of political power." And in Peking, the reaction was succinctly summed up: Spiro Agnew was "the God of Plague."

Such wild reactions had been partially expected. "There are very few people on the public scene who attack the sacrosanct institutions," says Agnew. "And when you do . . . when you imply that it's entirely possible that these predispositions on the part of the liberal community are not necessarily accurate, you immediately trigger a Pavlovian reaction." But while the reaction was somewhat predictable, its intensity was not. And equally unpredictable was the public response, overwhelmingly in

7

favor of Agnew. Turner Catledge puts it nicely in elegantly understated *New York Times*ese: "The nature and extent of public reaction to Mr. Agnew's strictures have been something not exactly expected." Agnew himself believes that media men "grossly misinterpreted public opinion. They probably thought that after I finished the speech, there would be legions rushing off to the defense of the television industry, instead of the great number who agreed with what was said."

And what precisely was said in that Des Moines speech, a speech which stirred up a controversy that continues unabated today? For one thing, he agreed with FCC commissioner Nicholas Johnson, himself a superdove with a hard-left tilt, that "the power of the networks may be greater than that of the federal, state, and local governments combined." Forty million people watch television regularly. There are three major television networks who split this audience among them. If the networks hold fast to only one set of ideas, one shared ideology, then their power to influence is enormous. Spokesmen for the networks, of course, try not to speak directly to the charge that their ideological stances are monolithic ("I don't even know what a liberal is," says the liberal Eric Sevareid, who most probably would find out were he to submit to psychoanalysis), and the response among the less rabid of them is to talk around the issue. Eric Sevareid, again, speaking in Phoenix, said that Agnew's complaint that the media was dominated by liberals was illogical. If it were true, he said, then the response showing overwhelming support for the Vice President's position demonstrates that the networks' attempts at brainwashing "must be very ineffectual — so ineffectual that I don't know why Mr. Agnew's so upset." But this is evasiveness, of course, an attempt to confuse the issue. Because people haven't been as ready to accept the network commentators' views as they would like, this doesn't mean that the commentators haven't been trying.

"The views of this fraternity do *not* represent the views of America," said Agnew, identifying the fraternity brothers as men "who live and work in the geographical and intellectual confines of Washington, D.C. or New York City — the latter of which James Reston terms the 'most unrepresentative community in the entire United States.' Both communities bask in their own provincialism, their own parochialism. We can deduce that these men thus read the same newspapers, and draw their political and social views from the same sources. Worse, they talk constantly to one another, thereby providing artificial reinforcement to their shared viewpoints."

Here again, Agnew hits the nail on the head. Once every few decades a politician appears who eschews circumlocution and evasion and says those things which most Americans know but despair of ever hearing expressed by their political leaders. Harry Truman, wrongheaded as many of us may think him, was one such politician, able to articulate directly and bluntly the half-formed thoughts of his constituents. Agnew is cut from the same mold. The charge of bias isn't startlingly new. But the description of the inbreeding which nurtures this bias has never in the past few decades been as graphically and simply presented. Anyone who has anything to do with the media — left or right — knows that the charge of intellectual incest is accurate. And just because Harry Reasoner comes from Iowa or Walter Cronkite from St. Joe doesn't make it any less true. Such men are now bona fide Easterners, and few of them would think of returning to the old hometown to take over Dad's business.

"Any journalist knows that his perspective changes as he moves into or away from that East Coast power center," writes David Broder, liberal *Washington Post* columnist, "in whose 'geographical and intellectual confines,' as Mr. Agnew said, influential people do read the same papers, go to the same cocktail parties and express the same thoughts." There are, as Agnew pointed out, three major TV networks, all headquartered in New York City, where national news policy is set. There are two newspapers in the United States — the *New York Times* and the *Washington Post* — which think of themselves and are accepted as national, or as Daniel P. Moynihan puts it, presidential newspapers. The people who work for the networks and for the newspapers and magazines know one another, drink lunch together, live in Connecticut or Long Island, ride the same commuting trains. (And try thinking seriously about the latest hot news out of Wichita when you spend four hours a day commuting on the Penn Central, a railroad which makes the Congolese National Railway look good.)

Periodically, of course, a writer will jet out to the provinces, spend a few days in a comfortable hotel lapping up booze and reading the local papers and getting a few interviews, then will jet back East to instruct the people he's just left on how they're thinking. But for the most part the media men live their lives in that tight little Northeastern corridor, a ghastly, cramped, decaying area, the urban barrenness of which no doubt explains why ecology and conservation are such important issues to Easterners.

Those of us who have lived in California have always resented this. California has, for instance, one of the loveliest pristine coastlines left in the world. Yet the Eastern media forever feature spreads showing the Nathanael Westish garishness of it all, even though photographers may have to drive fifty miles to find a hot dog stand. Then we come East, drive up that much-celebrated New England coastline, and find it to be one of the most sleazy, overcrowded strips north of Coney Island. Is

9

this, we wonder, the standard they use to judge California?

The life of the media man is an insulated life, safely wrapped in a geographical and intellectual and social cocoon, a life which makes it nearly impossible to really know what's going on out there (and this is just as true of my colleagues on the right as of those on the left. After just two years in New York I find that though I can keep up, I've lost my *feeling* for the way things are outside the cocoon. And that's disastrous for a writer). And it's indicative of the security provided by that cocoon that TV executives seemed so uniformly startled by the favorable public reaction to the Des Moines speech. They simply are not in touch.

And so ABC cribs from CBS which cribs from NBC. On any given day the very few news stories that are highlighted are invariably the same on all three networks. (I suppose you might argue that only six important things happen each day. But I doubt it.) The *New York Times* and the *Washington Post* do likewise (although the *Times* is rapidly losing ground to the *Post* in comprehensiveness) as do *Time* and *Newsweek*, both of which read as if they hold weekly joint editorial conferences. And so, the news fit to print is narrowly limited. And if you don't believe it, read the *Dallas Times-Herald* or the *Arizona Republic* or the *Los Angeles Times*, on balance, the best paper in the country. (Why is unclear, but the ideological stance seems less monolithic and the national coverage is much more comprehensive than that of the *New York Times* or the *Washington Post*, even though both claim to be national papers. Perhaps it has something to do with the time difference: Today's news in the East is still today's news on the West Coast. But in the East, West Coast news is yesterday's. Thus the big Western news stories are inevitably slighted by the national media.)

Read them, and if you're a habitual Eastern newspaper reader, see how much significant news you've missed. Or tune in some night on your shortwave transistor to the Canadian Broadcasting Corporation or Radio Australia or Radio South Africa and see how much news you've missed. Or visit California — Berkeley, say, when something like the People's Park crisis is blowing — and listen to a New York TV commentator read a completely distorted account of what you've just been watching.

"If television and radio were to become the instrument of a single opinion," writes Arthur Schlesinger, Jr., "this would constitute an obvious misuse of the airwaves and defiance of the Constitution." The Vice President agrees: "I am not asking for government censorship or any other kind of censorship," he stated flatly in Des Moines, thus insuring, of course, that the liberal media would claim he called for censorship. "I am asking whether a form of censorship already exists when the news that forty million Americans receive each night is determined by a handful of men responsible to their corporate employers and filtered through a handful of commentators who admit to their own set of biases."

Is there a media monopoly, as Agnew charges, controlled by "a tiny and closed fraternity of privileged men" who enjoy a concentration of power they wouldn't allow in government? Of course there is. Count the networks and the newspapers and the magazines and the executives who make them go. Is there a geographic centralization? Of course there is. And do the monopolists share a single view, which even Schlesinger warns us against? Of course they do. Pick an issue of the day, read the editorials in the *Times* and *Post*, listen to Dan Rather or Walter Cronkite or Marvin Kalb or Frank Reynolds or Eric Sevareid or Alexander Kendrick. Monolithic.

This is not to say that TV and newspaper people are consistently misleading or inaccurate. When they report state budgets or space shots or international squabbling or the national unemployment rate they can't often be faulted. But, as Edwin McDowell, conservative but scrupulously fair editor of the *Arizona Republic* puts it, "in those many grey areas where news touches on ideology, and in virtually all the areas of comment and analysis, the sentiment is overwhelmingly liberal . . . on issue after issue, only the liberal point of view is given the thorough, balanced treatment . . . which both points of view deserve [the liberal *and* the conservative]."

Many liberals, of course, would argue bewilderedly that there *is* no thoughtful conservative position on the issues of the day. Thus, perhaps, through ignorance, the media thought it was *true* that Carl McIntire's demonstrations for victory in Vietnam represented conservative sentiment rather than fringe sentiment. They might have believed it, but they'd never make the same mistake in distinguishing between, say, Rennie Davis and Teddy Kennedy, although both take what could easily be seen as exactly the same position on the war. The media has been scandalized at recent suggestions, growing out of Representative Ichord's investigations into peace demonstrations, that liberals have been less than scrupulous in aligning themselves with far-left revolutionaries during crazy days in Washington; there is no outrage expressed, however, when Dr. McIntire's counterdemonstration is treated as *the* rightist expression. Perhaps it's just that they can't distinguish between Bill Buckley and Billy James Hargis.

There are thoughtful conservative positions on every important issue. The welfare mess, for instance, has long been the center of discussion in journals of the right. And conservatives have *not*, despite innuendos to the contrary in the liberal media, opposed welfare because most

11

welfare recipients are Negro and conservatives are anti-Negro. The position has consistently been that welfare is debilitating, that recipients come to view it as a right, that when this happens, when welfare becomes institutionalized, there is little incentive for recipients to try to get off the rolls, that a whole generation grows up knowing the welfare way of life, and that politicians — John Lindsay is a prime example — work on these people as a constituency. And once a politician is assured of a solid bloc of votes from any constituency, he is not going to encourage the breakup of that constituency.

Thus, conservatives have long opposed the welfare system as anything more than temporary charity. And suddenly, liberals such as Nelson Rockefeller are discovering that Ronald Reagan's views make some sense after all. But this discovery comes a bit too late, of course, as do all liberal discoveries of conservative positions. Now that relief has become a right, it's going to take one hell of an effort to dismantle the system and build a new, more realistic substitute.

Similar conservative positions exist on every major issue. I don't claim they're all right, of course, and that some of them are not a bit crack-brained. But I do think that they have not been properly aired. And this *not* because there is a shortage of articulate conservatives, as is often claimed. Rather, these articulate conservatives simply don't get a national hearing because the media is informed by Schlesinger's "single opinion," and, in the Vice President's words, "a form of censorship already exists."

The charge of bias is a difficult one to make stick, partly because many of those who are biased don't know they're biased and therefore deny it flatly. The liberal position has long been the only position in the Northeast, where the media are headquartered, and many media people simply aren't aware that another exists. And then there's that other problem. Ideologues are as common as dandelions in liberal circles, and many of those who know they're biased believe they're right to be so, since they have a corner on absolute truth. (And it can be amusing to watch this moral absolutism at work among those whose whole gospel is predicated upon the notions of inevitable change, eternal flux. "Everything is relative," they tell us, displaying the heart of their doctrine. Yet they preach their social gospel with all the moral fervor of fundamentalist missionaries; one wonders whether this secular absolutism, founded on no verifiable moral code, is not an unthinking substitute for the religious absolutism no longer intellectually fashionable.)

But just occasionally, one of them will break ranks and admit the truth. Such was the case when Howard K. Smith gave his remarkable interview to Edith Efron in *TV Guide* (February 28, 1970). Despite the fact that he is respected by the Nixon Administration, Smith has never been doted on by conservatives, who like to point out that he presided over the tasteless ABC special a couple of years ago that prematurely wrote Richard Nixon's political obituary. Smith, conservatives remember, used as one of his analysts of Nixon's character Alger Hiss, the perjurer and Russian spy, without identifying him as such. Nevertheless, in 1970 Smith decided to break the liberal lockstep. His comments, although familiar to many, are worth quoting extensively here, coming as they do from one of the top men in the media, a respected insider of many years' standing.

Networks are staffed by liberals, a tradition carried down " 'from the time when liberalism was a good thing, and most intellectuals became highly liberal. Most reporters are in an intellectual occupation.' "

Smith believes, however, that contemporary liberalism has become a little less than a good thing. " 'Our liberal friends, today, have become dogmatic. They have a set of automatic reactions.' " Some of these reactions:

> *Race:* ". . . there is a substantial and successful Negro class. But the newsmen are not interested in the Negro who succeeds — they're interested in the one who fails and makes a loud noise. They have ignored the developments in the South. The South has an increasing number of integrated schools. A large part of the South has *accepted* integration. We've had a President's cabinet with a Negro in it, a Supreme Court with a Negro on it — but more important, we have 500 Negroes elected to local offices in the Deep South! This is a tremendous achievement. But that achievement isn't what we see on the screen."

Indeed it isn't. How much time, for instance, was allotted those school-bus overturnings in South Carolina? And how many shots do you remember seeing of those peaceful communities such as Willie Morris' Yazoo in Mississippi, where the schools have been integrated with much better grace than they ever will be in New York? And there may be just a bit more here than mere sensationalism. We all know by now, of course, as Vice President Agnew reminded us in Des Moines, that the media feed on unrest. As Daniel J. Boorstin, University of Chicago history professor, points out: "The development of radio, movies, and TV means that to be newsworthy almost by definition means to be violent. To attract attention on television there have to be people in motion or people hitting one another."

Or overturning school buses. But one wonders if there isn't something more. Have you *New York Times* readers noticed, for instance, how the *Times*men seem committed to ferreting out every single bit of anti-integration feeling in the South, how the *Times* emphasizes Southern recalcitrance? Read the *Times* carefully, and you're left with the feeling that the South is just as red-necked as ever, just as willing as ever to provide TV with good pictures by heckling beautifully dressed, frightened little Negro girls. But is it *really* like that? If you have the time to travel the South and talk to Southerners, you find that it isn't. Why this often frenzied whipping of the South, then? Well, listen carefully to Connecticut's liberal Democratic Senator, Abe Ribicoff. For the past few years now, he's been telling us that the North is committed to a double standard: integration for the South, segregation for the North. New York is one of the most segregated cities in the world, the squalor of its Negro slum schools unequalled by anything in deepest rural Mississippi. Teachers are assaulted daily: One New York school this year had to dismiss its female student teachers because they were being raped regularly on school property. Dope is peddled regularly on high school campuses; riots, beatings, and arson are the order of the day; and most of these schools close down as often as they open.

Yet this is played down. What is important is to integrate those schools down in Dixie. As with conservation, the high demands are made for other parts of the country. Scream with outrage when a Schlitz can floats down the Colorado River, but ignore the stinking sewer and junkyard that the lower Hudson has become. Rhapsodize about Senator Muskie's farsighted views on conservation, but forget the sewers he helped create in Maine. And ignore Senator Ribicoff's demands that Northerners also integrate their schools and keep punching away at the Confederates. The truth is, of course, that New Yorkers, especially of the affluent liberal variety, would no more think of sending their children to integrated schools than they would think of wearing white sweat socks to work. They're scared speechless of integration and would fight it to the end. And thus, perhaps, the technique of the *Times*. Keep the pressure on the South, minimize the problem in the North. Dixie's always been a fine whipping boy. And if we keep attention focused on them, perhaps the people out there won't notice our own hypocrisy. So do as we say, not as we do. "For too long," said the Vice President in Jackson, "the South has been the punching bag for liberal intellectuals."

> *Conservatives:* "If Agnew says something, it's bad, regardless of what he says. If Ronald Reagan says something, it's bad, regardless of what he says. . . ."

Two prime examples of this: Reagan's proposals for welfare reform and Agnew's proposals for diversity in higher education. In a speech enti-

14

tled "Education for What?" delivered in Baltimore in 1969, Agnew anticipated by two years ideas now being tossed around by educators such as Professor Ivar Berg, Associate Dean of Faculties at Columbia University. But because Agnew made the proposals, they received scant attention.

The Middle Class: "Newsmen are *proud* of the fact that the middle class is antagonistic to them. . . . Joseph Kraft did a column in which he said: Let's face it, we reporters have little to do with middle America. They're not our kind of people. . . ."

"Now, we have among us a glib, activist element who would tell us our values are lies, and I call them impudent," said the Vice President in Harrisburg, Pennsylvania. ". . . I call them snobs for most of them disdain to mingle with the masses who work for a living."

The Vietnam War: "The networks have never given a complete picture of the war. For example: That terrible siege of Khe Sanh went on for five weeks before newsmen revealed that the South Vietnamese were fighting at our sides, and that they had higher casualties. And the Viet Cong's casualties were 100 times ours. But we were never told *that.* We just showed pictures day after day of Americans getting the hell kicked out of them. That was enough to break America apart. That's also what it did."

"As a government official," said Agnew to the International Federation of Newspaper Publishers meeting in Washington, "I find it extremely frustrating . . . that only one side of the war is being emphasized by some of our most influential newspapers and television networks and that, overall, their coverage comes off slanted *against* American involvement in that war without any attempt at balance."

The Presidency: "The negative attitude which destroyed Lyndon Johnson is now waiting to be applied to Richard Nixon. Johnson was actually politically assassinated. And some are trying to assassinate Nixon politically. They hate Richard Nixon irrationally."

"In fact, the reporters *don't* like Richard Nixon," writes Gloria Steinem. "Richard Nixon is going down in history, alright, but not soon enough," editorialized the *New Republic* on its front page during the Cambodian hysteria. And the *New Republic,* you'll remember, was one of those periodicals that used to chastise the right for creating a "climate of hate and fear" in which political assassination became possible. But if there were another Lee Harvey Oswald or Sirhan Sirhan out there ready to take to heart the *New Republic*'s message, that Mr. Nixon's trip through history be speeded up, would the *New Republic* be willing to share the credit?

Smith's comments provide an outline for the issues in the battle between the Vice President and the media which began in Des Moines and continues to rage today. And the intensity of the conflict, I believe, and especially the intensity of the reaction to Agnew's criticisms, indicates that there is something more than politics involved.

Agnew's attack on the media was much more than that: It was essentially an attack upon a prevailing set of attitudes and beliefs which have determined the direction of American government for four decades. Agnew had criticized these attitudes and beliefs before, and continues to do so. But in Des Moines it all came together, thanks, ironically enough, to the ability of the media to provide dramatic exposure.

The national media, in matters philosophical, function as the propaganda arm of the American intellectual establishment, the basic premises upon which it operates being, as Howard Smith points out, popularized bite-sized bits of the prevailing liberal dogma. This dogma, although in its entirety never subscribed to by a majority of Americans, has nevertheless been central in shaping our national and international policies. But the reaction to the Des Moines speech proves that for the first time in decades, that dogma is in serious trouble.

A few years ago the Des Moines speech wouldn't have been taken seriously. Richard Nixon was seriously wounded by the media in 1960; Barry Goldwater was slaughtered. Both men, especially Goldwater, made many of the same charges. But neither could carry it off. And there was enough liberal confidence in 1968 to drive Lyndon Johnson from the White House. Indeed, by 1968 the press had become more powerful than the presidency or the legislature in shaping national attitudes and mobilizing public opinion.

"Young man," Lyndon Johnson told Agnew shortly after the election, "we have in this country two big television networks, NBC and CBS. We have two news magazines, *Newsweek* and *Time*. We have two wire services, AP and UPI. We have two pollsters, Gallup and Harris. We have two big newspapers—the *Washington Post* and the *New York Times*. They're all so damned big they think they own the country. But, young man, don't get any ideas about fighting. . . ."

But Agnew got precisely that idea and acted on it. And to the astonishment of everyone — conservatives as well as liberals — he escaped political assassination. Not for want of trying on the part of the media, of course. But when the dust of Des Moines had settled, the country was astounded to find Agnew still standing. And despite one of the most concerted media campaigns in history to discredit him, he continues to stand. Three years ago it probably wouldn't have been possible. But it was obvious that in 1969 something had changed.

"In any society the task of the elite is to supply the bonds that hold together diverse and potentially competing factions," editorialized the *Wall Street Journal* after Des Moines. "It is up to the elite to articulate and defend the values through which society judges what behavior is appropriate or inappropriate, how redress is properly sought, what decisions must be accepted as legitimate.

"Over the past decade — and this is the new factor — the American elite has not been protecting these social bonds but systematically assaulting them."

From the campuses, from the periodicals and newspapers, from the electronic media, the assaults have intensified, smashing at the fabric of our society, and these assaults are the logical result of a liberalism thrashing about in its death throes. People had grown increasingly uneasy, often desperate, as they watched their society come unglued. But there seemed no alternative, for most Americans had been conditioned, despite deep personal reservations, to believe that the liberal way, as it has become rigidly codified in politics, was the only *right* way. But then came Des Moines, and with it some sense of a possible new direction. And Des Moines and the speeches which followed frightened liberals badly, for they discovered that their hegemony was profoundly threatened. The reaction to Agnew demonstrates that many people — perhaps, in their various ways, a majority of people — have simply had enough.

This book will be about such things, about the new mood stirring in the country and about what I believe will be a new politics to grow out of it. The book will center around the speeches of Spiro Agnew, the things he attacks, and the reaction to the attacks. Although this will not be a book about the media per se, much of the discussion will center around TV and the press, for the national media are the most visible manifestation of the condition of contemporary liberalism.

The problem is that, because of the grip liberalism has enjoyed for several decades on the centers of opinion making, there has been little chance for choice. And because of its long term of power, contemporary liberalism has become ossified, reduced, as Howard Smith points out, to a series of unthinking reflexes. Any system of thought which stands too long unquestioned eventually grows inflexible; the tyranny of ideas can be the most oppressive tyranny of all.

Spiro Agnew may be a master politician, or he may simply be the right man in the right place at the right time. But this is irrelevant. What is important is that he has aired important national questions

17

which have long needed airing. This cannot be other than beneficial. Nothing is more dangerous in a democracy than deeply felt but suppressed grievances simmering over several decades.

Agnew may seem an unlikely leader in the attack upon the liberal hegemony. Less than a decade ago he was little known in his own state. In '68 the bumper stickers read "Spiro Who?" Now, as one distinguished conservative writer points out, "having succeeded in making his name an international household word, Agnew's 'style' — in an era when style is prized above all other political virtues — stands out less for his originality than his ability to state the obvious." Furthermore, says the writer, Agnew is a "politician of the middle class, and middle-class politicians (even those who learn their trade in the Maryland bizarre) are not remarked for their assaults on aristocracy, vested or otherwise. . . .

"The Agnew phenomenon confounds," he concludes. "Nevertheless, it grows with each new assault and is undiminished by each new counterassault launched by those vested aristocrats who see in him the incarnation of Babbitt, Gantry, and Berzelius Windrip — all, that is, which they were warned of in their youth about America-beyond-the-pale. So, to that extent, have Herblock and Huntley and Sevareid invented, because they needed, Spiro Agnew the 'kid' killer. But so, too, have tens of millions of Middle Americans come to believe that Agnew's assault is their assault; and the enemies he has made are theirs as well."

2

THE REASONS for the Des Moines speech were complex. The administration had been undergoing a heavy barrage of political criticism from moratorium marchers and from the media. But ever since he spoke out against Negro rioters in Maryland, Agnew had been undergoing a particularly offensive personal barrage from the press.

I first saw him at Palm Springs in December 1968. The occasion was the Republican Governors Conference, an easygoing affair designed to give the governors and members of the new administration a change to size one another up.

National Review had asked me to fly down from Berkeley to cover the conference. It was my first real assignment as a working journalist and I was particularly eager not only to watch the politicians but also to see some of the stars of the national press at work.

It wasn't inspiring. The politicians spent the week working out positions on touchy issues, jockeying for cabinet positions, making statements on national problems. There were statements on housing, statements on minorities, statements on fiscal policy, statements on foreign policy, statements on state–federal relations, statements on the cities. The press wasn't interested. The most common complaint: "There's no goddam news here." Controversy was what they seemed to mean. You got the impression that if Nelson Rockefeller were suddenly to take a poke at Ronald Reagan, or if Richard Nixon were suddenly to stub his toe during one of his patented suit-jacket-bunching waves and pitch headfirst down the steps of the presidential plane, why, there would by a story. But positions? Papers? Statements?

And so media men dog-paddled around the beautiful blue pool of the Spa Hotel, leered at teen-aged girls in bikinis, flirted with pretty waitresses, sweated away at paunches in the mineral baths, fought nervous hangovers, gorged on free food and booze which they complained about between gulps and swigs — and the food was wonderful, as was the booze; the press corps is treated by politicians like a bunch of touchy Arab chieftains — and filed clever stories. (I read the stories after returning to Berkeley. The single best account was by a reporter for the *Desert Sun*, a small Palm Springs paper. He wrote rings around his national colleagues.)

And then, on the sixth of December, a real story finally broke. Vice President Agnew arrived, the newsmen's hackles rose, and within a couple of hours the Vice President stubbed his toe. Or so the newsmen wrote it.

On the morning of the sixth, in a closed meeting of the governors and their immediate staffs, Agnew had made some wisecracks about certain periodicals. The *New York Times* and *Newsweek*, he is reported to have said, were more journals of execution than opinion. Both papers, said Agnew, were best suited to line the bottoms of birdcages.

And so, finally, a story you could get your teeth into. The first question at the subsequent news conference was: "Governor, would you care to talk about birdcages?" Excitement swept through the press corps. There was laughter, and reporters sat straighter, pencils poised, hangovers and indigestion momentarily forgotten. Agnew winced just slightly, his eyes hard and narrow as he looked at his questioner. "Birdcages provided no part of my formal presentation this morning," he said politely as he could in his flat, precise way, "and frankly I'm amazed that it would come up at an occasion as serious as this."

But the newsmen wouldn't let the matter drop. Agnew tried to give thoughtful and incisive statements on the major issues and the incoming administration's approach to them. But the statements were brushed aside and the reporters kept returning to the subject of birdcages. People reading the papers next morning must have thought it a pretty frivolous performance for a new Vice President.

By the time of the birdcage conference, Agnew had already had nearly enough. He had been the prime press target throughout the '68 campaign. Richard Nixon himself knew by '68 that the press hated his guts, a visceral almost instinctive hatred that he simply couldn't overcome. And so, unlike 1960 when, as Theodore White observes, the traveling press corps were in effect enthusiastically campaigning for Kennedy by purposely slanting their stories so Nixon always came off second best, Nixon decided to clam up. He kept press contacts to a minimum, and was extremely careful not to let his hair down, not to deliver one of those off-the-record remarks that would appear in the papers next morning. (One notable slip, however, was allowing Garry Wills to pump him. Wills, passing himself off as a conservative — he was in fact a conservative until he went to Chicago where, apparently, some kids were nice to him — insinuated himself into the good graces of Nixon's staff. The result: a tortured, malicious, virulently anti-Nixon book called *Nixon Agonistes*.)

The press corps would have loved to disembowel Nixon, just as they did in 1960 and 1964. But Nixon had decided to run a low-profile campaign. Part of the reason, of course, was the traumas the country had suffered during 1968. Unprecedented violence in the streets and on the campuses and two assassinations had left the nation badly shaken. Violence seemed to have become a fact of American life and there were very real fears that the fabric of American society had begun to unravel. The nation yearned for a return to something like normalcy, a spell of quiet and order so that we could find out what had been happening to us. Charisma was a dirty word in '68. The country had seen enough of it. Charisma, many people had begun to feel, inevitably attracts bullets.

But then too, of course, there were the national media men, the vast majority of whom are ideological liberals and thus automatically hostile to any conservatively oriented candidate, especially when that candidate had made the mistake of exposing the spy Alger Hiss, one of the establishment's old boys. So Nixon took the high road, kept the press at a distinct distance, and talked over their heads as much as possible directly to the American people. And so it fell on Spiro Agnew to be the prime target for the journalists' knives.

Agnew had moved rapidly from local to national politics, and because he had done so, he missed much of the basic training a conservative national candidate should undergo, especially in the area of dealing with the press. The working press begins with a built-in bias. The Republican candidate has to fight this bias in a way not required of the Democrat. In '68, the press, despite its bias, couldn't quite cotton up to Humphrey because of the spectacle he had made of himself at the Democratic convention, a production straight out of the theater of the absurd. And then during the campaign he continued in the Chicago pattern, claiming before one audience that he supported the war and LBJ, before another that he opposed the war, alternating between bouts of maudlin self-pity and near-hysteria. A Republican candidate performing similarly would have been blown straight off the front pages, of course. But Humphrey wasn't a Republican, and so the press just left him alone and concentrated on the most boostable aspect of his campaign, the performance of his number two man, Edmund Muskie.

Thus, from the beginning, it was Spiro Who versus Abe Lincoln. "If Agnew seems to be patrolling the low road for Nixon," mused *Newsweek*, the magazine that separates fact from opinion, "Maine's Ed Muskie, fifty-four, is riding an uncommonly high road for Hubert Hum-

21

phrey . . . he has been aiming his fundamental appeal to the best instincts of the electorate [translation: he appeals to liberals]. . . . Sweet reason has become his watchword."

Sweet reason seemed to slip occasionally, as when, for instance, Muskie called attention to the fact that Maryland, a state of which Agnew just happened to be governor, had the fourth highest crime rate in the country and "leads the nation in violent crimes." Now was that just coincidence? Or did Muskie mean to imply that Agnew was squishy soft on crime? If so, it sounds more like the low road than that uncommonly high one. But the question was never pursued. Instead, *Newsweek* congratulated the candidate on his "direct" approach to the law and order issue. "China blue eyes blazing, [Muskie] likes to twit those who blame the increase of lawlessness on the party in the White House."

Now this may well be even too much for liberals. "Sweet reason," "china blue eyes" which "blaze" as he "twits," all add up to some of the decade's silliest writing. But there was a purpose, that purpose being to set up Agnew, by contrast, as the heavy. Agnew is not Lincolnesque. Rather, he's "Sleek and self-contained . . . woodenly extending his hand to the small crowds . . ." sinisterly smiling "his tight smile" while delivering his "stock speech."

No china blue eyes for Agnew, marked for political assassination at his first informal campaign meeting with the Washington Press Corps. One newsman recalls the scene. At first the meeting went easily, Agnew confident and poised, discussing his political philosophy and his view of the role of the Vice Presidency. But this isn't the stuff that makes good headlines. What is needed is a birdcage or two. So a loaded question was lobbed at Agnew: "Did the Governor think Hubert Humphrey was soft on communism?" "Yes." And so the headline, written for Agnew by his interrogator:

AGNEW CHARGES HUMPHREY
"SOFT ON COMMUNISM"

A meaningless story, or course, the key phrase itself belonging to another era, the predictable charge of "McCarthyism" which inevitably followed equally anachronistic. Although politicians still fear the charge of "McCarthyism" (Agnew later said that had he known his off-the-cuff remark might "cast me as the Joe McCarthy of 1968, I would have turned five somersaults to avoid saying it."), it has become a knee jerk label, used by politicians of both parties only when the going gets rough and they can't think of anything sensible to say. Still, it's a favorite media word, and it's convenient, for it allows you by using it, as do all good clichés, to imply a whole bag of things without actually saying them.

Another of the all-purpose terms favored by the media is "racism." The Democrats and the pro-Democrat media professed to believe that Agnew meant dark racist things whenever he used such terms as "law and order," thus, oddly enough, using the very same technique which they designate by the term "McCarthyism." "I submit to you," said Agnew to his audiences, apparently determined to convince people that he was saying what he was saying, "that you know the phrase 'law and order' is a traditional phrase in this country. It doesn't mean bigotry. It means that no individual is going to decide for himself which laws to break and which to obey."

Now this is a problem which invariably haunts conservatives. Perhaps the most important single issue in the nation today is the issue of crime. Yet whenever a conservative mentions crime, he is accused of bigotry. And let's be quite clear here. What is meant is that, just as in the case of welfare reform, the conservative is constitutionally anti-Negro. When we attack welfare as an archaic, self-perpetuating, dehumanizing concept, we are really attacking the Negro, say the liberals, since most urban welfare recipients are Negro. And when we attack crime, they say, we are also attacking the Negro, since many urban criminals are Negro. The charge isn't true, of course, but many people, among them the media people, insist that it is. And so, because of this odd double-think, we find ourselves able to do very little to prevent crime. For if fighting crime is in reality fighting Negroes, few Americans will have the stomach for the battle, since even we middle Americans are not bigots.

Unless one maintains a twenty-four-hour guard, one eventually comes to believe what one is told, if told often enough. Thus, even the most conservative among us have come to feel a certain reticence about discussing without euphemism such subjects as crime prevention. The liberals, with the full backing of the media and scores of well-publicized presidential commission reports, have pretty well convinced most of us that it isn't the crime per se which is important, but that which caused the crime. And what causes the crime isn't some dark place in the soul of the criminal; it's the economic and environmental circumstances of his life. Thus we talk of root causes such as poverty and white racism. Eliminate these, we are told, and crime will also disappear.

Now this may or may not be true. But racism is a matter for theologians rather than for politicians to deal with, and the poor will always be with us. On the day that such inequities are finally eliminated, we shall also see the Second Coming. And for the victims of the muggers and rapists, this may be just a bit too long to wait.

And this is precisely the approach which drives conservatives up the wall. When a house burns, you immediately send for the fire department. After the fire is out, you try to find out what caused it. When you're laid low with a violent toothache, your first priority is to get the tooth pulled. You'd no doubt be very upset indeed were the dentist to tell you that he wouldn't touch the tooth because it was your own fault for eating fudge brownies. Cutting out fudge brownies will do nothing for a decayed tooth once it's begun to ache.

And thus it is with the liberal approach to crime. Search out the root causes while crime rages around you, and be easy with the criminal because it really isn't his fault. And thus we have incredibly light sentences or mistrials, and criminals are walking the streets almost as soon as they are apprehended. And, indeed, in such cases as the Black Panther trials, criminals are not only set free but are elevated to the status of folk heroes. It's nonsensical, cries the conservative, who tries to point out that the people who suffer from such laxity the most, are precisely the people the liberals want to help — the urban black ghetto dwellers. Most residents of, say, Harlem, would be absolutely delighted if the marauding criminals who terrorize black working people and prey on their children were kept behind bars.

But, given the liberal hegemony, it grows increasingly difficult to do anything to control the criminal. The first reaction of the media, for instance, just as it was the first reaction of liberal politicians, was to attack the police chief of Washington, D.C. for his handling of the May Day demonstrators in Washington last spring. Although the purpose of the demonstrators was to break the law, and although this purpose was announced time and time again by avowed revolutionaries such as Rennie Davis — who received all the TV exposure anyone could ask for — the first target of the liberals was the police chief. He didn't do anything *quite* wrong, but, opined people such as columnist Tom Wicker, if we scratch around long enough we'll discover he violated some constitutional rights. It's impossible for a black revolutionary to get a fair trial in this country, says Yale President Kingman Brewster. And he's right, as witness the trial of Bobby Seale, Black Panther leader. The jury let him off. At any rate, when Agnew spoke out against crime, it was *just* crime that he was speaking against. But the thrust of the press argument was that crime was a code word and that Agnew was a bigot, traveling the low road by appealing to other bigots. Hence the "Fat Jap" episode.

Agnew was walking through the press section of his campaign plane and spotted one of the traveling correspondents, a personal friend, Gene Oishi of the *Baltimore Sun*, sound asleep. Agnew grinned and said to no one in particular, "What's with the Fat Jap? Asleep again," employing a nickname long used by both Agnew and Oishi's fellow newsmen. Everyone laughed. Arriving in Honolulu for a campaign appearance four days later, Agnew was stunned to learn that the *Washington Post* had just featured a story implying that the "Fat Jap" crack was a racist slur. The story, it was learned later by an Agnew staff member, had been filed days before. But the *Post* waited to break the story until Agnew arrived in Hawaii, which has a large Japanese–American population. Agnew's campaign schedule was known days in advance. No other correspondent filed a word of copy mentioning the incident which by any fair standard of reportage was a nonincident. Coincidence? Perhaps. But the circumstances are such that a very good case could be made to support that charge that the *Washington Post* was actively campaigning against Agnew. And *not* just on its editorial page. And the accusation that was leveled, implicit in the story, that Agnew was a bigot, is perhaps the dirtiest that can be made in politics.

It should be remembered, however, that such charges are always *implicit*, the technique, as it has been named by one conservative commentator, "Judo Journalism." "Judo Journalists recognize the fact that understatement, rather than hyperbole, is the key to successful propaganda in a modern overcommunicated society," says the commentator, who points out that in contemporary political journalism, "a campaign charge that appears in overstated form is likely to be regarded with suspicion, even if true." Therefore, if you want to make your target out to be a bigot, you have to be a bit subtle, as was the *Washington Post* story.

Consider the story, which appeared in the *Washington Post* on September 23, 1968, under the headline NO FORMULA FOR PEACE, AGNEW SAYS. "Fat Japs" have nothing to do with the overall topic. But the final paragraph reads:

> Earlier, Agnew had astonished newsmen traveling with him, when he made a rare visit to their section of his airplane, pointed at a sleeping reporter of Japanese descent, who is, like Agnew, a second-generation American, and asked, "What's the matter with the Fat Jap?"

First, the placement. The story is about another topic and the Fat Jap reference is thrown in at the end, almost as if it were an afterthought. But it isn't, of course. Although it's apparently dropped in casually, it occupies the single most important place in the story, the ending, which often can be, as every writer knows, the most emphatic place in any short composition.

Now let's look at the sentence itself, a splendid example of the technique of "Judo Journalism" (I'm indebted to my conservative friend, who prefers to remain unnamed, for this analysis.)

Earlier	Three *days* earlier, in fact, but the idea is planted that the event took place earlier in the same day. Had the writer said precisely "Three days ago," the game would have been up before it started, because the timing of the story, coinciding with the Hawaii visit, would have been too obvious.
Agnew had astonished newsmen	The triggering phrase. The astonishment, which in fact did not occur, is the pretext for the story. It tells the reader that the reporter hasn't gone out of his way to react to the incident, such reaction being common among his colleagues. What the reader is to learn, then, is not to be shrugged off, as in fact it was by other newsmen.
when he made a rare visit to their section of his airplane	Agnew is distant, aloof, cold, not given to fraternizing with the press boys — which makes what's coming all that much easier to believe.
pointed at a sleeping reporter of Japanese descent	The atmosphere gets frigid. The nonidentification of the "sleeping reporter" makes what we are about to witness a hit-and-run case involving an innocent bystander. The Judo Journalist couldn't, of course, indicate in any way that *Agnew knew the reporter.* Even the designation "sleeping *Baltimore* reporter" would have been fatal to the writer's intention. This must be a *random* victim.

26

who is, like Agnew, a
second-generation American

An inspired touch. Here Agnew's own best defense is turned against him. Because Agnew speaks as a second-generation American, his remark seems especially insensitive and stupid.

and asked, etc.

ZAP.

Agnew was appalled, as was Oishi, by the way in which his crack was construed. In Maui, he did his best to explain:

> . . . A funny thing happened on the way to Hawaii. Maybe it wasn't so funny after all. Those of you who read your local papers are going to find that this vice presidential candidate, this son of a Greek immigrant, is being accused of an insensitivity to the national pride and heritage of other peoples. I submit to you that this is a rather ridiculous charge to make to a man who grew up in a neighborhood where his family was the only Greek family, a man who saw his father come home dead tired in the afternoon and climb down off a vegetable truck to be ridiculed by certain people who referred to us as "those Greeks on the block." Yes, we were sensitive in those days but thank God the United States has passed that point where we're drawn up so tight that we can't communicate with each other, and where our sense of humor is beginning to disappear.
>
> On the plane a reporter, whom I consider a friend of mine — because I never jest with my enemies — who happens to be Japanese, was asleep. I referred to him in certain slang, similar to the slang that people on athletic teams use affectionately among themselves, some of which wouldn't bear repeating. I don't think I said anything quite that harmful to my friend, Gene Oishi, and I don't think Gene Oishi took what I said in any sense of downgrading him. . . .
>
> Yes, I remember when my father first came here from Greece the word Greek was considered to be an epithet. Those very sensitive people, who were sensitive because they did not know how they were going to be received in the United States, because they were sensitive in that they didn't realize that this really was a free country. . . . They preferred to be called Grecians or people of Hellenic descent. But they got over that. They got over that because they moved up the line to where they had a sense of dignity and achievement and sophistication and assurance — just as the Japanese Americans, just as the Korean Americans and the Chinese Americans and the Polish Americans and everyone else — because the United States

27

is now reaching a point where your ancestry is simply an interesting point of conversation, not a slur, and we won't stop until we find that in this country of America, Negro Americans who have been so long discriminated against can feel the same way.

If I have inadvertently offended anyone I am sorry — I am truly sorry. To those of you who have misread my words I only say you've misread my heart.

The Vice President's speech was well received by the Hawaiians to whom it was addressed. But the pressmen remained unmoved. At this point in his career, Agnew still believed that sincerity, openness, and good-heartedness were sufficient. All that was necessary was to convince the media men that you really *were* this way. He still hadn't quite ferreted out the essence of snobbishness: the actual pleasure a snob takes in hurting.

And so, after the Maui speech, a deeply troubled Agnew sought out the *Washington Post*'s Richard Homan, who had broken the Fat Jap story. His intention was to talk to Homan on a man-to-man level, to convince him that "you've misread my heart." But, in the words of an eyewitness to the episode, "the *Post* reporter treated Agnew like a member of Louis XVI's court snubbing an outland peasant.

"Agnew was standing there in the plane aisle, saying, 'Dick, I'm really sorry you misconstrued what was meant to be a humorous remark, because — .' That was as far as he got. Homan just turned away and looked out the cabin window. All Agnew could do was breathe deep, shrug, and walk back to the front cabin."

3

IN A SPEECH delivered in Fort Lauderdale in 1970, Vice President Agnew explained why he had attacked a Neville Chamberlainlike university president, Michigan's Robin Fleming: "As for the vigor of my criticism of President Fleming, it was conscious — based on an old Cub Scout theory that the best way to put a tough crust on a marshmallow is to roast it."

No one has ever accused Agnew of being a marshmallow. His crust was already tough in '68. But by the time the press got through roasting him, it was very tough indeed. He was expected to learn several lessons, however. One was that the press wouldn't allow him to wisecrack as they would, say, a Jack or Bobby Kennedy. Conservatives are simply not allowed a sense of humor, and if they show one it is treated maliciously. Most of us probably remember Barry Goldwater's crack about lobbing a missile into the men's room of the Kremlin. The press professed to take it seriously and played it up as if it were a major foreign policy pronouncement. Or there was Goldwater's quip about sawing off the East Coast and letting it float out to sea — personally, I find it a most sensible suggestion and would like to suggest that we knock off welfare and use the funds to buy giant saws. Again, treated as a serious statement. And many of the critics claimed to see in it rampant anti-intellectualism, which tells you a great deal about how the people who live in the corridor think of themselves.

So lesson number one: No sense of humor. And closely related was lesson number two: The press is your link with the American people. If the press wants you to look bad to the public, you will look bad. At worst you'll come across as a bigot, at best an insensitive dullard. You're a Republican, which is bad enough. You have conservative instincts, which is even worse. So lesson number three: You're simply not what the people should have leading them, so you lie down in shame, lick the

29

hands of the media men, grovel for their approval, and take your defeat without whimpering.

This has too often been the pattern for conservative candidates and officeholders. But Agnew did what he simply wasn't supposed to do. He learned a different set of lessons and he applied them. Chief among them was the realization that because the media operates with an inbuilt bias, it is fruitless to try to curry favor with them, fruitless even to treat pressmen unguardedly as friends. (Agnew still slips here, as when for instance he had a bunch of reporters in for drinks last spring and gave them his off-the-record views on Red China. Off-the-record comments have always been treated reverently by older newsmen. There is no greater breach of professional ethics than to broadcast such views. The old school feels the same way about such comments as priests feel about confessions. But Agnew's comments were front-paged the next day.) The lesson which follows, then, is a simple one: Since you cannot trust a biased press properly to interpret and transmit your strongly held views to the American people, you skip the middlemen and go to the customers themselves, the American people. And in so doing, you might as well let the people know why, might as well roast a few of the media men in the same way they've been accustomed to roasting you.

Undoubtedly, then, Des Moines was the first big assault in a concerted counterattack, and because of '68 there can be little doubt that personal experience and disillusionment had a great deal to do with the zest with which the Vice President carried out his role. But there was a great deal more than personal pique involved. And that great deal more has to do with the whole dreary subject of Vietnam.

Richard Nixon had intentionally waged a low-profile campaign in '68, prompting one distinguished TV commentator, Frank Reynolds of ABC, to comment in his elegant unbiased fashion that Nixon was pulling his punches, fearful of displaying his "natural instinct" to go after his enemies with "club" and "axe."

From January to October 1969, the new administration continued, as it had during the campaign, to keep its profile low. The policy was a calculated one, designed, in columnist Joseph Kraft's phrase, to "wind down" the country's tensions, badly exacerbated by the Johnson years of media overexposure. Consequently, during his first months in office, Richard Nixon did little to reach his national constituency directly. As the year went on, however, it became clear that the plan was not working. The administration's message was being drowned out by the same media-directed cacophony that had laid Lyndon Johnson low. Compounding the problem was, as one administration official puts it, "the reemergence of the Camelot Restoration political–media coalition," reinforced by "members of the former Johnson Administration anxious to gild their roles in history."

CLIFFORD URGES TROOP WITHDRAWAL DEADLINE, screamed one typical headline. "That Vietnam was a 'litmus test' [as *Time* called it] for liberal media approbation can be seen by the ideological apotheosis of former Secretary of Defense Clark Clifford, onetime hawk, after he made his political deathbed conversion to dove in the late stages of the Johnson Administration," writes a conservative student of the media. "A decade ago, Rusk was the hero and Clifford, a behind-the-scenes political confidant of Democratic Presidents, was regarded with misgivings, if not distrust, by liberal ideologues. But by 1970, Clifford was writing *mea culpas* in *Foreign Affairs* quarterly for his former support of Johnson's Vietnam policy and receiving lavish tribute [from the liberal media]. . . . Clifford, not surprisingly, was among those pushed by the media for appointment to the Nixon cabinet during the interregnum period when print and electronic critics of the newly elected President, having lost the election, were determined to win *their* war [if not the country's] by means of editorial recommendations for cabinet posts." (Apropos of this last point, it's interesting to watch the same process at work in 1971, this time with recommendations for Vice President. The "dump Agnew movement," about which the media love to speculate, is just about as likely to occur as Clark Clifford was likely to get a cabinet seat.)

Now there is nothing wrong with a man changing his views, especially on an issue as depressing and complex as American involvement in Vietnam. Even as irritating and curmudgeonly a figure as J. William Fulbright can, I think, be viewed as sincere, despite the startling reversal of his position. One remembers his enthusiastic endorsement of the Gulf of Tonkin resolution: "The action taken by the United States . . . must be understood both in terms of the immediate situation and in terms of the broader pattern of communist military and subversive activities in Southeast Asia over the past ten years. On both levels the North Vietnamese regime is patently guilty of military aggression and demonstrably in contempt of international law."

That, you say, could well have been spoken by Curtis LeMay. But Fulbright finds himself in a dilemma, and one must hesitate to charge him with hypocrisy, for his dilemma is the honest dilemma of most old-line liberals. In international affairs the liberal doctrine has proven itself bankrupt, and the intensity of the new isolationism is a natural reaction to the complete breakdown of a long-held view of the world.

"The source of an effective foreign policy under our system is presidential power," said Fulbright in 1961, and quoted by Agnew in Cleveland in 1970. "This proposition, valid in our own time, is

31

certain to become more, rather than less, compelling in the decades ahead. . . ." Now, as most conservatives will agree, this was pretty much the foreign policy view held by all liberals from the forties down through the late sixties. Despite the efforts of conservatives such as Senators Taft and Bricker, liberal legislators encouraged for more than two decades the gradual erosion of the system of checks and balances between the legislative and the executive. Liberal theoreticians cheered whenever the executive expropriated a bit more power, jeered whenever those reactionary old mossbacks in the Senate attempted to hold on to their prerogatives. And so we entered the sixties with legislative power, especially in the field of foreign relations, badly eroded, more and more of it, thanks to the efforts of Senators such as Fulbright, centralized in the executive. And then along came Lyndon Johnson and suddenly liberals began to have a disquieting thought — suppose that this superstrong executive should be run by a bad man?

Liberals, of course, have never quite had the stomach to admit to what they have wrought, but badly stung by what they tend to think was LBJ's betrayal, they now work just as hard at calling for limiting the executive's power as they once worked to expand it.

This should not be unwelcome to conservatives, who have traditionally viewed the executive with extreme suspicion. But the *source* of the newfound liberal discontent rankles. The source, of course, is the war in Vietnam, and conservatives suddenly find themselves handed a war masterminded and expanded by two of the most liberal Democratic administrations in history. And now we're told it's *our* war and, as Senator McGovern instructs us, we have blood on our hands and should be ashamed of ourselves for not immediately apologizing to Hanoi and departing forthwith.

This can be most galling. I remember in 1966 attending a faculty party at the University of Denver. I was the only conservative there, and the only person there arguing against Johnson's expansion of the war. I mistrusted Democratic interventionist foreign policy under Kennedy and Johnson, I argued, because it dangerously undercut the effectiveness of an already badly enfeebled legislature. And there was something about the rhetoric of the Kennedy days — action for the sake of action, movement for its own sake, that reminded me very much of the activism of fascism. Vietnam, I was convinced then, as were many conservatives, was a trap, the wrong place at the wrong time. There were so many places where the issue had been clear-cut — Tibet, for instance, or all of Eastern Europe, when we should have acted. It may be heretical for a conservative to say so, but I even found slightly fishy the famous State Department white paper which Dean Rusk trotted out to prove that it wasn't civil war.

But as the war escalated the situation changed. Whether or not the State Department position has been accurate through the early sixties, it became accurate after Tonkin, when there was no longer any question about massive North Vietnamese intervention. Cynics may say, of course, that the Johnson Administration created the war it claimed it existed after the claim. This will be fought out by historians for years. But what is important at the moment is that the Democrats, misguided by one of the tenets of the liberal world view, got the nation into a war which could not be won. Before Tonkin we could have bugged out as rapidly as we liked. After Tonkin, when American troop strength climbed toward 600,000, it was too late. The war had to be wound down, because there was no hope that we could win the conventional war we were suckered into fighting, given the mood of the nation. And so the question became, how best to end the war and at the same time preserve national honor, realize as many of our goals in Vietnam as possible, and save the maximum number of American and South Vietnamese lives.

The Nixon Administration promised to end the war. And that is precisely what it set out to do. From nearly 600,000 American troops, the administration has dropped the number, at this writing, to something like 190,000. When you read this, the American troop level will probably stand at around 100,000. It would be almost logistically impossible to move faster and still avoid a Dunkirk. Yet the cry of the Cliffords and the Muskies and the Kennedys and Humphreys is that the President is not really ending the war because he hasn't set a specific date for getting all the troops out.

This is, of course, a ludicrous charge, almost as silly as the charges by Rennie Davis, who on a good day sounds remarkably like the gaggle of Democratic presidential contenders, that Richard Nixon is really widening the war. You simply *can't* widen a war by withdrawing troops, and it seems absolutely absurd to have to argue further. (And the word has gone out among the Democrats that they'd better mute that criticism just a bit, lest they be left in '72 without an issue. It would surely be hell to pitch your whole campaign at the troop withdrawal issue and then, come election time, find that there were only seven troops left.)

And so the Nixon Administration is ending a war started by and unsuccessfully prosecuted by liberal Democrats, and it must be galling indeed to find these same Democrats now trying, by some intellectual sleight of hand, to convince the nation that the whole thing was the fault of Republicans and conservatives. Especially galling when Hubert Humphrey claims that he was against it all along but didn't want to offend LBJ by saying so. Or when, as Vice President Agnew pointed out in Cleveland, Clark Clifford said in 1968: "We have no plan to reduce

33

the number of troops in Vietnam at all. . . . I could not predict the return of any troops in 1969. I want today to reiterate that position. We have not yet reached the level of 549,000 in South Vietnam. We intend to continue to build toward that level. We have no intention of lowering that level either by next June [1969] or at any time in the foreseeable future." A very firm hawkish statement, as the Vice President points out, ". . . as hawkish a statement as could be made in 1968." Yet immediately after the election of Richard Nixon, the dove feathers sprouted. Weeks after the election, Clifford wrote in *Life* magazine: "It is time now to end our participation in the war. We must begin the rapid orderly and scheduled withdrawal of U.S. troops from Indochina."

Unlike Fulbright's long laborious change of heart, this was an astoundingly rapid and unscheduled flip-flop, smacking strongly of the political functionary on the make. Nearly as startling was the conversion of Edmund Muskie, the man who led the successful attempt at the Democratic convention to put down the minority peace plank and who now campaigns on that plank. And who tells us, of course, that he, too, secretly opposed the war.

Richard Nixon believed at the beginning of his administration that the hypocritical politics-playing with the war issue would be so transparent that the majority of Americans would understand what was going on. But he hadn't reckoned fully enough with the media. The summer months of '69 showed that far from modulating voices, the low-profile technique had only emboldened his opposition. Would-be Democratic Presidents blanketed talk shows, monopolized headlines. Operating out of key communications centers across the country through September, organizers of the massive October 15th antiwar rally received free in television news coverage the equivalent of $10 to $15 million in advertising, promotional, and organizational costs.

The media villain in late '69 was anything that smacked of the military (this antimilitary emotionalism would reach its flowering in 1971, with the CBS special, *The Selling of the Pentagon*). Anything that related to "the military–industrial complex (known as "the arsenal of democracy" when we were fighting Nazis instead of Communists) was fair game for the media, which had a few years before ignored Barry Goldwater's charges that Robert S. McNamara's Strangelove policies were tending toward disaster. Across the country, TV camera crews played witting handmaiden to roving bands who, "responding to a higher law," vandalized draft boards, blew up Bank of America branches, burned down university buildings.

Antiadministration Republicans such as New York's junior Senator Charles Goodell (anyone remember him?) received extensive media coverage, while proadministration Republicans and Democrats were treated like the late-late show. When, for example, Congressman Richard Ichord, Democrat of Missouri, called a news conference to display photographs of the Communist massacre at Hue, he was virtually ignored by the same networks that a few days before had immersed viewers in coverage of a similar Capitol Hill showing of photographs taken at Songmy. And when 300 members of the House and 59 Senators endorsed the President's position on Vietnam, the event went unreported in the next day's Washington edition of the *New York Times,* the edition which brings most pressure to bear on Congress.

The noise level continued to rise, and the unrest it created was contagious, reaching its peak in the October 15th demonstrations. What had been programmed as a calm, cool administration stance now seemed something quite different — an administration on the defensive, jerky and jittery, always counterpunching, letting its opponents take the offensive and then responding in futile flurries.

"We're just not getting through to the people," said White House staff assistant and Pulitzer Prizewinning reporter Clark Mollenhoff after the defeat of the President's nomination of Judge Clement Haynsworth to the Supreme Court. (And there has seldom been a more shameful episode in the recent history of the Senate. Haynsworth was defeated *only* because he was a white Southerner, as arrant a piece of bigotry as has ever existed.) "By the end of October," says an administration official, "even the most ardent advocate of low-profile national leadership realized that the President could no longer stand above and beyond the battle for public opinion. If the administration was to avoid the fate of its predecessor, the President would have to renew the process of 'getting through' to his national constituency. Time had not worked in his favor. Now, he would have to reclaim his mandate, less than a year after being sworn into office, in the teeth of the most formidable opposition to any American national administration since that of the first Johnson."

It was obvious, then, that the low-profile technique had to be junked so that the President would have at least a fighting chance of getting his message, undistorted by the media, to the people who elected him. To carry that message, he selected Spiro Agnew. "Nixon," says one White House staffer, "comprehended the value of a vocal Vice President to a President like himself, one inclined to tactical conservatism and a go-slow approach when testing political waters." The President was hesitant to launch the full scale counteroffensive against his enemies personally. But he realized that the time had come to give his supporters some badly needed support.

Agnew was the logical man for the assignment, and from spring to autumn in 1969 he took to the stump, carrying the administration's message to local organizations across the country, getting the usual minimal media coverage traditionally accorded the utterances of Vice Presidents. But on October 19, in New Orleans, at a Citizens Testimonial Dinner, he gave a speech which rocked the nation, making page one of every newspaper and making Spiro Agnew overnight the country's most controversial political figure.

In New Orleans Agnew had decided to take the rhetorical gloves off. Given the cacophony raised by the critics of the administration and the new revolutionaries, he had decided that a public official, in order to get the hearing that should rightfully be his by nature of position and responsibility, had "to use strong language to get attention" — the same sort of attention that is automatically accorded, say, to an Eldridge Cleaver by the media. And so, in New Orleans, he landed the first of the pre–Des Moines stem-winders, a speech that, ironically enough, received the sort of media treatment that bore out his central theme, that "we are reaching a period when our senses and our minds will no longer respond to moderate stimulation."

We seem to be approaching an age of the gross. Persuasion through speeches and books is often discarded for disruptive demonstrations aimed at bludgeoning the unconvinced into action.

The young — and by this I don't mean by any stretch of the imagination all the young, but I'm talking about those who claim to speak for the young — at the zenith of physical power and sensitivity, overwhelm themselves with drugs and artificial stimulants. Subtlety is lost, and the fine distinctions based on acute reasoning are carelessly ignored in a headlong jump to a predetermined conclusion. Life is visceral rather than intellectual, and the most visceral practitioners of life are those who characterize themselves as intellectuals.

Truth to them is "revealed" rather than logically proved, and the principal infatuations of today revolve around the social sciences, those subjects which can accommodate any opinion and about which the most reckless conjecture cannot be discredited.

Education is being redefined at the demand of the uneducated to suit the ideas of the uneducated. The student now goes to college to proclaim rather than to learn. The lessons of the past are ignored and obliterated in a contemporary antagonism known as the generation gap.

A most thoughtful and provocative exposition, one that picks up the strands of all the issues leading to our contemporary malaise. But the media, of course, pounced on the punch line, the most strongly worded sentence in a strong speech, a sentence that would be taken out of context, amplified, analyzed, explicated, and then, in typical media fashion, treated as the topic sentence of the whole composition:

A spirit of national masochism prevails, encouraged by an effete corps of impudent snobs who characterize themselves as intellectuals.

There was nothing especially new in the speech. Agnew had said much the same things, speaking to the Young Presidents Organization on "Radicalism in Our Midst" in Honolulu and on "Rationality and Effetism" at Ohio State University. ("A society which comes to fear its children is effete. A snivelling, hand-wringing power structure deserves the violent rebellion it encourages," he said at Ohio State. At Honolulu he said: "A society which must constantly charge its batteries on great surges of dramatic and emotional confrontations is in deep trouble.") But suddenly, on the strength of a single sentence, he was center stage before the public, finally able to punch through at least part of the administration's message.

Reaction ran according to form: The people loved it, and the "Say It Again, Spiro" bumper stickers blossomed overnight. The snobs themselves were highly distressed, however, although some thinkers saw the performance as a breath of fresh air blowing away a couple of decades of cliché-riddled, senseless stock political oratory. "In fact," wrote Professor John Roche, former president of Americans for Democratic Action, "Americans have always looked on politics as a body contact sport and were by 1969 extremely bored by the one-sidedness of the match. Into this vacuum came Spiro Agnew. Actually, his first hard speeches were pretty mild, say, by comparison with any of FDR's assaults on his opponents. And by nineteenth-century standards, Mr. Agnew wouldn't even have made it into the big ring. But his victims responded as though they were en route to labor camps."

"It appears that by slaughtering a sacred cow I triggered a holy war," said Agnew to a group of Republicans in Harrisburg, Pennsylvania, eleven days later. Some had expected him to use the Harrisburg forum, deep in the heart of liberal Republican country, to soften his New Orleans remarks. But Agnew felt otherwise: "I have no regrets. I do not intend to repudiate my beliefs, recant my words, or run and hide. What I have said before, I will say again. It is time for the preponderant majority, the responsible citizens of this country, to assert *their* rights."

As had happened in New Orleans, the media focused on the striking phrases — "merchants of hate," "ideological eunuchs," "parasites of passion." And the result, again, distortion by omission.

We owe our values to the Judaeo–Christian ethic which stresses individualism, human dignity, and a higher purpose than hedonism. We owe our laws to the political evolution of government by the consent of the governed. Our nation's philosophical heritage is as diverse as its cultural background. We are a melting pot nation that has for over two centuries distilled something new and, I believe, sacred.

Then, back to the subject raised in New Orleans:

Now we have among us a glib, activist element who would tell us our values are lies, and I call them impudent. Because anyone who impugns a legacy of liberty and dignity that reaches back to Moses, is impudent.

I call them snobs for most of them disdain to mingle with the masses who work for a living. They mock the common man's pride in his work, his family and his country. It has also been said that I called them intellectuals. I did not. I said that they characterized themselves as intellectuals. No true intellectual, no truly knowledgeable person, would so despise democratic institutions.

It was as close as he would come to an apologia for the New Orleans remarks. He resented what the media had done to his speech: "There's a widely held misconception that I called students 'effete snobs,' " he commented on the TV program, *Firing Line*. "This is typical of the tactics of the media boys when they strip qualifications from your remarks as they repeat them. I said that some demonstrators were encouraged by an effete corps of impudent snobs. . . . But pretty soon it got to be that all of them were snobs — and the next thing I knew, all students were snobs. And then all young people were snobs. It's pretty hard to cope with that when it is picked up and repeated with the qualifications, as I say, stripped away. But it happens today in the media. I can vouch for it."

Nevertheless, Agnew accepted the risk, feeling it was better to be misrepresented than not to be represented at all. There was political danger in what was often abrasive language. But the chance had to be taken: "I gave a speech here in New York before the Boys Clubs of America," he explained on *Firing Line*, "a speech that I thought was a good one. . . . I thought it said something concerning the new anticulture, which I took pains to say did not apply entirely to youth. . . . That speech was conciliatory as far as not making a judgment about the propriety of the anticulture . . . [the speech] simply delineated its characteristics and stated the dangers that we would undergo as a

38

nation if everyone took it up — if everyone dropped out of responsibility, if no one wanted power. That speech attracted no attention. It got maybe a quarter of a column. Now, if I had written the speech differently, if I had written it in the hard adversary fashion [of New Orleans], I would have received a great deal of attention. . . . So, if you're going to be heard, you can't be heard by making speeches in a vacuum, and you've got to take certain risks of having them utilized in ways you might not desire, just to get the point before the public."

And so, no apologies for the effete snob speech in Harrisburg. Instead, Agnew used the Harrisburg forum to set the stage for the President's November 3rd Vietnam speech, a speech which was in turn to set the stage for Des Moines.

"Chanting 'Peace Now' is no solution, if 'Peace Now' is to permit a wholesale bloodbath," he said in Harrisburg. "And saying the President should understand the people's view is no solution. It is time for the people to understand the views of the President they elected to lead them."

And so the stage was set for the November 3rd speech, the reactions to which would prompt the Vice President to challenge the media to a duel, the end of which is not yet in sight.

4

RICHARD NIXON'S November 3rd speech was born partly of desperation and partly of determination. His message was a simple one: He
intended to bring the war in Vietnam to an honorable conclusion. But
he was desperate because the media simply refused to let him put this
message across. He was determined to do so, however. The print media
was a lost cause. "The administration," said *Time* after the speech, "now
seems committed to the politics of polarization. Vietnam is the touchstone of division, the litmus test of loyalty. There is nothing wrong with
the President's attacking his detractors; what is unsettling about Nixon's
current offensive is the weapons he has chosen and the way he does
battle. In his Vietnam speech, he honored the patriotism of his critics
— and then impugned it by remarking: 'North Vietnam cannot defeat
or humiliate the United States. Only Americans can do that." (Impugn-
ing or not, it's true.) David Halberstam wrote that the speech was "hard,
rigid, barren," something "from a time past," which "could have been
written by Rusk." Nixon was "playing games with the country on Vietnam."

The administration had expected such treatment from the universally hostile national papers and magazines. That's why the President
decided that TV, minus the customary press-conference format, provided the only means of going straight to the people without the interference of middlemen. And, indeed, such an approach had not always
been frowned on. Writing in the *New Yorker* shortly after John
Kennedy was elected President, Richard Rovere explained Kennedy's
similar views. "The White House knows . . . the structural flaws of the
televised press conference. It insists, nevertheless, that the President
will make as much use of TV as he can. He feels he must attempt direct
communication with the people because, in the first place, he wishes to
awaken and arouse them, and because, in the second place, he fears that

a predominantly Republican press will not deal objectively with him and his views."

In 1969 the basic situation was still the same, except that the Republican press had become a predominantly liberal press, staffed and for the most part run by people who were either trained in the Northeast or who had adopted the manners and attitudes of the corridor, members of what Irving Kristol has called "the adversary culture." And now it was a Republican rather than a Democratic President who was attempting to speak to his constituency in language they understood, over the heads of the interpreters. But now electronic journalism, like print journalism, had devised a method of distorting his words, a method that the Vice President was to call "instant analysis."

Those of us who saw the speech remember it as one of Nixon's finest performances, perhaps precisely because it so obviously was not a performance. The President was keyed high, tense, intent on convincing the people that he meant what he said, seeming almost on the verge of squeezing himself through the camera and into the living room if necessary. It was not a particularly graceful speech. It was too intense to be graceful. The message was direct. He would wind down the war, and we had his word for that. He would not allow national policy to be set by street mobs, and we had his word for that. He would also insure that we would not leave Vietnam in shame, and he promised us that too.

For the next two days the Gallup pollsters gauged the nation's reaction. It was overwhelmingly favorable. Seventy-seven percent of the people stood with the President. Not so with the TV middlemen, however. Immediately following the speech, the networks indulged in an orgy of analysis and interpretation. "Do you believe," asked ABC's Frank Reynolds of Bill Lawrence, "that there is possibly a full appreciation in the White House now of the depth of discontent with the war, the weariness, really, of the war." Seventy-seven percent of the people who heard the speech obviously weren't quite all that weary. But the media were very weary indeed.

If you saw the speech, then listened to the analysis, perhaps you shared my feeling, first of disbelief, then of outrage. I've never been an admirer of the President's rhetoric, but I believed that on that night he did his level best to explain his policies and to ask the American people for support of those policies, which, as President, he certainly has every right to do. But the networks came to criticize, to sneer and scoff. There was something incredibly cocky about it all, as if the media men had so convinced themselves of their infallibility and rectitude that they felt they had a perfect right to casually brush the whole thing off, much as if they somehow were finally responsible for the administration of the country, the President a mere interloper who just didn't understand his prerogatives.

The impudence was breathtaking, especially when ABC had the audacity to trot out W. Averell Harriman to analyze the speech. The use of Harriman as the newest electronic gimmick in a field preoccupied above all else by show-biz boffo stunned not only the Vice President. Leslie Stone, writing in the leftist British publication, the *Manchester Guardian*, makes what perhaps is the single most cogent criticism:

> No superhuman attempt at impartiality can hide the fact that many American newscasters are opposed to the Vietnam war. It will not take the most casual visitor to Washington who bothers to turn on his TV set very long to realize that CBS's Eric Sevareid would not be allowed to deliver his little homilies on British television . . . Neither would local newscasters like Tom Braden . . . and Frank Mankiewicz . . . get away with many of their value judgments in the context of a news programme.
>
> The keen rivalry between the political parties, jealously fighting to protect their own interests, helps to insure that under the British TV system a basic impartiality is maintained. It is hard to imagine the BBC allowing a former ambassador and politician [say Lord Harlech or Lord Gladwyn] to make adverse comments, however mild, immediately following a ministerial broadcast by [the Prime Minister]. But this is exactly what Agnew complains ABC permitted Averell Harriman to do after President Nixon's last TV address to the nation on Vietnam.
>
> In Britain the interview with Harriman [or his equivalent] would at the very least have to be balanced by an interview with a comparable figure on the other side: someone acceptable to the Nixon Administration or the Republican National Committee.

Precisely. What ABC did in effect was to take a cheap shot at the President. He didn't come to debate, he came to deliver an address. Harriman came to pick holes in that address before the public was allowed a decent interval to digest what was said. ABC attempted to digest it for them, and in the most hostile possible way, by bringing in an icon from the opposing party to do it. The last face the American people would remember seeing would be not that of Richard Nixon but of Averell Harriman.

Vice President Agnew was not to let Harriman creep away from the controversy in which he had tastelessly, and in a most unstatesmanlike fashion, allowed himself to become embroiled. Commenting on Harriman's instant-analysis, neopolitical criticisms, Agnew said in Des Moines: "A word about Mr. Harriman. For ten months he was America's chief negotiator at the Paris peace talks — a period in which the United States swapped some of the greatest military concessions in the history of warfare for an enemy agreement on the shape of a bargaining table. Like Coleridge's Ancient Mariner, Mr. Harriman seems to be under some heavy compulsion to justify his failures to anyone who will listen. The networks have shown themselves willing to give him all the airtime he desires."

Despite the fact that Harriman had made an error of taste and discretion, the old Camelot crew expressed horror at Agnew's treatment of him. But there was more to come. Harriman had allowed the statesmanlike mask to drop by playing petty partisan politics. And Agnew was not through with him. Harriman was a marshmallow deserving of a good roasting. And in Cleveland in 1970 Agnew continued to put a good crust on him:

In a speech six months ago [the Des Moines speech], I responded to Harriman's incessant carping at the President. For that criticism I have received the opprobrium of all those who revere Mr. Harriman as the epitome of a diplomat. I do not share that view.

As one looks back over the diplomatic disasters that have befallen the West and the friends of the West over three decades at Teheran, Yalta, Cairo — in every great diplomatic conference that turned out to be a loss for the West and freedom, one can find the unmistakable footprints of W. Averell Harriman.

It was Mr. Harriman as our Ambassador at Moscow who told the Polish Committee of National Liberation that the United States would not oppose Russian wishes on the Polish question — which effectively doomed any chance for the freedom of Poland, which of course is why the war had begun. A month after returning to the United States from his wartime chores in Moscow, Mr. Harriman was the grateful beneficiary of two fine thoroughbred horses — compliments of J. V. Stalin.

The disastrous wartime conference with the Soviets was not the last time that Mr. Harriman's penchant for trusting Communists has cost some peoples their freedom and others their lives. Speaking of the 1962 Geneva agreement — where Harriman bought the package deal of Hanoi and Moscow — Mr. Harriman stated, we got "a good agreement, better than I thought we would work out."

Mr. Robert Elegant of the Los Angeles Times describes it today a bit more accurately:

"The Geneva Agreement Ambassador Harriman signed in 1962 willfully ignored the certainty of Hanoi's using the [Ho Chi Minh] trail to invade South Vietnam — and made the conflict there inevita-

43

ble. . . . The Communists' chief channel for supplies and reinforcements, now doubly important . . . is sometimes — unkindly, but accurately — called the Averell Harriman Memorial Highway."

And so, Averell Harriman, failed statesman, partisan politician, and instant analyzer, RIP.

The White House mood the morning after the President's speech was grim. Averell Harriman's performance was bad enough. But especially galling were the comments of CBS's Marvin Kalb, who had the evening's last word on the question of whether Ho Chi Minh's response to a White House peace overture was inflexible or conciliatory. The President had just finished saying it was inflexible, and his interpretation was backed solidly by the State Department. "Kalb and the CBS State Department," cracks an administration official, "said conciliatory."

DAN RATHER: With me in our CBS studios are my colleagues CBS diplomatic correspondent Marvin Kalb and our national correspondent Eric Sevareid. Marvin Kalb, in your judgment, and let's preface this by saying, as always, this is a difficult bit of guesswork to immediately follow a Presidential address — what in your judgment is going to be the reaction in this country to the President's speech, and, after dealing with that, then overseas?

And here a brief break for this message. Notice what's going on here. You've just heard a speech by the President. You're trying to sort it out. You don't know precisely how you feel about the points he raised. But here, immediately after, is a gentleman supposedly much more knowledgeable in the field of political affairs than you, telling you how you'll react. Not much of a jump, really, to suggesting how you *should* react.

MARVIN KALB: Well, first, Dan, I'm not sure, but it seemed to me first that the speech cut no new ground. It seemed a soft-spoken straight-in-the-eye restatement of policy that clearly is not aimed at that group of Americans dubbed by Vice President Agnew as an "effete corps of impudent snobs."

Break again. The speech wasn't intended to "cut new ground." And it was aimed at the American public, *not* the impudent snobs. It wasn't intended, in other words, as an address to a convention of TV commentators.

KALB: Rather, it was aimed, as the President put it, at you, the great silent majority of my fellow Americans. Presumably those who do not demonstrate; those who want an honorable end to the war but have difficulty defining what an honorable end is and are willing to trust the President to get it.

Break: Notice condescending tone of voice. If you missed Kalb's performance, you can almost hear it dripping off the page. Gullible crew of trusting dolts, these unwashed nondemonstrating Americans, aren't they?

KALB: Those who are not so willing will point to the absence of a new announcement on troop withdrawals or a definite timetable for the total withdrawal of U.S. forces . . .

Break: Here we're being told precisely what to point to when we react to the President's speech. And funny, isn't it, that the things we're supposed to point to are exactly the things that all the liberal Democratic presidential hopefuls, plus men in search of cabinet posts in a Democratic administration, men such as Clifford and Harriman, also point to. If we didn't know better, we'd swear that Kalb and CBS were pushing the partisan liberal Democratic position. Here comes the clincher.

. . . and they may disagree with the President's judgment that the Ho Chi Minh letter was a flat rejection of his own letter. The Ho Chi Minh letter contained, it seems, some of the softest, most accommodating language found in a Communist document concerning the war in Vietnam in recent years.

And so that's what the viewer is left with. Marvin Kalb, student of Communist documents over the years, flatly contradicts the President of the U.S. And which judgment is freshest in your mind when the show signs off?

And finally, just before bedtime and hours before you'll be able to read the text of the President's speech in the morning papers, back to ABC, and that master of the anti-Nixon smear, Frank Reynolds.

FRANK REYNOLDS: . . . I think Mr. Nixon's a consummate politician. I think that around Christmastime he's going to announce a withdrawal of possibly more than 40,000 to 50,000 in a cut, and I think that Vice President Ky, whose crystal ball has been pretty good, said that by the end of 1970 there would be 180,000 Americans out of Vietnam. I think that if you're building for the 1970 election you don't blow your game all in one speech and I . . .

BILL LAWRENCE: The *President?* Playing *that* game?

Break. Here, no doubt, us we-my-fellow-Americans-gullible-silent-majority types are supposed to gasp. Revelation. Golly-wolly-crabgrass, Clara. Never thought of *that.* It's *politics.* And now, our beady little eyes sufficiently opened, back to eager Frank Reynolds, about to take up club and axe.

> FRANK REYNOLDS: Yes, and we must also recognize that this speech tonight is given just ten days before another great big demonstration that will be all over this town, you know. Apparently, Mr. Nixon has decided not to be influenced by that. It may well be that he feels there is more political advantage in giving the back of his hand to the demonstrators and standing up there as the embattled President holding firm against the onslaught of public opinion.

Now despite what Frank Reynolds thinks, a quarter- or a half-million demonstrators don't represent public opinion across the board. What they do represent is the opinion of a quarter- or a half-million demonstrators. And, of course, numerous TV commentators.

We can perhaps forgive Reynolds his statements, for the man has consistently proved himself unable to see beyond his own strongly held biases. What we have more trouble forgiving, however, is this deliberate attempt by opinion-makers who wield great influence to determine policies which the President had been elected to set. "I don't believe that the television commentators fathom their impact on the country, and they get careless — much more so than reporters," said George Christian, LBJ's former press secretary.

Carelessness or not, the Harriman–Kalb–Reynolds commentary alarmed the White House, because it threatened to blockade the one channel left for the President to communicate directly with the people who elected him. The networks had succeeded in turning a strained but desperately sincere attempt to explain policy and to ask for support of that policy into a mere self-serving political speech. The President's eye, according to Reynolds, was not on national unity but on the '70 elections. And Reynolds had the last word.

Believing that they couldn't possibly get a fair shake from the print media, Franklin Roosevelt and John Kennedy had both taken to the public air to reach people directly. But now the electronic media had finally developed a technique for dealing with the "fireside chat," a technique of instant analysis which could blunt and distort any presidential message.

Initially, the White House staff, because of the telegrammed outpour- •

ing of popular support for the President's position, was tempted just to ignore the critics and let the volume of printed messages speak for itself. But this would be an ostrichlike tactic, as LBJ's experience had proved. As one administration official puts it:

> The effect on prestige was cumulative, whittling, erosive: After every Johnson speech on Vietnam, public opinion surveys showed broad grass-roots support for his position. In time, however, his very physical authority as Chief Executive and Commander-in-Chief was diminished by exposure to a constant tug-of-opinion with his media critics and those political opponents, like Senators Robert Kennedy, McCarthy and Fulbright, favored by the liberal media.

White House staffers, deciding that above all else Nixon must avoid the trap LBJ fell into, recommended that the problem of media-bias be met head on by airing it before the people. The man for the job, it was agreed, was Spiro Agnew, Nixon's ambassador to Middle America.

Within twenty-four hours after the President's speech, work began on a major vice presidential speech on "The Responsibilities of Television." Agnew's schedule called for an address before the National Municipal League in Philadelphia that week, but the group, a public administration organization, was a bit too staid for the stemwinder Agnew had in mind. He did, however, touch upon the subject:

> The media have a tremendous obligation here as well. I recognize that the subtleties of everyday government cannot compete with axe murders. I know that reporters thrive on political controversy and publishers have to sell papers. But freedom should be tempered by responsibility. Great causes extolled on the editorial page are often lost by reporting strident opposition on the front page while supportive but less exciting news is buried somewhere between the tire advertisements and the obituary columns.

But Philadelphia wasn't the place for the big one. As it turned out, however, the administration found it couldn't afford to wait for precisely the right spot. The media had begun to beat the drums for the November 15th New Mobilization Washington Rally, and all signs pointed to the single biggest antiadministration demonstration the country had ever seen. If the administration was to beat the demonstrators to the punch, the speech had to be given immediately.

Weeks before, the Vice President had turned down an invitation to address a Midwest Regional Republican meeting at Des Moines. On the morning of November 12, as the first contingent of New Mobe marchers established their beachheads in downtown Washington to the delight of TV cameramen, the Vice President's office told Des Moines there had been a sudden change of plans and requested a meeting hall big enough for television camera crews. The word then went out to the networks that a big news story involving their interests was about to break. The advance notice resulted in an unprecedented massive national coverage of a vice presidential address and was crucial to the strategy of the speech. If Agnew's words were not carried directly to a national audience, his aides realized, the message would never come through. The interpreters would have a field day, and the next morning we would have been treated to headlines like "Agnew Calls for Censorship," or "Veep Vows to Muzzle Media."

In Des Moines the administration took the fight to the media, and after Des Moines there was no turning back. During the months to follow there would be a relentless attack on media bias, eventually forcing the networks, despite their battle cry of freedom of speech, to take a hard look at their practices. One network in particular, CBS, later decided to brazen it out and became, if anything, even more irresponsible. But on ABC the effect was salutary. ABC has now what is perhaps the best-balanced presentation of the issues of the day yet seen on TV. Commentary is always labeled as such, and there is always an attempt made to balance ideological positions.

The Des Moines speech was the most important vice presidential speech ever given, and it took the media, grown cocky and complacent over a couple of decades of basting in its biases, completely by surprise. Writes a student of the Administration:

> Coming as it did from an administration best noted for its ultracaution, the stroke had been bold and unexpected — least of all by the media. Though it was not surprising, considering the growth of media monopoly power in the twentieth century, that battle lines would form between America's political estate and its modern Fourth Estate, what did surprise was that when this confrontation finally occurred it was risked and undertaken not by a Democratic administration imbued with the anti-Eastern populism of the South and West; nor by an administration of the Left inspired by the antimonopolist gospel of a George Seldes; but, rather, by a conventional middle-class Republican administration desiring nothing so much as to keep the country and itself in the center of the road.

And so, ladies and gentlemen, to Des Moines, for the speech that shook the media world. Read it carefully, as objectively as you can. (See Appendix, p. 265.) Now, do you agree with the International Press

Institute in Zurich, a group that said Agnew presented "the most serious threat to the freedom of information in the Western world"? Or would you, as I do, agree with *New Republic* writer Bernard Hennessy, who observes in his opening sentence: "Just because Spiro Agnew has been wrong about everything else doesn't mean he's going to be wrong always." To which we respond, of course, that just because the *New Republic* has always been wrong about everything else doesn't mean that it won't occasionally contain a nugget of truth. And in Hennessy's analysis we find such a nugget.

> What did he [Agnew] say? . . . First, that Americans get most of their news and commentary on public issues from television. Second, that the decisions about what news and commentary to put on TV are made by a small number of men who are not *in any political sense* responsible to the public. Third, that such irresponsible power is dangerous because it's a threat to the open, free, and unrestricted dialogue that democracy depends on. Fourth, that there should be a wide, self- and public evaluation by, of, and about the power and performance of American TV. . . .

And even the *Washington Post*, which was later to show surprisingly strong critical judgment during the *Selling of the Pentagon* flap, demonstrated that it too was sometimes capable of being sensible. Richard Harwood and Laurence Stern warned their colleagues that the issue raised in Des Moines "is not going to evaporate in this country simply because publishers and network presidents wrap themselves in the First Amendment and sneer at Spiro Agnew. For the facts are that the media are as blemished as any other institution in this society and that there is growing public concern over their performance."

Spiro Agnew couldn't have said it better.

5

"MR. AGNEW," reported *U.S. News & World Report*, "in the first few days after his criticism of TV commentators, received more than 29,000 telegrams and seventeen sacks of mail. The communications were running roughly forty to one in his favor."

The public response for a time dampened the enthusiasm of the networks for battle. It's one thing to accuse the Vice President of attempting to impose censorship and then heroically to defy him, to the applause of your audience. But it's another to defy the wishes of that audience, especially when you discover that a vast majority of that audience hasn't been applauding at all. After all, despite the impression their executives' speeches give, TV networks aren't in the freedom-of-speech business. They're in the entertainment business, and their sole objective is to make money. Period. And when the audience isn't applauding, you worry about box office.

So for a time, the networks backed off, and it seemed that perhaps the Vice President's stated goal, to promote self-analysis and critical dialogue, had succeeded. On January 22, 1970, when the President delivered his State of the Union speech, there was little attempt at analysis, most network commentators content to summarize. "There is no doubt," said columnist Robert Novak, "that Mr. Agnew did scare the dickens out of the people on TV."

As the months passed, however, and as the media men continued to slap one another on the back and tell one another what fine, brave fellows they were, fear changed to defiance. Scarcely a day has passed since Des Moines that someone such as Norman Isaacs, president of the American Society of Newspaper Editors, who runs back and forth across the country screaming that he is being muzzled, doesn't give an address, widely covered by the media, of course, claiming that the media stand in the forefront of the fight for individual liberties. And so, inevitably, hopped up by their inbred hysterical rhetoric of rectitude and self-justification, the networks began to play politics again. In spades. And just as inevitably Vice President Agnew began again to counterattack.

The Vice President's primary target was CBS, for its "error and propagandistic manipulation" in three TV documentaries — *Hunger in America, Project Nassau* (filmed but never broadcast), and *The Selling of the Pentagon,* first shown on February 23, 1971. *Selling* especially galled Agnew, for he saw the whole thing as "a clever propaganda attempt to discredit the defense establishment of the United States." CBS, he charged, assembled officers' remarks out of context and then restructured them "to create a false impression." Interviews were obtained with "leading public figures under false pretenses." CBS, in short, according to the Vice President, falsified and distorted for clearly ideological purposes. The networks' response was, as usual, to charge Agnew with attempting to muzzle them. And, as a new wrinkle, they reran the show. Which the author sat through, like Brigadier General S. L. A. Marshall, who later described the experience in *TV Guide,* "With the aid of bourbon and branch water I managed to sit all aglow through the second showing . . ." The giggle juice helped me a bit, too, inspiring my notes, which I offer here all jaggedy, just as I took them, trying to capture that elusive something one writer has called "the rhetoric of the visual image."

> ROGER MUDD: Nothing is more essential to a democracy than the free flow of information. Misinformation, distortion, propaganda all interrupt that flow. . . .

Right on, Mudd. That's what Agnew says.

> MUDD: . . . The largest agency in our government is the Department of Defense and it maintains a public relations division to inform people of its activities . . . there have been recent charges . . . that the department is using those public relations funds not merely to inform but to convince and persuade the public on vital issues of war and peace. . . . CBS News set out to investigate these charges. . . . We began at . . . Armed Forces Day on . . . Fort Jackson, South Carolina. . . . The major event is a firepower display . . . they not only shoot, they also instruct.

And suddenly you sit a bit straighter, for the word *instruct* has been peculiarly emphasized in Mudd's introduction. *What* are people being

51

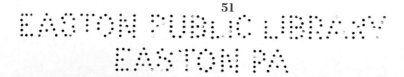

instructed in? *Who* is being instructed? Mudd's Southern-gentlemanly voice is suddenly cut by flat military tones.

INSTRUCTOR: The killing zone is fifty meters deep, fifty meters wide. . . .

The *killing* zone. So that's it. They're instructing people in *killing*.

MUDD: . . . The last part of the demonstration is known as the "mad minute.". . .

Your ears are assaulted by wild concerted firing, the soldiers unloading their weapons as rapidly as they can. Mayhem.

MUDD: [Tone icy, contemptuous] It would be hard to argue with that description.

And now the first doubts arise. Is this *really* an exposé of the Pentagon's PR division? Or is there something more involved, some deeper and more basic purpose?

MUDD: When the demonstration itself is over, another activity begins. The ammunition is gone but the weapons are not. Some of these are turned over to children.

My God. *Children.* Up to now you've wondered just what CBS was up to. It all seemed like damned good entertainment, and the citizens of South Carolina seemed to be getting a kick out of it, just like you get a kick out of any well-staged spectacle. But *children.*

FIRST CHILD: All right, Jack, here's a cool tank, man.
SECOND CHILD: I'm going over to the other tank.
THIRD CHILD: Get off —
FIRST CHILD: What are you doing?
THIRD CHILD: I'm going to shoot you.
SECOND CHILD: Ready — aim — fire!

Handsome, towheaded, clean-cut American kids. And they're being *instructed*, all right, instructed in *killing*. Kids. Killing. Aargh. And for the moment, at least, you forget about the whole PR angle and get the deeper message. Damn *all* those bloodthirsty military men. Now we zoom out to Peoria, to pick up briefly the comments of "a team of colonels touring the country to lecture on foreign policy." CBS "found

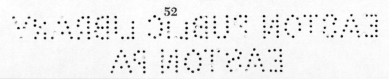

them in Peoria, Illinois, where they were invited to speak to a mixed audience of civilians and military reservists. The invitation was arranged by Peoria's Caterpillar Tractor Company, which did $39 million of business last year with the Defense Department." (Not true. The appearance *wasn't* arranged by the Caterpillar Tractor Company.)

. . . The Army has a regulation stating: "Personnel should not speak on the foreign policy implications of U.S. involvement in Vietnam."

Then comes the voice of a Colonel MacNeill, apparently doing just that, speaking out on implications of foreign policy:

COLONEL MACNEILL: Well, now we're coming to the heart of the problem — Vietnam. Now the Chinese have clearly and repeatedly stated that Thailand is next on their list after Vietnam. If South Vietnam becomes Communist it will be difficult for Laos to exist. The same goes for Cambodia and the other countries of Southeast Asia. I think if the Communists were to win in South Vietnam, the record in the North — what happened in Tet of '68 — makes it clear there would be a bloodbath in store for a lot of the population of the South. The United States is still going to remain an Asian power.

Break. Let me here briefly interrupt myself and jump ahead a bit. This last quote is one of the most controversial and has much to do with the charge of distortion levelled against CBS. "If the TV audience sensed that [these] five sentences, out of the mouth of Colonel MacNeill, sounded somewhat disjointed," says Claude Witze, senior editor of *Air Force* magazine, "there was good reason for it. They came from four different spots in the camera record. . . ."

CBS, in other words, took sentences from various parts of Colonel MacNeill's talk, then spliced them together to give the impression that the remarks had been made in sequence. Thus, the first sentence beginning "Well, now . . ." comes from page fifty-five of the briefing. The second sentence comes from page thirty-six, the next two from page forty-eight. The last two are the most controversial sentences in the sequence, flatly and dogmatically stating as they do the media-discredited domino theory. And, indeed, as they stand, they seem to amount to a clear-cut violation of the rule about not speaking out on the foreign-policy implications of Vietnam that Mudd warned us about. Indeed, within the short section, it is the *only* clear-cut violation of that regulation. One can, I think, say that those sentences ("If South Vietnam becomes Communist, it will be difficult for Laos to exist. The same goes for Cambodia and the other countries of Southeast Asia.") are essential to underscore Mudd's point, the point being that the "traveling team of colonels" regularly violates at least one standing Army regulation.

However, as is now well known, CBS tried a bit of skullduggery here. Colonel MacNeill did not in fact himself make that flat assertion. He was quoting Prime Minister Souvanna Phouma of Laos, but CBS rather carefully edited out the attribution. The full transcript actually runs this way:

> Now the Prime Minister is Souvanna Phouma, a very shrewd old man. He has an enormous problem on his hands today. Plain des Jarres has been completely reoccupied and he has about 740 to 750 [garbled] refugees from the eastern half of Laos — this brown area [referring to map] — which is held by the Pathet Lao Communists. They are being fed today in the Mekong River, primarily by Thailand, but the United States is also helping.
>
> Now Souvanna's position on North Vietnam was pretty clearly stated in November, 1967. He said that, "We can count 400,000 North Vietnamese in our country" — On his visit here last year, he raised the figure to 600,000 — "They fight beside the 15,000 Pathet Laos who are armed, paid, trained, and encadred by North Vietnam. By what right, what moral, do they assume the right to liberate us? If South Vietnam becomes Communist, it will be difficult for Laos to exist. The same goes for Cambodia and the other countries of Southeast Asia." Now we'll go back to the heavy red line we mentioned a few minutes ago, the Ho Chi Minh Trail.

Now read the statement as CBS presented it. There's a difference, isn't there? The colonel's statement as spliced in by CBS comes across as a flat personal assertion. But a reading of the full transcript shows that he never made the statement at all. He was quoting, and within the context of the quote, a wide-ranging situational briefing, the offending two sentences seem less assertive and less emotional.

What CBS has done, not to mince words, is to fake it.

When questioned on this point, Richard Salant, CBS news chief, was evasive. "In that same interview," he stated, "Souvanna Phouma gave a warning about going into Laos which the Colonel did not quote. . . ." Now this is a strange defense indeed. Why *should* the Colonel have repeated that warning? The implication in Mr. Salant's response is that the military views the North Vietnamese invasion of Laos in one way, ours in another. Yet, as *Human Events* Capitol Hill Editor Allan H. Ryskind points out, "Colonel MacNeill quoted the Souvanna statement in Peoria on May 14, 1970 — some eight months before the Laos incursion."

The CBS response to the various documented charges of error and misrepresentation always takes the same tack. You point to an obvious example, prove it, and CBS officials make countercharges — you want censorship, you want to muzzle the media, you're a threat to "the people's right to know." Thus the Vice President charges the network with acting in bad faith. The networks' response is never to attempt to *disprove* the charges. It is always, rather, to scream "intimidation."

But forgive this rather long station break. Back to *The Selling of the Pentagon.* Having discredited "the colonels," we now zoom out to St. Paul where, in a shopping mall, an Army display, Roger Mudd tells us, "emphasizes power, a recurrent theme in Defense Department public relations programs." *Power.* Aargh. And there're those *kids* again, good clean-cut towheads, getting sucked in (this time, we're also treated to a good boobish CBS-selected father, one of those middle-American fascist types). *Damn* those militarists. *Power. Kids.* Aargh.

Now a short quick look at some sharp flying by the Air Force Thunderbirds. Damned good show.

MUDD: The Air Force Thunderbirds flew 108 exhibitions last year in front of six million people. We were told that the Thunderbirds are supposed to attract volunteers, but what we found was a very elaborate commercial for air power.

And then on — but wait a minute, Mudd. Is that all? "We were told . . . but? . . ." Do you mean they *don't* attract volunteers? And how could that stunt flying *help* but be an "elaborate commercial?" And where's the proof such "elaborate commercials" don't attract volunteers?

Now a quick couple of shots showing Marine General Lewis Walt lecturing. An impassioned man, Billy Grahamish sort of delivery — a touch of the *South*, and we know what *that* means. Militarists, racists — get it? Now to a Green Berets demonstration:

GREEN BERET ANNOUNCER: Please pay particular attention to the hands, the elbows, the knees, and the toe of the boot, which are used to deliver killing blows to the vulnerable portions of the body.

MUDD: When it comes to sheer muscle, the legendary Green Berets are the Army's glamor exhibit. In twenty-one states last year, the Berets showed how people kill people sometimes. On one occasion, they showed about a thousand kids in New Jersey. When the Berets finished their act, the audience had its own turn.

CHILD: C'mon . . . no! Damn you . . . ow! [crying]

Get the message? "Killing blows," "how people kill people," "a thousand kids," then little towheads again, practicing killing, with animal screams of "kill" in the background. And end with a sobbing child. And you realize by now that *The Selling of the Pentagon* has really nothing at all to do with the Department of Defense's public relations program. The PR angle simply provides a way in, a way to structure the show. No, what we're seeing is a profoundly antimilitary film, an all-out artistic attempt to discredit the military and everything it stands for. And, I suppose, given the inbuilt bias of the Eastern media man, it would be difficult to explain to him why this might be *wrong*, why there might be a very real danger in undercutting the profession of arms.

The Vice President, speaking in Los Angeles last April, quoted a young Army major with a Purple Heart, back from two tours in Vietnam, who is leaving the service: "People don't respect the man in uniform any more. The nation doesn't support its fighting men. My wife has to explain to the kids that daddy's job isn't wrong, that it isn't something to be ashamed of. That's no way to live."

It's hard, I know, in 1971, to stand up for the military — hard because there seems no common language in use these days with which to build a convincing case. Such terms as "honor," "discipline," "courage," "self-sacrifice," "duty," "patriotism," are simply not understood or are understood as code words for some baser concept. Thus, for "patriotism" read "chauvinism" or "jingoism" or "sabre-rattling." For "courage" substitute "need to prove masculinity." For "discipline" read "Puritanism." And so it goes. Admiral Moorer, quoted by Agnew, says: "The American people can't have it both ways. They can't on one hand insist on an adequate defense against this buildup of capabilities on the part of potential enemies and on the other hand demean and degrade those in uniform."

Now this is a sensible statement, yet I'm not sure it shows a sufficient understanding of what's going on in the country. Most Americans don't demean those in uniform. But the opinion-makers do. Read any of the weekly magazines, any of the large daily papers. Story after story on race problems in the armed services, stories on the drug problem, stories on growing GI antiwar sentiment, stories on the massacres we have allegedly committed. Find me *one* story which praises the military in any way, show me *one* major TV network on which a pro or even a slightly favorable stance toward the military is taken, and, as a vice presidential speechwriter might say, I'll festively eat your fabulous fedora.

There is no doubt that the intellectual community has gone to war against the military. Why? I'm not at all sure. The majority of American intellectuals, I suppose, currently believe they pledge allegiance to a pacifist tradition, for one thing. And for another, the thrust of American intellectualism has always been leftward, and since all the major menaces to world peace today are mounted by leftist nations, I suppose they find the idea of having to take up arms against Marxist People's Republics abhorrent. There has always, of course, been an inability among American intellectuals to see what in reality goes on in Communist countries. When Hitler and Stalin signed their agreement to divide up Europe between them, American intellectuals couldn't (and still can't) believe that Stalin was anywhere near as bad as Hitler. Soviet murders have traditionally been explained away as necessary to "consolidate the revolution" (also, see the apologies for China and Cuba). And so, for instance, it seems perfectly consistent for Andrew Kopkind, writing in the *New York Review of Books*, to equate the Russian crushing of Czechoslovakia with the American intervention in the Dominican Republic.

But are American liberals really all that pacifistic? Would they scream too loudly, for instance, if we decide to intervene in South Africa or Greece, countries in which they profess to believe the horrors are just as great as they are, say, in a Soviet concentration camp?

No, it's not quite a pacifistic tradition. Remember, for instance, that as recently as the Kennedy Administration military men were honored by many liberals, and the Kennedy view of the world and our role in it required the cooperation of the military. And those of us who served in the fifties or even in the early sixties remember a much different attitude toward servicemen than the one that seems fashionable today. The country's pride in us resulted in pride in ourselves. We were somewhat cynical, of course — all troops are cynical — but we were proud of our function, and we had a great deal of self-respect. But given the mood of the nation today, that seems like a century ago.

I don't think the majority of American military men are totally disillusioned yet, but many of them are becoming increasingly demoralized. They are attacked on the campuses, assaulted by the national media, sneered at by the intellectual establishment. Given the strength of the concerted assault, led by those who control the information centers of the country, it would be strange indeed if there did not grow among many military men a feeling that they have been sold out by their countrymen, whose best interests they have pledged themselves to serve. And if a centurion complex ever takes hold among our career military men, we may find ourselves in the most dangerous period in American history.

The attack upon the military is largely due to conditioned reflex leftism. But there is always the danger of overideologizing, and much of the unthinking assault is simply the result of fashion. Fashion has a great deal to do with attitudes. It used to be brave to be brave. Now among the young it is brave to be cowardly. And just as the youth cult has steadily radicalized American campuses and their inhabitants, so too have the same attitudes crept into the media, where it is necessary to keep up in order to make money. And today it is fashionable to be antimilitary.

Vietnam, as usual, has a lot to do with it. Disillusionment with Vietnam, shared equally by students and professors and writers and talkers, has grown into a cult of disillusionment with all things patriotic. Once it was fashionable to support the war effort. Now it is fashionable to belittle it in every way possible, and the best way, apparently, has become to undercut the military.

This is obviously what CBS set out to do in *The Selling of the Pentagon*. And in so doing, it took a good snobbish swipe at all those middle American Babbitt philistine rotarian types who let themselves be hoodwinked by the military.

MUDD: Each year, the Pentagon runs special guided tours for over 3,000 influential civilians. . . . The guests are referred to as "major taxpayers." . . .

Focus on a fat face, a rather boobish looking cigar chomper. After a display of weaponry, one of the guests says: "At Fort Hood we were seated in the gunner's seat of the M–60 tanks, and we fired the rifles, and were told what excellent shots we were. . . ." "We fired tank cannon and recoilless rifles, . . ." says another. "It was fun to actually get your finger on the trigger," says a third, in tones intended no doubt by the producer to be unconsciously chilling. And always the closeup — fat cigars, bellies, blank expressions, the same technique of camera selectivity, really, that you notice in televised football, where one cameraman seems to spend the entire game looking for a pretty pair of legs or an interesting chest to zoom in on.

And now we're coming up on commercial time, but a few statements just before the break to keep us thinking. "One of the things I can personally see from this tour is that a lot of the statements that for example Mr. Fulbright and Mr. Proxmire make are absolutely baseless." "As we proceeded through numerous phases where we were personally involved," says the last "major taxpayer" just before the break, "my opinion has changed 180 degrees."

And there's quite a message for us to mull over. First, I suppose, we're to realize that these middle-American types are awful boobs. Just let them fire a few guns, mingle with the brass, and they're converted. To what? "I just wish that all the American people could see what we've seen. I think we'd find much less of this carping at the military and we'd find a lot more understanding." Understanding of what? Why, promilitary points of view, of course. And what's wrong with that? Well —. Well, we're never quite told. It's just *wrong*. The closest we get to an explanation of *why* it's wrong is when the fat cat criticizes Fulbright and Proxmire, both of whom are antimilitary. Since the man who made the statement is being satirized, his view lampooned, and since in his jackass wrongheaded way he attacks Fulbright and Proxmire, must be that the standard CBS uses to judge these things is the same standard embraced by Fulbright and Proxmire. There's just no *question* that those two could be wrong. Which sort of takes us back to where we started, doesn't it? That inbuilt liberal bias, always there, always following the current liberal trend.

Now back to Mudd, who chaperones us through a bunch of anti-Communist movies made by such organizations as CBS (he forgets to tell us that). His voice drips with scorn, his tone ridiculing those who could take such things as Communist menaces seriously.

MUDD: The Department of Defense believes that one of the best ways to save Americans from a red nightmare that comes true is with films like these. Although the Pentagon labels them informational, these films contain a high proportion of propaganda, as well as an obsession with monolithic communism. Tax money financed them all. . . . It has been more than a decade since the national policy of peaceful coexistence replaced the harsher rhetoric of the cold war years. But to the film makers at the Pentagon, 1946 seems to have lasted a whole generation.

You'll notice here that Mudd seems increasingly unwilling to let the pictures do the talking for him and seems bent on editorializing. And we owe him our thanks for ending the cold war and legitimizing the "national policy of peaceful coexistence." No doubt CBS will now draw up the official documents for the President to sign. Comments Brigadier General S. L. A. Marshall: "Mudd's most shining moment was when he ended the Cold War by CBS fiat, thereby felling at a blow the Pentagon jingoes who think it is still going, while failing to remark that two former Secretaries of State suffer the same illusion."

Now on to the Pentagon itself, and a chat with "a careful and respected adversary, Deputy Assistant Secretary of State Jerry Friedheim. He does not, of course, tell all he knows; he wouldn't have his job long if he did." So here's the liaison man with the press. Mudd, having already established that he will speak with a forked tongue, gives us a taste of this serpent's evasiveness. The first half-dozen sentences we hear him say run like this: "I can't discuss that at all." "I just don't have anything I can give you on that." "We'll have to check back and find that date for you." "Negative. It has not." His final comment: "That's correct." Not very gregarious, is he? Odd, though, isn't it, that while he gave numerous answers to questions, CBS decided to focus on the no-comment types?

Now, over to Assistant Secretary of Defense Daniel Henkin, the man in charge of Pentagon public relations and the most important figure interviewed in this section. The meat of his comments comes in two responses, well worth looking at not only because of what they say but also because of what CBS arranged them to say. And we can, believe it or not, thank the *Washington Post* for first publicizing this particular irregularity. What we *heard* was this:

MUDD: What about your public displays of military equipment at state fairs and shopping centers — what purpose does this serve?

HENKIN: Well, I think it serves the purpose of informing the public about their Armed Forces. I believe that the American public has a right to request information about the Armed Forces, to have speakers come before them, to ask questions, and to understand the need for our Armed Forces, why we ask for the funds that we do ask for, how we spend these funds, what we are doing about such problems as drugs — and we do have a drug problem in the Armed Forces. What we are doing about the racial problem in the Armed Forces, and we do have a racial problem. I think the public has a valid right to ask us these questions.

That's how we *heard* it. Now this is the way Henkin *really* answered the question:

MR. HENKIN: Well, I think it serves the purpose of informing the public about their Armed Forces. It also has the ancillary benefit, I would hope, of stimulating interest in recruiting as we move or try to move to zero draft calls and increased reliance on volunteers for our Armed Forces. I think it is very important that the American youth have a chance to learn about the Armed Forces.

Quite a difference, isn't there? The second response, which is the actual, undoctored one, makes a good deal of sense. Everyone wants to abolish the draft, move toward an all-volunteer army. Or so they say. So how better to attract young volunteers than to present as attractive a picture as possible, even if this requires a bit of PR pizzazz? Henkin's was an intelligent response, but it wasn't suitable for CBS. Deep down, one suspects, the hatred for the military has become so well rooted that they really no longer want an all-volunteer army or, for that matter, any army at all. Thus, an intelligent response, especially important because it speaks directly to one of the central questions raised in the show — *why* Pentagon PR? — is cut, and a stumbling statement on the *important* things — dope and race — is spliced in, a statement made elsewhere in response to a rather impudent leading question.

Now we get a Southern Congressman. Southerners are real safe targets, you know — racism, militarism, violence — all that sort of stuff. You'll never go broke attacking Southerners.

The victim is Louisiana Representative F. Edward Hébert, an outspoken critic of the media ("I'm one of those who believes that it's the most vicious instrument in America today"). Sin number one. Sin number two is that Hébert is a strong supporter of the military. And sin number three, of course, is that he is a Southerner.

MUDD: Using sympathic Congressmen, the Pentagon tries to counter what it regards as the antimilitary tilt of network reporting. [My God, Mudd, how could it come to a conclusion like that?] War heroes are made available for the taped home district TV reports from pro-Pentagon politicians. Here Representative F. Edward Hébert . . . asks Major James Rowe, a Green Beret and former POW, what keeps the Viet Cong fighting.

Star-spangled background, short-haired military type, Congressman Hébert, his deep South inflections striking, a shiny Southern bourbon non-Brooksy suit.

MAJOR ROWE: The support that the VC receives from the United States is the only thing that keeps them fighting.

MUDD: Later, Congressman Hébert, who is the new chairman of the House Armed Services Committee, asks Major Rowe for his reaction to a peace rally.

ROWE: I walked up and I heard one of the speakers yelling, "Down with imperialism, down with capitalism, down with the oppressive leadership in Washington. Power to the people." I heard the same thing from the Viet Cong, except there it was in Vietnamese and here it was in English. I looked around the crowd — I walked through the crowd, and I saw some VC flags flying from the Washington monument, I saw American flags with VC flags flying over the top of them. I saw American flags with the stars removed and a peace

61

symbol superimposed. I saw the red flag with a black peace symbol on it and then I heard one of my Senators say that "We are here because we cherish our flag." And the only thing I could think of in answer is what flag does he cherish?

After his four-paragraph hit-and-run job, Mudd moves on. But perhaps we should pause for just a moment, because someone is lying here. When Mudd says that the Pentagon "uses" sympathetic Congressmen and "supplies" war heroes, we are to assume that Hébert's interview is a typical example of this sort of manipulation. But, says Hébert, it's false from the word go. First of all, he says, the show was entirely his own idea, and it was *not* "planned to counter network TV reporting." It was planned by Hébert for his own local TV show in his district because he thought his constituents should see Major Rowe. Furthermore, Major Rowe was not "supplied" by the Pentagon. Representative Hébert picked him out himself, and the Major appeared at Hébert's invitation. In fact, says Hébert, the false impression was such that one first-rate reporter referred to it as an "Army-produced" film. "The interview," Hébert states, "was not an Army-produced film. None of the military services had anything to do with the film. The film was made here in the capitol and it was paid for by WWL-TV in New Orleans."

Strange, isn't it, to introduce an interview which has nothing to do with the Pentagon's PR division into a show purporting to expose the excesses of that division's operations? But, as has been mentioned before, the investigation of the PR division is only the ostensible purpose of the show. The real purpose is to take as many swipes as possible, from as many directions as possible, at the institution of the military and those who support it.

Thus the careful attention to Major Rowe's speech. Here Mudd doesn't need to editorialize. He knows that all right-thinking people will get the message. The major, like any true product of an essentially fascistic system, is against the dissenters. When he says that peace demonstrations give comfort to the Communists, we all know what *that* means. All together, now — McCarthyism. Agnewism. And that bit about the Senator cherishing the flag. The purest sort of smear, even worse than Agnew saying that Humphrey is soft on communism.

And no matter that there is a very real problem here for those honestly opposed to our involvement in Vietnam. The peace movement, many of us believe, has been captured by leftist organizations, an assortment of groups ranging from Trotskyite to Anarchist, but sharing one basic philosophical and social commitment — a commitment to Marxism. All of these groups not only oppose our involvement; they root actively for a North Vietnamese victory, just as they root for Communist victories in every Southeast Asian country. These are the people who seem to control the movement's funds, who provide the organizing know-how. Their program for the U.S. reads exactly like the North Vietnamese program for the U.S., and it is no mere coincidence that every massive antiwar protest is kicked off with a telegram of congratulations from the North Vietnamese and the Viet Cong.

No matter how much liberals prefer not to think about it, there is one inescapable fact underlying every antiwar protest. And that fact is that every such protest is seen by the Viet Cong and the North Vietnamese as an outpouring of support by the American people. The North Vietnamese say so freely, but apparently the drill is to make believe they don't.

And so, every time a sincerely troubled liberal marches, he finds himself, literally, marching under the banners of the Viet Cong. If you've ever attended one of these demonstrations, you'll know that the Viet Cong flag is everywhere. Thus it is very difficult indeed for a protester to separate the antiwar part of his protest from the pro-Viet Cong. People such as Major Rowe who have fought in Indochina and who have spent time as prisoners naturally see such protests as giving comfort to the enemy. And plain common sense argues that they have every right in the world to do so.

I am not insisting that I am right about the composition of the leadership of the peace movement, but I know absolutely that I am right when I say that Hanoi is all for bigger and better demonstrations. And I think this view should be accorded at least the same amount of respect as the views of Edward Kennedy — that these are just idealistic kids, it's a smear to link the peace movement in any way with anti-Americanism, that we are losing in Vietnam because we are morally wrong, that the U.S. military is consciously engaging in genocide.

Major Rowe's comments may not reflect the whole picture, but they certainly touch a part of it, and I find it just as objectionable to depict him as a fascist militaristic beast as CBS apparently finds it objectionable to suggest that peace demonstrations raise morale in Hanoi.

Now we're flying. As the program nears the end, most of the pretense has been dropped, and the show becomes more openly an antimilitary tract. The editorial thrust now becomes a simple one, boiling down to an attack on the war in Vietnam and the militaristic cast of mind which got us into this barbarous misadventure.

MUDD: Defense Department information machinery is well established in Vietnam, where a special language has developed that takes some time to learn. "Protective reaction" means the United States resumed the bombing of North Vietnam. "Selective ordnance" means napalm. "Defoliation" means nothing will grow there any more. A "civilian irregular defense group volunteer" is a mercenary. "Population resettlement" means getting villagers out of their villages, and "Military Assistance Command Daily Press Briefing" means this scene right here, which is popularly known among newsmen in Saigon as the Five O'clock Follies. The most popular phrase at these sessions, however, needs no explanation.

Strange. Mudd's contemptuous analysis of military jargon, and the horrors — from his point of view — that this jargon designates, sounds much like an analysis I heard an SDSer make a few years ago at Berkeley, before the radical-chic crowd caught on that it's fashionable to be antimilitary (American military, that is). But people like Mudd wouldn't keep their jobs long if they didn't keep up with the in-things. Mudd is a doctrinaire peacenik these days. His sideburns are also noticeably longer.

But on to this session, the most popular phrase of which needs no explanation.

ARMY BRIEFER: No comment. Nothing further to say.

FIRST REPORTER: Well, can you please tell us . . .

ARMY BRIEFER: I have nothing further to add to the statement read.

SECOND REPORTER: Why don't you answer my question?

ARMY BRIEFER: I repeat I have no comment.

Again, that's it. We discover later that the briefer gave numerous answers. CBS chose from among them only those of the no-comment variety. We never get to hear the text of that statement alluded to, and we're left with the picture of a barking, sullen, uncooperative servant of the military machine. No need for editorializing here. The image provides all the necessary rhetoric.

Now a disturbed ex–Air Force information officer, who ties everything up neatly for us, pulling PR, Vietnam, and militarism together.

TOLBERT: I feel that the military information arm is so vast, has been able to become so pervasive by the variety and the amounts and the way and the sheer numbers it's able to present its viewpoint to the American people. I think this attitude it was able to develop allowed Vietnam to happen. Had we not been able to convince the American people prior to Vietnam that a military solution was a correct solution, without a doubt and not to be questioned, we couldn't have had a Vietnam. I feel that if we allow this pervasiveness to continue, that frankly it could lead us to another Vietnam.

Now this is an extremely important statement, coming as it does just before Mudd's summary. And, if I may speak just a bit strongly, it's breathtaking in its idiocy.

First, as to the vastness and pervasiveness of this military information arm. We saw brief shows and exhibits in South Carolina, St. Paul, Peoria. How many such shows have *you* seen lately? I spent a month looking for one after the first showing of *Selling*. The nearest one to me, I discovered, was in North Carolina. So sure am I of this, that I'd like to issue a challenge to Roger Mudd right now. If he can, without searching for several weeks, find one of these spectaculars within driving distance of CBS studios in New York, I promise to grow a pair of media-man sideburns. If he can't, he is to get a crew cut. Pervasive they may be, although I can't find any. On the other hand, I can walk three feet from this typewriter and find CBS immediately. As can most of the other people in the country. All of which is a long way of saying that many more Americans are influenced daily by CBS than they are by an occasional military air show.

Then, Tolbert proceeds to tell us that we went into Vietnam because we were conditioned by the military. Absolute rubbish. We went into Vietnam because Presidents Kennedy and Johnson and their cabinets and the majority of our liberal legislators led us there. Kennedy and Johnson may have been unduly influenced by training films and lectures in Peoria. But the rest of us went because we generally tend to trust our elected leaders. That's what democracy is all about. Vietnam was primarily a civilian operation, conceived, produced, and directed by two Democratic civilian administrations run by people such as Robert McNamara and Clark Clifford. These men conditioned the military; indeed, most military men had grave reservations about the whole undertaking. Probably the only way we could have avoided Vietnam would have been to have an elected militarist like Douglas MacArthur, who abhorred precisely that kind of war. And please do remember, Tolbert, that a military man named Eisenhower kept us out of Indochina. It took a civilian, John Kennedy, to get us in.

And, finally, Mudd, his wrap-up statement epitomizing all the currently fashionable antimilitary clichés. The key section:

MUDD: Tonight we have seen violence made glamorous, expensive weapons advertised as if they were automobiles, biased opinions presented as straight facts. Defending the country not just with arms but also with ideology, Pentagon propaganda insists on America's role as the cop on every beat in the world. Not only the public but the press as well has been beguiled, including at times, ourselves at CBS News. This propaganda barrage is the creation of a runaway bureaucracy that frustrates attempts to control it.

I suppose, if you felt like it, you could fiddle a bit with this overeditorialized piece of rhetoric (the strongest points of which were not substantiated in the show itself) and come up with something like this:

On this broadcast we have seen, through selective close-ups and artistic juxtapositions, the U.S. military and the people who support it depicted as cretins who find violence glamorous; expensive weapons depicted as toys of the military, with no reference made to their necessity in a heavily armed and hostile world; biased opinions presented as straight facts or pictures. The notion of defending the country is held to be implicitly ludicrous, and CBS can see no connection whatsoever between foreign upheavals and wars and American well-being. Both the public and the press, which awarded this show an Emmy, have been beguiled, especially those among us who came away half-believing the Pentagon has anything like the day-to-day influence on the public that CBS enjoys. This propaganda barrage is the creation of a runaway monopoly that refuses to discipline itself and which there is no official way of controlling.

The Selling of the Pentagon was a very bad show, no major portion of which was free from distortion, misrepresentation, and outright falsehood. Its ostensible purpose was to investigate a PR operation. Its real purpose was to discredit everything military. And in the end, among those whose minds were already made up, those who mistake their biases for truth, it was a success.

Thus far it seems impossible to get any sort of straight discussion whatsoever from CBS. True, after the second showing, they allowed criticism from Vice President Agnew. But he was not allowed the time to present his case fully, and his request to be allowed to edit his own remarks was refused summarily. Representative Hébert was treated in a similarly perfunctory fashion. A questioner kept pushing him to say that producing the film constituted an "un-American act." After having the word "un-American" shoved at him sufficiently, he finally allowed as how it was — another instance, as in "Humphrey Soft on Communism," of letting your interrogator make his point by forcing you to use

66

his words. And we all know what the word *un-American* implies when used by a Southerner.

"Finally," as S. L. A Marshall puts it, "the best possible anticlimax was CBS News Chief Richard S. Salant's avowal of unimpeachable virtue, since morality, like chastity, is most dubitable when heaviest vaunted."

6

I DON'T mean this to be a chronicle of the transgressions of CBS. But I find the refusal of the network to speak directly to the charges made against it, and the way in which the refusal is made, and the nature of the charges themselves, to be highly significant. The attitudes underlying that adversary culture which the Vice President has made it his political work to examine and criticize.

A very strong bias exists among most members of America's intellectual establishment, be they professors, writers, artists, or media men. The reaction to being charged with this bias usually falls into three patterns: You can claim you are not biased, as do, for instance, people like Walter Cronkite and Richard Salant. But this response is always purely rhetorical — that is, you maintain that because I say I am not biased, I am therefore quite obviously not biased.

The second response is that of people like David Brinkley and an increasingly large number of trained newsmen like Thomas Winship, editor of the *Boston Globe,* who admit that they are biased, but necessarily so, since objectivity is not possible to human beings, and without objectivity there must be bias.

The third response follows quite naturally from the second — you quite readily admit to your bias, for you believe it is necessary. That is, you are *right,* your bias being the only sensible standard for conduct that you can discover. And because you are right, your job is to teach, to convince others of the rightness of your bias. Although the most honest, this last response is also the most dangerous, for the longer and more fervently you believe it, the more likely you are to confuse that bias with absolute truth.

In the Vice President's running battle with CBS, he has come up mostly against the first type, the first response being the least intelligent and the least intelligent of the members of the intellectual establishment tending to gravitate toward TV, an emotional rather than an intelligent medium. And it's not only the Vice President who gets emotional rhetorical treatment. When the *Washington Post* criticized CBS for its dishonest editing of *The Selling of the Pentagon*, CBS responded in much the same way it responds to Agnew. Richard Salant wrote a long letter of complaint, full of emotionalisms and catch phrases, without one substantive sentence. There are numerous references to the First Amendment, which Mr. Salant interprets so broadly that one suspects it covers the missing buttons on the shirts he sends out to Chinese hand laundries. He completely misunderstands the way in which the print media edit. (Example: If I found a quotation from Miss Twinkle Esther Clumb, in which she said, "John Lindsay has a heart of gold, a warm personality, and an IQ of forty-eight," I would probably, given my own biases and the biases of the periodicals I write for, quote Miss Clumb in this way: "John Lindsay has . . . an IQ of forty-eight." Now I've deleted a great deal, and I could be charged with distorting Miss Clumb's statement. But professional ethics require that I use that ellipsis, and any thoughtful reader will know immediately that something is missing. Television has nothing equivalent, and indeed, if *The Selling of the Pentagon* can be taken as typical, it goes out of its way to disguise the effect that an ellipsis automatically has in print.) And, as at the end of *The Selling of the Pentagon,* his refutation is entirely emotional and rhetorical.

"We believe," he tells the *Washington Post,* "as I have said publicly before [as if that made a difference], that *The Selling of the Pentagon* was edited fairly and honestly. Long after the useful and valuable debate on this broadcast has subsided and perhaps been forgotten we shall be editing other news broadcasts and other documentaries as fairly and as honestly. . . ."

That is the essence of Salant's second and, one presumes, unless the magic key is found, final comment on the show, and it's just as meaningless as his televised Checkers-speech refutation of the Vice President's charges made on March 18th in Boston.

Agnew, intent on showing that CBS had consistently acted in bad faith by routinely distorting significant sections of its documentaries, singled out, in addition to *The Selling of the Pentagon,* the CBS productions *Hunger in America* and *Project Nassau.*

"Many in this audience," said the Vice President, "may have been watching on the evening of May 21, 1968, when the attention of millions of Americans tuned to CBS television was drawn to the onscreen image of an infant receiving emergency treatment while a narrator's offscreen voice said:

"'Hunger is easy to recognize when it looks like this. This baby is dying of starvation. He was an American. Now he is dead.' "

Dramatic and heart-gripping. But a lie. The Federal Communications Commission reported: "Our postbroadcast investigation revealed that the infant who was filmed by CBS in the nursery, and who was shown in the relevant segment of the 'Hunger in America' program . . . was born prematurely . . . apparently as the result of a fall taken by the mother on the previous day. . . . The death certificate shows the cause of death as 'Immediate cause: Septicemia. Due to: Prematurity.' There is no evidence to show that either the mother or the father was suffering from malnutrition."

"Thus," said Agnew, "although the dramatic footage which opened the documentary *Hunger in America* may have served the network's purpose of whetting viewer interest, the baby shown 'dying of starvation' in fact died of other causes." In other words, CBS was caught faking it, and as the Vice President points out, much of the rest of the documentary was similarly faked. And what was Salant's response to this charge? Well, he implied that there may have been some irregularities, but hinted that some sort of investigation was still going on. CBS had, he assured us, "An answer for every one of the criticisms you've heard," but, he quickly added, he could answer "only a few charges" because of time. (Funny, isn't it, that the president of CBS News can't take a few extra minutes to clear things up once and for all, especially when the show has run past 11 P.M. anyhow, and there's nothing of any importance scheduled to follow it?)

One of the "few charges" that he chose to answer "involves," as Agnew says, "the participation of CBS personnel in an aborted effort to film a 1966 invasion of Haiti."

The whole astounding story of *Project Nassau*, as it unfolded before a House Commerce subcommittee, reads, as *Washington Post* staffer William Chapman puts it, "like a comic-opera cross-pollination of James Bond and Marshall McLuhan."

According to the House Report, CBS provided funds for the leasing of a sixty-seven-foot schooner which was to be used by the invasion force; reimbursed the would-be invaders for the expenses incurred in running the necessary guns to the jumping-off point; made payments to the leader of the conspiracy "with full knowledge of his identity and his criminal intentions." CBS, in other words, actually took part in an active conspiracy to invade a foreign country in order to get a hard-hitting documentary. As Representative John E. Moss (D., Calif.) put it: "When news becomes such a valuable commodity that it has to be manufactured and involves relations with other countries, it breaches any bounds of reasonableness."

"If these acts did not actually involve the network in the conspiracy

70

to violate the U.S. Neutrality Act," concluded the House Report, "they came dangerously close to doing so."

"Who can doubt," asked Agnew, "that had the evidence uncovered and the conclusions drawn by these investigative bodies related to any other industry or institution they would long ago have become, to coin a phrase, household words? The national media would have made them so — just as CBS even now seeks to exploit its purported 'findings' regarding the Pentagon." He continued:

> Yet when the industry and institution involved is itself a part of the national news media, a strange silence and rare restraint inhibits the people's right to know. So powerful is this inhibition that neither a cabinet member [Agriculture Secretary Orville Freeman, who was refused equal time by CBS to present a response to *Hunger in America*], nor an Executive agency [the FCC], nor a Congressional committee was effective in bringing to public attention [these] serious matters . . . My purpose here . . . has not been to pillory or intimidate a network or any segment of the national news media in its effort to. Rather it is, once again, to point out to those in positions of power and responsibility that this right to know belongs to the people. It does not belong to the national networks or any other agency, public or private. It belongs *to the people themselves*, and they are entitled to a fair and full accounting of the truth, and nothing but the truth, by those who exercise great influence with their consent.

Now the gauntlet couldn't be thrown down any more directly than this. And the Vice President's points are well taken. Surely, had the CIA or some other official agency involved itself in an abortive invasion of Haiti, there would have been no hesitation on the part of the networks in exposing the whole affair. Yet CBS simply refuses to discuss it.

The closest thing to a rebuttal came during that curious appearance after the rerun of *The Selling of the Pentagon* by Richard Salant. "We did *not* finance the planned invasion," he stated. "We did nothing illegal. No significant amount of money even inadvertently found its way to persons involved in the invasion plan." But the subcommittee has shown that CBS contributed more than $200,000 to the conspiracy. Now $200,000 may not be a *significant* amount. But it certainly seems just a bit more than pin money.

Again, let's remember what's going on here. The Vice President believes he has the goods on CBS. He documents his charges with specific examples. Yet the national media refuse to focus in on these charges, and CBS absolutely refuses to discuss the charges. And so, the best we can get for an answer is pure unsubstantiated rhetoric, plus a lot of vague references to freedom of speech and the "people's right to know."

"Finally," said Mr. Salant, after neatly avoiding specifics, "let me sum up our position regarding all those charges against CBS News: We can refute every charge. We are proud of *The Selling of the Pentagon*, and CBS News stands behind it. We are confident that when passions die down, it will be recognized as a vital contribution to the people's right to know."

All of which is worth, of course, precisely nothing. CBS continues to claim that it can refute all the charges brought against it. *Yet it never does so.* We are to trust their documentaries because they say we should. And as for "the people's right to know," apparently this doesn't include our right to know about what CBS is up to.

As of this writing, it seems unlikely that the Vice President will ever force the networks into any sort of hard self-evaluation. The rhetorical puffery with which CBS officials respond simply clouds the issue. When he attacks, he gets this in response.

Orates Dr. Frank Stanton, president of CBS:

"The Vice President's speech [in Boston] tonight is a vivid example of the traditional conflict between government and the free press which has marked this country's history." Notice the opposition set up here: Government as would-be censor, the press as carrier of the truth. And Agnew, of course, as the quintessential commander-in-chief of all those censors who want nothing more than to snuff out the torch of truth. Now Agnew is simply asking for a discussion of what appears to be conscious distortion. But Dr. Stanton refuses to acknowledge that CBS could possibly distort.

"CBS does not claim any immunity from criticism. CBS does not claim to be infallible. [If so, Dr. Stanton, then how about just one instance of CBS admitting to error?] But the Vice President's indictment is mistaken."

And now, for a moment, it seems as if the battle might be joined. Stanton says that Agnew's specific charges are false. But what does he offer as proof? Well, Agnew is wrong about *Hunger in America*, says Stanton, because Richard Nixon once praised it. But so did Agnew, before he found out about the fakery involved. And the primary reason he didn't immediately find out about the fakery was that the media refused to publicize the official report in any way.

Stanton similarly disposes of *Project Nassau* by pointing out that it "was abandoned and never resulted in any broadcast." Which answers nothing at all about CBS's involvement with the invasion force. And one suspects that had the preparations gone smoothly, CBS would have been there on the Haitian beaches.

72

Finally, the charges against *The Selling of the Pentagon*. Agnew was wrong, says Stanton, because "*The Selling of the Pentagon* has been praised by distinguished Americans from all walks of life." And that's the answer, in its entirety, the rationale being not much different than, say, arguing that Carmine DeSapio should never have gone to jail because on numerous occasions distinguished Americans such as Averell Harriman praised him.

But this is the sort of thing Agnew continually runs up against. Whenever he makes a specific point, the media respond with the most self-righteous sort of rhetoric, at times, as in this recent statement from Walter Cronkite, bordering on galloping paranoia.

"Many of us," said Cronkite, speaking to the International Radio and Television Society,

> see a clear indication on the part of this administration of a grand conspiracy to destroy the credibility of the press. . . . Short of uncovering documents which probably do not exist, it is impossible to know precisely the motives of this conspiracy. But is it too much to suggest that the grand design is to lower the press's credibility in an attempt to raise their own and thus even — or perhaps tilt in their favor — the odds in future electoral battles? . . . Nor is there any way that President Nixon can escape responsibility for this campaign. . . . He could reverse the antipress policy of his administration. . . . It attacks on many fronts. often reiterated but unsubstantiated charges of bias and prejudice from the stump, the claim of distortion or even fakery planted with friendly columnists, the attempts to divide the networks and their affiliates, harassment by subpoena.

Now on the surface this is a rather simpleminded statement. Imagine the reaction were any right-winger to talk of a shadowy "grand conspiracy," complete with secret documents which may or may not exist. This is precisely the sort of analysis that the liberals find so hilarious when uttered by someone such as, say, Robert Welch. And the assertion that administration spokesmen (read Agnew) reiterate "unsubstantiated" charges is equally absurd. There's plenty of evidence. It's just that the networks refuse to make an honest effort to refute it, thereby doing what the conspirators are accused of doing — damaging credibility. Attempts to divide the networks and their affiliates? Absurd. The affiliates grow increasingly suspicious of New York-produced network fare only because their audiences find it fishy. And as for "harassment by subpoena" — subpoenas wouldn't be necessary if the networks would openly speak to the charges leveled against them. All in all, then, a rather wild exposition, a model of imprecision. Cronkite charges that there is a concerted antimedia drive underfoot, yet adduces not one single shred of proof. Which is precisely, of course, what he accuses the Vice President of doing.

On another level, however, Cronkite's speech is an extremely interesting one, for he admits, not consciously, I think, to something that he would deny vehemently were it put to him in the form of a direct question. Mr. Cronkite, you might ask, is there among media a bias against the Nixon Administration? And does this bias affect the way in which network news is presented? No, we can assume that Mr. Cronkite would answer in the negative, perhaps explaining, as he did a year or so ago, that "The public does not understand journalism. They do not know how we work, they do not believe we can hold strong private thoughts and still be objective journalists." Now, aside from the elitist nature of this reply — the implication that the American people aren't able to assess intelligently what they see on the screen before them — this is an admirable statement. If true. This is not to say that I think Mr. Cronkite lies. Rather, I just think that he doesn't understand how completely nonobjective he and his colleagues have become, how clearly his bias shows.

Consider those points once again that he makes in his conspiracy theory, especially this key point which Cronkite uses to explain the administration's motivation in conspiring secretly to "destroy the credibility of the press." "But is it too much to suggest that the grand design is to lower the press's credibility in an attempt to raise their own and thus even — or perhaps tilt in their favor — the odds in future electoral battles?"

Now what precisely is he saying here? The administration attacks the credibility of the press in order to raise its own. But under what conditions could such a strategy work? Only, quite obviously, if the press were relentlessly hostile to the administration. If the press were not hostile, there would certainly be no political advantage in attacking it. Tilt the odds in their favor in future elections? The implication, quite clearly, is that under normal conditions, the press can be expected to be fighting the reelection of this administration. The odds, says Cronkite, aren't even. That's why the conspiracy. If this isn't a comprehensive admission of bias, I've never heard one. And perhaps it's no coincidence that those politicians most fervent in their defense of the national media also just happen to be Democratic Presidential candidates.

In Mr. Cronkite's defense, I think you can say that he just doesn't quite know what he's up to. For instance, he may not realize that he played a leading role in Chicago in 1968 in cutting up Mayor Daley. Cronkite doesn't believe that he is antiadministration; he just believes that the administration is always wrong. I have no doubt that he strives for objectivity. He just doesn't quite understand how strong his biases are. And I imagine the same is true of many of the more admirable of his colleagues.

Other media men, however, understand exactly what they are up to. Listen, for instance, to this typical explication of the role of the press by columnist Clayton Fritchey: "The press, in reflecting and often spurring public 'disparagement' of a disastrous Vietnam policy, has served democracy well. It has forced one jingoistic President to abdicate, it has turned Congress around and finally made a second President promise to withdraw most if not all the troops in Vietnam."

Mr. Fritchey's view of the real world is, admittedly, a strange one. Not until 1971 could the critics find one poll to support their contention that any large number of nonuniversity and nonmedia people actively opposed our Vietnam policy. Thus, the process was much more that of "spurring" than "reflecting." And it is misleading to say that the press somehow forced the President finally to decide to withdraw most of troops, when that's what he intended to do all along.

But the interest here lies not so much in misstatements as it does in Mr. Fritchey's rather arrogant definition of the function of the press. The press, apparently, is not a medium through which information about events is channeled to the public. There's a higher function, that function being to force jingoistic Presidents to abdicate when they don't follow the policies approved by the press, to "spur" public rejection of policies the press doesn't approve, to force Congressmen to change attitudes when those attitudes don't jibe with those approved by the press.

Now this is a rather heady role. In one paragraph, Fritchey sets the role of the press as that of driving Presidents from office, determining both legislative and executive policy, and dictating to the public how they should respond politically. This is much more than a mere Fourth Estate. Fritchey's press is a supraexecutive and legislative agency, into whose hands is delivered the responsibility for the well-being of the nation.

Exaggerated? Perhaps. But were they to take a look, I think the national media would see more of themselves in Fritchey's mirror than many newsmen care to admit.

7

"I SUBMIT," says the Vice President, "that it is the mission of the press to *inform* the public rather than try to *persuade* it; that the public, given sufficient information, can make a sound decision."

The function of the media man is a subject of raging debate today in the journalism schools and among members — especially younger members — of the national media. Central to the debate is the whole question of objectivity. For if, as the young turks of the media believe, the primary function of the press is not to inform but to persuade, then objectivity is necessarily a hindrance. When one sets out in proper missionary fashion to preach a gospel, another point of view interferes with the desired conversion.

Older journalists tend to stand by the concept of objectivity. Even Walter Cronkite, despite his strong unexamined biases always honest according to his own lights, said in 1969 at Yale: "Subjective journalism has its place, but not on the front page or in the television broadcast. . . . I abhor journalism which tries this new [subjective] approach." Herbert Brucker, *Saturday Review* media critic, writing shortly before the Des Moines speech, puts it this way: "Half a century ago . . . critics of objectivity were few . . . but today objective news has become anathema to young activists in journalism, to some of the rising generation university intellectuals and to others who also should know better . . . today's young journalists and some of their elders, do not see the issue in terms of what is actually at stake, unprejudiced news. Oblivious to this crucial point, they seem to see objective news as an obsolete convention that blocks progress toward a better world." And a better world, one might add, which is better only according to their subjective evaluations of what would be better. And this is always the great flaw in missionary zeal.

"Among the aberrations in today's mental climate," writes the distinguished journalist William Stringer in the *Christian Science Monitor,* "is the sinister suggestion that there is no such thing as objectivity — no objective truth, no objective history or sociology, not even an objective reporting of the news." "The argument," says Professor J. K. Hvistendahl of Iowa State in the *Quill* of Sigma Delta Chi, "is that with so much wrong in the world there isn't time for objective evaluation . . . that objective journalism should be phased out by commitment or activist reporting. . . ."

Turner Catledge, for two decades the chief news executive of the *New York Times,* a paper that increasingly swings toward advocacy journalism, expressed himself, on the occasion of his retirement, as deeply disturbed by the new subjectivity: A newspaper's most precious asset, he said, is its "believability." "If we ever get to the point where we lose believability . . . we'll just go back into a candidly partisan press — not partisan in party terms, but in terms of ideas. . . . I feel very strongly [about the attack on objectivity] and I'm terribly disturbed about it. These youngsters are very frank about it. They don't want to be responsible for just reciting the facts. They want to tell you what to think about it and what to do about it. That's advocacy."

And the problem with advocacy, of course, is that it inevitably must lead to distortion. As a political journalist with a strong bias I know this very well. (But in my case, of course, as in the case of *New Republic* staffers, for instance, bias is permissible, for we work for editorial magazines which clearly label themselves as such and which take predictable stands. We never attempt to pretend that we are not partisan, as do television commentators for CBS or writers for the news sections of the *New York Times.*) The new journalist who is committed to advocacy, says William Stringer, "believes he has a right to become personally and emotionally involved, and to write from his own committed viewpoint."

And what happens, one wonders, if this "committed viewpoint" is shared by *all* the new crop of journalists? Quite obviously, a monolithic point of view, in which only one side of a question is presented, that form of ideological censorship mentioned by the Vice President in Des Moines. (I remember reading recently a *Time* essay in which the writer somewhat pedantically scolded those of us who tend to use the singular — medium — and plural — media — interchangeably. The problem with this sort of sloppy usage, he pointed out, is that it leads to sloppy thinking, a failure to make the necessary distinctions between different forms of communication. Thus, he says, when we assail the "media," our careless use of the term ends in a loose designation of similar sins to dissimilar media. Well, perhaps. But given the increasingly monolithic point of view being embraced by all national forms of communication, it doesn't seem to make a hell of a lot of difference.)

Make no mistake about it. The assault on objectivity — although the debate within the profession has recently been somewhat muted, since the Vice President is making the same charges as the older journalists — is well under way. "Objectivity," says David Brinkley, "is impossible to normal human behavior." In Des Moines the Vice President quoted another network anchorman: "You can't expunge all your private convictions just because you sit in a seat like this and a camera starts to stare at you. . . . I think your program has to reflect what your basic feelings are. I'll plead guilty to that." This, of course, is Frank Reynolds, he of club and meat-ax fame.

"Objectivity," says New York parlor Maoist Andrew Kopkind, "is the rationalization for moral disengagement, the classic cop-out from choice making." And Mel Elfin of *Newsweek*, the magazine which has always sacrificed fact to opinion, states: "Objectivity is indeed a myth. The only objective book that has ever been written is the Manhattan telephone directory." (With an editorial attitude like this, one needn't spend too much time wondering why *Newsweek* consistently distorts in the way it does.)

But perhaps the definitive statement was delivered at the April 1971 meeting of the American Society of Newspaper Editors by Thomas Winship, editor of the *Boston Globe,* one of the few newspapers, according to Martin Nolan, a writer for the *Village Voice* (the leading practitioner, according to one conservative satirist, of that style called Smart Ass Left), which "retains the interest — let alone respect — of young people." And how do you reach Young People? Well, you throw objectivity the hell out the back door.

"I'd like to give my definition of objectivity," said Winship. "Objectivity is what we gave Joe McCarthy before a great group of reporters took their gloves off. . . ."

Sorry to interrupt. I'd like to see some hard proof of that objectivity in print. There were papers partisan to McCarthy, of course, but I remember the period quite clearly, for it was the period in which my interest in politics began. And I'll be damned if I remember any objective treatment of McCarthy in the national media. And just to refresh my memory I've been back through bound volumes of the weekly newsmagazines and the *New York Times.* Uniformly hostile. Even *Time* magazine, when Henry Luce was still around to keep it editorially coherent, didn't like McCarthy. I've been advised by friends not, for God's sake, ever to say anything that could be interpreted as slightly sympathetic to McCarthy in any book I write, for with the instinct of sharks, the reviewers will go straight for the offending passages. "McCarthy," says another friend, "was the rock upon which the conservative movement of the fifties foundered." Maybe, but I kind of liked him, if for no other reason than he made the right kind of enemies. So there, I've said it.

But back to the original point: Let no one pretend, for whatever reason, that the national media ever gave Joe McCarthy a fair shake. Even on his deathbed. Sorry. Back to Winship.

"Objectivity is what we gave cancer-producing cigarettes before the Surgeon General's report."

Sorry. Another interruption. Journalists have still another role here — intuitive fighters of disease. No one really was prepared to say before the report that cigarettes *did* cause cancer, any more than we are now prepared to say, until the evidence comes in, that holding toads causes warts. And indeed, there are many who *still* don't believe the link between cancer and cigarettes is certain. And without proof, how *do* journalists decide these things?

"Objectivity let the most unexplained war in history go on without challenge until one and a half million people were killed. [*The most* unexplained? How did the press handle the explanations, one wonders, of the War of Jenkins' Ear? And maybe, Winship, you just didn't *believe* those explanations.] Objectivity let industrial wastage almost clobber to death the face of America. [Well, a rather striking image, that clobbering a face to death. But a bit exaggerated.] . . . That's our definition of objectivity. I say it's spinach and to hell with it. . . ."

Well, if that really *is* our definition, I say to hell with it too. I've never really thought of the correlation between objectivity and spinach before, but now that Winship points it out — except, on second thought, I'm rather *fond* of spinach. Anyhow, let the man rant.

"We all know why objectivity as a debate is on the ASNE dance card this year. It's because ever since Agnew yipped at us, many editors have been more objective than ever. . . ." (Again, Winship, some proof.)

"Objectivity is such a nice trip for an editor. Every morning he swallows his little objectivity pill. It turns him off from all that paranoia among the long-haired kids in the city room who whisper dirty talk over the water cooler, words like 'Nader,' 'Hanoi,' and 'Panther.' . . . These young people still think the newspaper is one of the most effective instruments for social change. . . . Editors and publishers who continue to preoccupy themselves with this objectivity jazz will have as much luck keeping the establishment press afloat as they will selling Nixon as a folk hero to anyone under thirty-five."

And how many editors do you know who have been trying to sell Nixon as "a folk hero" to anyone of any age group, let alone that group who manage to sneak in under thirty-five, thereby in some mystical fashion, automatically, by benefit of age, cornering most of the world's supply of virtue. But there we have it. Winship may be a youngish fellow, or he may be one of those poor middle-aged types who believes that the kids really dig him (they like to call it, be they college deans or editors, "bridging the generation gap"). But whatever his personal disabilities, Winship lays it all out there. Objectivity, quite obviously, is that which leads to a liking for Nixon. The other quality, although never named apparently much superior to this objectivity spinach, instills in us a love for and appreciation of Nader, Panther, and Hanoi. Obviously much to be preferred. And the end of the newspaper, Winship instructs us, is to bring about social change. What sort of change? Apparently, that sort of change which will turn us from people like Nixon toward the Panthers, Ralph Nader, and the good people of Hanoi. I think I'll stick with spinach.

Spiro Agnew and the man who seconded his nomination at the 1968 Republican Convention, Mayor John V. Lindsay of New York.

After President Nixon's inauguration, Mr. Agnew chats with former President Johnson and former Vice President Humphrey.

An interview aboard Air Force Two.

1970 rally in Springfield, Illinois.

The Veep in his office.

Spiro Agnew arrives in the Congo.

The Vice President greeting the Queen of Thailand.

The peripatetic Mr. Agnew off on a world tour.

The Vice President arrives in Morocco. Standing with him are King Hassan's brother, wounded in the recent coup attempt, and the young Crown Prince.

The Veep and King Hassan of Morocco.

The Veep lunching with President Mobutu of the Congo.

A rainy arrival in Addis Ababa.

The Vice President leaving the Kenyan presidential palace after a successful visit.

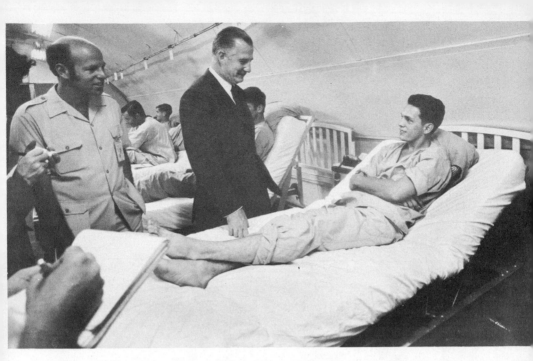

Visiting wounded G.I.s in Vietnam.

Mr. Agnew and Generalissimo Francisco Franco of Spain.

The Veep and Emperor Hailie Selassie.

Mr. Agnew reviews some crack Congolese Rangers.

The Veep says hello to two admirers.

Mr. Agnew addressing the Governors' Conference in San Juan, Puerto Rico.

Mr. Agnew and President Jomo Kenyatta of Kenya admire some roses.

Massive rally in Memphis during the "radic-lib" campaign.

Spiro Agnew accepts a bouquet in Seoul, Korea.

The Veep receives a spoof-gift from the Los Angeles County Board of Supervisors.

The Vice President addresses a group of 1970 White House Interns on the South Lawn.

Mr. Agnew arrives in Taiwan, Republic of China.

8

ALTHOUGH THE philosophers have been trying for centuries now, they have yet to resolve the question of whether objectivity is possible among men. But the national media people have settled the issue once and for all among themselves. Objectivity is not only impossible, but to strive for it is undesirable. And when Vice President Agnew insists that the function of the press is to inform rather than to persuade — that it should in fact be objective — the liberal response is direct and simple. Agnew's view is not only simplistic but dangerous as well, for if it were to prevail, the people just wouldn't think correctly. The American public is simpleminded, its instincts dark and untrustworthy. If you simply inform it, if you allow it to make its own decisions, you'll find yourself under a fascist regime within a decade. And so you teach it, since your own view of issues and events is somehow metaphysically sound and inspired.

In a piece entitled "The Era of Moroseness," printed in *Religion and Society,* the Vice President speaks of "the assaulting elite," who "can be found in every segment of society that helps to form the opinions of society at large: In the universities, in the media, in government, in the great professions. They are, for the most part, articulate and possessed of that smugness which comes only when one is dogmatically certain of one's essential rightness." And it is this absolute belief in their own rectitude which most aptly characterizes the people of the media.

The attitude of the media people toward the rest of society borders at best on the paternalistic. "Mr. Agnew," says Eric Sevareid, "would like those privileged to speak and write . . . to reflect the majority mood of this country. Not only do majority moods change, but the public mood of the moment is not necessarily in the public interest."

Now this may be a true, albeit an essentially antidemocratic statement, our country being founded on the conviction that the majority

97

do in fact have a better idea of what is in their own interest than do any of the minorities. And there are a couple of corollary statements which, if one accepts Mr. Sevareid's view, one must also accept. Mr. Sevareid is saying, of course, that the media are not reflecting the majority mood of the country because this is one of those historical moments in which the majority mood is not in the public's best interest. But then it must follow that there is a minority mood which is. And further, the group Mr. Sevareid refers to, "those privileged to speak and write," are somehow able to divine this minority mood and to promulgate it. Thus, if we follow Mr. Sevareid's reasoning to its logical conclusion, we find that if our society is to be a good one, its members must be prepared to follow the dictates of a prescient minority. It must be a nongovernmental minority, of course, because our government is made up of politicians, and politicians are men who, in order to attain office, must be receptive to the majority mood among their constituents. What is necessary, then, is an elite minority, which, being responsible to no majority constituency, can then decide what actions best serve the long-range interests. This attitude becomes dangerous indeed when it gains control of the country's media and through those media attempts to change the attitude it holds into national policy. Mr. Sevareid's view is a common one among "those privileged to speak and write." They do, in fact, think of themselves as a supragovernmental force for good and righteousness and from there as arbiters of national policy.

Up until the time of the publishing of the McNamara–Pentagon papers, the media's attempts at setting policy had usually remained implicit. They knew they were bucking a majority mood in their total opposition to administration policy.

"The delusion of the 'silent majority,'" wrote columnist Harriet Van Horne, "the regrettably large number of Americans who support Mr. Agnew's views, is that he is protecting the nation from the enemies within the gates: the liberals, intellectuals, editors, and commentators.

"In truth, it is we [liberal intellectuals] who have been fighting for the interests of the 'silent majority' all these years. The old analogy beloved by history professors was never more true. We are the canaries in the coal mines. It is we who first smell the poison gas. It is we who get the miners out in time. . . . It was the liberals, from the academic groves to the city rooms, who first sensed the damage being done our society, our youth, our very moral fiber, by the Vietnam war."

About this time the media began talking a lot about rotten moral fiber as if it were an objective fact of life, like air pollution or offshore oil slicks. And of course they attributed it all to the war. The business of sniffing gas, then, of detecting rot in the moral fiber, was one of the ways in which the media since 1968 have attempted to discredit our involvement in Vietnam. Yet even if we were to assume, for the sake of the argument, that an end to the war would remove the rot, there still remains the question of whether the media's ends can justify their means. For one must wonder just a bit about that gas that Miss Van Horne and her colleagues smell down in the mines. Isn't it just possible that they themselves might have helped manufacture it? Did Vietnam really rot our moral fiber or was it in part, at least, the work of the press? A chicken-and-egg question to be sure, yet it could be argued that the press has contributed significantly to the national demoralization they deplore. For to tell the country morning after morning, night after night, that its moral fiber is rotten is at best to extend the damage, at worst to create it. Furthermore, although it is impossible to assess the influence of the media on student rioters, we do know that television became their leaders' forum, the means by which they called their followers to action. Nor were they ever plagued, as was the administration, by unkind cutting and editing, by cynical or disparaging commentary on their actions. The hate and fear they preached was, at best, compared to the administration's, at worst not even acknowledged. If Rennie Davis and Abbie Hoffman are symbols of a rotten moral fiber, the media did little if anything to stamp out the rot.

A more recent example of the fact that the liberals feel that any means toward ending the war are laudable was displayed in their attitude toward William Calley. Now William Calley is a little creep who picked a baby up by its heel, threw it in a ditch and murdered it, and by imposing life imprisonment, the Army was telling its troops that this was the kind of action it would not countenance. But the liberal opposition to Calley's conviction sprang not from opposition to the penalty but from their fear that Calley's sentence would assuage national guilt and thereby allow the nation to continue in the course of action about which it had been feeling guilty.

Muckraking journalist Seymour Hersh, appearing recently on a national television show, bitterly protested the Army's action in bringing Americans accused of atrocities to trial at all. The reason? If the Army cleans house itself, it will take much of the steam out of the antiwar movement. An odd statement, coming from a man who claims to have dedicated his life to stopping the sorts of atrocities the Army is now investigating. And one might even argue that if the Army doesn't crack down, the atrocities will continue, thereby putting Mr. Hersh, given a choice between more atrocities and the moral outrage generated by these atrocities which fuels the antiwar movement, on the side of the perpetration of atrocities.

The media have worked hard to alter administration policy and bring an end to the war, nor have their efforts been limited to this country. For the same sort of poison gas the media detect within our own shores, they have also sniffed among the troops in Vietnam. And here again there is a suspicion that they might have manufactured some of the gas they claimed merely to have discovered. In fact some of the reporting became so biased that J. Russell Wiggins, former editor of the *Washington Post*, was prompted to give the following talk, as reported by Kenneth Crawford. The subject: How the modern media would have reported George Washington's crossing of the Delaware.

Television camera men would have focused their zoom lenses on the rag-wrapped feet of Washington's troopers. When it was over, microphones would have been thrust under the noses of stripling recruits to catch their answer to the question: "How do you feel about some of your buddies being lost in this sneaky operation?" The writing war correspondents would have salted their despatches with suggestions that the whole bloody venture was ill-conceived by an incompetent bloody commander, ill-executed by a badly trained and equipped army and predestined to fail.

New York editorial writers would have followed up with lamentations about the plight of Trenton's civilian population, driven from its snug houses into the cold on a sacred holiday, caught in the crossfire between Hessian defenders and attacking colonials, and forced into a fight against its will over a questionable cause: something about taxation without representation. Washington, instead of attacking, should have been negotiating. His occupation of Trenton and quick withdrawal showed that he was still engaged in search-and-destroy operations — "following the 'will-o'-the-wisp of military victory' . . ."

Whimsy, to be sure, but not without a significant basis in fact. Consider, for instance, this gem, already a classic, as it appears in a transcript of the CBS Evening News with Walter Cronkite on May 6, 1970. The Newsman is Gary Shepard. The occasion, our drive into Cambodia.

CRONKITE: Good evening. there was an indication today that North Vietnam may be launching a counteroffensive in response to the stepped up Allied military drive in Indochina. Communist forces, operating sixteen miles below Vietnam's Demilitarized Zone, attacked units of the 101st Airborne Division, killing twenty-nine Americans and wounding twenty-one, and those were the heaviest U.S. losses in any single engagement in almost two years.

100

At about the same time, the Allies opened three new drives into Cambodia. Gary Shepard was on the scene as one of the U.S. units prepared to strike into that country, and here is his report.

SHEPARD: Alpha Company, Third Battalion, 22nd Infantry Regiment, didn't know where it was going when it was thrown into the forward staging area at Tien Ngon, only five miles from the Cambodian border. All the men were told was they'd be moving out the next morning and to take enough C rations to last for three days. But then the news finally began to spread — tomorrow Alpha Company would be airlifted by helicopter into Cambodia, part of a task force of nearly 4,000 American soldiers who would attempt to wipe out a major North Vietnamese and Viet Cong base camp on the other side of the border.

The prospect of fighting the enemy inside Cambodia, and what it all meant, raced through each soldier's mind.

SHEPARD: . . . What are you going to do?

FIRST SOLDIER: I don't know. I'll tell you what. If I [indistinct] I'd just say I'm just going — I'm going — I'm going with them. I ain't going out. If they get about eight people staying I'm going to stay back, too, 'cause it ain't worth it.

SHEPARD: You realize what can happen to you?

FIRST SOLDIER: I don't care. I never even [indistinct]. Dishonorable, bad conduct, undesirable discharge — that don't mean that much to me. It means a whole lot to my father and my mother, see. This is why I'm here now.

SHEPARD: Are you scared?

FIRST SOLDIER: [indistinct] I was scared when I got my draft notice. Being scared ain't [indistinct]. Yeah, I'm scared. Who ain't?

SHEPARD: Time grew short. Other men of Alpha Company began to speak out as well, and it became apparent that there were few of them who really wanted to go.

SECOND SOLDIER: Most of us got very few ammo, and we're not really prepared. Just overnight notice for us, really. We're just really not prepared.

SHEPARD: When those choppers come in here in a little while and load you guys up and take you in there, are you going to get aboard, or are you going to stay here?

SECOND SOLDIER: Well, it really depends on my buddies. I'm all for what they — if they go, I'll have to go. It really don't do any good for just a few of us to stay. Got to get a lot of us.

SHEPARD: How many of the men here do you think really want to go in there today?

SECOND SOLDIER: Very few. But there's not enough — very many of them willing to stand up for what we know is right, but I don't know, if they'll [indistinct] about going into it.

SHEPARD: You say the morale's pretty low here in Alpha Company?

SECOND SOLDIER: Definitely. Very low.

SHEPARD: Why?

SECOND SOLDIER: Well, the way we've been getting pushed around. We don't get supplied like we're supposed to. They don't tell us what's going on or what we're going to do or anything. So it's definitely very low.

THIRD SOLDIER: We went on missions where the ARVN refused to go out, into their country. They refused to go out and fight, but yet still we fight. What makes a . . .

SECOND SOLDIER: If there were just a few of us to stay. Got to get a lot of us.

SHEPARD: How many of the men here do you really think want to go in there today?

SECOND SOLDIER: Very few. But there's not enough — very many of them willing to stand up for what we know is right, but I don't know, if they'll [indistinct] about going into it.

SHEPARD: You say the morale's pretty low here in Alpha Company?

SECOND SOLDIER: Definitely. Very low.

THIRD SOLDIER: What makes a — a hero? Courage? What makes a coward? Like, going to Cambodia, would that make us heroes? They don't want us there. If it was, that would be a different thing. Now, we're supposed to go through some village — village which — you can ask any officer around here — they don't even know where we're going. If they do they're not telling us.

SHEPARD: When the helicopters arrived to carry Alpha Company to the new war in Cambodia, there was some hesitation, but no one stayed behind. Each man moved out when he was given the signal, wondering perhaps what he would face when he jumped out of the helicopter across the border, wondering too whether he would ever make it back.

Gary Shepard, CBS News, at Tien Ngon, near the Cambodian border.

Not really too far removed from Wiggins' fantasy. The purpose of the canaries, quite obviously, is to discredit the allied operation, and anything goes. Notice, in the first place, how Shepard keeps asking how many of them want to go. An absolutely asinine question to ask a group of soldiers about to be airlifted into hostile territory. How many CBS newsmen at, say, 6:45 A.M., Monday morning want to go to work. Very few. "You say the morale's pretty low among the CBS newsmen this morning?" "Definitely. Very low." "Mr. Shepard, I notice you're still in bed. Are you going to go to work this morning?" "Well, it all depends on — I mean it's up to [indistinct] If all the other newsmen stay home I'll stay home too."

Except it's not really funny. Because for a newsman to wander, microphone extended, among troops about to begin an operation and to suggest to them in a man-to-man friendly sort of way that they all ought to consider a bit of mutiny, is almost criminally irresponsible. If the motive for such an interview were merely that mutiny makes good copy, it would be bad enough. But the thesis underlying Mr. Shepard's questions is quite obviously that no one wants this war, least of all the American fighting man. Were it not for our misguided policy of adventurism, these poor soldiers wouldn't have to fight. There's more than a hint, as the interview unfolds, that CBS wouldn't be at all heartbroken if the soldiers did mutiny. And if the newsman on the scene had had anything to do with that mutiny, well anything that gets us out of Vietnam . . .

When an act of near mutiny did finally occur, when five men suffering from combat fatigue refused immediately to return to the field after being ordered to do so by a green second lieutenant, the media treated the incident as definitive — as representing the mood of the troops in general. No attempt was made to put the incident in perspective, to remind the audience that such incidents have occurred in every war in which America has been engaged up to and including the Revolution. Why? "In my view," says Frank Shakespeare, head of the USIA, "it stemmed from the fact that . . . they [the networks] want out of Vietnam and they were totally opposed to our involvement . . . and they almost wanted to believe that maybe the American army would refuse to fight. It almost brought tears to my eyes to look at the way that incident was presented to the American people."

103

It didn't take a very sensitive nose, of course to smell the poison gas, mixed as it was with the odor of smoke and gunpowder which hung heavy over our campuses during the Cambodian invasion. In the Cambodian spring of 1970, as the campuses blew and students were shot at Jackson State and Kent State, the hostility of the media toward the administration on the Vietnam issue became hostility to the administration in every respect. For weeks the nation seemed poised on the brink of a major upheaval. But during this period, despite its pious admonitions to the administration to "cool your rhetoric," the media grew increasingly strident, semihysterical, whipping large segments of an already disturbed nation into a high-pitched frenzy.

The Vice President has always been open to attack, but during Cambodia he was a prime target indeed. James Reston even saw fit to compare him with Jerry Rubin. Jerry Rubin had been rabble-rousing on the Kent State campus just a few days before the explosion. "Until you people are prepared to kill your parents," he had screamed, "you aren't ready for the revolution. . . . Do you people want a diploma or to take this school over and use it for your own purposes? . . . It's quiet here now but things are going to start again." He was right. They did. Which is beside the point. The point is that next to Rubin, Vice President Agnew's speeches sound like Sunday morning sermons on brotherly love. Apparently James Reston could get just as upset when Agnew talked about impudent snobs as when Rubin called for parricide. It was an interesting reflection of the state of mind of the media during the spring of 1970.

There was more, of course. The *Atlanta Constitution* said of Agnew that he had "the grace of a drill sergeant and the understanding of a nineteenth-century prison-camp warden." And columnist Carl Rowan, who often knows better, used the following phrases in one unhinged column: Agnew "rose above his own laziness and ineptitude . . ."; (it's hard to see how anyone could look at the Vice President's record and deduce that he was at any time in his career either lazy or inept. In fact the thing that upsets Agnew's critics most is the vitality and success of his endeavors). Agnew is "a dumb joke — a sort of aberration of history . . ."; (then so is the silent majority for whom Agnew speaks. Surely Mr. Rowan doesn't think of the larger part of the American citizenry as "dumb jokes"). Agnew "has come to personify all the class conflicts, the racial hostility, the cultural and generational gaps that have transformed this society into a tinder box . . ."; (that's just sloppy prose, for in order to say that, you have to say that Agnew personifies the black ghetto youth as well as the hard-hat. A gap, after all, has two sides). Agnew is guilty of "calculated maliciousness," (he sets out to be evil) and would "prefer to pander to the prejudices of the most ignorant . . .

elements in society." (After a barrage like this I would say the composition of society's most prejudiced and ignorant members is open to question.)

President Nixon has always been troublesome for the media because he has a way of doing things that they would approve of if only he were a liberal. Since he is not a liberal, however, they are forced to manufacture reasons for not liking these things. But during the Cambodian invasion it was all very clear-cut, for Nixon was finally doing something that the media could wholeheartedly hate. "There is something so erratic and irrational," wrote the *Washington Post*, "not to say incomprehensible, about all this that you have to assume there is more to it than he [the President] is telling us." Now any professional, proficient in the use of words knows what's going on here. Words like "erratic" and "irrational" are loaded words, the connotations suggesting mental imbalance. Thus the President may not only be guilty of bad judgment; he may also be mad. And if not mad, then, as the final clause implies, a liar. And this from one of the most highly respected national newspapers in the nation. Its sister paper, the *New York Times*, exercised a comparative restraint, contenting itself with calling Cambodia "a military hallucination," and peremptorily ordering Nixon to withdraw forthwith. A *Times* columnist, however, Anthony Lewis, is less discreet: "The President of the United States, in a maudlin personalization and simplification of complex political issues, makes war the test of his own and the nation's manhood. . . . President Nixon has calculatedly chosen to widen the division among the American people, to inflame instead of heal." Here then are the motives of the President concerning the Cambodian incursion. To prove the nation isn't impotent. To prove he isn't impotent. And to inflame the electorate.

The President maintained a pretty low profile through the whole Cambodian operation, although it must have been an almost unbearably tense period for him. But there was one moment, just before Kent State, when the newsmen caught him off guard and Nixon spoke of the "bums who are burning down our campuses." Now on the face of it, you are not really going out on a limb when you call an arsonist, intent upon destroying public property, a bum. Some people might have even felt that the epithet was a bit mild. Not, however, the media. It took less then 12 hours before the "burning down" part of the statement had been deleted and Nixon had called everyone on campus who disagreed with him a bum. And it wasn't much of a jump from there to deciding that the President was responsible for the Kent State killings. Naturally when you call someone a bum he's going to get shot. Pete Hamill explains:

When you call campus dissenters "bums," as Nixon did the other day, you should not be surprised when they are shot through the head and the chest by national guardsmen. Nixon is as responsible for the Kent State slaughter as he and his bloodless gang of corporation men were for the antiintegration violence in Lamar, and for the pillage and murder that is taking place in the name of Democracy in Cambodia. . . . At Kent State, two boys and two girls were shot to death by men unleashed by a President's slovenly rhetoric. If that's the brave new America, I say to hell with it.

Much of the frenzy was brought on by deep personal hatred of Nixon and Agnew, of course. But the root of the reaction lies in the absolute conviction of the national media men that they should be allowed to determine national policy and that the President was usurping their function and doing it for them. And Cambodia is a dramatic example of the fact that the media people and the intellectual community in general make unreliable canaries. They smelled poison gas, this time from the White House. They knew that Nixon was widening the war. That once he was firmly entrenched in Cambodia, he would never leave. That the next step was all of Indochina. That at worst we would find ourselves fighting Red China, at best that it had destroyed any chances for closer ties. The canaries flapped wildly about the mine, banging their heads against the wall and causing panic and mayhem among the younger and less experienced miners. And when the dust had cleared, there was no gas there at all.

As we know now, Cambodia was a limited operation which achieved most of its goals. Supply lines were cut, base camps wiped out, and as a side effect, the Cambodian government, despite universal predictions that it would wither away and die, still stands.

The important thing about the Cambodian raid was that it was intended to make feasible the continued rapid withdrawal of American troops from South Vietnam. We have no evidence to show that it did not succeed in this primary goal, and much to suggest that it did. Yet the liberals simply could not buy this explanation, mainly, one suspects, because they loathe the idea that the Nixon–Agnew Administration is accomplishing something not accomplished under two of the most liberal democratic regimes in history — they are ending our involvement in the war. The Cambodian operation has proven, in retrospect, to be simply one more step in the orderly winding down. But the liberals refuse to see it as such; indeed, one suspects, they don't want to believe it.

Nixon and Agnew share conservative instincts. And so, despite the fact that they are carrying out nearly every wish expressed by the liberals for the past half decade, they will get no credit. As demonstrated by the reaction to Cambodia, no matter what they do they will be mistrusted and maligned. Every attempt to shorten the war will be viewed with suspicion, and when there are only those seven troops left, there will still be some diabolical intention to uncover.

It is clear now that the media won't allow Mr. Nixon to emerge easily as a man of peace. Any further temporary tactical maneuvers such as Laos or Cambodia, whether or not they are sincerely intended to facilitate withdrawal, will be viewed as widening the war. And as troops continue to leave, the new emphasis will be on how we are still really widening the war by bombing. And if all else fails, liberals will adopt the views of Rennie Davis, who assures us that Mr. Nixon is diabolically setting up a series of science-fictionish electronic sensors, which will enable us to bomb by remote control.

"Reporters and editors keep telling themselves and others that they have been more perceptive about this war than have the military and political leaders," writes Kenneth Crawford. "They may be right. But they have enjoyed the advantage of ultimate irresponsibility. In President Nixon's place, they would probably be doing about what he is doing. And history may be more approving of him than of them."

Eric Sevareid, then, thinks vague fuzzy thoughts about mood and public interest, Harriet Van Horne sniffs for gas and both of them try to set national policy. But it is a policy they would never be called upon to implement. They will never come face to face with the problems of the strategies for troop reductions or the intricacies of trade and diplomacy with other nations. Nor would they be in any way capable of handling these problems if they did. And more important is the fact that the media would never have to face the responsibility for the consequences of the kind of precipitous withdrawal they are calling for. The media are attempting to set a national policy which they need not implement, the consequences of which they will never be held responsible for. And to do so is, as Mr. Crawford points out, ultimately irresponsible.

The latest and most astonishing example of this "ultimate irresponsibility" is the publication of the McNamara–Pentagon papers, purloined top-secret accounts of the history of our involvement in Vietnam. The decision to publish the papers was, as Agnew put it with characteristic bluntness, "a cheap fencing action" (and he was speaking in the underworld rather than the sporting sense of that word). The media took administrative policy into their own hands in the most explicit and irresponsible way and only later discovered that there had been a very real danger that publication would destroy the secret plans for a meeting between Kissinger and Chou En-lai.

107

On the surface, one would expect the publication to help the Republicans, but there is already strong evidence that by the same transmutation that made Vietnam "Nixon's war," the apparent duplicity of two liberal democratic regimes will also be made into Nixon's duplicity. They will not believe that he sincerely wants to stop the war, and they will not give him credit for doing so. The snobs want the credit, and they will go to any lengths to appropriate it. Even to the length of publishing stolen secret documents.

And so if the controversy swirling around the McNamara–Pentagon papers proves anything, it is this: Liberal media types have finally made explicit that which up to now has been only implicit. They sincerely believe, with fanatical intensity, that they are the sole recipients of received truth, and that in times of national crises, they, rather than the government, should set national policy.

9

THE MCNAMARA–PENTAGON papers were put together in the sixties by a group of Defense Department functionaries, most of them liberal, most of them antiwar. But their value as historical documents is highly questionable, because the papers themselves were selective. Through another set of papers from the same files, Kennedy and Johnson could probably have been made to look like the thwarted men of peace they both claimed to be. And in fact, Lyndon Johnson believes that they were commissioned by Robert McNamara and were intended to be used by Robert Kennedy in his drive against Johnson for the Democratic presidential nomination. "The problem with the study," says one government official, "is that it is a prosecution brief masquerading as a dispassionate study." And John Roche dismisses the collection as "third-echelon chitchat." The papers, says William Buckley, "are nothing more than memoranda expressing attitudes; contingency plans; encyclopedic lists of alternative approaches to particular problems; routine exercises in the necessary dissimulations of government."

Nevertheless, although they are biased and although they never quite touch the heart of the whole matter — the process of presidential decision making — it would be disingenuous to dismiss the Pentagon Papers as inconsequential. Their effect has been profound. Not because people have read and digested them — only the compleat bureaucrat possesses the necessary immunity to boredom for that — but because of the way in which the media interpreters have chosen to use them.

Especially guilty of misinterpretation, says Walt W. Rostow, former special assistant for national security affairs to President Johnson, have been the writers for the *New York Times,* whose treatment of the papers Rostow calls "the shoddiest piece of journalism I've seen since I entered public life in 1941." "The *Times* headline writers, lead writers, editorial writers and columnists all went beyond the Pentagon

109

papers in conveying around the world the charges of deceit by the President, charges which are not substantiated by the papers themselves," said Rostow.

The papers have been used, quite simply, to discredit everyone connected with Vietnam. The purpose, obviously, is to rouse among Americans sufficient moral revulsion by attempting to convince them that they've been had, and by so doing to raise a popular outcry against the war. And at this writing at least, the operation has been successful. Shortly after the first of the documents appeared in the *Times,* the United States Senate, by a solid vote of fifty-seven to forty-two, adopted a resolution urging the President to pull out of Vietnam by the end of 1971. It was the first such resolution ever to win in the Senate. And according to polls, even Southern hawks are now demanding an immediate withdrawal. This is of course understandable, when the national media tell you flatly that two Presidents have lied in their teeth about the reasons for involvement and the nature of our response.

The temptation to make political hay is great. One thinks, for instance, of the shabby treatment accorded Barry Goldwater in '64, when people such as Herblock depicted him as a beady-eyed bomb thrower, opposed by Lyndon Johnson, the man of peace who, as he preached restraint during the campaign, had already made up his mind. according to media interpretation of the Pentagon papers at any rate, that the counsel of General Curtis LeMay to bomb them back to the Stone Age was the best advice. Or one is tempted to rehash the whole Tonkin incident. But to express public indignation and then to capitalize on the information disclosed in the papers would not only be fruitless but insincere as well. Most of us capable of following the news day by day already suspected that the Kennedys and Johnsons often spoke with forked tongues. Most politicians do, after all, with the exception of a few like Barry Goldwater. But even without referring to the Pentagon papers it can be reemphasized that the old truism of American politics — Democrats get us into wars, Republicans get us out — applies once again. And it is tempting to make that clear once more. The Vietnam war was conceived and mismanaged by liberal Democrat civilians, with only a couple of tame Kennedy house generals such as Maxwell Taylor representing the military in the planning. And perhaps now that the military is under such withering fire, it is worthwhile to remind Americans that the military involvement was only operational. Military men did *not* set policy under Kennedy and Johnson.

To its credit, the administration has not yet attempted to make political hay over the information in the Pentagon papers. But it could justifiably do so if it so desired, and it should do so if the President's genuine attempt to wind down the war and to cut American involvement continues to be treated as a Republican con game. There is nothing in the Pentagon papers which could possibly harm Nixon and, although liberals searched avidly for dark Republican secrets as the administration attempted to restrain publication, there were none, nor could they understand that Nixon acted because he genuinely felt that it was wrong to publish secret information no matter whom the information implicated and that he genuinely felt that the information disclosed, even though it had nothing to do with his own administration, might affect the credibility of the United States in the eyes of the world.

But still the attempt will be made to somehow discredit Nixon through the papers. Daniel Ellsberg, the fanatic who pimped the stolen papers, hints broadly that there are secrets, not as yet unearthed, that will implicate the Nixon Administration. But even without the papers to prove it, he assures us that he can sense a repeat of the 1964 escalation. How? Well, he can't quite say, but such types are big on divining moods through some sort of mystical process — the same sort of process by which it is determined that we are all collectively guilty and should do collective penance. Garry Wills, in one of his feebler columns, casts around for something good to say about Ellsberg and finally is forced to celebrate "the healthy return of a half-forgotten figure out of our history, the public penitent." It could be argued, of course, that it is in fact rather unhealthy to have men stumbling through the streets flaying themselves with knotted thongs, but this is what the liberal types would most like to see — Richard Nixon dragging his cross up Capitol Hill, trailed by a weeping nation. And this is precisely what Agnew, who doesn't find this kind of tendency healthy at all, means by "a national spirit of masochism."

Now the character of this "public penitent" is worth examining, for it seems to me that he represents a rather stunning epitomization of all the illnesses of twentieth-century liberal man and his institutions and attitudes.

Like all the young technocrats who planned and carried out the Vietnam war, Ellsberg was a "defense intellectual." His academic record at Harvard and Cambridge was brilliant. In the fifties, as Joseph Kraft points out, like so many of his type, he went to work for the Rand Corporation in Santa Monica, one of those think-tank operations that depend for their financial well-being on the Department of Defense. During the sixties, like so many others of his type, he was irresistibly drawn to Washington by the character of Robert McNamara, the think-tank technocrat's beau ideal.

Ellsberg himself seems always to have been a rather odd duck, variously described as an "intense, almost compulsive talker"; "messianic crusader" with "a martyr complex"; "a man driven" with a "bent for dramatization and self-dramatization."

One writer who knows him tells of his fear that he was constantly being followed and describes a party at which Ellsberg, for no apparent reason, appeared disguised as an Arab. Others tell of how Ellsberg seemed compelled to denounce his participation in DOD activities: "I come before you as a war criminal," he told one student audience. "I was participating in a criminal conspiracy to wage aggressive war," he told another. Such comments, coupled with the theft and delivery of the documents, led one writer to conclude that Ellsberg's role in the fencing operation derived from "his feeling of personal guilt and the need for expiation through action."

To many of those who knew him, in short, Ellsberg seemed — well — squirrelly. And when he appeared on a CBS special with Walter Cronkite on June 23, this impression was in no way modified. There was that strange secret smile, those funny anticipatory noddings, the constant wiping of the nose and chin, and above all, those eyes — extremely bright, the stare intense, constantly blinking — and just behind them a wary look, the look of a frightened deer as he watches the hunters through a thicket. Not too different, really, from some redundant Hollywood madman on the late show.

And then there are the strange delusions: 1971, he firmly believes, will see a replay of 1964. Nixon and Kissinger have secretly revived the notion of "escalation" and at any moment we can expect resumption of the bombing of North Vietnam. His decision, he tells us, was taken after a long struggle during which he carefully considered the conflicting concepts of moral judgments and legality, private morality and the public good. This isn't so alarming, of course, because most men at one time or another go through much the same sort of struggle. What is alarming is that Ellsberg seems absolutely certain that in his struggle he was representing the nation as a whole and that it is for him to decide just what would be most beneficial for us, a role usually reserved for madmen and the *New York Times*.

And so, because of what was known of the man, the oddness of his public personality, the lawlessness of his action, and his grandiose notion of his place in the cosmos, many of us were prepared to dismiss him as a loon. But this impression just doesn't hold up.

Ellsberg's appearance on the Dick Cavett show, for instance, was most impressive. One expected him, especially after the Cronkite show, to display psychotic tendencies. Yet here he seemed calm, collected, sincere, almost completely rational. Almost. His answers were lucid, thoughtful, despite an intelligent hour-and-a-half grilling. Only occasionally did something else peep through — a tendency to use terms such as "criminal" and "murderous" when referring to our actions in Vietnam, a strange allusion to a "sexist war," a statement that American "women and children" had always opposed the war.

On balance, it was an impressive performance. Yet just beneath the surface, something else lurked, obviously not lunacy, but something nevertheless that drove the man. Cavett perhaps came closest to bringing it above ground when he referred to a *Life* photograph taken in Vietnam which showed Ellsberg happily clutching a chopper, staring off toward what presumably were enemy positions, apparently waiting eagerly to let off a spray of bullets. Cavett asked whether he had realized that those bullets would kill someone, and Ellsberg, for one of the few times in the interview, was evasive.

And suddenly, if you were watching and listening closely, you saw it, and the references to women and children and the deep sense of shame and guilt which suggested mental illness all seemed to fit. Ellsberg wasn't mad. He had simply discovered emotions. Like so many of his counterparts in the world of the universities, the foundations, and the media, Ellsberg represents a relatively new type, the mid-twentieth-century liberal intellectual technocrat. Such men inevitably have followed similar patterns. They move from school to good university to graduate school to brief service stints in the officer corps to some sort of publicly or semipublicly supported organization such as the Ford Foundation or the Rand Corporation or to the media or to the universities, where they work with concepts, attempting to apply abstractions to the operation of systems. (In some cases, such as that of Robert McNamara, the route lies through the giant corporation, although it should be remembered that McNamara modeled his Ford operation on the think-tank pattern, and by so doing inevitably made enemies among the corporation's men of affairs.)

The life of the Ellsbergs is a heady one, for the models they create and the games they play can be large indeed, involving all of society and its citizens. Such men in a very real sense play God, and in the fifties and early sixties they came to be a whole new class in American society, and a most powerful one. It's hard to remember now just how powerful they were. In 1959 it seemed plausible to believe that every American citizen would one day be represented by an IBM card, and it was during the late fifties and into the mid-sixties that these people began to assume an increasingly important governmental function. Under the regime of Robert McNamara, especially, they took over larger and larger amounts of the work once reserved for men in the field.

As David Halberstam says in a *Harper's* magazine article, "The Programming of Robert McNamara": "He had come in at a dead run. By the time he was sworn in he had already identified the hundred problems of the Defense Department. He had groups and committees studying them. He had his people, the bright young men plucked off the campuses or the shadow government of the Rand Corporation and other think-tanks. They were cool and lucid, men of mathematical precision who had grown up in the atmosphere of the Cold War, students of nuclear power and parity and deployment whose very professions sometimes, to the humanist seemed uncivilized." Think-tank game playing replaced military strategy and tactics, and field commanders and the Joint Chiefs of Staff increasingly discovered that their decisions were being made for them in such places as the Rand Corporation in Santa Monica.

That this process was dangerous is nowhere better illustrated than in the mismanagement of the Vietnam war. The games players and the contingency planners often saw the large picture brilliantly. But they inevitably overlooked one important factor — the human.

McNamara simply wasn't capable of understanding or appreciating people who were not like himself. Halberstam relates a story that the newsmen like to tell. McNamara was in Vietnam on an inspection tour and on one specific occasion, "A Marine colonel had a sand table showing the terrain and was patiently giving the briefing. McNamara was not really taking it in; his hands were folded and he was frowning a little. Finally he interrupted: 'Now, let me see if I have it right, this is your situation: and then it came out from him — all numbers and statistics, this many friendlies on this many operations, this many troops to attack forty-eight percent of them after dark. The colonel was very bright and read him immediately, like a man breaking the code. Without breaking stride he went on with the briefing simply switching its terms. Out it came, all quantified, with percents and indices. McNamara was fascinated. Now the colonel's performance was so blatant it was like a satire and one of the reporters began to laugh and had to leave the tent. Later that day, the newsman went up to McNamara and commented on how tough the situation was up there. But McNamara wasn't interested in the Viet Congs. He wanted to talk about the colonel: 'That colonel is one of the finest officers I ever met,' he said."

And when Colonel Hacksworth, our most decorated officer, recently resigned his commission in disgust with the way we have operated in Vietnam, his harshest criticisms were reserved for those remote-control planners who had thought of everything except that one intangible element that invariably determines how well troops perform in the field — pride. It isn't that they consciously overlooked it, of course. It's just that you can't run something like pride through a computer, and there's no way of programming it into any strategic game you're playing.

The criticism perhaps most often leveled at Robert McNamara was that he was inevitably correct intellectually but invariably incorrect in predicting the outcome of the strategies he set in motion. The reason: McNamara simply didn't understand the human dimension or, more accurately perhaps, simply didn't believe in it any more than, say, the Marxist believes in such a thing as human nature. I believe McNamara came to realize this toward the end of his reign and his realization led to a particularly poignant understanding, finally, of how dismally he had failed.

"If the body was tense and driven," says Halberstam, "the mind was mathematical, analytically bringing reason from chaos, always reason. It was a mind that could continue to call on its mathematical kind of sanity long after the others, the good liberal social scientists who had never gotten beyond their original logarithms, had trailed off. Though finally, when the mathematical version of sanity did not work out, when it turned out that the computer had not fed back the right answers and had underestimated those funny little far-off men in their raggedy pajamas, he would be stricken with a profound sense of failure, he would at least briefly be a shattered man. . . .And so in the end the Great Statistician became himself a statistic, one more casualty of the war."

Part of the problem is one of insulation: the peculiar way in which the twentieth century has unfolded has led to the rise of groups and classes cut off from the daily life of the society and the majority of its inhabitants, and a consequent overdevelopment of one faculty, the intellectual, at the expense of others, such as the emotional. And when, in some period of stress, such as the present period, the McNamara or the Ellsberg realizes this, the result can be an extreme renunciation of the old way of behaving and the fervent espousal of a new.

Thus the peculiar intensity of Ellsberg's character as it transmits itself through the media. Unlike the majority of ordinary citizens, an Ellsberg has little experience of the whole range of experiences — mundane and tragic, embarrassing and hilarious, noble and profane — that form the development of man's character in society. The Ellsbergs are curiously insulated, protected from reality, and they develop hugely in one direction, but usually at the expense of others. But then one day it dawns. And the man of pure intellect suddenly discovers the whole welter of emotions that define human beings. And when he does, especially if he decides that his overdeveloped intellect has been misdirected, the renunciation is extreme, the act of expiation dramatic, and the man of pure intellect becomes the man of pure emotion. The man of pure intellect must by nature appear at times sadistic, for he understands little of harm to others. The man of pure emotion must by nature appear masochistic, for emotionalism in its purest form feeds on self-

115

suffering. The flagellant has become "the public penitent." Ellsberg, reacting to that picture of himself holding a machine gun, tells us just how puny one of the central tragedies of our time has become — the contingency planner suddenly realizing that his contingency plans, developed like games in a think-tank, can actually be applied in the real world.

10

ONE OF THE most impressive things about the nature of Daniel Ellsberg's public penance is that while he renounces all that he once stood for, his basic attitude seems to remain untouched. As think-tanker, he seemed sincerely to believe that he served the highest good possible. As a penitent, he continues to believe that he somehow, man alone, is able to decide what will most benefit the country. And underlying this attitude, there must be, of necessity, a basic, though no doubt undefined contempt for the average citizen and the average government he elects to represent him, a basic disbelief in the ability of this citizen and his government to formulate and execute coherent and intelligent national policies. This is, of course an essentially antidemocratic attitude, for all elitist attitudes are by definition antidemocratic.

Ellsberg is in the vanguard of Agnew's "assaulting elite," the prototype of the elitist man of the intellect. Less pure, but nevertheless marching to the same elitist drummer, are the men of the national media. When the *New York Times* decided to print the documents stolen by Ellsberg, *Time* magazine said: "Regardless of the legal issues [involved in the printing of the papers], the newspapers saw a higher morality in exposing the secret history of decisions that led to a dangerously unpopular public policy."

The men of words, when they join the men of pure intellect in an assault on their social system, play a significant role. To realize the type of society envisioned by elitists, the old society must be discredited. "This discrediting," writes Eric Hoffer in *The True Believer,* "is not an automatic result of the blunders and abuses of those in power, but the deliberate work of men of words with a grievance." And what is the nature of the grievance of the men of the *New York Times* and the *Washington Post?* "Whatever the type," writes Hoffer, "there is a deep-seated craving common to almost all men of words which determines their attitude to the prevailing order. It is a craving for recognition; a craving for a clearly marked status above the common run of humanity." The men of words, as Hoffer describes them, are the quintessential "snobs," as the term is defined by Agnew. But perhaps over and above the craving for recognition is a craving especially acute among American intellectuals — a craving for power, something that Americans have never been quite willing, to their eternal credit, to grant them. And so, frustrated in this craving, the intellectuals have in effect set up what one *National Review* editorialist calls a "counter government," a government consisting of university and think-tank intellectuals, certain liberal politicians, and media men. Their first task: to discredit the existing order, a task that falls first to the media men: "The preliminary work of undermining existing institutions," says Hoffer, ". . . can be done only by men who are, first and foremost, talkers and writers and are recognized as such by all." Hence the CBS attacks upon the system; hence the media assaults upon all aspects of our domestic and foreign programs; and hence such operations as the McNamara papers.

The growth of this assaulting elite as a class has been a gradual one. In certain senses it may be called an intellectual class. Intellectuals, says Professor Nathan Glazer, are people "who make a living from ideas. They live off ideas and they live for ideas. Politically, as we know, intellectuals have in general been critical of established institutions and values, sometimes from the right, much more often from the left. Only very rarely have they been conservative in the sense of approving of established institutions and values. Intellectuals possess most of the attributes of an interest group: They are concentrated in a limited number of occupations, they commonly share a certain orientation."

In the forties and fifties, Glazer points out, this group captured the universities. In the sixties they took the media. "The circulation of intellectual magazines has generally increased to an extraordinary degree," writes Glazer in *Commentary,* "while many of the mass magazines such as *Esquire* and *Playboy* regularly publish leading figures of the intellectual world . . . Publishing houses are now typically controlled by young editors, who have strong ties to the intellectual community. [This latter point particularly hits home. When I tried to peddle a proposal for a book on the Vice President, I was told by numerous major publishing houses that they wouldn't touch a pro-Agnew book. Now if I were willing to try an *anti*-Agnew book . . .] TV production staffs often share the concerns of intellectuals and increasingly even newspaper reporters are to be considered intellectuals. All this is only a natural consequence of the intellectual conquest of the campuses, since editors, producers, and reporters are almost always recruited from the campuses."

This tendency has been noted by others. The *Wall Street Journal*, commenting on the monolithically partisan political attitudes of the major media, puts it this way: "So far as we can tell, the chief reason for the trend toward uniform thought is a process of self-selection. Political views are not formed in a vacuum, but tend to be part of any individual's life-style. Thus, the people who become physicians are likely to be politically conservative, unless their life-style points them to psychiatry or medical school teaching, in which case they're likely to be liberal. In the same way, people attracted to establishment journalism and possibly the most sensitive and able of them, are likely to identify with the liberal wing of the Democratic party."

The ideological capture of our national information centers has been gradual, the process much like that which occurred in the universities during the fifties and sixties. During the fifties, the universities were the preserves of old-line leftist liberals who, as a matter of course, indoctrinated their students with comfortable Fabian notions which were, for the most part, accepted unquestioningly, their acceptance being a necessary requisite for admission into the intellectual establishment. These were not bad men. On the contrary, they tended to be gentle idealists who simply accepted on faith the prevailing notions of their day, and both the nature of the times and the nature of the beliefs made this acceptance easy. The loftiest notion of man in society, as it has been commonly held in the West, is essentially abstract, dealing with man as he should be, rather than as he is, in an ideal society, rather than the real society in which he finds himself. University life itself is an idealization rather than a microcosm, and the university professor tends to live among ideas, or abstractions, rather than in the reality of day to day life. Add to this the very real abhorrence of anything emanating from the right during the forties and fifties (the ghost of European fascism was still very much with us) and it seemed the most natural thing in the world for the academy to tilt consistently leftward.

It was a comfortable world, and as long as it remained an abstract world, it was not particularly dangerous. In the sixties, however, this comfortable condition was severely shaken by the New Left campus riots, and the academics began to question the validity of their roles. Detachment and criticism of the status quo had been the academic stance before the sixties, and this attitude, while often lending itself to first-rate parody, was valuable to society as a whole, serving as it did as a sort of national conscience. But in the sixties, detachment gave way to involvement, criticism to activism. As among journalists, the older notion of objectivity as a guiding principle—albeit an odd sort of objectivity that inevitably guided our thoughts leftward—gave way to a new subjectivity, the abstract practice of criticism giving way to direct and emotional attacks upon the system. Ideas and the life of the mind had seduced an earlier generation of professors, writes James Hitchcock, "but in the end the seduction seems an illusion, especially when others who never chose the academy, and the realm of thought — militant blacks, grape strikers, Latin American guerrillas, student activists — began to demonstrate that reality . . . is far more tractable to their deeds than to his [the liberal professor's] words." "Beyond the obvious and important changes," concludes Hitchcock, ". . . one radical thought has sunk deep into the universities' bones . . . this is the simple question whether the life of the mind is any longer a legitimate way of existence, and whether the search for truth is not a self-indulgent evasion of the searing demands for active life in society."

And so, in the sixties, as a new national spirit (which one might call the New Romanticism) grew, the professors increasingly eschewed their previous commitment to a life of the mind and took to the barricades. One may be, excusably, just a bit suspicious about how deep that commitment was initially. "Ideas," writes Dorothy Rabinowitz, analyzing the radicalized professor, are simply what one . . . talks about when one makes a contract with the university. He never did see what good they were — they never did him any good — and he had little difficulty yielding them up to the greater realism of the New Left revolution."

The social and intellectual incompetent described by Miss Rabinowitz is, of course, a familiar figure on most university faculties, and most of us who have spent time in academe know him well, that middle-class type whose ideas and attitudes are adopted for the same reason that he has taken up pipe smoking. But it is, I think, a mistake to write off the significance of the new subjectivity as nothing more than the manifestation of the deep personal bitterness felt by people who doubt the validity of their function in society. "If anything ail a man so that he does not perform his functions," writes Thoreau, "if he have a pain in his bowels, even . . . he forthwith set about reforming — the world." Perhaps. But it isn't that simple, of course. The Ellsbergs are obviously motivated by a good deal more than constipation.

The radicalization of the university campuses in the sixties had its effects beyond university towns. The central issue of the decade, the war in Vietnam, was at first a university issue. The talk-ins and teach-ins which represented the first tangible opposition to our Indochina policies were initially all-university affairs. The pattern at first was that of dedicated leftist–liberal professors instilling in their students a loathing of our national policies. But as the sixties proceeded, a curious reversal occurred. Suddenly a whole generation of indoctrinated students became the teachers and the professors discovered that in order to keep their liberal credentials up to date, it was necessary to sound as radical as their students. Thus, the older establishment–liberal teachers became radicalized and the university community became instead of a center of investigation and criticism, a center of organized activist opposition to the country's established government.

The radicalization of the campuses and the growth of a new adversary–counterculture spread among other segments of our society. At first, the antiwar, antinational New Left attitudes which became definitive in the universities were confined mainly to the academic world. When Berkeley erupted, the nonacademic men of the word, among them, for instance, the writers for the *New York Times*, were still urging support for our policies. But as the sixties passed, the attitudes of the nonacademic information centers became increasingly similar to the attitudes of the campuses, until, in 1971, editorials in the *New York Times* read almost exactly like the text of 1966 Berkeley New Left speeches. Today, when there is a massive antiwar march in Washington, we find the men of the national media approving wholeheartedly, and never mind the fact that the demonstrations are paid for and organized by various militant Marxist groups. It is no longer horrifying to the average leftist–liberal to be seen marching beneath the banner of the Viet Cong. The spirit of the New Romanticism demands national humiliation, and how better to satisfy this masochistic craving that to force us to crawl abjectly from Vietnam, our national pride humbled by a relatively small group of miserably equipped Asian guerrillas?

Almost imperceptibly, the national media, like our nation's universities, have become radicalized, and our centers of learning now can promulgate their ideas and attitudes through our centers of information. And thus, the counterculture has become a national phenomenon, and as the printing of the McNamara–Pentagon papers shows, the counterculture has set up a countergovernment.

The seriousness of this radicalization has best been discussed by Daniel P. Moynihan, in a *Commentary* article entitled "The Presidency and the Press." The media people, Moynihan points out, are not merely influential; they are potentially the most powerful people in the country because of their special relationship with government, a relationship, Moynihan points out, "that has no counterpart in other professions or activities. The relationship is one of simultaneous trust and distrust, friendship and enmity, dependence and independence. But it is the men of government, especially in Washington, who are the most dependent. . . . For the journalists are above all others their audience, again especially in Washington, which has neither an intellectual community nor an electorate, and where there is no force outside government able to judge events, much less to shape them, save the press. . . ."

The relationship, says Moynihan, has always been politely hostile. Both sides, however, the media and the government, have always been willing to abide by certain ground rules. Lately, however, this relationship has become extremely troubled, with the press willing to print, for instance, any information leaked by any self-serving bureaucrat who wants to damage the executive. A few years ago the *New York Times* thundered about types such as Otto Otepka who leaked information to legislative investigating committees. Today, however, the same *Times* shows no compunctions about reprinting stolen top-secret documents, righteously claiming as they do so that the people's "right to know" transcends any governmental need for secrecy. (And it's interesting how the President's announcement of his intention to visit China undercuts this argument among liberals. Obviously, had the Kissinger trip been announced in advance, the resulting political furor would have rendered such a trip impossible. So, since the *Times* and similar papers want us to recognize China, they don't criticize secrecy in this case. Obviously, this was an instance when it was better that the people didn't know.)

Why this new attitude? "The immediate answer is, of course," says Moynihan, "the war in Vietnam." But this is only a symptom, he continues, and even when the war ends, the problem will intensify. The problem, according to Moynihan, lies in the nature of the media and the types of men who make media work their profession: "Journalism has become, if not an elite profession, a profession attractive to elites. This is noticeably so in Washington where the upper reaches of journalism constitute one of the most important and enduring *social* elites of the city, with all the accouterments one associates with a leisured class."

This point, of course, came under heavy fire from the Washington press corps. But anyone who has spent time in Washington knows it to be true. Read the society pages and notice how many of the media men make the best parties. Eat a leisurely wine-soaked luncheon at the Sans Souci and notice how many of your fellow diners are media men (and notice their icy contempt for the Republican administration people who prefer steaks next door at The Black Steer to the French cuisine at the Sans Souci). Spend an afternoon at the National Press Club, enjoying one of those three-hour luncheons. The press has indeed become, on the national scale, an elitist profession. (And this might also explain why the media, although their muckraking desires have become increasingly heightened, are so bad at investigative journalism. One wonders, for instance, what in the world all those press men were

122

doing when Kissinger disappeared for three days behind the bamboo curtain. As in Saigon and Washington, one suspects, they were drinking long leisurely lunches and depending on press releases for their hard news. They do quite a job when documents "come into their hands" as with the McNamara–Pentagon papers. But they seem to fall down badly whenever hard, personal digging is required. One of the characteristics of an elite class is its air of languor.)

The national press, then, as Moynihan points out, has become an elitist class, an extension of the campus. The second serious problem, as Moynihan sees it, lies in the monopolistic nature of the national media, as outlined by Agnew in Des Moines, and the particular "mind–set" of the men who serve this monopoly. And compounding the problem is the nature of the audience for whom news is reported. "The two most important *presidential* (and therefore *national*) newspapers are the *New York Times* and the *Washington Post*. . . . Both papers reflect a tradition of liberalism that has latterly been shaped and reinforced by the special type of person who buys the paper. . . . There is a 'disproportionately' well-educated and economically prosperous audience. . . . Both the working-class Democrats and the conservative Republicans . . . have been pretty much driven from office among the constituencies where the *Times* and the *Post* flourish. . . . Thus they [the special liberal readership] help to set a tone of pervasive dissatisfaction with the performance of the national government, whoever the presidential incumbent may be and whatever the substance of his policies may be.

And this is especially true, of course, when the President is a Republican with apparent conservative tendencies. Given an elitist group serving an elitist group, given the breakdown in objectivity in the profession of journalism, and given an ideologically suspect administration, the result will inevitably be hostile reporting, no matter how hard the incumbents try to please. And, if necessary, as Moynihan points out in three well-chosen instances, the press will purposely distort to make the President look bad.

The results, says Moynihan, are most dangerous, resulting in a situation in which the national government has been placed "at a kind of operating disadvantage. . . . In the U.S. it is rare for government to succeed . . . and just as hard for government to appear to have succeeded when indeed it has done so." The government, in other words, cannot convince the nation of its success in any particular if a hostile press is determined not to allow it to do so. One prime example, of course, mentioned over and over again in these pages, is the war in Vietnam. Nixon is ending it, but the media don't want us to think so.

"The issue," says Moynihan, dismissing the specious charges by media men that the government is always attempting to muzzle them, "is not

123

one of serious inquiry, but of an almost feckless hostility to power." And too much of this, he believes, if it becomes simply a habitual reflex, may do immense damage to our social fabric. "American government will not only rarely and intermittently be run by persons drawn from the circles of those who own and edit and write for the national press; no government will ever have this circle as its political base. Hence the conditions are present for a protracted conflict in which the national government keeps losing."

What is at stake, in other words, is the confidence of the people in their elected government, or, in short, national morale. And here the government has certainly been losing, the press having launched, as Nathan Glazer puts it, an "assault on the reputation of America . . . which has already succeeded in reducing this country, in the eyes of many American intellectuals, to outlaw status. . . ."

Moynihan, summing up, picks one of the central strands of the Des Moines speech: "Further, there needs to be much more awareness of the quite narrow social and intellectual perspective within which the national press so often moves. . . . The national press is hardly a 'value free' institution. It very much reflects the judgment of owners and editors and reporters as to what is good and bad about the country and what can be done to make things better."

The belief in this latter function, acting to make things better, seems increasingly to preoccupy the national media. It was certainly in the national interest, they devoutly believed, to publish the McNamara papers. But the magnitude of the action taken also points to the great flaw in this attitude. It is essentially an undemocratic attitude in the most profound sense of the word. In a democracy the national interest and the governmental interest cannot be separated. The media are elitist, serving an elitist audience, propounding an elitist point of view. Because of the special relationship of government to the national media, this elitism can lead to incessant hostility, resulting, as in the case of the McNamara papers, in something very like "the treason of the intellectuals." And, as Moynihan points out, this inevitably must lead to tragedy, for, above all, democracy is government by ordinary men. "Whether or not ordinary men are capable of carrying out any governmental task whatsoever, ordinary men are going to be given the tasks. This is what it means to be a democracy."

But the question becomes, of course, whether the elitists will allow them to carry out these tasks and give them credit when they do so. The radicalization of the media is ominous. "Historians of the future," writes Andrew Greeley, "may look upon the 1960s as a time not when middle Americans deserted the intellectual ethnic group, but rather as a time when the intellectual ethnic group deliberately turned its back on its own mass population support and began a flirtation with radical groups whose ability to bring about social change was dubious, but whose moral rectitude — at least from the intellectual elite's point of view — was beyond question."

Thus, for instance, the radicalization of the *New York Times*. And thus, the McNamara–Pentagon papers. It is no accident that Ellsberg first approached the *Times*.

11

"THE AMERICAN majority may not be book intellectual but it is practical," said Vice President Agnew in Honolulu in 1969. "It may not be passionately committed to any ideology, but it is passionately against intolerant dogmatism."

In speech after speech Agnew has tried to draw public attention to the growth of the adversary culture. The danger, he points out, lies in the desire among the members of this culture for control of the political system, their desire not merely to participate but to direct. Elites are always dangerous, as the history of Europe sufficiently proves, and the continued growth of an intellectual elite in this country, opposed by definition to the whole notion of representative government, threatens to Europeanize the American experience.

"Nowhere at present is there such a measureless loathing of educated people for their country as in America," writes Eric Hoffer. And comments by leading intellectual luminaries seem to bear him out. "American society is ugly, repressive, destructive," says Professor Robert Woolf matter of factly, no doubt sure that all reasonable men of learning will agree. "The system is rotten and must be brought down," teaches Professor Richard Lichtman, one of Berkeley's finest. "I hate this rotten f——— country," screams a respected Berkeley student leader.

One of the reasons for the violent hatred of Agnew, of course, is that he actually attempts to defend this system so loathed by intellectuals. He calls himself a "frank advocate of the American system," and in speeches like this one in Philadelphia he goes to the root of the problem: "Several years ago, a foreign student addressing a college seminar was asked about his future plans. The young man replied, 'I want to return home to serve the country I love.' Fellow students gave him a standing ovation.

"But I wonder what the reaction would be if an American student at

126

an American college announced that he loved his country? Would there be applause or embarrassment? I suspect that many have been conditioned to be embarrassed by such an overt expression of patriotic sentiment. I would guess that many in sophisticated America consider love of country gauche or irrelevant.

"A double standard has emerged. We admire patriotism in others, but condemn it in ourselves. We seem to see everything about ourselves except what we have achieved. We forget this nation fought a bloody war to secure freedom for an oppressed minority. We forget that this nation was conceived and has continued as an asylum for the world's oppressed. We overlook the fact that today our country remains the first choice among the world's immigrants.

"Although we cannot be complacent about our faults, neither should we be apologetic about our strength. Yet apology appears to be becoming our national posture. We have seen attempts to pervert the liberal virtue of self-criticism to the national vice of self-contempt."

The same theme in Vermont: "The man who believes in God and country and hard work and opportunity is denounced for his archaic views. The nation which has provided more justice, equality, freedom and opportunity than any nation in history, is told to feel guilty for its failures." The same theme, in speech after speech: "The disease of our times is an artificial and masochistic sophistication — a vague uneasiness that there is something wrong with being patriotic, honest, moral, hardworking."

Such speeches inevitably send the phrasemakers up the walls, causing writers such as Garry Wills, his voice dripping contempt, to sneer at Agnew for "his optimism, his trust in 'the good old values,' and the rewards of American sobriety. . . ."

What is Wills getting at? Well, quite obviously, he believes that optimism is unfounded, that the old values are sham, that American sobriety never accomplished anything. It is unnerving to realize this, to realize that the loathing of our highly educated phrasemakers for the system has sunk in this deep. Why, one wonders? Why this automatic assumption among intellectuals that anyone who mentions such things as traditional moral values must be evil? And why the dogmatic insistence that our system is rotten, an insistence voiced most loudly by middle-class college kids who drive off to their revolution in Mustangs and can always count on good old Daddy for bail money, by affluent college professors and Leonard Bernstein types, and by highly paid television commentators — in short, the best fed, best clothed, best educated people in the world?

Eric Hoffer thinks he knows. "The 1960s," he says, "have made it patent that much of the intellectuals' dissent is fueled by a hunger for power." How else, asks Hoffer, to explain this measureless loathing of the intellectual for his country? "It is hard to believe," he continues, "that this savage revulsion derives from specific experiences with persons and places. . . . For those who want to be left alone to realize their capacities and talents, this is an ideal country."

But the problem is, of course, that the intellectual doesn't want to be left alone. He wants to shape and sway history, to make power, to run things — or, more precisely, to direct other people according to his notion of how things should be run. But in America, unlike Nazi Germany or fascist Italy or the Communist countries of the East, he's never been given his chance, has never, in Hoffer's words, "been integrated with or congenial to the politicians and businessmen who make things happen."

And so, frustrated in his dreams of power, realizing that they cannot be realized under the system as it exists, the alienated intellectual hopes, no doubt often unconsciously, for the collapse of the system, as do, for instance, to name a very few, the Kopkinds, the Lichtmans, the Chomskys, the Marcuses. And what in its place? Well, that's another problem. It can't be a democracy, for the people who can do things would never work for the abstractionists who can't. Why should a plumber, for instance, do what Noam Chomsky tells him to do at a wage determined by Chomsky? Because Chomsky has a Ph.D. and understands linguistics? Why should these qualifications make any more difference in a democratic society than the plumber's ability to unstop Chomsky's toilet? And what is the basis for assuming that Chomsky's skills are in some metaphysical way inherently superior to the skills of the plumber? Wouldn't it make just as much sense to argue that the plumber should actually be telling Chomsky what to do, since in any measurable way, the plumber has more to offer his society than the linguist?

Well, it's certainly quite a problem, the only solution to which seems to be to work for the sort of a society in which the intellectual can wield power, perhaps one of those good gray people's republics where the theoreticians run things. The plumbing never quite works, people save for years for a couple of pairs of shoes, there are chronic food shortages, and people queue up for hours for a handful of something they could buy buckets of with no waiting in any California supermarket. But at least the intellectuals would have the respect due them, and were there any argument, there's Mao's gentle thought — "power grows out of the barrel of a gun," and when people get uppity you shoot them. For the good of the state, of course. And also to insure that they keep working for you. After all, you can't do any of those things yourself, can you? But then you're busy thinking, and you shouldn't be expected to.

This contempt for the democratic man, the producer, is deeply ingrained in the American intellectual and, since this is the man for whom Agnew speaks, it also explains a good deal about the intellectuals' loathing of Agnew. Professor Charles Reich sees the working Americans as a sad lumpy lot, slopping around "in their sullen boredom, their unchanging routines, their minds closed to new ideas and feelings, their bodies slumped in front of the television to watch the ballgame Sunday."

An elegant sentiment from the author of the *Greening of America,* a quintessential elitist who lives his life cloistered in the academy, whose idea of work is to rap with the kids (sad enough in a middle-aged man) and write completely uninformed sappy books of sensibility designed to make those kids love him. Reich is an ass, of course, his book pure gush, his idea of the American workingman as deficient as his understanding of what's rattling around in the heads of the kids.

Reich's is a common attitude among the elitists, for even though the comfortable lives they live and the leisure they enjoy to write silly books is provided to them by the producers they loathe, they find it offensive that the American workingman simply can't seem to stay in the place they would like to assign him. When my first book appeared, I remember that Garry Wills, in a killer review, called me a "hard-hat with a degree." I found this phrase, and the attitude which informed it, particularly offensive, for I was proud of the fact that I came from a working-class family, that I had also been a hard-hat, and that I managed to earn a couple of degrees. This would not have been possible in most of the countries of Europe, for instance, or at least not nearly as easy. But the reaction wasn't so much personal. The important thing in Wills' statement seemed to me to be the underlying assumption that somehow it was wrong for a hard-hat to earn a college degree.

"Scratch an intellectual," writes Eric Hoffer, "and you find a would-be aristocrat who loathes the sight, the sound, and the smell of common folk." (And here let me add parenthetically that I realize it is dangerous to quote from Eric Hoffer. A few years ago he was the idol of the intellectuals. A self-taught man who scorned the academy and continued to do man's work on the dock, he could rightfully claim to be one of America's most original thinkers. And he was accepted as such, until one day the snobs came to realize that Hoffer wasn't just talking about true believers on the right. He also included the zealots of the left. Today his stock among leftist academics has dropped so sharply that I heard one, in typical tolerant liberal fashion, making fun of his accent.) Hoffer's favorite target is Herbert Marcuse, the academic revolutionary from San Diego, who has long lived comfortably in the California sun while hatching schemes to overthrow the system which makes his idyllic life possible. Marcuse, ironically enough, is a refugee from those European regimes set up by the intellectual theoreticians, and perhaps the very irony of his situation, the absurd divorce between his condition and the ideas he espouses, makes him the quintessential intellectual elitist.

"Professor Marcuse," says Hoffer, in a devastating piece of writing, "has lived among us for more than thirty years and now, in old age, his disenchantment with his country is spilling over into book after book. He is offended by the failure of egalitarian America to keep people in their place. He is frightened by 'the degree to which the population is allowed to break the peace and silence, to be ugly and to uglify things, to ooze familiarity and to offend against good form.' The vulgar invade 'a small reserved sphere of existence' and compel exquisite Marcusian souls to partake of their sounds, sights, and smells."

Herbert Marcuse, the very personification of the intellectual elitist. And yet, hilariously enough, the man is a Marxist, but with the reservation, of course, that the dictatorship of the proletariat should give way to the dictatorship of the student and the professor. A silly man, and an ungrateful man, the academic leader of a generation of well-heeled college revolutionaries who have never understood what it is to do meaningful work and take pride in that work. Snobs, both in Agnew's sense and in the sense once suggested by Lionel Trilling — people with pride in status but no pride in function.

"To a shabby would-be aristocrat like Professor Marcuse," concludes Hoffer, "there is something fundamentally wrong with a society in which the master and the worker, the typist and the bosses, do not live totally disparate lives."

Marcuse, of course, is an especially sad case. Yet he is revered in much of academe and at the very least respected among those word merchants dwelling just off the campuses. You'll surely never hear him referred to in the same contemptuous way, for instance, that people speak in their columns, their editorials and their classrooms, of the Vice President of the United States. Marcuse may seem an extreme example, yet in many ways his snobbery is typical, definitive of the attitudes held by the majority of our men of words. Consider one case, that of the eminently respectable liberal, Professor Victor Ferkiss, author of an acclaimed work called *Technological Man*. The astronauts, he loftily maintains, are "thoroughly conventional and middle class and essentially dull people who would make such nice neighbors and such unlikely friends." Just run that around your palate and savor it. "Could these," asks Professor Ferkiss, "be the supermen whom the race has struggled for a million years to produce?"

Unfortunately, Professor Ferkiss, despite his rather casual reference

130

to something sounding suspiciously like a neo-Nazi theory of genetics, is taken seriously by the snobs. Yet as I write this the astronauts are in the process of a third moon landing, while the intellectuals down below are providing the patter. The media men hold up their little capsule models to show us at just exactly what angle the astronauts will land; the astronauts are up there actually landing. And one is tempted to explain to Ferkiss and to the rest of the snobs who enjoy feeling superior to the astronauts, that the astronauts are their superiors in every possible respect — mentally, morally, pragmatically, physically. Each of them could outthink the Ferkisses in every measurable way. Each of them is capable of doing meaningful work, work which not only engages our imaginations and adds to the sum total of human knowledge, but also benefits our society materially and directly. Each of them is capable of bouncing the Ferkisses around like a volley ball, and each of them has a kind of courage the Ferkisses could never possibly muster. For you never have, nor will you ever, catch the Ferkisses up in those space ships. But they probably know this and the thought probably makes them just a bit bitter. Here are these nonacademic and therefore noncertified intellectuals doing the real intellectual work of our era. It's a little like the professor of American literature who can't write a novel and therefore hates Ernest Hemingway. But wouldn't it be nice for the snobs if they could convince enough people that what the race (whatever that is) struggled to produce was not these astronauts who would, after all make boring dinner guests and are therefore very basically lacking, but instead, themselves? And their dinner conversation is stimulating indeed. Then the snobs could get all these inferiors to work for *them* and wouldn't it be fun? Those bullies would never again kick sand in *your* eyes again. Right, Ferkiss?

In *The Temper of Our Times*, Hoffer writes:

Nothing so offends the doctrinaire intellectual as our ability to achieve the momentous in a matter-of-fact way unblessed by words. Think of it: Our unprecedented productive capacity, our affluence, our freedom and equality are not the end product of a sublime ideology . . . the skyscrapers, the huge factories, dams, powerhouses, docks, railroads, highways, airports, parks, farms, stem mostly from the utter trivial motive of profit. Equally galling is the fact that until now America has run its complex economy and complex governmental machinery without the aid of the typical intellectual. . . . Ironically, at a time when the world is becoming Americanized, the intellectual seems to be seceding from America . . . when you try to find out what it is in this country that stifles the American intellectual, you make a surprising discovery . . . what he cannot stomach is

131

the mass of American people. . . . The American intellectual rejects the idea that our ability to do things with little tutelage . . . is a mark of social vigor . . . when you talk to an American intellectual about common Americans it is as if you were talking about mysterious people living on a mysterious continent.

And this is certainly the impression that Charles Reich and his fellows give. The contempt for the average American workingman shown by the men of the word is astounding. Mayor Daley of Chicago in many ways is the spokesmen for a large number of working Americans. Yet look at how he was treated by the media in Chicago, when CBS invited him to present his views and then mocked those views by showing, unknown to the mayor, juxtaposed shots of street violence as he spoke. It may be bigotry when Mayor Daley heaps contempt on rioters. Yet there is just as much bigotry on the part of those college-trained rioters toward Mayor Daley, and certainly just as much reciprocal intolerance on the part of the media. The rioters were, if not completely excused, at least sympathized with, because they were unhappy with the system and wanted to change it. No attempt was made to excuse or sympathize with Mayor Daley because he was satisfied with the system and wanted to keep it. Yet Mayor Daley's sentiment is at least as valid as Abbie Hoffman's.

And how about that strange ambivalence in the intellectuals' attitude toward, respectively, blacks and what they call "ethnics"? Let Negroes riot in New Jersey, and no matter how widespread the destruction, no matter how wild the looting and violent the beatings, the intellectuals excuse it. "We must seek out the root causes," they tell us piously, and by so doing, condone the violence. Yet let the white workers of Gary or Cicero or Manhattan go on a rampage, then the Mayor Lindsays make headlines by calling for firm retaliatory measures. No root causes allowed here. The white workers aren't, after all, exotics. And let no one forget that during the last New York municipal elections, Mario Procaccino, the Democratic candidate for mayor, was the butt of jokes at a high-level gathering up at Yale because he was Italian and spoke with a pronounced Italian–American city accent. The boys had a good time with their ethnic jokes at Yale, the Alma Mater of New York's radical chic mayor, John Lindsay. But had Eldridge Cleaver been a candidate, you can bet your bottom dollar that they'd never have made fun of *his* accent, even though it's thick Arkansas-cotton-belt-minstrel-show black.

In a most perceptive essay appearing in the *American Scholar*, Michael Lerner, a leftist Yale graduate student, puts his finger on the problem. "Intellectuals," writes Lerner, "are able to assume that elite virtues are preferable to lower middle-class virtues across the board because they unconsciously restrict their idea of who should practice these virtues and to what end. . . . Blacks and students are expected to practice skepticism toward authority. If, on the other hand, the colonels, police, teamsters, longshoremen or garbage collectors practice prolonged skepticism toward constituted authority . . . then the elite semiradicals have a vague sense that something must be done."

The elite class, Lerner points out, believes "it can mock the politics of the policeman and the butcher while still living genteelly in the space between them. . . . There is little broad perspective in the words of the *New York Times* columnist [Tom Wicker] who wrote in sharp tones, 'Those are *our* children in the streets of Chicago.' That *Times* columnist did not understand a nation that approved of a police action in Chicago because its children were in the streets of Chicago, too. Its children were the police."

It is this elitist attitude, this attempt to exclude large segments of American society from full participation in government by systematically denigrating their views, that the Vice President has attacked in his most effective speeches. One such speech, for instance, given in Las Vegas in 1970, was occasioned by an editorial attack appearing in the *Las Vegas Sun*. It was a most typical media attack. The writer compared Agnew to Hitler, Stalin, and Mussolini, warned him, of course, to watch his rhetoric (this is a standard ingredient in all wild attacks on Agnew; the writers use language heated enough to peel wallpaper, then advise Agnew to cool *his* language), and then concluded: "The young intellectuals must never again permit a demagogue to so capture the hearts of the unthinking masses that the very foundations of the nation will be toppled."

The Vice President's response at the Nevada Republican Dinner was succinct, neatly encapsulating many of the points I've tried to make about the elitist point of view. "The single sentence says first of all that anyone who strongly stands up and speaks out for our principles is automatically a demagogue, secondly, that the people of Nevada, and by extension the citizens of the United States, are 'the unthinking masses' who, third, have to be led around by the nose by 'the young intellectuals.' "

Nowhere in the elitist view is there room for the aspirations and frustrations of the middle-class and blue-collar American. The emphasis is always on "the young, the black, the poor," and, of course, those affluent liberal types who dwell in the New York–Washington corridor. Thus, as a political phenomenon, Spiro Agnew has emerged as the voice of a long voiceless segment of American society, a segment which has

133

long sufferingly carried most of the nonproductive but highly audible segments on its back.

Agnew is antielitist. He is not, I think, anti-intellectual. In fact, a good case could be argued for Agnew as intellectual, as Max Lerner, for instance, has recently done. Consider the objects of his attacks, the things that rouse him. When he attacks the elitists in the media and in the universities, he does so because he finds their attitudes philosophically invalid, undemocratic. It is always an *idea* to which he responds, to the misuse of thought and words. If we accept Nathan Glazer's definition of an intellectual as one who lives for ideas, then I think we must see Agnew as an intellectual. It is the thought, the idea, that stirs him to action. ". . . as you all learn from your first course in philosophy," he says, "the difference between a free society and a totalitarian one is — the treatment of ends versus means."

(And this, of course, is the perfect response to those liberal media men who argue that their ends justify distortion.)

"In a totalitarian society, only the ends are important. The means to reach them, whether just or brutal, are irrelevant. In a free society, the means are just as important as the ends.

"The law is our means. . . . Structured law differentiates human civilization from animal anarchy. . . . I can claim no right as a human being or a citizen that you cannot claim equally under the law. . . . When any group asserts rights without commensurate responsibilities a privileged class emerges creating an atmosphere of abuse, paving the way to the ultimate abuse that is totalitarianism."

Vice President Agnew objects to civil violence, not because he finds the perpetrators of that violence personally offensive, although no doubt he does, but because their actions can lead, he feels, to the destruction of civilization.

And again: "Justice is founded in the rights bestowed by nature upon man. Liberty is maintained in the security of justice.' These two sentences are inscribed on a wall of the Justice Department building in Washington. I do not believe the first sentence is true.

I doubt that justice is founded in the rights of nature because we know that nature is not always just. . . . We might ask what justice exists in the jungle where carnivorous animals devour the weak and gentle? What justice is there in life where disease often cripples and kills the young and good?

What we regard as justice today does not exist by virtue of nature, but by the free will of mankind. Justice began the day we rejected the nature of savages and started something called civilization. Civilization progressed as we challenged and contested with the bestiality in ourselves. It advanced as we began to conquer the natural forces of fire, flood, famine, and disease. . . . If civilization is still a veneer, then civilized justice clearly requires constant, tender and protective care. . . . The citizens of this country are free to pressure Congress. They may petition and parade and protest before the President. They may howl and yowl and tax our patience. But when they move open rebellion into the courtroom, they remove from our midst all hope of justice.

Agnew is also interested in the psychology of the activist.

Emotion, formerly a person to person conduit, is now a closed circuit within the individual. The individual vicariously, and to whatever degree of involvement he wishes, tests love, hate, exhilaration, and depression by playing a spectator role disguised as an activist. For example, a militant demonstrator with a set of computer-fed beliefs can shout obscenities at me and charge my car, but really he has no *personal* encounter with me as an individual. His emotional experience is ersatz — entirely fake. A cause is his palliative for the competitive encounter of minds he secretly wishes to avoid. Dissent requires no dialogue — no assessment on either his or my part of the validity of his position.

All Agnew's best talks center on ideas, and as Max Lerner points out, Agnew may be the only politician on the American scene today of whom this can be said to be true. Yet there is the temptation to categorize Agnew as an anti-intellectual. And to an extent this is valid, insofar as we agree that there has grown up a certain class comprising university types, authors, publishers, and media men who share common attitudes and who think of themselves as belonging to the class called intellectual. Thus we sometimes use the word intellectual to describe members of a particular class, a special-interest group. When we do this, Agnew is of course properly labeled anti-intellectual. But when we return to the most basic definition, one who lives for ideas, then as good a case can be made for Agnew as intellectual as the case for, say, Arthur Schlesinger, Jr.

And even the emotional tone of Vice President Agnew's speeches springs from an intellectual decision.

The liberal media have been calling on me to lower my voice and to seek accord and unity among all Americans. Nothing would please me more than to see all voices lowered. . . . But I want you to know that I will not make a unilateral withdrawal and thereby abridge the confidence of the silent majority, the everyday law-abiding American who believes his country needs a strong voice to articulate his dissatisfaction with those who seek to destroy our heritage of liberty and our system of justice. To penetrate the cacophony of seditious drivel emanating from the best publicized clowns in our society and their fans in the fourth estate, yes my friends, to penetrate that drivel we need a cry of alarm, not a whisper.

What Agnew wants, in short, is a workable democracy. And a workable democracy is not possible when a nation's policy is set by elitists. Agnew is not anti-intellectual, but he is most definitely an antielitist, for elitism is completely antithetical to democracy.

12

BECAUSE OF the one-sided control of our national communication centers, the views of middle-America have little chance of being aired. Compounding the problem, as Nathan Glazer points out, has been "the inability of the American hinterland to develop spokesmen and leaders of substance."

The meteoric rise of Spiro Agnew to political prominence, however, suggests that the dearth of spokesmen for middle-America is ending. The enthusiastic response to his speeches indicates that Agnew may be, as Arthur Schlesinger, Jr. puts it, a "potential spokesman and leader of those Americans who feel that their views have too long been unrepresented in the national discourse."

Agnew has not, of course, been in a position to build a personal constituency, nor has he shown any desire to do so. The votes he attempts to win are for the administration he serves. But the intense reaction to his speeches shows that he has touched a nerve, and during his tenure as Vice President has, no matter how reluctantly, functioned as a lightning rod for as yet little understood political forces.

Something has been nudging around the edges of American politics for the past decade, and the political character of the nation has been shifting unpredictably. Traditional party alignments have been fractured, new groups, many still only roughly defined, find themselves unable to identify with the established organizations, and radical new ideas about man's relationship to his fellowman and to his government stir across the nation.

The new mood has been growing since the fifties, but few were aware of how deeply it had penetrated the political fabric of our society until 1968, when it crystallized during riots, conventions, assassinations. There was the new politics, on the one hand personified by Eugene McCarthy and Robert Kennedy and their neoromantic followers. And closely related was the emergence of an even newer politics, drawing its strength from the potentially explosive feeling of frustration among the white working and middle classes, a constituency that has remained silent and essentially nonideological during the preceding couple of decades. But suddenly, in 1968, they were heard from, and they came within a cat's whisker of throwing a considerable amount of support to George Wallace.

They were, and remain, deeply angry — angry at those politicians who invoked abstract panaceas and ended by creating national disaster areas of once respectable cities, angry because their families are preyed upon by criminals who seem to be coddled by the courts and wooed by politicians, angry because they believe they have been lied to, because they have been mocked and slandered. And they have a case. Go to see *Joe*. Look at the vicious cartoons printed in left liberal journals depicting the American workingman as a swag-bellied, beer-swilling, girl-ogling, kid-beating animal. (And let me add that I find this personally most offensive. I come from a working-class family, still carry a card in the laborer's union, and have also spent time on campuses. The majority of workingmen I've known are better read, more thoughtful, more polite, and certainly more impressive specimens than many of their campus cousins. I know a workingman who has read the *complete* works of Hardy. Few professors I know can make the same claim. And I'll give odds that if you drop in on a faculty party and then visit a workingman's bar, you're going to find the conversation in the bar a hell of a lot more enlightening than the faculty gossip.)

The workingman finds himself blamed by the men of words for many of our most serious national ills. Listen to that typical academic who complacently lays the responsibility for white racism at the feet of the workingman, while he himself, of course, keeps his own kids nicely cloistered in quiet little university-related schools. (Check out the faculties at Columbia or CCNY and see how many of them are willing to send their own children into New York's public schools.) Watch the initial bewilderment turn to anger when the workingman scrimps and saves and finally gets those kids to college, where the kids find their professors mocking every single standard and virtue that made it possible for them to get there. Watch the anger grow when the draft is modified, as the Supreme Court has modified it, so that any sharp student with a basic liberal arts education can fake his way out, while some apprentice or the boy who has begun working at a gas station must go instead, simply because he doesn't have a Contemporary Civilization reading list and the coaching of liberal arts professors.

What sort of system is it, the workingman wonders, in which the producers are expected to keep things running for those nonproductive types who can't make things run themselves but feel free to hold in contempt those who can? How must the workingman feel, as his sons die in Indochina, to be told by John Lindsay and the university and media types that the kids sneaking off to Canada are the ones really deserving of respect? Just what the hell sort of society is it, he wonders, in which an electrician's apprentice is held in lower esteem than a pot-smoking liberal arts major?

This is not to say that the workingman is anti-intellectual. Like Spiro Agnew himself, the average middle-American is, if anything, too respectful of the idea of the intellectual life. The standard media-peddled myth is that middle-Americans loathe university types. They do not. As anyone who has grown up in a working-class home knows, middle-Americans have tended in the past to worship at the altar of the educated man. There has traditionally been no higher ambition among such families than to send their sons to a university. And nothing causes greater pride than a son who becomes a professional man or a university professor. The middle-American did not begin to react against the university until evidence mounted that the campuses had become not centers of learning but rather staging areas from which a hostile new adversary culture launched assaults on American society.

In 1968, George Wallace understood all this. He knew what drove middle-Americans up the wall, and his pitch very nearly won their allegiance. To their credit, white workingmen didn't quite fall for it, although the temptations were great. I have talked to dozens of blue-collar workers, most of them union men, who told me that at the last moment they couldn't pull that Wallace lever because they feared that underneath it all he was a racist, something they could never be.

"We have done a grave disservice to the workingman by neglecting his central importance to our society," said Agnew in Baltimore, stating the basic view which defines his central role in the new American politics. Agnew's importance is that he gives middle-Americans somewhere to go and provides them with a voice. There is no lack of leadership for the other constituencies — the kids, welfare recipients, radical-chicers, academics, militant minorities. But the producers have few spokesmen, and increasingly few outlets within the system for venting their frustrations. The old FDR coalition has shattered, and the workingpeople of the country who, through their labor, have built up a considerable stake in the country's well-being (and are therefore, by the most basic definition, conservative), are searching out new alliances. It was tremendously significant that Jim Buckley, who during the 1968 Senatorial campaign had spoken out strongly against the minimum wage and for right-to-work laws, managed to capture forty percent of New York State's blue collar votes in 1970. The AFL–CIO gave its

139

endorsement, as expected, to Richard Ottinger, the Democratic candidate. But the unions gave the endorsement with no great enthusiasm and they never really opened up on Buckley as they could have done, never mounted the sort of last-minute, all-out campaign that just two years before had nearly sent Hubert Humphrey to the White House. The unions could have beaten Buckley had they desired to do so. It is most significant that they decided to offer only token opposition.

Buckley's victory in New York, in which the Vice President was most instrumental, was a landmark in American politics. The issue, for most of the campaign, was the social issue, and Spiro Agnew was the man who spoke most eloquently to it. People were tired of rioting, tired of seeing their tax dollars poured into bottomless programs which seemed to end only in bigger and better riots, tired of seeing college students marching under Viet Cong flags, tired of watching campuses blow up and burn down.

The social issue worked in New York, and well into September it appeared to be working in the rest of the nation. The "radic–lib" candidates seemed on the run everywhere, prompting Professor Harry Jaffa to observe "that as this campaign progresses, many Democrats will begin their addresses by denouncing Mr. Agnew, while devoting the remainder of their speeches to paraphrasing him." And they did just that. Out in Illinois, Adlai Stevenson suddenly was seen sporting an American flag lapel pin and calling for a crackdown on rioters. And up in Massachusetts, Teddy Kennedy began to sound like George Wallace with a Harvard accent.

But out in California the warning lights had begun to blink. Into October the Republicans seemed to be sailing confidently toward a smashing victory. Reagan, it was predicted, would beat Jess Unruh by a million and a half votes. His landslide victory would carry George Murphy back into the Senate, and the Republicans would take commanding control of the state legislature.

As October slipped by, however, the unemployment rate continued to rise. Down in Orange County, in the heart of Reagan country, where a new coalition between traditionally Democratic workingmen and conservative Republicans had been operating effectively since 1966, unemployment in the building trades passed twenty percent. Workers throughout California who, although once New Deal Democrats, were now conservatively inclined on the social issue, began to feel the economic pinch. By election day the economic issue was *the* issue. The specter of Herbert Hoover once again stalked the land, and traditional Democrats voted Democrat once more. When the dust settled, Reagan had won by only half a million votes (a dismal showing, given the complete disorganization and demoralization of California's Democratic Party, and given the incredibly inept campaign waged by Jess Unruh); George Murphy had been thumped by John Tunney, an unknown plagued throughout his campaign by an inability to say anything bright and an unnerving giggle; and the Republicans had lost control of the state legislature, a control they had been painstakingly building toward throughout the decade.

The pattern spread rapidly eastward. The message from the White House was to remain confident, to keep punching on the social issue and to ignore the economy. Richard Nixon's theory was that you never campaign on another party's issue, that you never let yourself become defensive. The Vice President's staff disagreed. There was no reason, they pointed out, to let the Democrats have the economic issue. The economy, after all, was in sorry shape because of the wild spending policies of two Democratic administrations. And compounding this was the economic displacement resulting from the winding down of the war. It would have been possible to restore the economy to full health immediately only by returning the war to the Johnson level.

"Consider this," said the Vice President. "The armed services have released 400,000 into the job market in the past twenty-one months . . . cuts in defense spending and the winding down of the war in Vietnam have reduced the number of jobs by 800,000." What, asked Agnew, would the Democratic critics "have done about this addition to unemployment — kept them in the army?" And how about defense spending. What would they have done about that — "raised defense expenditures?" And in addition, of course, there was the further irony that those Democrats most vociferous on the subject of the economy were the same Democrats who months earlier had been launching attacks on the military–industrial complex and on the war effort, attacks which must logically lead, if they were effective in their ends — as they were — to economic dislocation.

According to members of Agnew's staff, he wanted to tackle the issue head on, to carry the fight to the Democrats, to tell Americans that their economic discomfort was the direct result of Democratic policies. But the White House said no and Agnew, albeit reluctantly, stuck to the social issue.

This does not mean that Agnew for a moment considered abandoning the social issue. Rather, he simply considered it folly to ignore the omens that anyone who ventured outside the White House compound, where the picture of the world out there tends to grow fuzzy, could have divined. And when the returns came in, everyone belatedly agreed. Given the high hopes the Republicans had carried into the campaign, and given the crucial necessity for Republicans to approach parity in the number of Senators and Representatives, the '70 elections represented a political disaster.

Since 1970 there has been an attempt on the part of the media and among unfriendly Nixon supporters to pin the blame for the debacle on Spiro Agnew. His speeches, say the critics, were so hostile and divisive that they discouraged great numbers of voters from going Republican. But this, of course, is moonshine. Agnew points out quite correctly that it would have been impossible to divide the country any more deeply than it was divided in 1970. The problem was how to channel these divisions into meaningful political activity. Consider, he said on *Firing Line*, "the entire arena of American politics and our adversary system . . . when people run against each other for public office, they don't go around complimenting each other; they attempt to indicate that they have a better solution to the problems of this country . . . they imply, at least, and sometimes very forcefully, that the opponent has no solution — and, in fact, really is quite inept for the job he is seeking. So, we have our adversary system. . . . There isn't any such thing as a divisive aspect to campaigning over and above the natural divisions that result in a campaign. Most Presidents are elected with fifty-five percent or less of the vote, which means that forty-five percent were divided at the time of the campaign anyhow. And the whole process is a process of selection which implies in itself that it leads to certain divisions among the electorate. This doesn't mean that we should, of necessity, exacerbate tensions between people, but it does mean that we must avoid the tendency that's eulogized by the liberal philosophers . . . to always seek a benign nothing solution to the hard problems we face. And we should always avoid, they say, indicating our differences. I find that when you do that you don't solve any problems. People walk away from each other thinking they're in agreement, only to find out that they're really not."

Agnew's views on the politics of "positive polarization" are anchored in a deep faith in the two-party system. Under such a system, ideally, each party articulates clearly defined but different philosophies, methods, and goals. At some moments in history, those rare moments of absolute tranquillity, the parties will be much alike. But usually, there should be sharp contrasting differences, one party at one time speaking to the needs of an age, at another time the second party better interpreting the wishes of the electorate. But we have increasingly come to see in this century an homogenization, a blending of the two parties which makes it difficult, judging by actions, to tell Democrats from Republicans. Both seem intent on getting to the same issues first, and when they arrive, intent on taking identical stands. It is very difficult indeed, for instance, to imagine what a liberal Democrat would do that

Richard Nixon has not done. His positions on welfare, his attitude toward defense and disarmament, his views on economics, would seem perfectly consistent in the most liberal of Democratic administrations. And how mind-boggling it is that the first supposedly conservative candidate to reach the Presidency since the Nationalists lost the civil war should turn out to be the President most instrumental in legitimizing the Chinese Communist regime.

The problem, of course, is that with the blending of the parties and the fuzzing of legitimate differences, the two major political parties, racing to get to the accepted issues first, must necessarily end by being unresponsive to a large group of constituents, pandering instead to identifiable clusters of politicized bloc voters, such clusters, taken together, capable of providing narrow electoral victories. But those victories are getting tighter.

The American workingman was long considered the automatic supporter of Democratic candidates. The Democrats came increasingly to take him for granted, and the Republicans, despairing of ever weaning him away, just gave up. And so, ironically, although his bloc vote was the largest in the country, he came into the sixties finding that no one was talking to him any longer. His discontent grew to anger, and for the first time since the Roosevelt era he was ready to listen to non-Democratic politicians. It is to the credit of Spiro Agnew that he realized this and acted on it. For if one of the major parties is not willing to listen to the hopes and fears of the nation's majority group, members of that group will inevitably look to some other party. George Wallace's third party movement will not disappear until the major parties find some way of accommodating those Americans who listen to Wallace. And if they do not, we can expect the ranks of third and fourth party movements to swell, until such time that those narrow electoral victories will no longer be possible.

There is only one way to prevent this: The major parties must expand their bases. This is what Agnew understood in '68 and '70, and this is what he set out to do for the Republican party. In '68, he won the support of the border states for the Republicans and made significant inroads into the Southern vote. In 1970 he figured significantly in Jim Buckley's victory. The social issue was still *the* issue in New York State in 1970, and that blue collar vote that put Jim Buckley into office was the vote of the Agnew constituency. New York State gives the lie to the argument that Agnew's campaigning hurt the GOP. ("The Southern strategy worked in only one state — New York," quipped one columnist. And in a sense he was right. The Southern strategy was based on the social issue. And in New York, which didn't feel the pinch of the recession until much later, the social issue was the only issue.)

143

Agnew won new support for the party, the sort of support it had long despaired of ever winning. The economic issue lost it much of this newly won support in states such as California. But this has nothing to do with Agnew's campaign. The Christine Jorgensen crack, directed at Charles Goodell in New York and widely deplored by the media as excessive, didn't hurt Jim Buckley's campaign at all. But the state of the economy in California, a condition having no relationship whatever to Agnew's stance on the social issue, certainly hurt George Murphy's campaign. And had Agnew been given his head to speak out on the economy, many of those Republican incumbents who lost their seats believe that the results might have been different.

The dangers to Republicans in misreading the elections of 1970 are grave. If they decide that the Agnew campaign was at fault, rather than blaming the true culprit, the economy, they will draw back from taking those steps toward building a new constituency. Given the fact that there are more registered Democrats than Republicans, and given disturbing phenomena such as the recent defection of leading conservatives, it is difficult indeed to see how the Republicans can be overconfident about the '72 elections.

But perhaps, in the end, this may not be completely unsalutary, for conservatives had long deluded themselves that after the Goldwater debacle they had succeeded in winning major influence in the Republican party, only to discover that Richard Nixon really didn't think they were worth pampering after all, much as the Democrats once decided that they no longer needed to court the workingman. What seems increasingly necessary is some sort of new party alignment, one which can provide space for conservative and liberal, workingman and college professor.

As the demography of the party continues to change, as Kevin Phillips' "Sun Belt" increasingly becomes the center of national population and production, it seems likely that the two parties could change beyond recognition, one perhaps a sort of Republicrat party run by Nixonite conservatives and the Agnew constituency, the other essentially an urbanist–intellectual–academic–welfarist Demopublican party led by men such as John Lindsay or Edward Kennedy. It is difficult, I know, for many conservative Republicans to consider making common cause with, say the AFL–CIO. But the old labels have become meaningless, and whether the party remains the *traditional* party is irrelevant. What matters is that it provide an alternative.

Spiro Agnew's key role since 1968 has been to attempt to make the Republican party one which offers clear alternatives. He sees himself, and rightly so, I believe, as the ambassador of the common people to Washington, and he provides, at a time when it is most needed, a political channel through which the increasingly dangerous pent-up frustrations of middle-America can be released.

Unlike many of the rogue populists of the American past, with whom he is often confused, Agnew has no demagogic aspirations. He is today much the same man who fought for open housing in Maryland while at the same time scolding black leaders for irresponsibility. Agnew has remained consistent; it is the American political scene that has shifted wildly in the past few years. He considers himself neither a right- nor a left-winger: "I think I'm properly considered a part of the center," he said on *Firing Line.* "Labels are very difficult. I made some judgments in the course of my political career . . . which have been characterized as flaming liberal. I don't think they were; I think they were sensible. I think some of the things I'm saying now that are compatible with the views of the people who consider themselves very conservative are still sensible."

Agnew is quite right, I think, in his description of himself. He is not an ideologue: Like most Americans, he is conversative on some issues, liberal on others. He is also a man of conviction ("He is not as flexible as some," comments Arthur Burns, "but I would not call him inflexible. He has convictions. Should a man be flexible about his convictions?"). And one of these convictions is that the two-party system should be revitalized, that *every* American should be served politically by a major party responsive to his needs.

For too long, a great number of Americans, concerned over the increasingly erratic direction of the Democratic party, a party that once, they felt, served their best interests, have had nowhere to go, no avenue of political expression. They have been alarmed by the capture of their party by the elitists, the practitioners of the new politics of sensibility. But there has been no alternative for them. They couldn't go to Goldwater. And so they flocked to Johnson, only to find him ultimately powerless, finally hounded out of office by the phrasemakers. And then came Agnew. He made a few speeches, was properly chastised by the people of the word, and pronounced politically dead. But, incredibly he didn't lie down and take it and apologize for his impudence. Instead he punched even harder, accusing his critics themselves of impudence. For this, of course, they hate him, because he threatens their carefully constructed dreams of a new politics. ("Indeed," Irving Kristol has said, "one is often tempted to conclude that the cry for a new politics really amounted to little more than a demand for certain groups that the political process concede to them greater power and influence than they are entitled to under our traditional democratic formulas.")

In times such as this there can be no such thing as consensus politics. Our differences are deep and real and they must be aired politically rather than suppressed. For any one group in this society to argue, as the gas-sniffers have done, that its views are primary and should predominate is asinine.

Agnew, more than any other figure on the contemporary political scene, has blown the whistle on the elitists, has drawn attention to their attempts to establish an ideological hegemony. This country is *not* unified, and it is not necessary that it should be. What *is* necessary is that every group willing to try to live within the system be given a chance to make its views heard. Many underprivileged people and groups have found an outlet in the Democratic party. It is fitting that those productive citizens of middle-America be given the same opportunity. It is only through a system based on adversary politics, that we can judge the merits of the hopes, wishes, and complaints of *all* Americans. We have tended to worry a great deal about New Left revolutionaries. But such worries would seem puny indeed if middle-Americans, denied the sort of political release provided by a Spiro Agnew, decided to take care of things themselves. One hopes that the leaders of the Republican party can understand this.

13

SINCE I BEGAN this book, some of the central issues I discussed have been resolved, while others still hang fire. The McNamara papers controversy continues to sputter, and Daniel Ellsberg will soon be brought to trial, an affair that promises to be as dragged out and as inconclusive as the trial of the Manson family or the Angela Davis fiasco. But the steam has pretty well gone out of the issue, because the media people find themselves in an odd position. Just as they were most vociferously arguing the case for the people's right to know, Richard Nixon announced his China trip, a move which, as I mentioned earlier, they find it difficult to criticize. Had the plans been leaked in advance, they concede, the trip probably would have been called off.

The *Selling of the Pentagon* flap seems pretty well defanged. Representative Harley Staggers tried, and failed, to get his colleagues to vote to require CBS to provide Congress with all the materials relating to the production of the show. No one gave him much chance of succeeding, of course, since most Congressmen aren't willing to vote openly on the floor of the House for a measure which the media have made a pure freedom-of-speech issue. It is interesting, however, that most of those Representatives who voted against the measure but who took the floor to comment on it spent most of their time denouncing CBS for distortion. And shortly thereafter, Dr. Frank Stanton, head of CBS, issued an official memo to his news department forbidding it to continue the editing practices which led to the distortions. Stanton, in other words, by writing that memo, admitted that CBS had indeed been guilty of what it was charged with.

One thing remains the same, however, since I began the book. The media still loathe Agnew and have redoubled their efforts to drive him from the political scene. Their efforts have grown increasingly wild, at

147

times almost unhinged, as witness the press coverage of his 10-nation round-the-world trip.

In their attempts to analyze the *why* of the trip, they began by touching all the bases. First, of course, was the Dump-Agnew thesis. Since 1970, when the columnists began tentatively to suggest that Richard Nixon was thinking of getting rid of Agnew, there has been a daily stream of speculation about the '72 ticket. Most of it, of course, was media-inspired, the sources for the rumors always being identified as "sources close to" or "informed sources" or "high-ranking officials" or, limpest of all, "observers." This is an old media trick, intended to lend an air of authority to the webs you spin out of yourself.

However, there has also been in recent months some reason for the rumors above and beyond newsmen's fantasies, for there is one group of Nixon supporters who would love to see Agnew go. These are, for the most part, either ex-Ripon types, who want the administration purged of all conservative taints, or PR types who understand almost nothing about politics. These people are not in a majority in the party, and much of their gossip is, as John Roche said of the McNamara papers, third-echelon chitchat. Nevertheless, especially in Washington, rumors feed on themselves, and many of those who invent a rumor end up believing it.

There is no indication that Richard Nixon has even considered a change in the '72 ticket, and until he does all speculation is futile. As of this writing, Agnew will have the nomination if he wants it. But one thing is certain: The media men don't want him to get it. Thus the most popular rumor about the Vice President's 32-day trip was that it was intended as a farewell present from Nixon, preparatory to dumping him from the ticket. Given the nature of the trip, however — the places visited, the things done — the trip soon began to seem something less than a desirable present. So then the media decided that the trip was intended to appease kings, emperors, amirs, caudillos, and, in general, all those fascist types. And who better, of course, to send on such a trip than Spiro Agnew? And then the China announcement — Agnew's trip was obviously intended as a ploy to get him out of the country so that he wouldn't spill the beans about the trip in advance. But this one proved a little shaky, too, for the media men also argued that Agnew didn't know anything about the trip, and if he didn't know anything about the trip, it seemed just a bit strained to argue that he would tell anyone about it. And so, finally, the ultimate argument: Agnew's trip was intended as nothing at all.

No one, of course, except Agnew's press secretary and a few wild-eyed right-wingers, dared suggest that the trip was exactly what it seemed — a diplomatic trip, pure and simple, a trip intended to improve or cement relations with friendly countries, some of which hadn't received a great deal of American attention over the last couple of years, and all of which could understandably be expected to be nervous over our apparent new China policy.

But this was simplistic, of course. There had to be deeper and darker implications. And so the speculation about the purpose of the trip continued well after Agnew's return, the media men frantic to come up with an explanation that reflected the maximum amount of discredit on the Vice President.

Now one shouldn't be too surprised that the media men have had a great deal of trouble figuring out just why the Vice President took that trip, for if recent media performances prove anything, they prove that the men of the national press are singularly inept at investigative reporting — or for that matter, at seeing what goes on around them.

Recall, for instance, just how badly the press was faked out by Henry Kissinger's trip to Peking. Kissinger was tailed to Pakistan by the press corps whose job was to watch his every move, report his every action. Yet Kissinger disappeared for *three days,* and not *one* reporter had the nose for news or even the native wit to doubt his bogus cover story. Instead they contented themselves with eating well, drinking well, and writing cute little stories about the Montezuma's revenge with which Kissinger was supposedly afflicted. And the *Washington Post,* and one of our great national newspapers, summing up what was obviously its considered judgment of Kissinger's trip after he left Pakistan, printed a large picture of him squiring a stunning décolleté blonde around Paris.

One thinks also of the recent *National Review*–Pentagon Papers hoax. The editors of *National Review* sat down in their offices one afternoon, concocted a bunch of bogus documents written in perfect bureaucratese, and published them as the real thing. Anyone familiar with the magazine knew they were sham. And anyone unfamiliar with the magazine should have been at least slightly suspicious. But the men of the *Washington Post,* whose *job* it is to be suspicious, swallowed them hook, line, and sinker and reprinted sizable chunks. The *Post,* later discovering how badly it had been faked out, has nursed a bad case of sulks ever since. When eleven conservatives issued a statement withdrawing support from Richard Nixon, every paper in the country picked it up. Every paper, that is, except the *Post.* Their reason: It was signed by the editor and publisher of *NR.* Sort of like, I'll take my ball and go home, isn't it?

And meanwhile, we're still waiting for the *Post* to write one of their thoughtful editorials on the breakdown of investigative reporting, perhaps an editorial in which the phrase is necessarily redefined. Neil

Sheehan of the *New York Times* might provide a good model for that redefinition. Sheehan, you'll remember, has received most of the credit for the *New York Times* edition of the McNamara papers. And how did he do it? Well, there was thief and a Xerox machine. The thief xeroxed top-secret documents and either gave or sold them to the *New York Times* which, as soon as "this material came into our hands," as the *Times* always euphemistically puts it, turned it over to reporter Sheehan. Sheehan then wrote some biased summaries, the *New York Times* published them, crediting Sheehan for "investigative reporting," and now all Sheehan has to do is sit back and wait to be nominated for the Pulitzer Prize. Easy, when you're on the right side.

Asininity, with a healthy dose of malice, characterizes much of the press coverage of the trip. In a striking piece, read into the *Congressional Record* by N.Y. Congressman Jack Kemp, *Human Events* analyzes some of the more flagrant instances of media malice. The article, which devastatingly dissects *Newsweek*'s version of the trip, is worth reprinting in its entirety.

Nothing better demonstrates the validity of Vice President Agnew's charge of media bias than press coverage of his recent 10-nation round-the-world trip.

When you cover anything concerning Agnew, the drill is always to search out and highlight the gaffe. But gaffes were so scarce that *Time* magazine was forced to observe cryptically, its correspondent touchingly desperate, "In private talks and ceremonial functions, Agnew, from all available evidence, has performed flawlessly. Perhaps too flawlessly."

Now, how's that for criticism? If you were unkind you might even call it asinine. The asininity bug, in fact, seems to have bitten several of *Time-Life*'s stable of poetasters.

Hugh Sidey, for instance, sputtering around in *Life* for some new way to knock the Vice President, finally comes up with a couple of startling comparisons. The Vice President, he tells us, failed to live up to the standards of diplomatic deportment set by "Lyndon Johnson riding a bullock cart in India and giving the rebel yell in the Taj Mahal; and Hubert Humphrey calling hogs at a Vietnam livestock research farm and wearing his baseball hat on a ride down a river in Thailand."

Breathtaking. Agnew could have donned his Washington Senators baseball cap, ridden a bullock cart through the streets of Saudi Arabia, called hogs in the Congo, and ripped loose with a rebel yell in a mosque in Morocco. What a masterstroke it would have been for American diplomacy. Kings and emperors and amirs really love that sort of thing. And Mr. Sidey and his colleagues, we can be sure, would have written glowingly of such a performance.

But you can't really be too hard on poor silly Sidey. His predicament is that of most of the newsmen covering the trip: How do you make Agnew look bad when he performs almost flawlessly?

The answer, of course, is that you can't, unless you're willing to eschew facts and concentrate instead on distortion and ridicule. If he won't flub things up, you invent a fantasy in which he does so. And this is precisely what many media men set out to do, none more diligently than a scavenger called Andrew Jaffe, African correspondent for *Newsweek*.

The *Newsweek* account of the Vice President's trip, and especially his visit to the Treetops restaurant in Kenya, has become famous. Scores of columnists have used it as the definitive writeup, and it has been read into the *Congressional Record*, during which reading Jaffe's description of copulating rhinos, the best-known section of the piece, provoked an oddly salacious comment from a snickering U.S. Representative (and perhaps we should worry just a bit about the mental health of any man who seems to be turned on by the image of rhinos copulating).

It seems fitting that it was *Newsweek*. Among the organs of the national media, *Newsweek* has consistently shown the strongest symptoms of acute Agnewphobia. Presently they are lobbying mightily to get John Connally the No. 2 spot on the Republican ticket (only because, of course, like the Democratic National Committee, they love Richard Nixon and want him to have the strongest possible running mate in '72) and their previous hatchet jobs on Agnew have been among the most virulent. One such attack, similarly an ax job by a scavenger correspondent, actually prompted a letter of apology from the editor of *Newsweek* to the Vice President. The copulating rhino piece, however, is nonpareil in *Newsweek*'s anti-Agnew history.

There are seven paragraphs in the *Newsweek* article. Five of these contain errors of fact, conscious distortions, and dishonest omissions. The tone of the article is malicious, its method ridicule, its object to evoke contempt.

We are introduced to the Vice President "swinging his driver like a machete," "currently flailing his way around the world. . . ." His cargo plane carries two Cadillacs "for Agnew's dash from airport to hotel to golf course." We see him, when not "hacking up the local golf course," making ludicrous statements and giving and receiving ludicrous gifts and, despite all evidence to the contrary, generally making an ass of himself in the diplomatic world.

"Agnew has not made any serious *faux pax* so far," writes correspondent Jaffe, who openly hopes for better things (note the *so far*), "but he worked in many little ones." What are these little ones? Jaffe names four: "He called Arabia's King Faisal 'Prince Faisal,' referred to Jomo Kenyatta as Yomo Kenyatta, pronounced the name of Kenya itself the colonial way (*Keenya* instead of *Kenya*) and insisted that he is not going to any NATO countries on this round of diplomacy."

These are Jaffe's *only* substantive charges of blundering. And the substance is suspect indeed. The reference to "Prince" Faisal occurred on board Air Force Two, was quickly corrected by the Vice President himself, and would never have seen print had not a quick transcript been released to newsmen to facilitate their reports.

Thus, the charge that Agnew committed a *faux pas*, even a minor one, is false. It could only have been a *faux pas* had the reference been made before Saudi Arabian diplomats. (And this is why Jaffe can be called a scavenger. He joined the trip only briefly in Nairobi, relying completely on such news sources as unedited transcripts and casual comments from other reporters to flesh out his piece. He literally "scavenged" news.)

The Yomo pronunciation, the result of some erroneous spur-of-the-moment staff advice, was also quickly corrected. (Had the same pronunciation been used by, say, an Ed Muskie or a Ted Kennedy, you can be sure that *Newsweek*'s editors would have ignored the whole business—or picked up that pronunciation.) And as for *Keenya* versus *Kenya*, as many Kenyans themselves use the former as the latter.

The last charge, that Agnew "insisted" he wasn't going to visit NATO countries when he was, in fact, going to visit Portugal, is again an example of distorted scavenger reporting. The scene was a hectic plane-side news conference, at which scores of questions about Asia were being shouted. The last question, "What about NATO?" seemed, especially in the confusion, out of place. The response was automatic — we're not visiting NATO countries.

Again, there was a correct quick correction — we're talking about the Far East, we are going to Portugal. But once more, there was that unedited transcript for the scavenger to pick over.

And it's all irrelevant anyhow, for Jaffe hastens to inform us that Portugal, the only NATO country the Vice President chooses to visit, is also the only NATO country left that "still has large colonial holdings in Africa." And you know what *that* means.

Those are the substantive charges. Now on to some distortions. "Agnew spent under an hour with Haile Selassie. . . ." Fact: Agnew met Haile Selassie three times for over three hours. Agnew spent "all of 15 minutes with Kenya's Jomo Kenyatta and his cabinet. . . ." Fact: Agnew spent more than two hours and 45 minutes with Kenyatta.

He talked to the prime minister, met the vice president of Kenya, and played golf with the foreign minister, an outing characterized by Jaffe as "hacking up the local golf course." Jaffe forgets to mention that, in addition to the foreign minister, "hacking" along with Agnew were the vice chancellor of the University of Nairobi and the U.S. ambassador.

Much in the same vein is Jaffe's account of the Korean visit: The Koreans "shunted him off to the links." "Shunted" is a rather odd word to choose to describe an invitation by President Chung Hee Park to play 18 holes, an invitation extended on the *first* day after his inauguration.

Jaffe's choice of words is selective throughout. He tells us, for instance, that among what we are obviously to regard as rather absurd gifts, Agnew received from the Kenyans "a monkey skin robe." Nowhere is it mentioned that that "monkey skin robe" signifies the position of elder in the Kikuyu tribe and is one of the highest honors that can be accorded a foreign visitor.

We could go on like this for pages. *Newsweek* says there were four Boeing 707's flying the party. There were two. *Newsweek* says there were 141 people in the party. The Vice President's staff consisted of 15 people — 5 from his personal staff, 10 from the State Department. The Vice President has no control over the size of the Secret Service contingent and their numbers are never released.

There are numerous other instances of error. (The challenge, in fact, is to find an accurate statement or figure.) But the most objectionable section of the article is the one dealing with those rhinos. In

Kenya, Agnew's "main outing was to a nearby hunting lodge, where in company with his private physician and his pretty, red-haired secretary, he watched two rhinos copulating."

Now the "hunting lodge" is actually Treetops restaurant, an obligatory stop for visiting dignitaries. Treetops is built over a watering hole and a salt lick, a gathering place for Africa's great wild herds. On the afternoon and evening of the Vice President's visit, it is estimated that his party saw 101 Cape buffalo, 49 elephants, 16 rhinos, three mongoose, as well as waterbucks, baboons and numerous other animals.

So why single out those two rhinos? Why not say, for instance, that the Vice President and his party watched three elephants defecate? And why single out a personal physican and a pretty red-head to watch the rhinos with Agnew when, in fact, there were thirty-five people in the party, including, as Agnew's press secretary puts it, "one free-loading, free-riding scavenger correspondent from *Newsweek* who got a free ride up and a free ride back from Nairobi." (The eleven members of the press traveling with the party paid their own way from the United States. Jaffe is the only reporter whose way was paid.)

All thirty-five in the party, including the Kenyan ambassador to the U.S., the Kenyan minister of national parks, high Kenyan officials and U.S. diplomats, saw the rhinos copulate. Why not mention them too? Why, you'd ruin the innuendo. What innuendo? Ask that snickering congressman.

Newsweek bills itself as the magazine that separates fact from opinion and in their hatred for the Vice President — a hatred shared by many of the national media men since he held up that mirror in Des Moines and made them take a hard look at themselves — they've managed to make the separation complete. All opinion, no fact. But perhaps that depends on your definition. The organ of the Democratic National Committee, after all, is called FACT.

The depth of the media men's hatred for Agnew never came through as vividly as in the coverage of his trip. Shortly after the trip, four reporters — Peter Kumpa, diplomatic correspondent for the *Baltimore Sun*; Hays Gorey of *Time* magazine; Steve Gerstel, United Press International; and Edward O'Brien of the *St. Louis Globe-Democrat* — all of whom had traveled with the Vice President, appeared together at a public forum before a Washington Press Club group at the Statler-Hilton to discuss the trip.

Edward O'Brien gave an interesting stop-by-stop account of the trip and seemed generally grateful for the way the press corps had been treated. But the other three performances were incredible.

First came Kumpa, a man with a lurching, slurring voice, a voice that suggests all the worst qualities of Jimmy Breslin and W.C. Fields, with just a touch of the least pleasing nasalities of the late Fred Allen. Kumpa, it is obvious from a tape of the performance, was drunk — in fact, he says so: ". . . I've had more drinks than anyone else." (One of the things that the people who traveled with him most noticed about Kumpa was his chronic fondness for booze.)

"This was a lousy, dull trip," he says, because "we were traveling with a very shallow, boring man" who conducted himself "with absolutely no style and grace. . . ." Style and grace, and that from a slurring, rather pitiful man who continually feels it necessary to remind his audience, and perhaps also himself, that he is a "diplomatic correspondent." Loathing for Agnew literally drips from him as he maunders and mumbles. Agnew, he says, is "an introverted, ethnic middle-American. . . ."

And there you have it. Hatred for Agnew because he is "ethnic," because he is "middle-American." It is unnecessary for Kumpa to go further. He has made his point. The words "ethnic" and "middle-American" are pejorative, and obviously no man who can be characterized by them deserves to be Vice President.

And as you listen to Kumpa, the reason for the hostile reporting of the trip becomes clear. They *hate* the man, hate what he represents, and they will do everything in their power to discredit him. In that bumbling, boozy talk is encapsulated the spirit of the media, a spirit of impudent snobbery.

Gerstel and Gorey perform similarly, though perhaps a bit more soberly. Gorey is careful to go on record as believing the *Newsweek* account a cheap shot, although he milks it himself for titters by referring to the "the case of the copulating rhinos." Gorey points out that the trip was an evil one because Agnew visited only "dictatorships" (although, of course, he'd never think of denouncing Nixon's plan to visit the most oppressive dictatorship on earth) and concludes by stating that in his opinion Agnew's stature was not enhanced. He might also have added, of course, that the only way Agnew could have gained stature from the trip was by having the press traveling with him *say* that his stature was enhanced. Since the only way the American public had of knowing how the Vice President did was by reading the dispatches the press sent back about him, the press had the ultimate say in forming public opinion of the trip. If they said his stature was enhanced, it would be. If they decided his stature had been diminished, probably most people reading the dispatches would agree, since they have noth-

155

ing but the dispatches from which to form judgments. Awesome power indeed, and frightening, when you consider that that power is exercised almost solely on the basis of the personal and political biases of men of the quality of Peter Kumpa.

Steve Gerstel also gets some mileage out of the copulating rhinos. Agnew, he complains, was more "interested in relations between copulating rhinos" than in relations with the press. Gerstel makes the ritual denunciation of the *Newsweek* story, and then brings down the house with an insinuating comment about the image of Agnew watching the rhinos "while fondling his red-haired secretary. . . ." Gerstel says, of course, that he is merely passing along the image he carried away from the *Newsweek* story, but it is obvious that he relishes the transmission.

Gerstel, of course, may suffer from Kumpa's affliction. He says flatly, for instance, of that night at Treetops: "I was drunk. . . ." Lord knows, I would be the last man in the world to inveigh against alcohol. But I do think that perhaps an overfondness for booze plus distinct ideological bias might just manage to get in the way of fair and impartial, to say nothing of accurate, reporting. And this, of course, is to say nothing about the whole business of good taste and dignity.

The coverage of the trip has been, for many, the last straw. Victor Gold, Agnew's press secretary, a man highly respected among the solid professionals of the press, recently took the highly unusual step for a press secretary, most of whom shun controversy as if it were cholera, of calling the *Washington Star* personally to blast "the sloppy, rotten reporting" that characterized the coverage. The depth of Gold's anger and despair can be measured by the fact that he stipulated that he could be quoted, something that few press secretaries would dream of doing. It has become painfully clear to those around Agnew that they are going to have to set the record straight themselves. There are few among the impudent snobs and the large national newspapers and TV networks who are willing to strive for fairness or even good taste.

But Agnew's staff won't be able to do it alone, of course. The time is near when Agnew himself will once more have to take his case to the people directly, once again speaking to the American public over the heads of the media middlemen. And when he does, the chances are good that the response will be as enthusiastic as it was at Des Moines. Despite the determination of the media to ignore them, there are still a lot of middle-class Americans living west of New Jersey.

One hopes, when the next explosion comes, that the conservatives will be with him.

Many conservative Agnew partisans, of whom I am one, have noticed what we believe to be a distinct coolness in relations between the Vice President and many conservative spokesmen. This may, of course, merely be a manifestation of paranoia, an affliction not uncommon among people — especially writers — who concern themselves with politics. But many of us point to a rather conspicuous lack of favorable commentary in conservative journals. *Human Events* will defend the Vice President when he is attacked, and does reprint some of his choicer speeches. And the American Conservative Union's *Battle Line* did, several months ago, print a ringing endorsement of Agnew by Jeff Bell. Yet, despite these occasional salvos, there seems to be a discernible lack of enthusiasm among literary conservatives. For instance, Agnew has never been the subject of a thoughtful profile by a first-rate conservative writer as were Barry Goldwater or Ronald Reagan, and some of us believe that in the continuing media-inspired campaign to get Agnew off the '72 ticket, conservative attempts to scotch anti-Agnew rumors have been a bit less than wholehearted.

We may, as I say, be paranoid. But some of us believe that there is a tendency among members of the responsible right to keep pro-Agnew sentiments well under wraps, almost as if for some complicated reason it has been decided that he just can't be considered a full-fledged member of the family. At any rate, even though our sensibilities may be a bit too delicate, it seems time to make a conservative case for Spiro Agnew.

First there is the practical political case.

The basic argument is that it would be disastrous for the conservative movement and the Republican party were Spiro Agnew to be removed from the national ticket in 1972. Two considerations here seem paramount: Agnew's removal could alienate a constituency which seems to lie almost within the grasp of conservative Republicans — the blue-collar constituency; and his removal might insure the solidification of a new Dixiecrat South.

Both considerations, of course, are complicated by the recent conservative break with Richard Nixon. For some conservatives this step obviously represents a tentative break with the Republican party, as witness the fairly widespread flirtation with Senator Jackson. Now there is nothing wrong with this per se. Conservatives don't necessarily have to be card-carrying Republicans to be conservatives. But the thrust of contemporary conservatism seems consistently to have been toward a merging with contemporary Republicanism, the eventual goal being to make the conservative wing the most powerful wing of the party. To break with the Republican party now would be to undo decades of painstaking work, rendering such things as the Goldwater revolution, for instance, as monumental exercises in political futility and wasted effort.

Common sense argues that conservatives, even if they sit out the upcoming elections, will eventually have to align themselves again enthusiastically with one of the major parties if they are to continue to exert meaningful influence on national policies, and tradition argues that the party with which they align themselves will be the Republican party. The break could end in the formation of a completely new party, of course, but this seems unlikely. Odds run strongly against nonregional ideologically based splinter parties exerting significant national influence.

There was something hauntingly personal about the break with Richard Nixon, and to many of us not directly involved it seemed just that — personal. Despite the speculation, few of us are willing to read into it a meaningful break with the Republican party.

When Richard Nixon retires to San Clemente, there will still be a Republican party, a party which conservatives may need just as much as it needs them. And to insure that it will be a strong party in which conservatives will feel at home, it is necessary to keep men such as Spiro Agnew in high place.

Administration loyalists and disaffected conservatives still share certain common points of interest. One of these is the desire to prevent the Dixiecratization of the South. The South, including the border states, controls 175 of the 270 electoral votes necessary to elect a President. For Republicans, especially with California slipping into the doubtful column, a significant number of these votes is essential for victory. Even in defeat, a good showing is necessary, if the fragile new Southern GOP organizations are to avoid obliteration. The South today is being blitzed by a resurgent Wallace candidacy, and Spiro Agnew is the only major Republican figure (with the possible exception of Ronald Reagan) who can command strong Southern support. Thus, for Republicans, the situation is a simple one: dump Agnew and kiss Dixie goodbye. For disaffected conservatives, it may very well boil down to this: without Agnew on the ticket, conservative support tacitly goes to George Wallace. Wallace now makes it a point to speak to the issues raised in the conservative manifesto, his aim obviously being to drain as much conservative support as possible from the Republican party. Without Agnew to hold such support, the South will become a solid Wallace fief. And once that happens, given Wallace's undeniable political abilities, it will be very difficult indeed ever to win it back. Conservatives should think hard about whether they'd prefer an Agnew or a Wallace to speak for their movement in 1976.

Agnew's second great source of strength lies among blue-collar voters. The full impact of blue-collar support was not felt in 1970 because of the recession, during which working people who had strongly responded to the "social issue" suddenly saw the shade of Herbert Hoover

158

hovering over the ballot box and fled back to their traditional home in the Democratic party. It can no longer be a permanent home, however, given the capture of the party by liberal leftists, whose natural constituencies — welfarists, academics, students, media men — are anathema to blue-collar voters. Their votes have been up for grabs, and when the economy improves they will once again be nubile. Richard Nixon will probably never be popular among working people, but Spiro Agnew is.

There is, one senses, a great reluctance among many older conservatives and Republican regulars to join cause with working people. And because of Spiro Agnew's strong and special appeal, some traditionalists find him highly suspect. But this seems a case of confusing cause and reaction. Because blue-collar types respond to Agnew, some see in Agnew a strong populist streak. An examination of Agnew's rhetoric and the positions he espouses, however, reveal little of a populist nature. The response may seem populist, but the appeal is strictly conservative. James J. Kilpatrick, who has studied Agnew's speeches carefully, says that "never once has he stepped beyond the bounds of our political tradition."

Such reservations seem to many of us remarkably short-sighted. Republicans should realize that their party must expand if it is not to be a permanent minority party. And the blue-collar route, added to the South, represents the only realistic way of expanding. Conservatives must similarly seek new allies if they are not to remain an often ineffectual fringe group.

Given the necessity for expansion and the limited directions in which it is possible to expand, the idea of dumping Spiro Agnew makes little sense. There seem to be no good arguments detailing any specific ways in which he could hurt the ticket in 1972. And there are good arguments indeed detailing how he could help it. Among the possible new constituencies, Agnew has more support than any other Republican or conservative of comparable national stature. People such as John Connally are talked about as replacements, of course, since they conceivably could appeal to the same constituencies. But Connally is a wheeler-dealer Great Society Democrat, and Republicans and conservatives must expect that were Connally to achieve some measure of power, his ideas and programs would not differ from those of Lyndon Johnson.

From the point of view of practical politics, whether the viewer be Republican, conservative Republican, or conservative, Agnew seems essential to the '72 ticket. If the administration wins, Agnew will be the most important contender for the nomination in '76. If the administration loses, Agnew will still be highly visible in '76, an important figure commanding the loyalty of the new constituencies around whom conservatives could rally without fear of ideological embarrassment.

On the ideological level, there should be no doubt about Agnew. He is, as Kilpatrick points out, one of us, and one of us in the largest sense. As Jeff Bell puts it, "the Vice President is speaking to the moral malaise of the nation. He recognizes that the remedy for this malaise lies beyond politics in the realm of values — the values, patronized by the media and mocked by so many of our young, that have shaped and animated America and the West."

In a passage that seems to me to define precisely the crisis of our times, Frank Meyer once wrote: "Granted the highest development of freedom in the political order, a failure of the responsible interpreters of the intellectual, moral, and spiritual order would make freedom a useless toy by depriving men of standards by which to guide their lives."

It has become clear that the responsible interpreters have failed. And it is this failure that Agnew pinpoints in each of his major speeches, speeches which taken together make Agnew one of the most important articulators of the conservative ideal of our century, and one of the very few political conservative spokesmen of our age to touch the emotions of the common man.

And if this isn't enough, there's that appealing argument, perhaps best expressed in 1884 by Edward S. Bragg, seconding the nomination of Grover Cleveland: "They love him, gentlemen, and they respect him, not only for himself, but for his character, for his integrity and judgment and iron will; but they love him most for the enemies he has made."

Epilogue

I RECENTLY left the East Coast to live in Arizona, my stay in the East rounded off in a satisfying and oddly novelistic way.

In 1968, much against my better judgment, I moved my family from California to Connecticut. A few weeks before the move I had wise-cracked to a friend that the only way I would ever cross the Mississippi again would be with a rifle in my hands.

But a week or so later, William Buckley had invited me to dinner at Trader Vic's, where we drank delicious brown rum drinks and where I accepted a job as an associate editor of *National Review.*

Three years later I prepared to move my family to Arizona, where I had accepted a teaching job at Arizona State University. For three months I had been a temporary member of Vice President Agnew's staff. On my last day in Washington, the Vice President offered me a permanent job. I have never been so honored. Contractual obligations, however, and a belief that my family and I would be happier living in the West, dictated that I refuse the offer. It's the hardest thing I've ever done, not only because of the nature of the job but also because I admire the Vice President greatly.

And so, on that final day, I left the East—at Trader Vic's in Washington with the Vice President, over—you guessed it—delicious rum drinks. Artistically, a satisfying ending to my stay in the East.

Less satisfying to me at the moment, however, is what I consider to be one of the necessary drawbacks of this sort of book. My purpose has been to discuss some of the controversies which have swirled around agnew, to suggest some of the reasons for the intensity of those controversies, and to provide a definitive edition of his speeches. But in limiting myself to such discussions, I have neglected to provide a biographical portrait of Agnew.

Most Americans are now familiar with the career of Agnew the politician, a career that in itself proves that traditional American values of the kind Agnew champions still lead to success.

Spiro Theodore Agnew was Born on November 9, 1909, in Baltimore. His father, Theodore S. Agnew (né Anagnostopoulos), who emigrated from Greece in 1897, began penniless in Boston and ended a successful restaurateur in Baltimore.

Agnew attended Baltimore public schools and entered Johns Hopkins in 1937. After three years at Johns Hopkins he transferred to the University of Baltimore Night Law School, studying at night and working during the day to put himself through. His education was interrupted by the war, during which he served with the Tenth Armored Division as a company combat commander in France and Germany, earning the Bronze Star and the Combat Infantryman's Badge. After the war Agnew returned to law school, earned an LL.B. in 1947, and moved to Towson, a Baltimore suburb, where he began to practice law.

His involvement in politics began in the 1950s, when he worked in the successful Congressional campaigns of war hero James P. S. Devereux, a retired Marine brigadier general. In 1957 Agnew was appointed to the Zoning Board of Appeals of the Baltimore County Council, and in 1961 he ran for and won the office county executive, a position which in many urban areas such as Baltimore is equivalent to mayor of the suburbs. Agnew was the first Republican to hold the post since 1895. In 1966 he ran for governor against George "my home is my castle" Mahoney and clobbered him, taking 50 percent of the vote to Mahoney's 40 percent, in a state in which Democrats outnumber Republicans three to one. Agnew served as governor of Maryland until 1968, when Richard Nixon picked him for Vice President and John Lindsay seconded his nomination in an effusive speech in Miami. The rest, of course, is well known.

As county executive and as governor, Agnew's record was decidedly progressive, causing many liberals to embrace him as one of their own. Marylanders remember his tax reform measures, his tough water pollution act (still the stiffest in the nation), his open-housing law, his updating of the state's public accommodations law. Such measures were considered liberal, and Agnew, who refuses to let himself be ideologized, is still proud of them.

But then came 1968, and suddenly the country seemed to be tilting dangerously. Agnew claims that he hasn't changed since his early days in politics, and perhaps he hasn't. But the country certainly has, and a man who was a centrist in the fifties and early sixties finds that when he stands in one place for a couple of decades, the country slips leftward beneath him. And there was no more dramatic period of slippage than in 1968.

Already the memories of '68 have begun to fade. The widespread riots on campus after campus, the massive and often bloody demonstrations in the cities, the assassinations, seem curiously distant in 1971. Perhaps it is a false peace. Or perhaps the Nixon Administration has successfully carried out its mandate to cool the country. But for those of us who lived in or near the center of turmoil, 1968 will always remain a vivid year, perhaps the most dangerous in recent American history.

As 1968 unwound, each successive confrontation wilder than the last, it seemed possible that the structure of American society could collapse. And it was during this traumatic period that Spiro Agnew suddenly seemed, to many of his former liberal admirers, to change into a conservative. But the change was deceptive, for Agnew remained the same man he was before the national trauma. He believed strongly, and continues to believe strongly today, in the dignity of the individual and the necessity for providing him with every possible opportunity to better himself. But he also, unlike so many disillusioned sixties liberals, continued to believe that the American system was the single best system ever conceived for encouraging that improvement. Thus, although never denying, as his record as governor shows, that the system could be improved, he believed in dealing directly and forcefully with those who attempted to overthrow that system. Agnew understood, in other words, the difference between revolution and reform, a distinction that still eludes some of our most prominent academics.

Our system, Agnew believed, is based on the concept of the reasonable man, our social structure cemented by civility. Allow any significant number of people within the society to act uncivilly, unreasonably, and the whole structure is in danger of collapse, for democracy by definition cannot function under such conditions.

And so, when the unrest that began to spread across the country in 1968 reached Maryland, Agnew felt it necessary to act firmly. In April, a large group of Negro students from Bowie State College sat-in at the statehouse in Annapolis. When they refused to leave at closing time, Agnew ordered 227 of them arrested. Later, during the Baltimore summer riots, he unhesitatingly took the hard line. His firmness caught many liberals by surprise. But he had stated his position on selective lawbreaking on numerous occasions. In May 1968 he summed it up before a conference on police and community relationships in Baltimore. Obedience to the law is necessary, he said, because "defiance of law allows cynical leaders responsible to none to exploit the madness of the mob. Rapidly, civil disobedience falls prey to civil disorder. Passive resistance gives way to erosive force. Logical leadership is obscured by the demagogue's harangue.

"This phenomenon is apparent in our cities and on our college campuses where . . . ideals have disintegrated and legitimate causes have disappeared. And while no thinking person denies that social injustice exists, no thinking person can condone any group, for any reason, taking justice in its own hands. Once this is permitted, democracy dies; for democracy is sustained through one great premise: the premise that civil rights are balanced by civil responsibilities."

A clear statement of the creed to which Agnew has subscribed throughout his public career. There is social injustice, and it must be remedied. But social injustice can best be remedied by seeking recourse within the democratic structure, which was created for that purpose. Once you decide to operate outside the structure, once you decide to break certain of the laws that hold that structure together, you attack the structure itself rather than the injustices within it. If you sufficiently discredit certain laws, you inevitably end by discrediting the whole notion of laws, and by so doing you do nothing to stamp out social wrongs but rather destroy the means by which these wrongs can be righted. Thus the vulnerable democratic structure of our society is weakened, and a sufficiently weakened structure must inevitably collapse.

"What good are revolutions," asks Agnew, "if we are devoured by them?" And once we are devoured by them, once the structure of our society has collapsed, what can we do to prevent some sufficiently skillful demagogue from picking up the pieces and putting things back together again in any way he sees fit?

There is, of course, the counter argument, advanced by the Marcuses, who say that social evils are inherent in the structure itself and that the only way to be rid of them is to be rid of the system. There is no scientific way to disprove this argument. But if we accept it, then we have indeed become a people without faith.

These were the points that Agnew tried to make to Balitmore's reputable black leaders after he summer riots had devastated the city. The speech, a harsh one, caused great national comment, for Agnew accused the black leaders, many of whom walked out in outrage, of failing to exert the leadership necessary to counter the revolutionary calls to arms of black militants such as Stokely Carmichael and Rap Brown, who in '68 crisscrossed the nation, calling on the inhabitants of the ghettoes to rise up and overthrow the government, leaving in their wake a series of burned-out inner cities. Agnew spoke bluntly, as he always does, and perhaps he could have been more diplomatic. But diplomacy seemed a luxury in the summer of '68.

Yet a reading of the speech does not reveal quite the harshness that we have to come to believe it contains. It is, rather, a frank statement of belief in the American system and exhortation to the Negro leaders to attempt to share that belief. "Somewhere the objectives of the civil rights movement have been obscured in a surge of emotional oversimplification. Somewhere the goal of equal opportunity has been replaced by the goal of instantaneous economic equality. The country does not guarantee that every man will be successful, but only that he have an equal opportunity to achieve success."

For such passages was Agnew accused of insensitivity and harshness, and perhaps it is a measure of what has happened to us as a nation that a frank restatement of the ideas upon which our country was founded can cause us such acute embarrassment. Agnew's message was a simple one: Try it. It works. Critics, of course, saw it as a simpleminded statement by the son of an immigrant who had made it, implicit in their criticisms the notion that somehow it was *wrong* for him to have made it at all. And also implicit in the criticism is the notion that Negroes are different, that somehow it is not possible for them to make it in the same way that the Irish or the Chinese made it. Perhaps they can't. And perhaps it's true that their racial handicap is unique. But the success of the Chinese, who arrived in America under conditions very close to slavery and who suffered from a racial discrimination every bit as intense as the discrimination practiced against Negroes, would seem to undercut this theory. And who is to measure degrees of prejudice? Who is to say that the religious intolerance shown to Irish Catholics was any less intense than the racial intolerance shown to Negroes? There are numerous arguments, I know. But the white intellectuals who argue for the special condition of the Negro might do well to examine their attitudes for traces of paternalism and perhaps even a bit of reverse prejudice.

Agnew is not willing to concede that the Negro cannot rise through his own efforts, that the opportunities offered by the American system are not his to take. His position on race is a simple one: the American system makes no racial distinctions. There are bigots, to be sure, but bigotry is a blemish on the souls of individual men rather than an inherent flaw in the system. Destroy the system and bigots will still be with us. Keep the system, reform it, and bigotry will, as people climb the ladder, be rendered meaningless.

Agnew did not change in 1968. He remained progressive, insofar as he believed the system should be continually reformed in order to make it operate as it was intended to operate. But his attitude toward disorder remained quintessentially conservative: the system as a system was the best devised by man, and as such it must be retained. Agnew remained, in short, something larger than an ideologue—an American, nothing more and nothing less. "No ideologue," as even a *Newsweek* writer grudgingly admitted, "and certainly not a bigot, Nixon's understudy is a blunt advocate of most of the American verities—hard work, discipline, candor, and fair play."

It is a comment on our times that those "American verities" are so routinely mentioned in the most condescending tones, as if we all know that they really have no substance at all. Perhaps it is because Agnew

165

does believe in them that the intellectual community has reacted so violently to him, as if somehow his belief might discredit the fashionable view of the worthlessness of the American experience.

Yet there are others who show signs of responding, almost as if after a lifetime of continental cuisine, their palates jaded, they try in desperation a slice of apple pie. And find it delicious. Such people tend to approach Agnew warily, discovering as they move closer that although he says exactly the same things in private that he says in public, somehow there is an unexpected freshness about the man that tends to undermine their ideological hostility. To such people Agnew seems some sort of exotic, to be enjoyed for his originality. But what they see as originality is as homespun and basically American as that apple pie. What charms is the simple, straightforward, unblushing Americanism, an honesty directly rooted in those "traditional American verities."

There's no rush as yet to discover the best in Agnew (although were he a Democrat the stampede would be on, for Agnew would admirably fill the bill as the Harry Truman of the seventies), but a few of the connoisseurs have begun to edge closer. The most important of them is James Reston, *New York Times* columnist who blasted Agnew during Cambodian Spring.

Recently, Mr. Reston has begun to discover several rare qualities in Agnew; among them candor, courage, and loyalty. In a remarkable column, prompted by the never-ending speculation that the Vice President might not run again, Reston writes:

> Vice President Agnew has been accused of almost everything except a lack of saying right out what he thinks, and one of the attractive aspects of this compulsive candor is that he applies it to himself.
>
> He doesn't ignore the fact that this city is wondering about whether he will be the Republican vice presidential candidate next year, or pretend that speculation on the point is manufactured by his old antagonists in the Eastern liberal press.
>
> In fact, while he is more critical of the "effete snobs" of press and television than anybody else in this administration, he is also more available to them and more willing to discuss their problems and his than anybody else in the capital.
>
> Are people wondering about his future? Well, he says, he wonders about it. To him, this is a question for the President to decide. There is an illusion in this town, he says, that everybody fights for the ground he holds and struggles for power and position, regardless of private life, or the interests of the party, but he doesn't feel this way.
>
> He will do what he is asked to do, he says: get out, because home holds no terrors for him, or go on, if that is what the President wants him to do. It is interesting that he doesn't appeal primarily to the

Republican Party, where he has a stronger and more loyal conservative constituency than anybody else, including the President himself.

Whatever the President decides about a running mate next year, the vice president is not going to appeal to this conservative element in the party, which is startled by the President's new welfare, new economic, and new China and Soviet policies.

* * *

It would be very easy to do so. He obviously has his doubts about the wisdom of the President's pragmatic move to the left. He is much more ideological than his chief, but he is clearly not going to lead any charge against the President's policies, no matter what he thinks privately about it all, and he will undoubtedly leave the whole question about the Republican nomination of a vice president to Nixon.

On the question of a different Republican vice presidential candidate, if there is to be one, he is equally candid. Again, he defers to the President, but here he thinks the party in the nominating convention at San Diego will find that there are many Republicans who will want the job and feel that they have more claim on it than the Democratic secretary of the Treasury, John Connally.

If it comes to a change, then there will, he thinks, be many Republican senators and governors who will make the argument for themselves, in opposition to Connally. Party loyalty, he says, is a powerful influence in nominating conventions, and in a way, Connally is in a comparable position to Mayor John Lindsay, of New York: able and attractive, but a new convert in a different party, who will not be easily accepted by the party faithful.

* * *

From the Vice President's own point of view, it is a sensible and honorable position. He did not choose the role he has played as vice president. He has been the battering ram of the Republican Party, assigned by the President, and as such, he has been a divisive figure in American politics, always out front, scalding the opposition, and in the process, making enemies and loyal supporters.

But the amiable thing about him is that he understands all this and is prepared to accept the consequences. If his usefulness has been destroyed in the struggle, he is willing to accept it, and go back to Baltimore to his private life, or run again, or campaign for Nixon's re-election, even if he is dumped.

Not many men in the battle for personal, party, and national power would be quite as relaxed in the struggle as he is. It is easy to argue against his philosophy and his pugnacious tactics, but at least he says in private what he says in public, and since very few politicians in Washington risk such candor, he is not a man to be lightly dismissed in the coming struggle of the presidential campaign.

Candor, courage, loyalty—definitive qualities. Agnew is totally loyal to Richard Nixon, just as he is totally loyal to the people who work for him. And all he demands from them is that they reciprocate. And they do. It is some mark of the man's ability to inspire loyalty that he has retained so many of his original Baltimore staff. And it is indicative of his practice of putting personal worth ahead of ideology that his staff is as diverse as it is. Art Sohmer and Frank DaCosta, his chiefs of staff, have been with him since the Baltimore days. Both are ideologically neutral. Herb Thompson, his former press secretary and now chief speech writer, could probably best be described as a liberal of the old school that flourished just before the liberals lost their nerve. Dr. Jean Spencer, a University of Maryland professor and the special Vice Presidential assistant in charge of research, would rank as a liberal in anyone's book. Victor Gold, Agnew's press secretary, is one of contemporary conservatism's finest.

Yet despite these diverse attitudes, Agnew's staff works in remarkable harmony. There's none of the backbiting, none of the gossip that characterizes most organizations, especially political organizations. The reason: each of Agnew's staffers is absolutely loyal to him. Why this extraordinary loyalty? Agnew inspires it in those who know and work for him for a very simple reason: he personifies those "traditional American verities" that one hopes people like James Reston will rapidly rediscover before it's too late.

And there's another quality, one I experienced most directly—kindness. In 1970 I wrote a book called *The Kumquat Statement*, essentially a conservative view of the student unrest of the late sixties. I had run some professional risk in writing the book, for I had previously been known for writing tightly controlled satirical articles. In *The Kumquat Statement*, I decided to open up, however, to attack what I took to be the evils on campus and in society doing so emotionally as well as analytically. The result, to be expected when anyone on the right lets down his guard—some goddawful reviews. There were some surprisingly good ones—a brief but semisympathetic review in the *New York Times* and a strongly favorable review in the *Los Angeles Times*—but for the most part, in the larger papers, the reviews were killers. And I, of course, was depressed, authors being vain creatures (the very act of writing a book requires a disproportionate amount of hubris). And then one morning there was a call at my office from the Vice President of the United States. He had liked the book very much, he told me, as I sat there with my jaw hanging loose, not quite able to believe that the Vice President of the United States was calling me, convinced that the whole thing was a hoax. But I soon realized that is was real. The Vice President ordered a number of copies of my book to give as Christmas gifts, and later, when he attended a luncheon in New York given for America's top corporate leaders, he insisted not only that I attend but that I be seated next to him. Heady experiences indeed, for a youngish author of a first book. And what most impressed me was that there was no ulterior motive, I being in no position to do anything meaningful for him. Rather, it was simply an act of kindness directed at a writer still wet behind the ears.

Agnew's qualities as a man are difficult to describe without sounding soupy or sycophantish. There is that rock-hard integrity, hard to talk about simply because it is so basic, the kind of integrity that we once used to be able to take for granted in our best American men. But what should be automatically considered a virtue has led directly to many of Agnew's political difficulties. As I finish this, the speculation about whether Agnew will or will not run continues unabated. Where he to press the issue, Agnew could force the White House to make a statement. And given his widespread grassroots party support—a support, according to Barry Goldwater, greater than the President's—Agnew could probably, were he willing, as are most other Washingtonians, to play the game of political leverage, force that statement to be strongly affirmative.

But Agnew simply isn't that kind of man. He means it when he says he wants the President to consider his renomination in a "cold, hard, practical political way." And there is no doubt that there are "cold, hard, practical" politicians who would prefer not to see him on the ticket. Such men point to Agnew's recent relatively poor showing in the polls as sufficient reason for dumping him. But these polls were taken during the past summer, when Agnew had come under an unprecedented barrage of criticism, most of it unjustified, from the national media. And polls have a way of reversing themselves dramatically after a couple of good weeks, as witness the wildly fluctuating race in the Harris poll between Richard Nixon and Edmund Muskie. But aside from the temporarily unfavorable polls, there is still no hard evidence that any of the contenders for Agnew's position could add anything to the ticket beyond what he himself could provide.

The problem, of course, is that most of the most articulate speculators are anti-Agnew rather than proadministration, and there is a great deal of political naïveté in some of their more desperate speculations. The boosting of John Connally is a case in point. Connally, a long-time Democrat, would be viewed by Republican party regulars precisely in the same way that John Lindsay is viewed by Democratic party regulars. His popularity among Agnew's potential blue-collar constituency is nil, and his appeal in the South is highly questionable. In Washington, Texans and Southerners may seem similar. But in the South a Texan is viewed in much the same way that a New Yorker is viewed in New England—with profound suspicion. (Lyndon Johnson, the quintessential Texas, lost badly to Barry Goldwater in the South.) There is, of course, the argument that Connally could deliver Texas. Perhaps. But Agnew is highly popular in Dallas and Houston, and it seems highly unlikely that his presence on the ticket would lessen Nixon's potential Texas support in any way. And Connally would probably lose Nixon many of the votes across the nation that Agnew could deliver.

The rest of the speculation seems similarly to make little political sense. If the administration has finally decided to follow the suggestions of some of the President's advisors and write off the South and middle America and campaign strenuously for uncommitted liberal votes, then the discussion is academic, for Vice President Agnew will never appeal to liberals. But neither will Richard Nixon, and it will be politically tragic if he doesn't begin to understand this.

My own guess, and I know just about as much about it as anyone else —nothing (Richard Nixon is the only man who knows, and as of this writing he's not talking)—is that Agnew will be on the ticket in '72. He appeals to a clearly defined constituency in a way no other Republican appeals, and it is difficult to see where the administration could pick up votes without him that it could not pick up with him. And then, the President does owe him a strong vote of gratitude. He has done much of the administration's dirty work, and done it knowing that the media would pillory him mercilessly for having done it. He has watched the media boobize him, heard himself called a kid killer, and has taken it all, something extremely difficult for a proud sensitive man to do. His experience in county, state, and federal government has not been utilized fully during the first term, and he deserves four more good years to put his expertise to work. The Office of Intergovernmental Relations, for instance, representing an exciting new approach to relations between the federal government and local governments at all levels, is one of Agnew's pet projects. Yet during his first term in office it remained underdeveloped for Agnew spent most of his time on the stump. Yet there is nothing he would like better than to make it a going concern.

Agnew rendered a salutary service in taking on the intellectual establishment. It was something that had to be done and he did it effectively. For years matters such as bias in the national media simply weren't discussed. Now they're out in the open, and the media are taking the charges seriously. These days the TV panel shows are full of network types attempting to answer the questions asked first by Vice President

170

Agnew in Des Moines. A recent book by Edith Efron, *The News Twisters*, has caused an unprecedented reaction among the media men. Before Des Moines, it would have been summarily dismissed. But already, according to *Variety*, CBS has spent several hundred thousand dollars in an attempt to discredit the book. The networks, apparently, have decided to take a stand, and by so doing are being forced closely to examine their practices. The effect cannot be other than salutary, and for it we can thank Vice President Agnew. One hopes that the administration is properly grateful. Agnew has proven himself as a political infighter of the first caliber. He now deserves the chance to show what he can do in those areas—urban affairs, housing, intergovernmental relations—that most interest him.

As I write these last few lines, there are signs that the tide may be turning. The tone of many magazine and newspaper articles seems to be growing more sympathetic than anyone could have expected last summer. And most important, conservatives such as Barry Goldwater and Ronald Reagan, whose advice is not taken lightly in Washington, have spoken out strongly for Agnew. It just might be that he appeal of those "traditional American verities" will finally prove irresistible.

A few words about this book. As I had first conceived it, the book would have consisted primarily of text, with a few of the more important speeches appended. But the more I studied the Vice President's speeches, it increasingly seemed necessary to me to hold the text down and let the speeches speak for themselves. One of the problems with the Vice President's speeches is precisely that which makes them so effective—their quotability. So often the most striking sentences are taken out of context and headlined, while the body of the speeches gets lost in the subsequent publicity. For that reason, I have appended all of Vice President Agnew's speeches.

There have been other editions of the speeches, but none of them has been comprehensive, none of them carefully edited, and none of them published in hard cover.

The texts of the speeches included in this volume have been carefully checked against tapes, thus insuring for the first time a collection which includes all the changes and additions as they occurred during delivery. For this gargantuan task I owe special thanks to Stephanie Barry.

Special thanks also go to Dr. Jean Spencer, who will one day write the definitive speech on women's rights, and to Herb Thompson, a man whose friendship I prize. And to Victor Gold, Press Secretary to the Vice President, I owe a very special debt which one day I hope to be able to repay.

171

Speeches of the Hon. Spiro T. Agnew August 4, 1968 to June 25, 1971

Contents

179

August 4, 1968, Miami, Florida
Republican National Convention
Address by Governor Agnew

IF THERE is anything predictable in this unpredictable time, it is that from this convention will emerge not just the standard bearer of a grand old party, but the President of a brave new country.

We are a nation in crisis, victimized by crime and conflict, frustrated by fear and failure.

A nation torn by war wants a restoration of peace.

A nation plagued by disorder wants a renewal of order.

A nation haunted by crime wants respect for law.

A nation wrenched by division wants a rebirth of unity.

If there is one great cry that rings clear, it is the cry for a leader.

At this moment of history the Republican Party has the duty to put forward a *man* — a man to not only match this moment but to master it.

We have that man!

He has spent years building his party. He has spent a lifetime serving his country.

He has fought throughout his political career for principle and he has not hesitated to pay the price of unpopularity in standing up for principle.

He has traveled the continents taking America's message to the world. He has shared in the decisions which shaped for America the Eisenhower era of prosperity, untainted by war, dissension, fear, lawlessness, or the threat of fiscal and moral chaos.

He knows what is needed to be President and what a President needs to be.

But it is not only his record of yesterday, it is his voice for tomorrow that matches this man to this moment.

He says: "This is the moment of opportunity for America. We sense that opportunity when we put aside what's wrong with America and start looking at what's right with America." I believe that, don't you?

He says: "Let's stop apologizing for America's wealth and power. Instead let's use it aggressively to attack those problems that threaten to explode the world." Isn't that what this Party stands for?

He says: "Let's stop apologizing for the success of free enterprise and instead work at spreading and sharing that success."

He says: "Right now change rules America. It's time for America to rule change." Don't *YOU* believe that?

He says: "To a crisis of the spirit, America needs an answer of the spirit."

What is the spirit of this man who seeks now to answer the nation's call?

Ask the people of New Hampshire, Wisconsin, Indiana, Nebraska, South Dakota, Oregon — and they will tell you of a man who took his case to the people, and put his prestige on the line in every primary.

Ask the people with whom he shared power in Washington, and they will tell you of a man who has the wisdom to comprehend history, and the foresight to anticipate it; the confidence to make hard decisions; the courage to keep cool before one man in Moscow or a mob in Caracas.

Ask the people who have known him throughout his lifetime, and they will tell you of a man of warmth and wit, his perspective enriched by the private years.

Ask the people of this convention, and they will tell you of a man who helped lead this party to its greatest victories in the past two decades, and who stood by the party and its candidate in their darkest hour.

And when the American people are asked in November, they will speak too:

For a man firm in upholding the law, and determined in the pursuit of justice.

For a man who can negotiate peace without sacrificing life, land, or liberty.

For a man who had the courage to rise up from the depths of defeat six years ago — and to make the greatest political comeback in American history.

For the one man whose life gives proof that the American dream is not a shattered myth and that the American spirit — its strength and sense and stability — remains firm.

The final test of a man who seeks the presidency is not what he promises but what he can do; not what he says, but what he is.

The man I nominate tonight is a President.

When a nation is in crisis, and when history speaks firmly to that nation that it needs a man to match the times — you don't create such a man; you don't discover such a man; you *recognize* such a man.

It is my privilege to place in nomination for the office of President of the United States, the *one* man whom history has so clearly thrust forward — the one whom all America will recognize as a man whose time has come — the man for 1968, the Honorable Richard M. Nixon.

August 5, 1968, Miami, Florida
Republican National Convention
Address by Governor Agnew

LADIES AND GENTLEMEN, before I make these few remarks I would like to introduce my wife, Judy and half of my children, my oldest daughter and my, what I call my middle daughter, Pamela and Susan Agnew.

Mr. Chairman and my fellow delegates and fellow Republicans and my fellow Americans, I stand here with a deep sense of the improbability of this moment. Last night when I faced these microphones to place in nomination one of the truly great Americans of our time, Richard M. Nixon, I honestly had no idea whatsoever that I would be back on this platform to accept this nomination tonight. Obviously I have had no time to prepare a profound message.

But I do want to emphasize my awareness that I have with this high office — the challenge of this high office — accepted a tremendous responsibility to the party and to all Americans. What can I bring to this moment in behalf of our party and its great presidential nominee? Well, perhaps a few objectives borne of deep conviction. The objective to analyze and to help solve the problems of this nation without dependence on the canned philosophies of liberalism or conservatism. The objective to avoid the currently popular concept that the only purpose of government is to spend money, and that all spending in a good cause is worthy, whether or not it will get results. The objective that racial discrimination, unfair and unequal education, and unequal job opportunities must be eliminated no matter whom that displeases.

And I believe quite compatibly the observation that anarchy, rioting, or even civil disobedience has no constructive purpose in a constitutional republic. I look forward to sharing in an administration in which a President will entrust to his Vice President — with vital responsibilities for the great problems of the states and the cities, for I have a strong belief that changes must be made and that the Nixon Administration will make those changes.

I know — I am positive that there is a better way to balance the complex relationship between federal, state, and local government than is presently being exercised. I know that the federal government must work more constructively, more creatively, and above all more simply in meeting the problems of prejudice and poverty in our cities.

I know that there is a bright new world of ideas for cities, such as cultural, commercial, industrial centers and satellite cities, that we're only beginning to explore. I know that America is reaching for the frontiers of space and I am for it. But I also know we must treat generously the old, the sick, and the poor. We must help build independence and pride in the black community, and make black Americans partners in our system.

I also know that more important than words in this campaign and in the next administration will be action, the kind of action that follows from involvement in the problem, and from the closest kind of relationship with the people who are involved in the problems. In this campaign I will be speaking with those who even as I have been are dealing with these great problems every day, with the mayors, like my good friend, John Lindsay, the governors, the county executives and commissioners. And I will be searching out their views and their priorities.

One last word about the campaign we are about to begin. I am dedicated to a hard campaign, one that reaches into every area of the country and every set of circumstances, a campaign that brings the message of change to all the people of America, and that will lead from the top of the ticket to the bottom, to a great decision for change in November.

I feel that the Vice President must represent more than a region or an issue or a special interest. I feel that more important than where a lot of people live is what a lot of people think. I feel more important on a national ticket than a partnership of political expediency is an alliance of ideals. More important than contrast of views in a single focus. The American people are a great people, proud of their individuality and diversity, but still our strength is in unity, and now as ever a unity of leadership is imperative to restore the unity of America.

And unity in our relationship depends on unity of leadership. Richard Nixon offers that kind of leadership, and I am honored to share in it. Now I want to assure you of one thing. As a political animal and a relatively sensitive individual who hopes he will never lose his sensitivity, I am not unaware of what took place in this great convention hall at night — tonight. I am aware that the reasons that motivated it were not directed at me in any personal sense and were merely responsive of the opinions of those that took part in the nomination of that great governor of Michigan, whom I consider my personal friend, Governor Romney — those motives were simply to provide the strongest ticket for the Republican party in November.

I recognize also that a vice presidential nominee does not come to the successful fruition of his nomination by virtue of his personality or his attractiveness or his ability to generate a wave of enthusiasm on his own. He comes here because he is the selection of the man who does all those things on his own, the presidential nominee. And I am privileged that that great future President of the United States, Richard M. Nixon, has seen fit to invest in me his confidence to do the job. But I will not be satisfied, ladies and gentlemen, I will not be satisfied under any circumstances until I prove to you that I am capable of doing the job for the Republican party and the American people in November. I recognize —

I fully recognize that I am an unknown quantity to many of you. I can only tell you of my dedication to work for Republican tickets and Republican principles from now until the election.

And it is my fervent hope, my good friends, that when I visit your state you will allow me to contribute in the way you consider most beneficial, to that purpose that we all endorse, that we all aspire to, total change to a completely Republican-dominated political family — county, state, city, and federal in November.

February 5, 1969, Washington, D.C.
U. S. Senate Youth Program Luncheon

IT IS AN honor to greet so many of our nation's young leaders today. You are to be commended and congratulated for the quality of your leadership which has won you this trip to Washington. Along with all the honors and adventures and awards this week provides, you have a truly unique learning experience, a crash course in federal government.

You know we share this in common for I'm new to the halls of Congress, too, and in greater depth and detail I'm taking a crash course in the federal government. Of course, I've testified before Congressional committees, first as a county executive and then as a governor, but this is my first foray on the other side of the fence and I regard this learning experience as the most challenging and gratifying aspect of the vice presidency.

My theory is that as long as you are learning, you are living; and as long as you can learn, you are young.

There's an old saying that age is a mental not a physical state, and I'm inclined to agree with it. I think in some ways we overcelebrate the cult of youth in this country and in other ways we underemphasize its attractions. Sometimes individuals confuse growing old with growing up and this is a tragic error. For it is not the physical vigor of youth but its intellectual agility which is its greatest virtue. It is not only youth's aptitude for learning but its appetite to learn that is most appealing.

With more knowledge discovered during this century than in all the previous centuries of world history, all America and not just young America must adopt this appetite to learn. With ample evidence that of all the scientific knowledge which will ultimately sustain our present school age generation during their lifetime, seventy percent is as yet unknown and undiscovered, all of us must adjust to the idea that the learning process is not terminal but continual.

There are two ways for individuals to face the fact that there is no sure or secure knowledge. One is to be frightened or anxious that they cannot keep up with a world where change is the only constant. But fear polarizes and anxiety paralyzes, and dropping out doesn't prove a thing. The other way is to look at the knowledge explosion as a glorious challenge and approach it with a psychic passion. This is the most exciting era in history since the Renaissance and I am confident it will inspire individual distinction as great as any achieved by Renaissance man.

I think the majority of America's youth regards American life as a glorious challenge and you are well prepared for a life where you will be perpetually young because you are perpetually learning.

Certainly you're in the right place to see the learning experience in action. For our history, our progress, can to a great extent be credited to the clash of ideas in Congress. Out of intellectual impasse, time and time again, we have seen compromise create whole new directions.

Less than half a century ago — during my lifetime, and I want you to know there are

184

those who do not consider me an old man — the overwhelming majority of the members of Congress thought that government had no business in business; that government could not prevent abysmal depressions or skyrocketing inflations; that government might protect its people from war but not from poverty in their old age, ill health, or inadvertent unemployment.

You have grown up in an era where impossible dreams have become realities. What was science fiction to our generation is scientific fact to yours. So I imagine it's hard for you to conceive what tremendous changes have occurred not only in social programs but social thought in the past forty years.

But I can assure you if you had come to Congress half a century ago advocating Social Security and unemployment insurance payments and using a Federal Reserve Board or federal taxing power to heat up or cool down the national economy, you would have been considered a way-out radical. Yet, you have never known a life without these things, and even within your lifetime Congress has established Medicare to assure quality health services to our elderly and Medicaid for our lower-income citizens.

So you can see progress does come within the system and at an impressive speed. For our system is structured to achieve progress. It endures because it is founded upon one basic precept — no one has a monopoly on the truth.

The whole point to providing and preserving a free and open society is to assure all ideas may compete in Congress and in the intellectual marketplace for the country's mind. Every idea must be given every opportunity to be expressed and examined in the belief that ultimately the best will prevail.

If there is one reason why the elected official and the average citizen are so appalled by the kind of mind that extols violence or feels justified in closing down a college campus, it is because this is a totalitarian mind, a dogmatic mind. It presumes a monopoly on the truth and there is no greater menace to progress.

Our country is no stranger to violence, but in the Senate of the United States incidents of violence are rare. Yet the most brutal case bears retelling for its message. Five years before the Civil War, Senator Charles Pinckney Sumner of Massachusetts, an ardent abolitionist, was viciously beaten and crippled by South Carolina Congressman Preston Brooks. Now there were many passionate critics of slavery in the Senate at that time, but Sumner's attacks were singularly repugnant for their abusive content completely ignored the social evils existing in the North. This man sought to wield a one-edged sword of self-righteousness in a democratic forum sustained and defended by the two-edged sword of justice. As for the violent physical assault, it served only to reinforce Sumner's hatred with bitterness and the powerful Massachusetts Senator's revenge reverberated throughout the South during the Reconstruction period.

This is but one isolated example of how a closed mind or a closed society begets violence and how violence produces nothing but more violence or more repression.

Our open society offers legitimate avenues for creative dissent in recognition that progress is the product of debate. Diologue respects the right of others. Dictatorship does not. That's why ours is a system of checks and balances entrusting no level nor branch of government with absolute power. The President may propose, but Congress will dispose, and all legislative and executive acts at all levels of government are subject to the rulings of the Supreme Court.

There is another beauty to this system and this is the creative competition stimulated by the checks and balances. Throughout history where there has been a reluctant Chief Executive, Congress has taken the initiative and passed progressive programs. On those rare occasions when a lethargic President and quiet Congress coincided, the Supreme Court jarred them into action with landmark decisions.

Or if Congress was loath to see avenues of progress, a dynamic President emerged to point the way. Such was the case when President Theodore Roosevelt saw the America to be and sought an end to isolation-oriented foreign policy. "We have no choice as to whether or not we shall play a great part in the world," he told Congress. ". . . All that we can decide is whether we shall play it well or ill." Congress did not share this vision but the irrepressible Teddy ultimately prevailed and as mediator extraordinary President Roosevelt proved America could play its part well — as peacemaker in the world.

Although they're not blooming now, I'm sure you've been shown the cherry trees along the Potomac basin. These were a gift from the Japanese government to President Roosevelt for his role in settling the Russo–Japanese War. For his efforts President Roosevelt was the first American to be awarded the Nobel Prize for Peace.

Theodore Roosevelt was one of America's greatest Presidents, for he did not simply govern in the present, but perceived the future and prepared our country for it. It was under Teddy Roosevelt that the federal government took its first tentative steps toward social justice. It was the vision of the first Roosevelt that found fruition in the presidency of the second.

President Nixon often refers to President Theodore Roosevelt's maxim that this nation will not be a good place for any of us to live in unless it is a good place for all of us to live in. In the past decade, the Congress of the United States has led the advance toward social justice through landmark legislation.

Perhaps the progress has not been fast enough to suit some of us. Perhaps the pace has been too swift to please others. But we have moved forward. And we have advanced to a point that is good and new without destroying all that is good and old.

Now we stand at the threshold of a whole new era for America. An era we can perceive, but you may know. Yours can be an America respected throughout the world for its purpose as well as its power; an America revered for its wisdom as well as its wealth; an America honored for its moral spirit as well as its military strength.

Such an America is not decreed by will but evolved by work. This America is not arrived at by the acts of one Congress or the policies of one President, but achieved by the collective efforts of all our citizens. If this is the kind of America you want, you must share in its making. And I mean you, the acknowledged leaders of the young. I would be less than honest with you if I did not express my grave fear that the recent trend toward lawlessness, violence, and nihilism demonstrated by a small but strident minority of America's youth could engender a wave of reaction which would seriously impede social progress. The patience of the American people is just about exhausted. You, the responsible leadership, have the opportunity to ward off this reaction by condemning coercive force — *loud and clear* — and presenting alternative channels for positive contribution and constructive dissent.

We need not fear America's bright future will be prevented but we need not stand passively by and thus permit it to be postponed. I urge you to work actively, constructively, and courageously.

You are as President Nixon described you "better educated, more committed, more passionately driven by conscience than any generation that has gone before." I am confident that it is within your power to restore the country's perspective on youth, to share in the glorious challenge and lead in the "high adventure" of American life today. For all you have done, I congratulate you. For all you will do, I salute you.

February 15, 1969, Bowling Green, Ohio
Bowling Green University Lincoln Day Banquet

COMING TO Ohio has become a lot like coming home. This is my second "buckeye" run this week. I've spent so much time here since the start of the campaign that Governor

Rhodes ought to make me an honorary citizen — or at least give me the keys to the golf course.

Ohio is never in any political party's pocket. But it's full of sensible, practical, hardworking people — young and old — who want solutions to their problems, not just fancy explanations of them. And that's why Ohio was a good state for the Republicans this year. Ohio was crucial to our national ticket, and Ohio came through. This cradle of Republicanism has given birth to many American Presidents and victory to others. So as we pay honor to our first Republican President, may I pause to honor Ohio for our present Republican President. And to personally thank you for making my name a household word.

I might also say I feel at home not only because I'm in Ohio but because I'm on a university campus. Most people don't know that before and along with my political career, I taught for seven years at the University of Baltimore Law School.

The most bitter criticism hurled at me during my campaign for governor of Maryland was that I sounded too much like a college professor. I always replied that I hoped this would be the worst ever said of me. Those of you who followed the recent presidential campaign know that that hope fell somewhat short of realization.

Lincoln, whom we honor today, was in his own way very much an observer and teacher of the young.

Once a boy in Union blue came to the President asking for a promotion to captain. He was only sixteen, a fine soldier but too young for command. President Lincoln understood his impatience and his disappointment and comforted him with the words: "My son, continue to do your duty as you find it to do, and with the zeal you have hitherto shown, you will not have to ask for promotion. It will seek you."

President Nixon, too, understands the impatience of the young and finds in it the most promising sign of a promising generation. In their impatience, in their desire to participate, in their insistence on leading lives that are rewarding in quality as well as rich in quantity, they show themselves to be the finest crop of young people in our nation's history.

As President Nixon said in his inaugural: "We can see the hope of tomorrow in the youth of today. . . . They are better educated, more committed, more passionately driven by conscience than any generation that has gone before."

The President's enthusiasm for America's youth is well known. And there is gratifying evidence that the feeling is reciprocal. Immediately after the President's inaugural message, Peace Corps recruitment showed a sudden surge. It is obvious that our youth understand as our President understands, that "until he has been part of a cause larger than himself, no man is truly whole."

Today's young people are setting a pace and creating a pattern that is encouraging. In the past we used to say "Youth shall *be* served." Young people today say "Youth *shall* serve."

Of course we are all familiar with the minority of youth which unfortunately has come to dominate the majority of headlines. We cannot deny that an element of angry, alienated young people exists.

But the closed-minded shouters, who try to shut down college campuses as a way to claim attention they cannot gain through achievement, represent but a small percentage of our young. This does not mean that we should excuse or condone this brutalization of the right to dissent. Nor does it mean that we should tolerate the disruption of the academic community and the intimidation of those who seek only a quality education there. But it does mean we should recognize and reckon with this group in the proper perspective. We must avoid broad retaliatory measures that punish the innocent.

And although only a small number of America's more than seven million college students subscribe to the tactics of provocation, this does not indicate their endorsement of the status quo. Too many of our finest young people feel overpowered, overpatronized, and overprotected. I believe that most of our brightest young minds want big changes. But I believe also that they are willing to work for them *within* the system.

And the system must be ready to help them. We must listen to those who are prepared to speak with courtesy and good purpose. A "closed door" policy or mere lip service will only compound the problem.

At the same time, our young people must take note of President Nixon's words: "We cannot learn from one another — until our words can be heard as well as our voices."

I am sure you agree that our system is strong enough to accommodate dissent and to profit from it. Lawful dissent is intended to trigger the conscience, not to deprive others of their rights. Our system is flexible enough to take criticism and take it to heart.

But democracy cannot tolerate totalitarianism from any quarter. That includes the parricidal mouthings of a few highly-publicized malcontents. They constitute a violent movement that might be called, "know-it-all-ism." That movement combines the hatred and bias of the "know-nothings" of the past century with the "know-it-all" arrogance of modern day extremism.

We triumphed over the know-nothing-ism of North and South a century ago; we shall educate the know-it-alls today — in spite of themselves.

It is up to the public sector to define and defend that line that separates dissent from disruption. But it is up to the private sector — and especially to the family — to pave the way for a peaceful society. A lack of discipline in the home ultimately results in an undisciplined citizenry. The public sector cannot act in "locus parentis."

Our colleges and universities have an obligation here, too. College administrations must do more than offer courses on democracy; they must assure their students the "due process" which is an integral part of our democratic system. This means where abuses exist, ready avenues of redress must be available.

Student participation, where it can contribute to the quality of education, should be encouraged. But this must be developed in a manner that is constructive rather than disruptive.

We can take a lesson from history observed. Our university tradition began with two medieval universities. In Paris, faculty set up shop and students were the consumers. In Bologna, students set up shop and hired their teachers. The Bologna student-centered system lacked stability and, interestingly enough, educational "relevance." Ultimately, the university at Bologna survived by switching to the Paris system, putting the scholar in command.

A society as sophisticated as ours can establish practical, workable degrees of student participation. We can navigate some middle course without students locking teachers up or administrators locking students out.

Another middle ground which must be found is the place of the college in the community. Higher education can only benefit from a close, introspective look at such policies as "publish or perish" — ; an insistence on relevancy in curriculum; a voice for faculty below the professorial level; the proper balance in decisions between administrators and academicians. The middle ground appears to be somewhere between ivory tower retreat and settlement house immersion. There should be strong ties between the college and the community.

Certainly if our institutions of higher education have an obligation to rethink their relationships with students, all levels of government have an equal responsibility and opportunity here too.

Our young people are not only our greatest product, but our most promising resource. I don't mean this poetically for some point in the future, but for today.

If our local governments could but learn to harness the volunteer power of high school and college students they would have an enthusiastic work force money couldn't buy.

As governor of Maryland, I sought to energize and mobilize our student resources. Our nucleus came from student groups seeking a voice in setting state college budgets.

Quite often, young people fail to appreciate the budgetary dilemma of a governor with infinite good causes and finite resources. Abraham Lincoln brought home this point with humor when he described a struggle between his sons Willie and Tad. What was wrong between them, he said, was "just what's the matter with the whole world. I've got three walnuts and each wants two."

I urged the students to help their state and their campuses by doing their bit for the community. With student volunteers providing manpower on priority inner city projects, we could reallocate funds to higher education programs.

I sought to establish a youth corps with older students helping younger ones as tutors and recreational counselors, as big brothers and sisters. I feel it's not just enough to *demand* a say — you have to *deserve* it. Governments should make a way for students to participate and students should participate in a way that earns their say in state government. We want youth advisors and we want them to be more than armchair experts. We're looking for civic activists.

Every level of government would benefit from a student internship program comparable to the federal government's.

Actually, at the state level, I favor an even broader program extending from postgraduate to precollege youth. State governments are generally small enough to tailor summer work programs to the student's potential and will find it a valid investment. A good part-time internship experience in the present is a means of recruiting good full-time personnel in the future.

At the federal level our work is cut out for us. The first thing we should do is lower the voting age to eighteen. Not only because they're old enough to fight — but because they're smart enough to vote. I think it is illogical that in most states a girl is considered mature enough to enter a lifetime contract of marriage at eighteen, but not mature enough to vote.

Once our young people can sound off at the polls, I believe there will be less need to sound off in the streets. They'll have the chance to be counted where it counts.

Finally, I think we as a moral community must take heed of the disillusionment and disenchantment of our young. The young have a way of looking at reality with an honesty and freshness we cannot fail to appreciate. Hans Christian Andersen understood this when he wrote the wonderful story of the emperor's new clothes. Remember — no man in the kingdom, including the emperor, dared to admit he could not see the handsome cloth suit which the con man tailors said was invisible to those who were selfish, vain, and stupid. Only a little child in delightful candor piped up: "The emperor is naked."

Well, we have a veritable children's crusade telling us America can be an even better country. They are ready to go to work, and we must be ready to accept their contributions and to listen to their responsible criticism.

We must prove our system can change our world; and we must welcome all those who would change our world into our system.

President Nixon has put priority on including every American, young and old, in our system. White House staffers are already working on the ways and means to mobilize those who would serve as well as seek a better America. But let me make it clear that while the volunteer movement may be sparked by the federal government, it must be managed by the communities and manned by the private citizens.

We may propose ways to serve but only the people can dispose. For our young it means doing their own thing in their own way, on their own time. It means doing as well as demanding. It means contribution as well as confrontation.

Freedom depends on order — on laws, not violence. And to any who would destroy our freedom, I will take a lesson from the minister friend of Abe Lincoln, who sermonized: "I'm prepared to defend this Union till hell freezes over, and then I'll fight on ice."

We cannot afford self-delusion or delay. For as President Nixon says, "The American dream does not come to those who fall asleep."

I HAVE always felt that to be Greek is to be political, for the first great citizens' republic was formed in Athens and perfected by Pericles. And to be Greek is also to be philosophical, as ours is the heritage of Plato and Aristotle. Even more, to be Greek is to be involved. All this I learned from my father, who came from the town of Gargalianoi, who was political, philosophical, and very much involved.

There is no question that there is a special pride in national origin.

It's not the overwhelming factor in any American's background, but it is a gratifying, enriching, and contributing factor. Being part of a minority is being just a little different. Being set aside makes you strive for your family and yourself a little harder. There is a spur in knowing you have to make what's in you shine through the distractions of a different accent, or a different name, or a different look.

Of course there is a limit to this pride. There is a distinction between healthy self-respect and hopeless separatism.

We are proudly Greek and proudly American. But there is no question about which comes first. Our Greek heritage is something treasured from the past. Our American heritage is cherished for it represents both the present, the past, and the future.

We do not hesitate to plunge into the American mainstream and contribute to the total community. The melting pot of our nation works wonders. It builds unity out of diversity; all we have to do is give it the chance.

America doesn't ask any immigrant to divest himself of his identity, only to add to it. And as immigrants have added America to their identities they have also added to America.

We all talk a lot about the American dream. And to each of us it has special meaning. But the dream I have for America is of the day when national origin will become nothing more than a point of personal pride. Something we are sentimental about but not overly sensitive to. The time when ethnic epithets disappear and ethnic background becomes merely an interesting item for conversation. And the time we stop being so uptight that we are offended when someone jocularly says "How ya doing, Greek."

This day will come only with a wholehearted welcome of every minority into the mainstream. It will come only when we accept and insist upon every American having the right to be assimilated into and to participate in the community.

This after all is the promise of America. But it is a promise we have often failed to keep. We have paid *lip* service to values, yet denied *life* service to them.

In his inaugural address, President Nixon quoted President Franklin Delano Roosevelt's assessment of America's problems during the depth of the Depression. Roosevelt said, "They concern, thank God, only material things."

"Our crisis today" President Nixon said "is the reverse. We find ourselves rich in goods but ragged in spirit. . . ."

And let me tell you this is a far more serious thing. Government can come to the aid of its people when the crisis is material. But the people must come to the aid of their government when the crisis is spiritual.

President Nixon saw this when he said, "We are approaching the limits of what government alone can do. . . . What has to be done, has to be done by government and people together, or it will not be done at all. The lesson of past agony is that without the people we can do nothing; with the people we can do everything."

The problems facing America today, my friends, are urgent. Yet, rather than react to them with panic, we must respond to them through partnership. Our answer is partnership between the government and citizen; between black people and white people; between young and old; between labor and management.

We have the prosperity to invest in a better America. We have the technical genius to solve new and old problems. We have the chance to establish a life of abundance and opportunity for every citizen in this country; and to make this country a messenger of peace and freedom to the world. This is the life of "High Adventure" offered by President Nixon in his inaugural address.

"This is our summons to greatness. . . ." For almost two centuries America has been a citadel of freedom.

(I was moved when I heard those young ladies singing those patriotic songs. I happen to be one of those people who isn't ashamed to be moved, and I think the people in this room feel the same way. There's all too little of an admission that there is something within us when we hear and think about the greatness of our country that should be expressed, not suppressed or apologized for.)

President Nixon asks Americans to give freedom its full expression. He says "we can build a great cathedral of the spirit — each of us raising it one stone at a time, as he reaches out to his neighbor, helping, caring, doing."

We, the children and grandchildren of more recent immigrants, must be the first to respond to this challenge. For our forebears did not arrive in colonial America but industrial America. Their challenge was not the frontier but the tenement; the long hours, low wages, and occasional "lockout" by more settled society.

They struggled and they succeeded, and in their struggles and success developed a whole new set of ideas and institutions for this country. The labor movement; collective bargaining, factory inspection, pure food and fair trade laws — ultimately Social Security and unemployment insurance. These are milestones marking the progress not only of immigrant America but of all America's advance.

Now our country confronts another dynamic wave. This time it is a stirring from within rather than without. Old wrongs need righting, but new wrongs need avoiding. The bad people who use good causes as a vehicle must not prevail. At the same time, we are tested to see whether this country will live up to its promise of equality and opportunity; if we can deliver on spiritual values as successfully as we produce material goods; if we can be a nation respected throughout the world for its wisdom as well as its wealth, and for its moral spirit as well as its military strength.

I say we can make this America. I say that we are strong enough and secure enough to accept this challenge. We are every bit the men and women our ancestors who crossed the oceans in steerage were. We can make room for new ideas and institutions. We can build into America things that are good and new, and do it without destroying things that are good and old. We can offer our hands in help to those not as fortunate as ourselves. We can open our hearts to their problems and lend our individual talents and our organizational resources to their solution to those problems.

We can raise that "cathedral of the spirit" by calling upon the spirit that brought our families here from Gargalianoi . . . the faith that with work any dream is possible in America. We have inherited their strength and their spirit and their will. And we realize as our new President recognizes "The American Dream does not come to those who fall asleep."

And as I came here tonight I wondered what I can do to show the appreciation that I feel for the symbolic lift that the Greek–Americans of this country have given me. And I thought of my father. My father was a great man for education. The Worthington Chapter No. 30 of the Ahepa recognized this. They established a scholarship fund in the name of my father — a fund to send worthy students through universities here in the United States. But it occurred to me that I can do something a little different tonight and something that possibly can be the springboard for something big for the Society. I would like to be the first to send a young Greek boy through the University of Athens in the name of this Society. So I am proposing that this grant that I will make will be not in the name of my father, who was here in the United States and whom I had the pleasure to be with many, many years, but in the name of the grandfather I never saw, who was born in the town of Gargalianoi, who lived and died there. And incidentally, his name was the same as mine would have been if my father hadn't gotten smart and changed it. It is a little awkward here — Anagnostopoulos — although I've never run from it, I'm proud of

191

it. I think that it's appropriate that the young man who's selected be screened by the members of this Society and that he come from the town of Gargalianoi. So I will, with the help of this Society, provide sufficient funds to send such young fellows through the University of Athens. I hope this Society is therefore launched on an important new project.

February 24, 1969, New York, New York
American Management Association

A TURN of the century writer defined the ocean as "a body of water occupying about two-thirds of a world made for man, who has no gills." With all the millions of words written about the ocean and its fathomless allure, this precisely, if irreverently, reaches to the root of our problems.

Our nation, its history and greatness are inextricably linked to the sea. Ninety percent of our international commerce is transported by ships; seventy-five percent of our population lives in coastal areas. Fifty million people look to our coastal waters for recreation. All two hundred million Americans depend upon the ocean and its resources for life. Our national power, security, and defense require mastery of the sea. At the same time advances in international cooperation in the peaceful development of resources furthering the prosperity of all nations, can be achieved by unlocking the secret treasury that is the sea.

Millions of years ago life first emerged from the oceans. Now — to flourish — life shall return there. America has always looked to the sea and found success. Now it is time for fresh vision.

As chairman of the National Council on Marine Resources and Engineering Development, I welcome the opportunity to serve at this moment when we stand on the threshold of penetrating present mysteries of the deep and tapping the ocean's rich potential.

The Council, established by Congress in 1966, has a broad mandate to promote fuller realization of the sea's promise. The 1966 legislation assigned a leadership role to the federal government but anticipated a full partnership with state and local governments, and with industry and universities.

The fact that the American Management Association has devoted this briefing session to oceanology indicates private leadership's recognition of this important subject. I hope it also implies your readiness to participate in vital oceanographic programs.

The rich agenda for this conference reflects many of the facets of our national interest in the sea and underscores the importance of industrial involvement in all phases of our broadened ocean endeavors.

Last fall President Nixon stated that an integrated and comprehensive program in oceanography would receive priority attention by his administration. And as recently as last week, he urged that we now move forward to develop specific policies and programs. We recognize the key role of industry in marine affairs — in providing the necessary entrepreneurship, in developing the unique and complex tools that are needed in harvesting marine resources — and I can assure you that this administration is interested in a public–private partnership whether it concerns land, sea or air.

The development of a comprehensive oceanography program first requires coordination. The scope of marine science affairs delineated by Congress encompasses national security, foreign affairs, fishing, recreation, resource development, pollution abatement, transportation and trade, scientific research and exploration. Numerous federal agencies are involved.

The National Council on Marine Resources and Engineering Development will serve as the focal point and forum for this extraordinary range of important interests. All reports from both Republicans and Democrats give the Council high marks in mobilizing our resources, focusing attention on major policy issues, and stimulating ideas and action in all sectors of the marine community.

The President has explicitly requested the Council to provide advice on our ocean policies and programs — and where we go from here.

In response to that assignment and in accordance with its statutory responsibilities, the Council will continue to develop a comprehensive program of marine affairs; clarify agency responsibilities where they overlap; carry out long-range policy studies; and coordinate a program of international cooperation.

The President is deeply interested in firmly establishing America as a first-rate maritime power.

We intend to build on our existing technological readiness — the arsenal of ships, research submersibles, buoys, laboratories, instruments, and manpower developed since World War II — to the fullest extent.

We intend to rely upon our talented scientists and engineers.

We intend to blend together the wide and varied interests and capabilities of our states, our industrial and academic communities, and our federal establishment.

We intend to use the science of oceanology to serve the pressing needs of our society. The knowledge of the seas must be used to serve the cause of world peace.

And we shall pursue these policies — as the Nixon Administration shall pursue all national policies — with an emphasis on realism and a reliance upon the technological genius of our nation.

More than a decade of study and analysis has passed since Congress initially recognized the importance of a national marine program. In 1970 the International Decade of Ocean Exploration will begin. The past years have been a time of preparation, the present year should be one of organization, so that the next decade can be one of cooperation climaxing in realization of the sea's promise.

Yet, even as we explore the depths of the open sea in concert with other nations, we shall complement this effort with a decade of coastal development. Here our goal is to balance economic development with conservation of irreplaceable national resources.

As advisor to the President, the Council on Marine Sciences will give first consideration to recommendations of the Commission on Marine Science, Engineering, and Resources. This Commission was composed of distinguished Americans from many different areas — industry, banking, science, state governments. It had a set of Congressional advisors of both parties. It is to be commended for looking at our ocean interests in the broad perspective of the nation's stake in the sea and for adding a further dimension to our understanding of needs and opportunities. While some of the recommendations are controversial, there are cases where bold steps are needed to take advantage of emerging opportunities in this field.

However, apart from the particular points of controversy, the report provides a revealing balance sheet of what we know and what we need to do if America is to enjoy a leadership position in marine science.

We know that the world's ocean contains a storehouse of food critically needed in developing areas where malnutrition rages.

We need improved processes for manufacturing fish protein concentrate (FPC) and the development of marketing and distribution systems. For FPC can make significant contributions toward bringing these vast unused resources into the diets of protein deficient populations.

We know that the oceans provide an indispensable commercial highway with traffic growing at an ever-increasing rate. We know, too, that our existing ports and harbors cannot accommodate the larger and deeper draft ships that are rapidly entering service.

We need to incorporate new technology into our port system, and we need to integrate

193

this system into the transportation needs of the entire nation. The federal government must work closely with local and regional port authorities and industrial interests to achieve this goal.

We know that the seabed, and particularly the continental shelf, contains a reservoir of fuel and minerals for our expanding economy. At the same time, many of these resources are presently uneconomical to recover. Also, the recent oil spill near Santa Barbara was a grim reminder of related environmental hazards that we still do not completely understand, nor are fully able to control.

We need more knowledge in these areas and we need to develop sound national policies balancing environmental and economic interests.

Delay in this area could be devastating. Consequently, the administration is now reevaluating the government's offshore leasing policy for fuels and minerals and, with the assistance of industry, we will seek to develop a framework for managing this resource for the benefit of all of our citizens.

We know that the oceans provide us with a deterring shield to protect our country. However, we have no monopoly on naval technology.

Improved capability to operate in the deep oceans, developed jointly by the Navy and industry, is needed for our national security.

We know that the nation's future in the sea depends on an adequate supply of trained specialists, particularly ocean engineers and technicians, for the technological development of marine resources in the 1970s.

We need an expanded sea grant program to assist in fulfilling this need.

We know that the world's ocean has an important influence on global weather patterns. New technology is at hand to extend our capabilities to obtain the extensive observations required to understand and predict environmental conditions.

We need to continue our work with industry toward the development of buoys, spacecraft, and other platforms to collect oceanographic and meteorological data.

While particularly emphasizing these areas, I wish to point out that the administration is not unaware of many other aspects of marine affairs which deserve attention. The legal regime of the oceans and seabeds, the decline of our domestic fishing industry, the need for more adequate protection of life and property on the water and along the shores — these and many other problems will receive our earnest consideration.

Finally, I would like to turn to that part of marine environment which I know best — the coastal zone.

As past governor of Maryland, I claim considerable experience with the blessing and curse of coastal land. Maryland, as you know, is almost bisected by the Chesapeake Bay. The bay is 195 miles long and up to forty miles in width, and covers more than 4,000 square miles. It receives fresh water from the Susquehanna, Potomac, Rappahannock, York, James, and many other rivers, mixed with salt water tides from the Atlantic Ocean.

The shores of the bay are homes to four million people. It supports a commercial fishery resource valued at more than $65 million annually, one which provides a livelihood for 20,000 persons. It is a thoroughfare for more than 100 million tons of waterborne commerce each year and provides a prime location for industry, with easy access to markets, labor and transportation. It is a first class tourist attraction and recreation retreat for tens of thousands from all levels of our society. They flock to the bay to enjoy swimming, boating, fishing or sightseeing. Some 60,000 sport boats use its waters.

At the same time, the bay is the final repository of wastes from all these people and all these industries. Its shorelines are eroding at an alarming rate and some of its islands have disappeared within my memory. Its wetlands are being transformed to accommodate the needs of a growing population. Sediments washed from the uplands and excavated from navigation channels cover thousands of acres of the bottom of the bay.

We do not know in detail the effects of any of these activities, much less the complex interactions which occur. But we do know that the bay, and the rest of the nation's coastal zone, cannot continue to accommodate all of the diverse demands being imposed upon it at random and at an increasing rate, as it has in the past.

During my tenure as governor of Maryland, we developed and saw enacted the most massive pollution abatement program in the state's history. Even this program — which more than tripled all past efforts — is just the beginning of what must be done.

The problems of Maryland may be applied equally well to many of the bays, sounds, estuaries, and shorelines of all the coastal and Great Lakes states. The total resources of the coastal zone must be better managed. A system of management is needed that permits each use to be considered in its own right, but subordinate to the total economic, social, esthetic, and cultural needs of the people as a whole.

Over two years ago the Council began to examine the coastal zone, using the Chesapeake Bay as a case study. Congress has taken a number of initiatives to examine estuarine conservation and development. And the Marine Commission took a sharp look at the coastal zone and submitted many recommendations for improved management.

All of these considerations can contribute to a sound system of coastal management which takes into account national, regional, and local interests. Such a system should of course recognize the appropriate role of the states and private enterprise — seeking a harmony of compatible uses for the nation's sake. We will seek to put the federal house in order by strengthening coordination of federal programs in the coastal zone, by eliminating the conflicts and unnecessary overlaps resulting from the fragmentation of responsibilities and programs among more than a dozen departments, agencies, councils, and committees. We hope to increase public awareness of the need for wise management of coastal lands and waters. We will examine steps as to responsibilities of the individual states in the development of their coastal zone resources, and provide for closer collaboration between state and federal agencies.

In conclusion, I want to underscore that this administration will implement the full terms of the Marine Resources and Engineering Development Act. We are reviewing goals and programs of the prior administration. We are examining the Commission findings. And we will be developing a clear program of our own for the future.

I leave with you the words of an old Welsh proverb: "Three things are untamable: fools, women, and the salt sea."

This is a great moment for civilization — we stand at the threshold of taming the sea. Taming fools and women may take a bit longer.

March 21, 1969, Washington, D.C.
Plans for Progress National Conference

AS VICE PRESIDENT, I am deeply committed to the purposes of the Plans for Progress and — believe me — I know what minority employment means in this job.

The President has asked me to convey his genuine regrets that he is unable to greet you personally.

But you need only recall the words of his inaugural address to know the tremendous emphasis he places upon the problem-solving efforts of the private sector.

He said, and I quote: "Our greatest need now is to reach beyond government, to enlist the legions of the concerned and the committed.

"What has to be done, has to be done by government and people together, or it will not be done at all."

Plans for Progress exemplifies that partnership of government and people which is so essential and so effective to implement those plans.

Now as I was coming up here this morning, I picked up the remarks which had been

195

prepared for me, as is so often the case, and I read those remarks. It's a good predictable, harmless, non-controversy-provoking speech. I don't like it because I think that even though it's all those things I said it was, it's not going to tell you anything about what I feel concerning minority business enterprise — what my observations have been, what I think some of the directions that need to be moved in that are departures from those we are moving in should be, and basically where I think the problem lies.

So I'm not going to give this very safe, benign speech. I'm going to try to tell you in a few words — and they won't be well organized because frankly I haven't thought this thing through as far as presenting it to you this morning — but I think that what I say in a substantive way may be more helpful and more stimulating than what I would have said in the speech.

First of all, I think that people, when they think of minority businesses make the mistake and always think of some little hole-in-the-wall business. Whether it be a small restaurant or a laundry or a drug store or a grocery store or whatever the case where Uncle Sam and the big corporate giants out of the decency of their hearts and souls turn over a certain amount of money to a small, poor, struggling fellow and say, "Here, we're going to set you up in business. Now go to it. This is America, the place where the dream can be realized, and we think that if you've got what it takes inside you can create a business empire in due course."

You and I know that things just don't work that way. It sounds great on paper. But this direction has been the direction that all too unfortunately has been followed in some cases by the government and by the businesses that are established and functioning. And last year, it's my understanding, that out of some five thousand small business loans of the soft type — loans where the security was not such that a hard business scrutiny of the individual going into the business and his collateral would allow a bank to make such a grant — five thousand of these soft loans were given, and about ninety percent of them resulted not only in the failure of the businesses that they were supposed to have started but in the abject frustration of the people who tried to start those businesses in good faith.

Now why did they fail? They failed because they didn't have any direction; they didn't know anything about the businesses; they didn't understand the markets; they didn't understand the technique; they didn't have the collateral connections to financing that are required to expand a successful undertaking; and they could not compete in the market. And that's the most important point I want to leave with you today.

Just because a man, be he a Negro or a Mexican–American or an Indian, sets up a business in a community that's substantially composed of people of those races, doesn't mean those people are going to buy his product if the product isn't good. Moreover, he cannot succeed in the sense that we want to see minority business enterprise succeed, unless he has a market consisting of the entire strata of our population.

So basically, we've got to face one thing. That this is not charity on behalf — on the part of the consumer. This is a need to put out a competitive better product within the American system, that will let that business become competitive. To do that he must have recourse to the same public relations advertising techniques that big business has. He must have recourse to the same financing for his plan expansions. He must have recourse to the same market development techniques.

And what does he need to have these things? Well, it's very simple. He needs other people of his kind in those existing structures so that he will get equal treatment when he goes to expand his business. That's one thing he needs. The second thing he needs is an overwhelming awareness of the fact that he is not in a competitive posture when he begins, and must have continuing advice and assistance over the early months and years of the development of that business. And we've made a mistake by simply saying, as we've said in all of our social programs, "Here is the money — we've done our jobs." And then when he's not able to productively employ the money, we say, "Well, isn't it a shame. I guess he just can't handle it."

Well, it isn't his fault, ladies and gentlemen, that he can't handle it. It's our fault because we have not developed the proper techniques of assisting him in handling it. We have not, for example, provided the measures of opportunity within the existing corporate giants to bring along people of the minority races so that they occupy the positions that allow them to understand the "big picture" in the business world and to employ it in a competitive sense so they can take on the rest of their fellow workers, their fellow entrepreneurs.

And if I can leave you one question — one thought out of these short remarks, it's this: That business is a hydra-headed proposition today. There isn't any more small business where a person can set up a drugstore in a neighborhood, or a candy store where the people walk to get whatever product he purveys that day and walk back. This is the day when the people jump in their cars and go to the market that's most attractive. And you know the techniques that are used — the massive advertising campaigns; the price-cutting; the things that make it impossible for small business to compete for those markets.

So what I'm saying is we can't stop our efforts to start these small businesses. That's obviously the answer. But at the same time, there must be, on the part of the corporations in this country, a recognition that they must supply the corporate officers — the black, the Indian, the Mexican–American corporate officers who get a chance to see the super-structure of big business and to understand it, that they must bring these people along through their organizations. And they must provide the stock options that make those jobs so attractive. And then, when the minority business thrust begins to gather impetus and to roll, it's going to be because, when that lone black beginning businessman walks into a bank, let him have the option of walking into a black bank to get his money. Let him have the option of hiring a big public relations firm that's headed for, not the black market, but the market of the United States, but headed by a black man. Let him have the collateral assistance that we have. He can't have it overnight, but we've got to make a beginning.

And a beginning is not simply to set a man up in business and give him a handout and say, "This is enough to buy your plant and equipment. Now you're on your own." You've got to have a continued review and scrutiny of how that man is doing. It doesn't mean that you're going to come in and look over his shoulder. Tell him that he's not allowed to do this or that. But you can come in and say, "Now look, Joe, when we started our plant we tried that, and boy, it just doesn't work."

And this review has got to be a thing that is motivated and continuing all the time. And it's got to be done against human nature. What's against human nature? Setting up somebody else to be a competitor. That's human nature. But that's what we have to have to do if this thing is going to work. So these thoughts aren't in my speech, but they're thoughts that have been much on my mind as I've looked at what seems to be painted as the overwhelming success of minority business programs. I think we're just scratching the surface. We've got to move in a many faceted fashion. We've got to see that the opportunities don't just occur in certain areas of small business, but the receptivity of the business world at large, of the services that every business requires — the ancillary services — are provided for these minority business enterprises.

I think that can best be done by an organization like yours — the National Alliance of Businessmen cooperating with Plans for Progress. I think maybe you ought to sit down and think this thing through a little bit, see what you are doing about these black executives in your company or these Indian–Americans. Make certain that someone is assigned at the highest level to these new undertakings, to make sure those services — services for business that produce good markets — are there when a new business is begun.

And I'd finally hope that this organization would focus its talents for minority employment on a summertime thrust to employ disadvantaged youth in these jobs. I just announced a program, our first summertime program, on behalf of the President, in cooperation with the NCAA that will give 75,000 youth from inner city ghettos a chance at a day camp experience this summer on college campuses and university campuses of 140 institutions, universities in this country. The government is putting up 3 million dollars for this summer program. The NCAA is putting up a million and a half and the thrust will be toward a summer camp experience with sports and whatnot. But we're also going to have a job program for summer youth, and you might find some of your most talented people will come out of what can be developed in this regard. And I hope you do focus your talents in that direction.

Finally, I say in all humility and sincerity, I'm proud to be a partner in Plans for Progress. I hope I can contribute as much to you as you've contributed to the nation.

You've showed that the private sector determined to do a job can do it faster and better than government, but you have a long way to go yet, just as the government does.

But you have produced one thing — the greatest product this country can offer — and that's opportunity. And you have invested our nation's richest resource — its people. And if you're successful you will have supplied the ultimate human commodity — dignity.

March 28, 1969, Washington, D.C.
Presidential Classroom

IF WE FOLLOWED the tradition of the classroom, I would be here to teach; you would be here to learn.

But today I am going to break the expected pattern and ask you to join me in setting a new precedent.

I did not come to lecture you, but to enlist you in the volunteer movement sweeping this country.

In his inaugural address, the President said, "Our greatest need now is to reach beyond government, to enlist the legions of the concerned and the committed."

I issue you a blanket invitation by the administration to join "the legions of the concerned and the committed."

You are not too young to come to the aid of your country. In fact, America's responsible high school students are too bright, too educated, too dedicated to be left out of the action.

My experience as governor of Maryland justifies my confidence in your competence. In the spring of last year, I proposed the creation of a Youth Service Council to advise and assist the governor in developing special education and recreation projects. The response of college students was negligible, but the enthusiasm expressed by high school students was inspiring.

Further, the high school students did not await the consensus of their college counterparts, but on their own initiative went to work on some of the ideas which I had suggested.

Their response was sufficient to convince me that when we look for rich human resources, we should look to our resourceful high school students.

In saying this, I am not writing off any of America's young people. Certainly, the preponderant majority of our college students are better prepared, more willing to question and to contribute, than any generation of students that has preceded them.

While a radical campus element claims the most publicity, its notoriety is out of all proportion to its adherents.

Self-righteous in philosophy, destructive in tactics, the overblown rhetoric of the radicals attracts only about two percent of all our country's college students to its cause.

Not nearly as visible, but far greater in number, are the student activists. Equally intent upon changing our society, the student activists believe the best way to achieve change is by working within the system.

The radicals charge that the activists are sellouts to the system. But what is readily apparent is that while the *radicals* have been doing a lot of talking, the activists have actually been *changing* the system.

198

The system, I can assure you, is able to change. And society will change for the better at about the same rate citizens contribute their time and talent to improving it.

Right now, we have three major programs which not only thrive but survive on the vision of young Americans.

The Peace Corps, started in 1961, now has over 10,000 people working overseas in fifty-eight countries.

VISTA now has 5,000 full-time people working on educational and social projects in forty-nine states. It also has 1,500 specialists — lawyers, teachers, graduate students — working part-time for no money at all.

In the earlier days it was difficult recruiting young people for VISTA. Most wanted to go overseas and work in developing nations. But the pendulum of concern has swung to the problems here at home. Last year more than 100,000 people expressed interest in joining VISTA. Recruiting is up almost 100 percent.

The newest program, and in many ways the most promising, is the Teacher Corps. Now in its third year, the Teacher Corps last year attracted 10,000 applicants for its 1,300 positions.

The Teacher Corps' aim is twofold: To improve the instruction given to low-income children, and to train teachers in the special art of educating disadvantaged pupils. Participants in this program are organized into teams that are assigned to ghetto schools for two years. The teams are usually led by an experienced teacher and include college and high school graduates who intend to become teachers.

Over seventy-five percent of the first "graduating class" of Teacher Corpsmen decided to remain working in poverty areas, and fifty percent stayed on at the school where they had done their training.

The response to these programs reveals that the voluntary way has become a way of life for America's young.

It is my hope that this administration will build upon this fine record. We want to do more than maintain — we want to increase the involvement of *all* who care enough to contribute.

And one of the first steps will be to involve more high schools and high school students in the life of their communities.

Just last week, the administration announced a summer day camp program which will serve 75,000 disadvantaged youngsters this summer. The day camps will be operated on 120 college and junior college campuses in forty of the nation's largest metropolitan areas. Our goal is to provide a four-week respite of recreation and educational enrichment for young people whose only recourse would be the streets.

This year's program is designed for the ages of twelve to eighteen years. There is no question that we are not reaching all in this group or those but a few years younger — from eight to twelve years — who would gain so much from this experience.

The utilization of high school facilities and high school student counselors would be one way we could expand this program.

This is only one example of where you are needed and needed now. Let me offer a few others:

Hundreds of towns have no VISTA or Teacher Corps programs -— and there is need for local voluntary groups to fill this vacuum.

Few inner-city schools have enough tutors for remedial help or enough volunteers to supervise recreational programs.

Obviously, a high school sophomore could not tutor his counterpart, but there is no reason why you couldn't provide that extra hour of individual attention to a grade school student in desperate need of help. There is no reason why high school students with Red Cross lifesaving credentials could not serve as coaches and day camp counselors. There is no reason why a gifted young painter or musician should be barred from sharing his talents with others because of age.

Right now, too few disadvantaged children have anyone to take them on trips — to the zoo, the museum, the circus.

Too few have someone at home who has time to listen to their special problems, answer their serious questions, or provide the companionship that is so important to developing a child's sense of self and self-worth.

There is no reason why a mature, responsible high school student should not act as an aide on organized trips; or serve as Big Brother or Big Sister to a lonely, disadvantaged child. There is every reason why gifted teen-agers who care should be enabled to share their talents and express their concern.

The key is organization. Service centers must be developed to mobilize volunteers and match the people who want to help with the people who need help. Where training is necessary, training should be provided through an organized center.

Government — federal, state, or local — can assist in developing these centers, setting guidelines and standards for acceptable volunteer service. Perhaps even help in the provision of seed money for nuclear staffing, instructors, and supplies.

But private involvement need not await public initiative. Colleges and high schools can be centers of service on their own. Some already are. Perhaps your school already has a community service club or program underway.

Today, I would like to enlist you in a special project — a first step toward the national mobilization of high school volunteers.

I would like each of you to survey your high school as to the number of service programs underway and report to me by letter:

1. How many programs presently exist.

2. How many students are involved.

3. Outline the best, most effective program currently in operation.

Here, I urge you not to limit yourself to purely service-oriented projects. There may be related programs in human relations; crosscommunity dialogue; inter–high school cooperative efforts; police–community relations; or programs drawing upon your school's resources but sponsored by an outside civic or religious group. If you feel they are valid, or could have value, send them along.

Our goal is to develop a file of workable ideas for voluntary service involving high school students. Our plan is to assemble a booklet, built on your information, which we can disseminate to high schools throughout the country.

In order that this booklet may provide accurate guidance to high school students seeking to pattern programs after those proven successful in your own schools, I hope you will include substantial detail on the organization of the example you submit.

I urge you to elaborate on such specifics as the objectives of the program; the number of students involved; the faculty or administration supervision provided; the hours a week or month given to the project by students; recruitment procedures if any; and an organization chart reflecting the respective responsibilities of all participants.

Your letters will be the foundation of a move to enlarge the participation of high school students in vital community activities.

All across America we have students like you with a strong, sincere commitment to achieving a better world and a willingness to work toward this achievement. Your energy can produce significant changes in American society — and this administration intends to tap your energy, draw upon your talents, use the time you are willing to give.

But leadership still must come from you at the local level. The conscience of each community knows best what is needed and what needs to be done.

The administration can serve best by focusing attention on what our youth has done, can do, and is willing to do. We can serve as a clearinghouse for ideas by preparing publications like the one which will be based on your letters.

Both the President and myself have young people on our staffs deeply interested in expanding the opportunities for public spirited high school students. We are exploring ways to further understanding and participation.

The letters I have asked you to write are but a first step. But as the old saying goes: "Even the journey of a thousand miles must begin with a single step."

I hope you will take back to your schools the confidence in you expressed by the President in his inaugural. "We can see the hope of tomorrow in the youth of today.

. . . They are better educated, more committed, more passionately driven by conscience than any generation that has gone before."

Responsible young Americans are setting a pace and creating a pattern without precedent in this country. In the past we used to say, "Youth shall *be* served." Young people today say, "Youth shall serve."

The administration salutes this spirit and seeks your service.

April 23, 1969, Washington, D.C.

Ocean Science and Technology Committee of The National Security Industrial Association

DR. KIRKBRIDE, Mr. Weaver, distinguished guests and members of the OSTAC.

Mastery of the oceans has from the very first depended upon concerted action. The age of exploration of natural resources under the earth is virtually at an end. The age of exploration and the discovery of the new world really resulted from public–private partnership.

When Queen Isabella staked Christopher Columbus, she was ingeniously carrying forth tradition. When the British government developed a *quid pro quo* arrangement with the English East India Company, it was economically expediting national interests.

Now, there is nothing novel about public–private ventures into the unknown. While OSTAC is not to be invidiously compared to its sixteenth-century predecessors, it is to be commended for its early recognition of the ocean's potential for industry and for its ongoing efforts to clarify the appropriate roles of government and industry in realizing the promise of the sea.

The Committee's 1967 report presented a thoughtful justification that government should not preempt industry's traditional role in resource development. OSTAC's statement on the Marine Science Council's report and your general support of proposals for an agency and advisory commission on the oceans offer assurance that industry is aware of and concerned about oceanographic development.

Science and industry must emerge from peripheral activity to active — and even aggressive partnership with government, if we are to capitalize fully upon the resources of the sea.

This administration will pay attention to America's "seapower" in all its ramifications. We are aware that critical conditions exist.

The maritime stature of America — once a giant among commercial powers — has unquestionably diminished. U.S. flagships now transport less than six percent of our seaborne trade. And I think that's a frightening statistic.

Less than a third of a century ago, America's shipyards produced a fleet that provided the World War II lifeline to the free world. Today, our nation produces less than fifteen nonmilitary ships a year. Less than fifteen. Japan delivers two hundred annually.

The United States Navy remains the strongest in the world. Still the Soviet's recent penetration into the Mediterranean poses a powerful reminder that other nations are committed also to naval expansion. Evidence of a rapid Soviet buildup in missile-launching submarines was one of the underlying factors in the President's decision to proceed with the ABM System.

Beyond — and above — the compelling concern of national security is the specter of hunger and malnutrition which affects more than half the world's population. The nineteenth-century British political economist, Thomas Malthus, pointed out the inverse correlation between population and productivity. If an exploding world population is to escape a Malthusian destiny, we must better understand the resources of the sea: use them wisely; and replenish them frequently.

The coastal zone of the United States — a 17,000 mile ribbon around our nation — is plagued by a morass of social, legal, and institutional problems.

Fifty million people crowd our shoreline. This number will double within thirty-five years. The resulting pressures threaten irreversible environmental degradation accompanied by increasing social tensions.

Neglect of our nation's stake in the oceans is reflected in many prime ports where outmoded harbor facilities are unable to cope effectively with rapid advances in shipping techniques. Crime, corruption, squalid housing — every conceivable social ill — comes to thrive upon decay at our docksides.

Industrial wastes, discharged into waters ultimately emptying into the ocean, will increase sevenfold by 1980. If current waste handling methods continue unchecked, thermal pollution poses a new, not fully known factor.

Large segments of our fishing industry are in trouble. Once healthy fishing communities are now economically depressed. Obsolete equipment and techniques have caused America to slip from second- to fifth-ranked fishing nation. Peru, Japan, Communist China, and Russia all "out-fish" us.

Soviet trawler fleets virtually dominate the Grand Banks off our shores — fishing, researching the ocean depths and keeping us under electronic surveillance. Meanwhile, America does not have one modern long range trawler in service. U.S. seafood imports have soared from thirty-three percent in 1957 to seventy-one percent at present. Here we have an economic loss, a balance of payment loss, and of course a strategic loss.

While all these severe negative factors require an immediate response, there are positive justifications for "sea power" too.

The sea can reflect our hope for peace and international cooperation. While controversy may rage above its surface, the seabed remains open to all nations.

The oceans are indivisible. Currents, weather and water patterns neither know nor respect political boundaries. International cooperation is indispensable if mankind is to penetrate the sea's mysteries.

As all life emerged from the oceans eons ago, perhaps peace — the sole hope for life — may emerge from international oceanographic cooperation in the future. As the original stages of life were primitive, so these submerged steps toward peace may appear to some to be crude. But they do offer a new avenue we cannot neglect.

The sea promises hope for greater health — it is a pharmacopoeia barely known. Yet the little knowledge we possess reveals seagoing creatures have chemical resistance to fight cancer and to regulate the heart.

Weather and water are inextricably linked. Greater knowledge may forewarn of and ultimately prevent natural disasters.

The richest promise of the sea is humanitarian. Improved knowledge of sea biology would provide an estimated five to ten times larger food yield from the sea.

But before the dreams of tomorrow come the hard facts of today.

We must know more — much more; develop greater technical capacity; and harness more practical solutions.

If the resources of the sea are infinite, the resources of the United States government are of necessity finite.

Every investment in seapower must be tested against competing national priorities. Every budgetary consideration for the present must be sublimated to the issue of inflation.

While this administration is committed to restoring America's stature as an all-around seapower, this administration is also committed to a commonsense approach to government.

In terms of oceanographic research and development, future expenditures will be judged by this commonsense criterion. Just because something "could" be done beneath the sea does not mean it "should" be done beneath the sea. Only when the "could" and "should" coexist, should there be investment.

Government has a clear responsibility to evaluate the importance of large-scale experiments in the interests of national security or welfare.

Scientists must assist government in arriving at rational judgments. Scientific–industrial groups like OSTAC may be invaluable as interpreter of the issues to the general public and catalyst for action to the private sector.

Although partnership is our ultimate goal, government recognizes that it does have certain obligations to industry.

Imprecision in existing international law requires vigilance on the part of the United States government. The United Nations is seeking to develop a legal regime governing the development of the seabed's petroleum and mineral resources. The United States will continue to insist that any international arrangement must be supportive to private development of these resources. Further, the integrity of any investments made prior to international accord must be fully protected.

In the fields of international fisheries and maritime shipping, we shall attempt to strengthen the international rules governing ocean activities. We favor healthy, but not unbridled competition. Abrasive rivalry may generate conflict.

Turning to purely domestic programs, offshore leasing policies are currently under intensive review. Even before the Santa Barbara disaster, government had initiated studies to improve bidding and leasing arrangements.

Now, there is no need for me to belabor the value of the broad cooperation between industry and government on behalf of the national defense. I offer no apology for the presence of the so-called military–industrial complex so long as forces hostile to this nation continue to exist.

In addition, industry–government partnership ranges from the development of oil reserves in the Arctic to Tektite I — a sixty-day man-in-the-sea experiment — in the Virgin Islands.

A National Oceanographic Instrumentation Center was recently established by the Marine Council to serve government, the military, universities, and private industry. The Council will soon publish the first national inventory of marine research projects in catalog form.

Surveying these accomplishments, the complacent would be satisfied that we are making progress. I'm far from complacent. I'm far from satisfied. I concede that there's been progress, but I am conscious that much more progress must come.

In this tight budget year — I look to you, the scientist–businessmen, who understand the impact of inflation and the importance of ongoing ocean development — to increase initiative and private investment where the federal government cannot.

Many marine groups are unacquainted with one another in a detailed sense. There is a duplication of effort and a differing of views that is confusing rather than constructive. While your committee has done much to achieve industrial unity — you well know how much remains to be done.

Public and private investment in research to support America's marine industry is less than half a billion dollars annually. Compare this with "R" and "D" expenditures in other fields.

Production at present concentrates too heavily on the military oceanographic market. I urge you not to overlook the diversified opportunities in the civilian sector.

Certainly, for this year, we've reached a plateau on government investment in the marine sciences. It's my hope that industry will compensate through a broad alliance continuing and expanding private oceanographic efforts. Your leadership is imperative. And I offer just a few suggestions as to directions:

— Accelerate private investment in marine research.

— Recruit and train more oceanographers.

— Encourage universities and colleges to expand or develop ocean science programs.

— Consider methods where industry can cooperate with the National Science Foundation in realizing a genuine sea grant college system.

— Continue to manufacture ideas as well as hardware for government; because the oceanographer is not limited only by his hardware, he must have the ability to innovate and conceive of new directions.

I recognize that this places a tremendous responsibility upon you. But it will encourage government to be appreciative and increasingly receptive to your views.

From the largest defense contract to the smallest waterway chart, government has been doing a job for and with industry. Now — in this tight budget year — to paraphrase the words of a past president — this administration must ask what job will industry do for America and the oceans?

Thank you very much for this chance to be with you.

May 1, 1969, Phoenix, Arizona
Trunk and Tusk Club Dinner

MY SINUSES and I always look forward to coming to Arizona, where the sun shines brightly every day for the people who live here and even more brightly for the people who just visit here.

You have always been generous to me. Maybe because I was one dude Easterner who didn't turn his back on the man you sent throughout the nation in 1964 to stake his claim to the presidency. Maybe because I am a man who believes that American vigilance in defense of principle is no vice and an Alaskan dogsled in pursuit of publicity is no virtue.

My speech tonight is the one President Nixon approved for this occasion. It's somewhat short . . . beginning with my name, mentioning my office, and concluding with my serial number.

However, I plan to add a little something to it, just to see whether I have lost the knack for making a headline. After all, the press has to live too.

Besides, when you are thought to be too efficient, nobody pays any attention. It's only when you slip on the ice and end up with a bloody nose that the world takes notice.

Tonight, there are a lot of important things to be said. The first quarter of the new Republican administration have come and gone, and the stage has been set for the next three and three-quarter years . . . perhaps seven and three-quarter years.

In a relatively quiet way, we have drawn up a procedure for progress . . . believing that if we start on solid ground we will journey more safely through the dangers of our times . . . knowing that if we work our way carefully from war to peace, from division to unity, from doubt to confidence, that the result will be sensible and history will be merciful.

And if, at times, you hear the complaint that we are moving too slowly, reflect upon what happens when you rush too quickly into battle, with guns half-loaded and plans half-drawn. We did not come to Washington to repeat the mistakes of the past. We came to correct them and move forward — and we have come far already.

At Paris, in Vietnam and behind the scenes, the Nixon Administration has pressed ahead with its first priority — to secure an honorable peace in Southeast Asia.

In the Middle East, the administration has been exercising "preventive diplomacy" to avert a major crisis.

In Europe, President Nixon's trip to five nations fostered new unity within the Western alliance.

In relations with the Soviet Union, the Nixon policy of firmness without belligerence has paved the way for new channels of communication and new hope for accord.

In a moderate interim response to an act of aggression by a small, sword-rattling militarist, the President has demonstrated cool command under great pressure. He spoke in terms of facts, not threats. Reconnaissance flights have been resumed with military protection and as the president has said — a warning is given only once.

Inflation, the number one domestic problem, is being dampened by tactics of persistence and patience. The conscientious use of sound fiscal evaluation and application has been brought into play. The administration's $4 billion cut in the federal budget and its proposal to repeal the seven percent investment credit represent essential — and overdue — action to save the American dollar.

The executive branch of the federal government has been invigorated by new thinking. The National Security Council has been revitalized. An Urban Affairs Council has been established; an Office of Intergovernmental Relations and a Cabinet Committee on Economic Policy created.

Major federal departments are being revamped. The Manpower Administration in the Department of Labor has been reorganized. A minority business enterprise program has been instituted in the Department of Commerce. An Office of Child Development has been set up in the Department of Health, Education, and Welfare.

Federal regional field offices have been restructured with uniform boundaries, and interrelated federal agencies will be headquartered in a single city.

After almost two centuries marked by increasing inefficiency, the administration has taken post office operations out of politics. Competence — not party loyalty — shall be the future test for selecting postmasters. Further, far reaching reforms are under way.

A series of major crime control measures have been proposed. The President's primary target is America's primary culprit — organized crime.

Equality as well as efficiency is vital to a just, responsive government. The President has proposed progressive tax reform to assure that the most affluent Americans pay some tax and the poorest Americans pay none.

Perhaps the hardest — yet most vital decision — of the first quarter centered around the antiballistic missile controversy. The President, duly conscious of threatened imbalances jeopardizing national security — deeply desiring peace — took the *minimum feasible, responsible* action in advocating the Safeguard system.

This purely defensive protection of our deterrent retaliatory forces responsibly meets strategic requirements without the risk of provocation.

The Safeguard system itself is layered with safeguards for the American people. Its carefully phased stages of development along with its provision for annual congressional review afford absolute flexibility. Since Safeguard offers continuing research and development, it is the best approach for keeping all options open.

If we achieve a major *political* breakthrough — or if we reach the illusive but ultimate goal of disarmament, construction can be halted immediately.

If we reach a major *research* breakthrough — if a genuinely effective missile defense umbrella for the entire nation becomes feasible — it will be the result of Safeguard's research investment.

I am confident that the arguments over the ABM will not confuse the American people. They are not founded in substance. The Safeguard cannot be interpreted as provocative when the Soviet Union has already deployed its own ABM system around Moscow. In fact, the Soviet news agency has labeled it nonprovocative.

It cannot be regarded as unnecessary when we know the USSR is testing and developing powerful SS–9 ICBMs and expanding its missile-launching submarine fleet. It cannot be condemned as extravagant when it is much less expensive than the "thick" Sentinel system proposed by the previous administration.

In fact, one look at the President's revised 1970 budget reveals we are investing $5.8 billion more in domestic programs — in human and social spending — than sought the previous year.

The President cares about people and he has put cash on the line to prove it. Of the $8 billion increase in the 1970 budget — *seventy-two percent* went to human resource appropriations.

With vision and courage, the President has drawn new battle plans to help the poverty-stricken. Unsuccessful programs will be terminated. Marginally successful projects will be reformed to assure results commensurate with the tax dollar investment. Human problems are going to be solved with humane answers.

Arizona, for all its beauty, freedom, and productivity, knows human problems too. And of all human problems, perhaps it knows best the problem of the American Indian.

President Nixon has said, "The sad plight of the American Indian is a stain on the honor of the American people." To their eternal credit, the many good people of Arizona and many of their elected officials have worked hard and together to alleviate the plight of the Indians.

I am most familiar with the tireless efforts of your Senators Fannin and Goldwater who have privately and publicly advanced the cause of the American Indian. Their deep knowledge of the Indian as an individual has created a better understanding by Congress that Indians are people *not* tourist attractions.

The new administration is aware of this fact. The President has taken the position that henceforth government's approach to Indian problems will be based on interest in human beings rather than preoccupation with property management.

This position has long been advocated by Secretary Hickel, who as governor of Alaska has had different but fully equal experience in Indian affairs.

President Nixon's campaign commitments still stand.

"The special relationship between the federal government and the Indian people, and the special responsibilities of the federal government to the Indian people will be acknowledged.

"Termination of tribal recognition will not be a policy objective, and in no case will it be imposed without Indian consent.

"The right of self-determination of the Indian people will be respected, and their participation in planning their own destinies will be encouraged."

The President has already fulfilled his first specific pledge, the appointment of a full-blooded Indian to the Indian Claims Commission. More shall follow. The Indian people are producing fine leaders. They will be recognized.

As chairman of the Indian Opportunity Council, I recognize that on that council our Indian members are even more important than our cabinet members. They bring the voice and views of the Indian people directly to the executive office of the President.

I realize that there can be no monolithic solution to Indian problems. All the options and opportunities available to every American should be theirs. This includes the choice to assimilate or remain separate.

The Indian Opportunity Council is there to assure that those options remain open; to cut red tape where necessary, and focus prompt attention upon compelling matters.

It is my hope that we can seek and gain greater involvement of the private sector — of foundations and universities — in Indian problems.

It is my hope that the council will win greater awareness of the urban Indian whose troubles are often deep and desperate. All too often, the relocated Indian has fallen in the crevice between local services and the BIA; and for the uninformed this crevice can become a frightening chasm.

Finally, this administration recognizes that the ultimate answer to Indian problems remains with the Indian people. A really promising young leadership is rising. More Indians are in college today than ever before, and more are returning from college to the reservations to help their own.

Mature tribal leadership shall be given support, too. In every way possible, increased participation will be encouraged — but it will not be forced.

There will be no dizzying vacillations in policy to endanger security. There will be policies to foster independence and promote pride. The President recognizes the rich diversity of Indian traditions. Individualized answers must be developed to respect this diversity.

Above all, for the American *Indian*, for the American *poor* and for *all* Americans, this administration is determined to shape programs which fit *people* rather than expect *people* to fit arbitrary programs.

The message of the first quarter reveals this. Further, it reflects our President's determination to defend democracy; to restore principle; to inspire patriotism; to fulfill through *law* the promise of America.

What is that promise? Not easy life, not guaranteed success — but the *chance* to succeed and to live in peace.

This is what the President you supported promised. And this is what he shall deliver.

May 2, 1969, Honolulu, Hawaii
Young President's Organization

ORIGINALLY, I had planned to discuss the accomplishments of the administration to date and to concentrate, in detail, on the significance of the President's decision to proceed with the Safeguard shield as the minimum feasible, responsible action to redress a threatened imbalance in our strategic forces.

I feel the accomplishments of the President have indeed been impressive, and I believe the purely defensive Safeguard system does fit Secretary Laird's description of "a stepping-stone to peace."

However, that is not what is on my mind today. Any controversy over the equilibrium of international powers becomes a safe academic exploration when played against the panorama of criminal violence plaguing America's campuses.

A society which must constantly charge its batteries on great surges of dramatic and emotional confrontation is in deep danger.

A human body cannot endure under unrelenting, artificial excitement and stimulation — it will burn itself out. Likewise, a body politic, such as our constitutional republic, cannot forever withstand continual carnival on the streets of its cities and — the campuses of the nation. Unless sage debate replaces the belligerent strutting now used so extensively, reason will be consumed and the death of logic will surely follow.

What we have witnessed in the past weeks is not mere delinquency nor mere disruption. Both words dismiss too lightly the grave implications of campus disorders and the reaction to them that is reverberating across the country.

Not in every case, but in too many cases, we have young adults hell-bent on "non-negotiable" destruction.

We have college administrators confused and capitulating. We have sophisticated faculties distraught and divided over issues as basic as the criminality of breaking and entering; theft; vandalism; assault and battery.

We have a new breed of self-appointed vigilantes arising — the counterdemonstrators — taking the law into their own hands because officials fail to call law enforcement authorities.

We have a vast faceless majority of the American public in quiet fury over the situation — *and with good reason.*

207

Not one of these elements is constructive — compounded, they create first chaos, then repressive reaction.

The anatomy of violence is unpleasant and difficult to understand. We wonder how we reached this route. What lapse of logic allows a society to lose sight of itself?

I offer you a few answers, and I offer them from this framework — *there is damned little the federal government can do in this situation.* But if the people who can do something don't start acting — I *tremble* at the thought of what forces could fill this vacuum.

The first question that must be answered is: How did we get here?

Historically, we began with the highly legitimate civil rights movement, where civil disobedience was controlled and calculated to bring test cases before the Supreme Court. Intellectual, spiritual, civic, and political leaders hailed the cause of civil rights and gave little thought to where the civil disobedience road might end.

But as Supreme Court Justice Hugo Black *prophetically* wrote in 1966: "Once you give a nervous, hostile and ill-informed people a theoretical justification for using violence in certain cases, it's like a tiny hole in the dike; the rationales rush through in a torrent, and violence becomes the normal, acceptable solution for a problem. . . . A cardinal fact about violence is that once initiated it tends to get out of hand. Its limits are not predictable."

Psychologically, we began with permissiveness — again with the best of intentions — and moved again too far to an extreme. Parents deeply interested in proper emotional development of their children became enchanted with the advocates of permissive psychology. Traditional patterns of discipline and expectation were discarded in fear that trauma might scar the child's unfolding psyche.

At the same time, more families were having more children; more mothers were working; more money and more mobility were undermining traditional family organization. Permissiveness supplanted protectiveness. The vague insecurity of rootlessness could not be concealed by a facade of "togetherness."

Politically we began with the new politics which campus radicals have pushed to the furthest extreme. This not-too-extraordinary movement originated in the coalescence of the first two factors. Guilt over past injustices and the success of tactics revealed through the legitimate civil rights movement; plus a need for "belonging" — a sense of purposeful participation in something important which the family unit had failed to provide.

Irving Kristol capsulized the irony of the new politics: "Indeed, one often is tempted to conclude that the cry for a new politics really amounted to little more than a demand from certain groups that the political process concede to them greater power and influence than they are entitled to under our traditional democratic formulas."

The next question which naturally arises is this: Is there validity to claims pressed by the new politics? Or is there logic in the majority's demand for *responsible* participation?

I think the answer is self-evident. In America, constitutional government provides for elected officials responsible to their electorates to change the law. Accommodated defiance of the law allows cynical leaders responsible to none to exploit the madness of a mob.

Structured law differentiates human civilization from animal anarchy. Representative democracy permits change and prevents totalitarianism.

Democracy is sustained through one great premise: The concept that civil rights are balanced by civil responsibilities. My right to life, liberty, and the pursuit of happiness is secure only so long as I respect your right to life, liberty, and the pursuit of happiness. I can claim no right as a human or a citizen that you cannot claim equally under the law.

The two-edged sword of rights and responsibilities is the defense of a free society. When any group asserts rights without commensurate responsibilities, a privileged class emerges creating an atmosphere of abuse — paving the way to the ultimate abuse that is totalitarianism.

If no legitimate alternatives to reform exist, there is logic to revolutionary claims. But where a legal order, based on egalitarian standards and organized channels for change, is available, any action without the consent of the governed is no more than a dictatorial demand for irrational power.

I have no doubt that majority rule in this nation will prevail. The question is what kind of majority rule will we have in the wake of continuous assaults upon the established order?

This depends upon the steps taken by the diversive leadership elements within our country. The response of recognized authority — be it public or private — may very well determine whether the majority will support measures that are progressive or repressive.

It should be clearly understood that America's ruling majority embraces many minorities. Many myths about the American majority are without substance.

The political majority is neither all white, nor all affluent, nor all callous.

The American majority may not be book-intellectual but it is practical. It may not be passionately committed to any ideology, but it is passionately against intolerant dogmatism.

Finally, the majority is bewildered by present irrational protest.

In turn, the radical element involved in irrational protest merits inspection. In a modern society, the radical himself is in danger of becoming irrelevant. Aside from self-claimed romantic charisma, the radical's appeal is highly suspect in a democracy which responds to the electorates' demands.

In fact, radical movements simply cannot survive in a democracy without violence. If they submit to the rules and face the voters they either win and become the Establishment or lose and join the Establishment.

This is the dilemma of radicalism in a democracy and the situation as of now. Many of you heard Dr. Eric Berne discuss *Games People Play.* The name of the game the radicals play is "uproar" on a broad social scale. Radicals cannot survive without "uproar." The question is, will we play "uproar?" For as Dr. Berne probably noted, social dynamics depend on the willingness of all participants to play.

Do "We the People" enjoy "uproar?" Obviously, the answer is no! So, how do we stop without some kind of blanket repression which is just as obviously alien to the American tradition.

We begin by reaffirming our confidence in representative democracy. While we admit our society is far from utopian, we recognize our system *can* correct inequities and erase social evils.

We reassert the moral superiority of democracy. Our approach can be patterned after the low-keyed positivism of Winston Churchill, who said: "Democracy is the worst form of government, except all those other forms that have been tried from time to time."

The great moral strength of democracy rests with its refusal to equate politics with moral absolutism. In fact, morality is left to nonpolitical institutions — the home, the church, the school.

If — as radical youth complains — there is an absence of morality and purpose from modern life, it is because institutions *other* than government have failed.

Government has no place *providing* a preconceived set of moral values to the people. Rather in a democracy, government should *reflect* the values of the people.

This government is not going to be coerced into a moral dictatorship, and this government is not going to apologize for its absence of orthodoxy. If there is one absolute acceptable in a democracy, it is that freedom depends upon an utter rejection of absolutism.

Thus — it falls to the other institutions of our society to better do their jobs in imparting a moral framework and ethical focus for American life.

The family remains the fundamental institution. Parental discipline is the gateway to knowledge. The family alone can provide that bedrock security of the soul which enables the mature individual to look within rather than without for moral direction.

Organized religion — regardless of denomination — is an institution possessing a moral–ethical mandate.

Churches perhaps should question whether a little stronger emphasis should be placed on the philosophical rather than the congenial enrichments of religion. In his play *The Tenth Man,* Paddy Chayefsky gently jibes twentieth-century religion where the Little League spirit seems to have replaced God's righteousness as the main attraction for the congregation.

Certainly, the biggest revamping must come within the institution of education.

Aside from the small point that our primary and secondary schools should strengthen their curricula in civics so that even our youngest children learn that civil rights are balanced by civil responsibilities. I am talking about rethinking the purposes of education on the broadest possible scale.

Every sector of society should begin questioning present premises, shaping the total institutional form of education, *root and branch*. Is the four-year college program culminating in a B.A. degree in every case valid or necessary? Are there better means to the same ends — such as improved preschool programs, advanced secondary school curricula, sophisticated vocational education, and universal community college systems.

Does every high school graduate need or desire to spend four years in college? Is time invested in higher education solely for the college diploma? Is a college diploma a passport to a better job? Should education be a terminal process, or a continuing one? Is it not possible that the most relevant role of the college in the community could be enlarging the availability of enriching adult education?

Among the competing priorities for the public dollar, should the four-year college take precedence over establishing a system of day care centers for underprivileged preschool children, strengthening compensatory education, improving vocational–technical programs, and expanding community colleges to make two years of practical, usable higher education available to all?

Those are but a few of the questions every individual, every civic and business leader, every elected official and every academician should consider *today!*

Discussion should take into account the views of experts in diversive disciplines such as Dr. Bruno Bettelheim, who in recent testimony before the House Special Subcommittee on Education stated:

> . . . All too many who now go to college have little interest, ability, and use for what constitutes a college education. They would be better off with a high level vocational education which is closely linked to a work program which gives scope to their needs for physical activity and visible, tangible achievement. The complaint of many of these students is that nobody needs them. They feel parasites of society, and hence come to hate a society which they think makes them feel this way.

Equally important and most relevant to current campus disorders are the words of Bayard Rustin, pioneer in civil rights and present executive director of the A. Philip Randolph Institute:

> Everyone knows that education for the Negro is inferior. Bring them to the university with the understanding that they must have [the] remedial work they require. The easy way out is to let them have black courses and their own dormitories and give them degrees. . . . What in hell are soul courses worth in the real world? No one gives a damn if you've taken soul courses. They want to know if you can do mathematics and write a correct sentence. . . . A multiple society cannot exist where an element in that society, out of its own sense of guilt and masochism, permits another segment of that society to hold guns at their heads in the name of justice.

Present campus disorders demand such detailed discussion that they cannot be treated within the confines of today's speech. I only take note that when administrators and faculties capitulate before storm-trooper tactics they are not only doing a grave disservice to academic freedom but all freedoms.

The media comprise another American institution which must share in this drive for renewed responsibility. All too often the media have been too quick to assume that confrontation is a necessary catharsis to a sick society; to report wanton destruction in terms of noble causes; to publicize the least responsible leadership in any self-proclaimed crusade.

The Fourth Estate, which would rise in righteous fury against any demagogue attacking freedom of the press, has been far more gentle with demagogues preying upon the estates of others in the established order.

Finally, the institution of free enterprise is not without its share of obligations. In many ways the business community are meeting their obligations better and faster than the public realizes. Your efficiency in achieving "small splendid efforts" all too often goes unrecognized.

At the same time you share in the corporate failures of society to come to grips with some of our biggest problems.

How many businesses are moving past tokenism in minority employment? How many are taking the initiative in urban redevelopment and environmental rehabilitation? How many are out ahead — attacking problems in advance of requests or regulations from government?

For instance, how many businesses would be willing to abandon the four-year college diploma as a preferred criterion in executive hiring? Only with the support of business can we update the institution of education.

If our society is to defend itself from perpetual violent assaults, every institution must work together. For our society is the sum of its institutions. If the family fails, can we expect the school to succeed? If the school fails, can free enterprise compensate? If the media or the church do not inculcate conscience, should government fill the vacuum?

My answer is an emphatic no! Government's role is to enlarge opportunity and protect competing ideologies in the hope that the best will prevail. This is not to say government should not be moral, but that government's morality should be drawn from the traditional institutions of our society responsible for imparting ethics to the individual.

America is not yet two centuries old. In our evolution we have seen social, economic, and political progress without precedent in the history of the world. We have made this progress through freedom, through law and order structured by the world's oldest enduring constitution.

We have resisted every assault upon democracy by totalitarian forces from without. I am confident our society will defend itself from attempts to impose absolutism or create anarchy from within.

It is time for the Establishment of this country — governmental — educational — industrial and religious — to demonstrate confidence in themselves — to revitalize themselves — to recognize and be proud of the fact that they are integral and vital components of the greatest nation this world has ever produced.

I am not ready to run up a white flag for the United States of America, and I don't think you are either.

May 8, 1969, Provo, Utah
Brigham Young University Student Body

THANK YOU very much, Dr. Wilkinson, Senator Bennett, Congressman Burton, the many distinguished public officials from county, city, and state government here today, members of the administration, the faculty and the student body, your new student president, Mr. Kartchner, ladies and gentlemen.

I guess you'd like to know how I'm learning my new job. Well, Senator Bennett will tell you that I'm learning how to sleep with my eyes open in the Senate, also I've found out that the vice presidency is totally removed from politics. I learned that when I got my salary check last week through the Ford Foundation.

For me the Brigham Young campus offers a refreshing change of pace. Its virtues are readily apparent. Here the scenery is magnificent, the buildings are handsome, and you can still tell the boys from the girls. Now don't misunderstand me, I don't have anything against long hair, but I didn't raise my son to be my daughter.

When you read of campus violence day after day and when you survey a strident student minority, long on locks and lean on faith, there appears reason to despair. More Americans should learn about Brigham Young University. Our nation's largest private school does honor to the public spirit. Much credit belongs to President Wilkinson, to the Church of Jesus Christ of the Latter-day Saints, and to those who come to teach, and those who come to learn here.

The founder of this school, Brigham Young, once said: "The first great principle that ought to occupy the attention of mankind, that should be understood by the child and the adult, and which is the mainspring of all action, whether people understand it or not, is the principle of improvement."

Improvement is the purpose of education. It's the work of the school, the college, and the university. Improvement cannot be achieved in a condition of anarchy or uproar. Today, our colleges are under siege.

What we have witnessed in the past weeks is not mere delinquency, nor mere disruption. Both words dismiss too lightly the grave implications of college disorders and the reaction to them that is reverberating across the country.

Not in every case, but in too many cases, we have young adults hell-bent on "nonnegotiable" destruction.

We have college administrators confused and capitulating. We have sophisticated faculties distraught and divided over issues as basic as assault and battery, breaking and entering, theft or vandalism, all of which we understand to be crime.

We have a new breed of self-appointed vigilantes arising — the counterdemonstrators — taking the law into their own hands because weak and equivocating officials fail to call the law enforcement authorities.

We have a vast faceless majority of the American public in quiet fury and with good reason over this situation.

Not one of these elements is constructive — compounded, they create first chaos, and then repressive reaction.

The anatomy of violence is unpleasant and difficult to understand. Sometimes we wonder how we reached this route.

I offer you a few answers, and I offer them from this framework — *there is little the federal government can do in this situation.* But if the people who can do something don't start acting, I'm fearful of what forces could fill this vacuum.

I recognize that only a small minority — less than two percent — of America's six, nearly seven million college students participate in disruptive dissent. But the damage they do to the spirit of academic freedom — and, in fact, all freedoms — is vastly greater than their numbers. These students whose recourse to reform is demand rather than debate, lawlessness rather than logic, have the same philosophy as dictators.

Condemning the tactics of violence is not concluding that there is no need for change. But as you all learn from your first course in philosophy, the difference between a free society and a totalitarianism is one — the treatment of ends versus means.

In a totalitarian society, only the ends are important. The means to reach them, whether just or brutal, are irrelevant. In a free society, the means are just as important as the ends.

The law is our means. In America, constitutional government provides for elected officials, elected officials who are responsible to their electorates, the people who put them in office to change the law. Structured law differentiates human civilization from animal anarchy. Representative democracy permits change and prevents totalitarianism.

Democracy is sustained through one great premise: The concept that civil rights are balanced by civil responsibilities. My right to life, liberty, and the pursuit of happiness is secure only so long as I respect your right to life, liberty, and the pursuit of happiness. I can claim no right as a human being or a citizen that you cannot claim equally under the law. The two-edged sword of rights and responsibilities is the defense of a free society.

212

When any group asserts rights without commensurate responsibilities a privileged class emerges creating an atmosphere of abuse, paving the way to the ultimate abuse that is totalitarianism.

Now the time has come for America's colleges under siege to assert themselves. This is not to say we can't improve our colleges..I sincerely believe that every sector of society should question the present fundamentals that shape our systems of education. Certainly if even two percent of our students will resort to violence and a far larger percentage will stand silently by, perhaps even stand sympathetically by, we are failing somewhere along the line.

Compelling questions over the validity of our present system must be asked and answered.

For example, does every high school graduate need or desire to spend four years in college? Should education be a terminal process, or a continuing one? Is it not possible that the most relevant role of the college would be enlarging the availability of enriching adult education?

Among the competing priorities for the public dollar, should the four-year college take precedence over strengthening compensatory education, improving vocational–technical programs and expanding community colleges to make two years of practical, usable higher education available to all?

I think one of the most neglected fields of education in our time is that of vocational–technical training. And I think we've failed because we've classed this particular type training at the high school level alone. It seems to me that it should be possible to discern among certain students that their fortes lie not in formal education of the typical college type, but in vocational–technical training where they will learn a useful skill and be able to make an adequate living.

Discussion should take into account the views of such experts as Dr. Bruno Bettelheim, the renowned psychologist–psychiatrist at the University of Chicago, who in a recent testimony before the House Special Subcommittee on Education stated this:

> . . . all too many who now go to college have little interest, ability, and use for what constitutes a college education. . . . They would be better off with a high-level vocational education which is closely linked to a work program, which gives scope to their needs for physical activity and visible tangible achievement. The complaint of many of these students is that nobody needs them. They feel like parasites of society and hence come to hate a society which they think makes them feel this way.

Certainly, our institutions of higher education must take the initiative in asking the hard questions and in achieving internal reforms.

Many colleges and universities — the ones we do *not* read about — have developed legitimate and immediate methods for students to articulate their grievances.

These schools have done more than simply offer courses on democracy; they have assured their students of "due process" which is an integral part of our democratic system.

A society as sophisticated as ours can establish practical, workable degrees of student participation. We can navigate some middle course without students locking teachers up or administrators locking students out.

Another middle ground which must be found is the place of the college in the community. Higher education can only benefit from a close, introspective look at such policies as "publish or perish"; a voice for faculty below the professorial level; the proper balance in decisions between administrators and academicians.

An insistence on relevancy in curriculum is not an unreasonable request within bounds that are applicable and just. But when students simultaneously demand an increased social conscience on the part of the university, and an end to ROTC programs which some of them desire, there is an absolute lapse of logic.

What is the ROTC if it is not education to serve our country? I want to tell you that I am most disturbed about the lack of freedom on the part of those students who would like to learn the fundamentals of officer training in college, the lack of the ability of those students to have that training because a small dissident minority, who wants training of a specialized sort that it desires, refuses to stand still and let someone else elect what he wants to study.

Not only does that disturb me; I think it disturbs most people across the country. But when you consider that this country's strength in time of trial and turmoil has come from its citizen army, and that the freedoms that we enjoy we enjoy because we understand among our responsibilities as citizens lies the inherent, basic need to defend this country in time of crisis. And that defense comes best from our citizens and not from any elite, professional military organization. Oh, certainly we need the cadres of our military academies, but the balance that has always existed in our large citizen armies comes about because the people who are trained to lead those armies are basically civilians and not soldiers, and they respect and understand the need to get this country back to a peaceful civilian status as quickly as possible. And that's what we are trying to take out of our colleges today or the defense department will have to respond if there is no way to train officers in the colleges of this country. The defense department will have to create some other professional way to train them, and when that is done the sensitivity of the civilian soldier that I spoke about will be lacking.

Each college must determine its own middle ground somewhere between ivory tower retreat and settlement house immersion. In a recent article, journalist William Shannon delineated the role of higher education. And he said this:

It is to transmit knowledge and wisdom and to enhance them by research and study. The university is not a forum for political action. It is not a training ground for revolutionaries. It is not a residential facility for the psychiatrically maladjusted. It is not a theater for acting out racial fears and fantasies.

And I agree with those words. And he went on to say:

The university is a quiet place deliberately insulated from the conflicts and pressures of the larger society around it. Reason and civility are essential to its very nature because its aim is truth not power. Questioning and criticizing and listening must be done objectively, logically, and above all, lawfully. When administrators and faculties capitulate before storm trooper tactics, they are not only doing a grave disservice to academic freedom but all freedoms.

Finally, not only the institution of education but every institution comprising our society must share in this drive for renewed responsibilities. The family remains the fundamental institution. Parental discipline is the gateway to knowledge. Permissive parents do their children no favors because no self-discipline can come without discipline being there first. And it is a lack of discipline in the family that has led to the abusive conduct of the small minority of students that I talked about earlier.

The family alone can provide the bedrock security of the soul which enables the mature individual to look within rather than from without for moral direction.

Organized religion — regardless of denomination — is an institution possessing a moral–ethical mandate.

The conduct of Brigham Young University offers inspiring evidence of the serenity and strength which stems from strong faith.

The media — our free press — are not exempt from constructive introspection. All too often the media have been too quick to assume that confrontation is a necessary catharsis to a sick society; to report want and destruction in terms of noble causes; to publicize the least responsible leadership in any self-proclaimed crusade.

How many businesses, for example, are out ahead — attacking problems in advance of requests for regulations from government? The industrial community also needs to involve itself more heavily in these problems. It's the failure of the private sector to act which prods the public sector to enter.

Now, if our society is ever going to protect itself from perpetual, violent assaults, every institution must work together. For our society is nothing more than the sum of its institutions.

If the family fails, can we expect the school to succeed? If the school fails, can free enterprise compensate? If the media or the church do not inculcate conscience, should government fill the vacuum? My answer is an emphatic, "No!" Government's role is to enlarge opportunity and to protect competing ideologies in the hope that the best will prevail.

When I say that I don't mean to say that government should not be moral, but government's morality should be drawn from the traditional institutions of our society responsible for imparting ethics to the individual.

America is not yet two centuries old. It's hard to believe that we're that young a country. In our evolution we have seen social, economic, and political progress without precedent in the history of the world. We have made this progress through freedom, through law and order structured by the world's oldest enduring constitution.

We have resisted every assault upon democracy by totalitarian forces from without. And I am confident that our society will defend itself from attempts to impose absolutism or create anarchy from within.

The American system has never been stronger, never been more vital. The American conscience is awake, and the American spirit is very much alive.

May 30, 1969, Arlington National Cemetery, Arlington, Virginia
Memorial Day Ceremonies

ST. AUGUSTINE wrote: "The purpose of all war is peace." To this I would add the purpose of America is freedom.

Today we pay special tribute to those Americans who have contributed "above and beyond the call of duty" to preserve peace and freedom for their country.

These men have paid for our liberty with their sweat and sacrifice and personal pain. Our gratitude requires more than lip service; it commands life service.

We cannot honor our ideals or our veterans unless we honor our obligations to secure peace and freedom in America and throughout the world.

Neither peace nor freedom is lightly won. Together they compose mankind's most arduous task and noblest mission — commanding eternal vigilance and demanding internal strength.

Permanent peace depends upon freedom. For the nations of this world, peace is predicated upon self-determination. This is the right of people to govern themselves according to their laws within their boundaries.

For each nation in this world, peace is predicated upon personal freedom. This is the right of a citizen to lead his own life limited only by the laws of the land which preserve that same liberty for all others.

If the principles of peace and freedom seem simple, the processes to secure them are complex. Freedom requires much of the individual.

Thomas Jefferson once wrote: "If a nation expects to be ignorant and free, in a state of civilization, it expects what never was and never will be."

Thus, freedom depends upon education, and the endurance of free governments depends upon participation — the citizen's stake in upholding his society.

Still, the most important element of freedom remains its condition of universal equity. No man can be perfectly free unless all men are free.

As Abraham Lincoln said: "Those who deny freedom to others deserve it not for themselves and, under a just God, cannot long retain it."

So it is that our obligation to freedom extends beyond our consciences, our communities, and the borders of our country. For where there is no freedom, there can be no peace. Where men must serve masters not of their choosing, they will fight to unseat them.

It is in a nation where force supplants reason and in a world where might supersedes right, that war becomes a perpetual condition.

The only alternative to perpetual war is the patient pursuit of peace. This nation, consecrated to freedom, has no choice but to labor for liberty. Our motives are both selfless and selfish. For so long as men are slaves, our independence is in jeopardy. For so long as men are hungry, our prosperity is threatened. For so long as men are ignorant, our ideals cannot be fulfilled.

We cannot withdraw from our position of world leadership, and assume by turning our backs that our burdens will lessen. If we ignore our responsibilities, they will multiply.

All the agonies of past history have been perpetrated by those who feared and fled and failed. Sooner or later there is nowhere to retreat. A challenge conquered sooner — for all its sacrifices — proves far less costly.

Thus, when our citizens question why we defend the integrity of free nations in Southeast Asia, the answer is that we are defending not only their integrity but ours. If we allow the small and the weak to be devoured, the larger and stronger will infallibly become the prey.

Trace the history of the men we honor today and in its pattern one will find the reflection of a nation's enlightened understanding of the defense of freedom.

Little over a century ago, the battleground for freedom was our nation's soil. Not much more than two decades ago, the battleground spanned two continents and spilled over to a third.

Today, the battle continues but the enemy's thrust has been contained. An alliance of free nations has learned that you cannot compromise another nation's freedom to preserve your own. How many thousands of lives bought us this knowledge? To cast this wisdom away is to dishonor the memory of every man that lies here.

War is an agonizing alternative. There is neither progress nor civilization in chaos. If there is a message in twentieth-century conflict, it is the destructive futility of war and the need to secure freedom through other channels.

This country has worked toward this goal politically, economically, and diplomatically. The cannons were barely cooled in Europe and in Asia when we began. The viable democracies of our World War II enemies, as well as our allies, attest that in victory we were not vindictive, but kept our commitment to freedom.

Certainly this administration intends to carry forth that commitment, but in carrying it forth we will also perform our solemn obligation to those who lie here in Arlington — and to those who lie in other American cemeteries — here and abroad. We will not denigrate their sacrifices any more than we would desecrate their graves.

Some of these men died as heroes; some died without special recognition. But all of them lived and fought and were willing to die for freedom. We can do no less.

It is our fervent prayer that Americans may pursue freedom through peaceful service at home and throughout the world. But let friends and enemies alike know that the intensity of our convictions is deep enough and strong enough to fight — if we must — to preserve our legacy of liberty.

Freedom's cause is first served by fulfilling the promise of freedom, equality, and opportunity for every citizen in this country. Let us respond to the sacrifices of our servicemen by assuring that the principles they fight for abroad are vigorously practiced at home. While our soldiers secure the frontiers of world freedom, let us expand the heritage of democracy to new horizons in America.

Our country is young and vibrant and still free. Let us take comfort in our power and use it with purpose, and without apology.

Let us not shirk our responsibilities but stand resolute that free men and free governments "shall not perish from this earth."

June 7, 1969, Columbus, Ohio
Graduating Class of Ohio State University

PLUTARCH ONCE quoted a rational appeal by Augustus Caesar at the outset of an address to a young and impatient audience:

"Young men," said Caesar, "Hear an old man to whom old men hearkened when he was young."

The quotation is powerful, if for no other reason than its recognition that there is a time to speak and a time to listen — for both youth and age.

Today your kind invitation brings me here as a speaker — not a "know-it-all," but a frank advocate of the American system, who seeks only your thoughtful appraisal of his case.

Your generation is not the first youth who ever questioned the efficacy of a custodial generation. You are not the first to aggressively challenge the fundamental values of a society. Such challenges are normal, proper, and the basis of human improvement.

We are not in turmoil because of your testing. We are in trouble because my generation has apparently failed to define and defend either its achievements or its inheritance from past generations of Americans.

A society which comes to fear its children is effete. A snivelling, handwringing power structure deserves the violent rebellion it encourages. If my generation doesn't stop cringing, yours will inherit a lawless society where emotion and muscle displace reason.

A society which looks calmly into the logic or illogic of its youth's anger and ambition, accepting the rational and rejecting the immature, is alive. Ask yourselves which kind of society you want for tomorrow — tomorrow when you are the establishment.

My purpose is not to castigate youth nor discuss why the generations differ. They differ mainly because they develop consecutively, not concurrently. My purpose is to point out the case for American democracy and to challenge you to determine whether the advantages all Americans enjoy would have developed outside our free and enterprising system.

This nation was founded upon two great concepts — liberty and equality of opportunity. Our total political system has been structured to secure these precepts.

Our Constitution — the world's oldest enduring document designed to create a free and open society — guarantees a government by laws, not men. The individual is protected by its dimorphic thrust, extending civil rights on one hand and exacting civil responsibilities on the other.

The history of this nation is a lesson in the advantages of political freedom. A government formed with lofty purpose and the overall constitutional objective of human dignity has not run from the revelation of its hypocrisies but struggled over upward to match deed with word. Hard changes have been made because right is more important to us

217

than convenience. We know that real liberty means not just an equal opportunity to be equal, but an equal opportunity to be superior if one possesses the stuff of which superiority is made.

The record shows that human progress marks our history. We have not cowered before great contests. We have lost some, won many. Over the past centuries, slave labor and child labor and unfair labor practices have been outlawed. Discriminatory laws and invidious discriminatory practices have been repealed, overruled or abandoned.

All is not perfect. The purpose of our Constitution is not to promise perfection, but to establish a more perfect union. Happiness is not a universal condition among us. Our Constitution does not guarantee happiness. But ours is the only Constitution pledged to "the pursuit" of it. Our Constitution does not guarantee perpetual equality but only the vigilant maintenance of the opportunity to be equal or to excel.

Two centuries of a people's high dedication did not result from rhetoric but recognition that this country does offer the best way of life.

Democracy is above all a highly pragmatic system. It assumes truth is neither revealed nor absolute but arrived at through experience and open debate. It assumes all men have equal rights to publish their views and to affect their destinies. It assumes the more education society gives to its citizens the better the chance that they will hold enlightened views, pursue truth more perfectly and make individual and collective choices more intelligently. Enlightened views, truth, and intelligent choices breed progress.

Admittedly, no political system is perfect. Democracy's greatest flaw rests in its intransigent commitment to individual freedom. When social change depends on persuasion, rather than coercion, it comes slowly.

Totalitarian systems might deserve a higher mark if efficiency — not liberty — is considered the purpose of government.

The meteoric rise of Nazi Germany is an example of sometime totalitarian efficiency. Yet its success was short-lived. For one fact about tyranny is inescapable — as long as men serve masters not of their choosing they will struggle by any means to unseat them. If they succeed through force, chaos will ensue. There is neither progress nor civilization in chaos.

Winston Churchill has said it well: "Democracy is the worst form of government, except all those other forms that have been tried from time to time."

Even democracy is shaded by variances. American political democracy has retained its economic counterpart — a free enterprise system. Some successful democracies have opted for differing degrees of socialism.

The free enterprise system is perhaps the most arduous route, for it demands the greatest initiative from the individual. In my judgment, our results reveal rewards which justify that effort.

Socialism consciously creates economic equality by leveling the peaks rather than raising the valleys. A relatively equal income distribution may be artificially achieved. But in all too many cases, individuality is sacrificed and mediocrity becomes the standard. The right to excel is quashed by destroying the reason to excel. When security supplants excellence as the principal target, the goal of social planning is reduced to the lowest common denominator. In the absence of high goals and great dreams life becomes frustratingly drab and preoccupation with self gradually destroys the moral fibre of a country.

The free enterprise system is not without conscience. Its social goals envisage elevation of the valleys — bringing all to higher levels. Competition, not legislation, must be the principal instrument of achievement. Individual success is considered the foundation of social progress.

We believe that, just as truth and wisdom are the products of freely competing ideas, higher living standards for all result from competing economic forces.

The facts give confidence to our convictions. America discovers more, produces more, earns more, possesses more, and invests more than any nation in the world. Our young people are better educated, our elderly better cared for, and our impoverished better served.

218

This has not been the result of a single volcanic revolution. It has evolved through the perpetual orderly revolution which is embodied in the routine functioning of our political system.

I have lived half a century. Perhaps our accomplishments during my lifetime furnish a reasonable test of progress.

The breaching of scientific barriers has been phenomenal. I can remember when Charles Lindbergh landed his single-engined "Spirit of St. Louis" in Paris. Now I look forward to America's lunar landing next month.

The computer, the transistor, television, jet planes, radio astronomy, the laser, and nuclear energy were developments of the past fifty years.

In the last twenty-five years alone, mankind has acquired more scientific knowledge than in all of previous history. Ninety percent of all the scientists that have ever lived and worked are alive at work today.

Life expectancy has increased; infant mortality decreased. The dread diseases of polio, typhus, malaria, measles, small pox, pellagra, and rabies have been virtually eradicated.

America's ideas on social progress have made dynamic advances. In the year of my birth, the overwhelming majority of Americans thought that government had no business in business; that government could not prevent abysmal depressions or skyrocketing inflations; that government might protect its people from war but not from poverty in their old age, ill health, or inadvertent unemployment.

Today, we take for granted social security, unemployment insurance, and medical assistance programs. We use the federal monetary system to stabilize the national economy. We have a Securities and Exchange Commission to safeguard investments and a National Labor Relations Board to protect the rights of labor and management.

This year, this state alone will confer thirty-four thousand undergraduate degrees. This approximates three-quarters of all undergraduate degrees conferred in the United States fifty years ago.

Changes did not occur overnight, but progress that in the past took generations has been telescoped into decades and years. Reform in most cases has come peacefully and legally.

There is no reason to believe that this pattern of persistent and ever accelerating progress will not continue . . . no reason unless the vision of America changes.

There is great danger in confusing growing up with growing old. As America matures she need not grow old. Her vision need not become dim, nor her focus myopic.

I am reminded of a saying of Cicero:

"For as I like a young man in whom there is something of the old, so I like an old man in whom there is something of the young; and he who follows this maxim, in body will possibly be an old man, but he will never be an old man in mind."

I see no end to progress so long as there is freedom for every voice to be heard and every idea to compete.

I see no end to progress so long as successive generations test new leadership, new ideas, new purpose in the arena of free choice.

I see no end to progress so long as Americans refuse to accept either physical or spiritual barriers in this country, world, and universe.

Right now we have a choice. Will we treat all that is wrong with America as a challenge . . . or an indictment? Will we attack these problems or just weep over them? Will we condemn our institutions or correct them? Will we repudiate democracy because it moves slowly or revitalize it so its pace quickens?

The answers are far from self-evident. The jury is still out. I trust that the ultimate response will be positive. I trust that Americans understand history well enough to see in our imperfect past the promise of a more perfect future.

I trust we will not permit selfishness to narrow our vision or fear to corrode our confidence.

Today, we must decide anew whether to be bound by the illusory barriers of the past or to explore the potential of limitless boundaries in space, under the sea, and in human understanding.

This nation, I assure you, is not too poor in resources to meet this challenge. The question remains whether this nation is too poor and timid in spirit to test itself against all the perils of majestic undertakings.

The question remains as to whether the summation of a recent British study of the United States is right or wrong . . . it said: "The American people have lost the *will* to be world leaders."

The answer rests with all the American people and particularly with the new Americans represented by the Class of 1969. I pray your answer will be affirmative and your response strong.

June 8, 1969, Baltimore, Maryland
Loyola College Commencement

JUST BEFORE this century began, Theodore Roosevelt wrote of America: "We have no choice as to whether or not we shall play a great part in the world. . . . All that we can decide is whether we shall play it well or ill."

Today, despite significant changes, America confronts this challenge anew. The issue is no longer whether we shall be a great power . . . we are one. The choice is not between policies of isolationism or expansionism . . . both were discredited long ago. The decision is whether this country "conceived in liberty" and consecrated to justice shall fulfill those ideals for which it was founded and in which it has flourished.

The Class of 1969 . . . and those that shortly follow . . . may very well make that decision. For to you falls the choice whether to continue the struggle or surrender before the challenges to our nation's noble experiment in democracy: to assure "life, liberty, and the pursuit of happiness" to every individual.

The philosophical lines are being carefully drawn for you to consider. There are those who argue that in the grave problems of today, there is no place for individual initiative. There are those who see in poverty and injustice an indictment of all of democracy's institutions. There are those who charge that our society is corrupt because it is prosperous; guilty because it protects the majority; hypocritical because it specifies minimum moral standards.

This is the politics of despair which urges America not forward but inward. Its focus is a masochistic introspection tainted by unwarranted guilt and undermined by a totally unjustified lack of confidence in our democratic institutions.

"Look at poverty, prejudice, pollution, and ignorance," they seem to say, "and see in them not glorious challenges for a vigorous people to overcome, but the signals for a decadent people to surrender. Abrogate your commitments abroad and abdicate your responsibilities at home. There are no answers to these problems."

Countering the cries for capitulation are quiet voices of courage and hope. These are thoughtful Americans with a respect for history and a vision for the future. They do not deny that pockets of inexcusable poverty still exist in a land of plenty nor advocate a policy of complacency with injustice, prejudice, pollution, or ignorance. But they see in the flaws of today, the prod for tomorrow. They see in the general recognition of social evil how far we have come, and they sense fresh directions for us to follow.

Poverty was not so much an issue several decades ago because most of our citizens were not very prosperous. Therefore, the very poor were not such a glaring problem.

Prejudice was not so much an issue until rapid communication identified and condemned it. Ignorance and pollution were not considered real problems until our technology and our population advanced to the point where they could no longer be tolerated by a sophisticated society.

America must recognize its problems in their proper perspective — as unfortunate by-products of the tremendous progress this nation has made in the past half-century.

This is the politics of hope which articulates the healthy view that the world's most advanced and affluent society can correct inequities, eliminate poverty and expand opportunity to undreamed-of dimensions through reliance upon our enduring institutions of representative democracy.

Again, it was Theodore Roosevelt who captured the challenge of America — yesterday, today, and tomorrow — in these words:

"As it is with the individual, so it is with the nation. . . . Far better it is to dare mighty things, to win glorious triumphs, even though checkered by failure, than to take rank with those poor spirits who neither enjoy much nor suffer much, because they live in the gray twilight that knows not victory nor defeat."

In seven years our nation will enter its third century. The decisions "We the People" make this year may very well determine whether this shall be an occasion for celebration or whether our third century shall usher in an era of continual twilight or eternal dawn.

"We the People" have a great deal to do with our future for representative government is most sensitive to the mind of the nation.

Right now, America is poised at a spiritual crossroads with two currents of thought competing for our nation's soul. One cries for us to look inward; the other calls for us to move outward and move on.

I believe the dangers of the first are discernible. When Americans allow guilt to replace purpose as a primary motivating force, a malignancy is born. When Americans allow introspection to supersede obligation, our vigor is sapped. When Americans allow the easy way out to corrode our most basic convictions, our society is in mortal danger.

It is time for Americans to return to the hard, fresh realism and to the unique mix of optimism and pragmatism that made America a great power. It is time for Americans to remember that our political system remains the most free and flexible in the world. It is time to remember that within this century our society has produced every type of socioeconomic advancement from social security to polio vaccine; from radio and television to jet transportation; from the computer to the exploration of outer space. It is time to remember that our nation has met its obligations throughout the world by supporting every possible policy for peace from the Marshall Plan to the United Nations.

And it is time to take pride in our unprecedented progress and to understand that America went forward because America looked outward. Our achievements resulted from our refusal to accept a closing of physical or spiritual frontiers. We stand at the portal of important discoveries in space and under the sea — discoveries which will result in a better world for all people.

If we are not to sound taps for an era of American twilight, but reveille for a promising new day, we must evolve a new citizenship — twenty-first century style.

The citizen for America's third century must grasp the complexities of today. No longer can the simplistic standards to solve, to judge, to participate apply. The rapidity of change — environmentally, scientifically, and in every way, calls for an individualism more energizing and enterprising than ever known before in our nation's history. We must produce generations who not only have an aptitude but an appetite for change; who not only accept change but welcome it.

Education is our most powerful instrument. If we are to have an age of enlightenment, we must have an age of rational inquiry. Every citizen should be encouraged to reject slogans, labels, and cloudy oversimplifications from the past, and apply an uncluttered mind to the details of the problem. This means that where there are civil rights, so are there civil responsibilities. This means that freedom's first defense is government by laws not men. This means understanding that the greatest threat to individualism is absolutism and the greatest menace to progress is a monolithic society.

In the past year we have seen too many instances of self-appointed apostles of a new moral order seeking through force or violence to impose their will on universities. It has always been a free society's view that truth, not force, is the prevailing factor in progress. For this reason, our society has resisted philosophical absolutism just as vigorously as political totalitarianism. No one, no minority, no majority should dictate what should be thought or taught in this country. In *The Republic*, Plato aptly describes the state of a democracy drifting into anarchy as follows:

"In such a state of society, the master fears and flatters his scholars, and the scholars despise their masters and tutors; young and old are alike; and the young man is on a level with the old, and is ready to compete with him in word and deed; and old men condescend to the young and are full of pleasantries and gaiety; they are loath to be thought morose and authoritative, and therefore they adopt the manners of the young. . . ." Such a philosophy can easily lead to anarchy.

America is a pluralistic society where every option and every opportunity should be available to every individual. And this administration intends to uphold that precept.

We are not going to run America into the ground by closing frontiers and limiting horizons in knowledge or experience. We are going to do all it is possible for government to do to make way for the twenty-first century citizen.

We are going to put a premium on individuality. We are going to support voluntary action programs and provide incentives for private initiative — whether individual or collective — in national problems.

We are going to exercise what best could be termed constructive compassion — investing our resources in compensatory programs to build independence and buttress personal dignity. We believe in giving the minority businessman and the culturally deprived child a better than equal chance to make up for a less than equal start in life.

We are going to pursue complex problems with the patience of pioneers. We are going to experiment and explore both on this planet and in this universe in the confidence that all progress is linked to discovery and new knowledge.

We are going to pursue every alternative for peace. In terms of national security, this means focusing upon strong defenses rather than proliferating offensive weapons. In terms of international diplomacy it means an eagerness to move from an era of confrontation to a time of negotiation, fully understanding that permanent peace for the strong cannot be won by abandoning the weak. All of these things can be done by a free people's government.

Walter Lippmann wrote: "It is a mistake to suppose that there is satisfaction and the joy of life in a self-indulgent generation, in one primarily interested in the pursuit of private wealth and private pleasure and private success. . . . We are very rich but we are not having a very good time. For our life, though it is full of things, is empty of the kind of purpose and effort that gives to life its flavor and meaning."

Purpose surpasses prosperity as a life force. By purpose I do not mean the destructive, dogmatic protest that provokes confrontation — any more than I would suggest a life of mortifying, dismal sacrifice. Rather what Americans should strive for is the life of "high adventure" and individual excellence, which President Nixon spoke of in his inaugural address.

Government can but set the stage for such a performance — the role of America will be determined by the individual citizen. In a democratic society, government is no more than the sum of its individuals and their institutions. Today — as in the time of Theodore Roosevelt — only the American people can decide whether we shall play our part "well or ill."

This is the challenge of the Class of 1969 — as it was the challenge of the Class of 1899. I congratulate you in the confidence that your response will better the record of all your forebears.

222

June 10, 1969, Washington, D.C.
Address to Presidential Scholars

TODAY I offer not only my greetings and congratulations but those of the President. As you know, only the magnitude of the President's mission to Midway prevents him from being here.

The White House entertains many distinguished visitors from every nation in the world and every station of life. But our most honored guests are those invited because of their high personal achievement.

The Presidential Scholars are counted in this "most honored" category. And because you are young and because you are Americans, we are especially proud of you. It has become downright trite to tell you that *you* are the future of America. Probably because it's so true and obvious and inevitable.

Most truisms merit repetition and Plato — twenty-three centuries ago — said it best: "States are as men are, they grow out of the characters of men."

Therefore, it is gratifying to know that we have bright, young leaders like you and even more reassuring to know that you were chosen from more than a million potential candidates. I can appreciate the agonies of the Commissioners on Presidential Scholars as they were forced to pick the finest of the finalists. But we can all be more satisfied than sympathetic when decisions are difficult because there are so many superior alternatives to be considered.

The opportunity to address intelligent, responsible, receptive young people is at once a blessing and curse. There is so much I want to say; so much that should be said. Yet the danger of sounding pompous is all too apparent.

In the first place, I recognize that there is no point in decrying to you — our finest young citizens — the tactics of a small group of your contemporaries. It would be in the vernacular of the day — irrelevant.

In the second place, I believe we have to recognize that much criticism leveled at our generation by your generation merits consideration. Similarly, some criticism aimed at your generation by our generation is well founded . . . just as criticism that will be aimed at your generation by the next generation will probably be well founded. There's a promising ground for accommodation in our current disputes, and that's what makes progress.

So I am not going to stand up here and deliver a philippic on the sins of youth or eulogize the virtues of middle age. Rather, I am going to talk about ideas — yours, mine, and ours — and how to put them into action.

America is not a country given to dealing with abstractions. Usually, when we discuss ideas they are related to concrete issues. We don't believe that truth is revealed or absolute. We believe that truth is developed through experience. Our philosophy could be termed pragmatic and progressive.

Labels like liberal and conservative have little meaning when subjected to intensive scrutiny. For even the arch-liberal would be loath to relinquish our most enduring political traditions. The arch-conservative would not repudiate our most successful social reforms. Both agree on the ends of government — liberty, opportunity, prosperity, peace. Their agreement on ends makes for a stable society. Their disagreement on the means to achieve these ends assures that our society is not stagnant.

The purpose of organized society is collective progress. In a democracy, this can only be achieved if all members are in general agreement on certain minimal rules to progress. We call these rules law. But they are no different from the rules in any team sport. If all the players don't accept the basic rules of a game, they aren't playing that game. They're playing something else or they're playing at nothing.

The same applies to a political society. If everyone agrees to work within a just constitution, we have democracy. If everyone is compelled to obey a single leader, we have tyranny. If everyone agrees to go his own way, we have anarchy, and organized political society ceases to exist.

Today, the philosophy of anarchy has become quite popular with young dissidents around the world. Impatient with the problems at hand, they seek to destroy "the system" which they presume perpetrated or perpetuated these problems. Anarchists aren't interested in answers, only in creating some romanticized vacuum where goodwill prevails.

One thing we've learned about political vacuums — the good guys finish last. Where there are no laws to protect the innocent and the weak, they are devoured by the strong and unprincipled. Chronicles of all too many prisoner of war camps have provided us with hideous examples of internal lawlessness. The sixteenth-century philosopher, Thomas Hobbes, provided the classic description of life in a state of anarchy — "Nasty, brutish, and short."

Therefore, the first idea that must give way if we are to have progress is the idea of anarchy. Far better to work within the generous limits of our Constitution, for as Winston Churchill has said; "Democracy is the worst form of government except all those other forms which have been tried from time to time."

Once our willingness to play under the same rules in the same ball park has been determined, it is time to view the problems. I grant they are plentiful. But yours is not the first nor, I fear, the last generation to inherit what you consider more than your fair share of problems. My generation had the Depression and World War II, and after that the cold war and those first years of A-bomb anxiety. Although it's scant comfort indeed, be assured that you possess no monopoly on a problem-filled world.

Peace, the quality of our environment, the quality of our lives are the basic challenges. These embrace the problems of our cities, of poverty, of ignorance and prejudice. All are complex and pernicious. None will be simply or swiftly resolved.

Peace is foremost in every American's mind. Our goal should be nothing less than permanent peace. Too often America has won the war on the battlefield, only to lose the peace at the conference table. I think it's time that we learned from bitter history. Two centuries have passed since Immanuel Kant set the ideal ground rules: "No treaty of peace shall be esteemed valid in which is tacitly reserved matter for future war."

I think that your generation is right in asserting that civilized nations can find a better alternative than war to settle their differences. I think that our generation — with its greater experience — is right in asserting that peace cannot be a unilateral achievement. You can be sure that peace is the first priority of this administration. The President has traveled halfway around the world for only one purpose — to do everything that one man and one government can do to hasten the end of the war.

Your generation's impatience with the rate of national progress is also understandable. How you express your impatience may well determine the speed of our progress. When concern takes the form of bitterness and petulance, when dedication is dramatic but directionless, the audience is alienated. The reality of the matter is that it's not just what you say but how you say it that counts. I do not intend to debate whether this is good or bad. The point is that it's true for America, 1969. When dissenters look scruffy and behave deplorably, they are turning people off all across America. The slogan, "Get Clean For Gene," was not accidental in the McCarthy campaign.

Some young people I know equate Senator McCarthy's failure to win his party's nomination with a failure of the system. I think President Nixon proves just the opposite. If you play fairly and persistently you can triumph . . . and in reasonably good time. I believe young people have a real place in our political parties. I know our parties — both of our parties — are eager to tap the energy and idealism of youth.

We also have a better job to do in informing our young people of the opportunities available for them to work within our political system. A recently published study by the Advisory Commission on Intergovernmental Relations revealed that three-fourths of the 562 colleges and universities surveyed did not offer any course in state or local government. These are the levels of government closest to the people and most responsive to their needs. Here is where there is the greatest opportunity for individual impact on the system and our young people have a right to learn about it.

I cannot think of one branch of government — local, state, or federal — that does not welcome young people. There are many other harbors inviting the impatient who are willing to work hard. You have been briefed on two of the most demanding, VISTA and the Peace Corps.

Credit is due to the many young people who are turning toward careers in public service because they are more challenging albeit less lucrative than those in the private sector.

Once the present uproar on our campuses diminishes and the responsible majority of your generation takes command, we will have a far different perspective of America's future leaders. I think we will find them a new breed and an exciting one.

You have been given more in life, so you will demand more from life. You have been born in an era of dynamic change, so you will accept change as a glorious challenge. Your knowledge of war will stimulate your determination for peace. Your social awareness will heighten your civic activity. Your benefits from prosperity will enable you to extend as well as increase prosperity.

I salute you as individuals whose scholarship and leadership are a credit to both our generations. Today you number 121. My wish for America is that one day this country can claim 121 million young citizens just like you.

June 16, 1969, Miami Beach, Florida
Fifth Annual Conference of the Marine Technology
Society

ONE OF THE most gratifying and challenging aspects of my office is my role as chairman of the Marine Science Council. And I am aware of the role played by the Marine Technology Society in stimulating a large sector of our marine community to utilize the sea's resources for the benefit of mankind.

The theme of this conference reflects your recognition that America approaches a new threshold in our maritime history. We are anticipating a significant new decade in effective, intelligent use of the sea.

The past decade has been one of preparation. The present time is one of organization, so that the decade ahead may culminate in the realization of our aims.

To understand where we wish to go, it is well to remember from where we have come. In 1959, a National Academy of Sciences report awakened our nation to the vast potential of the sea — and startled our nation by assessing our efforts as both primitive and inadequate.

Congress responded with new support. The executive branch took steps to improve coordination through the Interagency Committee on the Oceans. Increased funds were granted. We began to strengthen our scientific base, expand our fleet, enlarge our resources in education and manpower.

In June 1966, Congress enacted a bill authorizing a long-term program to study and use the seas — the Marine Resources and Engineering Development Act. The Marine Science Council was formed to bring order out of the erratic progress and fragmented efforts of the twenty-three different federal bureaus involved with marine affairs.

As a result of the decade of preparation, we have increased funding for research and exploration by a factor of five. We have added fifty ships of 65,000 tons to our oceanographic fleet. The number of marine science graduate students has increased tenfold; we have six times as many Ph.D.s conferred in that field. Federal management has improved. Communication among governmental, industrial, and academic interests has dramatically improved.

We have made a beginning. We have an agency for organization — the Marine Science Council — which the President has not allowed to expire. We have a body of fresh, controversial recommendations from the Commission on Marine Science, Engineering and Resources. I do not say I agree with all their ideas. I do not say they will all be adopted. But the commission's work in compiling an inventory of long-term needs and opportunities has provided the President and Congress with a fundamental data bank and suggested direction.

I will be honest with you. This administration cannot rush full speed ahead into marine development programs. The realities of national priorities and continuing inflation demand executive discipline. All federal expenditures have undergone sharp review. In many cases we were forced to make painful reductions. Despite this, we intend to move with all deliberate speed. This administration has not been standing still.

Shortly after inauguration, the President requested the Marine Science Council to review the Stratton Report and recommend possible action. Comments from council members, the President's science advisor and the council's executive secretary provided the basis for proposals submitted to the President on March 27, 1969.

Six substantive areas were selected for immediate attention. Five of these probably can be implemented without further legislation. These are:

One: The establishment of a federal grant program; coastal zone laboratories; and regional port planning.

Two: The expansion of exploration of coastal and deep sea resources and weather forecasting services.

Three: Improvement of the U.S. fishing industry.

Four: The creation of national regional laboratories with a strong base of support.

Five: Leadership in defining a legal regime for the deep ocean floor.

Six: Initiation of a long-range federal contract program in basic marine technology.

As to the commission's recommendation to create a new independent agency — NOAA — the council has proposed and the President has concurred that it should be considered as part of a broad review of federal organization.

Positive, deliberate, and logical steps have been taken. Priority areas have been identified. The President has ordered the appropriate federal agencies to take these priorities into account in their planning for 1971 and beyond. Task groups have been established by the council to further refine and determine programs. The President's Advisory Committee on Executive Organization will give early attention to the question of NOAA.

This approach is the style of the Nixon Administration. Not to rush headlong into hastily conceived positions. Not to make promises that cannot be delivered. Not to make organizational changes for the sake of change nor invoke innovation to masquerade as improvement.

The measure of leadership is not the size of budget but the quality of management. This administration will not let history pass us by. We recognize the ocean's potential. We will not let our preoccupation with today's priorities block our vision for tomorrow. We realize that societies, which fail to look *to* the future, fail *in* the future.

In the years ahead we are committed to intelligent investment — investment that will result in ever-increasing dividends of progress.

In the decade ahead our advances should focus upon four critical areas — national organization; international cooperation; coastal zone development; knowledge accumulation.

National organization is imperative to achieve maximum results from frankly limited resources. We must be conscious of our objectives and establish a clear policy to realize them. Far better coordination of federal, state, and private efforts is required. Improved communication between all sectors involved in marine programs is essential.

If we cannot provide vast appropriations, we can at least prevent needless duplication. We can pool our information. We can provide incentives, enabling the industrial and academic communities to participate as partners.

International cooperation is the keystone to fulfill the peaceful promise of the sea. The United States' participation in the international decade of ocean exploration should underscore our policy of true partnership with all nations desiring to enhance knowledge for peaceful purposes. The international decade is an extraordinary opportunity for all nations to cooperate in a humanitarian crusade for knowledge. We shall work in the hope that the sea holds answers to the worldwide problems of hunger and disease.

The depth of the oceans like the infinity of space is a new environment. We cannot allow it to be contaminated by the vengeful conflicts of the past. We seek a seabed arms control treaty which will secure the ocean depths from weapons of mass destruction. We are willing to negotiate, freely and openly. But we cannot afford to negotiate from a position of weakness.

Last month our resolutions were introduced in the eighteen-nation disarmament conference in Geneva. Time and patience are necessary in complex diplomatic conversations. I am confident that with persistence, international accord will prevail.

The same patience and confidence must dominate our efforts to achieve a legal regime for the seabed. Our goal is not the fastest settlement but the fairest one. Our objectives should be agreements that can be permanent because they are just and constructive.

Development of America's coastal zone contains the greatest immediate benefit for our society. By the year 2000, seventy-five percent of our people will live within fifty miles of the coast. Right now, 150 million Americans live in coastal ports annually. Here we have the most to gain by doing something; the most to lose by doing nothing.

With all the investment made in marine research, more is needed to understand the resources of the coastal zone. It is urgent that we develop a better base of information to guide, preserve, and protect coastal zone development.

A sound system of coastal zone management must be achieved which will take into account national, regional, and local interests. The appropriate role for states and private enterprise must be determined. We should seek a harmony of compatible uses for the nation's sake.

Knowledge — more knowledge — remains the overriding factor in our conquest of this planet's last frontier. Every effort must be made to accelerate research and capitalize on present successes like the tektite program. We must recruit and train more oceanographers. We must encourage our universities and colleges to expand or develop marine science programs. The time has come to consider a genuine sea grant college system.

We have established a sound base. But it is a base *only*. We must press forward in both science and technology.

The decade ahead is filled with promise. The degree to which we fulfill that promise will be determined by our ability to improve national organization, international cooperation, coastal zone development, and marine knowledge in the years ahead.

As the decade begins we face grave problems in funding. But these problems should not affect our priorities in achieving rational management or international accord. These problems need not affect our determined leadership. Certainly these problems need not affect the private sector's very important role in marine affairs.

This administration will neither withdraw support from the marine field nor diminish the momentum which has built up over the past decade. It will deliberately develop a truly national marine program which will maximize the benefits to be gained, minimize the losses to be incurred, and be pertinent to the goals, aspirations, and problems facing our society today.

In closing, I believe all of us deeply interested in the development of our ocean depths would do well to move forward in the spirit of the Army Engineers: "The difficult we do right away. The impossible takes a little longer."

June 16, 1969, St. Petersburg, Florida
Pinellas County Republican Dinner

THE PROBLEMS America faces today are almost overwhelming. They are complex but they can be solved. There are answers, and this administration is determined to put those answers into action.

While I could talk generalities, I prefer to talk specifics — and to show you in detail how this administration is focusing the full power of the federal government on a very formidable problem — the problem is crime.

In the last ten years serious crimes against persons and property have grown 150 percent. Crime continues to increase at a rate close to nine times as fast as the national population. Ten years ago, one in every 150 Americans was a victim of a major crime; this year one in every fifty Americans will become a victim. If the current crime rate continues unchecked, ten years from now one in every fifteen Americans will be the victim of a felony. These figures indicate we must act now if we are to prevent a national crime crisis.

Already there are sections of cities where citizens fear to travel after dark. There are neighborhoods where stores are closed and padlocked, their windows protected by iron gratings even during the daylight hours. There are storekeepers and filling station operators and some frightened citizens who keep loaded weapons in deliberate violation of local ordinances. This is not the America we want.

The rising volume of crime cannot be traced to any single source. There is organized crime; there are crimes of violence; there are crimes of opportunity.

Conditions of poverty and impaction contribute to crime. Dope addiction breeds crime. A weakening of moral standards encourages crime. An inadequate system of criminal justice abets crime.

There are two levels on which government can and must attack crime. The first is the elimination of its underlying causes through environmental rehabilitation. But the struggle against poverty, slums, ignorance and prejudice — by its overwhelming scope — is difficult; and progress is admittedly slow.

The second level — while no less ambitious and complex — can be achieved more rapidly. This is the reform and revitalization of our law enforcement agencies, our correctional institutions, and our criminal judiciary system.

Here is where the President has launched his attack. Organized crime is our first target, for it is the evil parent of much individual crime. Organized crime smuggles in the heroin that turns humans into addicts compelled to steal or sell their bodies to continue their use of drugs.

Organized crime is not just involved with importing narcotics or the numbers racket. Its tentacles reach everywhere. It finances loan-sharking and the fencing of stolen goods. Its investments include efforts to infiltrate labor unions and corrupt public officials. More and more, organized crime is moving into legitimate businesses, subverting every aspect of our society. Organized crime is America's most vicious conglomerate.

The President is determined to tackle the biggest adversary first. He has proposed an expanded budget and an extensive program enabling the Justice Department to move decisively against organized crime.

The President has authorized the Attorney General to engage in wiretapping organized racketeers as permitted by law.

The President has authorized the Attorney General to establish twenty federal racketeering field offices across the nation.

The President has requested a $300 million appropriation in 1970, essentially for state and local law enforcement programs. Law enforcement remains primarily a state and local function. We recognize this and regard the federal role as one of providing leadership, coordination, and professional assistance.

New legislation is necessary to enable the federal government to reach into the citadels of organized crime. The President has proposed a new witness-immunity law; amendments to the Wagering Tax Act; legislation to make the bribery of police and public officials a federal crime.

Just as the causes of crime are multiple, so the solutions must take many forms. More money and manpower would be meaningless without better laws, modern equipment and a vastly improved criminal justice system. Each are links in a chain and no chain is stronger than its weakest link.

What point is there to putting more police on the streets if more arrests do not result in more convictions? What point is there in employing more prosecutors and relieving court congestion if our prisons are no more than revolving doors? We need court reform and prison reform. We need to attack organized crime and crimes of opportunity. Most of all, we need a public spirit that stands firmly against lawlessness.

Now I don't deny for a moment that poverty causes many crimes. I believe that public apathy encourages crime. While government can develop programs to counteract rising crime, only citizens can develop the attitude to combat crime.

Government can pay police officers, but only the public may provide the policeman with the respect, the cooperation and the prestige which any self-respecting person demands and our policemen certainly deserve.

The public must learn that the cop on the beat, the patrolman in blue, is on our side in the war against crime. His uniform is the uniform of our troops. A policeman's badge should command the same respect granted a soldier's green beret, a sailor's dolphin, or a pilot's wings.

Insufficient recruitment and a lack of respect for law and order are the major problems confronting law enforcement agencies today. And both these problems can be traced directly to the public's disinterest.

You as a citizen have as important a responsibility as your government has in fighting crime.

Only you can police your personal conduct to assure that no nickel, dime, or dollar is invested in the so-called innocent but nonetheless illegal vices.

Only you can develop within your home a reverence for the law and a respect for those who enforce it.

Only you can educate your children by example and by deed, giving credibility to your word.

Only you can commit yourself to become involved if it is necessary. Several years ago, a New York woman was stabbed nineteen times while her neighbors closed their windows to her screams for help — because they didn't want to get involved. No one wants you to be a vigilante. But citizens can and must report violations. You cannot abdicate nor limit your civic responsibility to uphold the laws of our land.

Only with the help of citizens can government move effectively against the environmental causes of crime in the community. Your initiative in eliminating slums and their lack of recreational or employment opportunities can make the difference.

I am confident we will conquer our national crime crisis. I am certain we can move swiftly with the support of an awakened citizenry.

Government can never be stronger than its people. It cannot be more committed to a cause than its citizens are committed. This is the challenge of democracy. Remember that — with all its imperfections, this *is* the challenge of democracy.

The administration you sent to Washington intends to fight crime on all fronts. We have the resources and the talent to triumph. And with the full support of the American people we will win.

July 15, 1969, New York City, New York
American Medical Association Convention

IN SPITE OF what we read in the papers, I know that most doctors are interested only in practicing medicine, not in playing politics. I know that many doctors across the country have suddenly found themselves in the position of defending their profession against unfair attacks.

I can sympathize with those of you who, after struggling for years to improve the health of this nation, now find few kind words written and few voices raised in your defense.

I believe that your record speaks for itself. I think that millions of Americans, who appreciate their family doctors and value the doctor–patient relationship, know your worth.

A nation is in sore need of perspective when so many opinion leaders nit-pick against a profession which in this century added more than twenty years to life expectancy; a profession which has virtually eliminated so many fatal, crippling, and debilitating diseases in this country and around the world.

Our medical profession has achieved this — not our politicians and not our press. Only years of grueling study and relentless research produced these results. And we betray every doctor — in and out of the AMA — when we deprecate your dedication.

Passion without perspective is, to my mind, one of today's ironies. Blindingly illuminated causes are pushed recklessly to the foreground and, if sufficiently dramatized, are accepted as all-consuming, all-important. We hear much of "relevancy," yet the relative values of issues are rarely considered. The diatribe of a campus radical gains more notoriety than the deliberations of thoughtful men on far weightier issues. Today, our highly literate nation seems to delight in sensationalism and to dwell on it to the detriment of more serious, pernicious problems that need solving.

Nowhere is this more clear than in the case of our environment. Unless a crusading writer like the late Rachel Carson captures the imagination of the nation, we are prone to neglect the persistent problem for the petty crisis of the moment.

You as doctors know this well. As swiftly as modern medicine discovers the means to prolong life, modern technology seems to devise ways to reduce its quality.

While enlightened man refuses to accept disease, he tolerates the erosion of his environment. Intelligent Americans — who would not live in unpleasant surroundings among hostile people — endure with bland indifference mildly poisoned air, polluted waters, and noise just below the pitch of madness.

A nation capable of catapulting men to the moon is in mortal danger of devouring its irreplaceable life-sustaining elements through simultaneous genius and foolishness.

The blessings of modern society are abundant and obvious. The curse of modern society is man's inability to eliminate — or at least to neutralize — the adverse effects of his own creativity. We are bringing a national plague upon ourselves. It is the plague of a polluted environment.

Now, the picture is not altogether bleak. The prognosis is not inevitably negative. Just as America can mobilize her resources to reach into space, so can she concentrate her talents on renewing and restoring the environment.

Our technological capability is unquestioned. Our ability depends upon our awareness of the problem and, of course, our commitment to its resolution.

Over the past decades, we have become increasingly conscious of the incipient damage caused by industrialization. At all levels of government, executive and legislative actions have been taken to combat pollution. But we've failed. We've failed to sustain the degree of awareness needed to support a sufficient long-term commitment.

Several deaths caused by a persistent inversion of smog may produce sporadic interest. For a few weeks the scientists who have long raged against air pollution win public attention. Then popular support dissipates as other controversial issues become fashionable.

Improving the quality of our environment is important enough to have our constant attention and our coordinated action. This type of persistence cannot be secured by occasional editorials. It requires nothing less than the leadership of the President.

Air and water pollution neither know nor respect political boundaries. Polluted streams pass through countries and cities. Polluted rivers cross many states. Increased numbers of cars, buses, and trucks emitting poisonous exhaust fumes freely move about the entire country. Ultimately, the problem becomes one that is, of course, national in proportion.

On May 19, 1969, President Nixon, by executive order, established the Environmental Quality Council as the focal point of present diverse and often uncoordinated activities geared to control and to improve our environment. The Council will provide the unified, organized approach the federal level needs to be prerequisite to the creation of the national policy.

At present, pollution abatement and prevention programs are fragmented among many departments — often with good reason. You know and I know that environmental problems cross many scientific disciplines and can only be attacked by cooperative action. Just as the Treasury Department, Commerce, State, and numerous agencies have specific responsibilities for monetary policy, many departments have related rather than competitive responsibilities for environmental quality.

Consider the problem of pesticides. Agriculture is involved because the survival of many crops depends upon the protection of pesticides. Their toxic dangers require the attention of HEW. And the Departments of Commerce, Interior, and Transportation — as well as the Atomic Energy Commission — have substantial interests in the problem.

There is no need to create another expensive superagency. The Environmental Quality Council affords a sane alternative for a coordinated approach. Here, the Secretaries of Agriculture, Interior, Commerce, HEW, HUD, and Transportation join under the chairmanship of the President. The President's science advisor acts as executive secretary. The Vice President acts as vice chairman. Problems are confronted at the highest level by men with the authority to act.

In modern society, the environment is the battleground of incessant competition. Every new residential or industrial development, every new highway or public improvement, may alter the environment to the detriment of some in our society. Every technological accomplishment may be accompanied by an aspect adverse to our surroundings. We don't always consume the elements of our environment, but we do degrade them. We convert them from life-sustaining elements to waste products. Relentlessly, irreversible actions threaten to diminish our environmental heritage.

I think a sophisticated society should be able to navigate a middle ground between industrial progress and environmental destruction. The Environmental Quality Council will develop rules and policies whereby the competition among uses of the environment can be examined and resolved to maximum social benefit.

On June 20th, the Council held its first meeting. It was agreed that it would deal with broad categories — air, water, lands, noise, and nuclear waste problems. Six committees chaired by cabinet secretaries were established to prepare policy recommendations in principal areas.

A beginning has been made. The significance of this first step cannot be overestimated.

Our environment is just as susceptible to purification as it is susceptible to contamination. Our ability to move swiftly and effectively is related directly to our national determination.

Many of you may recall the problems that came about because of detergents in the early 1950s. Initial detergent production relied on alkyl benzoate sulfate with a high foam stability that proved intractable to breakdown by usual wastewater treatment processes. By 1953 detergent production exceeded that of soap and it appeared that America's waterways were destined to be smothered by gigantic suds.

The situation was intolerable and government gave industry three years to develop a detergent susceptible to bacterial action during the treatment process. Industry met the challenge. Within the three-year limit, suitably modified detergents were under production. The message is clear. When America must do, America can do. When government must get tough, it can. When industry must invent or change its production or improve products, it can.

Right now we are moving toward an intolerable condition with regard to solid wastes. Recent estimates indicate municipalities must collect and dispose of a billion pounds of garbage every day at a cost of $3 billion a year. Every day industry produces an additional 600 million pounds of waste; agriculture contributes 12 billion pounds; and mineral wastes have reached 6 billion pounds. As a nation, we are threatened by a rather expensive burial in our own garbage.

The Solid Waste Act of 1965 — extended to 1970 by the past administration — assigned management responsibilities to both the Secretary of HEW and the Secretary of Interior. Other legislation in the field gives HUD and agricultural research to the development of a solution of this problem — the Department of Agriculture being involved concurrently. Commerce also has limited authority. Now, working together through the Environmental Quality Council, solid waste disposal has been targeted as an area requiring substantial improvement.

Not only will studies be made, but, in addition, proposals will be put forth to sustain or enlarge federal efforts in planning, research, control, and financing. Some will be rather sophisticated. Other concepts could focus upon simple means to counter what I call our throwaway philosophy. For instance, the possibility of again adopting the returnable bottle as a way to reduce solid waste volume merits serious consideration.

The point is that with the Council as the pivotal influence for the first time, environmental quality has moved into the Office of the President as a national priority. For the first time, the consciousness and the commitment — prerequisite to meaningful action — coalesce at the highest level. For the first time, the executive is not waiting to react to a new environmental crisis but is moving out ahead to prevent critical conditions.

In addition, the Council recognizes the importance of involving the states in developing national policy. Just as there is danger in becoming too narrow in focus to treat the symptom rather than cure the disease, so there is danger in assuming that a monopoly of interest resides in Washington, D.C. Just as we recognize the interdepartmental overlap of interest in environmental quality, we realize that the states, the regions and the metropolitan areas all have a stake in the decision-making process.

The newly formed Office of Intergovernmental Relations will assure that state and local governments are fully drawn into the planning dialogue. We now want to define a national environmental quality strategy in which all states will participate. Few states have scientific advisors who have an effective relationship with their governors. We are now considering the possibility of recommending that the President request that all states authorize the appointment of a strong science advisor to cooperate with the Office of Intergovernmental Relations and the Office of Science and Technology. His position would parallel that of the President's science advisor, and he would be effective in helping to shape federal action in environmental quality control.

Private professional organizations — like the AMA — will have a role to play in encouraging environmental improvement. You can bring the full force of your influence to bear in support of many of our programs. Too often in the past, the public health officer has been less appreciated than his counterpart in private practice. You can reverse this trend and work alongside public health officials in spirited partnership. Your increasing voluntary participation at the state and local level can result in greater public support for enlarged programs.

I guess the saving grace of environmental problems is their susceptibility to solution. As physicians, you have long raged against illness. You have crusaded for research and pioneered in preventive medicine. Now you can share in a great national crusade to bring about health outside the body. The environment is, after all, everything outside the skin. Without a healthy environment we cannot have a healthy civilization. Only with a benign environment can we aspire to the best life.

Right now we are pretty far from that beautiful environment that we dream of. Right now our task is far more fundamental. It must become the work of this nation to purify its air and water. With more people, more factories, more cars, we have more waste. We must run faster and faster just to keep position.

This administration's policy is to attempt to beat the treadmill; to anticipate problems rather than to react; to prevent rather than to eliminate. We feel we act upon a mandate as fundamental as the problem itself. It's the first mandate of humanity — the right to survive!

September 30, 1969, Chicago, Illinois
Chicago Executive Club

JUST AS there is a difference between making news and making history, there is a distinction between making history and changing civilization.

The ugliness you in this city endured during the 1968 Democratic Convention made news. The explosion of the first atomic bomb made history. The flight of Apollo II began the change of civilization. For man is no longer bound to this earth but a citizen of the Cosmos.

The implications of Apollo II are overwhelming. Think what the voyages of the last great age of discovery signified.

With the voyages of Columbus and Magellan, the era of Mediterranean civilization waned, the era of Atlantic civilization dawned. What did this exploration accomplish?

In political terms, it stimulated nationalism. In economic terms, it created a commercial revolution that in turn generated the industrial revolution. The revelation of so many people, cults, and cultures liberalized the mind of Europe. Above all, there was pride in the power of human achievement. Men realized the world of matter could be conquered.

The chains of medievalism were swept aside. The ancient motto of Gibraltar — "ne plus ultra" — "no more beyond" was changed. It became "plus ultra" . . . "more beyond." It was on this note of surging optimism that modern civilization began.

Comprehending all that the last great age of discovery produced, we have an obligation to continue the present one.

Within the light of our time and the limits of our nation's priorities, within the constraints of our budget and our commitments to our allies, we shall go forward.

Where government was the patron of the last great age of discovery, it is both the patron and the planner of the present one.

America's initial space objective was man's landing on the moon. The flight of Apollo II was the culmination of a decade of effort. It falls to President Nixon to determine the direction of America's next decades in space exploration.

Early this year the President created the Space Task Group to select some plausible directions. As chairman of the National Aeronautics and Space Council, I headed this study team composed of Dr. Lee DuBridge, the President's science advisor; Dr. Thomas Paine, administrator of NASA; and Dr. Robert Seamans, Secretary of the Air Force. Working with us were observers from the State Department, the Atomic Energy Commission, and the Bureau of the Budget; and from the possible user agencies, the Departments of Transportation, Commerce, Interior, and Agriculture.

On September 17th, after seven months of intensive study, we submitted our report to the President.

Our recommendation is for a balanced program — balanced in the sense that it places emphasis on *both* manned and unmanned missions to achieve *multiple* objectives in scientific development and technological applications.

Over the past weeks much has been written about the Space Task Group report. Yet I have found most commentary disappointingly incomplete. Understandable attention has been given the ultimate goal of a manned landing on Mars. But all too often this has been done at the expense of the more immediate recommendations. There has been a failure to distinguish between our suggested approach and that of the past Apollo program. Some of the most extraordinary, although less dramatic, features have been almost ignored.

The essence of the recommended program is balance. While the past decade was characterized by a rush to the moon, we propose a more deliberate approach. Manned missions will continue, but in a far broader perspective. The emphasis has shifted to intermediate accomplishment rather than one *final* objective. Where the last decade had a single focus — put an American on the moon — we now aim at five basic objectives.

First among these is applying space technology on earth to the direct benefit of mankind.

Present contributions of the space program range from its positive impact on the national economy — $35 billion in goods and services over the last decade — to the creation of the new commercial communication satellite industry.

The potential for world communication is staggering. Broad area satellite transmission of the future will enable people in Calcutta and Cairo and Chicago to talk to each other conveniently and inexpensively. Then, we will have the beginning of a true world community.

In the field of navigation and traffic control, we envision establishing a worldwide navigational network. By tracking ships' positions from a vantage point in space we will prevent marine disasters.

Weather satellites already provide superior forecasting. Ultimately, long-range (ten days to two weeks) prediction will be possible. Consider how a two week-advance notice on rain or frost will improve agriculture.

Earth resources surveying holds rich promise. Satellites equipped with special sensing systems will eventually be able to measure snow cover. This will help in management. Crop diseases may be detected in time so that corrective spraying can reduce wide area damage. The oceans may be scanned to pinpoint fertile fishing grounds.

Neil Armstrong's "one small step for a man" captured the imagination of the world. But the "giant leap for mankind" may prove to be these earth application programs which could — one day — save an exploding population from starvation.

Thus our primary concern is not landing men in any one place, but increasing the use of space capabilities to serve man everywhere.

During the past decade, we have successfully met a challenge to our technological leadership and now we have a space program and a capability second to none.

We have demonstrated our ability to respond to this challenge. We no longer need to conduct our program with outside pressures as a stimulus. We can instead seek the broadest possible participation of all men in our future endeavors.

There is a danger in letting our space program slip into a mere exercise of chauvinism. We cannot permit this.

Speaking before the United Nations, President Nixon pledged that America will take positive steps toward "internationalizing man's epic venture into space — an adventure that belongs not to one nation but to all mankind, and one that should not be marked by rivalry, but by a spirit of fraternal cooperation."

I doubt if any event has drawn the world closer than the flight of Apollo II which space communication satellites enabled the free world to witness together. Just as the discovery of the new world fostered pride in the old, let us pray that the exploration of other planets will forge unity on this one.

While the second objective of future space programs is international cooperation, the third must be the operation of military space systems to enhance national defense.

While the second objective aspires to cooperation in space, the third assures that there will be no blind reliance on good faith. There will be no vulnerability to those who would exploit the new capability. A limited military presence in space is important to national defense and should prove an invaluable force for peace in this world and beyond.

The fourth objective is the development of new techniques for operating in space. This is the prerequisite for all future deep space exploration.

Present space vehicles are expensive because they are expendable. New reusable, multipurpose vehicles must be developed to make space exploration economically as well as technically feasible.

A permanent space station and a space transportation system comprise our stepping-stones to the solar system.

The space station is envisaged initially as a permanent orbiting laboratory which can comfortably support six to twelve occupants for a considerable time. At a future date it will be expanded by attaching additional modules to house as many as fifty to one hundred men.

The space transportation system represents a major improvement over our present methods. Vehicles will be economical and flexible, capable of carrying passengers, fuel and even other space craft.

The system actually contemplates three components: an earth to low earth orbit shuttle; a reusable space tug to move men and equipment to different earth and lunar orbits; and a nuclear transport for geosynchronous orbit and deep space activities.

Development of this nuclear engine is underway. Initial tests have been successfully run and reveal we are advancing toward a major propulsion breakthrough.

The fifth and ultimate objective is manned exploration of the Solar System. Unmanned missions to Venus and Mars will serve as precursors to manned missions. Enlarging our knowledge of pure science and the lunar surface will occupy the early years.

Only after a firm base is built will we attempt to enter what could be irreverently described as the Buck Rogers stage of space travel.

However, those who avidly followed Buck Rogers and Lindbergh and Billy Mitchell should find NASA's proposal of grand tours into deep space irresistible. Unmanned flights are planned which use the juxtaposition of planets and their respective gravitational boosts to create a slingshot effect, driving spacecraft past several planets. In the late 1970s the outer planets will be so favorably positioned that unmanned, multiple planet "fly-by" missions will be feasible. In 1977 a "fly-by" of Jupiter–Saturn–Pluto is possible with a Jupiter–Uranus–Neptune "fly-by" to follow in 1979.

The manned landing on Mars is projected as a tandem effort with two teams of astronauts housed in identical linkable spacecraft with additional capacity should rescue be necessary. After the Mars landing, the manned crafts are scheduled for a Venus "fly-by" before their return to earth.

How soon America reaches the Buck Rogers stage is the President's decision. The Space Task Group deliberately avoided recommending a fixed time frame. Instead, three feasible alternatives were offered.

Option I would permit a manned Mars landing in the early 1980s and require a maximum annual expenditure of $9 billion by 1980.

Option II proceeds more slowly. The Mars landing would be targeted for 1986 and the maximum annual appropriation would be $8 billion sometime after 1980.

Option III defers the decision on Mars until after 1990, but still includes the base building elements of a space station and space shuttle. Here the financial obligation would briefly exceed the present $4 billion annual allocation, but generally fall below it.

The Space Task Group rejected two other possible programs of an extreme nature. One was to launch an all-out effort, the other to discontinue all manned missions at the conclusion of the present Apollo program.

My personal recommendation to the President endorsed Option II. This calls for continuing our present $4 billion effort through 1972 and reaching a peak effort of $5.7 billion in 1976. By that year the President must make the decision whether to go for the intensive decade culminating in a manned landing on Mars in 1986.

This position is conservative, for it holds the decision for planetary exploration in abeyance until our technological, scientific, and fiscal positions are better defined.

Two questions dominate all speculation over national space policy: Why space? And why Mars?

The latter is usually asked by those who endorse some space effort. Mars is a valid goal for reasons both logical and psychological.

Of all the planets in our solar system, Mars is the most earthlike. Mars holds the greatest promise of a capability to sustain human life. It is a potential resource and reserve.

More important for the present is the fact that the mind of America functions better when it focuses upon a clear target. Manned exploration of the solar system is too nebulous to capture the public's attention. A manned landing on Mars is as understandable a challenge to the citizens as it is to the scientist. It is a test that can be put in a time frame and its anticipation can be appreciated by all.

Public involvement with the national space effort is important. In fact, it is in part an answer to the first question, the question of those who oppose all space programs . . . why space?

The answer to this question is founded in the spirit of America. Our nation's history and progress have been inextricably linked with its yearning for the furthest frontier.

Those who would have us shut down the space program are doing more than depriving the world of a future Columbus or Magellan. For the Columbuses and the Magellans of this world will prevail. The passion for discovery will find a patron. Space will be conquered — if not by our nation then by some other.

Those who would deny America a role in the exploration of space are denying the most fundamental expression of American character.

We are a people who force frontiers. Call it the competitive spirit of a free society, or manifest destiny, or escape from the mundane problems of the ordinary. Commend us as a nation of pioneers or condemn us as a nation of adventurers.

Whatever it is, this hunger for the horizon has been our nation's spur to progress. America's greatness was born in its refusal to accept a closing of physical or spiritual frontiers.

To compare space programs with poverty programs is invidious . . . for they are different and respond to different human instincts. We will have poverty programs because we are humanitarian. We will have a space program because we are ambitious.

Civilized nations share in common their humanitarian desires, but few possess in such abundance the frontier vigor and pioneer spirit which brought our ancestors here in the first place.

Why space? Because it is in our blood as Americans. Because we believe that a better life lies beyond the horizon. Because we are citizens not of the old world but of the new one. Because ours is the heritage of those who broke the barriers of Gibraltar and entrusted to us their legacy of eternal hope — "plus ultra" — "more beyond."

October 8, 1969, Albuquerque, New Mexico
National Congress of American Indians

I HAVE looked forward to this day — to the chance to meet with you, to share in your Twenty-Fifth Anniversary celebration, to congratulate you — and especially your charter members, some of whom are here today — for your vision and leadership.

As impressive as your past growth has been, even more impressive are the prospects for your contributions to the Indian future. As never before, the nation is aware of Indian problems and the need for clear, decisive Indian leadership is urgent.

As a representative of government, I am especially interested in Indian leadership because I am convinced that the Indian people and their federal government must work more closely than ever before.

The President's statement, delivered to the last NCAI Convention in Omaha, still stands. This administration *opposes* termination. This administration *favors* the continuation of the trust relationship and the protection of Indian lands and Indian resources.

Let us now and forever put to rest all fears and begin positive action together. For every Indian problem there is also an Indian opportunity. Building upon that special relationship between Indian tribes and the federal government, we will solve the problems and open the opportunities.

There is no question that this special relationship will and must continue. It is its quality that should concern us most.

Not one of us who has responsibility can be complacent about Indian affairs. And no one who is sincerely interested will allow the plight of the Indian people to be used for publicity, politics, or personal advantage.

I see no merit in trying to place blame for the present situation. Too much energy has been diverted already to excuses for conditions of life that any sensitive person can see are inadequate.

You do not want our apologies and you do not need our explanations. You want and need action. And it is time for action.

There is a desperate shortage of job opportunity. Indian unemployment runs up to ten times the national average in this year of record employment.

— Housing shortages still plague more than half the families living in Indian communities.

— Schools for Indian children are underfinanced and deficient.

— Hardship invades almost every phase of individual and community life.

I do not have to go into details with you. You know the facts better than I. It is time to move forward. We must have improvement and a sense of direction.

This administration understands that there is no single solution to Indian problems. There is no such thing as *"the* Indian problem." A rich diversity of culture, language and background characterizes Indian communities across America. No single set of programs will fit everywhere.

This administration does not even expect complete uniformity and agreement among Indians as to their own goals or needs or desired programs. We must be flexible. For too long the Indian has been forced to fit a particular program. From now on the programs will be tailored to fit the particular Indian requirements. We will work with the Indian people on a community-by-community and tribe-by-tribe basis to develop programs best suited to local needs and priorities.

Indian tribes possess a unique and direct relationship with the federal government

237

which is derived from several sources. First, it is a legal relationship. Through treaty and law, Indian communities are entitled to certain services from the federal government.

As a result of the treaties, the Indian people surrendered their land to the federal government under certain unavoidable conditions of trust and good faith. The government undertook a sacred trust to finance basic programs such as health and education. In attempting to respond to their obligation, Congress has enacted much legislation affecting Indians. Some of it has been successful but too much has failed to carry out its objective.

It is important to remember that federal support of Indian services is, to a great extent, legally due the Indian community. These are not services offered at the pleasure of the government but solemn obligations to a people who accepted a good-faith settlement in reliance on governmental integrity.

Moreover, there is a formal basis for the special relationship between the Indians and their government. Congress, by establishing the Indian Claims Commission, acknowledged the integrity of tribes as legal entities. This created the way for the government to acknowledge debts and obligations to the Indian people.

Thus the special efforts to offset costs of certain services in Indian communities are the rights of the communities and the legal and moral obligations of the federal government. But there remains a crucial distinction that has been generally ignored for the past 150 years.

Government may have the absolute duty to provide services, but that does not necessarily imply that government must perform and administer those same services.

It is completely feasible that a service be funded federally but run locally. There have been some tentative approaches in this direction recently. But, in my view, these approaches fail to establish clearly the willingness of the government to consider local ideas and arrangements.

Most who observe the Indian scene use the word paternalism to describe government's relationship with the Indians. That may be true, but it is not necessary. We have never had a better opportunity to change this attitude.

One obstacle to a serious management effort on the part of some Indian groups arises from the fear that proposals for local initiative may become the first step in a federal pullout of funds and responsibilities. Study of Indian history certainly would cause a person to be suspicious. However, I want to reassure you that this administration recognizes the legal right of the Indian community to be provided basic services and the legal responsibility of the Federal government to finance them.

But while we urge greater local leadership, we will not force it nor use its immediate absence to deny assistance. The Indian people must have the right to accept or reject local control. In fact, no change in the operation of federally funded services should go forward without full local discussion and agreement. Adequate safeguards can be developed to guarantee that federal responsibilities are recognized and continued.

Some communities might want no part of change now. Others might prefer maximum local administrative authority and responsibility. A full range of alternatives should be available. Above all, the federal government must be ready at all times to respond to reasonable local determinations.

The National Council on Indian Opportunity — which, as Vice President, I chair — is one newly created agency to serve in developing new programs and proposals. Six American Indian leaders serve on the council by presidential appointment. They are full participating members whose voices and votes are equal to those of the seven members who are heads of major federal departments responsible for Indian programs. Mr. Chino, your distinguished President, Mr. Valandra, your treasurer, and Mr. Jourdain, one of your regional vice presidents, serve on the council.

This is the first time in the history of federal–Indian relations that the Indian people have had this type of official recognition and representation. It gives us a better chance of solving the problems because your leaders will be certain we understand them fully and will personally assist in the solutions.

I appreciate and support the NCAI endorsement of the council. Your statement adopted in Albuquerque last May read in part: "There is no other like body which gives

238

the Indian people such vital participation in the discussion and solution of their problems." I am confident that the future will bear out your faith.

Today it is realistic to talk of Indian communities as self-determining. More Indian youth are in college than ever before. More Indian leadership is serving the nation. A member of my personal staff — Woody Sneed, an Indian, a scholar and a White House Fellow — provides but one example.

Many an educated and dedicated Indian youth would gladly return to his community to administer important programs were the opportunity to do so truly available. But these young people are impatient with excuses and delays. They want real involvement, not mere tokenism.

The American Indian and the federal government have a clear agenda for action.

We must tap the wealth of talent among young Indian leadership.

We must resolve the unadjusted claims of native Alaskans.

We must come to grips with the problems of California Indians living on public lands without ownership.

We must attack the problems of Indians isolated in remote reservations which lack sufficient resources.

We must give priority attention to the increasing number of landless Indians now living in urban centers who seek to bridge two cultures in an alien environment.

We must capitalize upon the unique relationship between the Indian people and the federal government to solve these problems.

This administration recognizes that the time of oratory and tokenism is past. The time for action has come. The time for paternalism is past, the time for Indian leadership has come. The time for studies and promises has past, the time for solution and progress has come.

This week's NCAI deliberations will serve as a major source of guidance to Secretary Hickel, to Commissioner Bruce, to me, and to all concerned federal officials.

You are confronting vital issues on Indian rights, reservation development, tax status, and education. Out of these sessions will come creative ideas.

While we pay proper respect for the past, let us focus on the future. Let us achieve a partnership between the American Indians and their government that is productive and worthy of our highest efforts.

There is a new administration in Washington, a new awareness in the country. Together, we must draw upon both to create a new era of progress for the American Indian.

October 8, 1969, Denver, Colorado
National Association of Regulatory
Utility Commissioners

WHILE I confess limited knowledge of your complex field, there are parallels in our experience — for the management of government and the management of utilities both deal with power.

Whether power is literal and electric or figurative and political, it is born in conflict. To establish a political base or a power plant it is necessary to recognize and reconcile competing claims.

Electric power is directly related to our national security and prosperity. Our position as the world's most productive and powerful nation is linked to our position as the world's leading producer of electrical power. And like our position as a world power, our position regarding electrical power confers its burdens as well as blessings.

In response to these burdens, public service commissions — like all levels of government — have grown over the years. Their duties have expanded and their views as to their roles have enlarged accordingly.

Less than fifty years ago the federal government felt its role in domestic affairs should be minimal. No area was more sacred than that of the national economy where government's responsibility was to act as referee. Natural forces were presumed at work which neither man nor government could alter. The best that could be expected was to enforce the rules of fair play.

Less than fifty years ago fewer than ten percent of America's rural homes had electricity. Utility commissions — where they existed — were limited to act as referees. Their role was to secure the best possible service at the lowest possible cost to the consumer, consistent with a just and reasonable return to the investor.

We've come a long way. Today, the federal government has demonstrated that it has the right, the responsibility, and the intention to intervene in domestic affairs including the economy where it serves the national interest.

Today, with ninety-five percent of all rural American homes receiving electric service . . . and with the power needs of the United States doubling every decade, we see utility commissions evolving as activist agents of the public interest.

The best of our utility commissions are viewing their duties and responsibilities in the broadest possible terms. They are responding to a new sense of public ethics which not only guards the public's purse, but protects its environment. They are motivated by a social awareness that utilities must be developed, but only in ways that preserve natural beauty, our national heritage, and the quality of our environment.

As governor of Maryland, I supported our public service commission's battle to save the Civil War battlefield of Antietam from being marred by massive overhead power lines. Antietam, you may remember, was one of the bloodiest fights of the last century and the utilities cried it would be the costliest of this one. The ultimate resolution was landmark legislation empowering the public service commission to control underground power line construction to preserve historical sites, and, in specified cases, residential areas.

The utilities involved had an understandably ambivalent attitude. They cannot be faulted for measuring progress in the parochial terms of efficiently expanding service. "Progress," as one great manufacturer proclaims, is their "most important product." But all too often their approach is reminiscent of the preacher who chastised his congregation by sermonizing: "Brothers and sisters, if you all came to pray for rain . . . why didn't you bring your umbrellas?"

Whatever the feelings of utilities, there is no turning back from an increasingly vigorous role for utility commissions. You have developed a social conscience and you intend to exercise it.

There is much work to be done. The agenda for action is staggering.

Urban–suburban growth has resulted in demands for higher power loads with lower densities. Since we cannot substantially reverse demographic patterns, we are going to have to adapt to them.

Power development depends on water resources. Nuclear power has introduced the whole new problem of thermal pollution and we continue to confront the old ones of general pollution and ecological imbalance.

Competing claims on the environment characterize modern life. Every new residential or industrial development, every new highway or public improvement may alter the environment to the detriment of some in our society. Every technological accomplishment may be accompanied by an aspect adverse to our surroundings. We do not so much consume our environment as we tend to degrade it. Relentlessly, irreversible actions threaten to debase our environmental heritage.

The President has given recognition to the national proportion of this problem through the creation of the Environmental Quality Council. The problems of the environment have been elevated to a rank equaling national security in requiring presidential initiative.

A sophisticated society should be able to navigate a middle ground between industrial progress and environmental destruction. The Environmental Quality Council will develop guidelines and policy whereby the competition among users of the environment can be examined and resolved for maximum social benefit.

The need for research, planning, and cooperation is critical. We possess the science and technology to guide our decisions. It is urgent that we invest in and rely upon these instruments intelligently.

The Electrical Research Council has committed $4 million for a five-year research program. The Advisory Committee to the Federal Power Commission has demonstrated the potential of cooperation. These are examples of public–private initiative that must be multiplied in the future. Each of you is experienced enough in the conflicts of regulating power to know that selfish special interest reaches a self-defeating point of no return. Parochialism is futile.

There is every reason to encourage cooperation in your interstate relationships. There is every reason to continue to enlarge federal–state cooperation. There is every reason to insist on responsible planning within your states and become the advocate of research before the public and private sectors of this nation.

Power, as you know so well, is an extraordinary commodity. Whether it is political or electrical, power is only useful when it is handled sensibly. Overload an electrical circuit and the result is an electrical blackout. The same principle can be applied to our federal system. An overconcentration of power can cause a complete breakdown.

Over the past three decades this is just what has been allowed to happen. In the words of President Nixon: "A third of a century of centralizing power and responsibility in Washington has produced a bureaucratic monstrosity; cumbersome, unresponsive, ineffective."

We have entrenched social programs born in past decades of experiment that are totally discredited.

We have neglected to utilize state and county governments to the point that it is miraculous that they have not atrophied.

We have done so much *for* the people that their energy to do for *themselves* has diminished.

Too often groups in the private sector see a community problem and form a lobby to have government investigate it rather than have a citizen committee solve it on the spot.

Worst of all, some people are beginning to believe that unless government can find answers, there are no answers.

These internal attitudes can be every bit as debilitating as war or depression. In fact, the resilience of the American spirit in the face of external crisis is a known factor. We have proven that we can endure adversity. Ironically, today's question is whether we can endure prosperity? We have always shown that we can unite to defeat an enemy from without. Today's question is can we unite to defeat an enemy within?

This enemy is not some elusive fifth column but an intangible malaise that has afflicted our land. Its cause is not a failure of the citizen, but a failure of our institutions. Our challenge is now internal. It is a test of the flexibility of our institutions.

President Nixon has presented America with a blueprint for institutional rejuvenation. It is compelling in its basic drive to the heart of the problem.

Reform the welfare system so that it provides economic incentives and job training for the unemployed, and equity for the working poor. This will produce results for the taxpayer.

Reform the federal manpower training programs and turn their operation over to the states as fast as the states can prepare to handle them.

241

Reform the Office of Economic Opportunity so that it may function as a laboratory for social experiment rather than as a lobby for fledgling politicians.

Reform the federal tax structure to eliminate taxes for the very poor and tax loopholes for the very rich.

Reform federal food stamp programs because poverty is not only an economic condition but a medical one. Malnutrition robs young minds of initiative and ambition.

Reform the draft to achieve the equity of a lottery and the certainty of a single year's eligibility at an early age so that young American men can plan their future.

Reform the system of distributing federal funds so that state and local governments have additional discretionary resources through unearmarked funds and increased flexibility through the consolidation of the federal grants-in-aid program.

Reform the administration of federal field services to achieve efficient decentralization by establishing uniform regional boundaries and by delegating maximum decision-making power to the regional level.

Reform the federal government itself through the appointment of the first presidential council to recommend modernization of the executive branch since the 1953 Hoover Commission.

These reforms zero in on the basic malfunctions of major American institutions. They attack the impersonality, irrelevance and ineffectiveness caused by bigger government that is *not* better government.

They reach to the root of poverty problems . . . inadequate income and opportunity. The old saying that "the only difference between rich people and poor people is money" rings with truth. Poverty is a social problem with an economic solution. Cash alone is not the answer. But combine cash with work training and work requirements and you have a practical program.

These reforms are designed to reinforce major American values . . . individual dignity, opportunity, equity, and security. They reassert the rights of state and local governments and restore their resources to exercise these rights responsibly.

The President has called this program the new federalism and it is just that. It does not retreat to the past federalism of the "hands-off" and "laissez-faire" period. Instead, it diverts the tremendous power of the federal government into constructive currents to energize the states, the counties, and the cities.

It draws upon the strength and substance of the premise that it is those governments closest to the people that govern best. It restores power to the people by restoring power to those governments closest to them.

It revitalizes the American ethic of work and opportunity by rewarding work and enlarging opportunity.

It reestablishes the American principle of equality of opportunity. It reasserts the American confidence in individual initiative by encouraging and rewarding those who want to help themselves.

The new federalism is a domestic legislative package designed to prevent a national political blackout. It recognizes the dangers of a power concentration and decentralizes power to generate and redistribute dependable energy. It supplies new power for new productivity.

Above all, the President's program is a statement of unequivocal optimism. It is an action plan to stimulate initiative throughout the nation. It invites civic participation in the broadest possible sense.

It admits that all of this country's problems cannot be answered in Washington. But it affirms that all of this country's problems can be answered.

And these answers must come from the people. For in a *democracy* it is not the government but the people who determine the future. And within *our* democracy it is not what government has done for the people but what the people have for themselves that has made America great.

October 11, 1969, Montpelier, Vermont
Vermont Fund Raiser

I KNOW it is not the general practice to discuss deep subjects at party dinners. I know I could avoid serious issues, that most would expect me to in this setting.

But I also know that the time has come for this nation to face these issues or lose its soul. The time has come for America to grow up or be consumed from within.

There are those who justify evading hard truths about our society by saying that we live in an age of anxiety. Every age is an age of anxiety to those who live in it. I say we cannot be excused for tolerating an age of absurdity.

Think about the absurdity that abounds in our society.

In a time of prosperity, inflation has been allowed to devour prosperity.

In a time when mass communication could provide authentic culture, we eulogize pop culture.

We invest tremendous sums to make higher education available to the many, then permit our campuses to be closed down by the few.

Freedom of speech is fundamental to our liberty, yet we have accepted flagrant abuse of this right.

The man who believes in God and country, hard work and honest opportunity, is denounced for his archaic views.

This nation which has provided more justice, equality, freedom, and opportunity than any nation in world history, is told to feel guilty for its failures.

The time has come to call a halt to this spiritual theater of the absurd, to examine the motivation of the authors of absurdity and challenge the star players in the cast.

Who are the authors of the absurd? They are a strident few in our society who have conferred upon themselves a position of moral superiority.

The patent ridiculousness of a claim to moral superiority is apparent from the first. However, it is necessary to their purpose for they cannot argue their case on logic nor survive the safeguards of our democratic system.

So the authors of the absurd have set their scene outside of the system. Their drama cannot be played by the rules of representative government.

You are familiar with their works. The disruption of the 1968 Democratic Convention won the praise of some liberal critics. One extolled the spirit of the yippies as they sang: "This Land Is Your Land. . . ." He failed to comment on their incessant epithets — four-letter words — screamed through bullhorns; or their homemade bombs of human excrement; or their leaders' retreat to the safety of the rear when the inevitable arrests began.

Another masterpiece was the SDS closing down Columbia. It received such rave reviews that SDS repertory groups began opening revivals across the nation.

Then there were the never-to-be-forgotten one-night stands during the 1968 campaign as candidates — particularly the Democratic party's presidential candidate — were successfully shouted down. The fact that freedom of speech was denied was dismissed as of little consequence.

Who are the actors in this theater of the absurd? The willing and the unwilling, the exploiters and the exploited, are all used. And I mean *used*.

In Chicago, prime television time was provided a willing group which Theodore White describes as the "crazies." These are tragic segments of our community that need therapy, *not* publicity.

In politics we see most often the exploiter who uses absurd positions to advance his own failing career. A public official who minds his constituents' and the country's business has little chance for publicity. A public official who attacks the institutions he has sworn to serve makes news.

It is a sad comment that the headlines are won by those who attack our nation as an imperialist aggressor or attempt to justify violence as an outlet for the aggrieved.

Across the nation we see the exploited. They are students scared to go to class, and idealists who join movements against violence only to be used as pawns in violence.

They are parents who have struggled to send their children through college only to see their children high on drugs and low on moral standards.

They are our soldiers who are risking their lives abroad only to be cursed at home. They are our policemen who signed up to protect and serve only to be ridiculed and reviled.

They are citizens who want to work within the system and judge the issues on the facts, only to be told our system is corrupt and the facts irrelevant.

Now, the most absurd act of all is the act of accepting, excusing, or apologizing for this drivel. If the average American is to feel guilty, let him feel guilty for putting up with this kind of irrational behavior.

But never believe that we can dismiss these advocates of the absurd lightly. This country cannot endure constant physical confrontation. The clash of ideas must go on forever, but the clash of bodies brawling in our streets must cease.

When does it end? It ends when every individual and every institution in this country becomes conscious that this country is suffering from an acute citizenship gap — and moves to correct it.

The family must teach the values of self-reliance and self-discipline, which are the cornerstones of citizenship. Other institutions may supplement early training but they can never substitute for good parents.

Educators should review their curricula to see that attitude training is offered alongside academic courses. We must begin early to teach the distinction between liberty and license, and impress upon future citizens that civil rights are inseparable from civic responsibilities.

Local and state governments can provide positive channels for civic participation. Vermont's Youth Advisory Council offers an outstanding example. Your governor has taken the initiative. The best counter to radical students working outside the system is responsible students working within the system. Governor Davis has moved state government from a position of potential confrontation to one of cooperation.

The greatest reason for the citizenship gap remains the growth of the federal government. Big government means impersonal bureaucracy. When decisions are removed from the people, their sense of responsibility wanes.

The process occurred so slowly, its impact was so subtle, as to be imperceptible at first. Suddenly a sense of civic impotence gripped the citizen. He was powerless before the forces of big government. His contribution appeared unheeded by a paternalistic government. All that appeared left to him was his vote.

But in 1968 a vote was enough to change things because enough votes went to Richard Nixon.

The President has proposed reforms in government designed to restore the citizen to his rightful place in the American system — in control of his country.

Reform is our strategy to overcome the citizenship gap. President Nixon has presented America with a blueprint for institutional rejuvenation.

These reforms zero in on the basic malfunctions of major American institutions. They attack impersonality, irrelevance, and ineffectiveness caused by bigger government that is *not* better government.

These reforms reinforce major American values . . . individual dignity, opportunity, equity, and security.

They draw upon the strength and substance of the premise that it is those governments closest to the people that govern best. They restore power to the people by restoring power to those governments closest to them.

They revitalize the American ethic of work and opportunity by rewarding work and enlarging opportunity.

They reassert the American confidence in individual initiative by encouraging and rewarding those who want to help themselves.

If enacted by Congress, these programs will, in effect, put the citizen back in command.

Finally, I want to talk about the number one issue in all our minds — *peace*.

Where do we stand?

The President continues to act to the limits of his power.

1. By Christmas he will have brought 60,000 American boys home.

2. He is Vietnamizing the war.

3. He has reduced the draft call for October; canceled the draft calls for November and December.

4. Through these actions he has demonstrated the good-faith conditions asked by North Vietnam.

5. He has reduced the terms of settlement to a single criterion. Self-determination for the South Vietnamese people.

6. He has in public and in the Paris talks made countless proposals for peace. He has pledged to consider all proposals.

7. He has invited international initiatives. He has appealed to the UN nations to exercise their diplomatic influence to end this war.

What more can our President do? He cannot abandon the people of South Vietnam to slavery or massacre.

— He cannot repudiate our free nations' policy that the world's political boundaries shall change only through peace.

— To do this would not only dishonor our nation but invite world war.

Richard Nixon is ... always has been ... always will be — a staunch advocate for peace.

Those men who do not bear his terrible responsibilities repeat and repeat the same trite words:

— "We must try something new."

— Are they blind?

— Each day, each week, each month we try something new.

We have negotiated in good faith:

— We shall continue to negotiate in good faith.

And ... ladies and gentlemen ... we will *end* this war.

— It will not be terminated tomorrow.

— But it will be terminated with honor.

— It will be concluded so that our sacrifices will not have been made in vain.

— It will be settled so that no seeds are sown for further war.

245

I leave you with one thought. In 1970 we begin a new decade and in 1970 we have a national Congressional election.

I believe the Republican party must reach beyond specific issues to seek a moral mandate from the American people.

The Republican party must challenge the American people to reject absurdity so that the seventies may be a decade of principle, purpose, and common sense.

Our party affirms that America does have a position of moral leadership and that position has been *earned* by honor not power.

We believe that America has great work to do. We must make our cities livable, our environment pure, focus the power of our brilliant technology on the problems of hunger, health, and housing in America and throughout the world.

All this can only be done by a United States of America that is united in spirit as well as law.

For in a *democracy* it is not the government but the people who determine the future. And within *our* democracy it is not what government has done for the people but what the people have done for themselves that has made America great.

October 17, 1969, Cambridge, Maryland
Dedication of the Spiro T. Agnew
Mental Health Center

TODAY IS a unique experience for me. It is a day of great meaning for me — on many levels.

To know that this building will carry my name for many years into the future is an honor that I do not accept lightly. Being a household word is not quite as important as being a health word.

Not quite two years ago I gave the principal speech at the ceremony renaming the Chesapeake Bay Bridge for Governor William Preston Lane, Jr. I remember thinking at that time how much pride and comfort Governor Lane would haven taken in that recognition had he been alive to witness it.

So, I am grateful that you have allowed me to share in this day — and that you have excused me from paying the ultimate price for this privilege.

Finally, this building represents the fulfillment of a promise that I made to myself many years ago. One of my first responsibilities as county executive caused me to visit a locked ward at one of our state mental hospitals. I was shocked and shaken by what I saw — row upon row of human beings locked away by their society as well as locked within the sickness of their spirit.

On that day I made a private pledge that if I ever held the power to reduce the social tragedy that is mental illness, I would use that power.

As county executive I took the first tentative steps. Mental illness — although it afflicts an estimated one out of every ten Americans — is in itself a disturbing subject. Since we don't like to think about mental illness, we postpone the problems of the mentally ill and block them from our consciousness — perhaps a defensive gesture that psychiatrists understand better than we ourselves.

What we do not understand frightens us. While psychiatrists applauded my efforts to

246

establish the county's first community mental health clinic, many constituents were appalled. A program of community education became the necessary forerunner of a program of community care. Progress was impeded not only by the limits of our resources, but by the misapprehensions of our residents.

When I became governor, the Community Mental Health Act existed purely as a paper program. It was my privilege to recommend the funds to give it life. Here on the Eastern Shore and in Baltimore City, adjunctive to the University Hospital, funds were appropriated to build comprehensive mental health centers.

The community care concept is to treat the sick where illness overtakes them. This center will offer the full gamut of services, ranging from twenty-four hour emergency care to outpatient therapy. Community care tears down the walls of the institution. There are dangers in overstressing the institution. Unneeded care for the patient and an inflexibility of technique in the professional and semiprofessional personnel can result.

Community care permits the patient to be treated in his own environment. For the emotionally ill this is vital. Where circumstances are ideal, the love of a family is a therapeutic supplement. Where circumstances are far from ideal, a patient is helped to adjust to this reality.

Many forms of anxiety are the result of conditions we cannot change. By temporarily removing the patient from the conditions, we achieve the illusion of success. But the remote institution has a revolving door. A patient who functions well in the orderly environment of an institution may collapse when discharged to face the disorders of his real world.

All too often we have thought we were treating minds when all we were doing was retreating from conditions. Community care reverses this process. Cure depends upon adjusting the personality, not the environment.

In every way this comprehensive mental health center represents tomorrow. Its facilities are capable of not only treating, but preventing mental illness. It offers early care and individualized care. Its personnel can serve the community as educators, as well as analysts. Work in and of the community is the key.

We are finding this true of every aspect of modern life. The intimacy and immediacy of a community is most conducive to progress. I have always believed this, and I am gratified to be part of an administration which has put this belief into action. Our goal is to restore opportunity and resources to the states, the counties and the cities.

If the President's proposals for revenue sharing, welfare reform, manpower training, and grant consolidation are enacted by Congress, future governors will never confront the cruel decisions over conflicting priorities which I was forced to face as governor of Maryland.

Today symbolizes just the beginning of Maryland's new mental health and hygiene network. Once this system is operative, our present institutional approach will appear as archaic as the bedlams of the past century.

Mental illness and mental retardation occur more frequently, affect more people, require more treatment, cause more suffering, waste more human resources, cost more private and public funds than any other single health condition. While the cost of public institutional care is too little to help the individual much, it is too much if measured in terms of successful use of public health dollars.

We live in an age of anxiety. Emotional disturbance is an illness that will not disappear. Those of us who are strong enough — and fortunate enough — to function in our world must face the reality of mental illness and mental retardation. We must stop pushing the problems of the mentally ill to the back of our minds and to our legislatures.

Comprehensive community health care is the alternative. It has been proven effective. But private and public support of full programs must be forthcoming. This building renews my dedication, and I hope its success will stimulate further pledges by Maryland officials.

A man can commit his name to many causes, but only society can cause his name to be committed to public memory. You have done me great honor, and I am deeply grateful.

October 19, 1969, New Orleans, Louisiana
Citizens' Testimonial Dinner

SOMETIMES IT appears that we are reaching a period when our senses and our minds will no longer respond to moderate stimulation. We seem to be approaching an age of the gross. Persuasion through speeches and books is too often discarded for disruptive demonstrations aimed at bludgeoning the unconvinced into action.

The young, and by this I don't mean by any stretch of the imagination all the young, but I'm talking about those who claim to speak for the young, at the zenith of physical power and sensitivity, overwhelm themselves with drugs and artificial stimulants. Subtlety is lost, and fine distinctions based on acute reasoning are carelessly ignored in a headlong jump to a predetermined conclusion. Life is visceral rather than intellectual, and the most visceral practitioners of life are those who characterize themselves as intellectuals.

Truth to them is "revealed" rather than logically proved, and the principal infatuations of today revolve around the social sciences, those subjects which can accommodate any opinion and about which the most reckless conjecture cannot be discredited.

Education is being redefined at the demand of the uneducated to suit the ideas of the uneducated. The student now goes to college to proclaim rather than to learn. The lessons of the past are ignored and obliterated in a contemporary antagonism known as the generation gap. A spirit of national masochism prevails, encouraged by an effete corps of impudent snobs who characterize themselves as intellectuals.

It is in this setting of dangerous oversimplification that the war in Vietnam achieves its greatest distortion.

The recent Vietnam Moratorium is a reflection of the confusion that exists in America today. Thousands of well-motivated young people, conditioned since childhood to respond to great emotional appeals, saw fit to demonstrate for peace. Most did not stop to consider that the leaders of the Moratorium had billed it as a massive public outpouring of sentiment against the foreign policy of the President of the United States. Most did not care to be reminded that the leaders of the Moratorium refused to disassociate themselves from the objective enunciated by the enemy in Hanoi.

If the Moratorium had any use whatever, it served as an emotional purgative for those who felt the need to cleanse themselves of their lack of ability to offer a constructive solution to the problem.

Unfortunately, we have not seen the end. The hard-core dissidents and the professional anarchists within the so-called "peace movement" will continue to exacerbate the situation. November 15 is already planned — wilder, more violent, and equally barren of constructive result.

Is all this justified? Are we imperialist warmongers? Let's look for a moment at the President's policy in Vietnam in the light of political and military conditions as they were and as they are today.

The situation as of January 20, 1969

Military Conditions
— The number of U.S. troops to Vietnam was still increasing.
  (When the men on their way there on January 20 finally arrived, it reached an all-time high level in February.)
  We appeared still to be seeking a military solution.
— Military operations were characterized by maximum military pressure on the enemy, through emphasis on offensive operations.

— Progress in strengthening the South Vietnamese army was slow; not enough resources were being devoted to that effort.

Political Conditions
— We found only a general and vague set of proposals for political settlement of the war. While they called for "self-determination," they provided no specific program for achieving it.
— Mutual withdrawal of forces was provided for under the Manila Declaration which envisioned that the Allied withdrawal would be completed within six months of the withdrawal of North Vietnamese forces. But everyone knew at that time that the North Vietnamese were not about to pull out while we were still there.

The situation today

Military Conditions
— We have instituted a Vietnamization program which envisages South Vietnamese responsibility for all aspects of the war — coping with both Viet Cong insurgency and regular North Vietnamese forces — even if we cannot make progress in the political negotiations in Paris.
— We have offered the withdrawal of U.S. and Allied forces over a 12-month period, if North Vietnamese forces also withdraw.
— We have declared that we would retain no military bases.
— We have begun to reduce our presence in South Vietnam by setting in motion the replacement of over 60,000 U.S. troops (twelve percent of total troops, or twenty percent of combat troops). This is a meaningful act of deescalation.
— We have emphasized to our military commanders the requirement that losses be held to an absolute minimum, consistent with their mission to protect Allied forces and the civilian population.
(Casualties in the first nine months of this administration are one-third less than during the comparable period last year.)

Political Conditions
For the first time, concrete and comprehensive political proposals for the settlement of the war have been made:
— We have proposed free elections organized by joint commissions under international supervision.
— We and the government of South Vietnam have announced that we are prepared to accept any political outcome which is arrived at through free elections.
— We have offered to negotiate supervised cease fires under international supervision to facilitate the process of withdrawal.
— We have expressed willingness to discuss the ten-point program of the other side, together with plans to be put forward by the other parties.

In short, the only item which has been declared non-negotiable is the right of the people of South Vietnam to determine their future, free of outside interference.

Progress made to date in Vietnam:

— The enemy was unable to launch the summer offensive which everyone predicted for this year.
— The infiltration rate is down by two-thirds (which means that the possibility of an offensive this fall has receded).
— Casualties for the first nine months of this year are down one-third, as I indicated.
— The South Vietnamese army is larger, stronger, and more well-equipped.
— The influence of the government of South Vietnam has expanded substantially throughout the countryside. That government has made significant progress in coping with its domestic problems.

That is what is happening in Vietnam. There's a constructive program. What do the marchers in the Moratorium offer in place of that? Nothing. Absolutely nothing except an emotional bath for the people of the United States and this country can't afford to be torn to pieces by that kind of demonstrating in the streets.

Let us turn for a moment to a legitimate complaint of our young people — the draft.

The draft, at best, is a necessary evil — one that President Nixon wants to do away with as soon as possible. But while the draft is still necessary, our government has a moral obligation to make it as fair and as reasonable as possible. Our failure to do so mocks the ideals we profess so often.

What is it that makes our draft system so *unfair* and so *unreasonable*?

Essentially, there are two problems: first — the present system creates for our young men a long period of draft vulnerability, one which begins at age nineteen and stretches for seven long years — unless the young man is drafted sooner. During this time, his educational plans, his career, even his decisions concerning marriage and family are distorted by his inability to predict the impact of the draft. All of this constitutes a terrible pressure, a dark shadow which falls across the lives of young Americans at the very time when they should be greeting the opportunities of adulthood with the greatest sense of excitement and adventure.

Prolonged uncertainty is one problem with the draft. Unfair selection is the second. Though all are technically vulnerable to the draft, those who are able to go on to college and then into certain graduate programs or occupations are often able to escape induction. In short, the current draft system creates frustration and mocks justice; it is both unfair and unreasonable.

This is not my opinion alone. It is widely shared — by members of all age groups in all parts of the country. Two panels composed of distinguished citizens — one headed by General Mark Clark and one headed by Mr. Burke Marshall — have reached the same conclusion in recent years. So have the many leaders of both parties in the House and Senate.

Months ago President Nixon took the lead in the battle to reform the draft. On May 13, 1969, he sent a message to the Congress in which he asked that body to reduce the period of prime vulnerability from seven years to one year and to institute a fair, random-selection system. Under this arrangement, everyone would be eligible for the draft at age nineteen and would be randomly assigned a place in the order of call at that time. He would remain in a condition of prime eligibility for twelve months. If he were not drafted in twelve months, he would move into less vulnerable categories. Those who chose to take a deferment at age nineteen, to go on to college, for example, would do so knowing where they fell in that order of call and could plan their lives accordingly. They would then spend their year in the prime vulnerability group at the time they left school.

Few of the President's statements have brought more favorable reaction than his suggestions for reforming the draft. Despite the widespread dissatisfaction with the draft and despite the widespread praise which greeted the President's message — the Congress waited until this week to act. The House Armed Services Committee this week unanimously reported the bill favorably, and early House action is expected. Senate action will depend on prompt attention by Senator Stennis' Committee.

As Secretary Laird recently explained, all that is necessary is that one sentence be changed in the current draft law, a sentence introduced as a last-minute afterthought back in 1967. This single sentence now prevents the President from switching to the random-selection process. Now if they just take care of this one problem, if Congress takes care of that, the President can avoid doing it by administrative order which would eliminate the systematic inequity by scrambling the 365 days of the year and rearranging them so that birthdays fell randomly and the oldest in that year would not have to be taken. This is clearly the fairest system.

Certainly this is the time for the people to join the President in making their desires felt in this matter of draft reform. For if reform is frustrated, it will be a defeat not only for the President, but for the Democratic process. Above all it will be a retreat from the principles of reason and justice which we value so highly in this country, principles which we preach with great ardor to our young people, but which we have not yet achieved in our selective service legislation.

Among the inaccurate tirades against the present foreign policy of the United States is an oft-repeated allegation that we are mostly at fault for the strategic arms race with Russia.

If we examine the record of the past few years, it is quite clear that the United States has exercised considerable restraint in its strategic weapons programs, probably more than was prudent. Now, just listen carefully to these facts. You have heard it said on many occasions by Senators and Congressmen, for both parties, that the United States is responsible for this arms race.These are the facts:

— We built up to a force of about 1,000 ICBMs by mid-1967 and held it there;
— We began building the last of our forty-one ballistic missile submarines in 1965 and we have built none since;
— Even though President Kennedy was being pressed to deploy an ABM system as early as 1961, the U.S. refrained from a decision to deploy an ABM until 1967. And that was the time President Johnson suggested the Sentinel system. However, because of pressure, it was decided to modify the previous administration's ABM system to emphasize further that the U.S. deployment was not intended to be provocative to the Soviet Union, so we got the Safeguard system.
— We have stretched out a decision to deploy a new manned bomber for nearly a decade.

The Soviet Union's record should be judged against this background of U.S. restraint.

— The Soviets have already deployed sixty-four ABMs, and they are pursuing an active ABM development program today; they have more ABMs today than we will have by 1974, if the Safeguard program goes forward as planned;
— Their recent SS-9 tests with multiple warheads suggest that they are also pursuing a MIRV system; a development which is of grave concern to us;
— They have several ICBMs in development and production and have overcome our lead in deployed ICBMs; already this year they have started construction on upwards of 100 new ICBMs, and they show no signs of slacking off;
— They are continuing to build and deploy ballistic missile submarines and test new missiles for them;
— They are continuing to build up their air defense systems;
— They are developing mobile missile systems which move these ICBMs around the countryside.

In summary, they are active across the board in developing and deploying strategic systems.

Interest in arms control cannot be one-sided. It takes two sides to have a competition. I believe our record is clearly one of restraint. Moreover, since this administration took office, we have studied in detail every aspect of limiting strategic weapons.

— For example, for many weeks we have had a panel of experts examining in depth the possibilities and pitfalls in limiting the development and deployment of MIRVs.
— We have had another panel doing a detailed study of U.S. intelligence capabilities and our ability to verify compliance with an arms control agreement.

These studies have shown that clear cutoff points are very difficult to establish. For example, it would not be enough simply to ban MIRV testing in order to stop MIRV deployment. We would have to have collateral restrictions on the testing of most space and weapons systems involving multiple or maneuvering objects in order to have confidence that MIRV deployment was in fact banned. This makes a unilateral moratorium very risky.

Complex questions such as these cannot be resolved overnight. We look forward to discussing strategic arms limitation issues with the Soviet Union. We have asked them in April to set up a date for the talks. We asked them again in July to set a date for the talks.

We are still waiting to begin those talks on strategic arms limitations.

We gain nothing, and the prospects for successful negotiations are not advanced one iota by restraints which are not reciprocated. Why should the Soviet Union bargain seriously with us if they can have what they want without paying any price whatever? We would be playing Russian roulette with U.S. security if we failed to take the minimum essential steps to maintain our security.

Finally, we are beset with the accusation that this administration is insensitive to domestic needs; that we are not spending enough on the problems of the poor; and that we, in fact, do not have a domestic program.

The decisions and actions of this administration, since it came to office on January 20th, have been conditioned by the economic environment that we inherited. By Inauguration Day, 1969, the federal government had run for eight years an unbroken string of budget deficits that added more than $78 billion to the federal debt. The impact of these deficits on the national economy was far reaching.

By this past January, price inflation had been generated and propelled to the point where the cost of living was surging upward at a rate of five per cent a year. These price increases, coupled with tax increases, meant that the average American workingman had made no gain at all in real income in more than three years. For those below the national average — the Americans who live on pensions or fixed income — these three years had been even more difficult. These Americans were worse off economically in terms of real income in January of 1969 than they had been in December of 1965 — despite the growth in the economy.

The imperatives of this economic situation dictated to a great extent our legislative and administrative priorities.

We made initial cuts of some $4 billion in the proposed 1970 fiscal year budget. Later we made additional cuts of more than $4 billion to hold to our spending ceiling of $192.9 billion for this fiscal year. A short, tight leash on federal spending is the most effective means of controlling inflation — we are going to continue to use that leash.

We recommended an orderly phase-out of the surtax at the full ten percent for the second half of 1969 and at five percent for the first six months of calendar year 1970. Congress has so far only granted the first and most vital part of this request. We ordered a cutback of seventy-five percent in all federal construction; we have asked the states to cut back construction as much as they can; we have followed the restrained and restrictive monetary policy which our precarious economic situation requires.

While controversial and unpopular, I will agree, in the short-run to many Americans, these measures are essential to the long-run stability and security of the economy on which the well-being of the public sector and the private sector ultimately depend.

Even with a tight budget leaving little room for fiscal maneuver, we have come forward with legislative initiatives that break new ground in half a dozen areas that entail historic reform in others, and that will enable us to test a philosophy of government that rejects the old centralism that guided federal policy for most of the past four decades.

Among our recommendations to this first session of the Ninety-First Congress are:

1. The most extensive overhaul of the welfare system since the beginning of the New Deal. What a failure that welfare system has been. Just this week, we read that in the City of New York alone, there has been a $66 million waste of welfare money by giving it to people who are not even eligible to receive it under the AFDC program.

2. The beginning of a historic redistribution of power from the national capital to the state capitals and city halls through a sharing of federal income tax revenues with the states. Now I will agree that everyone talked about that for a long time, but this is the first time a President of the United States and administration have ever submitted legislation which will permit this revenue sharing to take place to reach within five years the level of $5 billion.

3. The first major reform of the Federal Tax Code in fifty years.

4. The first major reform of the Selective Service System since conscription became a permanent part of American life in 1948.

5. A major attack on organized crime and the narcotics traffic.

6. A concerted national effort to eliminate the vestiges of hunger and malnutrition from our national life.

7. Replacement of the 189-year-old United States Post Office Department with a government-owned corporation operating on business principles rather than political patronage.

8. The most extensive federal commitment to mass transit and aviation in history, a level of $10 billion in new spending for mass transit within the next twelve years.

Taken together, these recommendations represent our best judgment as to the priority of the competing and legitimate claims on the federal government. This is our assessment of where existing federal resources can best be distributed for the good of the country. If our diplomatic policies can produce an honorable peace in Asia, and our economic policies can halt inflation in the economy, we shall be able to take up at once other urgent needs of our people.

Great patriots of past generations would find it difficult to believe that Americans would ever doubt the validity of America's resolve to protect free men from totalitarian attack. Yet today we see those among us who prefer to side with an enemy aggressor rather than stand by this free nation. We see others who are shortsighted enough to believe that we need not protect ourselves from attack by governments that depend upon force to control their people — governments which came into being through force alone and continue to exist by force alone.

I do not want to see this nation spend one dollar more on defense than is absolutely necessary, but I would hate to see this nation spend one dollar less on defense than is absolutely necessary. Until the principle of open representative government exists among all nations, the United States must not abandon its moral obligation to protect by any means necessary the freedoms so hard won by past generations. The freedoms so hard won by the 400,000 Americans who made the ultimate sacrifice in dedicated belief that some things are more precious than life itself.

October 20, 1969, Jackson, Mississippi
Mississippi Republican Dinner

THANK YOU very much Dr. Moy, and thank you ladies and gentlemen. Both for that extremely warm reception and for the historic brick that came from the Church of the Redeemer and for that beautiful painting which I assure you that Mrs. Agnew and I will treasure. We are delighted to have it, and it will find a place of honor in our apartment. I wish we could hang it in the governor's mansion, but we don't have one with us any more.

Governor Williams, Reverend Clergy, Mr. Reed, Mr. Monger, Mr. LaRue, distinguished public officials of the state of Mississippi, the many distinguished guests we have sitting in the audience and the very gracious citizens of this fine state who have done us honor tonight.

It is good to be here on a happy occasion. My last trip to Mississippi — a few days after that terribly destructive storm had slammed into your coastal area — was not a pleasant one. Yet, in spite of the sadness and the shock I saw reflected in the faces of the people who met me at Gulfport, there was also an unmistakable attitude of quiet confidence and courage. Your public officials and private agencies deserve commendation for their magnificent response to a real crisis.

I want to say that I'm simply overwhelmed with the magnitude of this reception tonight, and I want to express my personal appreciation to Billy Monger and to the many people who are members of the Key Club and, in fact, to everyone here who is participating in this dinner tonight. I particularly want to thank my good personal friend, your governor, John Bell Williams, for his presence here under what might be characterized as rather unusual bipartisan circumstances.

And in the same bipartisan spirit, governor, I want to say to you that you deserve the commendations of the people of Mississippi and indeed the accolade of the entire nation for the way in which you pulled your state together in the face of a great natural disaster. The Governor's Emergency Council will stand as a tribute to the organizational abilities of your office for many years and I'm certain will provide for similar efforts as similar disasters must unfortunately strike this nation from time to time.

I also want to make a particular acknowledgement to Clark Reed, your chairman, whom as you already heard, is not just another chairman. He is one of the most important chairmen in the Republican Party in this country. He is a person to whom the President and his advisors and, of course, I listen to with rapt attention. Mainly because we don't get a lot of chin music out of Clark. We hear the truth even though it hurts sometimes.

After I talked to Governor Williams by phone shortly before the hurricane struck, and at the time it came, we were rather surprised that the course had deviated, and the hurricane came ashore where it did. We were expecting it in the area of Louisiana. I checked back and decided a few days after the crisis I should come down and review it firsthand. The President suggested that I do that and Governor Williams, Senator Stennis, Secretary of HUD Romney, and other officials met us at the airport. Some of us made a helicopter inspection of the coast. The devastation was almost unbelievable.

Soon thereafter the President asked me for a personal report, a detailed report, and I gave him the facts as I saw them. Believe me it would have been hard to exaggerate. He took immediate steps to correct deficiencies in our warning system and instructed me to move in every way to relieve the victims of the storm. His visit to Mississippi on September 8th demonstrated his concern, and the actions that he has directed show that the trip was not an empty gesture.

The President has allocated an estimated $60 million from the President's disaster fund for Mississippi alone. In addition, twenty federal agencies have mobilized men and money to assist the victims of Camille. The Corps of Engineers has moved 374,000 tons of debris and will spend before this clearance job is over $17 million. The military sent in 8,900 troops. The Third Army served 164,000 meals. The Department of Housing and Urban Development has supplied more than 1,600 mobile homes. The Small Business Administration anticipates providing $140 million in loans. The Department of Agriculture, Mr. Undersecretary, is delivering over 5.5 million pounds of food. We have and will continue to help Mississippi recover and rebuild.

I know that in spite of the magnitude of those efforts everything is not just perfect at the present time. After a storm of this magnitude, after a disaster of that scope, it is very difficult to have everything work out perfectly. But I can assure you one thing that with the help of the Governor's Emergency Council and the great organization here in Mississippi, and the dedication and conviction of the national administration to solve this crisis, we will continue to attack it until it does get solved and it is as perfect as humans can make it.

Speaking of rebuilding, one incident that occurred during my inspection trip, I must confess, irritated me considerably. At a news conference, I was asked to comment on the statement of an HEW official to the effect that no federal funds would be provided to rebuild schools which HEW decided were in violation of its desegration guidelines. Not only was this gratuitous determination by a minor official repugnant as an example of overbearing bureaucracy, but it was an insensitive slap at a people already reeling from a natural disaster.

I can assure you that that official has been disciplined and encouraged to correct the errors of his ways.

Now let me make it very clear at this point that this administration will never appeal to a racist philosophy. Every American is entitled to assessment on his personal merit regardless of his race or religion. However, a free government cannot impose rules of social acceptance upon its citizens. Just so I won't be misunderstood by the pundits who read so many things into my speeches I don't say I mean that to be social acceptance between members of the same race or religion or between members of different races and religions. The point is this — in a man's private life he has the right to make his own friends. Unfortunately, the legitimate cause of civil rights, a cause that I've fought very hard for in my state both as a county official and as a governor, has been all too frequently diverted, and even perverted, in this direction.

Very shortly the Supreme Court will consider a case involving desegregation of Mississippi schools. President Nixon is convinced that your public officials have made a strong case for additional time to implement the law without destroying quality education. The NAACP disagrees and has brought this case to compel immediate action. It is hoped that the result will provide a sensible solution.

Much has been made of the Nixon Administration's attitude toward the Southern states — mostly by the Northeastern liberal community. They've accused us of something, as you heard tonight, they call "The Southern Strategy." We have no Southern Strategy. We do have a conviction that the people of the United States, irrespective of their point of geographic residence, have an inherent right to be treated evenhandedly by their government.

For too long the South has been the punching bag for those who characterize themselves as liberal intellectuals. Actually, they are consistently demonstrating the antithesis of intelligence. Their reactions are visceral, not intellectual; and they seem to believe that truth is revealed rather than systematically proved. These arrogant ones and their admirers in the Congress, who reach almost for equal arrogance at times, are bringing this nation to the most important decision it will ever have to make. They are asking us to repudiate principles that have made this country great. Their course is one of applause for our enemies and condemnation for our leaders. Their course is a course that will ultimately weaken and erode the very fibre of America. They have a masochistic compulsion to destroy their country's strength whether or not that strength is exercised constructively. And they rouse themselves into a continual emotional crescendo — substituting disruptive demonstration for reason and precipitate action for persuasion.

This group may consider itself liberal, but it is undeniable that it is more comfortable with radicals. These people use the word "compassion" as if they invented it. "Compassion" is their weapon and their shield. But they apply compassion selectively. Crime is excused only when the criminal is "disadvantaged."

They're equally selective as reformers. Waste in the Pentagon is a national outrage. Waste in welfare and poverty programs is a matter to be overlooked. Ladies and gentlemen, if you don't think that there is waste in welfare programs just read your paper, and you'll find that a recent General Accounting Office survey uncovered the fact that $66 million in benefits were paid to people unqualified to receive them. This group I talk about is undeniably the group most likely to succeed with the SDS. Both groups proclaim their instant expertise. They both think that anybody with a contrary opinion is stupid. Both spend endless hours telling us what's wrong with America and neither offers constructive ideas on how to right those wrongs.

This is the group that believes in marching down the streets of America to protest the war in Vietnam to our President. They would never think of protesting the continuation of this war to the government that is actually continuing it — the government of Hanoi.

Finally these leaders on the New Left would have America abdicate its position of leadership throughout the world. The fact that this position of leadership was conferred — in trust and in respect — by the smaller and less powerful nations does not bother these men one whit. They would have us renounce our commitments and repudiate the 400,-000 American lives sacrificed to the cause of world peace during this century. They would have America turn inward and vegetate in splendid isolation.

255

These are the ideas of the men who are taking control of the national Democratic party.

And I suppose that's pretty much the reason why this is such a bipartisan dinner tonight.

I don't believe that the people of Mississippi want to travel that road. I don't even believe that the distinguished senior Democratic officials of Mississippi want to travel that road. Men like John Stennis and Jim Eastland have fought with great determination in Washington to preserve the strength and stability of this country. Often they have aligned themselves with the Republican party on important national issues. But they are too few and they cannot be effective as part of a national Democratic policy which has steered their party on a runaway course to the left.

That's why it is good to see so many people thinking Republican tonight. From what I was led to believe, Republican dinners in the Deep South didn't attract too many people, it seemed that the party loyal from ten counties might assemble and still have room for the rest of the state's Republicans . . . in the phone booth.

But I think this turnout proves definitely that some of Washington's political pundits are wrong. Before I came down here, one told me that Southern voters won't listen to Republicans . . . Southern voters won't support Republicans . . . and Southerners won't vote Republican . . . and he told me he was *never* wrong. And then he drove off in his Edsel.

The Republican party has faith in America. We see no gain in tearing this country down when we have so much to build. We may not agree with "participatory democracy," but we do understand civic involvement. We believe that the citizen should be in command of his community, we believe that civil rights must be balanced by civil responsibilities. And above all we remember that this country is a constitutional republic which elects its leaders to *lead* and not to placate the most vocal critics of the moment.

In my judgment, the principles of most of the people of Mississippi are the principles of the Republican party. Since the policy makers of the other party have repudiated these principles, does it not make sense that Mississippi should become a strong state in the Republican column? It not only makes sense, but it's happening. The success of this gathering proves beyond question that it is happening.

The Republican party does not believe that bigger government can masquerade as better government. It is time to call a halt to the charade that adds ten percent more bureaucrats to the public payroll and fifteen percent more spending to the federal budget and claims that these are answers to national problems.

Where previous administrations would spend money, we change systems. Where previous administrations advocate better answers manufactured in the White House, we provide resources to manufacture answers in the statehouse, the county courthouse and city hall. Where previous administrations did a lot of crying about lawlessness, the President is proposing legislation which handcuffs the criminal instead of the police.

To counter crime the President has nominated strict contructionists of the constitution to the Supreme Court. Chief Justice Burger now presides. And I am confident that Judge Clement Haynsworth will join him.

And I do not know what you have read about Judge Haynsworth down here. But I do know that he is a competent jurist and an honest man. A committee of the American Bar Association has reviewed the Haynsworth appointment and has endorsed and reendorsed it.

There is only one conclusion from the facts. Judge Haynsworth is not guilty of any impropriety — unless that impropriety is his place of birth and residence. The tragedy of the Haynsworth controversy is not the shadow it casts upon the Supreme Court, but the shadow it casts upon the motivation of some who have raised these various charges against him.

But this incident, ladies and gentlemen, is a comment on the tactics of our times. When a man makes an unpopular decision . . . or it's suspected that he may make an unpopular decision . . . he is subject to attack. If there is no basis in fact for the attack, suspicion will do. If there is no rational objection to the man, muddy him with insinuation and innuendo.

Well, this is frightening. This is alien to everything that we proudly call American. This

256

is why the country calls out for principled leadership. And this is why there's new life in the Republican party.

The Republican party has a place for every American who believes that flag-waving is better than flag burning.

The Republican party is making a pitch for every American who wants peace but refuses to be deluded that a dishonorable surrender to the bullies of the world can help achieve peace.

We look at law as inseparable from justice and we won't apologize for upholding, enforcing and respecting the laws of this land.

The Republican Party is the place for every American who cares for his fellowman — not by shouting from a street corner — but in the deeply personal sense of seeing that no man goes hungry, no child goes uneducated, no person grows old in poverty.

I believe that most of the people of Mississippi now belong in the Republican party. Further, I believe they can do the most good for Mississippi and for America in the Republican party.

A one-party system invites corruption. It is conducive to politics-as-usual and government-by-crony. A one-party system might be good for foreign dictators, but it has no place here.

This country thrives on competition. Competition in business means the best product at the lowest cost to the consumer. Competition in politics means the best government at the lowest cost to the taxpayers.

Now in closing, I'd like to leave you with a story about Senator Howard Baker. Tennessee used to be almost as strongly Democratic as Mississippi until men like Howard Baker took, quite literally, to the hills to sell the Republican party.

As Senator Baker was campaigning in the back country, he encountered an old man who listened thoughtfully to all he had to say. At the end of the rally, the old man approached the young senator and said, "You know, I've always voted Democratic because I think that's the way my grandfather would have wanted me to. But now I'm going to vote Republican because I think that's the way my grandson would want me to."

The time of our grandfathers is past. . . . But were those proud old men here today, they would probably have already reregistered Republican.

The time of our grandsons will soon be here. . . . Let us use our vote to make America a worthwhile legacy for them.

October 30, 1969, Harrisburg, Pennsylvania
Pennsylvania Republican Dinner

A LITTLE over a week ago, I took a rather unusual step for a Vice President . . . I said something. Particularly, I said something that was predictably unpopular with the people who would like to run this country without the inconvenience of seeking public office. I said I did not like some of the things I saw happening in this country. I criticized those who encouraged government by street carnival and suggested it was time to stop the carousel.

It appears that by slaughtering a sacred cow I triggered a holy war. I have no regrets. I do not intend to repudiate my beliefs, recant my words, or run and hide.

What I said before, I will say again. It is time for the preponderant majority, the responsible citizens of this country, to assert *their* rights. It is time to stop dignifying the immature actions of an arrogant, reckless, inexperienced element within our society. The reason is compelling. It is simply that their tantrums are insidiously destroying the fabric of American democracy.

By accepting unbridled protest as a way of life, we have tacitly suggested that the great issues of our times are best decided by posturing and shouting matches in the streets. America today is drifting toward Plato's classic definition of a degenerating democracy . . . a democracy that permits the voice of the mob to dominate the affairs of government.

Last week I was lambasted for my lack of "mental and moral sensitivity." I say that any leader who does not perceive where persistent street struggles are going to lead this nation lacks mental acuity. And any leader who does not caution this nation on the danger of this direction lacks moral strength.

Now let me make it clear, I believe in Constitutional dissent. I believe in the people registering their views with their elected representatives, and I commend those people who care enough about their country to involve themselves in its great issues. I believe in legal dissent within the Constitutional limits of free speech, including peaceful assembly and the right of petition. But I do not believe that demonstrations, lawful or unlawful, merit my approval or even my silence where the purpose is fundamentally unsound. In the case of the Vietnam Moratorium, the objective announced by the leaders — immediate unilateral withdrawal of all our forces from Vietnam — was not only unsound but idiotic. The tragedy was that thousands who participated wanted only to show a fervent desire for peace, but were used — yes, used — by the political hustlers who ran the event.

It is worth remembering that our country's founding fathers wisely shaped a constitutional republic, not a pure democracy. The representative government they contemplated and skillfully constructed never intended that elected officials should decide crucial issues by counting the number of bodies cavorting in the streets. They recognized that freedom cannot endure dependent upon referendum every time part of the electorate desires it.

So great is the latitude of our liberty that only a subtle line divides use from abuse. I am convinced that our preoccupation with emotional demonstration, frequently crossing the line to civil disruption and even violence could inexorably lead us across that line forever.

Ironically, it is neither the greedy nor the malicious, but the self-righteous who are guilty of history's worst atrocities. Society understands greed and malice and erects barriers of law to defend itself from these vices. But evil cloaked in emotional causes is well disguised and often undiscovered before it is too late.

We have just such a group of self-proclaimed saviours of the American soul at work today. Relentless in their criticism of intolerance in America, they themselves are intolerant of those who differ with their views. In the name of academic freedom, they destroy academic freedom. Denouncing violence, they seize and vandalize buildings of great universities. Fiercely expressing their respect for truth, they disavow the logic and discipline necessary to pursue truth.

They would have us believe that they alone know what is good for America; what is true and right and beautiful. They would have us believe that their reflective action is superior to our reflective action; that their revealed righteousness is more effective than our reason and experience.

Think about it. Small bands of students are allowed to shut down great universities. Small groups of dissidents are allowed to shout down political candidates. Small cadres of professional protesters are allowed to jeopardize the peace efforts of the President of the United States.

It is time to question the credentials of their leaders. And, if in questioning we disturb a few people, I say it is time for them to be disturbed. If, in challenging, we polarize the American people, I say it is time for a positive polarization.

It is time for a healthy in-depth examination of policies and a constructive realignment in this country. It is time to rip away the rhetoric and to divide on authentic lines. It is time to discard the fiction that in a country of 200 million people, everyone is qualified to quarterback the government.

For too long we have accepted superficial categorization — young versus old; white versus black; rich versus poor. Now it is time for an alignment based on principles and values shared by all citizens regardless of age, race, creed, or income. This, after all, is what America is all about.

America's pluralistic society was forged on the premise that what unites us in ideals is greater than what divides us as individuals. Our political and economic institutions were developed to enable men and ideas to compete in the marketplace on the assumption that the best would prevail. Everybody was deemed equal, and by the rules of the game they could become superior. The rules were clear and fair: in politics, win an election; in economics, build a better mousetrap. And as time progressed, we added more referees to assure equal opportunities and provided special advantages for those whom we felt had entered life's arena at a disadvantage.

The majority of Americans respect these rules . . . and with good reason. Historically, they have served as a bulwark to prevent totalitarianism, tyranny, and privilege . . . the old world spectres which drove generations of immigrants to American sanctuary. Pragmatically, the rules of America work. This nation and its citizens — collectively and individually — have made more social, political and economic progress than any civilization in world history.

The principles of the American system did not spring up overnight. They represent centuries of bitter struggle. Our laws and institutions are not even purely American — only our federal system bears our unique imprimatur.

We owe our values to the Judeo–Christian ethic which stresses individualism, human dignity, and a higher purpose than hedonism. We owe our laws to the political evolution of government by consent of the governed. Our nation's philosophical heritage is as diverse as its cultural background. We are a melting pot nation that has for over two centuries distilled something new and, I believe, sacred.

Now, we have among us a glib, activist element who would tell us our values are lies, and I call them impudent. Because anyone who impugns a legacy of liberty and dignity that reaches back to Moses, is impudent.

I call them snobs for most of them disdain to mingle with the masses who work for a living. They mock the common man's pride in his work, his family and his country. It has also been said that I called them intellectuals. I did not. I said that they characterized themselves as intellectuals. No true intellectual, no truly knowledgeable person, would so despise democratic institutions.

America cannot afford to write off a whole generation for the decadent thinking of a few. America cannot afford to divide over their demagoguery . . . or to be deceived by their duplicity . . . or to let their license destroy liberty. We can, however, afford to separate them from our society — with no more regret than we should feel over discarding rotten apples from a barrel.

The leaders of this country have a moral as well as a political obligation to point out the dangers of unquestioned allegiance to any cause. We must be better than a charlatan leader of the French Revolution, remembered only for his words: "There go the people; I am their leader; I must follow them."

And the American people have an obligation, too . . . an obligation to exercise their citizenship with a precision that precludes excesses.

I recognize that many of the people who participated in the past Moratorium Day were unaware that its sponsors sought immediate unilateral withdrawal. Perhaps many more had not considered the terrible consequences of immediate unilateral withdrawal.

I hope that all citizens who truly want peace will take the time to read and reflect on the problem. I hope that they will take into consideration the impact of abrupt termination; that they will remember the more than 3,000 innocent men, women, and children slaughtered after the Viet Cong captured Hue last year and the more than 15,000 doctors, nurses, teachers and village leaders murdered by the Viet Cong during the war's early years. The only sin of these people was their desire to build their budding nation of South Vietnam.

Chanting "Peace Now" is no solution, if "Peace Now" is to permit a wholesale blood-bath. And saying that the President should understand the people's view is no solution. It is time for the people to understand the views of the President they elected to lead them.

First, foreign policy cannot be made in the streets.

Second, turning out a good crowd is not synonymous with turning out a good foreign policy.

Third, the test of a President cannot be reduced to a question of public relations. As the eighteenth-century jurist, Edmund Burke, wrote, "Your representative owes you not his industry only but his judgment; and he betrays instead of serving you, if he sacrifices it to your opinion."

Fourth, the impatience — the understandable frustration over this war — should be focused on the government that is stalling peace while continuing to threaten and invade South Vietnam — and that government's capital is not in Washington. It is in Hanoi.

This was not Richard Nixon's war . . . but it will be Richard Nixon's peace if we only let him make it.

Finally — and most important — regardless of the issue, it is time to stop demonstrating in the streets and start doing something constructive about our institutions. America must recognize the danger of constant carnival. Americans must reckon with irresponsible leadership and reckless words. The mature and sensitive people of this country must realize that their freedom of protest is being exploited by avowed anarchists and commu-nists — yes, I say communist because a member of one of those committees is a member of the communist party and proud of it — who detest everything about this country and want to destroy it.

This is a fact. These are the few . . . these are not necessarily all the leaders. But they prey upon the good intentions of gullible men everywhere. They pervert honest concern to something sick and rancid. They are vultures who sit in trees and watch lions battle, knowing that win, lose or draw, they will be fed.

Abetting the merchants of hate are the parasites of passion. These are the men who value a cause purely for its political mileage. These are the politicians who temporize with the truth by playing both sides to their own advantage. They ooze sympathy for "the cause" but balance each sentence with equally reasoned reservations. Their interest is personal, not moral. They are ideological eunuchs whose most comfortable position is straddling the philosophical fence, soliciting votes from both sides.

Aiding the few who seek to destroy and the many who seek to exploit is a terrifying spirit, the new face of self-righteousness. Former HEW Secretary John Gardner described it: "Sad to say, it's fun to hate . . . that is today's fashion. Rage and hate in a good cause! Be vicious for virtue, self-indulgent for higher purposes, dishonest in the service of a higher honesty."

This is what is happening in this nation . . . we are an effete society if we let it happen here.

I do not overstate the case. If I am aware of the danger, the convicted rapist Eldridge Cleaver is aware of the potential. From his Moscow hotel room he predicted, "Many complacent regimes thought that they would be in power eternally — and awoke one morning to find themselves up against the wall. I expect that to happen in the United States in our lifetimes."

People cannot live in a state of perpetual electric shock. Tired of a convulsive society, they settle for an authoritarian society. As Thomas Hobbes discerned three centuries ago, men will seek the security of a Leviathan state as a comfortable alternative to a life that is "nasty, brutish, and short."

Right now we must decide whether we will take the trouble to stave off a totalitarian state. Will we stop the wildness now before it is too late, before the witch-hunting and repression that are all to inevitable begin?

Will Congress settle down to the issues of the nation and reform the institutions of

America as our President asks? Can the press ignore the pipers who lead the parades? Will the head of great universities protect the rights of all their students? Will parents have the courage to say no to their children? Will people have the intelligence to boycott pornography and violence? Will citizens refuse to be led by a series of Judas goats down tortuous paths of delusion and self-destruction?

Will we defend fifty centuries of accumulated wisdom? For that is our heritage. Will we make the effort to preserve America's bold, successful experiment in truly representative government? Or do we care so little that we will casually toss it all aside?

Because on the eve of our nation's 200th birthday, we have reached the crossroads. Because at this moment totalitarianism's threat does not necessarily have a foreign accent. Because we have a home-grown menace, made and manufactured in the U.S.A. Because if we are lazy or foolish, this nation could forfeit its integrity, never to be free again.

I do not want this to happen to America. And I do not think that you do either. We have something magnificent here . . . something worth fighting for . . . and now is the time for all good men to fight for the soul of their country. Let us stop apologizing for our past. Let us conserve and create for the future.

November 11, 1969, Philadelphia, Pennsylvania
National Municipal League

FROM ITS birth, the National Municipal League has been consecrated to the concept of a dynamic American democracy where citizenship is an exacting obligation; government, a service; and politics, an honorable profession.

The founders of the National Municipal League understood that the citizen was central to the system. In a time of political corruption, they retained their faith in democratic institutions. They were reformers, *not* radicals . . . and, as reformers, they would stand apart from many in the present generation of critics because of their insistence that failure was not the fault of the system, but the citizen.

In a dissertation on the causes of young radical dissent, the distinguished University of Michigan professor, John W. Aldridge, states: "Although the necessity for reform is the ostensible and conscious reason for their protests, one notices how vague the militants are about the precise nature of the measures they wish to be taken; how much more articulate they are in the demands for confrontation than they are about the concrete issues of confrontation."

Charles J. Bonaparte expressed the prerequisites of reform very well: "If you wish to secure for the community a better government, you must make the community deserve a better government, and show it deserves it by getting it."

Men like Theodore Roosevelt, Charles Shurz, Charles Eliot and Louis Brandeis, who founded the Municipal League, and you, who carry it forward today, know that workable democracy will not appear on demand, but must be deserved. Freedom is earned, not given. Citizenship involves more than voting and paying taxes. Reform requires a positive program. What held true when the National Municipal League was formed seventy-five years ago, hold true today. Progress is predicated upon the existence of constructive alternatives to replace what is being discredited and abandoned. It is not enough to see corruption and to condemn it. Work must begin — not end — with a call to "throw the rascals out."

And the work of the National Municipal League, as well as the work of its founders, began with faith in America — its system and citizens. Those men had deep, enduring confidence in the resiliency of our institutions and the destiny of our nation. One word could describe their attitude, and that word was patriotism.

It was not just jingoistic pride, but something far more profound, that inspired the vision of a Theodore Roosevelt and the perception of a Louis Brandeis. They were sophisticated men in the best sense, and they were "socially aware" by the best of contemporary standards.

Several years ago, a foreign student addressing a college seminar was asked about his future plans. The young man replied, "I want to return home to serve the country I love." Fellow students gave him a standing ovation.

But I wonder what the reaction would be if an American student at an American college announced that he loved his country? Would there be applause or embarrassment? I suspect that many have been conditioned to be embarrassed by such an overt expression of patriotic sentiment. I would guess that many in sophisticated America consider love of country gauche or irrelevant.

A double standard has emerged. We admire patriotism in others, but condemn it in ourselves. We seem to see everything about ourselves except what we have achieved. We forget that this nation fought a bloody war to secure freedom for an oppressed minority. We forget that this nation was conceived and has continued as an asylum for the world's oppressed. We overlook the fact that today our country remains the first choice among the world's immigrants.

Although we cannot be complacent about our faults, neither should we be apologetic about our strengths. Yet apology appears to be becoming our national posture. We have seen attempts to pervert the liberal virtue of self-criticism to the national vice of self-contempt.

Some weeks ago a professor named Robert Paul Wolf wrote in review of a book called *The Making of a Counter-Culture:* "American society is ugly, repressive, destructive and subversive of much that is truly human." He contended that this view of American society "is now acknowledged to be true by virtually every sensible man and woman." Now, most Americans, and certainly most sensible Americans, don't share that view.

The point is that while there is a lot wrong with America, there is a lot more right with America. Our strengths outweigh our problems. Our potential is vast, and the time we waste on negative introspection could be far better invested in positive action.

Just because America has not implemented all the ideals of the Declaration of Independence and the Constitution does not mean that we should stop trying. Our inadequacies should be a spur to improvement. If ever American society totally achieves its ideals, it will do so because those ideals have become unchallenging and ludicrously low. In the case of a self-renewing society, each generation establishes a new and higher set of ideals. Our notable failures should not diminish our noble aspirations, but rather fuel our determination to close the distance between what is and what should be.

While I concede that some of our institutions and establishments are in serious need of change, there is no reason to believe that our free system of government will in any way impede democratic responsiveness to this need. Today's dissidents misdirect their fire when they attack the system. They should instead use the system to reform the institutions and establishments.

To those who question the validity of our system, the answer is participation in the processes of democracy. To those who question the social worth of the free enterprise system, the answer is to make business more responsive to the problems of society. The alternative to alienation is involvement.

In speaking of the lack of pragmatic involvement of the young today, Professor Aldridge links it to a tranquil, undemanding personal life. Continuing, he says: "Difficulty brings more of our essential humanity into play than tranquillity does and so heightens our responsiveness to life."

Involvement is the theme of your convention, and it must become the goal of our nation.

Today I intend to focus on the rich potential of private involvement. I recognize that this audience is fully conversant with the substance and purpose of the President's domestic proposals to achieve "the new federalism." So I want to draw upon my past experience as a governor and county executive to cite some immediate problems which you can best solve.

The private sector has historic precedents for initiative. As far back as the dawn of written history, the private sector has always led. Education was a private institution before it was a public one. This was true in a broad sense of welfare and health, until the twentieth century. Only after private citizens discern and respond to needs does the public sector adopt or extend programs. This pattern continues today. Public kindergartens, day care and community health centers, are recent derivatives of private pilot projects. Your first challenge — as citizens — is to scrutinize institutions, isolate problems, and develop solutions.

The first item for action is education in citizenship. The foundation of good citizenship depends upon the inculcation of individual responsibility at an early age. There is little doubt that our generation has failed to carry out this basic requirement. In a devastating indictment of us as parents, Professor Aldridge castigates the permissive attitudes of post–World War II parents: "It is scarcely surprising that . . . the beneficiaries of all this love and attention and self-sacrifice should have grown up contemptuous of us, or convinced that really we were dead all along, and only they are alive. . . . So we taught them by our example and by our obsequious treatment of them to have no consideration or respect for adults and a grotesquely inflated respect for themselves."

Discipline is an essential precursor to self-discipline. Self-discipline is a prerequisite to productive citizenship. Since discipline and specific personal responsibility were not required in the home, imparting essentials of good citizenship was left to the schools.

I regret to say that the trend in early education was similarly not in the proper direction. There was downplay of competitive engagement among students and the way was all too frequently provided for the young student to avoid his responsibilities on the basis that he just wasn't up to them.

The centralization in junior high schools and high schools created an impersonal environment which did little to stimulate the warm interpersonal relationships conducive to citizen involvement. Added to this, there was a scarcity of formal teaching in the practicalities of citizen obligations. The curriculum was deemed adequate if it simply narrated the concept of our federal system. What it should have done was to make clear that no other system depends so heavily upon the participation of people. It should have stressed that a majority of observers on the sidelines will produce an inferior political leadership and an uninvolved electorate will be pawns for the manipulation of a minority of political activists.

It is time that we establish training in citizenship as an educational priority and set about investigating the means of making it an integral component in our educational process.

Not only our young, but our present generation of mature citizens, have much to learn about citizenship. In a recent survey made in Montgomery County, Maryland — a Washington suburb considered to be one of America's more educated and affluent subdivisions — two out of every three citizens could not name their county councilman. We cannot begin to talk about responsive government until we know whom we must hold responsible for governmental action or inaction.

In modern computer-oriented society, there are few severe shortages of reliable public information. However, there are formidable deficiencies in publicity and public relations techniques. And, fortunately or unfortunately, most of our citizens are conditioned to the dramatic Madison Avenue approach. Like it or not, the fact is that, until we produce a new generation of civic-oriented consumers, we can serve the total community best by following advertising techniques.

Skillful presentation will not betray the integrity of a school bond bill. It is not beneath a businessman's or a candidate's dignity to launch an attention-catching campaign, and neither should it be beneath the dignity of civic groups. As a governor, I saw the magnificent work of a constitutional convention — led by one of your council members — fail at the polls because of inability to excite the electorate. We stood by our principles and the usual public information resources. Our opponents stood by a good "fear and fury," hard-sell, radio campaign and defeated a superb document.

The media have a tremendous obligation here as well. I recognize that the subtleties of everyday government cannot compete with an axe murder. I know that reporters thrive on political controversy and publishers have to sell papers. But freedom should be tempered by responsibility. Great causes extolled on the editorial page are often lost by reporting strident opposition on the front page while supportive but less exciting news is buried somewhere between the tire advertisements and the obituary columns.

During Maryland's constitutional convention, debate over regional governmental provisions was dull until enlivened by an occasional outburst of irresponsible rhetoric from one of the convention's foes. In Baltimore County, a critical urban renewal loan became newsworthy as a result of the shenanigans of its opponents. The cumulative impact of controversy in daily dosages confuses and frightens the average voter.

Political participation remains the citizen's most effective lever. All too often citizens are reluctant to involve themselves in partisan politics. Entrepreneurs, who have never carried a precinct, have a condescending attitude toward politicians who have never met a payroll. Some think of politics as messy and believe that the best people should be above it. To say that politics is beneath us is to say that democracy is beneath us. A failure to participate in politics is a sign of ignorance, not innocence.

Anyone who does not work for good candidates is a dropout from democracy. He not only abdicates a basic responsibility; he neglects a major opportunity.

You know that I am an outspoken critic of disruptive politics, of provocative techniques and of that small percentage of Americans who advocate destruction of our system. I am also an enthusiastic supporter of responsible participation for the young. I have continuously urged lowering the voting age to eighteen. As governor of Maryland, I proposed a Graduate Corps — a comprehensive student internship program for state and local governments. With the cooperation of college leaders I was developing a Governor's Youth Advisory Council.

Right now I would wager that there are proportionately more young faces around the White House than around any city hall or county courthouse in the country. It is good business to draw new talent and energy into the governmental community, just as it is good business to draw the innovative ideas of youth into the industrial and professional communities.

We know that there is a silent majority in this country. This is the majority that President Nixon addressed on his Vietnam policy last week, and the majority which responded with such resounding support.

There is also a silent *young* majority who go to school, and to work, and to war, if necessary. There are the nonshouting concerned; the nonradical responsible; the noncomplacent constructive activists of the under-thirty generation. Their idealism is disciplined by reason.

The presence, integrity, and commitment of the silent young majority is overshadowed by the strident minority who arrogate unto themselves voice, virtue, and power out of proportion to their numbers and even more out of proportion to their abilities. The silent young majority must be recognized. They must be given outlets for their concern, opportunities for their ideas, and responsibilities equal to their capabilities. The silent young majority is challenged to make itself heard, to come to its own defense. And we — the older majority — are challenged to accommodate them within all our institutions.

The young American community wants to be involved. The American business community must be involved. It is time to think of industrial development in terms of human resources. Businessmen must be challenged to relate enterprise to environment — and profit to people.

America's most successful businesses are challenged to do more than share the wealth. We are asking them to share their know-how and their capital to stimulate minority businesses; we are requesting that they broaden their employment base. Our goal is to turn capitalists into catalysts — catalysts for moving those on welfare rolls onto payrolls, and for moving those already employed up the ladder.

Finally, there is the need for increased involvement of the citizen as a volunteer. Despite all the noise about America's selfish establishment, the facts prove that the silent majority is a deeply concerned and active majority. There are more than a million voluntary hospitals and private foundations — service organizations, civic groups, and fraternal clubs.

The Gallup poll has estimated that sixty-one million adult Americans would be willing to contribute 245 million man-hours every week to voluntary activities. There isn't a social problem that hasn't been solved sometime and somewhere in America. American volunteers have tutored dropouts, trained the unskilled, counseled juveniles, taught illiterates, and found jobs for the unemployed. In establishing the National Program for Voluntary Action, the President has provided a new way to tap and direct the talents of the public spirited citizen.

There is work in this country — great work for every individual. Because our potential is so great and our problems are so many, we cannot help but be impatient with unproductive idle protest.

The mob, the Mobilization, the Moratorium have become somewhat fashionable forms of citizen expression. But each suffers from the same flaws that prompted the founding of the National Municipal League. They are negative in content; disruptive in effect. They inflame emotions rather than stimulate solutions. Protest is every citizen's right, but that does not ensure that every protest is right. It simply protects every citizen's lawful protest, be it right or wrong.

Ultimately, the popularity of mass street demonstrations will wane just as we saw mass violence wane over the past year. And for the same reason — they are pointless. Turning out a few hundred thousand people in a nation of two hundred million proves nothing in the way of a public mandate. We can speed the demise of carnival in the streets by withholding our sympathy. We can blunt its adverse impact by seizing the initiative.

The body politic of America's not able to survive on adrenalin any better than apathy. We are a mature nation, which means that we should be able to navigate a moderate course without being trapped on the shoals of mediocrity.

This is the challenge of the decade ahead. It is very much your challenge. Now, as never before, we have the opportunity to turn the power of America to great humanitarian purposes. I believe that this nation has a moral obligation to prove the virtues of a free system and meet the exacting standards of free citizenship. If this is patriotism, it is also a spirit of positive action. It is a mandate for involvement and a means of restoring a sense of community to our people.

Unless we are united in spirit and dedicated to our system, we will languish and eventually backslide. It is our freedom that makes us respected throughout the world — not our wealth; and it is our regard for the freedom of others which makes us invincible — not our military strength.

Because the intolerant clamor and cacophony rage about us, let us not be afraid to raise our voices in spirited defense of the most successful society the world has yet known. In this time of danger, it is an alarm we sound — an alarm that must be audible to be heeded. I, for one, will not lower my voice until the restoration of sanity and civil order allow a quiet voice to be heard once again.

November 13, 1969, Des Moines, Iowa
Midwest Regional Republican Committee Meeting

TONIGHT I want to discuss the importance of the television news medium to the American people. No nation depends more on the intelligent judgment of its citizens. No medium has a more profound influence over public opinion. Nowhere in our system are there fewer checks on vast power. So, nowhere should there be more conscientious responsibility exercised than by the news media. The question is . . . are we demanding enough of our television news presentations? . . . And, are the men of this medium demanding enough of themselves?

Monday night, a week ago, President Nixon delivered the most important address of his administration, one of the most important of our decade. His subject was Vietnam. His hope was to rally the American people to see the conflict through to a lasting and just peace in the Pacific. For thirty-two minutes, he reasoned with a nation that has suffered almost a third of a million casualties in the longest war in its history.

When the President completed his address — an address that he spent weeks in preparing — his words and policies were subjected to instant analysis and querulous criticism. The audience of seventy million Americans — gathered to hear the President of the United States — was inherited by a small band of network commentators and self-appointed analysts, the *majority* of whom expressed, in one way or another, their hostility to what he had to say.

It was obvious that their minds were made up in advance. Those who recall the fumbling and groping that followed President Johnson's dramatic disclosure of his intention not to seek reelection have seen these men in a genuine state on nonpreparedness. This was not it.

One commentator twice contradicted the President's statement about the exchange of correspondence with Ho Chi Minh. Another challenged the President's abilities as a politician. A third asserted the President was "following the Pentagon line." Others, by the expressions on their faces, the tone of their questions, and the sarcasm of their responses, made clear their sharp disapproval.

To guarantee in advance that the President's plea for national unity would be challenged, one network trotted out Averell Harriman for the occasion. Throughout the President's address he waited in the wings. When the President concluded, Mr. Harriman recited perfectly. He attacked the Thieu government as unrepresentative; he criticized the President's speech for various deficiencies; he twice issued a call to the Senate Foreign Relations Committee to debate Vietnam once again; he stated his belief that the Viet Cong or North Vietnamese did not really want a military takeover of South Vietnam; he told a little anecdote about a "very, very responsible" fellow he had met in the North Vietnamese delegation.

All in all, Mr. Harriman offered a broad range of gratuitous advice — challenging and contradicting the policies outlined by the President of the United States. Where the President had issued a call for unity, Mr. Harriman was encouraging the country not to listen to him.

A word about Mr. Harriman. For ten months he was America's chief negotiator at the Paris Peace Talks — a period in which the United States swapped some of the greatest military concessions in the history of the warfare for an enemy agreement on the shape of a bargaining table. Like Coleridge's Ancient Mariner, Mr. Harriman seems to be under some heavy compulsion to justify his failures to anyone who will listen. The networks have shown themselves willing to give him all the airtime he desires.

Every American has a right to disagree with the President of the United States, and to express publicly that disagreement.

But the President of the United States has a right to communicate directly with the people who elected him, and the people of this country have the right to make up their own minds and form their own opinions about a presidential address without having the President's words and thoughts characterized through the prejudices of hostile critics before they can even be digested.

When Winston Churchill rallied public opinion to stay the course against Hitler's Germany, he did not have to contend with a gaggle of commentators raising doubts about whether he was reading public opinion right, or whether Britain had the stamina to see the war through. When President Kennedy rallied the nation in the Cuban Missile Crisis, his address to the people was not chewed over by a roundtable of critics who disparaged the course of action he had asked America to follow.

266

The purpose of my remarks tonight is to focus your attention on this little group of men who not only enjoy a right of instant rebuttal to every presidential address, but more importantly, wield a free hand in selecting, presenting, and interpreting the great issues of our nation.

First, let us define that power. At least forty million Americans each night, it is estimated, watch the network news. Seven million of them view ABC; the remainder being divided between NBC and CBS. According to Harris polls and other studies, for millions of Americans the networks are the sole source of national and world news.

In Will Rogers' observation, what you knew was what you read in the newspaper. Today, for growing millions of Americans, it is what they see and hear on their television sets.

How is this network news determined? A small group of men, numbering perhaps no more than a dozen "anchormen," commentators, and executive producers, settle upon the twenty minutes or so of film and commentary that is to reach the public. This selection is made from the 90 to 180 minutes that may be available. Their powers of choice are broad. They decide what forty to fifty million Americans will learn of the day's events in the nation and in the world.

We cannot measure this power and influence by traditional democratic standards for these men can create national issues overnight. They can make or break — by their coverage and commentary — a Moratorium on the war. They can elevate men from local obscurity to national prominence within a week. They can reward some politicians with national exposure and ignore others. For millions of Americans, the network reporter who covers a continuing issue, like ABM or Civil Rights, becomes in effect, the presiding judge in a national trial by jury.

It must be recognized that the networks have made important contributions to the national knowledge. Through news, documentaries, and specials, they have often used their power constructively and creatively to awaken the public conscience to critical problems.

The networks made "hunger" and "black lung" disease national issues overnight. The TV networks have done what no other medium could have done in terms of dramatizing the horrors of war. The networks have tackled our most difficult social problems with a directness and immediacy that is the gift of their medium. They have focused the nation's attention on its environmental abuses . . . on pollution in the Great Lakes and the threatened ecology of the Everglades.

But it was also the networks that elevated Stokely Carmichael and George Lincoln Rockwell from obscurity to national prominence . . . nor is their power confined to the substantive.

A raised eyebrow, an inflection of the voice, a caustic remark dropped in the middle of a broadcast can raise doubts in a million minds about the veracity of a public official or the wisdom of a government policy.

One Federal Communications Commissioner considers the power of the networks to equal that of local, state, and federal governments combined. Certainly it represents a concentration of power over American public opinion unknown in history.

What do Americans know of the men who wield this power? Of the men who produce and direct the network news — the nation knows practically nothing. Of the commentators, most Americans know little, other than that they reflect an urbane and assured presence, seemingly well informed on every important matter.

We do know that, to a man, these commentators and producers live and work in the geographical and intellectual confines of Washington, D.C. or New York City — the latter of which James Reston terms the "most unrepresentative community in the entire United States." Both communities bask in their own provincialism, their own parochialism. We can deduce that these men thus read the same newspapers, and draw their political and social views from the same sources. Worse, they talk constantly to one another, thereby providing artificial reinforcement to their shared viewpoints.

Do they allow their biases to influence the selection and presentation of the news? David Brinkley states, "objectivity is impossible to normal human behavior." Rather, he says, we should strive for "fairness."

267

Another anchorman on a network news show contends: "You can't expunge all your private convictions just because you sit in a seat like this and a camera starts to stare at you. . . . I think your program has to reflect what your basic feelings are. I'll plead guilty to that"

Less than a week before the 1968 election, this same commentator charged that President Nixon's campaign commitments were no more durable than campaign balloons. He claimed that, were it not for fear of a hostile reaction, Richard Nixon would be giving into, and I quote the commentator, "his natural instinct to smash the enemy with a club or go after him with a meat-ax."

Had this slander been made by one political candidate about another, it would have been dismissed by most commentators as a partisan assault. But this attack emanated from the privileged sanctuary of a network studio and therefore had the apparent dignity of an objective statement.

The American people would rightly not tolerate this kind of concentration of power in government. Is it not fair and relevant to question its concentration in the hands of a tiny and closed fraternity of privileged men, elected by no one, and enjoying a monopoly sanctioned and licensed by government?

The views of this fraternity do *not* represent the views of America. That is why such a great gulf existed between how the nation received the President's address — and how the networks reviewed it.

As with other American institutions, perhaps it is time that the networks were made more responsive to the views of the nation and more responsible to the people they serve.

I am not asking for government censorship or any other kind of censorship. I am asking whether a form of censorship already exists when the news that forty million Americans receive each night is determined by a handful of men responsible only to their corporate employers and filtered through a handful of commentators who admit to their own set of biases.

The questions I am raising here tonight should have been raised by others long ago. They should have been raised by those Americans who have traditionally considered the preservation of freedom of speech and freedom of the press their special provinces of responsibility. They should have been raised by those Americans who share the view of the late Justice Learned Hand that "right conclusions are more likely to be gathered out of a multitude of tongues than through any kind of authoritative selection."

Advocates for the networks have claimed a first amendment right to the same unlimited freedoms held by the great newspapers of America.

The situations are not identical. Where the *New York Times* reaches 800,000 people, NBC reaches twenty times that number with its evening news. Nor can the tremendous impact of seeing television film and hearing commentary be compared with reading the printed page.

A decade ago, before the network news acquired such dominance over public opinion, Walter Lippmann spoke to the issue: "There is an essential and radical difference," he stated, "between television and printing . . . the three of four competing television stations control virtually all that can be received over the air by ordinary television sets. But, besides the mass circulation dailies, there are the weeklies, the monthlies, the out-of-town newspapers, and books. If a man does not like his newspaper, he can read another from out of town, or wait for a weekly news magazine. It is not ideal. But it is infinitely better than the situation in television. There, if a man does not like what the networks are showing, all he can do is turn them off, and listen to a phonograph."

"Networks," he stated, "which are few in number, have a virtual monopoly of a whole medium of communication." The newspapers of mass circulation have no monopoly of the medium of print.

"A virtual monopoly of a whole medium of communication" is not something a democratic people should blithely ignore.

And we are not going to cut off our television sets and listen to the phonograph because the airwaves do not belong to the networks; they belong to the people.

As Justice Byron White wrote in his landmark opinion six months ago, "It is the right of the viewers and listeners, not the right of the broadcasters, which is paramount."

It is argued that this power presents no danger in the hands of those who have used it responsibly.

But as to whether or not the networks have abused the power they enjoy, let us call as our first witnesses, former Vice President Humphrey and the City of Chicago.

According to Theodore H. White, television's intercutting of the film from the streets of Chicago with the "current proceedings on the floor of the convention created the most striking and *false* political picture of 1968 — the nomination of a man for the American presidency by the brutality and violence of merciless police."

If we are to believe a recent report of the House Commerce Committee, then television's presentation of the violence in the streets worked an injustice on the reputation of the Chicago police.

According to the Committee findings, one network in particular presented "a one-sided picture which in large measure exonerates the demonstrators and protesters." Film of provocations of police that was available never saw the light of day, while the film of the police response which the protesters provoked was shown to millions.

Another network showed virtually the same scene of violence — from three separate angles — without making clear it was the same scene.

While the full report is reticent in drawing conclusions, it is not a document to inspire confidence in the fairness of the network news.

Our knowledge of the impact of network news on the national mind is far from complete. But some early returns are available. Again, we have enough information to raise serious questions about its effect on a democratic society.

Several years ago, Fred Friendly, one of the pioneers of network news, wrote that its missing ingredients were "conviction, controversy, and a point of view." The networks have compensated with a vengeance.

And in the networks' endless pursuit of controversy, we should ask what is the end value . . . to enlighten or to profit? What is the end result . . . to inform or to confuse? How does the ongoing exploration for more action, more excitement, more drama, serve our national search for internal peace and stability?

Gresham's law seems to be operating in the network news.

Bad news drives out good news. The irrational is more controversial than the rational. Concurrence can no longer compete with dissent. One minute of Eldridge Cleaver is worth ten minutes of Roy Wilkins. The labor crises settled at the negotiating table is nothing compared to the confrontation that results in a strike — or, better yet, violence along the picket line. Normality has become the nemesis of the network news.

The upshot of all this controversy is that a narrow and distorted picture of America often emerges from the televised news. A single dramatic piece of the mosaic becomes, in the minds of millions, the entire picture. The American who relies upon television for his news might conclude that the majority of American students are embittered radicals, that the majority of black Americans feel no regard for their country; that violence and lawlessness are the rule, rather than the exception, on the American campus. None of these conclusions is true.

We know that television may have destroyed the old stereotypes — but has it not created new ones in their place?

What has this passionate pursuit of "controversy" done to the politics of progress through logical compromise, essential to the functioning of a democratic society?

The members of Congress or the Senate who follow their principles and philosophy quietly in a spirit of compromise are unknown to many Americans — while the loudest and most extreme dissenters on every issue are known to every man in the street.

How many marches and demonstrations would we have if the marchers did not know that the ever-faithful TV cameras would be there to record their antics for the next news show?

We have heard demands that Senators and Congressmen and Judges make known all their financial connections — so that the public will know who and what influences their decisions or votes. Strong arguments can be made for that view. But when a single commentator or producer, night after night, determines for millions of people how much of each side of a great issue they are going to see and hear; should he not first disclose his personal views on the issue as well?

In this search for excitement and controversy, has more than equal time gone to the minority of Americans who specialize in attacking the United States, its institutions, and its citizens?

Tonight, I have raised questions. I have made no attempt to suggest answers. These answers must come from the media men. They are challenged to turn their critical powers on themselves. They are challenged to direct their energy, talent and conviction toward improving the quality and objectivity of news presentation. They are challenged to structure their own civic ethics to relate their great selling with the great responsibility they hold.

And the people of America are challenged too . . . challenged to press for responsible news presentations. The people can let the networks know that they want their news straight and objective. The people can register their complaints on bias through mail to the networks and phone calls to local stations. This is one case where the people must defend themselves . . . where the citizen — not the government — must be the reformer . . . where the consumer can be the most effective crusader.

By way of conclusion, let me say that every elected leader in the United States depends on these men of the media. Whether what I have said to you tonight will be heard and seen at all by the nation is not *my* decision; it is not *your* decision; it is *their* decision.

In tomorrow's edition of the *Des Moines Register* you will be able to read a news story detailing what I said tonight; editorial comment will be reserved for the editorial page, where it belongs. Should not the same wall of separation exist between news and comment on the nation's networks?

Now, my friends, we would never trust such powers, I've described, over public opinion in the hands of an elected government — it is time we questioned it in the hands of a small and unelected elite. The great networks have dominated America's airwaves for decades; the people are entitled to a full accounting of their stewardship.

November 20, 1969, Montgomery, Alabama
Alabama Chamber of Commerce

ONE WEEK ago tonight I flew out to Des Moines, Iowa, and exercised my right to dissent. This is a great country. In this country every man is allowed freedom of speech — even the Vice President.

Of course, there has been some criticism of what I had to say out there in Des Moines. Let me give you a sampling.

One Congressman charged me with, and I quote, "A creeping socialistic scheme against the free enterprise broadcast industry." Now this is the first time in my memory anybody ever accused Ted Agnew of having socialist ideas.

On Monday, largely because of this address, Mr. Humphrey charged the Nixon Administration with a "calculated attack" on the right of dissent and on the media today. Yet, it is widely known that Mr. Humphrey himself believes deeply that the unfair coverage of the Democratic Convention in Chicago, by the same media, contributed to his defeat in November. Now, his wounds are apparently healed, and he is casting his lot with those who were questioning his own political courage a year ago. But let us leave Mr. Humphrey to his own conscience. America already has too many politicians who would rather switch than fight.

There were others who charged that my purpose was to stifle dissent in this country. Nonsense. The expression of my views has produced enough rugged dissent in the last week to wear out a whole covey of commentators and columnists.

One critic charged that the speech was "disgraceful, ignorant and base," that it "leads us as a nation into an ugly era of the most fearsome suppression and intimidation." One national commentator, whose name is known to everyone in this room, said "I hesitate to get into the gutter with this guy." Another commentator charges that it was "one of the most sinister speeches that I have ever heard made by a public official." The president of one network said that it was an "unprecedented attempt to intimidate a news medium which depends for its existence upon government licenses." The president of another charged me with "an appeal to prejudice," and said that it was evident that I would prefer the kind of television "that would be subservient to whatever political group happened to be in authority at the time."

And they say *I* have a thin skin.

Here indeed are classic examples of overreaction. These attacks do not address themselves to the questions I raised. In fairness, others — the majority of critics and commentators — did take up the main thrust of my address. And if the debate they have engaged in continues, our goal will surely be reached — our goal which is, of course, a thorough self-examination by the networks of their own policies — and perhaps prejudices. That was my objective then; and that's my objective now.

Now, let me repeat to you the thrust of my remarks the other night, and perhaps make some new points and raise some new issues.

I am opposed to censorship of television or the press in any form. I don't care whether censorship is imposed by government or whether it results from management in the choice and presentation of the news by a little fraternity having similar social and political views. I am against — I repeat, I am against censorship in all forms.

But a broader spectrum of national opinion *should* be represented among the commentators of the network news. Men who can articulate other points of view *should* be brought forward.

And a high wall of separation *should* be raised between what is news and what is commentary.

And the American people *should* be made aware of the trend toward the monopolization of the great public information vehicles and the concentration of more and more power in fewer and fewer hands.

Should a conglomerate be formed that tied together a shoe company with a shirt company, some voice will rise up righteously to say that this is a great danger to the economy; and that the conglomerate ought to be broken up.

But a single company in the nation's capital holds control of the largest newspaper in Washington, D.C., *and* one of the four major television stations, *and* an all-news radio station, *and* one of the three major national news magazines — all grinding out the same editorial line — and this is not a subject that you have seen debated on the editorial pages of the *Washington Post* or the *New York Times*.

For the purpose of clarity — before my thoughts are obliterated in the smoking typewriters of my friends in Washington and New York — let me emphasize I am not recommending the dismemberment of the Washington Post Company. I am merely pointing out that the public should be aware that these four powerful voices hearken to the same master.

I am raising these qeustions so that the American people will become aware of — and think of the implications of — the growing monopolization of the voices of public opinion on which we all depend — for our knowledge and for the basis of our views.

When the *Washington Times-Herald* died in the nation's capital, that was a political tragedy; and when the *New York Journal-American*, the *New York World-Telegram and Sun*, the *New York Mirror* and the *New York Herald-Tribune* all collapsed within this decade, that was a great, great political tragedy for the people of New York. The *New*

York Times was a better newspaper when they were all alive than it is now that they are gone.

And what has happened in the city of New York has happened in other great cities in America.

Many, many strong independent voices have been stilled in this country in recent years. And lacking the vigor of competition, some of those who have survived have, let us face it, grown fat and irresponsible.

I offer an example. When 300 Congressmen and 59 Senators signed a letter endorsing the President's policy in Vietnam it was news — it was big news. Even the *Washington Post* and the *Baltimore Sun* — scarcely house organs of the Nixon Administration — placed it prominently on their front pages.

Yet the next morning the *New York Times*, which considers itself America's paper of record, did not carry a word. Why?

If a theology student in Iowa should get up at a PTA luncheon in Sioux City and attack the President's Vietnam policy, my guess is that you would probably find it reported somewhere in the next morning's issue of the *New York Times*. But when 300 Congressmen endorse the President's Vietnam policy, the next morning it is apparently not considered news fit to print.

Just this Tuesday, when the Pope, the spiritual leader of half a billion Roman Catholics, applauded the President's efforts to end the war in Vietnam, and endorsed the way he was proceeding — that news was on page 11 of the *New York Times*. But the same day, a report about some burglars who broke into a souvenir shop at St. Peters and stole $9,000 worth of stamps and currency — that story made page 3. How's that for news judgment?

A few weeks ago here in the South, I expressed my views about street and campus demonstrations. Here is how the *New York Times* responded:

> He [that's me] lambasted the nation's youth in sweeping and ignorant generalizations, when it is clear to all perceptive observers that American youth today is far more imbued with idealism, a sense of service, and a deep humanitarianism than any generation in recent history, including particularly Mr. Agnew's [generation].

That seems a peculiar slur on a generation that brought America out of the Great Depression without resorting to the extremes of either fascism or communism. That seems a strange thing to say about an entire generation that helped to provide greater material blessings and more personal freedom — out of that Depression — for more people than any other nation in history. We have not finished the task by any means — but we are still on the job.

Just as millions of young Americans in this generation have shown valor and courage and heroism fighting the longest and least popular war in our history — so it was the young men of my generation who went ashore at Normandy under Eisenhower and with MacArthur into the Philippines.

Yes, my generation, like the current generation, made its own share of great mistakes and great blunders. Among other things, we put too much confidence in Stalin and not enough in Winston Churchill.

But whatever freedom exists today in Western Europe and Japan exists because hundreds of thousands of young men of my generation are lying in graves in North Africa and France and Korea and a score of islands in the Western Pacific.

This might not be considered enough of a "sense of service" or a "deep humanitarianism" for the *"perceptive critics"* who write editorials for the *New York Times*, but it's good enough for me; and I am content to let history be the judge.

Now, let me talk briefly about this younger generation. I have not and do not condemn this generation of young Americans. Like Edmund Burke, I would not know how to "draw up an indictment against a whole people." After all, they are our sons and daughters. They contain in their numbers many gifted, idealistic, and courageous young men and women.

But they also list in their numbers an arrogant few who march under the flags and portraits of dictators, who intimidate and harass university professors, who use gutter obscenities to shout down speakers with whom they disagree, who openly profess their belief in the efficacy of violence in a democratic society.

Oh yes, the preceding generation had its own breed of losers — and our generation dealt with them through our courts, our laws, and our system. The challenge now is for the new generation to put their own house in order.

Today, Dr. Sidney Hook writes of "Storm Troopers" on the campus; that "fanaticism seems to be in the saddle." Arnold Beichman writes of "young Jacobins" in our schools who "have cut down university administrators, forced curriculum changes, halted classes, closed campuses, and set a nationwide chill of fear all through the university establishment." Walter Laqueur writes in commentary that "the cultural and political idiocies perpetrated with impunity in this permissive age have gone clearly beyond the borders of what is acceptable for any society, however liberally it may be constructed."

George Kennan has devoted a brief, cogent, and alarming book to the inherent dangers of what is taking place in our society and in our universities. Irving Kristol writes that our "radical students . . . find it possible to be genuinely heartsick at the injustice and brutalities of American society, while blandly approving of injustice and brutality committed in the name of 'the revolution.' " Or as they like to call it — the movement.

Now those are not names drawn at random from the letterhead of an Agnew-for-Vice-President Committee.

Those are men more eloquent and erudite than I. And they raise questions that I have tried to raise.

For we must remember that among this generation of Americans there are hundreds who have burned their draft cards and scores who have deserted to Canada and Sweden to sit out the war. To some Americans — a small minority — these are the true young men of conscience in the coming generation. Voices are and will continue to be raised in the Congress and beyond asking that amnesty — a favorite word — should be provided for "these young and misguided American boys." And they will be coming home one day from Sweden and from Canada, and from a small minority of our citizens they will get a hero's welcome.

They are not our heroes. Many of our heroes will not be coming home; some are coming back in hospital ships; without limbs or eyes; with scars they shall carry the rest of their lives.

Having witnessed firsthand the quiet courage of wives and parents receiving posthumously for their heroes Congressional Medals of Honor, how am I to react when people say, "Stop speaking out, Mr. Agnew, stop raising your voice."

Should I remain silent while what these heroes have done is vilified by some as "a dirty and immoral war" and criticized by others as no more than a war brought on by the chauvinistic, anticommunism of Presidents Kennedy, Johnson, and Nixon?

No. These young men made heavy sacrifices so that a developing people on the rim of Asia might have a chance for freedom that they obviously will not have if the ruthless men who rule in Hanoi should ever rule over Saigon. What is dirty or immoral about that?

One magazine this week said that I will go down as the "great polarizer" in American politics. Yet, when that large group of young Americans marched up Pennsylvania and Constitution Avenues last week — they sought to polarize the American people against the President's policy in Vietnam. And that was their right.

And so it is my right, and my duty, to stand up and speak out for the values in which I believe. How can you ask the man in the street in this country to stand up for what he believes if his own elected leaders weasel and cringe?

It is not an easy thing to wake up each morning to learn that some prominent man or some prominent institution has implied that you are a bigot, a racist, or a fool.

I am not asking any immunity from criticism. That is the lot of the man in politics; we would not have it any other way in this democratic society.

But my political and journalistic adversaries sometimes seem to be asking something more — that I circumscribe my rhetorical freedom, while they place no restrictions on theirs.

As President Kennedy once observed in a far more serious situation, this is like offering an apple for an orchard.

We do not accept those terms for continuing the national dialogue. The day when the network commentators and even the gentlemen of the *New York Times* enjoyed a form of diplomatic immunity from comment and criticism of what they said is over. Yes, gentlemen, that day is past.

Just as a politician's words — wise and foolish — are dutifully recorded by the press and television to be thrown up at him at the appropriate time, so their words should likewise be recorded and likewise recalled.

When they go beyond fair comment and criticism they will be called upon to defend their statements and their positions just as we must defend ours. And when their criticism becomes excessive or unjust, we shall invite them down from their ivory towers to enjoy the rough-and-tumble of public debate.

I do not seek to intimidate the press, the networks, or anyone else from speaking out. But the time for blind acceptance of their opinions is past. And the time for naïve belief in their neutrality is gone.

But, as to the future, each of us could do worse than take as our own the motto of William Lloyd Garrison who said: "I am in earnest. I will not equivocate. I will not excuse. I will not retreat a single inch. And I will be heard."

December 3, 1969, Washington, D.C.
Remarks to Governors and Their Families

IT HAS FREQUENTLY been stated that the strength of a nation depends upon the strength of its people. But people are not born strong. A young person draws his strength from the teaching and example of those closest to him. In most cases this means the family. So it would not be inaccurate to say that the strength of a nation depends upon the strength of its families.

The President of the United States is a family man. Because he is, and because he believes you are family-oriented, we are here today — as the French say, *"en famille."*

Since so many of you have brought your youngsters with you, today I would like to talk about young people, about the silent majority and the vocal minority of youth. I would like to discuss shallow demonstrations and profound demonstrations, and a way for men and women of goodwill, and of all ages, to begin to bridge the generation gap.

For some time now, I have been speaking out against the cause that some people have been demonstrating about. As a result, I have been charged with being "against the right to demonstrate."

For some time now, I have been reminding parents and young people alike that self-respect begins with mutual respect, and that order in society begins with discipline and authority in the home. As a result, I have been charged with being "against young people."

(I've also made a couple of speeches about the media, but nobody paid any attention to those.)

Now, anybody who knows me, or has taken the trouble to read what I have to say, knows that I respect the right of dissent in America, and knows that I admire and respect the great majority of young people in America today.

But the fact of the charges illustrates a phenomenon of our times. Too many of us are unwilling to argue a point but are too willing to point at an arguer. Too many of us stand ready to evade a debate by challenging the motives of the debater. Why bother to come to grips with a real issue, they ask, when a straw man of your own offers such an inviting target?

That kind of evasion results in "ricochet rhetoric" — when people do not respond to what is said, but to what other people say you meant. There is nothing wrong with joining an issue, but there is something very definitely wrong in two sides deliberately missing each other's point.

That is why there is so little real communication between those who demonstrate and those who are the targets of demonstration. That is why what should be a "meaningful dialogue" has become all too often a cacophony of meaningless monologues. That refusal to approach an issue with an open mind, that refusal to entertain a spirit of compromise — that is what is building barriers between the young and the not-so-young, between an outspoken minority and a soft-spoken majority. That is the barrier we must begin to dismantle — from both sides.

Freedom of speech is useless without freedom of thought. And I fear that the politics of protest is shutting out the process of thought, so necessary to rational discussion. We are faced with the Ten Commandments of Protest:

Thou Shalt Not Allow Thy Opponent to Speak.
Thou Shalt Not Set Forth a Program of Thine Own.
Thou Shalt Not Trust Anybody Over Thirty.
Thou Shalt Not Honor Thy Father or Thy Mother.
Thou Shalt Not Heed the Lessons of History.
Thou Shalt Not Write Anything Longer than a Slogan.
Thou Shalt Not Present a Negotiable Demand.
Thou Shalt Not Accept Any Establishment Idea.
Thou Shalt Not Revere Any but Totalitarian Heroes.
Thou Shalt Not Ask Forgiveness for Thy Transgressions; Rather Thou Shalt Demand Amnesty for Them.

In the face of these Commandments of Protest, how do we establish communication? How do we reach out without caving in? How do we talk *to* each other instead of just *at* each other?

Fortunately, the true believers in these Commandments are relatively few. And fortunately, we have an administration in this country ready to listen to the legitimate needs of the young, and even more important, ready and able to respond to those needs in significant ways.

You have already seen this morning how we are tackling the problem of dangerous drugs, which are more of a threat to our young people than any other segment of the population. And right across town this week, a White House Conference on Food, Nutrition, and Health is taking place; this administration has thereby provided a forum and a focal point for constructive controversy on a subject of deep concern to millions of our committed young people.

To a young person's question, "What have you done for us lately?" the obvious answer is "reform the draft." Certainly this long-overdue reform ends the terrible uncertainty that hung over millions of young lives. By and large, most young people of draft age can now make plans for their lives with a big question mark removed. And now that the President has demonstrated his credibility in this area, I think most young people believe he means what he says about an all-volunteer army in the future, and an end to the draft.

But let us look beyond the issues of immediate concern to young people, and look into the events of the past month that may affect their lives for years to come:

275

— We have signed a treaty that limits the spread of nuclear weapons, and reduces to some degree the threat of holocaust to future generations. The diplomatic negotiations that led to this signing are for historians of the future to detail, but there was far more to the signing of the Nonproliferation Treaty than the stroke of a pen.

— We have announced our intention to return Okinawa to Japan, in a generous rather than a grudging spirit, thereby laying the basis for a harmonious long-term relationship with the third most important industrial nation in the world, and increasing the chances for stability in the Far East in the generations to come.

— We have unilaterally renounced the use of germ warfare, and by setting this example to the world, we have added to the environment of peaceful negotiation as we lessen the terror of war to future generations.

— We have begun Strategic Arms Limitation Talks with the Soviet Union, and the depth and extent of our preparation for these talks cannot help but impress the other side of the table with our seriousness of purpose. And on the outcome of these negotiations hang so many of the hopes of tomorrow's generation of Americans.

Consider for a moment what those four acts last month mean to young people in America: The NPT, the return of Okinawa, the renunciation of germ warfare, the opening of the SALT talks.

I believe that when future historians look at the month of November 1969, they will not consider it to be the month of the March or the month of the Moratorium. I believe they will consider November 1969, to be a turning-point in the history of the twentieth century — a month in which President Nixon led the way toward world peace.

Since I mentioned the demonstration of last month, let me address myself to the focal point of the protest of so many of our young people: Why are we Vietnamizing the war in an orderly way — why don't we just pull out right now?

Here is the straight answer: We are being steadfast in Vietnam because we do not want the next generation of Americans to have to fight another war. If America were to cut and run, we would be cutting the chances for peace in the seventies, and running out on the children in school today who would have to fight a war tomorrow.

This generation is charged with the responsibility of dealing with the real world, with life as it is. The power and pressure and suspicion of the real world cannot be dispelled by wishful thinking, or by turning inward, or by doubting our ideals, or by blaming ourselves for all the ills of mankind.

By following the path of appeasement, this generation could accomplish "peace in *our* time." But we say to the next generation — "We are just as much concerned with peace in *your* time." We refuse to accept a solution that says "Peace Now — Pay Later." Because it is our children — the younger generation — who would have to pay later the price of surrender now.

More than anything else, the desire to transmit a better and a safer world to the next generation motivates the men at the center of decision today.

Why are we overhauling our welfare system — if not to build a better life for children who would otherwise be doomed to lives of poverty?

Why are we taxing ourselves at the highest rate in America's history — if not to avoid the deficits that would bankrupt the next generation?

Why are we turning the flow of power away from Washington and back toward the states — if not to enable the adults of tomorrow to have a greater say in managing their own destinies?

This is our way of "demonstrating." This is our demonstration of good faith toward the young Americans who are far more the objects of our hopes than our fears.

In this demonstration, the only signs we carry are the signs of the times — the hard evidence of action, the deeds you can see and the reform you can feel.

And the march we are most interested in is the march of progress — the progress that comes from respect for each other, respect for our free institutions, respect for new ideas.

I believe that we will see young people tomorrow dedicating themselves more profoundly than by the simple drama of demonstration. I believe we will see them involving themselves in community action against pollution — organizing cleanup brigades, but-tonholing civic and political leaders, pressing their cause with cogent argument, and mobilizing support by the power of their example. By working within the system, they can change the system.

Why do I believe this? Because sooner or later, you face the choice in life between getting something off your chest and getting something *done*. That's the choice that determines maturity.

I think the vast majority of the young activists in America are mature enough to want to get something done. In that cause — as in every positive cause — they will find an administration, and an older generation, with them all the way.

December 10, 1969, Baltimore, Maryland
Theodore Spiro Agnew Scholarship Fund Dinner

I AM GRATEFUL for your presence tonight. More than an honor to me, it is a profound tribute to the memory of my father. Many of you knew him, knew the kind of man he was and knew that such men are rare in any community — at any time.

I am proud to say that I grew up in the light of my father. My beliefs are his and my father believed deeply in America. My father was deeply involved in the life of the Greek community, for this, to him, was part of being an American.

"My Brother Ahepans" he said eight years ago, "Who better understands the true value of freedom and dignity than *we* . . . who are the direct descendants of the authors of those principles — the Ancient Hellenes? Who better understands the true value of freedom and dignity than *we* who have matured and prospered in the workshop of democracy, the United States of America?"

This Ahepa-conceived Scholarship Fund is particularly appropriate to honor my fa-ther's memory, for he cherished education as the key to a better life. That belief is Greek as much as it is American.

Pericles, the father of the first democratic state, said in the fifth century before Christ, "Athens is the school of Hellas." The Athenian ideal was that of the free citizen in the free state. But a state of freedom was never a state of ignorance. Education was, and always will be, integral to civilization.

As Pericles said, "The grave impediment to action is . . . not discussion, but the want of that knowledge which is gained by discussion preparatory to action." Courage from conviction distinguishes the free and civilized citizen.

To Socrates, to Plato, to Aristotle, all education served the soul. The Golden Age of Greece gave birth to the concept that public education was prerequisite to intelligent citizenship. Twenty centuries before Thomas Jefferson, Aristotle connected the public and private interest with cultivation of the mind as a free society's ultimate aim.

Never was there a separation of individual and collective good nor was there a distinc-tion between a life of pleasure and a life of civic fulfillment. The Athenian spirit was not only to live but to live well. Civic duty was an honor, and a life balancing work and comfort was the goal. Neither property nor prosperity were vices, only their misuse or a misunderstanding of their value was deplored.

This is our Greek heritage — deeply philosophical and political — and while the world has grown in technical prowess, it has never surpassed the Athenian ideal of free citizen-

277

ship. Ancient Athens remains the school of civilized nations. And from ancient Athens we can draw lessons of good and evil applicable today.

The rise and fall of all free nations mirrors the rise and fall of Athens. The overall lesson is that freedom and the good life are demanding possessions. To use them well and possess them permanently, discipline and education are required.

If I am known to raise my voice in criticism, it is because I see danger in our nation's course. Because America, like ancient Athens, can become foolish and corrupt; because a life of ease is not synonymous with a life of fulfillment; and because no generation can confer wisdom upon its children. Each generation must work to earn its own.

Heraclitus, one of Greece's earliest philosophers, perceived that all is flux. Change is the only constant. Arcesilaus, the skeptic, said, "Nothing is certain, not even that." Is this not true of today? Power is ephemeral and no excuse for conceit. Freedom, prosperity, moral and military strength are evanescent, not eternal. They cannot be secured once and then forgotten but must be carefully and continuously cultivated.

Education is the source to replenish a free society. America understands renewal and reform. We labor to renew our cities and reform our government. Yet we have left education — the source — relatively untouched. Of course, we have expanded and multiplied educational opportunities. We have had added preschool programs, community colleges, and enlarged universities to multiversities. But we have not sufficiently probed to the essence of the pure institution, and this explains much of our present problem.

By inclination, Americans think quantitatively. We are appreciators of the bigger. The danger in this lies in possible error in the original assumption. If what we are doing is not right to begin with, quantitative adjustments compound the wrong.

We have sometimes failed to perceive that as times change, we must not only change our programs but our premises governing education. Albert Einstein once defined education as "that which remains after you have forgotten everything you learned in school." Yet the American public continues to think of education as a terminal process limited to the youthful years of life. In a society where skilled laborers must learn new techniques six times before retirement, where fifty percent of technical engineering knowledge becomes obsolete within a decade, where seventy percent of all knowledge that will serve our present student generation during their lives is as yet unknown and undiscovered . . . it is time to stop regarding education as circumscribed by a particular period of a lifetime.

We must stop developing educational programs for twelve years, or sixteen, or twenty years, and start creating programs that gear themselves to useful, satisfying lives.

In the first place, the penchant for clustering higher education in the postadolescent decade adversely affects the human spirit. We are consigning a huge group of our young citizens to an academic limbo totally alien to their human instincts. Whether we realize it or not, whether we intend it or not, we have created a disenfranchised social class called youth.

How? Although our young population — between the ages of eleven and twenty-five — has not grown disproportionately, the proportion of young people in school has increased dramatically. High school attendance has doubled in two decades; ninety-four percent of our young people attend high school; seventy-five percent graduate from high school; and in higher education, the growth is even greater. College enrollment has tripled in twenty years; forty percent of all young people attend college for at least a year. Including advanced technical training, the figure approaches fifty percent.

By pricing teen-age labor out of the market and expanding secondary and higher education, we have stretched postadolescent dependency a full ten years. While the age of physical maturity has declined, we have confined a generation on campuses at a point in life when their fathers and grandfathers were supporting households. We have subsidized youths' education at the expense of many of their human rights. And society, in many cases, has forced its youth into an academic mold alien to their aptitudes or inclinations. The distinguished psychologist, Dr. Bruno Bettelheim, writes of higher education's debilitating effect;

"What makes for adolescent revolt is the fact that a society keeps the next generation too long dependent in terms of mature responsibility and a striving for independence . . . all too many who now go to college have little interest, ability, and use for what constitutes a college education. They would be better off with a high level vocational education which is closely linked to a work program which gives scope to their needs for physical activity and visible, tangible achievement. The complaint of many of these students is that nobody needs them. They feel parasites of society, and hence, come to hate a society which they think makes them feel this way."

In our reverence for education and our desire to do right by our children, we have inadvertently denied this generation's right to participate as mature citizens. The damage it does to the individual is no greater than the damage it does to the university. Denied political participation in the real community, the youth seeks to politicize the only community he has, the academic one. This defeats the purpose of the university which journalist William Shannon notes:

". . . is to transmit knowledge and wisdom and to enhance them by research and study. The university is not a forum for political action. It is not a training ground for revolutionaries. It is not a residential facility for the psychiatrically maladjusted. It is not a theater for the acting out of racial fears and phantasies."

As we demean, we pervert. Consider the single problem of those black students, trapped by the best intentions into a situation where he cannot compete. The demands for black studies, black dormitories, special black grading systems, are often smoke screens evading the basic failure in black primary and secondary education. Brandeis professor and former presidential aide, John P. Roche, sees black separatism on the campus as a last-ditch attempt for survival by culturally deprived students who have been admitted to college just because they came from inner-city ghettos. They are bright, but unprepared to compete with their highly articulate classmates. Without swimming lessons, they have been dumped in the mainstream and they are not going to drown without a struggle. Bayard Rustin, pioneer in civil rights and executive director of the A. Philip Randolph Institute, takes a harder line:

"Everyone knows that education for the Negro is inferior. Bring them to the university with the understanding that they must have [the] remedial work they require. The easy way out is to let them have black courses and their own dormitories and give them degrees. . . . What in hell are soul courses worth in the real world? No one gives a damn if you've taken soul courses. They want to know if you can do mathematics and write a correct sentence . . . an element in that society."

The point remains that we have neglected the real problem of compensatory education for the shallow solution of sympathy. And there are other equally compelling areas of neglect.

We have neglected vocational and technical education for the elegant ornament of liberal arts. Certainly the social sciences are important but they are not sacrosanct. And in our society, which needs skilled labor, we must restore the manual arts to their rightful place of esteem. We have done a grave disservice to the workingman by neglecting his central importance to our society. We have failed his appetite for the arts, his preparation for leisure, and, in many cases, his need to renew his skills.

If we are not going to have revolution within our educational community, we will be wise to take a revolutionary look at our institutions of education. We should not be reluctant to ask daring questions or consider bold solutions. Is the four-year college necessary in all cases? Are there better ways to combine secondary and undergraduate programs? To accelerate graduate work? Or to space it out over the years? Should we invest more in adult education and enrichment? Are present primary and secondary school programs creating enough outstanding citizens — citizens with an appetite for learning and an aptitude for service to others?

The answers require courage and cooperation from every sector of our society. There is little point in questioning the value of graduate degrees in the soft sciences if business-men continue to treat these degrees as keys to open the inner doors to better jobs. There is no point in discussing black studies without an objective ordering of educational priorities by the black community. There is no hope for major academic reform without the support of America's academicians.

There is no chance for change if parents revere the college degree as a symbol of their parental success. Until every interest group reappraises its attachments to existing institutional forms, we cannot achieve a new structure.

Today's students have an obligation, too, to question radicalism and demands for relevance as satisfactory answers. Revolution is ridiculous and relevance often an excuse for more amusing and less arduous involvement. Where is this drive for reality in the demand for nongraded courses? The real world distinguishes between excellent and mediocre effort. Is doing one's own thing ennobling or selfish; profound or simply vacant?

Finally, I think government has an obligation to review its many programs affecting youth and ask itself whether it is doing a good job or even what it intends to do? Right now, this administration is taking a hard look at youth policies. We are looking at the ways we have prolonged the period of dependency . . . disenfranchised our young adults . . . discriminated against noncollege youth and directed others, in disregard of their desires, into higher education.

We are saying that many young people have cause to complain. They are alienated — not by our hypocrisy, or racism, or the war in Vietnam — but by our best intentions and inappropriate institutions. There claims of hyprocrisy, racism, or immoral wars are not borne out by the facts. Their frustration at being held apart from responsibility and reality is understandable.

The educational community should ask whether encouraging ever increasing numbers of young people to attend college — when forty percent already do — benefits the lower half of the intelligence scale. We should question whether society's demand for college attendance compounds social antagonisms between those who go and those who do not. For if everyone is expected to attend college, life will only be harder on those who simply cannot achieve in an academic setting.

The federal government should reevaluate those policies which protract dependence . . . civil service age requirements, restrictive apprenticeship programs, present age limits on voting and public candidacy.

We should question whether some programs do, in effect, discriminate against the working young . . . such as the Peace Corps and VISTA which could benefit greatly from their marketable skills.

All of these questions should be asked not in the fear that we are out to destroy popular education, but as a positive search to broaden educational opportunities and to make our educational institutions fit the public rather than make the public fit the institutions. The threat to education does not lie in asking these questions, but in not asking them.

The challenge of American education from the cradle to the doctoral degree is our most important work. Our nation's future depends upon it, for as the Greek maxim goes, in the face of youth we find the future. America need not falter like ancient Athens if we learn from ancient Athens. We can retain our vigor and replenish our power by renewing our institutions.

Hope brought my father to America, and in honor of his limitless hope, the Theodore Spiro Agnew Scholarships will be bestowed. Because he was a child of Greece, they will go to youths of Greek descent. And because he was a citizen of America, their recipients will study here.

For as my father revered his Greek heritage and, like Pericles, saw Athens as the school of Hellas, so he would want . . . as we want . . . America to be the school of free men everywhere.

Above all, this scholarship is established in the spirit of my father's legacy to me — his painfully accumulated knowledge that — the principles of freedom need and deserve our constant protection — that we must work to make democracy live.

January 26, 1970, Washington, D.C.
National Council on Indian Opportunity

IN HIS State of the Union message last Thursday, the President said:
"Our land, this land that is ours together, is a great and good land."
None of our citizens have known this truth more directly, or known it longer, than the first American.

They lived off the land, used the land, revered the land. Ground and water and sky were sacred. It has taken the rest of us one hundred years to learn what the Indians knew from the beginning. Now at last we do know it, and, as the President said:

> Restoring nature to its natural state is a use beyond party and beyond factions. . . . Clean air, clean water, open spaces — these should once again be the birthright of every American.

A reverence for nature is inherent in the culture of the American Indian. Just as deeply inherent in the culture we, as much later arrivals, brought from our European homes were the ideals of liberty, equality, fraternity. We are now learning the importance of the Indians' respect for nature; they however have not yet benefited from the ideals supposedly ours: "liberty and justice for all." Indian people are still our most poverty-stricken Americans — and it is outrageous that this should be so.

It is my purpose and the purpose of this council to attack that raw truth and to do so effectively within the term of this administration.

In September of 1968 President Nixon set forth policies he would pursue to assist the American Indians to reach the goals they have set and will set. Basic to his program are three key principles:

I. The special relationship between the federal government and the Indian people and the special responsibilities of the federal government to the Indian people is acknowledged.

II. Rather than "termination," our policy objective is that the right of choice of the Indian people will be respected, and their participation in planning their own destiny will be encouraged.

III. Indian people will be fully consulted before programs under which they must live are planned.

As special consultant to the President, Leonard Garment wrote to an Indian spokesman last November:

> Officials must begin by listening to Indian voices speaking on their own terms . . . the process of listening must be begun on the local level . . . the Indians voices heard must . . . embrace . . . elected tribal officials, grass roots spokesmen, Indian organizations of all perspectives, urban Indians, Indian youth and those many other voices not heard before . . . the process must be as open as possible.

The National Council on Indian Opportunity provides the chance for federal cabinet officers to work directly with Indian leaders in:

— carrying out the policies of the President,

— carrying out new policies developed in consultation with Indians,

— encouraging full use of Federal programs by Indian people,

— apprising the impact and progress of Federal programs for Indians,

— suggesting ways to improve such programs.

First of all, it is absolutely essential that each cabinet member of the Council assures that his department has the necessary mechanisms and procedures which will provide the full and complete consultation with Indian people called for by the President. This should be done in cooperation with the Council.

The Indian members of the Council have met twice in preparation for the meeting today, and I should like to devote the major portion of our session to considering their comments and recommendations. It is my understanding that among their recommendations will be one relating to the subject of consultation.

The President has also called for increasing the authority and responsibility of Indians over programs affecting them and has cited the following examples:

— Independent Indian school boards, funded at government expense for each government-run school.

— Tribes should be urged to take over reservation law.

— Road construction and repair activities should be under Indian management.

— School service contracts for running school buses or for operating a school lunch program, should be funded as they are now but should be an activity of the Indian people themselves rather than of the federal government.

However, as I stated during my speech to the National Congress of American Indians in Albuquerque in October 1969, while we urge greater local leadership, we will not force it nor use its immediate absence to deny assistance. The Indian people must have the right to accept or reject local control.

Members of the Council are of course aware of the problems of interest to American Indians. Indians suffer limitations, disabilities and indignities that few disadvantaged groups in America suffer in equal measure; their unemployment rate is ten times the national average; 95% of their housing is inadequate, etc. The Federal members of the Council must ensure that all appropriate employees of their departments are also fully aware and keenly sensitive to these facts.

Economic opportunity on Indian reservations offers special problems and on the other hand very special opportunities. In this area the President has once again set forth very clear guidelines for us to build from:

The economic development of Indian reservations will be encouraged and the training of the Indian people for meaningful employment on and off the reservation will have high priority.

My administration will promote the economic development of the reservation by offering economic incentives to private industry to locate there and provide opportunities for Indian employment and training.

The special development problems of smaller reservations will also be recognized, and the administrators of government loan programs will be encouraged to take businessmen's risks in sponsoring Indian enterprises.

Off the reservation, many Indians, some of them unwisely relocated by the federal government, have not been successfully assimilated and find themselves confined to hopeless city reservations of despair because of lack of education and skills. I am advised that Indian center facilities are of particular assistance to Indians attempting to make the adjustment from life on the reservation to the complex environment of our urban areas. These centers offer Indians an opportunity to obtain information and guidance on how they can best utilize the public and private programs designed to assist them as well as providing a focal point of help from all interested parties. I want the appropriate departments to examine their various programs to assure that they are fully supporting such Indian centers and to make recommendations as to how they can be improved and additional ones established.

The Council has repeatedly received complaints that off-reservation Indians are denied assistance from federally supported programs. The principal reason given for this denial is that since they are Indians, the Bureau of Indian Affairs is responsible for them and they are therefore not eligible to participate in the program in question. This, as we know, is incorrect; however, many persons in our regional and field offices apparently don't understand that fact and it is imperative that this situation be corrected. With several exceptions, the BIA's responsibility is limited to the Indian reservation. American Indians living off the reservation are as entitled as any other American citizen to participate in any and all federally assisted programs. The Council's staff has prepared a suggested memorandum, to be found in your folder, which could be used in correcting this problem.

Programs designed to assist Indians encounter the same difficulties as other federal programs: coordination problems, poor delivery systems, and the lack of flexibility to meet varying circumstances.

First with respect to the problem of coordination. In 1957 the total federal outlay for Indian programs was about $78 million, nearly all of which went to the Interior Department. Today our federal expenditures for Indians total over $.5 billion with nearly half of this amount going to the six departments, other than Interior, represented at this table today.

This Council must provide the guidance for improved coordination and we must take advantage of the opportunities provided by the new regional offices and the Regional Councils of the Departments of Labor; Health, Education, and Welfare; Housing and Urban Development, and the Office of Economic Opportunity. I have requested the Bureau of the Budget to examine how the eleven BIA area offices may better coordinate their activities with those of other departments in the new regional offices. Assistant Director of the Bureau of the Budget, Dwight Ink, will make report on the progress being made in that area.

The President has stated that we are to eliminate needless bureaucratic levels which insulate decision making from the Indian people. This directive goes hand in hand with our efforts for expanded consultation with an involvement of Indians and with the President's desire to decentralize decision-making authority. Secretary Hickel may desire to specifically comment on this aspect especially in view of the malignment of the BIA.

The diversity of the characteristics of 290 Indian reservations also requires special approaches to the critical needs of education, health, and housing. I understand that in New Mexico the Pueblo Indians want to build their houses of abode and other indigenous materials, yet our federal programs require them to use other types of material in order to qualify for federal assistance.

The number one disease among Indians is now *otitis media* (middle ear disease). Its inadequate treatment results in loss or impairment of hearing and it is most prevalent among young children — sixty-three percent of reported cases being among children five years of age. However, we have no discrete program for its prevention and treatment, and research in this area is to be discontinued.

The members of the Havasupai tribe at the bottom of the Grand Canyon rank among their most urgent needs a third and fourth grade so their children will not be required to leave home at the age of eight. Right now their children are among the 9,000 Indian children under nine years of age who are at boarding schools living away from their parents.

283

These comments are not meant as criticisms of the respective departments but only as illustrations of our need to constantly reexamine our programs in terms of the particular needs of Indian people.

The Council meeting today offers the opportunity to focus on these problems, take inventory of our accomplishments and our failures and plan for a better day for the American Indian. I should now like to have brief reports from the federal members of the Council and then turn to the Indian members for their comments and recommendations.

February 12, 1970, Chicago, Illinois
Lincoln Day Dinner

WE ARE MET to commemorate the birthday of Abraham Lincoln, sixteenth President of the United States. The man whom we honor is remembered and revered as few statesmen in the history of the world have been — as no other American has been. He became the central figure in the most tragic drama of our national life; yet he came to be regarded with affection by the best of those who had fought against him, and by their posterity. Because of what he was able to do, we are able to celebrate his birthday as one nation. Yet the wisdom of his political acts has been fiercely disputed, and the justice of them has been denied by historians as much as by the hot-blooded political partisans of his lifetime. No one, least of all Abraham Lincoln himself, ever thought him infallible. In a curious way Lincoln has become a symbol of human imperfection, struggling to do right as God gave him to see it and as he felt it within his own heart.

It is a melancholy fact that more Americans died as a result of the commands issued by Lincoln, as Commander-In-Chief of the armed forces of the United States, than by any other President. But Lincoln could in truth say that he never placed a thorn in any man's bosom. Lincoln was of that rare breed of extraordinary men who make ordinary men like ourselves feel kin to him and to each other. In his struggle with poverty, with business failure, with political defeat, with the death of his mother in early childhood, with the death of his children in their youth, of his friends in their prime, he knew the sorrow closest to the heart and which, more than anything, links us all in a common humanity.

But Abraham Lincoln was not only a man of sorrow. He was also a man of indefatigable jest. During his presidency he was probably more criticized for his jokes than for any other single thing. Not, I should add, because the jokes were not funny, but because it seemed to his critics that the President should never be anything but solemn. Actually, it was only by his sense of humor that Lincoln found relief from the terrible burdens that otherwise would have crushed him. As in the great Shakespearian tragedies he loved, the comic interlude was needed to relieve the desolation of the catastrophe that surrounded him and to prevent his sensitivity from becoming cynicism, a change that happens too easily to men at the summit of power.

It is always instructive to seek parallels between the times of great men and our own times — and between their difficulties and ours. Lincoln's political life was dominated by the evils of Negro slavery, sectional antagonism and, finally political disunion and civil war. Ours has been dominated by international conflict, by world wars, and by racial and social turmoil. The Civil War ended chattel slavery and the threat to the Union, but it accelerated the industrial revolution that ushered into being the urban America whose problems beset us now.

In 1838 — in what now appears as an idyllic era of the American past — Lincoln said that the American people lived under a government "conducing more essentially to the ends of civil and religious liberty than any of which the history of former times tells us." That these same American people imperfectly appreciated the blessings of their government was the theme of his speech. I think we can say the same today. Ours is still the freest government on earth; and we are still a restless people, dissatisfied and unappreciative of our freedom. Perhaps it is the nature of a free people to noisily exploit their freedom rather than to quietly count their blessings. We hear little of the discontent that lies, we know, behind the Iron Curtain. When voices do rise there, as they did such a short time ago in Czechoslovakia, they are soon silenced. Much of our dissatisfaction is the effect of our freedom; dissatisfaction breeds progress no less than protest, and we would not have it any other way. Nevertheless, we may declare with confidence that if ours is not a perfect form of government, it most certainly is the best there is; and we challenge critics not merely to point to its flaws, but to tell us what they would put in its place.

No one long in this world who is not a natural tyrant expects to have his own way in everything, or even to have it altogether in anything. A free society is one which is more or less successful in equalizing the limitations on us all in the interests of a civilized existence. The only worthwhile freedom is freedom under law, because freedom without law results either in anarchy or despotism. The principal source of law under our form of government is majority rule. But to arrive at a majority, many compromises must be made among many opposing points of view; and minority rights must be respected. No one is, or ever should be, perfectly satisfied with the results of law in a free government because such law by its very nature embodies concessions to opinions with which we differ. But this does not give anyone the right to flout the law.

In 1861 a dissatisfied minority attempted to withdraw from the rest of the American government of which it was a part, because it had failed to gain the majority in a free election. Civil disobedience in a free government — except for the nondisruptive testing of the legality of the law itself — whether that disobedience takes the form of secession, trespassing upon private or public property, the disruption of a college campus, the refusal to pay taxes, or the refusal to obey the order of a court — is a placing of oneself above the law and implies a superiority to the law-abiding. This is not only arrogance, but constitutes a denial of the equality pronounced in the Declaration of Independence, to which equality Lincoln rededicated the nation in the Gettysburg Address.

The limits upon free action in a free society are well expressed by the saying that one man's right to swing his fist ends where another man's nose begins. And the limits upon free speech are equally well expressed by the saying that no man has the right to falsely shout "Fire" in a crowded theater. In despotic governments some men swing their fists as far as they wish; and they shout what they will without contradiction. But the price, let us remember, is that others have their faces smashed and their voices silenced. Those who denounce without self-restraint the limitations upon personal freedom in our form of government are more likely to curtail than to perfect that freedom.

Nowhere in today's United States is freedom more actively under discussion than on our campuses. This is as it should be. Although one could wish that the discussion would be somewhat more acute and dialectical; that more of men's minds, and less of their angry passions, were involved. A university is a community with its roots in two essentially different worlds, and the many paradoxes and tensions in higher education arise from this fact. Every university, every academic community, has its existence in a time and a place, in a nation, and a specific part of a nation. But, as its name suggests, it also belongs to a universe that is larger and different from any political community. A university is cosmopolitan, and its members are fellow citizens of the republic of arts, sciences, and letters that is beyond all nationality. When physicist meets physicist; mathematician, mathematician; classicist, classicist; they are joined with each other by a common good which is their vocation. And that vocation knows no boundaries of political geography, of civil law, of religion, or ideology. It is essential to the scientist and scholar that his work be restricted by nothing that might impede the discovery or recovery of truth in his field. But this does not prevent the free scholar or scientist from recognizing his indebtedness to the free government which appreciates and protects his independence. The free university should be loyal to the free society, while carefully protecting and preserving its autonomy.

I'd love to be able to go onto some of the embattled college campuses and speak to an audience that came to listen and absorb what I had to say. Unfortunately, today this is not possible. Because the dissidents, the dissenters — those who would rally favor for their point of view not by dialogue and discussion, not by moving closer together through an eventual accommodation of viewpoints of disparity — these will not allow the free interchange of information and will bus their supporters for the purpose of disruption from one college to another. It only takes a small group to make it impossible for anyone to be heard. And I believe it's one of the tragedies of our times, that the many fine students, the preponderant majority of students who would like a chance to hear principals in public life give vent to their opinions and possibly to engage in dialogue and discussion, are prohibited from doing this by those who characterize themselves as intellectuals but remain the most visceral people in the world.

As imperfect as any institution of this world, the university is nonetheless governed by the ancient and reasonable principle that the doctors, or qualified teachers of each discipline, lay down the rules for admitting people to study in their field; and they decide what courses should be pursued by apprentices and journeymen in order that in their turn they many become masters and doctors. Where methodical instruction and extended training are needed to become qualified, it is right and proper that men should be treated as unequal. For example, it is not right that the unqualified should sit on boards of admission to decide who is qualified to receive instruction in institutions of higher and professional learning. Neither a university, a business firm, nor a labor union should ever discriminate among applicants for membership upon any basis other than aptitude for learning and practicing its craft. But it should discriminate upon this basis. Among applicants to a medical school, those best able to become medical doctors, in the opinion of experienced medical doctors, should be chosen in preference to any others. Anyone can see why this is true, because everyone knows that when he is sick, or his loved ones are sick, he wants the best possible medical assistance and nothing else.

But we should remember that it is no less important for society that all the other vocations, in the professions and the liberal arts, have the same guidance of the untrained by the trained minds. For those who think that there should be ethnic quotas, or race quotas, or socioeconomic class quotas in the admissions to colleges or universities I would address this question: When next you are sick, do you wish to be attended by a physician who entered medical school to fill a quota or because his medical aptitude was high? When next you travel by jet airplane, do you want to go in a plane designed by engineers selected to fill a quota or by aptitude? When next you build a house, do you want an architect selected for architectural school by aptitude or by quota?

By some strange madness, we find the thought seriously entertained among men in responsible positions in the academy itself that the exigencies of society are such that the untrained should help choose those to be trained and that membership, whether as students or teachers, in institutions of higher learning should be determined fundamentally by considerations other than aptitude either for teaching or learning. Of course, the criterion of competence has in the past sometimes been honored more in the breach than in the observance. But surely that is no reason to abandon it, as happens when the concept of what is erroneously called "open admissions" makes its way among some of our supercilious sophisticates.

Another less apparent but entirely pernicious and debilitating result of the use of quotas or "open admissions" is the automatic creation of a vested interest in making such selections turn out reasonably successful. The same pressures which operated to bring about the favored admission status to those admitted because of race, socioeconomic class or ethnic background continue to operate in favor of their successful completion of the studies undertaken. Given an equal number of enrollees of each type, should the ratio of "quota" graduates to "aptitude" graduates be unfavorable, a strong presumption is created that the average "quota" enrollee is less intellectually suited to the skill sought than the average "aptitude" enrollee. This conclusion is repulsive to the liberal philosophy, even though it may be true.

The first and highest obligation of a university is to perform its own functions well, according to the laws of learning itself. For it is in the institutions of higher learning that the arts of civilization in their highest reaches must be preserved, enhanced, and transmitted.

Let me digress just a moment to say this: I'm concerned, as I've said to many academic friends of mine, that some of the most outspoken of the academicians of today seem to believe that anyone who is not continually cloistered in a college campus is unable to think things through at all clearly. I've found all too frequently that those who are professional intellectuals, as they call each other, would seem to feel that the attention of a master's degree or a Ph.D. degree relieves them from any necessity for continuing the learning process in the later years of their lives. And I would submit that learning is a continual process and that much good can be accomplished by the continued cultivation of these fine academic minds if they would simply at times leave their cloistered environment and come into the political areas of life with an attitude of learning rather than an attitude of dictating the course of society.

All that we in the political community hope to achieve must find its justification in the flowering of the human spirit as it confronts the mysteries of existence — of the universe — in those activities that transcend the political life. And our best political leaders, like Abraham Lincoln, are those who, amidst turbulent change, not only preserve us from destruction but remind us of the need we have for a saving wisdom of the permanent things.

February 20, 1970, Minneapolis, Minnesota
Republican Dinner

IN OUR LIFETIME we have seen the term "states rights" used all too often to escape responsibility. We should stand up and cheer when a state demands its right to assume responsibility. In our lifetime we have seen too many standards lowered everywhere and money will never buy back what we have lost. You have a beautiful state, and you live here, and you want your children to live here. Who has a better right than you to preserve and protect your land? And finally, there is the letter of the law which will be interpreted, but I would say that the spirit of the law is clear. It calls for clean air and pure water. It stands as our commitment to stop destroying in the name of progress what we cannot replace.

The President has proposed that we go no further, and the administration has moved from the defensive to the offensive. We are not going to sit back and wait for this earth to be destroyed, or go out with Band-Aids to patch gaping wounds. We are going to plan and prevent. We are going to stop problems before they start. And, without taking sides in a legal controversy, it seems to me that that's what the Minnesota case is all about.

This is indeed a happy day to be a Republican. Indeed, most Democrats today find conditions in their Party intolerable. I would sooner play golf in the Hope Desert Classic with Doug Sanders than be a Democrat today. As a matter of fact, I think Doug Sanders would rather play golf with me than follow the trail now being blazed by McGovern, Fulbright, and Harris and company.

Today, the Democratic party is caught up in a schizophrenic convulsion. Webster defines schizophrenia as a psychotic disorder characterized by loss of contact with environment and by disintegration of personality. What is happening to the Democratic party certainly fits that definition. Because truly it is losing contact with its environment and its personality is disintegrating. What is the natural environment of a political party if it is not the majority of its members? What is the personality of a political party if it is not the sum of the enduring principles under which it has prospered and progressed? Why do I say that the Democrats are caught in a schizophrenic convulsion? Only because their national party leaders, in a curious rush to accommodate left-wing extremism, are ignoring the principles of rank-and-file Democrats across this nation. These party leaders, and you don't have to go any further than the front page of your local paper to find out who they are, show a weird desire to suck up the political support of organized dissidence by excusing and rationalizing their outrageous antics. And, in their apologies for the obscenities, the destruction, and the anarchy repeatedly evident in the conduct of these malcontents, they assign a high moral cause, an attempt to invoke the public compassion for the relatively few weirdos whom they broadly describe as the young and the black and the poor. Well, ladies and gentlemen, the average American just isn't going to buy that kind of nonsense. And ladies and gentlemen, the overwhelming majority of the thoughtful young and the thoughtful black and the thoughtful poor are going to recognize those gyrations for the self-serving political declarations they are.

I was sickened, but not really surprised a few days ago, when I read the pronouncements of certain political luminaries relative to the conviction of five of the Chicago Seven. In that trial, the State faced the most calculatedly disruptive and provocative tactics ever mustered to confuse a criminal proceeding. What was threatened was our entire constitutional system of justice. Fortunately for America, the system proved equal to the challenge. The implications, vilifications and obscenities, the posturings and spectacular dramatics, the irrelevant political mouthings, only delayed and did not deter the administration of justice. And, in the end, that jury came in with an American result. It saw through the theatrics and the distractions of counsel who forgot the canons of ethics. It saw through the importuning and the keening against the American system which has survived nearly 200 years of vigorous appraisal. Yes, it eventually saw those defendants stripped of their altruistic disguises for the anarchists and societal misfits that they really are. And in rendering its verdict, that jury stood firm and resolute against the threats of an angry, irrational mob; and I say thank God for a system of laws that made that jury possible.

Returning to the great liberal national leaders of the opposition party, there's scarcely an aberration that can be committed in the name of individual freedom that will not provoke their sympathy. Burners of college, company, and draft board records trigger their instant sympathy because the wicked establishments must be made to reckon with the ultimate sin of being an unashamed part of a free competitive society. Assailants of policemen, stoners of firemen are given the tut-tut treatment by such statements as: "We don't condone such conduct, but we understand the years of deprivation that make them act that way." Looters, rioters, shatterers of acres of plate glass are described by these liberal thinkers as: "people caught in the excitement of the moment who do not realize what they are doing." Deserters and draft evaders who have fled to Canada and Sweden are characterized by them as: "some of our finest and most concerned young people." Yes, these new-way politicians also lament the accumulation of evidence to convict

288

criminals, abhor the censorship of blatant pornography, deny the conventional idea that success constitutes a reasonable objective in life, question the efficacy of our constitutional system, hate the military–industrial complex, adore teachers who fawn over juvenile delinquents and reject the idea that the American public is capable of doing anything for itself without massive governmental assistance.

Well fortunately for us, most Americans, be they rich or poor, black or white, young or old, male or female, college graduates or self-educated, saints or sinners, are not about to let themselves be enveloped and suffocated by such a society. And for that we Republicans are very grateful, because that's the reason our party is on the way up.

And now my friends, that I've stated, I hope with reasonable clarity, what the party of Lincoln and Nixon doesn't stand for, let me state what it does stand for. Look back to 1968, and see a country besieged by doubt and division. We had a credibility gap, we doubted that our government was telling the truth. Worse, we had a confidence gap. We doubted that our nation's leaders were capable of solving our problems: Vietnam, inflation, violence in our cities. Division was apparent and abrasive, visible and violent. In the month of April 1968 alone there were riots in 125 American cities. College campuses became embattled citadels. In August the Democratic National Convention served as the climax of a decade of dissent transforming the city of Chicago into a grand-scale guerrilla theater. Adding to the spiritual sickness were staggering facts. The crime rate had risen sharply during the '60s. The Democratic administration had spent $57 billion more than it took in to bankroll the worst inflation in our government's history. And, in the background, more and more of our young men marched to Vietnam every year.

President Nixon rose to take his inaugural oath knowing what must be done. He had to make the people understand the existence of formidable forces. He had to make people believe in their government and in themselves and to trust each other again. The President had to engage the conscience and gain the confidence of two hundred million Americans. Incredibly, he has done this. How has he done this? First, through truthfulness he has established his credibility with the American people. Second, through his programs and proposals, he has restored the confidence of the American people. Today, one year into this administration, two-thirds of our people rate the performance of our President as good. In foreign affairs we have seen significant new directions in the past year. We've seen a move away from paternalism and toward partnership in our relations with other nations. And on the overriding issue of Vietnam, we have seen an increased understanding of our involvement and the implementation of a plan of disengagement. Our troops are coming home, and I can report from my recent tour of military installations in Vietnam that the Vietnamese army is growing in numbers, competence, and confidence.

Just a few days ago, the President issued a 40,000-word statement of our foreign policy, the most comprehensive statement of foreign policy issued ever by a President of the United States. It isn't only that the President, in this doctrine, saw fit to delineate, with particularity, the course that he has chosen for the United States to follow as its Chief Magistrate. It's that he has defined and let the American people know of the systems he uses to make his judgments. He has downgraded the bureaucratic system of having a solution presented to him by the Department of Defense or the Department of State. He insists upon the presentation of all alternatives by the National Security Council which has been reactivated and better staffed than ever in its history. And out of the alternatives, the President makes the decisions, and so far — I think you'll agree with me — that the foreign policy of the United States of America has never been better understood and has never gained the confidence of so many citizens of the world. He has implemented balanced budgets and a realistic fiscal policy and monetary policy to slow the course of an inflationary psychology which has almost engulfed us. Those restraints are beginning to take hold, and as you can see, prices and costs are beginning to come down.

And, as you can see, the President has steadfastly resisted activities which are formally known as "jawboning," even though there's a great temptation in labor negotiations to insert himself as a persuader in these matters. But the President feels that the United States of America is composed of leaders in all segments of our life, labor and management, who understand the problems of this country and the problems of their particular undertaking. And that government is best that seeks to encourage the responsible members of our community to negotiate and bargain and solve their own problems. And in this philosophy, he is gradually, with a firm hand, bringing our economy under control.

We've also seen the enactment of draft reform, ratification of the Nuclear Nonproliferation Treaty, the opening of Strategic Arms Limitation Talks with Russia, and the first budget in two decades in which the spending for human resources exceeds spending for military defense. And to those who tell you that the military establishment is in control of this country, I would point out that this year's defense budget is the lowest percentage of our gross national product in the past twenty years.

There was, of course, the question of our government's ability to solve problems at home. Again the President's response combined truth and action. He acknowledged that failures existed, failures that could not be corrected by the old habit of merely increasing federal spending. He proposed New Federalism, a package of unparalleled domestic reform. Yes, I said domestic reform. The party that now criticizes our party for failing to make constructive suggestions on the democratic scene hasn't had an original thought in the past twenty years. It's simply been more and more and more of the New Deal, and the same programs, and escalate the amount of money. The President has moved in and begun to weed out those programs that don't work. He instituted a postal reform that will put our post office on a sound basis, a welfare reform — the first undertaken ever — which will bring to the working poor some subsistence, and which will provide incentives for getting out of the welfare routine for those who would like to raise themselves from that condemnation of maintaining a dependent status forever. He has instituted revenue sharing to give the states of this nation a chance to set their own priorities in spending money that the federal government sends back to them; which, of course, originally came from its own taxpayers. And, he has submitted an unprecedented crime package consisting of eighteen bills which now lie languishing in the Congress because of the inactivity of the opposition party.

Yes, as Republicans, we can take pride in our administration's progress. I think we can feel that a new era is dawning for our party. Why else would so many people as are here tonight be interested in the Republican party? We are the open party, the umbrella which welcomes a broad spectrum of views. And we're going to see that umbrella sheltering a lot of new people in the future. And as Republicans, we must have the candor to admit, even as we take pride in our accomplishments, that much remains to be done and that this is no time for complacency.

The Democratic leadership has grown complacent in power. The Republican party has the great potential today. We write off no one. We have no regional strategy. You know, it makes me laugh when I hear "regional strategy" or "Southern strategy." Look at the results of the last election. One of the candidates, situated in the South, received votes only from certain Southern states. Another candidate, who lives pretty close to where we are, received just about ninety percent of his support from a few Northeastern industrial states. *But Richard Nixon received his support from states all over these United States. Now will the real regional candidate please stand up!*

Yes, and we want the young voters who want to do something more than talk about what is wrong with the system. We want those who want to change things from within, and we say to them, "Come along with us." We want those Democrats, of whom I spoke earlier, who have been dispossessed by their national leadership. We want those who believe that the principles which unite us as citizens are greater than the economic, ethnic or regional interests which divide us as individuals. In 1970 we have a message to get across to the people of this country. The Republican party is ready, willing, and able to provide leadership. It is more interested in people's principles than their politics. Forget past labels and look at our logic. We believe that citizenship begins at home and that government begins at the local level. As Republicans, we're confident of our abilities and optimistic about our future. We are not the party that tears America down. We are the party which wants to build America up. And we believe in law and order, and justice as the proper basis for progress, just as we believe that reform is the proper basis for change. If people believe these things, they belong with us. Let's go get the votes!

290

February 21, 1970, Atlanta, Georgia
Lincoln Day Dinner

THIS IS the time of year when the Republican party pays respect to Lincoln, who acknowledged the human imperfections that were inherent in his mortality and tried so hard to overcome them. Tonight also happens to be the eve of Washington's birthday, and one cannot help but reflect on the differences in their times, one from the other, and even sharper distinctions between both of those periods of history and American life today.

In leading your thoughts in this direction, I don't suggest the obvious comparisons of technology, pure scientific knowledge, or economics. These conventional indicia of what we popularly characterize as man's progress have been calibrated literally thousands of times by qualified historians. But every little attention has been focused on the severe, and I believe, the dangerous changes in fundamental attitudes of human beings to each other.

Perhaps the more sophisticated, and certainly the more cynical of our contempories, would say that the concept, popular in both Washington's and Lincoln's day, that men are basically decent, was illusory and has been swept away — the cynics would say that the greed of man, that his hypocritical and crass nature — are now clearly revealed for the first time in the rigid examination of a frank, open, and realistic intellectual community. I cannot believe that what the cynics say is true.

Now there is something to be said for the destruction of self-serving naïveté if the real world is ever to be improved. But I, for one, cannot believe the often-expressed thesis that our country's course is presently directed by leadership — leadership across the spectrum of the establishments — political, military, and industrial — that leans toward no higher cause than self-gratification.

Human relationships were more immediate and direct in Washington's time; and to a slightly lesser extent, the same was true of Lincoln's time. Today, the compacted busyness of modern life and our preoccupation with impersonal activities masquerading sometimes as emotional experiences, create a rather sterile, laboratorylike environment for developing mature human beings. Is it then so surprising then that so many of us have become robots emotionally, conditioned to Pavlovian reaction when properly or perhaps improperly stimulated by those who we have been led to believe are opinioned leaders?

Emotion, formerly a person-to-person conduit, is now a closed circuit within the individual. The individual vicariously, and to whatever degree of involvement he wishes, tests love, hate, exhilaration, and depression by playing a spectator role disguised as an activist. For example, a militant demonstrator with a set of computer-fed beliefs can shout obscenities at me and charge my car, but really he has no *personal* encounter with me as an individual. His emotional experience is ersatz — entirely fake. A cause is his palliative for the competitive encounter of minds he secretly wishes to avoid. Dissent requires no dialogue — no assessment on either his or my part of the validity of his position.

In similar comparison, charity has become a computer operation. What satisfaction is there in writing a check to a gargantuan impersonal charitable fund, generally thinking principally of the deductibility of the contribution for tax purposes? What value is that compared to the personal satisfaction of an anonymous delivery of food to a hungry family you personally know? That was charity in Washington's and in Lincoln's day, and it did a lot more for the soul of both the giver and the receiver.

The point I am trying to make is that the detachment of modern life — the increasing interpositioning of machines between direct human contacts — the fear of really knowing one another without a guarantee that no one will be hurt or disappointed — has brought about what is fundamentally a false impression of a brave new world.

We need now, more than anything else, to seek the answers to the difficult questions within each of us. We must abandon the cozy idea that we can turn a dial, or refer to an opinion maker for a quick, easy solution to our interpersonal problems. If you and I disagree, it is not so important that you are right or I am wrong as it is that you persuade me by logic and argument that that is so. Disengagement and street demonstration are an extension of the modern fear of *intellectual* confrontation. I believe that physical confrontation cannot be a productive substitute for debate. I believe that men of good will and intent must sit down with each other to *solve problems — not to act in the theater of public opinion.*

In our country today, there are great issues which require the best effort that each of us can muster within him. The problems cannot be solved by simple slogans such as: "Peace Now" or "Freedom Now." We must first define peace and freedom in the context of our mutual rights and responsibilities.

My individual freedom stops where your nose begins, so far as the swinging of my fist is concerned. My right to demonstrate my disagreement with a law does not give me the privilege of interfering with the rights of other people.

Now a certain kind of peace could have been obtained immediately in World Wars I and II and in Korea by simply announcing our withdrawal and declaring that we would dispute the aggression of the enemy no longer. And the same is true in Vietnam.

But if we are honest with ourselves, we know that peace must protect our children and our grandchildren — not just buy time for us. We have offered to negotiate a reasonable settlement of the Vietnamese war. In that offer continues to be ignored, we must disengage in a manner commensurate with the ability of the South Vietnamese people to contain the aggression.

Tomorrow some commentators and editorialists will probably wonder how the tone of this speech can be reconciled with my blunt criticisms of student radicals and other sympathizers with violent dissent. The liberal media have been calling on me to lower my voice and to seek accord and unity among all Americans. Nothing would please me more than to see all voices lowered — to see us return to dialogue and discuss and debate within our institutions and within our governmental system — to see dissatisfied citizens turn to the elective process to change the course of government — to see an end to the vilification, the obscenities, the vandalism, and the violence that have become the standard tactics of the dissidents who claim to act in the interests of peace and freedom.

But I want you to know that I will not make a unilateral withdrawal and thereby abridge the confidence of the silent majority, the everyday law-abiding American who believes his country needs a strong voice to articulate his dissatisfaction with those who seek to destroy our heritage of liberty and our system of justice. To penetrate the cacophony of seditious drivel emanating from the best publicized clowns in our society and their fans in the Fourth Estate, yes my friends, to penetrate that drivel we need a cry of alarm, not a whisper.

And if the hippies and yippies and disrupters of the system in Washington, disrupters of the systems that Washington and Lincoln as Presidents brought forth in this country, will shut up and work within the framework of our free system government, I will lower my voice. And if the Black Panther party will disclaim its publicized purpose of violence and overthrow of our elected government by force and will run candidates for election in the traditional democratic fashion, I will lower my voice. If the SDS, the RAM, and the PLP will transfer their allegiance from Mao Tse-tung and Castro and the Viet Cong to the United States of America, I will subside to a more professorial tone.

So, therefore, in the traditional and popular phraseology of the new left, I am offering these initiatives to restore a sane method of mediating the volatile controversies that envelop us as a nation.

Let us never be persuaded that the vicious reactionaries of our society are more than a small minority. Let us not fall victim to their tactic of attempting to identify themselves as the young, the black, and the poor.

I look upon the youth of today of every race and creed as a fountainhead of ideas, as an infinite reservoir of knowledge containing energy of solar dimensions. All of our hopes for the future are with them. We need them in the Republican party.

I would hope the wayward few will cast off the blanket of filth and confusion; the dependency on drugs and artificial stimulants; that they will shed their negative thesis and return to the pursuit and, in time, and yes, to the realization of the American ideal.

Our answer today is the same as the answer in the days of Washington and Lincoln. Let the forces of logic and reason continue to shine strongly so that the fog of confusion and specious rationalization can be swept away. Let the people who made the United States a great nation continue to bequeath it to those who will make it greater. And let the few, the very few, who would desecrate their own house be made fully aware of our utter contempt.

February 24, 1970, Phoenix, Arizona
Trunk and Tusk Club

THE GATHERING here in Phoenix, Arizona, is a partisan one. We can be justly proud of our partisanship for President Nixon has accomplished much in the past year.

It is tempting — and indeed it may be fitting — to give a partisan speech before a partisan audience. Tonight, however, I would like to forgo that temptation and talk to you and all Americans about a national problem.

I refer to calculated assaults on our last bastion of individual rights, the administration of justice.

The trial of the Chicago Seven — or eight, as the original docket read — has now been concluded. The jury has reached its verdict, the judge has passed sentences, and the appeal procedure has begun.

This trial served as the stormy footnote to the turbulent 1968 Democratic National Convention. The trial itself should have tested the constitutionality of the 1968 Civil Rights Act. I say "should have" because that issue may have been obscured by the contest of personalities and a script written for drama rather than the administration of justice.

I do not intend to comment on the conduct of the trial nor the finer points of law. The point is not what these particular men — judge, advocates, defendants and spectators — did in this particular time. What is significant is what disruption does at all times to the system of justice.

I contend that if our courts are not sanctuaries of dispassionate reason we cannot have justice. We cannot have social or civil progress. Emotional demonstration and guerrilla theater must end at the courthouse door. The rights of petition and assembly do not extend into the halls of justice although they are appropriate when lawfully exercised outside. Within the courtroom, dissent must be orderly and supported by logic. The rule is persuasion, not intimidation.

As Supreme Court Justice Hugo L. Black cautioned in 1966:

> Once you give a nervous, hostile, and ill-informed people a theoretical justification for using violence in certain cases, it's like a tiny hole in the dike; the rationales rush through in a torrent, and violence becomes the normal, acceptable solution for a problem. . . . A cardinal fact about violence is that once initiated it tends to get out of hand. Its limits are not predictable.

A corollary conclusion is . . . violence rewarded breeds further violence and perpetual violence ultimately produces a brutal counterreaction.

Civil disobedience, at best, is a dangerous policy, since it opens the path for each man to be judge and jury of which laws are unjust and may be broken. Moreover, civil disobedience leads inevitably to riots, and riots condoned lead inevitably to revolution. This is a clear and present danger today.

"Justice is founded in the rights bestowed by nature upon man. Liberty is maintained in the security of justice." These two sentences are inscribed on a wall of the Justice Department building in Washington. I do not believe the first sentence is true.

I doubt that justice is founded in the rights of nature, because we know that nature is not always just. Each generation of youth discovers the beauty of nature anew and is stunned by the magnitude of it, perhaps to the extent of confusing beauty with justice. Yes, nature is beautiful. But it can also be brutal and predatory.

We might ask what justice exists in the jungle where carnivorous animals devour the weak and gentle? What justice is there in life where disease often cripples and kills the young and good?

What we regard as justice today does not exist by virtue of nature, but by the free will of mankind. Justice began the day we rejected the nature of savages and started something called civilization. Civilization progressed as we challenged and contested with the bestiality in ourselves. It advanced as we began to conquer the natural forces of fire, flood, famine, and disease.

No, I do not believe that natural rights or human rights or even legislated rights can flourish without sufficient definition and protection under a judicial system.

For so long as we have free will, so long as we attempt to separate right from wrong, we are contributors to our own destiny or our own doom.

No natural or human right is enforceable except as a civil right. It is only when society acknowledges it as a right and backs it by the power of the state and the respect of a majority of its responsible citizens that that right exists.

If we consider the time it has taken civilization to progress from primitive savagery to sophisticated jurisprudence, we realize some amazing facts. Five hundred million years of evolution preceded the present state of civilization. Barely 2,500 years have passed since the early laws of Moses and Hammurabi established the foundations of justice. Only seven centuries ago, the Magna Carta produced the principle that a nation and its leaders would "deny justice to none, nor delay it."

So those who condemn civilization for not having moved fast enough are wrong. At the same time those who would be complacent are just as wrong. A look at Nazi Germany, Communist China or Castro's Cuba proves that ten centuries of civilized progress can be destroyed overnight.

If civilization is still a veneer, then civilized justice clearly requires constant, tender and protective care. Out of progress have come some painful lessons. We have learned that there must be a framework for justice. In America, the Constitution provides the ground rules for freedom, justice and order. The Constitution establishes basic rights and in doing so imposes corresponding responsibilities. The Constitution also establishes a representative government empowered to enact laws and Courts which may rule on them.

Laws may conflict with other laws and with constitutional rights. Constitutional rights supersede laws. The Courts alone can resolve these conflicts. They stand independent of all other branches of government. Federal court judges are appointed for life to secure their personal independence from past, present and future influences. Society has encased its courts in these protective layers because it values justice. Justice depends on dispassion and compassion as well a knowledge of the law. But passion has no place in the courtroom. Raw passion has never contributed a thing to the administration of justice.

Nor has pressure. The citizens of this country are free to pressure Congress. They may petition and parade and protest before the President. They may howl and yowl and tax our patience. But when they move open rebellion into the courtroom, they remove from our midst all hope of justice.

The case of the Chicago Seven proves this point. The trial could have provided a significant test of the constitutionality of the 1968 antiriot law.

As it happened, the outrageous courtroom conduct totally obfuscated the constitutional question. Instead of a clear test of law we saw a perverse display of arrogance, vilification, and childish braggadocio.

The Chicago Seven were not interested in the Constitution nor in improving justice. Defendant Abbie Hoffman said, "This trial isn't about legal niceties. It's a battle between a dying culture and an emerging one."

Except for one traumatic lapse, the Civil War, our culture has peacefully evolved for 181 years at an almost revolutionary speed. We have moved from a concept of "laissez-faire liberty" to a recognition that liberty requires continuous care. We have learned that it is not enough to say all men are equal and all enterprise, free. We must assure equal opportunity and secure fair play.

During the course of this century alone we have restricted the "anything-goes liberty," which led to robber barons and watered stock; which permitted monopolies and prevented labor unions. We have advanced individual liberty by providing social security, unemployment insurance, collective bargaining, medicare, and medicaid. We have struck down laws giving sanction to discriminatory practices. We have witnessed an unprecedented — and some feel excessive — protection of individual liberties. Moreover, and perhaps more importantly, we have enacted laws affording equal opportunity where the motivation was humanistic and compassionate, not legalistic.

This peaceful revolution has, to a great extent, been the product of our courts. The courts are the operating rooms of freedom where cancerous invasions of individual and group rights are excised by trained judicial surgeons so that the patient — our free society — can survive. And while the operation is performed on an antiseptic atmosphere, the patient does not remain in quarantine. He returns to everyday life strengthened and more vital.

Our courts do not need lectures from self-appointed social critics. They do not need the antics of the guerrilla theatre. They do not need lawyers who confuse themselves with disciples of a new cult. They do need skilled advocates to be catalysts to the cause of justice and reporters who have not predetermined the guilt or innocence of the accused.

The courts have been put above and beyond the rough and tumble for a reason. The judicial branch does not represent a majority nor a minority, but all society past, present and future. Elected officials in the executive and legislative branches are directly responsible to their electorate, they are subject to pressure. The judiciary is independent. The Supreme Court is responsible to its own conscience and to posterity. The courts are a bastion in defense of individuals and minorities. But decisions are made to favor the majority not the minority but to fairly interpret the Constitution and laws of the United States.

The case of the Chicago Seven concerns neither the right of the majority nor the minority. It concerns the rights of society to be protected against a mob. It points once again to the dangerous confusion between a minority and a mob. A responsible minority has rights and any law-abiding political minority has the right under our Constitutional system to persuade our people to make it a majority.

A mob represents neither a political majority nor a minority. A mob is a mob — unruly, mindless, passionate, inchoate, coercive and oppressive. It represents only a dangerous threat to democracy, individual civil rights, and progress. It invites tyranny and repression.

Today's left-wing extremists like to invoke the revolutionary principles of our nation's founding fathers as their precedent. There is no parallel. That is the New Left's Big Lie.

The founding fathers rebelled against a system which deprived them of the right to be represented and the right to dissent. Today's revolutionary has both of these rights. But lacking a constructive purpose, he finds no logical way to bring others to his point of view. So he engages in destruction for the sake of relieving his frustration with himself.

The founding fathers proposed a positive system of government . . . the most superb social organization in human history. Today's radical thought is solely negative and nihilistic in content.

Those who advocate revolution and those who encourage them pervert the ideals of our founding fathers and distort the facts. Those who smash windows and seize university buildings destroy by their injustice whatever justice their cause ever had.

If we confuse these people with legitimate political minorities, we do a cruel disservice to every minority group in this country.

If we romanticize the revolutionary's role in present America, we diminish the efforts of every responsible, conscientious citizen.

If we capitulate before their terroristic tactics, we endanger the fabric of our freedom.

We stand at an extraordinary moment in our nation's history — a moment which demands nobility from ordinary men.

We are challenged to exercise calm in the face of moral outrage.

We must enforce the law with dispassion and disregard the provocation of passion.

We must distinguish the mob from the minority and not find any minority guilty for the sins of a mob.

We must not tolerate abuse nor violence by a mob yet continue to assure the rights of petition and public assembly.

These are formidable challenges for humans without inexhaustible patience. In a time of incessant confrontation, it is all too easy to begin to hate. It is all too effective to initiate repressive measures. Yet, if we fall prey to hate and repression, the mob has won. Destroying a mob is relatively easy; the difficulty lies in not destroying ourselves.

One of the wives of the convicted Chicago defendants said, "We will dance on your graves." We cannot let this happen any more than we can permit our court rooms to become circuses; our campuses, bedlams; our streets, battlegrounds.

We are not going to retreat to Dark Age repression and we cannot go forward to enlightenment without sanity and reason.

So we are going to stand our ground with patience and dignity.

The months and years ahead will not be easy. But no one has ever said that freedom was easy. And I am confident that our culture will emerge stronger and wiser for the test.

Confrontation is not novel to our citizens; only its form is new. We have faced dictators before . . . only they had foreign accents. Now we face an enemy within, and, as Abraham Lincoln said: "If destruction be our lot we must ourselves be its author and finisher. As a nation of freemen we must live through all time, or die by suicide."

Ladies and gentlemen, suicide is alien to the American spirit. Ours is the spirit of John Paul Jones; we "have not yet begun to fight."

February 26, 1970, Washington, D.C.
National Governors' Conference

YESTERDAY THE President spoke to you briefly and specifically about a few facets of the administration's domestic program. I believe you could easily detect in his remarks an awareness of the difficult financial burdens that state government faces. At no other level of government have built-in program increases left less resources for the implementation of new programs. And notwithstanding the rigid disciplines which had to be imposed on the federal budget to brake runaway inflation, the President has moved to commit more federal assistance, and federal assistance in a more flexible form, to state government than ever before.

The beginnings in revenue sharing, in the fight against pollution, and in the welfare reform await the action of Congress. Whether these programs are passed as offered or whether they're modified, they will have an effect on your ability to finance the growing burdens of state government.

But the administration's recognition of the formidable difficulties faced by the States has a mirror image — the governors' recognition of the equally difficult problems faced by the administration.

I want you to know that we are very grateful for your cooperation in our fight against inflation. In September, when we met last, the administration sought your aid through a voluntary cutback in nonessential construction. Your response was prompt and substantial. The states collectively have reduced or deferred $1,084,000,000 of planned highway construction. Other deferred capital construction has exceeded $1,009,000,000. So you have shared in cooling inflation by putting a potential $2 billion multiplier on ice.

Obviously, you merit and have the plaudits of this administration and the gratitude of the nation. With this one responsible act you've done more than your share in the war against inflation. You've given life and proof to the federal precept. You've demonstrated that state governments are willing and capable of disciplining themselves and of cooperating in the nation's interest. And you have proven that those who would counsel for federal supremacy, or advocate the bypassing of state governments because they are careless and insensitive about problems outside of statehouse politics, are totally wrong. In one act, you have put down four decades of slander about state government.

In terms of our nation's history, I believe your prompt, voluntary policing of your own spending will be remembered both as a blow struck to restore a balanced federal system and as a pivotal factor in a year-long crusade to combat inflation.

Yesterday, you heard the President touch briefly on the environment and reiterate the administration's commitment to the fight against water pollution. We will never be able to clean up our waters without adequate waste water treatment facilities. Our proposed new $10 billion joint federal–state program for the construction of such facilities represents one of the most important direct steps we can take to begin the restoration of our environment. This new program proposes to allot federal matching funds of $1 billion per year for four years, and is expected to induce the expenditure on a local level of $6 billion in that same period.

I want to emphasize several points from Secretary Hickel's statement of yesterday to your Committee on Natural Resources and Environmental Management.

First, $10 billion is the amount of funding we can look forward to. It should be enough to do the job. If it proves inadequate, the President has said that he will seek more.

Second, the federal government will meet its reimbursement commitments. I want to make it clear that for the fiscal year 1970, the states will receive $800 million as a total appropriation — out of which they will have the option of using their monies for new projects or reimbursement of old projects if they are at least twenty-five percent complete. In succeeding years beginning with fiscal 1971, twenty percent of the amount of money totally authorized will be allocated for reimbursement by regulation of the reimbursable commitments have been met.

Third, for those municipalities unable to finance their share of waste water treatment facilities, a new environmental financing authority will be structured to help meet that need.

Fourth, the new program will permit allocation of federal matching funds on both population density and pollution density.

Fifth, and this is a much desired innovation, we will provide in the program the highly significant reform of comprehensive river basin planning.

Thus, the three R's of restoration, reform, and renewal described by the President are all evidenced in our new water pollution control program.

In addition to capital construction deferrals and the financing of the difficult battle against water pollution, there are probably a hundred other matters of specific executive decision which I might move to and discuss with you at this time. They'd all be familiar to you, they'd all be controversial, they'd all have been discussed many times before. Basically, the solution to these problems depends on a constant search for modification and adaptation by professional governmental administrators such as yourselves.

After the long working sessions at this and other governors' conferences, you do not need me to preach about subjects you thoroughly understand and which you will eventually solve by hard work, patience and the long process of compromise. Rather than weary you further with recitals geared less to your enlightenment than to the display of what ex-governors such as I like to think of as accumulated gubernatorial wisdom, I would like to touch briefly on a generality that I feel is of vital importance, even though often lost in the specific frenzies of modern government.

I refer to the most solemn unwritten obligation of a governor — that of leading the people of his state, and through his statements, molding opinion. Somewhere amid the sometimes exciting, sometimes tedious intricacies of the sophisticated governmental structure of a modern state, the elected leader must disengage from the manipulation of *things* and consider the *spirit of the people* he is elected to serve.

At no time in our history have we seen a greater preoccupation with the machinery of government, a greater fascination with the ideas of the "In-Group" of bureaucrats and professional experts, and less attention to the true functions of leadership, which form the only real reason for the people of a sovereign state to designate one citizen to give them direction and hope.

It's easy to mistake great activity and a proliferation of high-sounding programs for leadership. No one knows better than a governor how tempting it is to spend hour after hour in staff level meetings discussing tax formulas, federal–state contributive ratios, education and health budgets and other important details — not to mention all the varieties of unimportant trivia which wash through the sands of the great departments, propelled by the pumps of countless career public servants dependent on activity more than progress to justify their existence.

No one knows better than a governor, who digs his way through reams of paper — through memoranda ad nauseam — through studies and consultants' reports ponderously redundant — how easy it is to get caught in the "make-work" climate of modern government. I used to sit in my office in Annapolis and occasionally look up at a portrait of some ancient predecessor and wonder what it was like before the typewriter and the duplicating machine visited these miserable torrents of minutiae upon us — before committees and study groups and lobbies, convinced of their unique knowledge and the originality of ideas born and discarded from the time of George Washington down, thrust themselves upon us. I'd suspect that these early executives had more time than we to devote to creative thought and the assessment of the direction of their constituents.

Today, we have a dangerous delusion — words masquerading as decisions, activity masquerading as progress, and nonproductive dissent masquerading as constructive debate. It is easy to be deceived into thinking that because we are busy we are making progress. To the contrary, I would suggest that the destructive forces gathering strength in the country today are equivalent to enormous headwinds on the nose of the ship of state. Our engines are flailing, but we're not getting very far very fast. Until we accept the necessity of facing our leadership obligations and stating a direction for our people, we will continue to lose ground.

What is the greatest issue today? It's not the war in Vietnam, it's not inflation, nor the environment. It is not an issue that you even hear discussed in its stark and simple enormity. But it is, nonetheless, the overriding and compelling issue in the United States today. Simply stated, it is: "Will the government of this country remain in the hands of its elected officials or will it descend to the streets?"

It is not unusual, nor should it be distressing, that individuals of monumental ego among the failures of our society should attack everything fundamental to our free culture. They're simply lashing out in all directions because they cannot bear to face their individual inadequacies. Neither should it overly concern us that certain brilliant but sequestered academicians are criticizing the government. This has always been so, and probably will always be so. Sometimes it even does some good. Also, we should not seem surprised that the neophyte political ambitious loudly champion all causes of the least affluent. That works beautifully until they get elected and have to represent all the people.

Why then, if these political phenomena are standard to a democratic government, should we be disturbed about them today?

The answer lies not in the fear of the kooks or demagogues themselves, but in their current respectability. Never in our history have we paid so much attention to so many odd characters. Twenty-five years ago the tragicomic antics of such social misfits would have brought the establishment running after them with butterfly nets rather than television cameras. It's in this inordinate attention to the bizarre, this preoccupation with the dramatic, this rationalization of the ridiculous, that we threaten the progress of our nation.

It's time for the political, business, and academic leaders of this country to lead a figurative march back to normalcy. There are, and always have been, political risks in speaking out; but the silence of our leaders when confronted with outrage is being construed in the country as uncertainty and even in some areas as sympathy for these assaults on the fundamental nature of our culture.

Courts are becoming carnivals; laws are flouted. Criminals commit their despicable acts against society in the name of political activity.

Gentlemen, I propose that all of us elected to positions of governmental responsibility should speak out forcefully and directly against the outrageous patterns of conduct which have become so fashionable of late. Whether or not one agrees with every ruling that the judge made in the recent Chicago trial is not the point. The point is that a handful of oddballs deliberately set out to politicize a simple criminal proceeding and to disrupt the most basic protection of our society — the dignity of the courts. The point is that the new technique of judicial disruption is spreading like wildfire throughout the country. The tactic is to provoke and inflame in the hope that overreaction will obliterate the true nature of the proceeding.

The spread of revolutionary conduct, as you are well aware, is not limited to the courtrooms of this nation. We find it in our educational systems and, in fact, beginning to spread from college to high school to junior high school. We find it invading every governmental body that depends upon constructive citizen participation. The purpose is clear and obvious — to immobilize and incapacitate the normal procedures of our constitutional government.

What can we do? We can exert our governmental authority to protect the people who placed us in these positions of responsibility. This requires firm decisive action and a willingness to withstand the criticism of the liberal community who are presently so blinded by total dedication to individual freedom that they cannot see the steady erosion of the collective freedom that is the capstone of a law-abiding society. This, of course, means acting within the law.

Of equal importance, we can begin to lead American opinion. I am convinced that the overwhelming majority of Americans will follow the lead of their governors and other elected officials if we will just launch a campaign to exert the force of public opinion to drive these bizarre extremists from their preemptive positions on our television screens and on the front pages of our newspapers. There are more valuable subjects to be covered in the public interest.

Let us move vigorously to deeply involve our citizens in the traditional American fashion. Let us establish constructive dialogue and debate to replace the nonproductive disengagement and dissent. Above all, let us react automatically, briskly, and effectively against the threat of violent revolution and recognize it for the clear and present danger it constitutes.

THE NATIONAL Alliance of Businessmen provides proof that the private sector of this nation has a real commitment to improve the chance that every citizen has to earn a share in the bounty of America.

There is no activity which attests better to that philosophy than NAB's efforts to achieve fuller economic opportunity for those who presently participate the least — the minorities, the undereducated, and the handicapped.

In the past we have often fallen short of reaching national goals because of a preoccupation with the government solution. We have relied too much on government's abilities and too little on the proven effectiveness of private enterprise. This overemphasis on the importance of governmental spending needs to be brought into perspective. It is important that we promote public understanding that over seventy-five percent of our GNP is privately spent and that with that seventy-five percent goes an almost equivalent ability to finance the solutions to our nation's domestic problems.

The NAB indicates an exceptional understanding of the proper leadership role for the private sector.

I do not for a minute underestimate government's companion role. It includes the need to sustain a proper environment for economic growth and the need to provide selective catalytic action in areas where private initiative is lacking. A benign environment for economic growth requires a definitive national policy which will allow us to reap the maximum benefit from our national and human resources.

As the President said at his dinner for your board of directors and your metropolitan chairmen, he is deeply grateful for your efforts. All of us in the administration feel the same. We pledge our continued support and offer the prospect of increased assistance through the President's proposed Manpower Training Act and Family Assistance Program.

As you meet here this week to formulate your plans for the coming year, I request that you consider several basic problems which we often acknowledge, but fail to directly address. I am referring to the interplay among the problems of urban, suburban, and rural areas — and our need to stop compartmentalizing those problems. Urban problems, for example, will never be solved until they are attacked on a metropolitan basis.

I have been particularly concerned with the fact that relatively speaking we continue to neglect the poor youth of our rural and suburban areas. By no means do I think we are doing as much as we could for those in our cities, nor that we should do less for the cities in an effort to balance our approach. However, it is important to realize that in an urban–rural comparison of health and education facilities and income levels, we find major disparities with rural America consistently in the disadvantaged position.

As chairman of the President's Council on Youth Opportunity, I have had the opportunity to be particularly aware of NAB's Summer Youth Program. The Council is establishing a pilot project wherein we anticipate being of more assistance to your summer program as well as your broader year-round effort for the hard-core unemployed. We are seeking to enlist a larger role for the state and suburban governments in providing opportunities for poor youth. Through state and suburban governments we are hoping to reach youths in need of help who live in the rural and suburban fringe as well as providing a new or expanded dimension to the central city itself.

For the first time on a pilot project basis, we will provide funds for state youth coordinators who are to assist the governors in coordinating and stimulating the public and private sectors' efforts in youth opportunity programs. We are also making every possible effort to enlist county governments to join with the cities in comprehensive metropolitanwide youth opportunity programs. NAB, from its inception, recognized the need for a metropolitan approach. You are to be commended for your foresight and perception, and I hope that the NAB regional and metropolitan chairmen will work closely with the state and local government youth coordinators.

Unfortunately, too few persons have recognized the need or demonstrated the willingness to participate in comprehensive metropolitan approaches to the problems in our cities. These city problems may be isolated in a geographical sense; however, it is clear that their effect permeates the entire metropolitan area and the entire metropolitan area should assist in eliminating them.

The suburban dweller who turns his back on city problems and claims that he should not financially contribute to their solution is closing his eyes to the direct relationship between the economic viability of his county and the city. All of the profitable beltway industries and the dramatic mercantile growth in urban counties can be attributed to their positioning around the city hub. Without the railhead, the port, the airport, the trading center, and the location of primary industry within the city, suburban business and industrial growth would be impossible.

At one time I was an executive of a metropolitan, suburban government where the people were rather reluctant to participate in city problems. I pointed out on many occasions that earnings taxes and devices to impose a burden on a certain segment of the peripheral residence were unrealistic. And that, in fact, the entire periphery — the entire suburban bedroom counties, regardless of whether they contained individuals in those homes who worked in the city or not — should contribute to the sustenance of the city mainly because, as I pointed out just now, there is no doubt that the going business communities of that county are dependent upon their relationship to the city for their existence. And they would never be there were it not for the fact that this city provided this stimulus to create the business-oriented atmosphere that makes success possible in the bridges.

Therefore, there is an interdependence and an obligation to the city that must be faced by the suburban dweller whether or not he works inside or outside that city. The cities have problems, but they are everybody's problems.

Dr. Pat Moynihan, Counselor to the President, has stated:

> Poverty and social isolation of minority groups in central cities is the single most important problem of the American city today.

I agree. But I add that this is everyone's problem, whether he lives in our out of the city.

There has been the assumption on the part of many that because the primary problems of race and poverty are found in the ghettos of urban America, the solutions to these problems must also be found there. These ghetto-oriented programs tend to ignore the geographic distribution of resources throughout metropolitan regions. Resources needed to solve the urban poverty problem — land, money, and jobs — are presently in scarce supply in the inner cities. They exist in substantial supply in suburban areas but are not being sufficiently utilized in solving inner-city problems.

Since the end of World War II as much as eighty-five percent of urban employment growth in metropolitan areas has taken place in the suburbs. Housing starts in the suburbs have increased from sixty percent in the '50s to seventy percent and above in the 1960s and in the larger metropolitan areas nearly eighty percent.

Ghetto-oriented programs, by their exclusive concern with solving problems within inner cities, are not taking advantage of these suburban and urban fringe resources. As a result, ghetto residents are denied the income gains and improvements in housing quality that would result from freer access to suburban jobs and land.

The cities must create new opportunities in the ghettos; and they must create decent environments in the areas that are now slums and ghettos. But these goals cannot be effectively met until there is broad utilization of all of the resources of metropolitan regions. Through your help we must improve the linkage between the central city labor forces and areas of expanding job opportunities.

I am concerned that the restrictive ghetto solutions may in effect constitute a subtle form of racism. Allowing members of our minority groups to find possibilities for decent housing, income, job, and educational opportunities only in a limited geographical area that is already, or is destined to become, a minority enclave encourages segregated living and the development of racial hostility.

Solutions to the nation's urban problems call for continued attention to the task of rebuilding cities and for building new cities on the nation's nonmetropolitan land supply. In addition to these programs, however, the need now is to focus public attention and action on the opportunities immediately available in suburban areas for jobs and for the development of housing at costs and rental levels affordable by the disadvantaged groups of urban America. I urge your help in making this need known and a continuation of your efforts to meet this need.

The concept of providing fuller economic participation to members of our minority groups must not be limited to job opportunities alone. It has been an article of faith in the United States that each individual with sufficient personal energy and initiative has the right to attempt to get into business for himself. The foundation of our economic system has been the astounding number and variety of small businesses. Many immigrants to this country, including my own father, have been able to earn a stable base for their families from an investment of small amounts of capital and large investments of their personal energies.

But something has obviously impaired this participation in economic and social escalation through business ownership for some groups of Americans. Almost ninety-seven percent of our nation's businesses are owned by the white majority. The remaining three percent are owned by persons from the 30 million black, Spanish-speaking, and Indian citizens who together make up almost fifteen percent of our population.

Even in the neighborhoods occupied predominantly by minority groups, the businesses are owned by people who live elsewhere. The businesses which are owned by blacks, Indians, and Spanish-speaking Americans are frequently underdeveloped by mainstream business standards. Most are small service and retail operations. Of our total businesses in retail trade, 3.6 percent are owned by minority persons. Of the banks, only .04 percent are owned by minority persons and of the life insurance companies only .2 percent. As a total, minority ownership represents less than ½ of 1 percent of the total assets of business ownership.

What are the causes for such a tragic omission from the benefits of free enterprise ownership? The root cause and their effects are complex. The neighborhoods in which many of the existing minority business enterprises exist are challenge enough to survival. The absence of new initiatives stems from a lack of individual qualifications, a paucity of business heritage, a lack of opportunity, a deficiency of capital, and the absence of supervisory know-how in the minority communities.

A venture into minority business is even riskier than a venture into small business generally. The minority enterprises are usually marginal and are undercapitalized. They have limited markets and restricted locational opportunities — many times artifically imposed by discrimination from the majority community.

With unskilled business personnel, they are handicapped in overcoming these built-in impediments. Unusually subject to vandalism, pilferage, and robberies, the minority businessman finds that insurance is sometimes completely unavailable and usually unobtainable at realistic rates.

Starting with such handicaps, it is obvious that the potential minority business entrepreneur is going to need something more than a bank loan. He is going to need the type of assistance which can come only from the private sector — marketing skills, a knowledge of organizational and personnel procedures, accounting and purchasing know-how, advertising and public relations expertise — all of which make the difference between profit and loss.

One year ago, the President created the Office of Minority Business Enterprise in the Department of Commerce to coordinate the efforts and resources of federal departments and agencies with private enterprise to assist and encourage additional business ownership by minority group members. That office has created or has suggested several key

302

methods through which the special resources of the private sector can be made available to minority enterprise. Two of the most productive methods deserve your close attention.

The MESBIC (or Minority Enterprise Small Business Investment Companies) approach offers a means for business to involve itself firsthand in developing minority business. The MESBIC's program is expected to produce $1 billion in new minority capital by fiscal 1971.

The other method, the turnkey spinoff relationship, allows the fledgling firm to have firm market support in addition to the investment of advice and money from the mother company. It can be a symbiotic relationship, with the new company learning to compete without assistance and the parent company receiving a quality product from a committed supplier.

It is expected that Secretary Stans is going to describe these programs in detail as he moves around the country during the coming year, and we certainly hope they're going to meet with a high degree of success in overcoming these ridiculous proportions of minority, small business ownership.

I request that, where at all possible, you and your company make available these needed resources of talent and expertise to a minority enterprise and that you make them available as long as it takes to assure the emergence of that minority business as a successful venture. It is also essential that you not regard such an undertaking as a social program. Everyone concerned must never lose sight of the fact that he is building a business.

The new firm will be anxious to achieve independence from the sponsor and may sometimes attempt to do so long before it is prepared for such a move. This will exert a pressure on the sponsor's management which, if too readily accommodating, could well put the new firm in great jeopardy. You undoubtedly will be required to endure problems, frustrations, and delays which you would not contend with in your own business. You may ask why you should commit your company to such a difficult undertaking let alone one which may create competition for you.

The answer is simple. You cannot afford to do otherwise.

March 9, 1970, Washington, D.C.
Nineteenth Annual Congressional Banquet,
Order of Ahepa

WHENEVER I speak to my brother Ahepans, I am reminded of one of the chores my father assigned me to do when I was a boy. As you know, he was once Secretary of the Worthington Chapter 30 of Ahepa, in Baltimore. It was my job to help fold the meeting notices and address and stuff the envelopes.

Later on, in my teens, when he was president and then district governor, I would help him write his speeches. He liked to speak of his pride in his Hellenic heritage, and of his pride and delight in being an American in a century when the great democratic principles laid down in ancient Greece were best expressed in this land of opportunity.

His speeches were never covered by television, but television hadn't been invented yet so I can't complain about that. At least he had one critic — my mother — but she was also his biggest fan.

One central point that he would make in those speeches that we worked on together has a special relevance to what I would like to talk to you about tonight.

He spoke of a "spirit of community" that existed within the Americans of Greek descent, and his life reflected a powerful example of that spirit.

Like so many others, my father lost all he had in the Depression. He went to work hauling vegetables, starting at 3 a. m. most mornings, to restaurants and food stores in the Baltimore area. He went into competition with the big suppliers of vegetables, who were able to offer better and faster service than he could ever offer. But he found customers, because of that spirit of community. These customers were men who were willing to give up the convenience the big suppliers had to offer, because in those hard times they were anxious to help a small supplier get started to earn a living.

The men who ran the restaurants — mainly those of Greek extraction, most of them immigrants to this country — who bought those vegetables understood something about human dignity. They were not giving a man charity, they were giving a man a chance — and it was a charitable spirit that moved them to endure whatever inconvenience it cost, it was the kind of charity that never demeaned the recipiet. And of course, when my father got back on his feet fiancially, he made sure that the help he gave others was the kind of help that enhanced rather than destroyed a man's self-respect.

That brings me to my subject tonight. Quite frankly, I want to enlist your help in a cause — a cause central to our desire to set this nation on a new path toward greater dignity of the individual.

You may have heard recently that the House Ways and Means Committee overwhelmingly approved this administration's *Family Assistance Plan*. That plan was designed by President Nixon to end the scandal that has been the welfare system in this country. I say "scandal" advisedly.

The way our welfare system encourages idleness is a scandal. The way our welfare system actually breaks up families is a scandal. The way our welfare system robs human beings of their dignity — binding succeeding generations in a lifetime of despair — is the worst scandal of all. During my years in county government and as governor of Maryland, I spoke out frequently for reform of the welfare system. One of the first conversations I had with the President was about the problems of the welfare system.

The President was determined to end the welfare scandal, to reform a system that failed the taxpayer, insulted the working poor, and placed people on a treadmill of dependency.

We call the new plan "workfare," rather than welfare, because it encourages people to work.

Under the old system, a poor man who is working can look across the street at a family on welfare getting more for not working than he makes at his job. In bureaucratic language, the rage that he feels is described as a "disincentive." In plain English, it is an open invitation for him to quit work and live on welfare. If a man can make more for his family on welfare than he can make working, you can bet that many men will quit work, sit back, and watch the soap operas on television all day.

With workfare, the "disincentive" is removed. A family with a working member will always get more than a family without a working member. Work will always be rewarded, which — let's face it — is why most people go to work.

Under the old system, every dollar you earned was subtracted from your welfare payments. This amounted to 100 percent taxation, and the social planners who dreamed this up forgot that a profit motive is a powerful thing. But under our system, you keep fifty cents out of every dollar you earn as you work your way out of poverty, and a welfare recipient who goes to work is better off than one who does not. It didn't take a genius to figure this out — which makes you wonder why it's never been suggested before.

To put a program like this into operation, we are going to have to put a lot of people who are "working poor" — people who are struggling to get themselves out of poverty — onto the welfare rolls. We are proposing to add to their incomes to establish the basic principle that "it pays to work."

Here is where we run into opposition from some people who — quite properly — are concerned about adding to the welfare rolls and adding to the amount of money the government spends on welfare.

When you talk about not being able to afford the initial cost of welfare reform, it reminds me of the man who refused to put water on his burning house because his water bill was too high already.

I suppose I'm for this welfare program. A lot of columnists and editors, who up to this point hadn't made up their minds, are going to be against it because I'm for it. As far as I'm concerned many of them react to this sound of my voice like a mother who is harried and distracted and she hears her children in the backyard and they're talking too loud and she rushes out and says "go see what Willie's doing and tell him to stop."

Speaking of columnists, I'm trying very hard to get along with them. I want you to know that. Just yesterday I tried a new approach that seemed to work very well on one who'd been particularly nasty in his criticism of what I say. I treated him like a gentleman. I guess not many people had ever tried that on him.

Now to put a program like this new welfare plan into operation, we're going to have to put a lot of people who are "working poor" on the rolls as I've said. And the addition to these working poor to the list of those who receive benefits lays down the principle that it pays to work, that work is rewarded in America, that it is in your own self-interest to get a job. This is a principle that is intensely valuable to American society, and it is well worth the cost all by itself.

Second, look at the people it helps. It helps the man who is not looking for a handout, but who is trying to make ends meet by himself, who just cannot quite make it. These are the proudest poor, the people who are striving in the best American tradition. This offers a boost to the man who is already trying to climb, and we all know that there can be no better investment toward ultimate independence and self-reliance.

Third, we have introduced — at long last — a work requirement into the welfare system. Every single able-bodied adult — who doesn't have preschool children or sick adults to care for at home will be required to register with the Secretary of Labor for work or work training.

Fourth, we are bolstering this family assistance plan with a whole new approach to manpower training — one that does not cost more money, but will deliver more jobs. For example, in cities all across the country, we are introducing a computerized job bank — a modern way of matching available jobs to men with the training to handle those jobs. And we are adding to our day-care center facilities, to make it possible for more welfare mothers to go to work while their children get good supervision.

And fifth, our program will surely save money in the long run. Within the next four years, if the old system were to be allowed to mushroom the way it has been, the cost to the taxpayer would be more than a billion dollars more than our family assistance plan — with none of the incentives toward work.

Those are some of the sound, sensible reasons that the Ways and Means Committee decided that our plan for welfare reform — for "work-fare" — was worthy of support.

So when you hear someone say "The Nixon proposal will add two million families to the welfare rolls" — see it in perspective. It is the only way to stop the downhill slide toward a welfare state — by rewarding the poor who are willing to work.

And when you hear the charge "it's going to cost over four billion dollars" remember the cost of what the present system would be, if allowed to continue to balloon. We have to pay the start-up costs — the turnaround costs — if we are to start to get people moving off welfare rolls and onto payrolls.

Why am I making this case to the people here in this room? Because I know you understand, as well as anybody in this world, the "spirit of community," the need to help somebody help himself. Especially in the face of the permissiveness that afflicts so much of our society, you understand the importance of building self-respect, self-reliance, the dignity that comes from earning a dollar.

305

And there is a second reason. To put it bluntly, Greeks love to talk politics, and to take part in politics. We are born activists — and we know the difference between an activist and an agitator. Your help now, your active support of welfare reform is urgently needed. I don't have to tell you how to mobilize your support, or how to spread the word that it is welfare reform now or handouts forever.

In receiving your Socratic Award tonight, it is fitting to recall a point made by Socrates at the end of his life. As he lay dying, his last words were reported to be about a debt that he owed — he wanted to make sure that a man who had given him some food would be repaid.

In the same way, we all have debts to repay to our fellowmen, in return for the opportunity our society has given us. To the helpless, we owe sustenance; to the able-bodied, we owe opportunity and training.

As we repay that debt, let us never forget what the dignity of work can do for a human being.

One reason the silent majority is so silent is this: They're too busy working to make a lot of noise.

All too often today, we see some young people — by no means all, but some — who take refuge in postgraduate study not to get a better education, not to prepare themselves for productive lives, not even the draft — but to avoid going to work.

We see some welfare rights organizations denouncing our family assistance plan, not because it doesn't help the helpless, but because it requires able-bodied people to go to work.

We see some employees arriving at work in the morning with their minds fixed on the coffee break; we see people starting their careers with one goal in mind — early retirement; we see some union leaders promising their membership a golden era of a twenty-hour week.

I submit that the people with a phobia about working are missing one of the greatest satisfactions of life. The quality of life will not be determined by how much time off we have, it will be determined by the quality of the work we do.

Certainly, a menial job with no future, a dead-end job, would depress anybody and direct him away from work. That is why we, as a nation, must open up opportunities for people to fulfill themselves to the full extent of their potential.

And that is why this administration is guided by what could be termed a work ethic.

We refuse to accept the kind of sustained unemployment that existed in the first five years of the sixties — which, many people forget, ran close to an average of six percent.

We refuse to accept a manpower training program that trains people for dead-end jobs, creating resentment and discontent.

We refuse to accept a welfare program that penalizes the worker and tempts him to quit.

And we refuse to permit some unions to ration opportunity, as if it belonged to them alone — because opportunity in America is everybody's birthright.

To the able-bodied person who says "the world owes me a living," we say: Mister, you're wrong.

But to the person willing to work who says "this nation owes me a chance," we say: Friend, you're right.

That's the work ethic that guides the leaders of this country today. It does not make government the "employer of last resort," providing meaningless make-work jobs; it does make government responsible for enforcing equal opportunity, for ending discrimination based on race, sex, or any other unfair basis, and for managing our economic affairs in a way that permits solid growth without inflation.

We owe it to ourselves, and we owe it to our children, to reinstill this work ethic that builds a nation and builds a man's character.

This is no impossible dream. On the contrary, this is the American Dream and it is up to every one of us — in and out of government — to be sure we make this dream come true.

In utilizing our great resources to help people, we must not forget the admonition of Socrates: "A horse cannot be safely used without a bridle, or wealth without reflection."

April 13, 1970, Des Moines, Iowa
Iowa Republican Statewide Fund-Raising Dinner

FIVE MONTHS to the day have passed since I visited Des Moines to present a few thoughts about the network news. It is a pleasure to be back — I enjoy visiting famous battlefields, especially when the outcome of the conflict was decisive and served a useful purpose.

Tonight I hope to cover more completely a subject touched upon in my Lincoln Day remarks in Chicago — the disturbing trends in administrative and admissions policies of America's colleges and universities.

With regard to the determination of curricula and the hiring and firing of college professors, I stated in Chicago that the desires of students should not be the controlling factor. However, it cannot be validly argued that students' views on these matters are of no value in making educational judgments. Students, the consumers of knowledge, are in a unique position to assess the effectiveness of educational policies. Therefore, their views should be considered and be an ingredient of final decisions by the educational establishment.

From the light of experiences in the last decade, it would seem to me that Professor Sidney Hook hit the nail on the head in his recent book, *Academic Freedom and Academic Anarchy*. He stated:

> There are no compensating advantages in the risks incurred when students are given the power of educational decision. "That is why with respect to the . . . demand for student rights, we must say: "Consultation, yes — decision, no."

Tonight I want to give you my views in greater particularity on the subject of college admissions, and this time I come armed with supportive quotations from distinguished administrators who are equally concerned about this problem.

The American system of colleges and universities, ladies and gentlemen, is the envy of mankind. It belongs not just to the professional educational community, but to all of us. When decisions begin to represent a definite trend that may drastically depreciate those national assets, then all of us have an interest at stake; all of us have a right to be heard — indeed, a duty to speak.

When one looks back across the history of the last decade — at the smoking ruins of a score of college buildings, at the outbreaks of illegal and violent protests and disorders on hundreds of college campuses, at the regular harassment and interruption and shouting down of speakers, at the totalitarian spirit evident among thousands of students and hundreds of faculty members, at the decline of genuine academic freedom to speak and teach and learn — that record hardly warrants a roaring vote of confidence in the academic community that presided over the disaster.

We in public life who criticize, however, should make that criticism constructive. This I intend to do. I feel as much as anyone that there should be expanded educational opportunities for deprived, but able, young people in our society. The difference is that I favor better preparing them — with additional governmental assistance — in some form of prep school rather than tossing them into a four-year college or university curriculum that they are not equipped to handle. And I do not feel that our traditional four-year institutions should lower their sights or their standards for the sole purpose of opening their doors wider.

Now, there are two methods by which unqualified students are being swept into college on the wave of the new socialism. One is called a quota system, and the other an open admissions policy. Each is implemented by lessening admission requirements. They may be equally bad.

Under a quota system, a specific percentage of the student body must consist of minority or disadvantaged students regardless of whether they can meet the existing standards for enrollment. If they do not apply, they must be recruited.

Under an open admissions policy, a college deliberately opens its doors and expands its enrollment despite the inability of many of the applicants to meet minimum standards.

There are distinguished, even brilliant, men with grave reservations about the wisdom of either of these policies. The historian Daniel Boorstin is one of them. Speaking in Tulsa last June, he carved his views in sentences more emphatic than my own.

> In the university all men are not equal. Those better endowed or better equipped intellectually must be preferred in admission, and preferred in recognition. . . . If we give in to the armed demands of militants to admit persons to the university because of their race, their poverty, their illiteracy, or any other nonintellectual distinctions, our universities can no longer serve all of us — or any of us.

Professor Boorstin argues his case on behalf of the integrity of the university, but there are also other arguments against racial quotas, not the least of which is that of simple justice.

For each youth unprepared for a college curriculum who is brought in under a quota system, some better prepared student is denied entrance. Admitting the obligation to compensate for past deprivation and discrimination, it just does not make sense to atone by discriminating against and depriving someone else.

Another argument against easy admissions was summed up in the testimony of Dr. Clark Kerr of the prestigious Carnegie Foundation's Commission for the Advancement of Teaching in testimony before the House Education Committee. He said:

> Some institutions have brought in students too far below the admissions standards with the result that it ended up in frustration for the student. . . . It's bad policy to start someone on a path when you know he can't reach the end of the road.

Is it understandable that I wonder why the remarks of Kerr and Boorstin were greeted with respectful editorial silence by the same tribe that came looking for my scalp after Chicago?

We can see the visible results of weak and insufficiently defined educational policy in the growing militancy of increasing numbers of students who confuse social ideals with educational opportunities. John Roche, a former Special Consultant to President Johnson, a syndicated columnist, and a professor at Brandeis, observed the phenomenon on his own campus. In my opinion, he analyzed it correctly. Last year he wrote as follows about the violence emanating from black student militancy:

> Sociologists and others have had a field day explaining the sources of this behavior, but I do not believe the problem at Brandeis, San Francisco, Swarthmore, or wherever trouble has erupted is terribly complex. We created our own difficulties the day we (and I mean the liberal academicians) decided that a college or university should double as a settlement house. Once the decision was made that Negro or "culturally underprivileged" youngsters should be admitted to first-class colleges, without the usual prerequisites, the escalation began. . . .
>
> All this special black admission business has, of course, been conducted with a brass band, as college and university administrators and faculties congratulate themselves on their radicalism, on their willingness to rise above white racism. In fact, what has happened in most instances that have come to my attention is sheerly cosmetic: nobody has actually worried about the anguish of the poor Negro kids who have been dumped into a competitive situation, have been thrown with inadequate preparation into water well beyond their capacity to swim.

In criticizing my views on racial quotas following my speech in Chicago, the *Cleveland Plain Dealer* said:

"In the prestigious Ivy League, the schools admitted freshman classes last September that were ten percent Negro . . ." and it added approvingly, "This represented a huge increase in black enrollment."

But, is this a really good thing — and if ten percent is good, would twelve or fifteen percent be better?

President Clifford Lord of Hofstra, in a speech last December, aired his own doubts about a policy of "open admissions."

"This can be a very expensive process for the private institution, financially and academically," he noted. ". . . There is the additional and critical question of the educational desirability of mixing those who are qualified by modern standards for work in a particular institution and those who came in under an open enrollment program."

A Ford Foundation education expert, Mr. Fred Crossland, registers more than just doubts; he thinks this ten percent quota today is impossible to attain.

According to the Office of Education, though blacks constitute about twelve percent of our college age population, they account for only six percent of all high school graduates. Mr. Crossland adds that only about half of this six percent is capable of handling a college curriculum. Where does this leave the *Plain Dealer's* ten percent? Says Mr. Crossland:

"Given present standards, it's preposterous and statistically impossible to talk about boosting black enrollment to ten percent even over the next five years."

What makes Mr. Crossland's unequivocal statement so timely is that just two weeks ago — after twelve days of heat from striking militant students at the University of Michigan — President Robben W. Fleming agreed to nearly all their major demands — the first of which was for a ten percent black enrollment by 1973.

Now let me read you what a distinguished member of the Michigan faculty said about the President's action. He is Gardner Ackley, the economics professor who served as Chairman of President Johnson's Council of Economic Advisers. According to the *Ann Arbor News*, this is what Professor Ackley told a faculty meeting:

"This has been a very tragic year . . . which has seen the beginning of the destruction of this University as a center of learning. . . . It is being destroyed by its own faculty and administration.

"The University's administration," he said, "is unwilling or unable to resist the destroyers. . . . However ridiculous or worthy the cause, it will win in proportion to the willingness of its supporters to disrupt the life of the University.

"University facilities are now available for . . . promoting any cause, no matter how obscene or revolting.

"There is no reason. There is only power."

According to the *Ann Arbor News*, Professor Ackley received a standing ovation; and there were shouts of "Bravo" from his colleagues.

The surrender at Ann Arbor is not dissimilar to the tragic surrender of Italian academic and political leadership to the demands of rebellious students two years ago for open admissions to the universities of all high school graduates.

The results have been instructive, to say the least. Measured in diplomas granted annually — the number has jumped, in just a few years, from 28,000 to 40,000 — the reform is a success. But these are bargain-basement diplomas — and total Italian employers advertising for college graduates are careful to specify that the degree must date back to 1967.

In a few years' time perhaps — thanks to the University of Michigan's callow retreat from reality — America will give the diplomas from Michigan the same fisheye that Italians now give diplomas from the University of Rome.

President Lord of Hofstra, who, as I stated earlier, expressed his serious reservations about mixing "open enrollment" students and academically qualified students, feels nevertheless that this might be a good policy — for institutions other than Hofstra. Is it with tongue in cheek that he said:

"It seems to me that the wholly or largely tax-supported institutions such as the State University or the City University have got to pick up this ball and carry it . . ."

309

One gets the distinct impression that Hofstra will not be picking up the ball and carrying it any time soon.

But the public institutions are not without impassioned defenders — like Irving Kristol — who believe it a major tragedy to impose upon quality institutions of higher learning, such as the city colleges of New York, a social burden of assimilation and uplift that they are neither designed nor equipped to shoulder.

Writing in the *Public Interest* last November he warned:

> . . . black militants are demanding that many more [and eventually all] black students who are graduated from high school be admitted automatically to the city colleges regardless of grades or aptitude, or whatever and [New York's Upper East Side and Suburban Elite] which in any case sends its youngsters out of town, thinks it is being "constructive" when it meets this demand at least part way — i.e., when it grants to poor black youngsters a college diploma in lieu of a college education. . . .
>
> The city colleges are one of the most valuable — perhaps the most valuable — patrimonies of New York. The Jews took them over from the WASPs and used them to great advantage; the Irish and Italians are now participating and benefiting; the Negroes and Puerto Ricans will very soon be in a position to inherit this remarkable system of higher education. But as things are going now, their inheritance will be worthless.

These institutions — the widening avenue of advancement for the young natural leaders in New York's community — are, in his words:

> . . . being transformed — degraded is not too strong a term — with the approval and consent of the elite, into four-year community colleges, with all academic distinction being remorselessly extinguished.

If these quality colleges are degraded, it would be a permanent and tragic loss to the poor and middle class of New York, who cannot afford to establish their sons and daughters on the Charles River or Cayuga Lake. New York will have traded away one of the intellectual assets of the Western world for a four-year community college and a hundred thousand devalued diplomas.

The central mission of higher education is intellectual, argues Dr. Lincoln Gordon of Johns Hopkins University.

To the extent universities deviate from that objective, we are devaluating a national asset that many foreign leaders believe has given America a unique advantage over the nations of the world.

I agree with Dr. Gordon. Any attempt to subordinate the great universities of this country to social goals for which they are ill-designed and ill-equipped can only result in tragic losses to both these institutions and the nation.

Perhaps the country has already marched too far under the banners of the slogan, "Every Man A College Graduate," to abandon it now. But maybe not. Perhaps there remains a "via media," a middle way, that will both preserve the integrity and quality of America's colleges — and advance the cause of minorities and the disadvantaged.

Assuredly, the first step along such a road was taken a few weeks ago by President Nixon when he called on the nation to make a historic commitment:

> No *qualified* student who wants to go to college should be barred by lack of money. That has long been a great American goal: I propose that we achieve it now.

Certainly, no young man or woman with ability and talent should be denied, by the ancient and traditional barrier of poverty, the opportunity to advance to the limits of his capacity. Not in this wealthy country in 1970. To allow that to happen is to tolerate an unnecessary individual tragedy which, when multiplied, amounts to a national tragedy.

Nor can we let talent go unnoticed. A perpetual national search should be conducted to locate within every community every child of ability and promise. When located, they should be given special attention — to advance them to limits of their potential and to prepare them for leadership in their communities and in society.

We must also recognize the needs of the unprepared and underachieving child and of those who do not begin to show promise academically until later in high school. Where necessary — and it is often critically necessary — substantial programs of compensatory education must be developed. Extra summers of study, extra years of academic preparation must be provided at public expense. For there can be no doubt that we must compensate for the deprived environment.

For these students I believe we must have more community colleges and special preparatory schools, to insure to the late-blooming, the underprepared, and the underachieving student every educational opportunity.

But I make this distinction: Preparatory and compensatory education do not belong in the university. Students needing special educational services — who do not meet the standards and requirements of institutions of higher education — should not be encouraged to apply — in the first instance — to such institutions.

Rather than lower the standards of higher education, we must raise the level of the student's preparation and achievement, so that he may not only one day take his place in the colleges and universities of this nation, but successfully hold that place in active, healthy competition with other students.

This, I believe, is the kind of commitment that can and must be made to balance the scales and insure full equality of educational opportunity.

But, a firm commitment to equality of opportunity must not result in the dilution of that opportunity. For colleges and universities to deliberately draw into a high academic environment students who are unqualified intellectually or whom the primary and secondary schools have conspicuously failed to prepare is to create hopes which are doomed to disappointment.

Moreover, the cluttering of our universities, already too large in many cases, through the insertion of high school level semesters for the accommodation of those unqualified for the traditional curriculum is a major cause of campus inefficiency and unrest. The number of students on college campuses has increased by 400 percent in three decades and is expected to reach nearly ten million within five years. In 1940 only two universities in the country had more than twenty thousand students; today, sixty universities can claim that dubious distinction.

Rising student enrollments have been forced to exaggerated heights by a combination of underlying social pressures. Within the awesome statistics of bigness lie the heart of the justified complaints of many college students today — complaints about absentee professors — about the plastic facelessness on campus — about the decline and disappearance of the personal teacher–student relationship — about ill-equipped graduate students teaching courses for which undergraduates have paid $60, $70, and even $80 a credit — about being matriculated, administrated, graded, and graduated by computer.

I do not accept the proposition that every American boy and girl should go to a four-year college. Even now, with nearly eight million students on the campuses of this country, there are tens of thousands there who did not come for the learning experience and who are restless, purposeless, bored, and rebellious.

College, at one time considered a privilege, is considered to be a right today — and is valued less because of that. Concentrations of disoriented students create an immense potential for disorder.

The Chairman of the Sociology Department of Columbia University, Professor Amital Etzioni, recognizes the phenomenon, deplores its inevitable and undesirable by-products — the depersonalization of the campus and the threat to academic quality because of massive enrollments — but sees no certain solution.

Writing recently in the *Wall Street Journal*, he contends that the lowering of admission standards results in the presence on campus of pressure groups with — and I quote:

... a social ideology and a political organization to further demands for easy promotion and guaranteed graduation.

If one tries to enforce select admission or academic standards, he risks being labeled a racist, and he lays himself open to campuswide attacks . . .

The goal of college education for everyone is now too widely endorsed both by white middle-class Americans and minorities to stop the high-schoolization of colleges simply by trying to uphold the old standards . . .

If we can no longer keep the floodgates closed at the admissions office, it at least seems wise to channel the general flow away from four-year colleges and toward two-year extensions of high school in the junior and community colleges.

And, of course, that is what should be done.

Consistent with this philosophy, I favor the sort of procedures in high school that screen out the best students and make greater demands upon their greater talents.

In some areas, such ideas have been discarded as reactionary. But if we accept Jefferson's concept of a "natural aristocracy" among peoples — then that is as true for every race and community of man. It should be our objective to find, to nurture, and to advance that natural aristocracy through the rigorous demands of intellectual competition.

To require a student of genuine ability to sit for hours in a classroom with those neither able nor prepared, and to permit him to be intellectually stalled at the level of the slowest, is a cruel waste of his God-given talents.

In Washington today there is a single black high school — Dunbar — which once trained this natural aristocracy with unrivaled success. Two decades ago, eighty percent of its graduates went on to college, a higher percentage than any other school in the District of Columbia. That high school numbers among its graduated federal, district and appellate judges, the first black general in the American Army, and a United States Senator.

After the Supreme Court decision of 1954, however, this school under prevailing educational nostrums was allowed to become just another school in the inner city. Today, it ranks at the bottom of District of Columbia schools in the percentage of graduates going on to college.

In my opinion, Dunbar High School was sacrificed by the levelers and the ideologists on the altar of educational egalitarianism — and I cannot believe that the black people of the capital or the nation are better for the loss.

My remarks here tonight have been extended — I am sure they will also strike some of my critics as pure heresy. As soon as they come clacking off the news wires into the horrified city rooms of the East, my friends on the editorial pages will start sharpening their knives and dancing around the typewriters. I ask no favors — but make one recommendation. Read my remarks through just once at least, before turning to the keyboard. Sometimes, that can improve the editorial.

Thank you and good night.

April 17, 1970, Washington, D.C.
Republican Leadership Conference

I WOULD LIKE to take a few minutes tonight to speak to you about something that is of critical importance to the President and to every Republican officeholder in the country.

On March 18th the most important financial center in America came abruptly to a standstill. A city of more than eight million people was crippled. New York City was dragged over what Postmaster General Blount has called "the rim of disaster" by a postal work stoppage.

That illegal action or the threat of it soon spread to every major city in America. Finally the President was forced to put members of the armed forces into New York City post offices to avert catastrophe.

I think it's most unfortunate to have to use federal troops in this manner. I know that most Americans feel this way, and certainly no one feels more this way than the President. I consider the necessity of such an action a real tragedy.

But the greater tragedy lies in the fact that all this might have been avoided. The work stoppage should not have happened. It really didn't have to happen.

The Postmaster General has been warning the Congress and the country for more than a year that the present postal system carried within it the seeds of its own destruction. He warned that the system had to be changed. Men of good will on both sides of the aisle recognized the wisdom of this warning, and supported the effort to bring a change. And this was not, I assure you, a partisan issue.

But there were those who sought to make it a partisan issue. It was not a political matter, except to those opportunists who wanted to make it a political matter. It was a public matter. It was a matter which questioned whether or not this country is going to have a workable mail service.

But the change was delayed. It was delayed in no small measure by those shortsighted few who found the status quo was most compatible with their own political needs, and they chose to ignore the needs of 200 million Americans. Finally it became a situation which would tolerate no further delay. Anyone who supposes that what happened on March 18 can't happen again is simply deluding himself. The need for action is just as clear as is the cost of inaction.

By a rapid and judicious response to the postal emergency, the President and the Postmaster General succeeded in minimizing the damage and in getting the men back to work.

The agreement announced at the White House yesterday between the Postmaster General and the representatives of the unions would:

— Convert the Post Office Department into an independent establishment in the executive branch of the government, to operate as a self-contained system, with continuity of responsible management, with appropriate control over postal rates, and with a workable means of borrowing capital in the private market;

— it would provide a framework within which postal employees in all parts of the country can bargain collectively with postal management over pay and working conditions; and

— finally, it would increase the pay of postal employees by eight percent, over and above the governmentwide increase of six percent, and would shorten the time required to reach the top pay step for most of the postal jobs.

Now, this plan is going to require both the economies of postal reform as well as a postal rate change to pay for the wage increase. But the increase is an equitable one. It is in accord with the President's efforts to get a noninflationary pay increase for postal employees.

Reorganization will afford economies on the order of a billion dollars a year.

It will produce more rapid and more reliable mail service.

It will permit an equitable pay increase for the postal worker.

And it will permit collective bargaining with binding arbitration.

The bill which the administration has sent to the Congress provides for all this.

It's now up to the Congress to act. The President has done all that he can do. The

313

Postmaster General has done all that he can do. But these men cannot make law. Only the Congress can do that.

Now, what does this mean in terms of the upcoming elections?

It means that the President is upholding his promise that this will be a reform administration. He's moved across the broad spectrum of the government to bring reform. But the Post Office Department, by its visibility, by its long tradition of political manipulation, and by its very immensity, is going to provide one of the most outstanding examples of governmental reform in this century. I believe it's entirely in order to emphasize this.

I think it is entirely in order to point out the political costs that are involved here. It is the Republican party which is sacrificing patronage; it's the Republican party which is putting the needs of the people ahead of the needs of the politicians. And when the vote comes in the Congress, I don't think it will hurt a bit for us to point out, where necessary, that some Congressmen voted in the public interest and some voted in their own political interest.

The issue of reform is essential to the success of this administration. The people want reform. They want their dollar's worth from the federal government. And I think we must make it clear to them that we're going to have to return men to the House and the Senate who support the President on this score. A Republican reform President is going to have to have a Republican reform Congress if he is going to succeed. And anybody who thinks the Democrats are going to uproot this labyrinth of boondoggling bureaucracy which they have so painstakingly constructed, just to give the people better government haven't been around Washington politics very long.

Now let me pause for just a moment to say a word about a remarkable man. When the President decided to overhaul the Postal Department, when he was looking for a Postmaster General, I knew he didn't have any illusions about the magnitude of the task. It was a formidable one. It was one which required great dedication and great purpose and great courage. To do that he chose a man who can achieve these things, and we're fortunate to have that man in our Cabinet . . . Red Blount.

I suppose in some ways it's redundant for me to add my thoughts to those of the President's concerning the safe return of the astronauts from a very precarious situation. But I think, to some extent, what I'm about to say is complementary to the remarks of the President, so I will continue with my remarks on this as planned.

Apollo 13 is down from space, and the world's people, friend and foe alike, are relieved that three brave men are safely returned to earth. Among our adversaries and even among our most courteous competitors, one suspects that a certain quiet elation exists because the uniquely successful American space program has shown a flaw. But this is an understandable human reaction from teams who are tired of chasing the team that wins the pennant year after year. Because we are an open society, because we do not cloak every high-risk undertaking in secrecy, because we clearly state our objectives, our shortfalls are quite visible.

For the same reason, our successes are documented and are not dependent on self-serving declarations after the fact. We like our system. We take our chances and revel in our triumphs and we suffer through our failures.

So it's not surprising that once the exhilaration of the rescue of our interdependent explorers has subsided, Americans will feel uncomfortable that the mission failed. But what is difficult to understand is the defeatism that is already beginning to show among some of our own people.

Many of those who smugly basked in and vocally approved of that amazing string of cosmic victories are now wondering aloud whether we can afford to continue these costly experiments. The fair-weather friends of the space program are quietly disengaging and looking for a safer vehicle to satisfy their urge for vicarious high adventure. The clever little pontificators who so fluently spoke the exciting language of NASA now solemnly predict great difficulties ahead for our space program. And the old_____ — they're always there — are undoing the escape hatches and readying the lifeboats for a quick exit. And the social levelers of the new left are "I told you soing" all over the place and demanding that the space budget be sucked down into the nearest slum.

314

To abandon the manned space program because of a technical breakdown — a breakdown which in its own way did more to demonstrate the resiliency and the versatility of human beings than a hundred routine successes — would be a shortsighted tragic blunder.

Suppose the first airplane mishap had caused those pioneers to throw up their hands and quit trying to fly. Well, a great many of you wouldn't be in Washington, D.C. tonight. And even if you were, you'd be dead tired and irritable after several days of riding.

But what I'm trying to point out is that we must never be afraid to take a risk; to take, in Neil Armstrong's words, "a giant leap for mankind." Great gains require equally great risks. To live, even in monotonous comfort, without even a dream realized or an ambition fulfilled is to vegetate.

Our lives, all of our lives, are better because brave men risked their lives to implement the dreams of mighty intellects who preceded us. So when we share this glory of the brave men who push the spirit of America to new frontiers, let us never forget that with the prospects of glory goes the risk of failures. As Americans we should proudly take that risk and stand by our country in good days as well as bad ones.

But this has not been a bad day. Our astronauts are safely home. Their courage and their discipline were exemplary. The magnificent work of the entire Apollo team deserves our highest accolade. Yet the point remains stark and clear: When men reach for the stars, there can and probably will be many disappointments along the way. There may be tragedy, there may be despair. But men will continue to reach because God made them that way, and for that we can all be grateful.

April 28, 1970, Fort Lauderdale, Florida

TONIGHT, AT the risk o being further charged with divisiveness, insensitivity, and mediocrity, I want to continue my discussion of the deterioration of American values in many of our institutions of higher education.

Let us not be naïve enough to believe that there are no seeds of revolution in the rebellion that radical young people describe as "the movement." Let us be candid enough to face the fact that the spawning ground and sanctuary of "the movement" is the American university. Few institutions are more vital to a free sofciety; none is so susceptible to capture and destruction by the radical or criminal left.

Before some of my detractors are tempted to skip blithely to the conclusion that I am labeling all college students as members of the criminal left, important distinctions must be drawn.

I am *not* talking about the overwhelming majority of college students who are on the campus to learn, nor am I talking about the majority of faculty members who find it increasingly difficult to teach in a spreading climate of disruption and disorder. But I am gravely concerned that their majority will soon become a minority unless some strong swift steps are taken by administrators who up until now haven't shown much heart for counteraction.

The vulnerability of the academic community to exploitation by the radical or criminal left is based on the communal spirit and identity of interest of its members. Each year a malleable swarm of new undergraduates enters the hive and is immediately caught up in peer customs and permeated by peer opinions.

For them, all the ingredients of a new independence coalesce. Parental supervision is removed or greatly diminished; the heady wine of intellectual elitism courses through

315

their veins. More than anything else, they resemble probationers of some esoteric organization — eager to the point of sycophancy to do all the right things and make all the right noises so that they will be accepted into the group.

And the group to which they feverishly seek admission has unfortunately become alienated from the values and institutions of our society. The most vocal and well publicized members of that group are committed to radical change. Small wonder, then, that each year a new group of impressionable consumers falls victim to the totalitarian ptomaine dispensed by those who disparage our system.

The real pity is that many of the students of our universities really feel that the theatrical radicals are the architects of a brave new, compassionate world. Spiced with "rock" music, "acid," and "pot," the old Marxist idea of regulated equality without effort becomes exciting, and they assail the institutions of the free enterprise system without beginning to understand them.

The true responsibility for these aberrations and the nurturing of arrogance and contempt for constitutional authority rests not with the young people on campuses, but with those who so miserably fail to guide them. I can well understand the attitude of the majority of the student body at Yale University when most of the Yale faculty votes to endorse a strike in support of members of an organization dedicated to criminal violence, anarchy, and the destruction of the United States of America.

And when the President of that respected University describes the election of a President of the United States by the people of the United States as a "hucksterized process" under which they could not expect much better "whichever package was bought or sold," it is clearly time for the alumni of that fine old college to demand that it be headed by a more mature and responsible person.

President Brewster of Yale has also stated that he does not feel that black revolutionaries can get a fair trial within our judicial system. I do not feel that the students of Yale University can get a fair impression of their country under the tutelage of Kingman Brewster.

What kind of mentors are we entrusting our young people to when two college professors are convicted of brutally beating a third because of his political beliefs? When a former associate dean at a major university is charged with setting fires on the campus? When faculty members join students in acts of property destruction and encourage discourtesy to guest speakers on the campus?

Most of these young people who depend upon the ideology of "the movement" for moral and mental sustenance will in time find themselves as well nourished as a new baby on a diet of cotton candy. At that point, they will return to the enduring values just as every generation before them has done.

But unfortunately, there is a much smaller group of students who are committed to radical change through violent means. Some of these may be irretrievable; all will require very firm handling.

Within their ranks are the students who last week hurled stones at the home of the President of Penn State University, the students responsible for the arson at the University of Kansas, the score of students at Cornell who, wielding pipes and tire chains, beat a dormitory president into unconsciousness.

This is the criminal left that belongs not in a dormitory, but in a penitentiary. The criminal left is not a problem to be solved by the Department of Philosophy or the Department of English — it is a problem for the Department of Justice.

The journalist, I. F. Stone, recently stated that:

> Statistics on bombing from cities around the country suggest that we may be entering the first stages of an urban guerrilla movement.

I confess to being comforted that there is little likelihood that reality will ever intersect with the rhetoric of Mr. Stone.

He hurries on to suggest that far-reaching political reforms can coax the bombs and rifles out of the hands of the criminal left. His is a traditional and historically fatal error.

Black or white, the criminal left is interested in power. It is not interested in promoting the renewal and reforms that make democracy work; it is interested in promoting those collisions and conflict that tear democracy apart.

In the current student year there have been twenty-five separate acts of sabotage against ROTC installations on campuses; there have been seventy-eight separate incidents of arson; the rate of violence and the volume of damage now exceeds that of the spring of 1969.

The question I raise tonight is how the university is to survive the current crisis.

My answers are not complete — the subject is complex. But some rules, it seems to me, are clearly dictated by experience.

First, the era of appeasement must come to an end. The political and social demands that dissidents are making of the universities do not flow from sound basic educational criteria, but from strategic considerations on how to radicalize the student body, polarize the campus and extend the privileged enclaves of student power.

Let me quote you Mark Rudd of the SDS in one of his more coherent comments:

> Let me tell you. We manufactured the issues. The Institute for Defense Analysis is nothing at Columbia. Just three professors. And the gym issue is bull. It doesn't mean anything to anybody. I had never been to the gym site before the demonstrations began. I didn't even know how to get there.

When peace comes through appeasement and capitulation to the likes of Rudd, by trading away sound educational principles and the safeguards of academic freedom, the peace thus purchased is not worth the price. That sellout is intellectual treason. Better a confrontation than a cave-in.

Second, a concise and clear set of rules for campus conduct should be established, transmitted to incoming freshmen, and enforced — with immediate expulsion the penalty for serious violations.

The rule of reason is the guiding principle in an academic community, and those who apply the rule of force have no business there. For the good of the academic community, they should be booted out.

Third, as I stated in Des Moines, it is folly for universities confronted with their current crisis in our turbulent times to open their doors to thousands of patently unqualified students.

A recent survey sponsored by the Carnegie Commission on Higher Education indicated that less than one-half of the more than 60,000 university and college faculty members polled favored relaxing normal academic admission standards for minority group applicants. And almost three-quarters of the 60,000 did not favor relaxing normal academic standards in appointing minority group members to the faculty.

I am going to pause on that note for a moment. It is not a daily occurence to find my opinions shared by such a large number of the academic community. I now await patiently the second thoughts of the columnists and commentators who dismissed my recent speech at Des Moines and my comments at Chicago as knee-jerk racism and reaction.

Just as I argued then that our colleges, simply by opening their doors, cannot solve the problems created by discrimination and deprivation in the central city; so, also, those colleges cannot succeed by becoming circus tents or psychiatric centers for over-privileged, underdisciplined, irresponsible children of the well-to-do blasé permissivists.

It was that first point I stressed in my remarks two weeks ago in Des Moines.

Mr. Gardner Ackley, whom I quoted in that speech, asserted his words were taken out of context. Yet, the text of his statement is nestled now in the cocoon of the Congressional Record. It reveals Mr. Ackley as a bird of the feather — on the issue of defending the university against radical tyranny. Mr. Ackley flies in tight formation with the hawks.

Criticism of my speech also came from Italy where it was contended my charges about the University of Rome were unsubstantiated. If that be the case, my apologies — but the source of my facts was an analysis in the *Washington Post*. That is where the diplomatic protests should be lodged. And if any of the information that the *Post* printed was in error, I am sure they will come forward with their usual prompt retraction.

Finally, my remarks also met with acid criticism from Michigan University President Robben Fleming, of whom I had been severely critical. "Your facts were wrong," charged Mr. Fleming; but the facts are these:

Two months ago, the militant Black Action Movement at Michigan made non-negotiable demands, including the enrollment of nine hundred black students by fall of 1971, a full ten percent black enrollment by the fall of 1973; to thereafter increase until black registration was proportionate to Negro population in the State of Michigan.

When the demands were not met fully and precisely, BAM, supported by SDS, struck. For twelve days classes were disrupted, furniture and windows broken, and students and teachers intimidated and assaulted by black and white radicals. Fires were set in campus buildings. Local and state police, mobilized to restore order, were kept away on the directive of President Fleming.

Twelve days after it began, the strike ended. The concessions granted were indistinguishable from the demands.

At the strike's end, a spokesman announced, "BAM has called an end to the strike, but the revolution is only started."

To President Fleming the agreement may be a "bold commitment" for Michigan; to me it looks like the kind of settlement intimidated garment manufacturers used to "negotiate" with Louis "Lepke" Buchalter. President Fleming has set a target that will almost be impossible to reach without impairing the quality of his institution. Moreover, he has greatly expanded the power and influence of a militant organization that is flushed with a victory gained by having crippled his school. The plain truth is that Fleming buckled under to a few squads of kid extortionists.

As for the vigor of my criticism of President Fleming, it was conscious — based on an old Cub Scout theory that the best way to put a tough crust on a marshmallow is to roast it.

Our colleges and universities are charged with a grave duty — to preserve and broaden the intellectual heritage of our nation and civilization and to educate the leaders of that nation and the world in this and the next century.

In the past that slice of national responsibility seemed to be sufficient. No longer. Today, the glamor stocks are the war against poverty, the war against racism, the war against pollution, the war against war; and the colleges and universities want a piece of the action. Selling short their traditional portfolio, they are buying into the high flyers.

But, in committing resources to these political and social ventures, for which they are totally unprepared; the colleges must necessarily neglect their prime responsibility in which they are highly expert. They will get a measure of glamor and headlines — and the approval of students who prefer campaigning to studying. But one day the crash will come; and this country will wake up with a serious loss in net educational worth.

So, one of America's problems is that her great institutions are neglecting their callings and, like the French Army in 1914, marching off singing and cheering into the kind of political and social battles for which they are ill-trained, ill-armed, and ill-equipped. If they persist, they will be cut to pieces.

Fourth, no negotiations under threat or coercion.

Fifth, no amnesty for lawlessness or violence. This last canon is crucial. Once an individual has deliberately and consciously violated the criminal law, he should be removed from the academic community, which is not equipped to deal with the argument of force, and left to the larger society which has both the aptitude and determination for the task. A crime is no less a crime because it is committed in an ivy hall in the name of academic freedom.

Sixth, any organization which publicly declares its intention to violate the rules of an academic community and which carries out that declaration should be barred from the campus. The university is a community with its own rules; and one of these is that reason

318

governs and ideas prevail on their merits, not on the number who can be massed behind them.

Two years ago, at the time of the violence at Columbia, President Nixon said that the Columbia disorders were

> The first major skirmish in the revolutionary struggle to seize the universities of this country and transform them into sanctuaries for radicals and vehicles for revolutionary political and social goals.

He counseled Columbia to rid itself of any student organizations involved directly in the violence.

"If that student is either rewarded or goes unpunished then the administration of Columbia University will have guaranteed a new crisis on its own campus and invited student coups on other campuses all over the country."

Columbia ignored the counsel and granted a general amnesty, an amnesty received with contempt, jeers, and a stream of four-letter epithets from the militants who had held out for it.

Now, two more years have passed and the commonplace seizure of campus buildings has been pushed off page one by the burning of campus buildings.

Civil disobedience has degenerated into criminal violence. From sit-ins, we have moved to clubs, bricks, bottles, and guns — to violent clashes with police — to burning the Bank of America.

It is late in the day — but it is not too late to save the colleges and universities of this country from the future the anarchic dreamers have in store. It will take courage and it will very probably involve the kind of confrontations understandably distasteful to men of thought.

The prescient professor of philosophy from New York University, Dr. Sidney Hook, traces the seeds of the current disorders back to 1964. A year ago, in *Saturday Review* he wrote:

> Shortly after the riotous events at the University of California at Berkeley in 1964, I predicted that in consequence of the faculty's refusal to condemn the student seizure of Sproul Hall, the administration building, American higher education would never be the same again, that a turning-point had been reached in the pattern of development. I confess, however, to surprise at the rapidity of the change, if not its direction, and by the escalation of the violence accompanying it.

American higher education has never been the same since. The toehold of the antidemocratic left at Berkeley has become an established beachhead in both universities and the larger society.

Campus anarchy that might have been nipped in the bud at Berkeley with a single act of administrative decisiveness and faculty courage — can now be contained only at considerable cost. But the sooner the price of saving the universities is paid, the better.

Seventh, we must look to how we are raising our children. In the *New York Times* columnist Tom Wicker made a lugubrious lament that those were "our children" in the streets of Chicago giving the Bronx cheer to the Conrad Hilton. To a degree Wicker is right — and the fact that we raised some of the crowd that was out there in Grant Park is one of the valid indictments of my generation.

But precisely whose children are they?

They are, for the most part, the children of affluent, permissive, upper-middle-class parents who learned their Dr. Spock and threw discipline out the window — when they should have done the opposite.

They are the children dropped off by their parents at Sunday school to hear the "modern" gospel from a "progressive" preacher more interested in fighting pollution

319

than fighting evil — one of those pleasant clergymen who lifts his weekly sermons out of old newsletters from a National Council of Churches that has cast morality and theology aside as not "relevant" and set as its goal on earth the recognition of Red China and the preservation of the Florida alligator.

These parents not only indulged their children; they indulged themselves — leaving Junior alone night after night with his favorite babysitter — the TV tube. By the time the average child reaches eighteen years of age, he has spent something like 18,000 hours squatting mesmerized before the make-believe world of television. Now undeniably, he learned some good things there, but they cannot substitute for parental guidance. Unfortunately, he also learned that instant gratification can be had with a proper admixture of credit cards, fast automobiles, cigarettes, pills, toothpaste, deodorants, and hair dressing.

Today, by the thousands — without a cultural heritage, without a set of spiritual values, and with a moral code summed up in that idealistic injunction, "do your own thing," junior — his pot and Portnoy secreted in his knapsack — arrives at "The Old Main" and finds there a smiling and benign faculty even more accommodating and less demanding than his parents.

For a decade these colleges and universities have undergone a barrage from the underground press, films, plays, manifestos, novels, and even mass magazines; the theme of which is that American society and all its institutions — business, the army, the government, the universities — are irrational, racist and corrupt.

Glorifying direct action and violence, these publications have as their pervasive emotions — contempt for Western culture and hatred for the United States. Undeniably, this stream of opinion has been influential on the campus. Is it any wonder that in 1970 some are easily radicalized by the SDS?

Eight, we must look to the university that receives those children. Is it prepared to deal with the challenge of the nondemocratic Left?

To most academicians the traditional enemy has always been on the Right. The sixties showed how pitifully unprepared the academic community was for an assault from its ideological rear.

They had best learn how to deal with it, for their survival is at stake. One modest suggestion for my friends in the academic community; the next time a mob of students, waving their non-negotiable demands, start pitching bricks and rocks at the Student Union — just imagine they are wearing brown shirts or white sheets — and act accordingly.

Ninth, let us support those courageous administrators, professors, and students on our college campuses who are standing up for the traditional rights of the academic community, against what the *New York Times* rightly calls the "New Fascists." Their number is growing.

Last week President Eric Walker of Pennsylvania State University along with his wife was driven from their home by rock-throwing students. He has pledged no amnesty for the thugs responsible, his trustees are behind him; and the country will be well served if he stands by his guns.

The country will support these principles — and from the recent survey of the Carnegie Commission on Education, college faculties themselves have had a bellyful and are ready to act as well. Eighty percent interviewed said these campus disorders were a threat to academic freedom; three out of four said that students who disrupt the college should be suspended or expelled. Can it be that within the faculty lounges there is also a Great Silent Majority?

One final thought about academic freedom and the true liberal philosophy. Neither can be reconciled with the coarse repression by the New Left of other points of view. The rude shouting-down of guest speakers is totally incompatible with the presence of intellectual excellence. Therefore, we must presume that intellectual excellence is no longer present on campuses where another viewpoint cannot be expressed, analyzed, and debated. And it is not enough to defend by saying that the disrupters are in the minority.

Because if intellectual excellence were present, it would never abide such animal conduct.

It is one of the tragedies of our time that faculties and students sit in catatonic trance while the raucous militants destroy academic freedom.

When will they awaken?

April 29, 1970, Ithaca, New York
Statement of the President of Cornell University

IN A SPEECH delivered last night, the Vice President of the United States, Spiro T. Agnew, made a brief reference to "the score of students at Cornell who, wielding pipes and tire chains, beat a dormitory president into unconsciousness."

No such incident has ever occurred at Cornell University. No incident even remotely fitting this statement has ever occurred at Cornell University. It is incredible that the Vice President of the United States should publicly make such a statement for which there is absolutely no basis in fact.

April 29, 1970, Washington, D.C.
Statement from the Office of the Vice President
in Reply to the President of Cornell University

THE BEATING of a dormitory president by students wielding tire irons and chains occurred this month at the University of Connecticut rather than Cornell.

It was at Cornell University this month that the African Studies and Research Center was destroyed by fire, probably arson, that small groups of students vandalized the bookstore, that university authorities had to obtain restraining orders to prohibit violence, that these orders were tested by SDS and the Black Liberation Front with no action taken against them.

It was at Cornell this month where numerous bomb threats were received by campus authorities, where a Molotov cocktail was thrown through a window of the University Library and where Molotov cocktails were discovered in other buildings.

The Vice President regrets that he misplaced the location of the beating of the dormitory president at Cornell rather than at Connecticut.

Herbert L. Thompson
Press Secretary to
the Vice President

May 4, 1970, Washington, D.C.
American Retail Federation

IN SEVERAL recent speeches I've called attention to the grave dangers which accompany the new politics of violence and confrontation which have found so much favor on our college campuses. Those dangers were not imaginary. And today, at a state college in Ohio, the powder keg exploded resulting in tragedy that was predictable and avoidable. At this point the assignment of fault will not restore the young lives wasted. In any event, we must have the most effective and impartial investigation.

All of us as parents are grieved and shocked by the tragedy. And our sympathy for the affected relatives is deep.

The speech that I am about to deliver was prepared long in advance of this sorrowful event. There are those who will relate portions of it to today's misfortune and claim that it shows a certain insensitivity. And yet today's events make the truth of these remarks self-evident and underscore the need that they be said. They're not meant to apply to Kent State University nor to any specific institution of higher learning. They address themselves to the general malaise that pervades America today — the malaise that's used for violent demonstration instead of debate, and for confrontation instead of conciliation.

In recent years there has been a developing uncertainty about the relevance of America's basic institutions to the traditional American values. This questioning was good because human imperfection makes the process of self-examination necessary to progress.

Unfortunately, the legitimate and constructive debate over our institutional efficacy has, in too many cases, degenerated into a thoughtless attack on our system and in the traditional values that have kept us pointed in the right direction during the past two centuries. Tonight I want to call attention to those fundamentals as they relate to the dominant characteristics of the American people.

This has never been a nation of Pollyannas. We have been realists right from the first. We have known that the world is not perfect. We have, in short, always been concerned that what has been called "the best that is possible among mortal and finite, diverse and conflicting men" must prevail.

Yet along with our realistic attitude, we have always been characterized as a people of good will. We are an essentially optimistic people. We have been blessed with a land unparalleled in its fruitfulness; we have a population unsurpassed in its inventiveness and creativity; our institutions have been able to keep pace with our changing times without sacrificing basic principles. We have *thought* and *worked* hard, and have always felt a sureness about our nation.

There is one more sense in which we have been a people of good will. As a nation traveling the road through time, we have been among the most charitable and among the most selfless. We have aided friends and former enemies. We have never harbored long animosity against any nation or group of nations. Our feelings toward other nations have been and are today feelings of respect, of warm affection where possible, and of strict propriety where necessary.

American history, in general, has, in short, been "an era of good will" — not because we have never had problems, but because we have always felt, even in the midst of the worst problems, that the essential greatness of our people, of our institutions and of our national principles would eventually transcend and triumph over the problems of the moment.

And this has been true — until now.

Now we find ourselves with part of our people — a great part, I am convinced — contributing to the continuation of good will. But another part of our nation — small in number but strong in influence — delights in a calculated, consistent, and well-publicized barrage of cynicism against the principles of this nation as it is now constituted. And they have created "an era of moroseness."

I refer not merely to those tomentose exhibitionists who provoke more derision than fear, nor do I refer to the paranoids and cases of arrested development who have attempted to destroy our system of higher education. These are dangerous — but they are *obviously* dangerous. They make no bones about their hatred of our society, their contempt for traditional morality and their delight in the unbridled passions that lead them to their orgies of violence.

Hating what they call "middle-class" justice, they will openly disrupt a courtroom; hating capitalism, they blow up a bank; hating law, they will attack law enforcers.

Now these are dangerous and heinous crimes. But the very fact that they are openly committed makes them easy to identify and easy to contain.

No, it is not these unfortunates of whom I speak. I speak instead of those who perform a more subtle but infinitely more dangerous kind of violence — a philosophical, intangible violence. They are not at the bottom of the social ladder — indeed, many of them were born on the social ladder and have a very great say about who is to climb on which rung. They are not poorly educated — indeed, they are probably among the most formally educated people who ever lived. They are not necessarily young. And very few of them are black. They do not break laws. In many cases, they help to make them or to carry them out.

They can be found in every segment of society that helps to form the opinions of society at large: in the universities, in the media, in government, in the great professions. They are, for the most part, articulate and possessed of that smugness that comes only when one is dogmatically certain of ones essential rightness.

They want no part of perpetuating an era of goodwill that has characterized America since its beginnings. They have instituted their own era — "the era of moroseness" — about our nation.

A perceptive editorial in the *Wall Street Journal* put it this way:

> In any society the task of the elite is to supply the bonds that hold together divisive and potentially competing factions. It's up to the elite to articulate and defend the values through which society judges what behavior is appropriate, or inappropriate, how redress is properly sought, what decisions must be accepted as legitimate. . . .
>
> Over the past decade — and this is the new factor — the American elite has not been protecting these social bonds. It has been systematically assaulting them.

For the first time in history a great nation is threatened not by those who have nothing — but by those who have almost everything. As a nation are we strong enough to deal with the violent revolutionaries in the streets? Are we strong enough to deal with those who want to seize power? Yes.

But what of those *in power* who make insidious attacks on the philosophical and religious ideals of Western civilization? What of those who, entrusted by our society with passing on to the next generation what have been called the "traditions of civility," choose to publicly hold those traditions up to scorn — and usually at a profit?

What of those in public life who are delighted to travel anywhere in the nation as long as they get an opportunity to tell a college audience that the greatest danger this nation faces comes from law enforcers rather than from lawbreakers?

And what of those who "either out of ignorance or out of calculated political cynicism" pander to the ignorance and the fears of those who are all too willing to believe that the criminal who throws a bomb at a bank is a hero and the policeman who gets killed while trying to stop him is a pig?

What of those who, presumably in possession of all their faculties, write articles calling for open revolution and are either too ambitious or too addled to understand what they have written?

Some of the politicians in this country, in their feverish search for group acceptance, are ready to endorse tumultuous confrontation as a substitute for debate, and the most illogical and unfitting extensions of the Bill of Rights as protections for psychotic and criminal elements in our society. The mayor of New York not long ago said, and I quote:

> We have seen all too clearly that there are men — now in power in this country — who do not respect dissent, who cannot cope with turmoil, and who believe that the people of America are ready to support repression as long as it is done with a quiet voice and a business suit.

Now *my* view of the problem is this:

> We have seen all too clearly that there are men — now in power in this country — who do not represent authority, who cannot cope with tradition, and who believe that the people of America are ready to support revolution as long as it is done with a cultured voice and a handsome profile.

These are not matters which are merely subject to the private interpretation of events. They are matters of what has been called the "public philosophy."

And what is this public philosophy? Walter Lippmann defined it in this way:

> . . . [It is] that body of positive principles and precepts which a good citizen cannot deny or ignore . . . the art of governing well has to be learned. If it is to be learned it has to be transmitted from the old to the young and the habit and the ideas must be maintained by the seamless web of memory among the bearers of the tradition, generation after generation.

This "seamless web of memory" has been maintained for long centuries of Western civilization. But in our own time, some of the bearers of that tradition have betrayed their trust, have told the young and the poor that if their grievances, real and imagined, are not immediately resolved, society must be remade overnight.

And that is the insidious nature of what I have been describing. The very ones we have entrusted to pass on to our children the traditions of civility have mocked those traditions, have held them up to ridicule, and given a generation the stone of cynicism where they should have offered the bread of intellectual life.

As one great upholder of the traditions of civility said "We laugh at honor — and are surprised to find traitors in our midst."

Yet, it is true; we have listened to those elitists laugh at honesty and thrift and hard work and prudence and logic and respect and self-denial; why then are we surprised to discover we have traitors and thieves and perverts and irrational and illogical people in our midst?

There is no greater problem confronting the American people than this. There must be an intellectual, philosophical counterattack made against the cynics, the moral relativists, the creators of this "era of moroseness."

In our colleges, in our pulpits, in our forums, we must once again hear the principles of Western freedom defined, and defended, rationally, openly — yes, and proudly. The cynics have held the center stage in our intellectual life for too long. I believe that there are in our nation academicians and professionals whose intellectual credentials equal and surpass those of the smug purveyors of mockery and scorn — and that the "traditions of civility" can be saved by their efforts.

Let us have public debate of the principles upon which this nation and our civilization is built. Let us hear once more, in departments of philosophy, in public forums, the proud voice of reason, of tradition, of respect for legitimate authority and human freedom — for the public philosophy.

President Nixon has made the defense of those traditions the operating principle of his administration. I consider this to be the most significant accomplishment of the administration. In defending the traditions of civility, of reasoned change and rational progress, we are defending not only our nation and its future, but the future of the world.

If we allow the philosophical heritage of the West, the religious traditions of our Judaeo–Christian heritage to be mocked without challenge and to be scorned without debate, then nothing we have built is worth the keeping.

The time has come for those scholars, teachers, and thinkers who believe in these traditions to mount an intellectual counterattack. We have great truths to defend. We have the arguments with which to defend them.

What is more urgent than this, the salvation of the principles of our civilization?

May 8, 1970, Boise, Idaho
Idaho Republican Dinner

I JUST CAME from watching the President at the news conference on television that Art Linkletter mentioned. I watched the President who is gravely concerned with his responsibility to be a President to all the people — not just part of the people, not just the people who voted for him — but all the people. I saw him trying very hard to penetrate a blanket of emotion that seems to have settled over this country in the past few days, to strip away the reactions that have developed so that people would be able to see the logic in a great decision — a momentous decision, a courageous decision.

The speech that I'm going to give tonight was distributed earlier today — particularly in the East where the time difference made distribution necessary at an earlier moment — has become highly controversial in its opening. Some of you may have already heard of this, because some of the things that are said in the beginnings of this speech relate, in part, to the emotion that the President spoke of tonight.

Now, this speech was prepared before the national scene became so tense. And some of you who are students of my rhetoric will be surprised to know that I did not author these controversial paragraphs. They have been released, and I will not apologize for them; the content of them is in accordance with my thinking. . . .

Now, I heard the President say tonight in responding to some questions about the way I phrase my convictions . . . that he would not muzzle me. And I haven't heard from him; I haven't talked to him. The only message I got was relayed by Mr. Haldeman today when he told me that the President wanted me to be certain that I knew that he had made no criticism or made no attempts to suppress what I wanted to say. But the President did say this [tonight]: "When the situation is hot, I would hope that the people on my team will profit by my advice and know that that's the time that the rhetoric should become cool."

Now, this is an example, ladies and gentlemen, of a great leader. A man who does not lead by mandate, a man who does not impose his will upon you, a man who lets you know that he's solidly behind you and, at the same time, while being supportive, attempts to indicate through the depth of his experience a concern that you will possibly learn something from his long experience.

I don't intend to be so opaque or stubborn that I can't learn a little bit too from that experience. And even though, as I said, this speech has been distributed in total, if my abandonment of the first two pages of this speech in some small way will help to cool the volatile situation in the United States, I'm going to do it.

So tonight I am not going to deliver the parts of this speech that some may criticize as being a little too pithy, but I will begin with the substance of the matter. And I hope, in this way, that all of those who are involved in the tremendous wave of emotion that's sweeping the country at the present time and manifested itself in the various demonstrations will exercise the kind of self-restraint that I, through the example of one of the greatest Presidents of the United States, am going to impose on myself this evening.

The North Vietnamese have maintained major sanctuaries in Cambodia. While Prince Sihanouk was in power, we refrained from attacking the Communist bases despite the military problems that they posed. We did this because of Cambodian neutrality, because the base areas were kept confined and because the Communist forces in Cambodia were held somewhat in check by the Cambodian government's control of supplies into the base areas. In the period immediately following the coup, when the Lonnol government took over, we planned no change in this policy.

By April 20, 1970, the situation had become much more serious. The Communist forces had spread out from the base areas and were pressing into Cambodia. With the benefit of the doubt, however, their moves could still be interpreted as widening the frontiers of the bases and improving their defensive positions. So we therefore counseled restraint to our Vietnamese allies and did not change our policy in the hopes that the situation would stabilize and that we would be no worse off than we were before Sihanouk was overthrown.

In the President's speech of April 20, he pointed out the Communist escalation in Indochina and warned against actions that would threaten the security of our forces. He nevertheless proceeded to announce the further withdrawal of 150,000 Americans; and the policy of restraint along the Cambodian/South Vietnam border was continued. The President also took the opportunity to strongly reiterate our continuing preference for a negotiated settlement fair to all parties.

Within several days of that speech, and in the face of our restraint and our warnings, the Communist response became painfully clear. They moved out from the confines of their bases with the clear intent of linking them up in a bold attempt to change the border area from a series of isolated enclaves, dependent on the government for rice supplies, into a solid band of self-sustaining territory stretching all the way to the sea.

Suddenly we faced the prospect of Cambodia becoming one large base area for attacks along the 600 miles of Cambodian/South Vietnamese border. This development would have permitted complete freedom of action to an enemy which could then move his forces and supplies rapidly across the entire length of South Vietnam's southern flank. No longer would their supply routes be confined by the restrictive characteristics of the Ho Chi Minh Trail. They would have open access to ports, roads, factories, and equipment to build up and sustain their forces. They could attack our forces in South Vietnam from these expanded sanctuaries and attack them with impunity. We thus faced a greatly deteriorated military situation from that which existed even on April 20th. And, ominously, the Communists were challenging both our warnings and our credibility.

On April 30th, the President in his address to the nation described a critical military and psychological problem. He outlined the basic options and why he had chosen to move against the source of the trouble. We could not stand idly by and suffer the military and psychological consequences. Nor did we wish to launch a massive aid program to Cambodia which we really didn't think they could absorb. Such a course would probably not have been decisive and would have tended to involve us more directly in Cambodia.

So instead, the President chose important but limited measures. These measures are an inseparable function of our efforts in Vietnam, although they naturally provide corollary benefit to the Cambodian regime. These operations concern only territories long occupied and controlled by foreign Communist forces and the areas are quite sparsely populated. The operations should last only six to eight weeks at which time our forces will definitely be withdrawn back to South Vietnam.

Contrary to the arcane interpretations of the decision by some media commentators, the principal target of the operations is not personnel but the enemy's logistical infrastructure. This has been nonsense what has been stated in the press — quite a bit of nonsense about a supposed failure to find a Communist headquarters. We had originally and still have no expectation of capturing the actual headquarters personnel, nor do we know that they are in any one area at a given time. Their headquarters personnel move around in those two base areas plus an area of South Vietnam that adjoins them. The probability was always that the personnel would have left by the time our troops moved in. But our objective was to destroy their communication facilities and, above all, to destroy their supply dumps. And this objective we are achieving and expect to complete.

Let me stress that the significance of these base areas is not personnel, but the supply depots and communications network that have taken them a period of many months to accumulate. With the start of the rainy season, it will take many more months to rebuild the essential logistics bases. This operation, if successful — and it is being quite successful — will buy at least eight months during which these base areas cannot support military operations in South Vietnam. And even this assumes that we would not attack the bases once again. It will now be far harder for the enemy to sustain major operations. And this should mean fewer allied casualties and should afford the opportunity to consolidate pacification gains, improve ARVN readiness, and thus help us to hold to our schedule for the withdrawal of American troops. From now on, the Communists must worry about the security of these base areas, forcing a basic change in their calculations concerning supply routes and disposition of their forces.

As a corollary, but not unimportant benefit, these actions are providing a major morale boost for the ARVN who are conducting their largest-scale operations to date and for our own forces who have long been quite frustrated by the Communist immunity in the base areas.

Allied operations to date are proceeding with considerably greater success than anticipated. Casualties have been light and we are already beginning to turn up significant caches (including some supplies donated by American peace groups). The amount of supplies uncovered thus far is in itself surprising since we did not expect to uncover the major supply areas at the outset. Our initial objectives are to secure the territory. And the careful searching for the heavily camouflaged installations will, of course, follow later.

The evidence will mount daily that our efforts are meeting with success. And in that regard, I would like to give you some figures that I got from the National Security Council staff just this afternoon to give you some idea how successful these operations are being.

Since we jumped into the sanctuaries in Cambodia, we have taken 1,004 prisoners of war; the enemy killed in action amount to 3,607; we have captured 256 suspects; we have taken 4,511 individual weapons, most of them in their cosmoline or preservative, not even out of their crates yet. We have captured 644 crew serve weapons. We have destroyed 1,662 bunkers. We have captured 2,052,000 pounds of rice — that's enough rice to feed 45,610 men for a month. We have captured 1,327,000 rounds of small arms ammunition — rounds that could kill Americans and South Vietnamese troops. We have captured 1,603 mortar rounds and 440 large rocket rounds as well as 3,777 small rocket rounds. We've destroyed 124 trucks. We have captured 1,148,981 rounds of rifle ammunition above the small arms ammunition that I mentioned and 179,000 rounds of machine-gun ammunition.

The United States in this operation has lost in action fifty-three Americans thus far. The South Vietnamese have lost 179 of their troops.

Now, in addition to those figures that I've just given you, just this afternoon, two tremendous new caches have been uncovered. They haven't even begun to count this material. And on the basis of the incomplete count, you can add to those figures that I've given you another 2,000,000 rounds of small arms ammunition, another 60 large rockets

327

and another 2,000 mortar rounds. So you can see what a debilitating thing it is for the enemy to have, in the initial days of an operation of this type, this many supplies that have been laboriously accumulated, transported down the Ho Chi Minh Trail and in through the captured Port of Sihanoukville. And it's a blow that's going to cost them very dearly and save a great number of American lives.

A lot of operations today are proceeding with considerably greater success than has been anticipated. And we think that the successes we have realized so far are by no means all that we are going to achieve. As we get into a more minute examination of these areas and penetrate the camouflage of the more sophisticated installations, I'm sure we're going to find additional gains will be realized.

The reaction overseas has been mixed just as here at home. It is interesting to note that the closer the nation is to the scene of the action, the stronger the support for the President's decision.

The Cambodian government itself has expressed "satisfaction" with the U.S. decision to "aid in the defense of Cambodian neutrality, which has been violated by the North Vietnamese." The Cambodian government also "expresses its gratitude to the United States government and respects what the President said in his speech to the Nation." And it is interesting to note, because not many people realize this and this question came up when the President was briefing some of the Congressional leaders, that the Cambodian government attempted to complain to the Security Council of the United Nations about the invasion of the North Vietnamese; and unfortunately, the Security Council faced a veto by the Soviets and would not take up the question. And also — unfortunately — the International Control Commission which is the organization that is to check to see whether the 1964 Geneva Accords are being performed satisfactorily, presently under the control of the Indian government, would not go in there without the consent and cooperation of the Soviet government. So even though Cambodia has protested that that part of its territory has been taken over, it's impossible to get the International Control Commission in there because of a imminent Security Council veto in the United Nations.

Now, most of the countries in Southeast Asia have expressed their understanding of and approval for the President's action. Some of them have done this privately and some have done it publicly. This, of course, comes as no surprise to me, because on my Asian trip, I found that all Asian leaders emphatic in their desire that the U.S. not allow the Republic of Vietnam to be overrun by the Communists. Many of them expressed in various words the thoughts of Prime Minister Lee of Singapore, who urged that the United States not withdraw in such a way that would destroy the "climate of confidence" which United States' actions had created up to that point in Asia. Another prominent Asian leader privately commented on the so-called "Domino Theory." I suppose you've heard of that; and you know that some of our more knowledgeable people, who comment frequently on foreign affairs, are not exactly in accord with its conclusions. But in Asia, you find it's in accord with their conclusions. This particular leader said, "The Domino Theory may have fallen into disfavor in the West, but those of us in Southeast Asia have no doubt about its existence "After all," he said, "my country is one of the dominoes."

The reasons for this necessary decision should be understood by all. They are, as the President indicated:

— As Commander-in-Chief, he had to act to protect allied forces now in Vietnam and those remaining after our next withdrawal.

— It was necessary to ensure continued progress in our Vietnamization program and in the pace of our withdrawals.

— It was necessary to increase our chances of shortening the Vietnam war and our involvement in it.

There reasons should be clear, but I should like to point out with special emphasis one reason that may have been obscured in some minds. Unfortunately, those protesters and commentators who have cried doom and defeat in an almost unprecedented intemperance, may have confused the effect of our resolve in Hanoi and in other equally important capitals. We intend to make clear to the enemy that they cannot repeatedly ignore our warnings and escalate their attacks in Indochina. We intend to reaffirm our credibility and decisiveness when these qualities have been sharply questioned not only by Hanoi but by others. The relevance to the Middle East situation should be obvious. We intend to ensure that there are no miscalculations in Southeast Asia and elsewhere around the world which could lead to dangerous confrontations in the future.

Now, lately the conviction has steadily grown abroad, that overpowering pressures exist in this country to force us to come to terms with other countries on their terms, rather than other countries coming to terms with us on a basis of reciprocity. This has never been the attitude of this country in the past. It must not, in the interests of peace, be our attitude today.

Of course, the desirability of attaining peace cannot be the subject of either intellectual or partisan political debate in this country. The only controversy can be on the means of achieving that peace. The objective of all of our activities in Southeast Asia is and must always be the attainment of peace. If, however, peace is to be anything but a cruel illusion, it must rest upon foundations of stable security for each nation concerned and an equilibrium for the area. It is just that stability that is being successfully established by the Vietnamization program. It follows that we must continue to make every effort to persuade the Communists to return to substantive negotiations. A negotiated settlement remains our primary goal. We must, of course, be watchful that in our conception of such negotiations, and in the methods by which we seek to bring the Communists back to them, we are in fact strengthening not undermining the foundations on which a lasting negotiated peace can be based.

The President is determined to end this war with a just peace. We would all prefer to achieve this through negotiations, and our actions in Cambodia should improve the prospects for that solution. We will not have serious discussions so long as the enemy believes it can ignore our warnings and reject our flexible proposals for a settlement based on mutual interest. I should like to emphasize in special measure also that we are not increasing our demands at the Paris talks. All of our negotiating offers remain on the table. And if I may depart for just a moment to let you know one thing that I think most people in this country don't understand about our peace offer.

You've heard the proponents of immediate withdrawal say from time to time, how can we expect the North Vietnamese and the Viet Cong to agree to mutual withdrawal and elections if the Thieu government which they claim is repressive, is in charge of those elections. Well, we have not insisted that that be the case. We have offered to the North Vietnamese and the Viet Cong governments as part of a settlement — and the Thieu government has joined in this offer with us — that the elections that take place will be supervised by an international control group of sufficient strength to oversee the entire elective process.

Now, with that kind of guarantee for a free election, there is no reason why we cannot negotiate a settlement if the North Vietnamese are sincere in their stated purpose of allowing the people of South Vietnam to determine their own destiny. But we get no answers from them unfortunately.

If the negotiations continue to be blocked, and the Communist delegation does no more than to continue to read statements from Senator Fulbright at the negotiating sessions, then we shall pursue Vietnamization and withdrawals. With the continuation of massive support from the Soviet Union and other states in North Vietnam, a stable security equilibrium will not be established between North and South Vietnam until the Vietnamization program is completed and until we have withdrawn the last combat troops, and South Vietnam is allowed to stand on its own.

A lasting peace can never be made on the basis of threats. Our actions in Cambodia are not intended to threaten or to intimidate the Communists. They demonstrate instead that we shall end this war with a just peace without depending upon the good faith of the Communists.

I should like to conclude with a comment upon the observation of Mr. John Hughes of the *Christian Science Monitor*. He has observed that Asians feel that the moment of truth has arrived for the American public. The Communist mood is viewed as clear, solid, and determined. The President is confronting that mood and "it is the mood of the American people, not the Communist people, today that is the critical factor."

So this is indeed a moment for the nation to stand firm. I am certain, in my own mind, that our ability to achieve a just peace depends more than anything else on the character of the American people and that character must find expression in a firm spirit. I am confident that that spirit is there.

May 9, 1970, Stone Mountain Park, Georgia
Dedication of Stone Mountain Memorial

MY FELLOW WESTERNERS, my fellow Easterners, my fellow Northerners, my fellow Southerners:

We stand here together today because we are all fellow Americans.

At a moment like this, we are reminded that whatever our place of birth, whatever our accent, whatever our party or political bent — we stand united as a people, proud to be countrymen and grateful for our common heritage.

Half a century ago, an American President was called upon to dedicate a monument to Confederate soldiers at the National Cemetery in Arlington.

This is what Woodrow Wilson said as he declared a chapter in American history ended: ". . . I bid you turn with me your faces to the future, quickened by the memories of the past, but with nothing to do with the contests of the past, knowing, as we have shed our blood upon opposite sides, we now face and admire one another."

With Wilson, all Americans of today can stand "shoulder to shoulder to lift the burdens of mankind in the future and show the paths of freedom to all the world."

I do not come here today solely to dedicate this magnificent monument to three great Americans.

I come here representing the President to reaffirm our faith in the fact that we are one nation — drawing strength from our diversity and drawing even greater strength from our unity.

It is significant that this monument is so close to Atlanta. No American city has ever suffered more in war, and no American city has made more progress toward a spirit of genuine brotherhood.

The men we honor here today — Lee, Davis, and Jackson — were bonded together in war, and now are bonded together for the ages on a great mountain of granite.

It is well that we consider some of the principles they stood for, principles which know no limit in time or region.

In the life of General Jackson, the principle that permeated his brilliant military career was, above all, *loyalty*. When surgeons amputated Jackson's left arm to try to save his life, General Robert E. Lee sent this message: "While you have only lost your left, I have lost my right arm." It is fitting that he is enshrined in granite alongside his Commander.

In the life of Jefferson Davis, the principle that will be remembered most is *dignity* in defeat. In the twenty-four years of his life after the Civil War, the quiet dignity of this

American triumphed over all those who would abuse him. It would be well to remember, too, that when religious intolerance caused some to attack Judah Benjamin, Davis elevated him to his Secretary of State.

In the life of Robert E. Lee, we see an example of the highest principle of all — *honor*.

Lee was a man for all seasons and a man for all sections. His military genius and his personal integrity caused him to be offered the command of two great opposing armies. This man, who opposed slavery and who opposed secession, chose to accept the leadership of Confederate forces because he could not honorably, as he put it, ". . . raise my hand against my relatives, my children, my home."

During the war he earned the devotion of the troops he led, and the deep respect of the men on the Union side. He was an American gentleman, a man of honor, and a man of nobility.

But it was the Lee *after* Appomattox that our own generation would do well to remember. He asked that every Southerner unite in "the allayment of passions, the dissipation of prejudice and the restoration of reason."

It was Lee who followed the great tradition of Jefferson and devoted the remainder of his life to education. It was Lee who urged, in words with such meaning for us today, "the thorough education of all classes of the people."

The college he led now bears his name, and it is appropriate that two citizen-soldiers who were both Virginians are linked forever in our minds at Washington and Lee.

Of all his words, this statement of Robert E. Lee should be graven in granite and impressed upon the minds of everyone in every region and this land today: "Abandon all these local animosities and make your sons Americans."

That, to my mind, is the theme of this gathering today. How do we, as a people, "make our sons Americans"?

First, we must recall those principles of loyalty, dignity, and honor that shine through the lives of the men we commemorate today. These are not just old virtues — they are the bedrock of idealism that underlies our hopes for future generations.

Next, we must overcome the new slavery — the willingness of some to become slaves to their passions, devoid of reason and individuality.

Third, we must set aside the evils of sectionalism once and for all. Just as the South cannot afford the discriminate against any of its own people, the rest of the nation cannot afford to discriminate against the South. But we must not forget that each locality and region may call upon its own traditions and its own special character in making its sons Americans.

Most of all, we shall make our sons Americans by behaving as Americans ourselves — compassionate and generous to our fellowman, protective of our individual liberties, determined to bring peace and freedom and order to our homeland and to the world.

I do not believe that what is past must always be prologue; if we turn aside from our past divisiveness, we can truly say as one nation: What is past is past.

The South that will make its greatest contribution to the American dream is the New South.

This New South rejects the old grievances and the old political appeals to the worst in us.

The New South embraces the future, and presses forward with a robust economy fueled by industrial development.

The New South interprets the doctrine of States rights in new ways — ways to make State and local government closely responsive to the needs of people close to home.

That is the new and enlightened spirit of the South envisioned by Robert E. Lee a century ago when he urged his countrymen to make their sons Americans.

Today, young men of the South and young men of the North are fighting side by side in Vietnam. These young men, from South Carolina to South Dakota to South Chicago, are upholding the standards of honor that make it possible for a great nation to bring some order to a threatened world.

The President has determined that there must be no close sanctuary from which these young men can be attacked.

The Oval Office in the White House has never been, and can never become, a sanctuary for anyone who wants to flee from his responsibility.

Let no one here or abroad mistake disagreement with disunity: We are reminded here today that we have paid too great a price for being one nation to let ourselves now come apart at the seams.

May 22, 1970, Houston, Texas
Texas Republican Dinner

LATELY YOU have been exposed to a great deal of public comment about vice presidential rhetoric and how I should "cool it." The President is getting this advice daily from many quarters . . . some of them inside the government. But mostly it has come from persons who have been in the target area of some of my speeches. Nowhere is the complaint louder than in the columns and editorials of the liberal news media of this country. It almost pains me to call them liberal, because they're really the most illiberal, self-appointed guardians of our destiny. And what they'd like to do is run the country without the inconvenience of submitting to the elective process as we in public office must do.

The President has refused to curb my statements on behalf of this administration's policies, or to tell me what words to use or what tone to use in my speeches. And on my part, I have refused to "cool it" — to use the vernacular — until those self-righteous people lower their voices a few decibels. This, I am sure, they are unwilling to do. There is too much at stake in the nation for us to leave the entire field of public commentary to them.

I can assure you that some of these pundits make my rhetoric seem tame. Here are a few recent, random samples I have collected to share with you tonight. These I am quoting are the people who never tire of telling a President how he should run the nation's affairs. I hope you will overlook the slightly hysterical tone of some of their comments. They are overwrought because their advice is not heeded by the President with any degree of regularity.

The *Washington Post*, which constantly urges us to lower our voices, said after the President's detailed address to the nation on his decision to clean out the enemy sanctuaries in Cambodia:

"There is something so erratic and irrational, not to say incomprehensible, about all this that you have to assume there is more to it than he is telling us."

The *Post* may as well have come right out and said that it thought the President had lost his sanity. Words like "erratic, irrational, incomprehensible" are not ordinarily used to describe a carefully studied military decision by the nation's Commander-in-Chief.

And when the President referred to some college-based criminals as bums — these were people who had burned up a professor's life work — the *Post* was beside itself. It fulminated as follows, and I quote:

"A gratuitous clop . . . a page from Vice President Agnew's copybook . . . campus unrest is simply being fanned and exploited by the administration. . . . Hate the dissidents, excoriate the 'bums,' see if you can match Mr. Agnew in hurling names at them."

That was the hysterical view from the *Post*'s ivory tower where that master of sick invective, Herblock, also works. He reached a new low with a cartoon showing a National

Guardsman in the aftermath of the Kent State tragedy with a box of live ammunition — each bullet bearing a phrase from my speeches. Except one. That bullet was labeled "college bums" in honor of the President.

And they ask us to cool our rhetoric and lower our voices.

Meanwhile, at the other end of the Washington–New York axis, the *New York Times* was thoughtfully contemplating events.

A "military hallucination," it called the President's decision; and it sternly warned one and all: "If the President does not promptly pull back from this dangerous adventure, Congress will have to assert its constitutional powers of restraint."

The *Times* columnists were less restrained. Anthony Lewis, writing from London, said: "The President of the United States, in a maudlin personalization and simplification of complex political issues, makes war a test of his own and the nation's manhood. . . . By this action President Nixon has calculatedly chosen to widen the division among the American people, to inflame instead of heal."

And Tom Wicker, the soft-spoken boy wonder of the opinion molders, said with disdain: "Whatever his motives and his policy, Mr. Nixon relied heavily, in his appearances before the nation, on deception, demagoguery, and chauvinism."

James Reston, the *Times*' premier columnist, writing from Washington on May 10, after the weekend of student demonstrations, saw fit to equate me with Jerry Rubin as an extremist. Mr. Reston did not bother to amplify on this comparison.

But so that the *Times* and its editors and columnists can be kept in proper perspective, I would like to quote you a few comments that the incendiary Mr. Rubin made on the Kent State campus one month prior to the confrontation that brought the student deaths there. The *Akron Beacon Journal* reported that he told an audience of 1,500:

"Until you people are prepared to kill your parents you aren't ready for the revolution. . . .

"The American school system will be ended in two years. We are going to bring it down. Quit being students. Become criminals. We have to disrupt every institution and break every law. . . .

"Do you people want a diploma or to take this school over and use it for your own purposes? . . . It's quiet here now but things are going to start again."

To suggest that I am guilty of this type of incendiarism is in keeping with the irresponsibility that the *Times* manages to achieve on its editorial pages. And it is appropriate that the slur be cast by Mr. Reston, who delights in calling other people demagogues.

Earlier, the *Times* had deplored what it called "the administration's open exploitation of fear and discord" and had said "there is a disturbing appeal to the nation's lowest instincts in the present administration's descent to gutter fighting."

And they ask us to cool the rhetoric and lower our voices!

While the President's move on behalf of our troops in Vietnam caused shivers at the *Washington Post* and *New York Times*, it brought apoplexy in some of the other misnamed bastions of liberalism in this country.

The *New Republic*, in a rare front-page editorial, said this week: "Richard Nixon is going down in history, all right, but not soon enough. . . ."

It used such terms as "transparently phony . . . fraud . . . mean contempt . . . driven . . . disorderly . . . secretive . . . dangerous" to describe the President's actions.

"How is this country to get through the next two-and-one-half years without flying apart?" the magazine asked.

I. F. Stone's Bi-Weekly, another strident voice of illiberalism commented: "The race is on between protest and disaster. . . . The only hope is that the students can create such a Plague for Peace, swarming like locusts into the halls of Congress, that they stop all other business and make an end to the war the No. 1 concern it ought to be. The slogan of the striking students ought to be: Suspend Classes and Educate the Country."

During the frenzy following the Cambodian action, which news media invective helped fan instead of cool, it was not even safe to visit the South.

Some of you may recall that I substituted for the President in dedicating the massive new Stone Mountain Memorial to Generals Lee and Jackson and Jefferson Davis near Atlanta on May 9th.

The *Atlanta Constitution*, which doesn't care much for me anyway, decided I was unfit for the honor. They put it in stronger terms, saying it was "a shame and a disgrace" that I was making that address.

The editorial continued:

"Honorable men ride that rocky ledge. . . . Spiro Agnew has none of those redeeming qualities. He has the grace of a drill sergeant and the understanding of a nineteenth-century prison camp warden."

Not even the *Arkansas Gazette*, which views me with varying degrees of horror from its position on the extreme left, has matched the rhetoric of that tribute. Or at least, I haven't seen it if it has. I only see those clippings from the *Gazette* that are forwarded to me by Senator Fulbright. . . . And sometimes Martha Mitchell.

Life's expert on the presidency — or I should say its leading expert, Hugh Sidey — pictured the President as acting from "a kind of splendid and angry isolation in the Oval Office, a deliberate defiance of a large and growing number of Americans and their institutions."

Mr. Sidey was even less charitable about the Vice President.

"For weeks now," he said, "Agnew, more than Abbie Hoffman or William Kunstler, has dominated the headlines with a torrent of abuse that served mainly to call attention to all that is bad in our society — or what he takes to be bad . . . laving about with that big careless brush of his against the administration's lengthening list of enemies."

Now I leave it to your judgment. Who is the real critic of America today? Who rails against our system and our institutions — suggesting we are a racist, imperialistic society? Is it *Life* magazine or the Vice President?

But for pure unbridled invective, you will have to look far to beat that of the excitable columnist, television commentator and former ambassador to Finland, Carl T. Rowan. Mr. Rowan might once have used diplomatic language, but he long ago lost the art and his rhetoric is anything but cool.

In one recent column about me, he employed these phrases: "rose above his own laziness and ineptitude," "a dumb joke — a sort of aberration of history, he has come to personify all the class conflict, the racial hostility, the cultural and generation gaps that have transformed this society into a tinderbox," "calculated maliciousness," "prefers to pander to the prejudices of the most ignorant and selfish elements in society." I guess he means you, ladies and gentlemen.

And Mr. Rowan could not resist joining Herblock and others in suggesting that I had something to do with the deaths of the Kent State students.

Quote: "Incredibly, even as four Kent students lay in the morgue and others lay critically wounded in hospitals, the Vice President's trigger-happy tongue was still firing buckshot."

But the most vicious attempt to transfer the blame for the Kent State student deaths that I have read was in the illiberal *New York Post* by columnist Pete Hamill. Listen to his irrational raving:

"When you call campus dissenters 'bums,' as Nixon did the other day, you should not be surprised when they are shot through the head and the chest by National Guardsmen. Nixon is as responsible for the Kent State slaughter as he and the rest of his bloodless gang of corporation men were for the anti-integration violence in Lamar, and for the pillage and murder that is taking place in the name of democracy in Cambodia. . . . At Kent State, two boys and two girls were shot to death by men unleashed by a President's slovenly rhetoric. If that's the brave new America, to hell with it."

Or if you care for a distaff view from that same organ, here's Harriet Van Horne:

"The President's . . . TV presentation of this decision was, moreover, maudlin, crafty and stained by fulsome sentiments."

Ladies and gentlemen, you have heard a lot of wild, hot rhetoric tonight — none of it mine. This goes on daily in the editorial pages of some very large, very reputable newspapers in this country — not all of them in the East by a long shot. And it pours out of the television set and the radio in a daily torrent, assailing our ears so incessantly we no longer register shock at the irresponsibility and thoughtlessness behind the statements.

"But you are the Vice President," they say to me. "You should choose your language more carefully."

Nonsense. I have sworn I will uphold the Constitution against all enemies, foreign and domestic. Those who would tear our country apart or try to bring down its government are enemies, whether here or abroad, whether destroying libraries and classrooms on a college campus or firing at American troops from a rice paddy in Southeast Asia.

I have an obligation to all of the people of the United States to call things as I see them, and I have an obligation to the President to support his actions in the best manner that I can. I will continue to choose my own words, and I set the tone of my speeches. As he said at his recent press conference, I am responsible for what I say. And I intend to be heard above the din even if it means raising my voice.

Nothing would be more pleasing to some of the editors and columnists I have quoted tonight than to have me simply shut up and disappear.

Nothing would be more pleasing to those on the campus whose motives I have challenged. They are, for the most part, not the great body of students who are trying honestly to get an education. They are rather a small hard core of hell-raisers who want to overturn the system for the sake of chaos alone. They burn, pillage, and destroy because they rebel against their lack of creativity. Although they are few in number, they have had a shattering impact. Unfortunately, they are encouraged by an equally small number of faculty members who apparently cannot compete legitimately within the system or do not choose to do so.

It is my honest opinion that this hard core of faculty and students should be identified and dismissed from the otherwise healthy body of the college community lest they, like a cancer, destroy it.

Peaceful dissent, yes! Violence, no!

Reasonable debate, yes! Street rioting, no!

Orderly change, yes! Throw out the system, no!

Some others who would be just as pleased if I lapsed into a more traditional vice presidential silence are in the Congress — the isolationists in the Senate, who seek at every turn to thwart the President's efforts to conclude this country's involvement in Vietnam, in a manner which will prevent that part of the world from falling to Communist aggression. These Senators are well intentioned, and most of them have been on the Washington scene far longer than I, but I'm afraid this has narrowed their viewpoint. They should get out in the country and maybe out in the world a little bit. It would improve their vision and their sense of reality. Most Americans, I believe, fully realize that this country can never again withdraw to its shorelines and survive. That is the lesson of history that some have failed to learn or have too soon forgotten. The President desperately needs a Republican Congress to replace these neo-isolationist views and remove the willful obstruction of his programs.

Finally a word about another group that has received some attention in my speeches — the electronic news media. I have tried tonight to be specific in my criticism. I realize I have left out many who are in the business of second-guessing the President and who should have been included. I hope we can get around to them later. But I also recognize there are many in the news profession — a group upon whom the country has to depend for an honest report of what is going on in this world — and that they are attempting to live up to this responsibility, most of them successfully. I exclude them totally from the criticism I make here. And I compliment them for doing their jobs well under strong counterpressures, often within their own offices and among less responsible colleagues.

It does bother me, however, that the press — as a group — regards the First Amendment as its own private preserve. Every time I criticize what I consider to be excesses or faults in the news business, I am accused of repression; and the leaders of the various media professional groups wave the First Amendment as they denounce me. That happens to be my amendment too. It guarantees my free speech as much as it does their freedom of the press.

I was interviewed about a week ago, at a time when there was a great amount of conjecture about whether I was going to be asked to subside in my comments by the

President. I was interviewed out on the West Coast, and one of the reporters asked me, "Is the President going to muzzle you?" And I said, "How can you suggest such a thing? You've been accusing me of suggesting repression. You've been accusing me of suggesting that possibly in an indirect fashion there should be some curbs on what is said among the media." Of course, that was absolutely false. I never suggested such a thing and don't intend to. But the point is that they were suggesting a muzzle for me which would deprive me of my right to free speech at the same time they were attempting to controvert some of my statements into an implied thought that they should not be allowed total freedom of press.

I feel this way, there's room for all of us — the Vice President and the Press — under the First Amendment. There's room for our divergent views. And let's continue to express them.

Thank you.

June 3, 1970, West Point, New York
Graduating Class of U.S. Military Academy

IT IS an honor to address you on your graduation day and to speak also to those classes you have helped to train as well as to your families and friends. There is an intense sense of shared pride in you, not just among those here, but among most other Americans who believe deeply in the traditional values of this country. A great deal depends on you and on what you will accomplish.

While it would be an honor to give the commencement address at West Point in any year, it becomes especially meaningful to me at this time. These are years of great national confusion, much of it contrived confusion brought about by a clever, sustained assault on America's system and institutions. This is a time when application, achievement, and success are derided as callous, corrupt, and irrelevant. This is a time when the criminal misfits of society are glamorized while our best men die in Asian rice paddies to preserve the freedoms those misfits abuse. This is a time when the charlatans of peace and freedom eulogize foreign dictators while desecrating the flag that keeps them free.

No one need tell you that this is a difficult time, especially for those who serve their nation by defending it in a world which many wishfully view as less dangerous than the recurring hard realities reveal it to be. But difficult times are not unfamiliar to our Army — indeed, they may be said to be the customary circumstances of the American soldier. To these recurring challenges generations of West Pointers have brought courage, strength, resolve, and dedication as strong and dependable as the rock foundations of these Highlands. I believe these qualities are founded in the solidity of the West Point experience. What makes it so solid and so valuable is what I would like to turn to first.

West Point fosters an ethically informed and achievement-oriented system of values. It is based on a belief instilled in each man that demonstrated merit will be rewarded, and likewise that .shortcoming will be penalized. Since the system is run by human judgment, it is not perfect; but it still remains valid to a high degree. This idea of life "played by the rules" may very well be the most important part of the West Point experience. It is reflected in nearly every aspect of cadet life, from academics to standards of personal conduct, to leadership and military aptitude. There is constant recognition that education for high public responsibility has two purposes: first, to teach; second, to remove and reorient those whose talents are incompatible to the skill sought or those who lack the personal commitment to succeed.

The constant testing and challenging which are integral to cadet life implement the second principle. To survive, one must have both the talent and the heart to continually rise to the occasion, to meet the requirement, to produce under pressure with no prospect of respite. Those who excel are rewarded with more difficult leadership responsibilities, advanced and enriched academic challenges, and opportunities for independent effort. Those who fall short must look elsewhere for a career.

This kind of orientation is indispensable to men in training for the defense of the nation, where a good try that fails is not enough. Equally important, the training is coupled with ethical values which emphasize that the means must be as admirable as the ends. The result, ideally, is a high-principled and achievement-oriented leader who can get things done.

A man so constituted can have enormous impact upon those he interacts with in his professional and personal life. He is a man who has made the transition to maturity. He has accepted the discipline and standards of an institution he believes in and transformed them through self-discipline into standards of achievement that are with him for the rest of his life. The strength of this system of values seems to me to be the solid contribution of West Point. Her graduates have influenced the Army, and indeed the nation as a whole, with these beliefs.

Our hopes for you who are graduating today stem from America's great need for the perpetuation of such values. There is a need for balance in one's concept of his role in society. With such balance "doing your own thing" includes being responsible for your own actions. It means being self-controlled, self-motivating, and self-correcting. It means feeling a sense of obligation to make the most productive use of one's given abilities and opportunities, no matter how modest or extensive they may be.

It also means recognizing the individuals responsibility to others — to the unit he serves, to the colleagues who share his hardships, disappointments, successes, and ultimately, to his oath of office and the nation he represents. This kind of responsible maturity recognizes the possibility of genuine differences among reasonable men, approaches their reconciliation with earnest goodwill, and exercises restraint in pursuit of one's own legitimate goals so as not to interfere with others in pursuit of their own.

You are going out into an Army today that has borne the brunt of a lonely and difficult war, far from home, and in the face of open and hostile lack of support from a minority of our citizenry. Despite that, our deployed forces have stood between our Vietnamese allies and powerful enemies who were on the verge of enslaving them. They have simultaneously fought the big battles, advised and trained Vietnamese forces helped them mobilize and expand, reequipped and armed them, and protected a remarkable series of genuinely free elections resulting in the formulation of a constitutional government in the midst of war.

All of this has been done without complaint by a magnificent Army of military professionals, citizen/soldiers and mobilized reservists. In the midst of the hard, tough going they have also found time and heart to turn to the Vietnamese with compassion and brotherhood. This is the side of the story you seldom see reported. Our soldiers have tended the sick, helped build schools, fed children, collected and distributed clothing, and done a thousand other things which said, "I care." You can go out into this Army and assume the positions of leadership entrusted to you with gratitude, pride, and humility.

In these days, in which we hear so much talk about involvement, you can also take pride in a profession which exacts the ultimate involvement — an unlimited commitment in the service of something greater than self. As John Gardner has pointed out, the geniuses of history have been "characterized not only by very high intelligence, but by the desire to excel, by perseverance in the face of obstacles, by zeal in the exercise of their gifts." We have need of such future in our nation.

A leader in today's world needs a strong resistance to adversity. He needs also to realize that leadership in a free society, unable to call on authoritarianism, must rely all the more heavily on the persuasive and inspiring example — on the authority of superior competence, and the impact of demonstrated and effect dedication and concern. He must lead by resisting and rejecting a way of life in which reckless agitation becomes an end in itself, and in which the institutions that have made the Republic possible are being gradually destroyed in the name of improving it.

At any level of responsibility a leader must be motivated by legitimate objectives, must have the wisdom to choose policies which will advance them, and the moral courage to pursue those policies even in the face of opposition. Particularly is this true when there are requirements for contradictory goals such as peace *and* security, and the existing situation presents only the options of peace with tyranny or security through war.

All our knowledge of the history of the world indicates that conflict is rooted in the nature of man. Perpetuation of the hard-won elements of civilization and the ideals of a society of free and responsible men will not come about through happenstance. Only if we are prepared to defend our freedom can we expect to retain it. That preparedness includes not only the means of defense but also the will to resist aggression.

General Pershing wrote in his final report as Commander-in-Chief of American Expeditionary Forces in World War I that "our armies were conscious of the support and cooperation of all branches of the government. Behind them stood the entire American people, whose ardent patriotism and sympathy inspired our troops with a deep sense of obligation, of loyalty, and of devotion to the country's cause never equaled in our history."

I believe that a nation possessed of that kind of resolve and common purpose in pursuit of noble ends is indomitable. The lack of that kind of support leaves the United States a precarious existence in this dangerous world. We are privileged to be citizens of a remarkable nation. Probably no other in any time has been so generous with its wealth, so sympathetically concerned with the affairs of all mankind, so unselfish in making sacrifices so that others could continue to enjoy freedom.

Our armed forces have turned back aggression in Europe and Asia. Our partnerships with other nations committed to peace and freedom have done much to prevent renewed violence. In the wake of conflicts not only our allies, but our former enemies as well, have prospered with our assistance. The Marshall Plan and the successor foreign aid programs have provided billions of dollars to those in need in other parts of the world. The success stories of West Germany, Japan, and South Korea would not have been possible without America's help.

We often lose sight of the essential grace and nobility with which America has played her role as a great power. We should not let preoccupation with our problems diminish our pride in our wonderful country. Certainly we have problems, and they command all of our abilities and earnestness of purpose.

We will, no doubt, always have problems of one kind or another. That is the human condition. We are constantly in process of becoming. But the man who devotes all his best efforts to moving us toward our ideal, not the one who stands aside loudly bewailing the distance yet to go, is the true producer. And it is the sum of the contribution of millions of people who in their daily lives do the best they can, then try to make that best a little better, that establishes the national character. Given this, we can meet our problems with optimism and goodwill bolstered by remembering all that is right with America.

There is an important lesson in this for each of you as you approach your first assignments. Your years at West Point have been, in many ways, an idealization of life. You have been privileged to consider, under the tutelage of one of the best schooled and motivated faculties in America, all manner of things of the broadest compass. Matters of national policy have been discussed with you by many of the most senior officials of the government. From this somewhat rarefied atmosphere you move now as the young leaders of our troop units to close daily contact with a multitude of problems and challenges.

You may feel some pain in making the transition. You may feel that you are at the bottom of the funnel. You may often find yourself with too few men, not enough spare parts or gasoline, and too many requirements to be met. But you will make do, you will get the job done, and you must never doubt that your individual actions are significant.

At this time, as we move toward an Army of volunteers, the quality of Army life is all-important. This administration is committed to providing major improvements in pay, housing, and other benefits. But what *you* must provide, and it is perhaps the most important factor of all, is an environment and a way of life that our best people will find challenging, meaningful and satisfying. There are no magic schemes for achieving this. It is largely an intangible result of the bond between a commander and his men.

People like to be in a good outfit doing a worthwhile job. They like to be challenged and find, in meeting the challenge, that they are more than they thought they were. They like to work for someone who is bright but not overbearing, understanding but not permissive, ambitious but not callous. They respond to loyalty, enthusiasm, encouragement, and goodwill. You individual actions, then — the kind of man you are and the kind of inspiration and example you set — will be extremely important.

Even more important will be the cumulative impact of all of you as a class. Going as you are to many parts of the world and to nearly every major unit, you will have a very real and immediate influence on the quality of Army life. Coming at this particular time in our national life that influence may be every bit as important as anything you will do individually or collectively in more senior positions in the years ahead.

You are embarking upon careers that offer challenge and opportunity in abundance. You will deal in what may practically be viewed as the primary indispensable: survival of the sovereign nation. You will find little ease and fewer tangible rewards than you deserve. Much of what you will be called upon to do will be dangerous, arduous, or unpleasant. But it will matter, and you never need doubt that you count — for what you do or fail to do will make the difference.

We all have need for purpose in our lives and for authority as well. Happiness cannot be pursued as an end in itself. It comes, as the Greek philosophers recorded long ago, only as a by-product of giving our best efforts for a cause in which we can believe. West Point teaches this, not only as an abstract theory, but as a satisfying and meaningful way of life. It accounts for her solidity and for our high hopes as you go forth today. I am proud of you for achieving this goal, and wish for you all good luck and Godspeed in the years ahead.

June 11, 1970, Washington, D.C.
Annual Conference of U.S. Attorneys

IN HIS State of the Union Address to the Congress, President Nixon said:

"We have heard a great deal of overblown rhetoric during the sixties on which 'war' has perhaps too often been used — the war on poverty, the war on misery, the war on disease, the war on hunger. But if there is one area where the word 'war' is appropriate it is in the fight against crime. We must declare and win the war against the criminal elements which increasingly threaten our cities, our homes, and our lives."

I believe it is appropriate before this audience of United States Attorneys, who are appointed by the President as the federal prosecutors and are thus in the vanguard of the war on crime, to focus the spotlight of publicity on some of the "criminal elements" referred to by the President.

Those elements are truly the enemies of our country.

They weaken its moral fiber by purveying illegal drugs and pornography.

They weaken its will by instilling in our citizens a fear of walking the streets at night — a fear of every approaching stranger.

They weaken its governmental structure by corrupting weak public officials and framing others. In one way or another, they affect local political processes.

They weaken its economy by infiltrating legitimate businesses and labor unions, by cheating on taxes and by other frauds.

These then are the enemy:

The organized criminal: the Mafia chieftain and his henchmen, the labor racketeer, the drug pusher, and the smut peddler.

The street criminal: the rapist, the robber, and the burglar.

The white collar criminal: the tax cheat, the embezzler, the dishonest repairman, and the dishonest businessman.

Like all who would threaten the life and health of this nation, they must be fought with every weapon available and consistent with out Constitution.

Under our Constitution, the primary role in combating crime is assigned to the states. But the recent massive increase in crime and the growing interstate scope of its operations have prompted the nation's leaders, of all political persuasions, to take a new look at Washington's responsibilities. The federal government is today committed to strengthening state and local law enforcement authorities through financial and technical assistance on an unprecedented scale. From a modest beginning in 1968 the Law Enforcement Assistance program has grown to the extent that we have asked the Congress to provide nearly a half-billion dollars for the next fiscal year.

We think that results are beginning to show. There are some encouraging signs.

Much of this is due to the tireless dedication of you and your staffs. You are filling, arguing, trying, closing, and handling the appeals of many more criminal cases, even though the whole process has become more difficult. Justice is coming more swiftly and surely, and more effectively.

We have also seen that as a result of more police exposure, crime rates in the District of Columbia have declined for five consecutive months. FBI statistics show that for the first time in several years the rate of increase in violent crime in the country decreased in 1969.

Please do not let me mislead you. The amount of crime itself did not decrease. It was up over 1968. Nevertheless, the downward turn in the rate of increase is encouraging and, as I have indicated, it is a start.

The federal government does have a special responsibility in the fields of organized crime, illegal use of narcotics and dangerous drugs, and the proliferation of pornographic materials, because of the interstate dimensions of these problems, and because of the high mobility and the international implications of organized crime and illegal drug operations. And for much the same reasons, we have a growing interest in the white-collar crime problem.

The administration's declaration of war on organized crime was made in President Nixon's message to the Congress on April 23, 1969. Organized crime is America's principal supplier of illegal goods and services, such as narcotics, illicit drugs, prostitution, pornography, and unlawful gambling. Its principal income comes from these sources. But it is increasingly operating in the fields of legitimate business. To insulate its activities from governmental interference, the syndicates systematically attempt to corrupt public officials and to exercise local political influence. In some cases they are successful. To control markets and supplies, they infiltrate labor unions. To curtail competition with American free enterprise, they use blackmail, extortion, tax evasion, fake bankruptcy, fraud, and other unscrupulous means to reap exorbitant profits.

As you know, we have made great progress in our efforts to mobilize against organized crime. Thirteen of the twenty strike forces of prosecutors and investigators recommended by the President are now on duty at strategic locations throughout the country, and the other seven will be soon established. Indictments and prosecutions of key syndicate leaders are on the upswing. We are beginning to make the Federal presence felt in the underground.

The success of these federal strike forces prompted the President to create, on June 4th of this year, the National Council on Organized Crime. Under the chairmanship of the Attorney General, this Council will formulate an effective, coordinated national strategy for the elimination of organized crime.

The President's statement, at the time of this council's creation, goes to the very heart of the problem we face today — it is a message which all Americans should heed:

"Organized crime in the United States has three goals: exploitation, corruption, and destruction. When it cannot directly exploit, it seeks to corrupt; what it cannot corrupt, it seeks to destroy. Its degrading influence can be felt in every level of American society, sometimes in insidious, subtle ways, but more often in direct acts of violence and illegality. It is a malignant growth in the body of American social and economic life that must be eliminated."

Unfortunately, the legislation needed to effectuate the President's program has not been provided. The antigambling statute, the witness immunity statute, the wagering tax law amendments, and the organized crime control measure which the President urged the Congress to enact are still not law. Although three of these proposals have been passed by the Senate, not one has gotten out of committee in the House of Representatives. On behalf of the President I urge the House to hasten action on these needed reforms.

Sadly, I must report that the administration's proposals on drugs, on pornography, and on crime in the District of Columbia are in much the same status. I don't believe that I need to go into detail with you about the enormity of the drug problem, the seriousness of the District of Columbia's problems, and the necessity for stopping the flow of pornography into American homes.

Our federal law enforcement agencies have made progress in these problem areas with the weapons available to them. But they need more. Despite special presidential messages to the Congress on these problems, the needed legislation has not been enacted. Congressional action is imperative.

I know that we do not have to ask for renewed dedication on your part in the anticrime program. I am sure that we have your complete support.

But I would like you to take back to your communities the concept that the war against crime must be more than a governmental effort. It requires the concern and efforts of all Americans. For ultimately, it is the community which must be the bulwark against the deterioration of the security of our homes, our parks, our streets, and our places of business.

As individuals and as members of a community, each American must work to create an environment in which criminal behavior is not a feasible alternative to lawful productivity — indeed, we must make it clear to those who doubt it that lawful productivity is the only possible course.

The lack of community involvement in our urban centers unquestionably contributes to the fact that so much of our criminal activity occurs there. But this association is not a necessary consequence of density. An attack on local officials, on places of business, on those basic institutions which are vital to life and freedom in this society is, ultimately, an attack on each citizen. In the absence of citizen concern, suspicious activities go unnoticed, crimes are not reported, victims receive no aid. This is a high price to pay for anonymity and a hesitancy to get involved.

But we are all involved. Every citizen must be encouraged to continue to make a meaningful contribution to the war on crime. And government officials at the local, state, and federal levels must continue to encourage the cooperation of citizens and community groups in this urgent undertaking.

Gentlemen, I sincerely implore you and your staffs and all other dedicated Americans responsible for the operation of our criminal justice system not to despair at the enormity of the task ahead of you. For I think that now, in this new decade, there is much to be encouraged about. I think that we can see some light.

There is national leadership committed to control of crime.

There is government commitment at all levels — Federal, State, and local.

And there is greater support and assistance on the part of all responsible citizens. They have let us know of their concern and they have offered their support. This is no doubt the most valuable aid available to you.

Our task is to convince these criminal elements — whether they be violent or outwardly gentle, gross, or polished — that the America of the seventies is aroused — and that we are going to apply the law evenly and justly in an all-out war against crime.

MEMBERS OF THE International Federation of Newspaper Publishers:

It is a pleasure to welcome you, the leaders of the World's free press, to our nation's capital. I bring you greetings from President Nixon and his sincere wishes that you will have a pleasant stay and a productive conference. I understand that this is only the second time in your twenty-three-year history that you have held your annual meeting in the United States, the other occasion being ten years ago in New York City. We are very glad to have you with us.

When I was invited last fall to deliver this opening address, I had not then achieved my present degree of notoriety as a newspaper critic. I want to assure you that that reputation is somewhat exaggerated — as occasionally happens with public officials who'd dispute with the press. Were that not the case, I am sure that your hosts from the American Newspaper Publishers Association would have withdrawn their invitation long ago.

While government and the press are natural adversaries — in your countries, I'm sure, as well as in this one — I think you will find in the course of my remarks that we are in agreement on more things than we are in disagreement.

First, the matter of freedom of the press. It is the underlying principle of your organization. I strongly believe in it. Without a free press, the Free World that we know and strive to protect would not long exist. It is one of the principal freedoms that sets us apart from Communist countries.

In our country freedom of the press is bound together with freedom of speech, freedom of religion, and the right to assemble and peaceably petition the government — all within the First Amendment to our Constitution. We Americans assiduously protect all of those freedoms.

As my friend J. Howard Wood, Chairman of the Board of the *Chicago Tribune* Company, said in an address to your federation in Tel Aviv in 1967, "In the United States all direct and obvious attempts to silence newspaper criticism of government have been eliminated." He also pointed out that in addition, and I quote him, "We have outlawed the more devious censorships of the early days, such as the licensing of printers and publishers and the taxing of the press into bankruptcy."

In short, no government official in the United States today could by any method — devious or otherwise — succeed in any effort to impose any form of restraint on freedom of the press.

Now, my differences with some of the news media in this country have come not over their right to criticize government or public officials, but *my* right to criticize *them* when I think they have been excessive or irresponsible in their criticism. As the news media have often pointed out, I am not really expressing any new thoughts. It's just that most of my predecessors, and many of my colleagues, have found it more comfortable to rock with the criticism than to return it.

I hope that former President Lyndon Johnson will forgive me for disclosing one bit of advice he passed along to me, shortly before I was sworn in as Vice President. I had known him during the preceding two years while I was governor of Maryland and, in the wake of a hard campaign for Vice President, was discussing with him some of the problems that lay ahead with the national press. He sympathized completely but warned me against what he called "taking on" the press.

"Just remember this," he said, "they come out every day; you don't."

But problems of public officials with the press go back, at least in this country, to the beginnings of life in the Republic.

In almost any discourse on journalism or freedom of the press in this country, you will hear quoted often these words by Thomas Jefferson, the author of our Declaration of Independence and our third President. He said:

The basis of our government being the opinion of the people, the very first object should be to keep that right; and were it left to me to decide whether we should have a government without newspapers, or newspapers without government, I should not hesitate a moment to prefer the latter.

That often-quoted statement by Thomas Jefferson was made in 1787 *before* he became President of the United States.

Listen to this lesser known observation from midway in his first term in 1803. He said:

Indeed the abuses of the freedom of the press here have been carried to a length never before known or borne by any civilized nation.

And four years later, midway through his second term, he said:

Nothing can now be believed which is seen in a newspaper. Truth itself becomes suspicious by being put into that polluted vehicle.

Gentlemen, that disenchanted view of the press by one of the founders of America's freedoms makes my well-publicized rhetoric pale by comparison. I cannot agree that newspapers are all that bad.

But I do believe firmly that with freedom goes responsibility and that you cannot enjoy one and ignore the other.

Incidentally, I congratualte your federation for having recognized among its basic principles that "a sense of personal responsibility, freely assumed by newspaper managers and publishers, is one of the essential guarantees of the independence of the press."

I now speak of responsibility in perhaps a broader sense, one of obligation to the public that you serve. To me, in its simplest form, it means telling both sides of the story — something that has gone out of vogue in some of the major news organizations in America but which I hope is only temporarily in eclipse. The price for not presenting both sides of a story is loss of credibility as a public institution. It is a heavy price to pay for a fleeting exercise in power or influence. Because a newspaper, like a politician, has lost everything when it loses its credibility.

As a government official, I find it extremely frustrating, for example, that only one side of the Vietnam war is being emphasized by some of our most influential newspapers and television networks and that, overall, their coverage comes off slanted against the American involvement in that war without any attempt at balance.

We see paraded daily all of the reasons we should not be involved and none of the reasons that we should be involved.

We read of alleged American atrocities of civilians in a hamlet called My Lai, but virtually nothing of the even more atrocious slaughter of Vietnamese civilians in the major city of Hue by the terrorist enemy invader.

We read and hear horrified accounts that the United States has equipped South Vietnamese soldiers to fight in Cambodia. There is virtually no mention of whom they are fighting — namely, the *Russian-equipped* North Vietnamese, who have invaded that country by the thousands as they did in South Vietnam and Laos.

When I raise some of these points in discussion with media groups, the answer is, "We are *only* concerned with America's involvement. We do not circulate in Hanoi." [Or "We are not seen or heard or read in Hanoi."]

Gentlemen, this is my point. *Hanoi has no free press* to tell the world of its atrocities if you don't do it. And Americans or Europeans, Asians or Australians cannot make a valid decision if you do not attempt to give them *both* sides of the story.

I submit that it is the mission of the press to *inform* the public, rather than try to *persuade* it; that the public, given sufficuent information, can make a sound decision.

In fact, I'd like to go back to that original quote of Jefferson's in this speech. There was a line in it that always gets chopped off in the traditional journalism-speech quotation but

343

which puts the whole thing in better perspective. Jefferson wasn't arguing for newspapers in lieu of government in 1787, but he said if it ever came to that, "I should mean that *every man should receive those papers, and be capable of reading them.*"

In other words, what Thomas Jefferson meant was, give all the people the *complete* information and trust them to decide. Don't try to do it for them.

The complete reporting of the news has become even more important with the almost overnight transformation of global communications. The world's major newspapers are transported by jet aircraft among the world's most influential capitals and major cities in one day or at most in two days. They are read by foreign leaders, editors and broadcasters and they have an immediate impact on current issues.

Television by satellite has given mankind instant visual communication. When man steps on the moon, or is in trouble in space, it is known instantly around the world. By the same token, the earthquake in Peru, the flood in Rumania, bring an instantaneous response of assistance from sympathetic earthlings around the globe.

If there is to be any balance in informing the people of the free world, it will come from you — and from the radio and television stations in your countries. It will definitely *NOT* come from the controlled media in countries that are hostile to my country and to yours. In those countries information unfavorable to them will be suppressed; information favorable to them will be played up.

I am sure that many things contribute to the making of America's image abroad — the coverage of our nation by your own newspapers, the wire services, the American news magazines with their large overseas circulations, television, and films. But the portrait often is distorted.

Our government has a continuing indication that people visiting the United States almost uniformly find us *less* violent, *less* racist, *more* ordered, *more* friendly, then they had been led to believe.

I hope that will also be your experience during your visit this year. If it is, you might well ask yourself: Why is this so?

Thank you, and have a pleasant stay.

June 23, 1970, Hot Springs, Arkansas
National Sheriffs' Association

I AM PLEASED to be with you at this assembly of sheriffs from all parts of the nation. As a former county executive, I know something of the burdens you bear and challenges you face as the local guardians of a lawful and just society.

It is appropriate that I use this opportunity to discuss with you one of the greatest crises facing law enforcement officers and in fact facing all us as a nation. That crisis is drugs — and particularly the drug problem with respect to youths.

At no risk of exaggeration, it may be said that this society is being caught up in and carried along by a steadily mounting wave of drug abuse. Consider these facts:

— In all of last year, customs officers seized 624 pounds of hashish. In the first three months alone of this year they seized more than double that amount. Their first quarter haul was equivalent to 400 tons of marijuana.

— 10 billion sedative dosage units will be produced this year . . . the equivalent of fifty for every man, woman, and child in the country. One-half of this supply will get into illicit markets.

— It is estimated that over one-half million citizens are now dependent on non-narcotic drugs — sedatives, stimulants, and the like. A recent study has shown that twenty-one percent of all students have tried amphetamines, with the family medicine cabinet being a major source of supply.

— There are now perhaps 200,000 heroin addicts in the Nation, with recruitment growing fastest among the under-twenty-ones.

— Estimates put the number of those who have smoked marijuana at between eight and twenty million persons.

This is, of course, only the leading edge of the problem. It says nothing about the amount of drugs escaping customs officers, the arrests not made, or the drug abuse from the back alleys to the most affluent homes which remains surreptitious and unreported.

The alarming fact is that we may be just in the first stages of this collective national "trip," as the slang expression goes. It is expected that the use of all forms of drugs in the next decade will increase a hundredfold.

We are, in fact, in the midst of a drug culture that threatens the future of our society if we do not act quickly, forcefully, and intelligently to bring it under control.

Millions of men and women in the United States turn daily to their physicians for tranquilizers, pep pills, and sleeping pills. Still more millions turn, with the encouragement of massive advertising campaigns, to the corner drug store to buy a variety of medicines to calm their nerves, put them to sleep, or keep them awake. We as a country have hardly noticed this remarkable phenomenon of *legal* drug use. But it is new, it is increasing, and the individual and social costs have yet to be calculated.

The youth of our nation, being energetic and adventurous, have in large numbers turned to new sources to get drugs. Many of these sources are illegal, and the drugs obtained from them are also in many cases illegal. Our young are experimenting with drugs of great potency and great danger. Their participation in illegal channels of securing drugs has brought them into serious and, in many cases, tragic conflict with our criminal justice system.

Ten or twenty years ago the criminal justice system was dealing with illegal drug use primarily in America's ghettos where the problem is still particularly acute. But now it is much broader. Young people from outside the ghetto are involved with drugs in unprecedented numbers. In the last five years, urban drug arrests have risen 280 percent; suburban drug arrests have gone up 1056 percent! By far the greatest increases are among those under eighteen.

Although law enforcement agencies have responded vigorously, they are everywhere confronted with new problems which are not solved by the old approaches. The twelve-year-old "heroin pusher" and the sixteen-year-old "marijuana dealer" are now commonplace.

In order to cope effectively with this problem we must acquire much greater knowledge than now exists about these drugs and get that knowledge before the public as dramatically as possible. Once we do this, your job as law enforcement officers will become much easier.

The now recognized menace of LSD offers an excellent example of what I am talking about. Experimentation and use of this mind-blowing drug was on the increase until recent evidence came to light that it would produce damage to chromosomes and result in malformed babies. This new knowledge apparently has brought about a sharp reduction in the drug.

Heroin in particular is a drug with which you, as law enforcement officers, are concerned. Your focus in the past has been on the heroin addict, who often turns to crime

345

in order to support financially his costly, illegal habit. But many of those who become hooked have graduated from marijuana to the use of this more virulent form of addiction. While medical treatment for heroin addiction improves, it does not lessen the menace to society. We must find better ways to get across the message of the dangerous and self-destructive nature of this drug and get it across before our young people become enticed to using it. And this involves reaching parents as well as the young.

President Nixon, recognizing the fact, stated last December that there would be no higher priority in this administration than seeing that the public is educated on the facts about drugs.

Accordingly, he has taken these steps:

— He's established a new $3.5 million program to train school personnel in drug abuse education.

— He's created a National Clearinghouse for Drug Abuse Information giving the public one central office to contact.

— He's modified the Law Enforcement Assistance Administration to allow large cities to apply for funds to be used for drug education as well as law enforcement.

— He's embarked upon an expanded campaign of public service advertising against drug abuse.

— And he's supplemented by $1 million the funds for increased research into the effects of marijuana on man.

Along with better public understanding of the drug problem, there is need for more realistic laws. The administration has also recognized this need and has moved forcefully to correct the problem.

In the past, numerous young lives have been ruined because of the law making possession of marijuana a felony, with sentences for the possession of marijuana often more severe than those for involuntary manslaughter. Such a law invites circumvention and every circumvention undermines public respect for the law.

Under the Controlled Dangerous Substances Bill proposed by the President, present inequities would be eliminated and penalties would be more closely tailored to the crime. There can now be a second chance for a youth who has taken a misstep and has been charged with possession of marijuana for personal use. This would be in the discretion of the judge. On the other hand, tougher penalties would be meted out to drug profiteers. A dealer could be sentenced from five years to life and would also face a mandatory fine of $50,000 and forfeiture of property.

This legislation has passed the United States Senate and is now before the House of Representatives, where it has been facing a delay in the Interstate and Foreign Commerce Committee. It might help if you gave your Congressman a nudge and helped us dislodge it.

The administration also has moved forcefully to improve enforcement. All of you, of course, are familiar with the massive raid of this past week: 139 persons in ten different cities were arrested. It is estimated that the ring involved handled thirty percent of all heroin sales in this country and seventy-five to eighty percent of all cocaine sales. It was the largest federal narcotics raid in our history.

But this is just the beginning of the crackdown planned by Attorney General Mitchell. The enforcement personnel in the Bureau of Narcotics and Dangerous Drugs have been increased by twenty-five percent this year and are expected to increase by an additional seventeen percent in the next twelve months. In customs, a supplemental budget approved by Congress will provide $8.75 million for 915 additional men and new equipment.

There are some of the proposals that the Nixon Administration has made or is now considering in the area of drug abuse. They are good proposals. But as every one of you knows, laws will not be enough to handle this problem. This is a problem primarily of individual citizens. And it is a problem that demands for a solution not only knowledge, but also courage. Let me give an example. Most people admit that heroin and LSD and methadrine are dangerous. But a lot of people say that marijuana is different, that it is no more dangerous than alcohol. And they say, in fact, that the older generation is hypocritical when it drinks whiskey but registers shock at the smoking of marijuana.

And that is the kind of problem I am referring to. We are not hypocrites. We have made our mistakes, and some of them we have admitted, and some of them, perhaps, we have not admitted as quickly as we should have, because of pride. But we have given our best efforts to our country and to our children, and we must not allow ourselves to be dissuaded by arguments that depend on a false reading of our motives.

We must stand up for things that we believe are right and talk out against those things we consider wrong, even if occasionally we are found to be in error. In our opinion, marijuana is dangerous. It is not just the grown-up equivalent of alcohol. Alcohol has been known for thousands of years and it has won the approval of peoples and governments, at least the acquiescence and its use. And that is the difference. Marijuana too, has been known for thousands of years but in every single nation of the world that has had a long acquaintance with marijuana and its consumption, the use of this drug is prohibited by law. That is a striking fact. It may not be a proof of marijuana's danger, but it is a weighty historical point, and I believe that, until strong evidence to the contrary is brought forward stronger than we now have, certainly we must assume that this drug is dangerous. And knowing that, we must have the courage to stand up and say to our children, No, pot is not the equivalent of whiskey. It is harmful, and that is why we forbid it. We do not forbid it out of whim, or out of point of personal taste, but because in our best judgment; it is dangerous.

We forbid it by passing laws. And these laws, as well as many others, are enforced by you men here today. And, gentlemen, I should like to say one thing now that I feel very strongly: If we are to preserve freedom in this country, if we are to make certain that the people in this country have recourse to a law-abiding, legal society that is within the contemplation of the framers of the Constitution, then the burden of law enforcement must fall on men like you, our local law enforcement officials. I say this because you men are accountable to your own communities, you in particular, because most of you are elected officials. But this is also true of the police officers who work together with you, because they are appointed by men who are elected and are therefore accountable to their communities. And this is the kind of law enforcement, the law enforcement that is answerable to its community, that is the fundament of freedom.

For when community control is removed from law enforcement and the burden of keeping peace is placed upon the national government, then there is a serious danger of overcentralization of authority. But there will never be a need for such overcentralization of authority if you men continue to serve your communities as well as you have in the past, and as well as you serve them today.

Your work is hard, and especially in the last few years you have been exposed to a form of abuse that is appalling. You are often called upon to prevent anarchy in the streets. And when you do your job, you are often called fascists and pigs. Yet I wonder if your detractors have even stopped to think that if you did not enforce the law at the local level, an anarchy so ferocious would result that in the end the citizens of this nation would turn in desperation to a tight and brutal centralization of authority simply to ensure their bodily safety? This tight and brutal centralization of authority is what we never want to have, for it is the base of fascism. You are the men who stand against it.

And I wonder if your detractors have ever considered the dignity of your work? We hear a lot today about meaningful work and about service to others. Yet what could be more meaningful than helping to keep violence out of one's own community? And what could be a greater service than saving the life of a fellow citizen? This is the work that you men do, and you can be proud of it. You can be proud in the knowledge that if you did not do your work and discharge your duties, your fellow citizens would be in danger, and they might suffer or die. That's a knowledge that few men can boast, and it gives you dignity.

We hear a lot about peace nowadays. But what peace is more important to a man than peace in his own streets? And you are the men who keep that peace. You make our communities safe and you guard our liberty against the invasions of anarchy and the invasions of central power. You are the men who receive unending abuse and do not quit your posts. You are the men who give the people of this nation every day, right in their own neighborhoods, an example of service and selflessness and sacrifice. I, for one, am grateful, and I thank you.

July 9, 1970, Denver, Colorado
Education Commission of the States

THANK YOU very much, Governor Tom McCall. I don't know whether it's proper to thank Governor McCall for that introduction or not! I'll have to think about it awhile and see what it really meant.

Governor Love and other distinguished governors; members of the various state agencies and other officials connected with education; ladies and gentlemen.

I didn't come here, Tom, to lay any rhetoric on this distinguished audience. So I want to disabuse you of that notion if that's what was running through your mischievous mind when you made that introduction.

I'm serious about this particular speech because I think that it's seldom that a Vice President has a chance to address an audience as aware as this audience. And I think that today there are things that need to be said and perspectives that need to be emphasized.

We live in an age of impression and image. The complexity of our national life makes it impossible to gain much of our knowledge by directly doing or directly observing. Except in the hard sciences — where we are often able to recreate in the laboratory conditions close to the natural ones which existed at the source of knowledge — we are heavily dependent upon the judgments and opinions of other people.

This is what makes "communication" such an important factor in the modern world. More and more — in making our own judgments about issues and people — we are deeply affected by the impressions and images and opinions conveyed to us by those we think are in a better position to know.

Educators are among the most important "communicators" in our society. And I believe that it is important that everyone involved in education realize how great an effect he can have on the morale of our country. If educators are positive in their approach to the problems our country faces — if they place our liabilities in proper perspective along with our assets — they will have a positive effect on the search for solutions. If they are constantly negative, they risk producing little except despair.

I believe that this matter of approach on the part of educators is of more importance than ever in these times when there is such an extreme concentration on the negative. We are constantly bombarded with strident cries of what's wrong with America — and this has led too many people to believe that this great country is in the grip of anarchy, panic, repression and despair.

Fortunately, you know and I know that it just isn't so. And let every American be assured that it is not going to be so.

First, let's look at just a few examples of the progress that this great country has made in the past fifty years — since 1920.

In 1920, the population of this country was 106 million — half what it is today.

Life expectancy in the United States was fifty-four years; now it is more than seventy.

The Gross National Product was 89 billion dollars; today it is more than 900 billion dollars and within this decade it will rise to a trillion dollars.

Fifty years ago today women were not allowed to vote — the Nineteenth Amendment to the Constitution was not declared operative until later that summer.

Fifty years ago today there was no regularly scheduled radio broadcasting anywhere.

Let me dwell for a moment on the field that is of most interest to you — education.

In 1920 there were 311,266 young people graduated from high schools in the United States. This year the number — in a population that merely doubled — was ten times greater.

Ninety-four percent of young Americans who are of high school age are attending high school, nearly twenty percent more than in 1950.

Institutions of higher education in this country conferred 53,516 degrees in 1920; this year they conferred more than one million.

The percentage of college graduates among our people is more than twice as great as that of any other country in the world.

In 1920 six percent of our population was illiterate. Today illiteracy has almost disappeared.

We have the greatest system of education the world has ever known and we intend to preserve it and improve it.

I want to stress that word *improve*, for here, too, perspective is most important. When I talk about the positive side of our system of education — when I say it is the greatest in the world — I am not saying that there is nothing wrong with it. We know that it is in need of reform and renewal, and that's why President Nixon last March sent to the Congress two historic messages on education reform. The President called for a new focus on educational research and experimentation, and a new approach to the problem of financing education; he called for expansion and redirection of student aid, for new emphasis on community colleges and vocational education, and for a general reassessment and reinforcement of our system of education.

One of the subjects the President discussed in these messages was the issue you have chosen as the general theme of your meeting this year — accountability. He said that it is in the interest of school administrators and schoolteachers as well as in the interest of their pupils that accountability be clarified. The President's position on this was consistent with the general view in this administration that the best government can be delivered by the entity closest to the people. He said: "Success should be measured not by some fixed national norm, but rather by the results achieved in relation to the actual situation of the particular school and the particular set of pupils. . . . I am determined to see to it that the flow of power in education goes toward, and not away from, the local community. The diversity and freedom of education in this nation, founded on local adminsitration and state responsibility, must prevail."

To give you a general sense of the priority this administration places on education, I would like to quote just one further paragraph from the President's message to the Congress on higher education. He said:

"No element of our national life is more worthy of our attention, our support, and our concern than higher education. For no element has greater impact on the careers, the personal growth and the happiness of so many of our citizens. And no element is of greater importance in providing the knowledge and leadership on which the vitality of our democracy and the strength of our economy depend."

I have two reasons for citing this administration's concern about education. First, I know how interested you are in this field. And secondly, I want to make the point that when I say we should see the positive side of life in the United States, I do not mean that we should blind ourselves to the need for improvement in many fields. What I am saying is that our view should be balanced.

The examples that I have cited of progress in education and other fields — and there are many, many more — serve to remind us of how much has changed, of how much general improvement there has been in health, wealth, education, communication, social consciousness, and in every aspect of life in this land in the last half century. That progress has made this the greatest nation on earth — and we should never allow ourselves to forget that basic truth.

Despite these fundamental long-term gains in life in these United States, there is a tendency abroad in the land to cry doom. This tendency emerges in different forms at different times — without the regularity but with the same rasping effect as the seventeen-year locust.

Take the case of the local government body in Massachusetts which deplored "the calamities of the present unjust and ruinous war" and foresaw "the dissolution of all free government and the establishment of a reign of terror." And consider the act of a state legislature which tried to rally the people to form a national "peace party." It called upon opponents of the federal government's policy to "let the sound of your disapprobation of this war be loud and deep." While there was a move in the Congress to cut off funds for the war, the President was said to be "insidious," "devious," "prevaricating," and "Machiavellian." And a Congressional orator shouted that the President and his supporters were plunging over a precipice and drawing the country after them.

Does all that sound a bit familiar? Well, all of it was said during the administration of James Madison early in the nineteenth century. And despite all of the alarms, all the protest, all the doubt, the United States of America survived and went on to greatness.

In 1842, Charles Dickens visited the United States and decided that "the nation is a body without a head and the arms and legs are occupied in quarrelling with the trunk and each other. . . ." And if you think that some American writers sound the knells of despair today, listen to Walt Whitman one hundred years ago. He wrote: "Never was there, perhaps, more hollowness at heart than at present, and here in the United States. Genuine belief seems to have left us. . . . The spectacle is appalling."

I cite these pieces of the past to make the point that today's outcry from the negativists should be heard in the perspective of history. They've said it before, and they will say it again. And — as in the past — the vast majority of Americans who want to see their country advance will continue their positive and constructive words and deeds, and will help the United States to go on to new greatness.

There was a difference in how that rhetoric of ruin was heard then. The orator in the Congress to whom I referred was Daniel Webster—and his speech was considered so inflammatory that the text wasn't published for nearly a hundred years. The words of Dickens and Whitman were read at the time by only a few. Today it's all there on the evening news in full color — and perhaps even in bulletins before that. But we can trust the American people to separate truth from advocacy and, if I may divert an expression, to go "right on."

We hear a constant clamor today over economic conditions in the United States. And let us admit, the economy is in a sensitive state. We are battling an inflation that has been burning for more than four years. And we are trying to bring about the rare combination of stable growth and high employment. Let me say to you today that we are winning that battle.

One of the reasons we are winning it is that the U.S. economy is the strongest and soundest and fairest that the world has ever known. Never in history has more wealth been more fully shared by more people than in the United States today. Let's look at a few basic facts:

After making full allowance for higher taxes and inflation, the average real income of Americans is higher this year than ever before.

The typical American family can buy nearly twice as much with its annual income as it could in 1950.

Unemployment has risen in recent months — and we must reduce it — but it is a full 25 percent less than it was in 1961.

The average income of the individual American is nearly twice that in any other country of the world, and many times the income in most countries.

While we worry about the poverty that still remains in this country — as we should — let us not overlook the progress that has been made in our attack on this problem. Since

1950 — in an increasing population — the number of people living below the poverty line has decreased about 35 percent. Yet, some poverty still persists, but never has any nation done so much, so successfully, to reduce the ravages of poverty. And we are determined to reduce the ranks of the poor until they reach the irreducible.

I have no doubt about the strength and potential of the United States economy. Some say that too much affluence is at the base of many of our country's problems. This is a theory that reaches back to John Adams' adage that "Human nature cannot bear prosperity." I say we will learn to bear it — and enjoy it, too.

Now, let's look at another issue before the country today — one that I've been somewhat concerned with. Some of my interpretations about it have been, I believe, misconstrued. And I speak of the issue — dissent. We should appreciate the fact that more than in any other country in the world peaceful dissent is recognized and protected in America. And let us keep our historical perspective about dissent. This country has weathered it before in a way that is largely forgotten. Who remembers that there were more than 300,000 draftees who refused to report for service in World War I — more than ten percent of the total number inducted — and that more than 16,000 slackers, delinquents, and evaders were arrested in one roundup in the New York City area in September of 1918? The United States survived that genuinely serious manifestation of dissent and went on to become a greater nation.

The status of minority groups is a matter of constant concern — and rightly so. But I can report to you that in every one of the categories that I have listed — real income, education, standard of living — the gains, which have been substantial for all our people, have proportionately been greater for blacks than for whites. For example, the proportion of Negroes earning middle incomes has more than doubled since 1950 and the proportion of black students in colleges has increased more than fifty percent.

There has been another kind of progress in America that we must not overlook. In recent years appreciation of the arts and interest in the humanities have broadened and deepened all across the United States. Attendance at and participation in the performing arts and the programs of the nation's museums have increased manifold. This is a happy trend, because it carries with it both the reality and the prospect that more and more Americans have and will have a greater share in the full richness of the nation's cultural life. As in every field, a challenge is present here: There is a growing need for more help for the arts and humanities from both the public and private sectors, and I am confident that this help will be forthcoming.

This country's dramatic advances in science are know to all the world. The historic achievements of our space program are the most spectacular example, but there are many other achievements that are less widely hailed but nevertheless of the highest significance for the future of mankind.

There is a relatively new issue that is the center of intense interest among our people today: the environment. At base it must be said that our enormous success as a productive and affluent society has created much of the environmental problem. There was a time when smoke pouring from a smokestack was a welcome sight — it meant jobs for men who needed them and products for consumers who wanted them. Using the factory in a symbolic way, as it relates to the problems of the environment, it can be said that our challenge now is to upgrade the jobs, improve the products and eliminate the smoke. We accept that challenge. The same American ingenuity that helped to create the problem can lead the way to overcoming it.

No issue is of greater moment in 1970 than the war and the prospects for peace. The problems involved in foreign policy are perhaps the most complex and most difficult of all. But in recognizing the difficulties, let us not disregard achievement. We have completely reversed the flow of United States' involvement in the war in Vietnam; we are helping the South Vietnamese to improve their capability to defend themselves; and we are bringing our fighting men home. We will end this war with honor.

World tensions remain — and will remain. The Middle East continues to be a powder keg. But these are challenges to be met, not causes for despair. In the midst of tensions we are as of right now in meaningful and serious negotiations with the Soviet Union on limitation of strategic arms.

We often hear today the assertion that we must change our national priorities. The fact is we *have* changed our priorities. In the federal budget for the next fiscal year, for the first time in twenty years, we will use more of our resources for social needs at home than we will for military and defense purposes.

While much of the progress I have been discussing is often measured in quantitative terms, there is a qualitative side to nearly all aspects of it. In no other country of the world at any time in history has there been so much respect for liberty, freedom of conscience, justice, human dignity, and human fulfillment as there is in the United States today. The fact that we are still concerned about protecting these elements of freedom should not be taken as a sign that they have been diminished but rather as evidence of what a high value we place upon them. Yes, some injustice does persist, but never has any people had so great a commitment to justice for all. More Americans today are doing more to help their neighbors than at any other time in history.

In speaking of the progress we have made, I am by no means suggesting that we do not face serious problems in this country. It is good news that we recognize our problems and we are more sensitive to them than any people in the history of mankind. It is good news that we are not satisfied with the progress we have made.

As we go forward in our attacks against what's wrong with America, we should never forget what's right with America. Let us see and treat the blemishes, but never let them blind us to the beauty.

As we make progress on these fronts, many will say this is not enough; we must have *more now.* Such impatience, when it gets out of control, produces only negative results. But when it runs in constructive channels, it can help to add that extra measure of spirit which will enable us to meet the challenges of our time.

Let us confront out shortcomings, not with anger, but with determination.

Let us commit our resources, not with reckless impatience, but with urgent care.

Working from the sound and solid base that is the American condition today, and recognizing the very real problems the nation faces, the Nixon Administration is moving forward on a course of reform, restoration and renewal. The goal of this policy is to make the America of the seventies and beyond a land in which we have assessed both our successes and our failures with sound judgment — and have moved to enhance the good and root out the bad.

This should — and will — continue to be a society of great expectations. As we go forward into the seventies, we must — and we will — see more of those expectations become realities.

We will preserve and we will enlarge the American dream.

We will nourish and we will refresh the American spirit.

We will enhance the quality of life for all Americans.

We will prove — once again — that in America the voices of despair are ultimately stilled by the clear fact of progress.

It's been a privilege for me to address this distinguished audience today.

August 17, 1970, Miami, Florida
Veterans of Foreign Wars

I WOULD like to speak to you today of a rising threat to everything our servicemen have fought to accomplish in Southeast Asia — a threat embodied in the Hatfield–McGovern Amendment.

Should this proposed Amendment become law, unless America declares war, President Nixon would be forced to end any military aid to Laos and to halt all military operations in South Vietnam — twenty weeks from today. Every American soldier, sailor, marine and airman would have to be out of Vietnam by June 30 of next year — ten-and-a-half months from today.

Hatfield–McGovern is a blueprint for the first defeat in the history of the United States — and for chaos and communism for the future of South Vietnam. The *Washington Post* was generous to call this amendment "reckless." It is worse than that; if adopted by the Senate and passed by the House, this publicized "Amendment to End the War" in Vietnam will go down in history as the amendment that lost the war in Vietnam and destroyed the chances for freedom and peace in Southeast Asia for the balance of the century.

Nothing less is at stake.

But, if this amendment, and any similarly irresponsible proposal which may be offered, can go down in humiliating defeat for its sponsors in the Senate — then this nation will *not* go down in humiliating defeat on the battlefields of Southeast Asia — I promise you that.

Today I have a simple question. I am here to ask you, as fellow Americans, and fellow veterans — can the President of the United States count on your support?

The charges I have already made here are among the strongest since I took office as Vice President. But no more dangerous proposal has been presented to the American Congress in those nineteen months — or in nineteen years for that matter. While I do not question the patriotism of the sponsors of this amendment — I do deeply question their wisdom, their judgment and their logic. They are horribly wrong — and if their grave error is enacted into law, generations of Asians and Americans will suffer for their tragic blunder.

Let us look at the inevitable consequences should Hatfield–McGovern be enacted.

First, the amendment would be a final lethal blow to the Paris peace talks. Any vestige of hope that the enemy will negotiate with Ambassador Bruce at Paris would disappear overnight — for the last incentives for the enemy to talk seriously would be gone. He would have gotten what he came to Paris to get — a fixed final timetable for all Americans to get out of South Vietnam. Why should the enemy offer concessions to the United States for something Senators Hatfield and McGovern and their allies will give him free of charge in four months?

Should this amendment become law, and all American military operations in Southeast Asia cease by December 31, the immense burden of this war would fall immediately and totally upon South Vietnam. The government and people there would confront, alone and all at once, the completion of the enormous tasks of creating a stable democratic society, promoting economic and social reform, fighting an internal war against guerrillas and defending their nation from invasion from three frontiers.

Though South Vietnam has made enormous strides in development in recent years — today she could not carry those burdens alone. No developing nation could.

Hence, the result of a unilateral, precipitous American abandonment of South Vietnam would be the collapse of the government, chaos in the country — and ultimately the kind of communism that literally decimated the civilian population of Hue in the Tet offensive.

The Rand Corporation estimates that if communism prevails in South Vietnam, 100,000 Vietnamese who placed their faith in us will die for that error in judgment. Douglas Pike, the nation's foremost expert on the Viet Cong, estimates three million South Vietnamese could lose their lives in the bloodbath following a Communist victory.

Assuredly, this is not what Senators Hatfield, McGovern, and those supporting them want — but that is what they are inviting.

They say their amendment will provide for transport and a refuge for Vietnamese who would fear for their lives when the Americans go. But how — and where? Do Senators Hatfield and McGovern have in mind opening up Oregon and South Dakota to resettle the refugees? Hardly. And the place for these men and women who believe so deeply in freedom that they will become exiles rather than submit to the Communist yoke is not Oregon or South Dakota — it is South Vietnam.

It is clear from their mention of "provision" for refugees that Senators Hatfield and

McGovern have considered that the collapse of South Vietnam will indeed be one consequence of their amendment. But have they considered the consequences of that collapse?

One wonders if they really give a damn.

If South Vietnam collapses then victory and success go to the hard-liners in Hanoi and Peking who counseled belligerence and war instead of peace and negotiation.

If South Vietnam collapses then 285,000 Americans will have suffered and 43,000 will have died for nothing. An American Army, undefeated on the field of battle, will come home in humiliation because impatient pacifists in the Senate lost the war. What will be the reaction then when the American people wake up to learn that the thousands of lives and billions in taxes over a decade had been spent only to find national humiliation and disaster at the end of the road?

Will they then reward the blind impatient politicians who could not see the war through its final hours — and so snatched, for America, military defeat from the jaws of political victory?

If South Vietnam collapses, then Southeast Asia is gone. Those who do not believe in the domino theory, as the President has put it, have not talked to the dominoes. Already Cambodia is half-occupied by North Vietnamese and Viet Cong. Laos is half-occupied by North Vietnamese and Pathet Lao. Thailand is fighting its own Communist insurgency, aided and encouraged from without. Does any rational man believe these countries — or Malaysia and Singapore at the end of the peninsula — can survive if South as well as North Vietnam should come under the rule of militant Communists?

Have the isolationists in the Senate pondered the full consequences of America's defeat in South Vietnam — and freedom's defeat in Southeast Asia?

Looking down the road to the year 2000, we see most Asian nations on the threshold of technological maturity; we see an Asia that contains sixty percent of all humanity; we see a world in which there are ten Asians for every American.

Are the isolationists content to let that Asia go by default to the Communists because they lacked the perseverance to see this through?

Well, we are not, my fellow Americans and my fellow veterans — and the President is not — and together we shall see this war through to an honorable end that will do justice to the sacrifices of all our sons.

Have the isolationists considered the impact of the abandonment of this one ally upon America's other allies around the world? Could any nation put trust in the word and capacity of the United States — if we slink home, defeated, from the battlefield of Southeast Asia?

The lessons for nations like Germany and Japan — even India — would be clear: The inescapable conclusion would be that the United States cannot be counted upon in the crunch and nations must depend upon themselves to survive. The nonproliferation treaty would be forgotten as every state rushed to develop its greatest possible deterrent. If collective security is a failure in Vietnam — who will place confidence in it in Europe or the Middle East?

As I stated moments ago, while I do not question the patriotism of the Senators I criticize, I do question their wisdom, their logic, and their judgment — and I question also their sense of justice.

Some of the same Senators who bewailed a Democratic President's lack of power in foreign policy ten years ago now contend that this newly installed Republican President has too much power.

Some of the same Senators who supported the "peace plank" at the Democratic National Convention in 1968 now condemn a President who has taken more risks for peace than that plank contained.

Some of the same Senators who were silent while a Democratic President sent 532,000 American soldiers to Vietnam are obstructing and undercutting a President who is bringing 265,000 Americans home.

What is there in the record of this President to justify the attitude and actions of these Senators?

When President Nixon took office there were 532,000 American troops in Vietnam. He did not send more troops in — he started bringing the boys home. He pledged in June of last year to bring home 25,000 troops; they have come home. He pledged in September to bring home 35,000 more; they have come home; he pledged in December to bring home 50,000 more; they have come home. Every promise he has made to the American people about the war in Asia, he has kept. American casualties are a third of what they were in 1968; time is now on the side of the allies, not the side of the enemy; and still they malign his policies and his performance.

The President has turned the war over to the South Vietnamese as rapidly as they have become prepared to shoulder the burden.

To proceed slower than that is to break faith with the American people. But to move faster than security dictates is to risk the lives of our men and invite a victory for communism that tens of thousands of our lads died to prevent.

And no matter what the McGoverns and Hatfields propose — the President is not going to take those risks with the lives of American men.

The Senate sponsors of Hatfield–McGovern cannot win this war; they cannot conclude an honorable peace, but they can lose this war — as well as guarantee the ultimate failure of the uneasy peace to follow — if they convince enough of their colleagues to support their amendment.

They argue in the Senate that the Cambodian decision underscores the need to place limits and restrictions upon the President — to force upon him a timetable for withdrawal. I do not agree with that assessment. In my view, the President's decision to enter Cambodia and capture and destroy those tons of enemy arms and ammunition that would otherwise have been killing American men was an act of courage and the finest hour in the Nixon Presidency.

The Cambodian decision does not argue for putting shackles upon this President. It argues eloquently the case that the Senate should leave the President alone to exercise his Constitutional powers as Commander-in-Chief and determine what is necessary to protect the lives of American men.

Senator Fulbright now seeks a larger role for his committee in the conduct of foreign policy — but where the President decided and acted in a matter of hours to protect American lives — it took Mr. Fulbright and his colleagues seven weeks to decide on a simple amendment. His is a history of querulous "fuddy-duddying."

Many of the men in this great organization trace their military service to their country back to World War I. Yet, today, we see abroad in our land and in the halls of Congress the voices of that same shortsighted isolationism that lost the peace after World War I and helped to bring on World War II.

Let us not again forget the lesson that for the United States, there is no security in a retreat from the world. Let us not again force an American President to make in deepening despair the kind of statement that Woodrow Wilson made in St. Louis just 10 months after the armistice in France:

If [the Covenant of the League of Nations] should ever in any important aspect be impaired, I would feel like asking the Secretary of War to get the boys who went across the water to fight, together on some field where I could go and see them, and I would stand up before them and say, "Boys, I told you before you went across the seas that this was a war against wars, and I did my best to fulfill the promises; but I am obliged to come to you in mortification and shame and say I have not been able to fulfill the promise. You are betrayed. You fought for something that you did not get.

"And the Glory of the Armies and Navies of the United States is gone like a dream in the night, and there ensues upon it, in the suitable darkness of the night, the nightmare of dread which lay upon the nation before this war came; and there will come sometime, in the vengeful Providence of God, another struggle in which, not a few hundred thousand fine men from America will have to die, but as many millions as are necessary to accomplish the final freedom of the peoples of the world."

Let us never force an American President to say that again.

September 2, 1970, Portland, Oregon
American Legion National Convention

GOVERNOR McCALL, Commander Patrick, Mr. Don Johnson, Mrs. Davidson, honored guests and my fellow Legionnaires — especially those people from Maryland I know.

I'm proud to be at this distinguished gathering. Thank heaven the people here aren't so sophisticated they long for an American defeat.

As you know, I've just returned from an Asian tour during which I visited many countries including Vietnam and Korea. I brought back many messages from our brave troops there to some of our more dovish Senators. The soldiers asked me to deliver those messages personally because you're not supposed to send that stuff through the mail.

After I leave here, at the President's request I'm going to stop in Texas and brief former President Johnson on my Asian trip. Then I return to Washington.

First, let me thank you for your support — in the great, nonpartisan tradition of the American Legion — for the administration in its efforts to bring about a just and lasting peace in Vietnam, and in the world.

Having just returned from Asia, I can say that these efforts now hold great promise of success.

I would like to thank you, in particular for your support of the President's difficult decision on Cambodia.

Those who opposed the move into Cambodia four months ago thought it would prolong the war, increase American casualties, and jeopardize our troop withdrawal program. When the President made it — and I can say this with authority, because I sat in those councils — he did so precisely for the purpose of achieving the opposite results.

Having just been in Vietnam and in Cambodia, I have seen what the results have been. And it can be said now that this decision was one of the important turning-points in this long and difficult war.

The success of the Cambodian venture has assured that our program of troop withdrawal can go forward. The process of Vietnamization has been greatly strengthened. The President said that by destroying enemy supplies we would reduce American casualties. And American casualties are down. In fact, two months have now passed since the end of the Cambodian campaign — and the number of Americans killed in action in those two months since Cambodia is the lowest for any two-month period since February 1966 — the lowest, that is, in the last four-and-a-half years.

Now, let there be no mistake what our goal is in Vietnam. Our goal is peace — a just peace. I can understand the impatience of those who cry out for "peace now" — but let's not have "peace now" if it means "pay later" with a bigger and more terrible war. By achieving a peace that discourages aggression, that gives the South Vietnamese a chance to find their own way and determine their own future, we'll increase the chance of a peace in the Pacific that can last through this final third of the century.

America's veterans now know all too well that this nation has been called on now to fight four wars in the space of only half a century.

From the standpoint of the United States, it is significant to note that three of those four wars have come to us from the Pacific.

For the balance of this century we can do better — and we must do better. By ending the war in a way that discourages future wars, we can greatly increase the chances that for the balance of the century we can in fact have peace in the Pacific, and peace from the Pacific.

But as we talk about the war in Vietnam, let us not forget the man who's had to fight the war, and whose sacrifices will have helped secure the peace.

We who came back from World War II, from Korea, were honored for our service in wars that the overwhelming majority of our countrymen supported.

Today's veteran — the Vietnam veteran — comes back to a country deeply divided by a war that he has been called on to fight.

He comes back to find many saying that the war is immoral. Yet never has America fought for so unselfish a purpose. We have not sought any treaties nor any bases. The shores of the United States itself were not immediately threatened, as they were in World War II. And the man himself went, not because he wanted war, but because his country called on him — just as other soldiers, in other wars have answered their country's call.

Just as I did. Just as you did. Whatever our own views on the war, we should be proud of our young men who have done their duty, and who have served in Vietnam. I have noted with dismay that some political leaders who have themselves been critics of the war have lamented that our best young men have gone to Canada. The best are not those who ran off to Canada, but those who went to Vietnam.

In the months ahead, we will have many men coming home from Vietnam. But we must recognize that it will be necessary for the United States to keep many men in uniform for a long time to come.

Serving in the armed forces in peacetime has not, traditionally, been a calling that has commended the measure of respect in this country that it deserves.

In fact, we find among many today a tendency to look with disrespect at men who wear the uniform — whether as members of the peace forces abroad or of the peace forces at home. It's time we gave those men the respect and the honor they deserve — because it is their service that enables the rest of us to live in peace.

Speaking now not just of Vietnam but of the larger subject of world peace, I also want to thank the American Legion for its vigorous and steadfast support of a strong national defense.

This is probably the first time in the Legion's long history when continuing widespread national support for a strong defense was even a serious question.

The spirit the Legion represents is what has kept America strong — and what has kept the peace.

The real peace lobby today is composed of those who maintain the peace, not those who disturb it.

One of the great strengths of America is the essential determination of her people that what must be done will be done — resisting the temptation of the easy way that seems an easy way out, but is actually only an easy way in — into more wars, more tragedy and more human suffering.

Faced with a challenge to the peace, it may seem easy — and it may seem tempting — simply to walk away from the challenge, or to pretend that it doesn't exist, or to dismiss it as simply "cold-war rhetoric." This provides an excuse for not meeting it. But though excuses may be good in the short run, they're no good in the long run. In the long run we're judged purely by results.

Americans have fought three wars in a generation — four in half a century — not because we like war, not because we wanted war, and not because we coveted foreign dominions, but because the aggressions of others drew us into war. The goal of the real peace lobby now is to ensure that this next generation can live without war. And in order to insure that goal, in order to achieve that effort, we have to concentrate on the strengths of many for the security of all of us.

What principally has averted war on a global scale since World War II, what has given security to the billion-and-a-half people who live in the free world, has been the strength of the United States of America.

We didn't ask for this responsibility. But because of what happened in World War II, we were the ones who had this strength. We held an umbrella of strength over Western Europe, Asia, and the new nations of Africa — not for the purpose of dominating those nations, but rather for the right to defend free people who want to chart their own future without outside interference.

Now, to be sure, the world has changed. Devastated nations have been rebuilt. New nations are growing stronger. There have been shifts in the power relationships. The United States is no longer the dominant power that it once was — meaning not that we are weaker, but that others are stronger, including our friends as well as our potential adversaries.

Therefore, we have both a need and an opportunity to establish new kinds of partnerships, in which America continues to assist other free nations. But they themselves play the primary role in their own defense.

The solid rock on which the new Nixon Doctrine is built, however, remains the continuing strength of the United States.

One aspect of maintaining that strong defense on which, once again, I wish to thank the American Legion for its strong support, has been the decision to go ahead with the antiballistic missile.

We were faced last year with a difficult decision — a very difficult decision. The Soviet Union, with its tremendous buildup of land-based missiles and missile-carrying submarines, had been closing the gap and moving ahead in some categories. We had either to settle for an inferior position — with all the dangers that would have posed to the future security not only of the United States, but of the world — or do something. What we decided to do was to build defensive weapons system.

That system was not for the purpose of threatening anyone else, but rather for the purpose of ensuring that we could not be successfully threatened.

Now we have demonstrated our good faith by indicating that we are willing to limit that system if the Soviet Union will limit its own system.

There's been a great deal of talk about "reordering priorities." We have reordered priorities. Others claim we haven't gone far enough. Faced with the desire to do something more domestically, the automatic answer of many is: cut defense.

We take a different approach. We begin by asking: What is the minimum level of military expenditures that we can set without jeopardizing the peace of the world? Then we say: Let's cut to that level — but no further.

We recognize that the first priority — the one that makes all else possible — is peace, and peace depends on security.

We all want that peace. The question is how do we achieve it — and what kind of peace do we achieve?

We seek a world — and a nation — in which each country, and each person, shows a decent regard for his neighbors' rights, for his neighbors' privacy, for his neighbors' dignity.

The principle of mutual respect is threatened abroad, and therefore we have to maintain a strength sufficient to preserve it.

The principle of mutual respect is threatened here at home, and therefore we have to be firm in defending it.

The real advocates of peace, ladies and gentlemen, are those who respect the rights of others, not those who infringe upon those rights; those who seek accommodation, not confrontation.

One of the tragedies of life in America today is that when we speak of maintaining peace, we do have to speak not only of peace abroad, but of peace at home.

We find bombs exploding not just in Vietnam, but in our own cities.

We find many of those who most loudly condemn "the system" violating those basic human decencies, those patterns of mutual respect for the rights of one another, on which a free system rests.

Those of us who have worn this nation's uniform in the past have worn it proudly — and when we have saluted the flag, we have done so proudly. We believe in what that flag represents.

And that belief and that pride did not leave us just because we changed to civilian clothes.

We know the country has its faults, but we also know it has great and enduring strengths — and one of those strengths is the best system yet for correcting our faults.

There are some who look at the faults, and cry that "the system" has failed. Their problem is they just don't understand the system.

Those who condemn "the system" in America call it unresponsive; they claim that it only protects the status quo.

They couldn't be more wrong.

The American system is the greatest engine of change and progress the world has ever seen. The American system has produced more goods, more widely distributed than any other system, any time, any place. It has given more people more true freedom — in the sense not only of political freedom, but in the sense of freedom to work at jobs of their own choosing than any other system, any time, any place. And it provides the best means yet devised by man of directing progress not toward the ends that some arbitrary authority might choose, but toward the ends that the people themselves choose.

In preserving the American system, we are defending the ideal of freedom. We also are preserving a process of change — a process that gives each person the right to be heard, and lets no one voice dominate.

Ours is a system rooted in law. It is based on respect for law, and on laws that deserve respect — and also on respect for those who have the responsibility for upholding the law.

At the very heart of the American system is respect for the rights of others — and we have built a body of laws designed to protect those rights. And that's precisely what the bulk of our laws are all about.

We don't brand murder and arson and rape just as an excuse to put people in jail. We do it to protect the right of the ordinary citizen — the noncriminal — not to be killed, not to have his house burned down, nor to be assualted.

By the same token, we have laws that have the effect of limiting the way in which opinions can be expressed. We have a first amendment that guarantees the right of free speech and free assembly. But smashing windows, burning offices, assaulting people in the streets, are not acts of speech or assembly. Those are trespasses on the equally sacred right of others to be safe in their lives and their property, and in the free enjoyment of their liberty.

Confronted with a choice, the American people would choose the policeman's truncheon over the anarchist's bomb. But true peace lies neither in the bomb nor the truncheon. It lies in that pattern of mutual respect and mutual forbearance that is the essence of a civilized society. That pattern is what has to be strengthened and maintained.

America hasn't survived for nearly two centuries, and become the world's richest nation, and its strongest, because we were weak or dispirited or because we had a "system" that didn't work. The other free nations of the world haven't turned to us time and time again to help preserve their freedom because we held freedom lightly. When we poured out our resources to help the poor and the disadvantaged, it hasn't been because we didn't care. As we have erected new batteries of legal safeguards for the rights of minorities, it hasn't been because we were racist or bent on oppression.

We have done all these things because the heart of America is good, and because its arm is strong — and because we believe in liberty and justice, not just for a favored few but for all people.

We have done them because our "system" is good — and we have been able to do them because our system works.

So let's not be bowled over by those who dismiss "the system" — or dismayed by their pessimism about the future.

Let's look instead at the great promise — the real promise — that the future holds for this country of ours.

We are going to have peace in Vietnam.

We are moving slowly, surely, and with steady purpose toward a world in which we can have peace in the last third of this century.

We are moving toward the time when we can limit the awesome growth of arms, and devote more of our resources to meeting the needs of our people here at home.

Because of the enormous and increasing wealth that our system produces, we can move not only against those ugly blotches that its excesses have produced — fouled air, polluted water, scarred landscapes, urban congestion — but also toward better health care, better education, greater and more rewarding job opportunities, and a level and a quality of life that no one in the world would ever have dared dream of only a short time ago.

The thing we have to remember is not simply to sit back and let government do it, but rather for all of us to pitch in together — for each of us to recognize that he has his own "thing" to do.

"The system" — our democratic system, here in America — is not a something-for-nothing machine. It requires that each of us contributes. Its base is not government. Its base is people. Its great strength is not the great strength of government, but the strength of the people. And its guiding genius is not the genius of government, but the fundamental wisdom of 200 million Americans — old and young, East and West — who time and again have demonstrated that the real needs of people are best understood by the people themselves.

As we strive to restore and maintain the peace — both abroad and at home — it is important that we maintain it in a way that preserves liberty, and that encourages the flourishing of those richly humane values that lie at the heart of the American spirit and the American experiment. But this we can do together, and in so doing we will find once again that what divides us is far less that what unites us.

In that spirit, as we approach the future, we can do so confident of the basic strength of the American people, and the basic goodness of the American system. This will be preserved and in turn will preserve our liberties and those of our children.

It's been a privilege to address you this noon.

September 10, 1970, Springfield, Illinois

PEOPLE OF ILLINOIS, this noon we formally open the national campaign to determine the leadership of the seventies — a campaign to determine which party will control the next Congress of the United States. This is, of course, profoundly important to the future of every American. Because the Illinois campaign is not an isolated campaign; and the election here is not an isolated referendum.

It was right here in this state — and let me speak from my heart about him — that one of the finest public leaders I've ever known, your great singular, very lovable Everett Dirksen served in the Senate. He long and ably represented the state of Illinois, and he led his party with great distinction. I wish simply to say how proud I am to be speaking today on behalf of Ralph Smith who will carry on the great Dirksen tradition.

Here in Illinois, and across America this fall, there is occurring a second critical phase in the historic contest begun in the fall of 1968 — a contest between remnants of the discredited elite that dominated national policy for forty years and a new national majority, forged and led by the President of the United States — a contest to shape the destiny of America.

Some months ago, discussing the bitterness and violence of the last decade, the *Wall Street Journal* wrote, and I quote:

"The source of [America's] pathology is in the American elite."

Said the *Wall Street Journal:* "In any society the task of the elite is to supply the bonds which hold together diverse and potentially competing factions. . . .

"Over the past decade . . . the American elite has not been protecting those social bonds but systematically assaulting them . . . the message pouring out of our most prestigious universities, our most respected media, our largest cultural centers, our most successful political party . . . [is] that American society is utterly undeserving of respect. . . ." So said the *Wall Street Journal.*

As the stream of contemptuous commentary has poured forth from America's old elite, small wonder it has been embraced by the disgruntled who seek the reason for personal failure everywhere but in themselves.

The objective, then, of this campaign 1968 is not simply to win or hold offices; it is also to give America a new leadership — a leadership of faith, courage, and optimism. It is to replace those who moan endlessly about what is wrong with their country with men and women of the wit and will to stand up and speak out for what is right about America.

And, ladies and gentlemen, this means sending to Washington men of the character, courage, and vision of Paul Findley, your Congressman, and John Anderson, the Chairman of the Republican Conference in the House of Representatives and Les Arends, the whip of the Republican Party in the House. It means returning Senator Ralph Tyler Smith to the Senate to serve alongside your able senior Senator, Chuck Percy. And let me say, Chuck, how pleased I am that you were able to accompany me to this distinguished gathering of Illinois citizens today. Ralph Smith is needed by his nation. And because your country cannot afford any more ultraliberals in the United States Senate, he is needed more than usual. There was a time when the liberalism of the old elite was a venturesome and fighting philosophy — the vanguard political dogma of a Franklin Roosevelt, a Harry Truman, a John Kennedy. But you know, and I know that the old firehorses are long gone. Today's radical–liberal posturing in the Senate is about as closely related to a Harry Truman, as is a chihuahua to a timber wolf.

Ultraliberalism today translates into a whimpering isolationism in foreign policy, a mulish obstructionism in domestic policy, and a pusillanimous pussyfooting on the critical issue of law and order.

Now, consider its record in foreign policy. While congressional isolationists have ceaselessly prattled about peace, our President has been moving to achieve it.

Today, America is moving to ratify the Geneva agreements forbidding chemical and biological warfare. American negotiators in Helsinki and Vienna are working toward agreement to halt the arms race. American diplomacy has produced a cease fire in the Middle East which, while obviously tenuous, we hope will lead to a meaningful peace talk. America has reversed the course of involvement in Asia. Where the past administrations sent 535,000 troops to Vietnam — President Nixon will have almost half of them home by next April.

These achievements, however, have not mollified for a second the caterwauling critics in the Senate. When the President ordered destruction of the enemy sanctuaries in Cambodia, the radical–liberals (I call them radic–libs) called his decision "ghastly." They said it would "increase American casualties" — that it would "lead us to the borders of China."

Though events have proven them all wrong, not one has stepped forward to admit it.

We did not go "to the borders of China." We went twenty-one miles into Cambodia and were out in sixty days, precisely as the President promised. American casualties did not go up; they went down, precisely as the President predicted. Ten days ago, when I was in Saigon, American casualties had fallen to the lowest level in four years. And what on earth is "ghastly" about a decision that guarantees the withdrawal of American forces and saves the lives of American men?

One of the great questions Illinois will help to answer in November is this: What kind of men will help to determine America's foreign policy? Will it be Fulbright and his faction in the Senate? Or will it be the stand-up Senators like Ralph Tyler Smith to help the President of the United States?

At the time of the peace-at-any-price demonstrations, a year ago in the streets of Washington, David Broder of the *Washington Post* wrote as follows, and I quote:

"It is becoming more obvious with each passing day that the men and the movement that broke Lyndon B. Johnson's authority in 1968 are out to break Richard M. Nixon in 1969."

Ralph Smith's opponent, should he win, would join the ranks of those benighted men; his election would strengthen that misguided movement. On the other hand, the election of Senator Smith would return to the Senate a man whose presence there strengthens the hand of a President who has brought us closer to a just peace than any analyst would have predicted possible twenty months ago.

In domestic policy as well, this campaign presents us with a clear choice — between the troglodytic leftists who dominate Congress now, and the moderate, centrist and conservative supporters of President Nixon — between the tried irrelevant liberalism that made the Ninety-first Congress a citadel of reaction — and the New Federalism of the 1970s.

Within the framework of that New Federalism, the President has proposed: consolidation of the multibillion-dollar maze of federal grants-in-aid; a historic overhaul of the chaotic, demeaning, bankrupt welfare system; an unprecedented sharing of federal tax revenues with states like Illinois. These things are innovative; they are new; they are dramatic; and they deserve the support and applause of the American people. Nearly a year ago, the President also proposed that a cost-of-living escalator be written into the Social Security Act to protect twenty-five million Americans from the scourge of rising prices. Last February he sent Congress the most far-reaching legislation any President has ever proposed to deal with air and water pollution. Not one of these initiatives has returned to the President's desk to be signed into law — not one of them.

The President's adversaries in Congress apparently prefer *no* legislation to *new* legislation bearing the name of Richard Nixon. As a matter of fact, if anyone wants to paint a picture of Congress this year, I'm pretty sure it would have to be a still life.

My far-left friends in Congress never tire, never weary of telling me *they* are the Good Samaritans; that *they* are more sensitive to the needs of the impoverished; *they* are the chosen representatives of the poor.

Well, we believe in representing the poor too; and we do; but the time has come for someone also to represent the workingmen of this country, the Forgotten Man of American politics; white collar and blue collar; and the President and I are applying for that job — just as Ralph Tyler Smith is applying for it here in Illinois.

That is why we have acted to increase unemployment benefits and extend them to nearly five million American workers; that is why the President proposed three billion dollars for manpower training; that is why new health and safety standards have been advanced — and enacted in mining and construction; that is why forty-six computer job banks have been establihsed; that is why working families — as well as welfare families — would benefit from the President's family assistance program; that is why low-income workers have been exempted from federal income taxes.

Rejected and written off by the old elite — the workingman has become the cornerstone of the New Majority. We are also asking in the election the support of the working-women of America, whether they labor in home, factory, or office — or just breach the ramparts at McSorley's bar in New York.

There is a new deadlock of democracy today — between a progressive president, carrying out his mandate for reform, and a reactionary Congress in the grip of bitter men who forfeited that mandate. Look over the timecards of the Ninety-first Congress; they explain a great deal about its performance. In 1969 members put in only fifty to sixty percent of the hours they spent in session in the first year of Presidents Kennedy or Johnson. The congressional goldbricking has been monumental, and public esteem for Congress last March sank to its lowest depth in five years.

Nowhere has this Congress been more derelict than in its ho-hum, business-as-usual attitude to the President's program to control and reduce the crime and filth in our society.

Sixteen months ago, the President proposed the toughest bill in the nation's history to uproot the corrupting influence of organized crime. The bill still sits there, languishing in Congress.

Fourteen months ago, the President asked unprecedented power for the Justice Department to crack down on the narcotics merchants who are growing rich destroying the lives of thousands of our young people. That bill, too, just sits there, languishing in Congress.

How many children, my friends, must we pick up out of the gutters and alleys of our great cities, dead of overdoses of heroin, before Congress finally decides that maybe it's time to act?

Sixteen months ago, the President sent to Congress three measures to safeguard your homes and families from the pornographic filth being sent unsolicited through the mails.

Portions of one bill were written into the President's postal reform; but the others have been lost in the shuffle by an apathetic congress.

How do you fathom the thinking of these "radical–liberals" who work themselves into a lather over an alleged shortage of nutriments in a child's box of Wheaties — but who cannot get exercised at all over that same child's constant exposure to a flood of hard-core pornography that could warp his moral outlook for a lifetime. I think it's high time that these radic–libs put their own houses in order. It's high time these ultraliberals put *their* priorities in order.

Last March, the President proposed that the transportation and use of bombs and Molotov cocktails be made a Federal crime, with penalties to match the crime. People are dying today, because of these bombs — but Congress has yet to be jolted into action.

These bombings reached a new plateau of horror just last month with the death of the graduate student at the University of Wisconsin. The moderate *Wisconsin State Journal* said it well in a single paragraph:

". . . it isn't just the radicals who set the bomb in a lighted, occupied building who are guilty. The blood is on the hands of anyone who has encouraged them, anyone who has talked recklessly of 'revolution,' anyone who has chided with mild disparagement the violence of extremists while hinting that the cause is right all the same."

On this question of domestic violence and disorder, I contend that the testimony of Ralph Smith's opponent disqualified him for the U.S. Senate.

Just listen for a minute to what Senator Smith's opponent said in December of 1968. He said that the report of the Chicago disorder, and I quote him:

"Speaks eloquently of the results of denying the parks for peaceful assembly and peaceful protest. The storm troopers in blue were the result."

Any public official, especially from the State of Illinois, who still believes the riots at the Chicago convention were the result of quote "denying parks for peaceful protest," has no business in the United Senate.

Any individual who, in these times, will slander the men of the Chicago police force by calling them "storm troopers in blue," ought to be retired from public life.

In the last eight months alone seven policemen, men from that force this gentleman branded the "storm troopers," have died in the line of duty — most of them shot to death by urban terrorists.

And, by the way, it is certainly time that somebody stood up in a public forum and spoke the truth — that the enduring and grave injustice done by that convention was not done to the demonstrators in the streets; it was done to the good name of the great city of Chicago, and its mayor, Richard J. Daley.

Whenever the President or I raise the anticrime issue the chorus comes back from Capitol Hill: "Repression, repression, the Nixon Administration wants repression." Well, that's either slander or stupidity. No citizen who respects the law need fear anything from this government. No administration is more committed to the civil rights of every American. But, the President's definition of "civil rights," encompasses the right of black Americans to be secure in the central city, the right of small businessmen to be free of violence at the hands of drug addicts, and the right of the women of this country to be free to walk the streets and parks without being attacked or molested by hoodlums and thugs.

Clearly those civil rights are not going to be restored until we get a new Congress that cares about law and order.

But there are presidential initiatives that *have* succeeded on Capitol Hill; there are issues where Congress *has* been forced off dead center, thanks to the overtime of men like Senator Smith.

Selective Service has been reformed. The draft is now as just and equitable as we can make it, short of our dream and goal of a volunteer army. The United States Post Office has been completely overhauled. The food stamp program has been extended to cover nearly all of America's poor. Historic airways and airports legislation that will benefit businessmen and vacationing workingmen for generations has been enacted.

Not for 120 years, not since Zachary Taylor, has a first-term President taken office with both Houses controlled by hostile majorities. Even with this massive opposition, however, the President has been able to inaugurate a new era of restoration, renewal, and reform. Give him a Congress to work with and you will bring on an era of prosperity and progress, the like of which America has never seen.

And plainly, very plainly, Ralph Smith is just the kind of Senator we need in that Congress. Though a man of but a few years experience in the national legislature, Ralph Smith is already among the most effective members our party has. Twice in the last six weeks Smith Amendments have been added to major legislation. The first calling for a limitation on huge agricultural payments to save the taxpayers millions of dollars and the second came only yesterday when Ralph Smith proposed and the Senate adopted an amendment to study and determine the effects of pollution upon human beings. And that is fine work indeed by a brand new member of the United States Senate.

I believe that it is about the economy that the weeping and wailing of the Congressional left-wing has been loudest — and least convincing. When President Nixon took office, the nation had run seven straight budget deficits totaling 57 billion dollars; prices were rising at the fastest rate since the Truman Administration; interest rates were the worst since the Civil War; a ten percent surtax had been imposed on business and labor; and the real take-home pay of American workers had not risen a dime in three years.

Today, much of that has been reversed. The surtax is gone. Short-term interest rates have dropped. The wholesale price index is declining. Business indicators are reading their best gains in fifteen months. Inflation is being brought under control.

After twenty months, as America has moved away from war and toward peace, the President has steered the economy successfully over some rocky terrain. We appear to be back on the highway again. But we ought never to forget our narrow escape. When the President took the wheel in 1969, the economy had been clocked at well over a hundred in a thirty-mile zone and was headed straight for the cliff.

Because of the way they raced the engine of the economy, the ultraliberals in Congress should have had their licenses revoked in 1968. Until they demonstrate a little more judgment and maturity, they shouldn't be given the keys to the car again.

For twenty months, the President has fought the unpopular fight for an honest budget — fought it against a fraternity of Big Spenders who will never be housebroken of the habit of spending more money than we can afford.

Last month Congress raised the President's education bill $453 million. They raised his housing bill — $541 million. When the President proposed an unprecedented ten-billion-dollar sewage treatment plan — the junior Senator from Maine rallied at his desk to raise him $15 billion. Now for that Senator, who is not widely known for advocating the taxes to pay for his spending schemes, playing with billions of taxpayers' dollars can be a lot like playing Monopoly. Everybody has a good time, and nobody gets hurt.

The problem is when that Senator and his friends *did* have control of the federal budget in the 1960s, tens of millions of Americans *did* get hurt, and they are still getting hurt — because when that Senator and his friends thought they were playing with Boardwalk and Park Place, they were really playing with the savings and income, the hopes and dreams, of the whole American people.

If this Congress is turned just ten more degrees toward the radical left — then the President's efforts to protect your income and savings will be overridden, and this country will go off on another spending spree like the last one. Prices will shoot up; interest rates will rise; and taxes will go through the roof. And you will end up with a bloated bureaucracy in Washington that will make the featherbedding of the current big spenders look like the work force at the corner drugstore.

If any of you are regular readers of the liberal Eastern press — the organ grinders of the old elite — you will probably read on your editorial pages tomorrow, "That terrible Mr. Agnew has done it again."

Don't let this bother you, because it certainly does not bother me. When you have been head-to-head with our Korean ally for six hours of tough negotiation — you are not likely to be stampeded off the range by an editorial writer for the *Washington Post*.

Let them run right up the wall. We are going to be out with the other "happy warriors" on the campaign trail this fall — roasting marshmallows along the way.

Long ago, President Lincoln wrote words with profound meaning for all of us today: "The dogmas of the quiet past," he said, "are inadequate to the stormy present. The occasion is piled high with difficulty and we must rise with the occasion. As our case is new, so we must think anew, and act anew."

And we too shall rise with the occasion; and we too shall think anew and act anew. For our goal is not less than to give the new men and the new thinking a crack at these challenging new times.

Yes, there will be hard going. There will be harsh criticism; there may be political casualties. But our cause is far more important than any individual who may be a part of it, including a Vice President.

And in this fateful collision of political philosophies, we can say as Churchill did in a collision of arms:

"I avow my faith that we are marching toward better days. Humanity will not be cast down. We are going on — swinging bravely forward along the grand high road — and already behind the distant mountains is the promise of the sun."

September 10, 1970, Casper, Wyoming
Wyoming Republican Dinner

WHAT A DELIGHT and privilege to be in your beautiful Wyoming this first day of the 1970 campaign.

And what a pleasure to be on the platform with my valued friend, Stan Hathaway. As he said, we came to our governorships together and shared ideas along the campaign trail. As a matter of fact, we even underwent a common experience that we refer to jokingly as the "charm school." This was a school for gubernatorial candidates conducted by the Republican party in Colorado and right away I recognized that Stan had some very unusual talents. Stan has been a great man for Wyoming and a great leader among the other governors. He is as energetic, candid, and decent *out* of Wyoming as he is *in* Wyoming. He just doesn't know how to be any other way. Professionally, his efforts to attract new industry to the state and, at the same time, to keep your environment clean have won national acclaim. I know the people of Wyoming are proud of Stan, and I know they are going to reelect him, and I know he is going to continue to do an outstanding job as the governor of this outstanding state. Because, after all, he follows another distinguished Republican governor, your present Senator Cliff Hansen, who is the greatest.

I have to tell you a funny story about that. When I first came into the distinguished halls of the Senate, I didn't realize what a constricted life the Vice President was supposed to lead there. The distinguished majority leader, Mr. Mansfield — after he had welcomed me to the Senate in a very friendly fashion and after the minority leader had spoken also — said, "I ask unanimous consent," (that's the way that the Senate does it's business; anything can happen when you have unanimous consent) "that the Vice President be allowed two minutes to respond." And that's the longest time I've ever had to venture an opinion in the Senate since.

But unfortunately, I have people like Cliff Hansen and other stand-up Republican Senators who speak the peace for the President and for me. And heaven knows we respect and admire and count on them. Cliff, we're awfully glad you are there. And the reason we have Stan Hathaway and Cliff Hansen is because the state of Wyoming has a real gungho Republican organization under Bud Brimmer and I want to express my appreciation to him tonight for his work as State Chairman.

Yours is a stand-up-and-be-counted state — one that gave President Richard Nixon in 1968 a resounding vote of confidence. For that we remain both proud and grateful. Tonight I have come to report on our promises to you — our pledge to brake inflation, to reestablish law and order, to begin the redistribution of power from the Federal Government back to the states and the people of this country.

I report tonight that, to the maximum of his ability, the President has kept his word. He has taken all the executive action within his power; he sent to Congress measure after measure to achieve his goals. And now it is perfectly plain that a recalcitrant Congress blocks the path between the President and fulfillment of his commitments to the people of the United States.

That is why I am here in Wyoming tonight — to suggest how we can best attain those objectives for which we worked together in the fall of 1968.

So I gladly and I emphatically speak up for the election of John Wold to the United States Senate. Actually the proposition is a simple one. You elected President Nixon to lead this nation in 1968. Now I hope you will send to Washington another Senator, one who can be depended upon to work with Cliff Hansen and your President to carry out our common aspirations for this country.

Two of the great issues confronting this country are: the war in Vietnam and the state of the economy. The first issue is preeminent because it involves the lives of American men.

Twice I have been into the farthest reaches of the Pacific in the last year — both times as the personal emissary of the President and both times, therefore, at public expense.

Last year John Wold was also in Southeast Asia. But not at government expense. He went there, not on a government tour, but paid his own way to learn firsthand the problems of American policy in this divisive war. This is the kind of personal drive, of commitment, of concern, that we need in Washington — that you of Wyoming need in the next man you send to the United States Senate.

Let's briefly recall some of the positions taken and some of the legislation proposed by Wyoming's next Senator.

John Wold, as your Congressman, has proposed no fewer than two dozen measures to preserve the environment and to conserve our national heritage. He has fought, far more than most other Congressmen, to prevent the use of the United States mails as a transmission belt for pornography. John Wold has introduced his own legislation to control the traffic in narcotics and drugs that is ravaging an entire generation of our young people. And I can certify this — on his anticrime proposals, the President of the United States has had no stronger supporter in either House of Congress than John Wold of Wyoming. If we had fifty more men like him in Congress — in short order the cities of this country would be a lot safer to walk in and to visit. And on the paramount question of peace with honor in Southeast Asia, this stand-up legislator — in a time of demonstrations, of disorder, and of violence — has stood foursquare behind the President of the United States. And on that issue above all others, that's exactly where you want your Congressman to be in this day and age.

On my way here this evening, a fellow stopped me and asked if I could think of any reason why John Wold should not be in the Senate of the United States. I said the only reason I could imagine was that we need to save that seat in the House of Representatives.

But then it didn't take me long to remember that we have Harry Roberts, whom I referred to earlier and who will probably go down in posterity as Harry Taylor Roberts, running for John's seat. And Harry Roberts is going to win, too. I think he looks a little like Robert Taylor anyhow. So, I suggest that you of Wyoming have every reason to send us John Wold as your next United States Senator because that House seat is going to be very capably in the hands of Harry Roberts.

On the other great domestic issues, this fine Congressman, John Wold, has won his spurs for the Senate.

Take federal spending.

Now, I hardly need to tell you that this problem of controlling federal spending has become critical. If we fail in this, runaway inflation will resume. Prices and interest rates will skyrocket again, and new taxes will become inevitable. In any case, I regard government indulgence of inflation as a breach of faith with the American people. For you know and I know that inflation is a thief. It steals away the value of the savings that the working person puts away; it robs him of the purchasing value of the dollars that he earns.

So I deeply feel that inflation is far more serious than a political issue alone — it is very much a moral issue. We intend — with the help of men like John Wold — to keep faith with the workingpeople, the retired people, yes, and the poor people of this country. We are determined to do whatever is in our power to see that their income, and their savings, and their insurance are not cynically stolen away by fiscal irresponsibility and political profligates.

History abounds with tragic accounts of countries that were too witless to stand up to inflation. When prices rise faster than the incomes of workingpeople, the confidence ebbs in their country's economy, and soon their confidence in the integrity of their government is lost. When that last trust has been forfeited, virtually all is lost.

So let's focus briefly on the problems, the economic problems and the reasons behind them that the President has been moving so energetically to solve.

While economists disagree on almost everything, they do seem to agree that the basic cause of our current inflation is caused by the huge budget deficits incurred before President Nixon took office in 1969. These deficits totaled — and I don't suppose I need remind you of this in those eight years — $57 billion. In fiscal year 1968 alone, we overspent our income by $25 billion. That one year we went deeper in debt than we have ever before in any entire administration since World War II.

So now you are paying more for your food and clothing and your children's books and shoes because fiscally myopic and politically irresponsible men were unwilling to live within the limits of federal income during a time of furious economic activity.

I think the trend to spend far more than we could afford is symptomatic of something deeper in our society.

This is part of a philosophy that says "anything goes." It is an outlook toward life that loves the dance but hates to pay the piper. It is a belief that — no matter what we do to it — the American free enterprise system will keep delivering an ever-higher standard of living.

But you know that in life, just as in economics, things just don't work out that way. We cannot abuse our economy, we cannot strain our system to the breaking point, not without expecting a reaction.

So we are now going through a great awakening. Millions of Americans are opening their eyes to the consequences of the wild ride of the sixties. And we are determined that the American people march into the seventies with their eyes open.

And that's why we lay it on the line — that's why we level with the people about spending. You pay for what you get — people in Wyoming know that there is no such thing as something for nothing. You pay for that spending and you pay in terms of higher prices and higher taxes.

That is not a message the radical economists or the promissory politicians like to hear. But it's the truth, and the American people are mature enough, yes, and intelligent enough to hear it. We're going to tell it to them.

Now let me depart from my prepared text tonight to comment on a fascinating phenomenon taking place on the political scene.

As you know, there has been a covey of confused Congressmen way over on the left over there fighting the President for the past two years. These radical–liberals have taken over the Democratic party in Congress. But now we come to election time and a strange political alchemy is taking place. Since the views of the radical Congressmen are so completely at variance with the majority of Americans — their constituents — they have begun a mad scramble to the center. All of a sudden the radical–liberals are fulsome in their praise for the police. All of a sudden a notorious Senate dove deserts his old allies on the McGovern–Hatfield amendment, flies the coop because he's up for election. And all of a sudden, today in Chicago, the Democratic National Chairman denounces what he calls, and I quote, "extreme and irresponsible statements by members of his own party." He realizes that when it comes to weakness and permissiveness that dove has turned into an albatross.

But, my friends, don't ever let this stampede to the center fool you. The new election-time patriot is still our old undependable friend, the radical–liberal. The overnight hard-liner on crime is still that old bleeding heart, not worried about his heart but his seat.

Now these men, these sheep in wolves clothing, are trying to pull the fastest switcheroo in American politics. But I intend to blow the whistle on them from Maine to California and they are not going to get away with it.

Now in fairness I do not include any Wyoming candidate in this tight cove of confused Congressmen. The Nation can be thankful that Wyoming does not produce many radical–liberals. But I do part company with John Wold's opponent on one of the critical issues of our time — big spending and the inflation that follows it. He is a big spender and that's an undeniable fact.

If you would like hard proof of this fact, let me urge you to study a new analysis of the spending record of all Congressmen. This is compiled every two years by an independent, nonpartisan group, and it separates the spenders from the savers on the key votes of the past session.

Here's how John Wold's opponent stands: When it comes to saving money, he has one of the lowest economy records in the Senate — a rating of twenty-five percent. That means, of course, that three times out of four, when he had a chance to choose between spending and saving, he chose to spend your money.

In contrast, here's how John Wold stands: When it comes to saving the taxpayer's money, he has one of the highest economy records in the House — an economy rating of ninety percent. Nine times out of ten, and that means, of course, nine times out of ten he cast his vote against the big spending that drives up prices and taxes.

Now, it isn't often that voters are presented with such a stark contrast in spending philosophy. John Wold has proven he will strongly support the President's fight against inflation — and we need him now more than ever to turn back the tide of federal spending.

There's another point, too. In 1966, John's opponent laid heavy emphasis on his party affiliation with the President of the United States. He said, and I am taking this quote from the *Rocky Mountain News,* "A state . . . should realize that when you have a Democrat in the White House, you need to have Democrats in the Senate."

Well, he can't have it both ways. Today we need men in the Senate who will support our President.

Now, many people ask: Why does the Vice President of this Republican administration come to Wyoming to speak for a man running against a Democratic incumbent who has supported that administration on some important occasions? And I will tell you why.

It is because the election of John Wold's opponent would help to guarantee that those who oppose the President up and down the line in Congress stay in their positions of majority power. It is because the election of John Wold's opponent would be a defeat for those who want to rein in federal spending and curb inflation. It is because the election of John Wold's opponent would help to leave in the positions of power in the Senate the same radical liberals — the radic–libs who control that body today and who have already seized many of the levers of power in the Democratic party. That is why a victory for John Wold is necessary in the great State of Wyoming on the third of November.

And now, my Wyoming friends, let me just say this: If your concern is foreign affairs, as well as of sound fiscal management, just remember this: If you can change the makeup of the Senate this fall, in January you will change the chairmanships of every committee in the United States Senate. And so you see, a vote for John Wold is a vote for new leadership of the Senate Foreign Relations Committee. We surely agree that would sit well in most places in the United States. It would serve America's interest, believe me — it would do wonders for the United States Senate. And just think, then we wouldn't have to have two State Departments anymore. Now we have one at Foggy Bottom and then one that's just foggy in exile on Capitol Hill.

My friends, in these times we hear a lot about women's rights. I recall that the territory of Wyoming gave women the vote a half-century ahead of the rest of the Union. That's the kind of political pioneering we need right now. By giving the nation another Senator who will help our President achieve the goals which we promised and you approved two years ago, you of Wyoming can — and I believe you will — set the example and lead the way for the rest of the country.

September 14, 1970, Las Vegas, Nevada
Nevada Republican Dinner

IN CASE any of you didn't have a chance to see your children today, let me just say that I met them all at the airport — and they're wonderful kids.

I'm really glad you could all make it tonight, and I hope you didn't mind your forced bus ride.

Just the other day, in San Diego, I started the Come-Lately Club. Its membership consists of those men in control of the opposition Congress who have for years winked at disorder and in this Congress have blocked the President's anticrime legislation. But now that election time is near they suddenly lift high the banner of law and order.

Just today we enrolled our newest member. He denounced campus radicals and compared them to the Palestinian terrorists. His blast at what he called the "apostles of force" sounded tough. But it did not sound at all like the man who was saying it. Now, who do you suppose is the latest to lash out at what he calls "the campus commandos"? None other than that newest member of the Come-Lately Club, Senator Ted Kennedy. Kennedy Come-Lately — it's about time.

Those of you have followed this campaign know of our efforts to win a victory over radical–liberalism — in the election booth in November where victory should properly be won. The press has asked me for an example of this radical–liberalism in American life — and I am delighted to say that on my arrival — the *Las Vegas Sun* has come forward as a candidate.

As Bill Raggio indicated, in its front-page editorial today, I was compared with Joseph McCarthy, Hitler, Stalin, and Mussolini — in a piece that said I should watch my rhetoric. Now the editorial concluded with this thought, and I'd like to quote this to you and I'd like your thoughtful attention to it. This is taken from that editorial:

"The young intellectual people must never again permit a demagogue to so capture the hearts of the unthinking masses that the very foundations of the nation will be toppled." Here you have it all, my friends — the contemptuousness, the elitism, the condescension toward the good people of this country that are the hallmarks of the radical–liberal.

That single sentence says first of all that anyone who strongly stands up and speaks out for our principles is automatically a "demagogue; secondly, that the people of Nevada, and by extension, the people of the United States, are quote "the unthinking masses" who have to be led around by the nose by the "young intellectuals."

Well, people of Nevada, I don't believe that we are "unthinking masses" and I don't believe that we need any "young intellectuals" to tell us how we should conduct our lives. I believe the people of America and the people of Nevada have the independence, the intelligence, the judgment, and the wisdom to make up their own minds — and let's send the so-called "young intellectuals" back to the ivory towers where they belong.

Just because a man works hard, pays his taxes, obeys the laws, does not walk around with a sign demanding surrender now — that does not make him "unthinking". On the contrary, he is thinking a lot more sensibly than the young intellectuals or their older admirers who look down on him.

Just because a man is a member of the Great Silent Majority of Americans, he does not become what the old Marxists used to call "the Masses". On the contrary, he is far more of an individual than those who follow the foolish fads of phony intellectualism.

Not only will the great silent majority of Nevadans be thinking, they will be voting — and they will be voting for the men who respect their judgment and value their support: men like Bill Raggio.

Because these men will stand behind a President who believes the American people are not the masses of some reactionary regime, but the good solid, independent citizens of a great Republic.

Now as I indicated previously, I am here tonight for one basic and critical purpose — to enlist your help in helping yourself, by making some changes in the Congress of the United States.

If you want to take the "opposition" out of "opposition Congress," you have it in your power to ride the opposition out of office this November — and I believe you will.

And if you want your State House run by a man who understands the will of the people and the value of a tax dollar — you'll elect Ed Fike to be your next governor — and I believe you will do that.

President Nixon and I campaigned across this country two years ago, promising you and all other Americans to bring back a respect for law in this society. The FBI figures show we've made headway — last year, for the first time in five years, the rate of increase of crime was cut in half.

But thirteen of the fourteen crime bills that the President has urged Congress to enact are still held hostage in committees of the Congress. What you need — what America needs — is a new Congress that will stand up on this issue, a Congress that will give us the laws we need to protect the American people.

I don't need to tell you the people of Nevada about Bill Raggio's record as a crime fighter. He served twelve years as the district attorney in Reno. In 1964, he was chosen the outstanding prosecutor in the entire United States. He was fair to the accused — but he was equally fair to the victims of crime. He respected his responsibility to the victims of crime. That's what *you* want. And that's the sort of fair-minded, tough-minded, level-headed man that President Nixon wants from Nevada in the Senate of the United States.

As a man from Maryland, it's not becoming for me to tell the people of Nevada how to vote. But I feel free to say this: Because we have a hung-up Congress, the progress you want, and the progress we promised, have been stymied by unnecessary politicking. And if you think this politicking these past two years has been bad, just imagine the backbiting we'll have these next two years if we're given another opposition Congress. Why, with their eyes on 1972, they would obstruct our President — and obstruct your interests — every step of the way.

Bill Raggio and I share another concern — one of the major issues in our country today — the drug problem. I know this troubles every Nevadan, and it probably concerns Bill Raggio because of his invaluable experience as a prosecutor more than for any other reason.

Tonight, therefore, I would like to discuss a broader aspect of this terrible drug problem . . . one that you not only will recognize, but more important, one that you can do something about.

This is a Republican gathering, and you and I are proud to be partisans. But I want to discuss with you tonight a matter that transcends politics, a social issue of concern to every American. So, I'll hope you'll forgive me if I leave the partisan talk that generally attends this type of gathering and underscore most seriously and honestly a very terrible, a very overriding problem in our society that needs our direct attention.

Our America is made up of many cultures. They reflect our diversity as a nation and make us unique as a nation. But there is one rapidly growing culture that contributes nothing to our well-being and, indeed, threatens to sap our national strength unless we move hard and fast to bring it under control.

I am talking about the *drug culture* that pervades our adult population and is spreading like cancer through our youth.

When I speak of the "drug culture" I refer to a much wider circle than those who are actually hooked on drugs. I refer to those who are adopting "escape" as a way of life, who seek a release from human responsibility by pretending there is some world other than the real world.

There are millions of Americans, young and old, who believe that if the music is loud enough, the distractions are strong enough, the sedatives and the stimulants are active enough, they will drown out their frustrations and loneliness. By yielding to pressure to conform from their friends, they are creating a rigid establishment of their own, building an altar to alienation.

Tonight I would like to identify this culture, show some of the unlikely ways it disseminates its propaganda, and finally, point out some of the action you as citizens can take to reverse the trend and help its victims cope with the world we all live in.

There are two reasons why the growth of the drug culture especially concerns us today:

Number One: Although the drug problem is by no means only a youth problem, our youth is involved and involved to a degree never known before. The abuse of drugs extends to children, eight, ten, and twelve years old.

Number Two: America's present drug culture poses the danger of mind-eroding chemicals previously unknown to man, and relatively easy to produce.

We have arrived at this culture partly because society's natural resistance has been broken down by the "pill popping" of adults who fancy they need a pill to get to sleep and another pill to wake up in the morning. This, coupled with growing adult alcoholism, was all that some of our younger citizens needed to do some experimenting on their own.

It should not be surprising, then, my friends, that in recent years so many young people have been drawn into the drug culture. It is, after all, the "in" thing to do among their friends. And it has been urged on them by some of their foremost heroes.

Consider, as one example, the influence of the drug culture in the field of music.

A generation that shocked its parents by doing the Charleston has no right to mock the development of progressive jazz, and the people who were hep to swing are wrong to look down their noses at those who are now hip to folk-rock. Much of today's popular music is complex, much of it is exciting, and some lyrics use the images of poetry far more adroitly and skillfully than the old moon-and-June routines of Tin Pan Alley.

But in too many of the lyrics, the message of the drug culture is purveyed. We should listen more carefully to popular music, because at its best it is worthy of more serious appreciation, and at its worst it is blatant drug culture propaganda.

I do not suggest for one moment that there is a conspiracy among some songwriters, entertainers, and movie producers to subvert the unsuspecting listener. In my opinion, there isn't any. But the cumulative impact of some of their work advances the wrong cause. I may be accused of advocating "song censorship" for pointing this out, but have you really heard the words of some of these songs?

One of the hits of the 1960s, registering more than one million dollars in sales, was a record entitled, "With a Little Help From My Friends."

The key lines are this,

> "I get *by* with a little help from my friends,
> I get *high* with a little help from my friends. . . ."

It's a catchy tune, but until it was pointed out to me, I never realized that the "friends" were assorted drugs with such nicknames as "Mary Jane," "Speed," and "Benny." But the double meaning of the message was clear to members of the drug culture — and many of those who are tempted to join.

Or this one, called "White Rabbit":

"One pill makes you larger and one pill makes
  you small
And the ones that mother gives you don't do
  anything at all.

Go ask Alice when she's ten feet tall. . . ."

There are scores of such songs: The titles themselves often whisper or shout the message. Listen to these: "The Acid Queen", "Eight Miles High," "Couldn't Get High," "Don't Step on the Grass, Sam," and "Stoned Woman." These songs present the use of drugs in such an attractive light for the impressionable, that "turning on" becomes the natural and even the approved thing to do.

And all the while that this brainwashing has been going on, most of us have regarded it as good, clean, noisy fun.

I am sure that very few, if any, station managers in America would deliberately allow the use of their radio facilities to encourage the use of drugs. Few parents would knowingly tolerate the blaring of a drug-approving message from phonographs in their homes. And few musicians intend their "in-jokes" and double meanings to reach past the periphery of pot users. But the fact is that the stations do, the parents do, and the musicans do.

Music is only one medium used by the drug culture. Strong approval, or at least an indulgent attitude, also comes across in certain movies, books, and the underground press of more than two million circulation.

A popular recent movie — I will not name it here because I don't want to promote it — has as its heroes two men who are able to live a carefree life off the proceeds of illegal sales of drugs. When they come to a violent end, the villain, it turns out, is an allegedly repressive society. No sympathy is wasted on the wrecked lives of the people who bought their drugs and financed our heroes' easy ride.

I feel as a reviewer did in the *New York Times*, who writes about the trend toward movies that exalt violence, flirt with pornography, promote pot, and glorify the seamy side of life: ". . . the filmmakers' sensibilities are so jaded, their senses so atrophied, that I doubt they would even feel the swift kick they so richly deserve."

And, my friends, we can expect more of this for one good reason: There's money in it. Look at the exploitation of music festivals, run by men who use young people as props in pot-smoking, acid-dropping events. These parasites of the drug culture care nothing about human rights; they're interested only in movie rights.

Fortunately some of the networks, motion picture companies, magazines, and newspapers are beginning to counter drug abuse with excellent documentaries, dramatic productions, and articles. These can help to educate the nation to the dangers involved. But far too many producers and editors are still succumbing to the temptation of the sensational, and playing right into the hands of the drug culture.

Recently I had a letter from a Philadelphia physician who described, and I quote: "the apparent irresponsibility of the press in glamorizing, or at least rewarding with sensational publicity, diverse psychopathic behavior."

His letter continued:

The point which needs stressing is that both addicts and persons with addiction-prone personality, are immensely gratified by any publicity, and especially by dramatic and sensational publicity. They are, and they feel that they are, shallow and inadequate and unimportant, but now that suddenly everybody is looking at them, discussing them, considering their imagined grievances, they are important. . . . One can see how publicity given to drug "festivals" will attract vulnerable personalities, perhaps not yet addicted.

It is time that we wake up — that we listen to and understand what's going on in the drug culture. It's time that we counter this propaganda with the truth.

What, you may ask, is our Nixon Administration doing to counter the drug culture? As the "happy warrior," Al Smith, used to say: Let's look at the record.

Our President, in the last two years, has more than doubled the sixty-six million dollars being spent on drug control when he took office. Substantial increases have been made in enforcement personnel at the Bureau of Narcotics and Dangerous Drugs and the Bureau's overseas personnel has more than doubled.

He has moved through international diplomacy to dry up the major sources of supply from foreign countries and has cracked down hard on enforcement at home.

The roundup last June of 139 persons in a ring handling thirty percent of the heroin sales in this country was the largest narcotics raid in our history.

Our proposed Dangerous Substance Bill would mete out tougher penalties to drug profiteers. A dealer could get from five years to life, and would face a mandatory fine of $50,000 and forfeiture of property.

For the most innocent victims of drugs, the President has proposed a massive effort of research, educational and legal reform. It includes a fifty-three percent increase in spending on drug research, double for rehabilitation, and four times more for education and training since he took office.

Our administration also has created the first National Clearinghouse for Drug Abuse Information; to cooperate with responsible people in the mass media who understand the need to combat the new slavery of drugs.

Beyond all these specific actions, many of us in public life have been saying some things that have gone unsaid for too long.

When we allow a creeping permissiveness to permeate every aspect of our relations with our young people, we are not helping them — we are hurting them.

Those who indulge violence and condone lawbreaking in the name of any cause, are not helping to bring us togehter — they are helping to drive our society apart.

And those who close their eyes to the pernicious influence of any form of drug — for fear of being out of step with the times — are dismally failing their own sons and daughters.

If this hard sense brings down upon us the label of being "squares," then we will just have to live with it — because it is up to each one of us to squarely face up to the responsibility of being mature human beings.

What, then, can you of Nevada do to help?

First, you can open your ears and open your eyes to the drug culture's message. It gets by largely because good citizens don't notice it, or because the message is too loud to hear. The propaganda will wither under the light of pitiless publicity.

Second, you can set an example within your own family of firmness with understanding of the kind of authority with compassion that will prevent the loneliness that makes people run for the escape hatches of the drug culture.

Third, you can send Bill Raggio to Washington — a man with the know-how, and the determination to back the President in his fight against crime, against senseless disorder, against the foolish philosophy of "anything goes."

And finally, you can help expose the drug culture for what it really is — not a form of protest, but a form of surrender; not a rebellion of the spirit, but a demeaning acquiescence to a form of spiritual slavery, not an expression of individuality, but just the opposite — a craven conformity to an unnatural fad.

It was Ralph Waldo Emerson who coined the phrase "do your own thing" in his essay on self-reliance. And this was his message: "Whoso would be a man must be a nonconformist."

This nation was built by aggressively independent individuals, not by conformists.

Those of all ages who embrace the affectations of the drug culture, who speak its language and wear its trappings and hail its heroes, all too often make a pretense of individuality. But, they are locking themselves into a depressing life-style of conformity that has neither life nor style.

I deeply believe that the American spirit is still too strong, still too independent, to buy a uniform that turns into a straitjacket. That is why I believe more and more of our peopl,e will reject this evil and invidious culture that turns people into robots. For this, we do not need "a little help from our friends": We need a little help from our conscience.

This is, in effect, what I believe the American people voted for two years ago. Now in this election year, the time is ripe to complete the job we started then: To give us a Congress in Washington that will help the President keep his word to you to end a war with honor, to curb inflation, to stop the rise in crime, to help strengthen the character of American society.

Let us, this election year, sweep out the salons of sellout in foreign affairs. Let's retire the opponents of reform in domestic affairs. Let's vote *out* the vacillators on violence and crime. Let's vote *in* the man with the backbone to turn back the tide of weakness and permissiveness in our national life and in our personal life.

That is how the drug culture will be defeated. That is how the character of the American people, in its dignity and fierce individuality, will triumph again.

September 15, 1970, Albuquerque, New Mexico
New Mexico Republican Reception

STILL ANOTHER hijacking was attempted today in San Francisco — you've probably read and heard — and was aborted. It was aborted because of the quick thinking and the courage of the guard who chanced to be on the airplane. This, we believe, will serve as a deterrent and should also serve as a warning to any others who may be thinking of hijacking an American plane.

Let it be understood by everyone that, thanks to the President, there are now guards riding U.S. aircraft. And they will deal sternly with hijackers. Their guards are under instruction, when necessary, to be prepared to shoot to kill.

Since my opening campaign speech in Springfield, Illinois, my friends of the traveling press have been asking for a fuller definition of "radical–liberalism." These reporters — I assure their Eastern editors — have done their job; and, best I can tell, they have gone at it with enthusiasm.

Herb Adderley, recently of the Green Bay Packers and now of the Dallas Cowboys, never covered a receiver as closely as they have covered me.

Just last Saturday, when playing golf with Doug Sanders in California, I was coming up on the tenth green when the voice of the press cried out from the rough, "Mr. Vice President, who are the radical–liberals?" I three-putted that green.

On through the back nine and later in the locker room, they continued their hot pursuit. But the question is legitimate. And tonight, in part, they — and you, too — will have the answer.

But to keep this contest of 1970 a clash of philosophies rather than of parties or personalities, I shall continue to hold off — for a time at least — the naming of the men themselves. I think the people of this country will eagerly make their own judgments about who these men are.

But of these individuals, I should say this first of all: They are not evil, not insincere, not unpatriotic. It would be dead wrong to say they are. One of the most troublesome aspects of this problem is that they believe very sincerely, very deeply in the course they have been following. But in the year 1970 their philosophy is out of step with the times.

It makes them neoisolationists in foreign policy at a time when neo-isolationism openly invites Communist aggression. The same philosophy makes them obstructionists in Congress at at time when America's need is for progressives who will cooperate with our President in initiating an era of restoration, renewal, and reform. The same philosophy makes them social permissivists at a time when America just can't stand more permissiveness if this society is to control the radicalism tearing at its roots.

Make no mistake. This radical–liberalism that infects our Congress and poisons our country is at best a bizarre mutation of the Democratic liberalism in the great Wilson, Roosevelt, Truman, and Kennedy tradition.

To measure the distance the new breed has departed from the enduring principles of the Democratic party, one need only hear again the eloquent words of President John F. Kennedy:

> . . . the adversaries of freedom plan to consolidate their territory — to exploit, to control, and finally to destroy the hopes of the world's newest nations, and they have ambition to do it before the end of this decade. It is a contest of will and purpose as well as force and violence — a battle for minds and souls as well as lives and territory. And in that contest, we cannot stand aside.

You will never, ever, hear that kind of statesmanship and determination from the radical–liberals posturing about today in the United States Senate.

As for the great and long American tradition that "politics stops at the water's edge," they have rejected that with impatience and contempt.

Let us contrast two men. When Richard Nixon was out of office through the years of the 1960s, he always defended American foreign policy when he was beyond our shores. At home he never undercut the President's efforts to win an honorable peace.

Yet, when President Nixon made the courageous Cambodian decision to protect American lives in Southeast Asia — the Democratic candidate of 1968 publicly accused the President of committing an act of "open aggression." If that's the new Hubert Humphrey, I prefer the old.

As for the radical–liberals — they make the evening news, and they make their living by openly and flamboyantly undercutting the President's efforts to win a just peace in Asia.

But some good Democrats will say in response — this is only Mr. Agnew, and he is a partisan Republican. I implore these good people (and there are millions around this country) to listen to the voices of reason and concern within their own Party.

Within the last month, the governor of South Carolina has expressed his "grave apprehension" at the direction of the Democratic Party, warning, "I do not think our people are ready for a political party of extremism."

Just last week, the chairman of the Democratic National Committee belatedly urged the party to purge itself of extremist elements.

Two weeks ago a lifelong Democrat, the head of the nation's largest labor organization, stated:

> [The Democratic party has] disintegrated. . . . It is not the so-called liberal party that it was a few years ago. It has almost got to be the party of extremists in so far as these so-called liberals or New Lefts, or whatever you want to call them, have taken over the Democratic party. As they take it over and they move more and more to the left — and I mean way over to the left — I think more and more are going to lose the support of our [labor] members.

Now those are the words of a leader who supported the Democratic party throughout his lifetime. And the other quotations, each containing the word "extremists," are from concerned Democrats, terribly concerned over the course that their own party is taking.

375

That is not the voice of the Vice President — that is the voice of a man whose organization has long furnished both a substantial part of the manpower and the war chest for the Democratic party.

The great collision of philosophies in 1970 will help to shape the destiny of our country — it will almost surely determine which faction will take control of the Democratic party. That is why, here in New Mexico, Republicans and Democrats alike have a vital stake in the political defeat of the incumbent and a smashing triumph for your next United States Senator — Andy Carter.

But there are other ways to draw a bead on the radical–liberal. He is the kind who delays or weakens or opposes every anti-crime bill the President sends up — at least until public pressure becomes irresistible.

He supports every effort to undercut the President's authority in foreign policy.

When the President asks for the money and weapons needed to maintain America's strength and commitments abroad, he will hint darkly that the President has been taken over by the military–industrial complex.

When the President uses force — as in Cambodia — to protect American lives, the radical–liberal gets almost hysterical.

He excuses campus violence as the inevitable and justified response of the alienated — but he luridly denounces the reaction of workers and the peacekeeping efforts of the police as harbingers of fascism.

He will bemoan the rise in prices — but vote for every spending bill that comes down the pike.

In the Senate he wants America to welch on all her commitments to the peoples of Asia — but he acts the jingo in the Middle East — blind to the truth that America's credibility is not something that can be destroyed in one corner of Asia and is expected to survive anywhere else in the world. Either our word is good, or it is not — and when we give our word, then it sticks through the tough times as well as the good times.

The radical–liberal will not get exercised over the presence of hard-core pornography at the corner drugstore — but don't let him catch your son praying in the public schools.

The radical–liberal will not hesitate to demand immediate use of the 82nd Airborne to integrate the schools of a Southern state — but he will buy his house so far out in the suburbs that you have to take the Metroliner to get there.

The radical–liberal will want your child bused clear across town to meet someone's notion of proper racial balance — but his own kids will be off to Pennsy Prep.

Such, my friends, are the radical–liberals in the Congress of the United States. They destroyed a President from their own party, Lyndon Johnson; now they are trying to destroy another, Richard Nixon. But they are going to fail. Because in 1970 Democrats, Republicans, and Independents, moderates, centerists, and conservatives are going to join together to administer the political defeats that they so rightly deserve.

I have watched the radical–liberal move through the Capitol corridors with the aloofness of one who has had a private revelation — that the system founded by our forefathers is no longer of any count.

No matter that this great republic has persevered through two centuries of enormous progress. No matter that the American representative democracy has produced the most flexible and free economy in all the history of man. No matter that individual freedom has been advanced for millions and then tens of millions to a degree previously unknown on this earth. No matter that Americans enjoy the greatest abundance of any people in recorded time. No matter that the spirit of generosity pervades this people as it has no other since history began. No matter — the radical–liberal looks on all this and says the system is increasingly unjust and corrupt.

Without any mandate, without any plebicite, the radical–liberal will posture as spokesman for the young, the poor and the black — though most of these Americans do not know who he is and would not like him if they did.

The radical–liberal will tell you that if the war goes on, the best of our young people will scurry off to Canada. He will tell you that the real heroes are the ones who refuse to serve in the armed forces of the United States.

376

Those may be the heroes of radical–liberals — but they are not our heroes.

Our heroes are the American youth who respond to their country's call, who do their country's bidding in a time of crisis. Our heroes are those who have sacrificed years and some their lives in as selfless a cause as any nation has ever undertaken.

A very mysterious transition is presently in progress as more and more of these radical–liberals read the mood of the American people they disguise their identity, and, lately, they have started coming to town masquerading as moderates.

Over this weekend, we had a fresh new recruit to the advocates of law and order. A young Massachusetts Senator enlisted suddenly, lashing out at student radicals as "apostles of force," "campus commandos." He compared them to the Palestinian terrorists. How surprising — and how interesting — that this Senator should now come charging in from the far left of the political spectrum toward the center, where the President of the United States has been all the time and where he stands today.

And this is significant. For this is a Senator who as much as any other in American political life has always had his political course charted out for him in advance by those faithful navigators — the professional pollsters.

But by their past words and deeds we shall know them — these people who drift in strong directions under the pressure of the poll.

The Senator who rose in the world's greatest deliberative body to say that this "chamber reeks of blood" will have a hard time convincing us he is a moderate man.

The Democratic chairman of the Senate Foreign Relations Committee who said that: "[The United States] ought to welcome North Vietnam's preeminence in Indochina" will not be forgotten. And when he is retired from that chairmanship there will be bipartisan rejoicing all over America.

I predict that the economic journalist and self-appointed Democratic party theoretician who wrote that, "[socialism] describes what is needed . . . the Democratic party must henceforth use the word socialism," has advised his last President.

As for that Democratic candidate for the Senate who describes himself as a "revisionist Marxist," he needs to be informed by the voters in November, in a massive way, that America just won't have Marxists in the United States Senate.

As for that former Attorney General who publicly accuses President Nixon of appealing to "fear and hatred" and who says, and I quote, "I'm like [Black Panther] Bobby Seale in many ways: maybe not in as many ways as I should be" — the American voters should guarantee that he never holds another elective office as long as he lives.

The criticisms I have made tonight are blunt and stern — but they are valid and they are true, and I believe they are necessary.

I ask that these radical–liberals be removed from office — not because of personal animus — but because they are the nation's major roadblock for the remainder of this century both in our quest for world peace and in the progress we must make at home.

And I am not here simply to speak out against radical–liberalism. I am here to speak out for all the domestic programs the President has offered that sit idle in the hands of an indifferent Congress. I am here in Albuquerque to ask the people of New Mexico to return your outstanding Congressmen, Manuel Lujan and Ed Foreman, to Washington where they will stand with our President — and to send Andy Carter to tip the balance back toward responsibility in the United States Senate — to make that Senate again a chamber of which all Americans can be deeply proud.

Respect for Congress has dropped to its lowest point in five years — we in the executive branch do not like that or want that. We want a cooperative Congress working with the President for peace and progress — a Congress that will stand tall again in the eyes of the American people. Ed Foreman, Manuel Lujan and Andy Carter will help make it that kind of Congress again. And I am here, as an ex-governor, to speak on behalf of a fine candidate — the next governor of the great state of New Mexico — Peter Dominici.

In Springfield, I closed my speech with a statement of hope made in this collision of philosophies that Winston Churchill made once in a collision of arms.

I'm going to close with that quote, but before I do I want to depart, just for a moment, from my text to say this to you. The Republican party and the people of New Mexico, who have an interest in the destiny of the Republican party as the party of responsibility in this state, recognize that sometimes in party circles there are grave contests and tempers flare and things aren't too good. But I'm delighted to see that in spite of the fact that in this state there has been a very, very active and energetic primary election. I'm delighted to see that the standard-bearer of the Republican party in your state is seated at this table to support the nominees of the Republican party here. And I'm proud that he's here. I want to say thanks to Dave Cargo. Governor Cargo and I served together as governors. We came to our governorships at the same time. We attended the same functions. We became close friends as our families did. I have tremendous personal respect for him, and I'm just so pleased that he is part of the team effort that's going to put the candidates that I've named — your fine nominees — into the offices they seek this November. So let's all get out there and work together to elect Republican candidates this year.

Now I want to close with that quotation from Winston Churchill that he made in the terrible struggle in massive collision of arms when at the beginning of it the people were terribly confused about the course the world should take — about the propriety of the actions that he advocated. And he said:

> I avow my faith that we are marching on toward better days. Humanity will not be cast down. We are going on — swinging bravely forward along the grand high road — and already behind the distant mountains is the promise of the sun.

It's been a great privilege and a pleasure for me to be here in New Mexico at this most important function as the campaign in November draws to its inevitable close — the election of all Republican candidates of this great state. Thank you.

September 16, 1970, Grand Rapids, Michigan
Michigan Republican Dinner

TODAY I was saddened as I watched an able and gracious lady — interested only in serving her country in the United States Senate — courageously endure the most rude, crude, and lewd heckling imaginable. My concern was not only for her, but for my fellow Americans, living and gone, who have invested so much effort in maintaining a fair, honorable and free nation.

Why has this come about? It has come about partly because radical–liberals in the government and in the universities have cultivated the garden of irresponsible protest. It has come about partly because Senators like Lenore Romney's opponent have condoned a disrespect for law and for American institutions.

The obscene voices at the airport in Saginaw, however, I know and Lenore knows, are not the true voices of the people of Michigan. The true voices of this state came from the vast majority of that crowd, and from the clear majority of the young people there — young people whom Lenore and I met and shook hands with as we moved along the fence. The one comment I heard most often — and Lenore heard — as we went along that fence was this: "They don't speak for us, Mr. Vice President; they don't speak for Michigan.

I know that is the truth. The people of Michigan believe in the right of free assembly — without having that assembly widely disrupted. The people of Michigan believe in the first amendment right of speech — without having that speech shouted down by radicals chanting obscenities. And the people of Michigan are going to make their feelings known this November — when they put into office men and women who will both respect and defend our rights, our traditions and our institutions — men and women like Bill Milliken, the Governor of Michigan — and Lenore Romney, your next United States Senator.

The obscene shouts of an arrogant few will never in the State of Michigan drown out the quiet voices, young and old, of dignity and decency.

Let me add this. Today in the Field House at Kansas State University in Manhattan, Kansas, the President of the United States showed Americans of every persuasion the kind of dignity and determination with which to face down the tiny minority of know-nothings on the American campus.

I am glad to be back in Grand Rapids, where you gave the Nixon–Agnew ticket such a warm and friendly reception in 1968.

I really can't think of any more appropriate place to visit in this first full week of the 1970 campaign than the home district of a future Speaker of the House of Representatives — Jerry Ford.

Make no mistake about it, ladies and gentlemen, this is the primary goal of this national campaign — to give President Nixon a Congress ready and able to work with him in carrying out the mandate you gave him in 1968.

And no one would appreciate that more than Jerry Ford. Jerry has the experience, the drive, and the legislative savvy to do the job. All he needs are the horses — good, strong steady Republican horses.

I have seen him in leadership meetings with the President. As he's told you, we sit in these meetings together nearly every week. I have seen him called upon for advice in critical situations. And I have heard him deliver his judgments coolly, sensibly, and persuasively.

If you could see him in action behind the scenes, where the pressure of national affairs separates the men from the boys, you would know why I am traveling all around this nation in this campaign: I'm traveling to get more all-Americans like Jerry Ford to support the President in Congress in the years ahead.

Important to the success of any state campaign is the man at the head of the ticket. You are fortunate, here in Michigan, to have a man with the ability and solid experience of Bill Milliken.

Of course, you are all aware that Michigan is the land of leadership. When the chips are down, we know we can turn to a freshman Senator whose talent and brainpower have catapulted him to one of the most responsible leadership positions in American government — I refer, of course, to a gentleman with whom I had a telephone conversation today — Bob Griffin. He would be here tonight but for the fact that he's busy on important legislation in the Senate and our distinguished minority leader of the Senate — Senator Scott of Pennsylvania is out in the hustings, so Bob Griffin has to stay there and watch the store.

Bob would be the first to admit, I think, that the Senate offers plenty of room for improvement.

There is something to be said about President Theodore Roosevelt's remarks: "When they call the roll in the Senate, the Senators do not know whether to answer 'present' or 'not guilty.' " These days, though, Teddy's remarks would be considered "polarizing."

Michigan has a splendid opportunity this year to help us reverse the political balance of the Senate — to break the grip of a little band of unwilling men who are holding back the will of the people. You have a first-class candidate to do this in Lenore Romney.

I have known Lenore well since she was Michigan's First Lady. She is profoundly concerned with the well-being of people. She is totally dedicated to public service. And if anybody is tempted to underestimate the power of a woman, let them talk to Senator Margaret Chase Smith — and Senator-to-be Lenore Romney.

You won't find Lenore Romney, for example, exculpating draft dodgers . . . voting against crime control . . . cooing with political doves who seek to sabotage our effort to secure an honorable peace in Southeast Asia . . . you won't find Lenore Romney voting for wild spending that drives up the cost of living . . . or saying that marijuana should be legalized.

It's incredible, really, that the opposition party of this state would formally embrace resolutions favoring a unilateral pullout of all of our forces from South Vietnam by Christmas of 1970 — thereby accepting an American defeat.

It is hard to believe that the platform of the Democratic party of this state urges the granting of amnesty to draft evaders who are in prison or who have fled to Canada. In effect, they vote no confidence in our men who are doing their duty, and put their blessing on those who shirked their duty.

Any political leadership that far out of touch with the people is not worthy of holding elective office — state or national.

This idea of welcoming home the runaways did not originate here in Michigan. On February 25, 1969, Senator Edward Kennedy proposed a commission to explore the granting of amnesty to draft evaders. This Senator, who today finds it popular to rail against the "campus commandos," last year pointed out that — and I quote: "Many times in our history we have, as a nation, been magnanimous enough to grant amnesty."

Rest assured, my friends, that there will be no amnesty for draft dodgers. There are great choices in life. Millions of young Americans chose the path of courage, and more than 40,000 of them died for their decision. The few hundred slackers who chose another path are just going to have to live with the consequences of their decision.

I make that point tonight, ladies and gentlemen, to illustrate a larger choice that faces our entire society.

There is a segment of our society that embraces amnesty as a way of life. This segment is represented far beyond its number in the United States Senate.

When a decision is required to keep America strong enough to encourage a peaceful world order, a little band of Senators can be counted upon to come down on the side of weakness.

When a decision is needed to restrain federal spending to hold down the cost of living, this same little band of unwilling men is sure to decide against the President and against the interest of all the people.

When a decision is needed to crack down on lawlessness, to sweep the dope peddlers and thugs off the streets of America, this little band of men says no.

This little band of radical–liberals has long marched behind banners that say "police brutality" and "repression" — at a time when innocent human beings are being brutalized by crime, and the civil rights of millions are being repressed by fear of senseless violence.

This little band of men is guided by a policy of calculated weakness. They vote to weaken our defenses; they vote to weaken our moral fiber; they vote to weaken the forces of law. They were raised on a book by Dr. Spock, and a paralyzing permissive philosophy pervades every policy they espouse.

These are not evil men. They are not disloyal men, or unpatriotic men. And, with the exception of election time, when they trim their beliefs to appear to be more in accord with the will of the people, these are not insincere men. They deeply believe that permissiveness at home and isolation abroad would be the best course for our country.

But because these men are so wrong about America, they are doing great wrong to America. And that is why they must be driven from their positions of power.

You might wonder why, in a democratic society, this little band of unwilling men is so confident that it can get away with frustrating the will of the great majority of Americans.

I think I know the reason. They believe they will automatically be returned to power every six years by a force more powerful than any other force in politics — the force of habit.

They believe that the American workingman, who supported them years ago, will go down the line, in FDR's phrase, "again and again and again."

Well, this year the apostles of the old political order are due for a rude awakening. The working people of America will no longer be taken for granted.

I am convinced that George Meany is absolutely right when he says that the American workingman is the captive of no party. More and more, the American workingman is turning away from the people who have sold out his interests; more and more, he is turning to candidates who understand his needs and respect his views.

Never forget this: The only kind of government that works is the kind that respects people who work.

This is the man who has built America — with his heart and his mind and his hands. He is proud of his country. He properly resents seeing it run down by people who have never had to work as hard as he does.

He and his sons have served proudly in our armed services. Many of them have fought, and some have died in Vietnam. He does not appreciate the suggestion by some Senators that this sacrifice be thrown away. He respects the flag.

This forgotten American has strong family ties and keeps faith with his religion. He is fed up with the tired rationales and the general permissiveness that have brought rioting in the streets and on the campuses. He is fed up with watching college buildings destroyed in the name of academic freedom — especially when the wanton destruction drives up the tuition he must scrape to pay.

He does not enjoy being called a bigot for wanting his children to go to a public school in their own neighborhood.

For too long, this American has been forgotten — but on this election day the forgotten American won't forget.

I speak of the backbone of America — the workingman, earning between $5,000 and $15,000 a year, supporting his family with no handouts from Uncle Sam. He has to fight and scrimp to make ends meet; often he moonlights at a second job, or his wife works to supplement the family income. His real wages didn't go up one thin dime in the second half of the sixties, thanks to higher taxes and inflation, the legacy of his former political friends.

The President has acted responsibly and effectively to curb the runaway inflation which was brought on by $57 billion in consecutive budget deficits in the spending spree of the sixties. We have strong evidence now that he is succeeding, and that we are now on the road toward full employment with reasonable price stability.

Lenore Romney's opponent and some of the other knee jerk spenders in Congress have constantly contributed to this problem. They are still trying to pile on more spending than the country can afford. Mrs. Romney's opponent alone has sponsored bills that would add $17 billion to the national debt.

Crime is another matter of prime concern to the workingman where this administration is moving aggressively, but has been hamstrung by Congress. The President has sent fourteen crime bills to Capitol Hill, thirteen of them last year. Only one has come back for his signature — the District of Columbia Crime Act which should produce dramatic results on a local scale, and serve as a model for similar local legislation across the nation.

Despite this "ho-hum" attitude in Congress, the national crime rate was curbed last year through strong administrative efforts and better local law enforcement. The FBI report issued last month for 1969 showed that the increase in serious crimes nationwide slowed down last year — for the first time in five years. And in cities over 250,000 the increase in serious crimes was cut in half. That's not enough — but that's progress.

I am sure Lenore Romney will continue reminding Michigan audiences that her opponent was one of only four Senators who voted in 1968 against the Omnibus Crime Bill. This legislation needed to fight crime was passed despite the opposition of this Senator from Michigan, and it brought $1.6 million to Michigan last year for improved law enforcement.

Our administration has also undertaken a host of other programs of great importance to the workingman. Let me document a few of these.

— We asked for nearly $3 billion for manpower programs to provide skill training and employability development to well over one million unemployed or underemployed workers.

— We installed forty-six computer job banks to serve metropolitan areas in thirty-three states. These help job seekers to find out quickly what jobs are available throughout an entire metropolitan area.

— Our Department of Labor has undertaken strong efforts on behalf of minority-group workers.

— Income tax relief will be granted to lower income groups under the Tax Reform Act of 1969.

— Well over a million heads of families who work full time but whose annual income is less than the poverty level — the so-called working poor — will qualify for assistance under the Family Assistance Act.

— Improved health and safety standards for workers are now before Congress.

— The administration has proposed equal opportunities in higher education for children in families below the $10,000-a-year level — to be achieved through a combination of grants and loans. For the first time in our history, no qualified student would be denied higher education because his family could not afford it.

— We have succeeded in providing unemployment insurance protection for almost five million additional workers.

— Improved retirement benefits were included in the Social Security Bill signed recently by the President.

These are all long strides forward for the American workingman and woman, taken at the initiative of President Nixon and, in most cases, pushed through a reluctant Congress.

But let us not delude ourselves, as our opponents do, into thinking that there is a monolithic bloc of votes that can be labeled "The American Worker."

And let us not delude ourselves, as our opponents do, into thinking that any group of individuals votes strictly on the basis of group self-interest.

When political pundits look at the workingman, they say with their usual absolute certainty that the Republican appeal is on the social issues, while the Democratic appeal is on the economic issues. I submit that today's conventional wisdom will turn out to be tomorrow's mistake.

I believe that we have a powerful case to make on that "gut issue" called "The Pocket-book Issue."

That case is based on one single unpleasant fact that everybody hates to face. Let me give it to you without the frills: The only time the Democrat leaders have been able to bring about full employment is during a war or during preparations for a war.

I'm sorry if that hard fact upsets the squeamish, but it happens to be true. And once you have said it out loud the first time, it becomes easier to say again: "The only time the Democrat leaders have been able to bring about full employment is during a war or during preparations for a war."

Therefore, to use a phrase of Dickens, they brought about "the best of times and the worst of times" — both at the same time. That is not an economic record that merits pride.

This administration, on the other hand, offers the American workingman something new and different — prosperity in peacetime, and without a runaway inflation.

Right now, today, we can point to an economy that is headed upward while a war is heading downward. We're not talking "pie in the sky." We're talking about solid, measurable progress toward a goal that the opposition never was able to achieve.

Just the other day, a survey of almost two hundred leading economists showed an overwhelming agreement with our policies. Production is on the rise, and that will surely mean more jobs. And since it will take place in peacetime, that will mean less inflation and more real take-home pay for more workers.

We do not belong on the defensive when it comes to jobs and real prosperity for the working man. Just the opposite — the record of 1970 offers greater economic hope than the average family has ever had before.

Remember this: The hardest times are the war times. The American people are ready to trade a helmet in for a hard-hat any day.

One great difference between this administration and previous administrations is this: We put the interests of all the people ahead of any special interest.

We don't say, "Stick with us, and you'll get a better deal than your neighbor." Instead, we say, "Think as Americans first, and then as American workers, or American employers, or American veterans or housewives or suburbanites or whatever."

If there is a "new politics" abroad in our land, that is it. The old way of assembling majorities by appealing to people by ethnic group or social class or region is doomed to defeat.

Ours is a more inspiring message. We say, "Whoever you are, whatever you do, wherever you live — think of yourself first as an American, and support what is best for the whole country."

Idealistic? Maybe. But there is a streak of idealism that is part of the American character, and it has not been preempted by highbrows or longhairs.

The American worker doesn't need politicians to tell him that unemployment is higher now than it was when we were spending ten billion dollars more to support a wider war. He knows it, and we know it.

But he also knows that something had to be done to restrain a runaway inflation that snatched away his pay increase. He knows that the big spending that sounds so good to specific groups on the receiving end has to come from somewhere — and it's the worker who pays, in higher taxes and higher prices.

Most important of all, the American worker knows that what is best for the whole nation is best for every single American in it.

And now, at long last, we have a President in Washington with the courage to do what is best for all the people.

The forgotten American is forgotten no more.

We remember who pays the taxes. We remember who has had to fight the wars. We remember who makes the automobiles, builds the plants, and makes this country run.

And by our action to end this war with honor; by our action to slam the brakes on the cost of living; by our action to crack down on the racketeers and thugs who prey on honest people; by these actions on behalf of all the people, I believe we have earned the strong support of the working people of America.

One important way to improve the quality of life is to enhance the dignity of work. To do this, we must show a new and decent respect for the decent people who respect the law, respect the flag, respect their neighbors, and have earned respect for themselves.

Let me say it again — the forgotten American is forgotten no more. And as long as he joins in sending Senators and Representatives to Washington like Jerry Ford and Lenore Romney, who will stand shoulder to shoulder with the President of the United States, he will never be forgotten again.

September 25, 1970, Milwaukee, Wisconsin
Wisconsin Republican Dinner
THE AGE OF INDULGENCE

THERE WAS a newspaper headline here in Milwaukee a few days ago that read: "Milwaukee Braces for Agnew Visit."

I suppose the same writer will proclaim tomorrow: "Vice President Leaves, Milwaukee Heaves Sigh of Relief."

I come to Wisconsin, my friends, to speak up for two fine men. One is a man who is best equipped to carry on the tradition of good state government so well established by your present governor, Warren Knowles. Governor Knowles leaves behind some big shoes to fill — and the best man to fill them is Jack Olson.

Wisconsin is one of the leading states of the nation in real effort to clean up the air and water; it has set new standards in the streamlining of state government, making it manageable and responsive; it has aggressively expanded job opportunities through planned economic growth, and has dramatically improved its statewide system of education.

This is the kind of dynamic state administration that has earned your confidence, and that record will be strongly carried forward under Governor Jack Olson.

My other reason for being here tonight is to lend my support to a new face on the American political scene, a man that Wisconsin and the nation will come to know and deeply respect in the years ahead: John Erickson.

This is a time when teamwork between the President and the Senate of the United States is absolutely essential. John Erickson is a man who intimately understands the meaning of teamwork.

This is a time when our young people need firm moral guidance as seldom before in our history. John Erickson is a man who knows how to inspire young people and marshal their energies in constructive causes.

My friends, consider the choice before you:

A vote for John Erickson is a vote to support the President in his effort to bring about an honorable peace in Vietnam; a vote for his opponent is a vote to return a man who has increasingly sought to tie the President's hands in making a peace that will discourage future wars.

A vote for John Erickson is a vote to remove from the chairmanship of the Senate Foreign Relations Committee the leader of a little group of unwilling men who would take us down the road of appeasement: J. William Fulbright.

And a vote for John Erickson, my Wisconsin friends, is a vote to support President Nixon's drive to hold down excessive federal spending, the kind of spending that drove up your prices and drove up your taxes during the spending spree of the sixties.

Make no mistake about it: John Erickson's opponent, despite his flamboyant press clippings about slashing national defense, is a certified big spender. He has shown, time after time, that he cannot or will not vote to hold the line against the rising cost of living. You sent Richard Nixon to Washington to break the back of a runaway inflation — and I think you will agree that the President deserves the support of at least one Senator from Wisconsin in his fight to hold down the cost of living.

We have real progress to report on the inflation front. You saw the figures just the other day — that the cost of living rose less in the past month than in any time in two years. Over a longer term, it can be shown that inflation has been slashed by two-thirds. And inflation is being curbed, for the first time in recent history, without a recession. Production is going up; interest rates are coming down; unemployment has been held below the early years of the sixties, before the wartime buildup cured that problem but announced the arrival of one infinitely worse.

All this economic progress, all this slowing of inflation without recession, has been accomplished despite the freewheeling spending efforts of Senators, like John Erickson's opponent, who have fought the President every step of the way.

Think about it. If these big spenders have their way, all we have fought for in these past two years will be lost, and we'll be off to the races again — and the prices in your supermarkets will once again go through the roof. Let's learn by our experience, and send men like John Erickson to the Senate.

My friends, from time to time in this campaign of 1970, I will be departing from the customary political themes to discuss trends in American life that go beyond politics. Last week I discussed some of the overlooked aspects of the drug culture that is spreading through the nation. Tonight I would like to reflect with you on a subject that profoundly concerns every one of us — indeed, one that underlies many of our present problems.

My subject — my target, if you prefer — is permissiveness.

The man who's going to be your next Senator was a coach. And as I was thinking about permissiveness in this country, and the loss of willingness to discipline ourselves, I remembered another coach who used to live in Wisconsin. I'm sure you know whom I mean: Vince Lombardi. He didn't believe in taking it easy. He didn't believe in sliding through. He believed in hard work, discipline, self-restraint, and sense of purpose. And that is my theme this evening.

The most overworked cliché in American politics today is this: "We must reorder our priorities."

Although many people do not realize it, in the past two years we have drastically reordered our priorities.

For example, consider how much Americans as a people spend on our military needs compared to what we spend on all levels federal, state and local, both public and private, for education.

Three years ago, we were spending far more on defense than we spent on education —over 25 billion dollars more to make us strong than to make us more knowledgeable.

Today, in a dramatic turnaround, America is now spending more on education than it spends on defense.

This fact, I submit, is solid evidence that this nation is reordering its priorities on the grandest scale imaginable. Internationally, with the Nixon Doctrine, we are reordering our priorities as well — changing our emphasis to require our allies to bear a greater share of the burden of their own defense.

Socially, our priorities are changing, too. Not long ago, it was said that one-third of the nation was "ill-clothed, ill-housed, ill-fed;" today the fraction of our population living below the poverty level is down to one-eighth, and that figure is shrinking all the time, despite the rise in population. As the percentage in poverty drops, we will be concerning ourselves more with helping the workingman who is neither poor nor well-to-do, who provides most of the muscle and much of the backbone of the nation, and who has until recently been the forgotten American.

But there is one area in which our priorities have not changed as yet, and it happens to be the area that most urgently needs a change.

I am talking about our priorities not as a nation, but as individuals. I am talking about putting first things first in our own minds.

Before we as a people can properly address ourselves to any national issue, each one of us must address himself to this personal issue: how can we reinstill a sense of discipline in our thinking?

Discipline is a harsh word. But my friends, there is no greater need in the American body politic today than the need for discipline.

Here is what I mean. During the past generation, a philosophy of permissiveness has permeated American life.

In our schools, the ability to adjust became more important than the ability to excel.

In our courts, the rights of the accused became more important than the rights of the victims.

In our legislatures, the temptation to spend exceeded the willingness to tax.

In our culture, the need to protect free expression overrode the need to restrain bad taste and outrageous vulgarity.

In our society, the need to escape was exalted and the need to cope was demeaned.

In our families, the desire to give our young people a more pleasant life overcame the responsibility to give them firm guidance.

In short, we have gone through a debilitating, enervating age of indulgence. Can we say as a result that the upcoming generation is any happier than the previous generation? Is it more productive, more responsible, more capable of human dignity?

I think not. More of our young people are alienated than ever before; more are lonely; more are inclined to drop out of society; more are inclined toward violence. This is not only my assessment; it is theirs as well.

The age of indulgence cannot find an alibi in the war in Vietnam. In the past twenty-eight years, we have had fourteen years of war; it is not the special affliction of today's youth. And student unrest is a problem in countries that are not at war at all.

The simple fact is this, much as sociological soreheads hate to admit it: This pervasive policy of permissiveness has turned out to be a tragic mistake. The age of indulgence has eroded personal responsibility and corrupted discipline. It has replaced respect for authority with fear of repression. And that, my friends, is not progress toward greater freedom and justice. And freedom and justice are essential goals in a democracy.

Recently, I heard of a case that illustrates the insecurity of some parents. In one community, parents got together to compare notes on some rules to be set for their teen-agers — how late they could stay out, habits of dress, that sort of thing. But instead of coming to any conclusions, they invited in their children and held what amounted to an adversary hearing negotiating rules of conduct.

Now, it is a good thing for parents to consult their children about their opinions, and to hear out their suggestions — but it is the height of insecurity to turn the dining room table into a bargaining table. Parents and young children should not be in a labor–management relationship.

Let me give you some everyday examples of the kind of permissiveness that has insinuated its way into our behavior.

A permissive parent sees his child come to the dinner table wearing dirty clothes, his hands unwashed and his hair unkempt. The parent finds this offensive and turns to Dr. Spock's book — which has sold over 25 million copies in the past generation — for guidance. He reads this on that subject: "As usual, you have to compromise. Overlook some of his less irritating bad habits, realizing that they are probably not permanent." The thing to be carefully avoided, says our foremost authority on children, is "bossiness".

Who do you suppose is to blame when, ten years later, that child comes home from college and sits down at the table with dirty, bare feet and a disorderly faceful of hair?

Another example: A sociology teacher looks at a failing examination paper of a favorite student. The teacher considers how active the student is in extracurricular work, or what a contribution he is making to intergroup relations on the basketball team, and the teacher passes the student on up to the next grade.

Years later, when that student is unable to cope with the advanced work in his class, who is to blame when he demands an end to examinations, or control of the curriculum, or a voice in choosing faculty?

One more example, a little more topical: A college administrator observes a student deliberately breaking a window in an otherwise peaceful demonstration. The dean is delighted that the extent of the destruction is small; he doesn't want to cause an uproar by suspending or expelling the offending student. So he forgets about it. Who is to blame, months or years later, when that student participates in the burning of an ROTC building — or even worse?

In my view, in each case the individual breaking the rules bears part of the blame — but a full share of the blame also lies with the permissive parent, the permissive teacher, the permissive administrator.

I do not go along with those who would absolve every individual from the consequences of his actions, blaming "society" for every wrongful act. That philosophy of holding everybody responsible actually holds nobody responsible, and it provides the rationale for an unconscionable — and ultimately cruel — leniency. An extensive hunt for "root causes" in poverty or parental divorce is often launched by people whose permissiveness is often the root cause itself.

"The fault, dear Brutus, lies not in our stars but in ourselves. . . ." The cause of campus violence, my friends, lies not in an alienated generation but in the individuals in both generations that have made a fetish out of indulgence.

Consider for a moment the easy automatic responses that have been substituted for discipline:

First, there is the *hero–villain lineup*. To many of us, and especially to many young people, the world appears divided into good guys and bad guys, white hats and black hats. If somebody is not with you all the way, he is against you. If McGovern is for it, it has to be right; if the President is for it, it has to be wrong. If a liberal proposes it, it is probably good; if a conservative, it's probably bad. It is unthinking, instinctive, Pavlovian — and colors much of the political criticism today.

Second, there is the requirement for *instant gratification*. The decree that infants should be fed on demand and not on a schedule has been elevated to dogma up to age thirty. Now many say that patience or even prudence is not a virtue, it is a weakness; if satisfaction cannot be guaranteed right now, this minute, then the system is sick and unresponsive and needs major surgery instantly.

Third, there is *geneaphobia*, the fear of another generation. The idea is all other groups in society are linked up in a conspiracy to frustrate the legitimate demands of youth. The other generation refuses to "listen" or "communicate" — which most often means they refuse to follow suggestions. Of course, the established order does have ways to block radical change — but this conspiracy theory holds that every other group is consciously in cahoots against youth per se. Of course, geneaphobia works both ways — and we often see the same automatic rejection of young ideas by an older generation that is equally unfair.

Fourth, the *intellectual double standard*. Here are a few:

— Seniority and tenure are right in a university and wrong in a Congress, because a university is a special place.

— Shutting out views that oppose yours is right, and others shutting out your views is wrong, because what you say is the revealed truth.

— Senator Fulbright's record on civil rights is inconsequential because he is a dove, but other Senators are hypocrites for bowing to home state political pressures.

— Cyclamates should be taken off the market because we do not have proof that they are harmless, and marijuana should be legalized because we do not have proof that it is harmful.

— Public disagreement with government policy is legitimate dissent, but public disagreement with dissent is illegitimate repression.

The hero–villain lineup; the requirement for instant gratification; geneaphobia; and the intellectual double standard are four cheap substitutes for discipline.

They offer the lazy mind, or the mind made lazy by the age of indulgence, a shortcut to a conclusion. They require no original thinking. They demand no rigorous reasoning. They introduce no dissonance to a comfortable pattern of beliefs. The boilerplate is ready; the stereotype is set.

The abdication of the responsibility for thoughtful inquiry has always been a danger to democracy. James Bryce, in *The American Commonwealth*, written almost a century ago, put his finger on the source of many political and social beliefs:

These beliefs when examined, mostly resolve themselves into two or three prejudices and aversions, two or three prepossessions for a particular party or section of a party, two or three phrases or catch words suggesting or embodying arguments which the man who repeats them has not analyzed.

But the path of true scholarship, the path of the devoted seeker after truth, has never been the path of least resistance. That path is hard; genuine inquiry is by its nature upsetting to the man searching for his own answers.

That is why I believe so many college administrators are failing their students today; that is why so many parents are failing their children today.

By failing to demand disciplined thinking, by permitting these shortcuts to substitute for discipline, they delude themselves into believing they are helping the younger generation, and they expect to be popular by appearing to be "with it."

387

In reality, however, their permissiveness harms rather than helps young people cope with life, and the administrators earn only the young people's scorn. They deserve that scorn.

Discipline is a necessary precursor of self-discipline. A person who has been encouraged — even forced — to think for himself will not become a member of a mob; he will not slip into the easy comformity of the drug culture; he will not mock his ingrained values by shouting obscenities at men he disagrees with or by flying flags upside down.

I have been traveling the length of this land in recent weeks with a double mission: Specifically, to help elect men to public office who will lean hard against the trend toward permissiveness, and who understand its terrible consequences in terms of disruption and violence. More generally, my mission is to awaken Americans to the need for sensible authority, to jolt good minds out of the lethargy of habitual acquiesence, to mobilize a silent majority that cherishes the right values but has been bulldozed for years into thinking those values are embarrassingly out of style.

And yes, occasionally I use colorful language; but you cannot awaken people with a whisper. Of course I seek to make my views heard; a call to intellectual combat cannot be issued by a flute; it needs a trumpet. John Maynard Keynes put it this way: "Words ought to be a little wild, for they are the assault of thoughts on the unthinking". And of course I am often met with outraged reaction; I am challenging the very articles of faith of people who get their opinions secondhand.

The charges of polarization, of divisiveness, of repression and censorship are only the defense of minds too shackled by old shibboleths to rise to the stimulus of disciplined argument. Among all those who have leaped to challenge my motives, very few have risen to counter the points I have raised. Why? Because reasoned argument requires preparation and effort, and too many of the old opinion leaders are out of the habit of making a rational argument.

The adversary political system we have developed provides the perfect format for such discussion. Let's use it. The academic freedom that now needs new protection from disruption on campus offers the best climate, for hard logic, for rational discourse. Let's make them citadels of reason and disciplined thought again.

The kind of intellectual that America needs so badly today is the man who has been trained, disciplined, to use his own mind to arrive at his own conclusions — not to buy his opinions with his morning newspaper or to slavishly mimic the postures of some other intellectual.

The kind of student America needs today is one who is not only ready to challenge conventional wisdom, but is willing to invest the effort to challenge the conclusions of his fellow-students and himself.

The kind of teacher and college administrator America needs today is one who will preserve a climate of reason against any disruption, and provide both the enthusiasm and the caution that will give birth to a life of the mind.

The kind of parent America needs today is one who will refuse to indulge sloppiness in thought or even in dress, and who will provide the firm moral base on which a young person can build his own life.

The kind of political leadership America needs today is the kind that will do its homework, think through its problems, and come up with reforms and fresh approaches to help people help themselves.

I have seen the way the President of the United States approaches a problem. He demands the exposure of every feasible option. He then considers the consequences of each alternative: in human terms, in money terms, in terms of his overall political philosophy. He probes for answers, and will not tolerate slipshod analysis from anyone. He puts his own disciplined mind to work. And when he makes a decision, you can be certain it is one that has weighed all the risks and opportunities and new ideas. And it was that disciplined thinking when the chips were down that did far more than most people realize in averting a war in the Middle East last week.

He knows he can not always be right, but he also knows that he will be right a lot more often than a man unwilling to think it through for himself. A man who prefers to adopt the views of the opinion makers and who would like to govern without the inconvenience of standing for election.

Every one of us should be willing to do his homework in the matters important to each of us as individuals. The age of indulgence is at long last coming to an end; the time of individual responsibility is at hand.

Just as past permissiveness led to alienation and disorder, I am confident that the new sense of responsibility that is taking hold today will lead to greater self-respect in every American, and a far deeper mutual respect between generations.

My Wisconsin friends, if you agree that this state and nation need the kind of leadership that can move us toward those goals, then you will elect Jack Olson to be your governor, and you will send John Erickson to the United States Senate.

September 29, 1970, Sioux Falls, South Dakota
South Dakota Republican Luncheon

LADIES AND GENTLEMEN: In two weeks I have campaigned in ten states — and one issue dominates this election: Will the radical–liberalism that controls the Senate of the United States prevail in the nation — or will America be led into the future by the moderates, centrists, and conservatives who stand behind the President of the United States?

Fred Brady and Dexter Gunderson, your Congressional candidates — and especially Frank Farrar, your excellent governor — are men the President needs at the national level, and at the highest level in this state — if the President is to carry out the mandate the people of South Dakota gave him in 1968.

Before he left for Europe, President Nixon told me that South Dakota was among the crucial states we must win this fall.

For Frank Farrar, your governor is one of the men on whom he is counting to help bring about an historic change in the political landscape of America. With his unprecedented program to share federal tax revenues with states like South Dakota, the President needs in the governor's chair a man who shares the philosophy of the New Federalism, a man who shares his deep belief that we stop concentrating power in Washington and start returning it to the states and the people; a man who knows the needs of South Dakota a man with the ear and the confidence of the President of the United States — a man like Frank Farrar.

And if we are going to defeat once and for all the radical–liberalism that has seized control of so many leadership positions in the Democratic party, we need also more men like Fred Brady and Dexter Gunderson in Washington.

The President has proposed fourteen major pieces of anticrime legislation — legislation all America voted for in 1968; legislation all America needed in 1969 and 1970, yet legislation obstructed and blocked in Congress by radical–liberals. Put men like Dexter Gunderson and Fred Brady in the Congress — and every one of those bills will become a law America needs in the first months of the Ninety-Second Congress.

Now, because it is the truth and because it is necessary to say so — let me say that one of the foremost national leaders of radical liberalism — and its chief fund-raiser today — is the junior Senator from South Dakota.

When the President nominated two federal judges — Southern judges who stood for law and order and against busing — Senator McGovern attacked both men and hurled at one the ugly charge of "racist."

When the President asked for Congressional support for an honorable peace in Vietnam — your junior Senator voted time and again to restrict his power and tie his hands.

When the President asked for the necessary military wherewithal to negotiate with the Russians from strength — not weakness — at Helsinki and Vienna, your junior Senator voted to deny him what was needed and what was asked.

His voting record is 100 percent on the radical–liberal index. He does not represent the people of South Dakota who elected President Nixon; he represents his ultraliberal friends back in Manhattan and Georgetown.

But let us look also at the statements made in recent years that place your junior Senator squarely in the radical–liberal camp.

Last June, in Hanover, New Hampshire, he stated that the greatest threat — I repeat — the greatest threat to American foreign policy is the philosophy of "anticommunism."

I don't believe this represents the thinking of South Dakota. Every good American should be both an antifascist and anticommunist, and any individual who says that "anticommunism" is the dominant threat to our foreign policy does not know the world he lives in and does not belong in the United States Senate.

When the President made his courageous decision to clear the Cambodian sanctuaries of enemy troops, this junior Senator accused the President, and I quote, of a "betrayal of the humanitarian principles of the American people." This is a gross misrepresentation and an inexcusable slander of the President of the United States.

And because this great contest this year is not between Democrats and Republicans — but between the President's philosophy and the radical–liberals who obstruct him at every turn, I am right now calling on the Democratic candidates for Congress in South Dakota — both of them — and Mr. Kneip, as well, to repudiate all these statements and to repudiate the leadership of the Senator who made them.

Barely a day passes that this Senator does not accuse me of dividing the country. Yet, he himself sabotaged his own Democratic President; he himself contributed mightily to the bitter division in his own party that led to the confrontation in Chicago. This Senator who helped destroy a President of his own party is trying to destroy President Nixon. With your help, my friends, we will deny him that macabre pleasure.

When his recent amendment — a blueprint for American defeat in Asia — was overwhelmingly turned down by his colleagues, your junior Senator stood up and cried, and I quote: "This chamber reeks of blood."

I know that Dexter Gunderson, Fred Brady, and Frank Farrar join me in rejecting that kind of language and that kind of politics — and I again call upon each of their opponents to make their position known.

Nor is it only in foreign policy that the views of this Senator are wrong; he has also done much to morally disarm America in dealing with disorder and violence and crime. When the militants were massing in the streets of Chicago and hurling obscenities and epithets and rocks and excrement at the police — this Senator said and I quote, "Emptyheaded cries for law and order carry an undertone of racism."

With this kind of accusation of racism, every time we demand that the law be obeyed — how can we ever return to the rule of law in America?

You will recall the trial of the so-called "Chicago Eight" who spent weeks disrupting the courtroom and shouting obscenities at the judge who tried them. Well, when that trial was over — and the sentences were imposed this was the comment made by Senator McGovern:

That trial was deplorable — a disgrace to the court and our judicial system. . . . Our fundamental liberties are denigrated when a judge, even though he may have been insulted and have an intense personal dislike for the defendants, is allowed to ignore this presumption on the basis of an apparently capricious conclusion that the men on trial are "dangerous."

There we have it in its pristine majesty — the double standard of the radical–liberal. There we have a blistering attack on a federal judge, with only a word in criticism of the seven defendants and their attorneys who use every obscene means imaginable to provoke the Judge and to disrupt the trial. But the conduct of the defendants fails to provoke critical comment by the junior Senator from South Dakota.

But let me turn now from the individual to another example of political extremism over the past weekend — an example provided by the most radical–liberal organization housed within the opposition party . This past Sunday, the ADA, an organization dominated by radical–liberals, made this blatant charge: Referring to the deaths at Kent State and Jackson State, the ADA said, and I quote:

"The President and Vice President sanction official lawlessness."

My friends in South Dakota, that is a bald-faced lie. The President and I condemn now and have repeatedly condemned the use of violence in this society — by anybody and any time. The course of action for the millions of good Democrats across this country is now clear.

Ask your Democratic candidate in this election whether or not he utterly repudiates that statement and that organization — and if your Democratic candidate is getting either an endorsement or support from the ADA — he does not deserve your support.

But let me turn now to a matter of national attention this past week: Last weekend the Scranton Commission after months of painful gestation, went into the final hours of labor, and gave birth to a two-pound report on student unrest. The rejoicing in the Eastern Liberal Establishment continues unto this very hour.

In seriousness, my friends in South Dakota, there are today — as inevitably there was certain to be — two separate reports from the Scranton Commission on Student Unrest.

The first is the report itself as released on Saturday and presented to the President. The second is the "Scranton Commission Report" which the nation has come to know and accept as the final verdict — for which we can thank the self-appointed interpreters and translators on the commission, and within the nation's "academic–journalistic complex," who rushed before the cameras to tell us what is said.

These two reports, the real one and the cosmetized one, are vastly different.

For the vast majority of Americans — that second report will be the only report — and therefore I must address myself to what "its" conclusions were:

First, the American people have been led by this truncated and distorted report to believe that the primary need for restoration of order on the American campus is for the President of the United States to exercise greater moral leadership. This is an unfair, outrageous and unacceptable charge to make against a President who has time and again spoken out in defense of dissent — time and again spoken out in unequivocal condemnation of violence and disorder wherever it occurs.

Let me tell you also about the kind of moral leadership I have witnessed from this President.

When a President is not panicked by the cries of a strident minority and resolutely pursues a policy that will bring peace without surrender — that's moral leadership.

When a President makes the painful decisions to restrain a runaway inflation and stands by his guns despite widespread predictions of failure and demands for crippling controls — that's moral leadership.

When a President resists every outside pressure to impose his will on college campuses, in the knowledge that academic freedom must be defended from within — that's moral leadership.

When a President reorders the national priorities so that spending for defense is, for the first time in two decades, billions less than what is spent to meet human needs — that's moral leadership.

When a President risks his personal popularity and political future in taking the action needed to protect the lives of our men in Vietnam by cleaning out enemy sanctuaries in Cambodia — that's moral leadership.

Moral leadership, my friends, is not in exhortation alone — it is also in courage to decide what is right and to do what is right.

391

By what he has done in times of crisis; by what he has done at the risk of unpopularity; by what he has said when it needed saying; by — first and foremost — the power of his example, the President of the United States has exercised moral leadership the likes of which this nation has not seen in many a year.

The second conclusion of the contrived second report — the one purveyed by press and TV to America — is that somehow, because there is a war going on, and because there are remnants of injustice and racism and poverty in America — there is, therefore, some explanation or justification for antisocial conduct and disorders by disaffected students. This is totally false and utterly unacceptable.

Students — no matter how idealistic they are or claim to be — comprise but four percent of America's population. And while that four percent has the same right to be heard as anyone else — it has no greater right to be heeded. And, assuredly, students have no more right than anyone else to disrupt our institutions when they deem it a proper form of protest.

No minority of the electorate has any special claim to direct our national policy; that policy is not going to be directed by any self-appointed or self-anointed elites; it will be directed by the elected leadership of the American people. Nor do I believe that the collective tantrum known as campus disruption is any more tolerable today than it was in other years.

The third conclusion the media conveyed to the country out of that report was that men in the public arena should be extremely guarded in what they say and what they do — lest their criticism of militant students bring about more antisocial conduct on the campus.

The suggestion that vigorous public condemnation of antisocial conduct is somehow, ex post facto, a cause of that conduct is more of the same remorseless nonsense we have been hearing for years. If that were true, those who have remained silent or indulgent in the face of academic anarchy would be the heroes of the last decade — whereas history will identify them along the major causes.

It is not those who vigorously condemn student violence and disorder — but those who encourage it or condone it — on whom the burden of guilt has been rightly placed by the American people.

And what of the actual report itself? After hearing interim verdicts handed down almost nightly on the network news by the more publicity conscious members — the nation did not expect much from the report — but in some particulars it cannot be faulted.

Assuredly, there is a great deal within it with which everyone can agree. First and foremost, it takes an unequivocal stand against violence. Second, much of the historical analysis makes a contribution to an understanding of the decades-long roots of the present unrest.

But in the indiscriminate fashion in which it diffuses and dilutes responsibility, in the total unfairness of the most widely publicized recommendation, in the thinly veiled rationalizations for student disruption, the report comes out, in its overall impression, imprecise, contradictory, and equivocal. It is sure to be taken as more *pablum for the permissivists.*

The commission condemns, with an even hand, the disruptions by students that have very nearly destroyed many American colleges and the vigorous public denunciation of those disruptions by academicians and public men who were alert to the danger long ago.

The commission rebukes those who outspokenly condemn campus disorder and violence — while it exempts from criticism those public officials who have excused, condoned, and encouraged disruption for an entire decade.

The commission tells us that many students believe ours is a corrupt repressive society engaged in an immoral war — but the commission could not muster the moral courage to declare the utter falsehood of that charge. And the commission lacked the moral vision to condemn that intellectual elite whose attacks on our institutions and society as racist and repressive have led students into believing this nonsense.

392

With its call for a cease-fire, the commission assumes a posture of neutrality as between the fireman and the arsonist.

The university disruptions of the last half decade that have undermined academic freedom in this country are blamed on everybody and everything in this society, when the blame belongs squarely on the disrupters themselves and their apologists in the larger community.

And again, the primary responsibility for maintaining academic freedom within a campus community does not belong on the steps of the White House — as some commissioners suggest — it belongs on the steps of the university administration building and at the door of the faculty lounge. The United States is not the policeman of the world — and the President cannot replace the campus cop.

Look at the history of violence and disruption on the campuses today. As the commission report points out, the campus at Berkeley was the victim of student disruptions four years before Richard Nixon ran for the Presidency, and long before I was a household word — even in Baltimore County. Disorders and disruption precluded the appearance of President Johnson on almost every American campus and in many cities — long before Richard Nixon won the election of 1968. The presidential campaign of Vice President Humphrey was disrupted time and again by student militants — well before this administration took office.

To lay responsibility for ending student disruptions at the doorstep of this President — in office twenty months — is "scapegoating" of the most irresponsible sort.

There are scores of American colleges and universities where students, faculties, and administrators have maintained without interruption a climate of academic freedom. Where that has happened the academic community deserves *total* credit — neither President Nixon nor I can take any credit for that success. But neither do we accept blame for those academic communities where students and faculty and administrators have failed to maintain peace or an open forum for ideas.

We find in this report also one after another recommendation for how the President should reorder our national priorities in a way that suits the commission — and the student protesters. As I have stated: He has already done so. And, ladies and gentlemen, let me say that the determination of the priorities of the United States will be made by the elected President and elected Congress of the United States — they will not be determined by any small and unelected elite.

While we defend the right of every American including every student to be heard, we will not evaluate the validity of protest on the decibel count of the protesters. There are people in society with legitimate complaints who protest loudly — others with equally legitimate complaints who dissent quietly.

We shall assess the complaints against national policy and claims on our national resources — on what we deem to be their merits — not on the tactics of protest used to advance them. Disruption of a campus does not mean the cause is right — and a quiet voice of disagreement does not mean that voice is wrong.

The commission recommends massive increases in federal aid to colleges and students. That sounds to me suspiciously like a call for a payoff. Besides, federal aid for colleges and universities in recent years has more than doubled. And let me reiterate: *The President and the Congress* — in the federal budget — shall determine if funds for higher education are more important on the national agenda — than funds for the health care of our elderly, funds for our national defense, or funds for the retraining of workers.

Nowhere is there within this report — that I can find — the clear-cut statement that *anyone*, not just faculty, in a campus community who disrupts that community — no matter how grand or idealistic his cause — should be expelled from that community; no ifs, ands, or buts.

Nor can one find in that report the justified recognition of the enormous contribution of the workingmen and women of this country, whose taxes have built most of our great colleges and universities and who have rights within those institutions as well.

We hear a great deal of talk about our universities not being responsive. They *should*

393

be responsive to students and faculty, true. But alumni and taxpayers have certain rights within them as well, and it is time their legitimate protest about what was going on is heard as well.

Let me conclude my brief remarks about this report with a statement by Dr. Sidney Hook, a very perceptive man, an academician who has talked sense throughout the incursion of disorder in our academic institutions. Dr. Hook said:

> The history of American higher education is a history of change. Violence has never played an appreciable role in that history. It need not play a role today if it is recognized that the primary function of higher education is the quest for knowledge, wisdom, and vision, not the conquest of political power; that the university is not responsible for the existence of war, poverty, and other evils; and that the solution of these and allied problems lies in the hands of the democratic citizenry and not of a privileged elite.

September 30, 1970, Salt Lake City, Utah
Utah Republican Dinner

IT IS A pleasure to be back in Utah.

Last year I addressed the student body at Brigham Young and received a most cordial and civil welcome. The atmosphere there is a far cry from the destructive rampages that have been managed by a strident minority on some of our East Coast, West Coast, and even Midwestern campuses.

At Brigham Young the faculty is still in charge of the campus and, in another sense, the students are in command of their faculties. It is a place where a national officeholder — a controversial one at that — feels he can go and say his piece and not be shouted down.

Today I had a very unusual experience in an otherwise hospitable welcome from the people of Salt Lake City. I was speaking very close to the hotel in a public place and there were some young dissenters present who were utilizing the traditional means of disrupting a speech.

Now I don't know where the idea came to these young people that this is a way to demonstrate their intellectual acuity, but it seems to have become fashionable to attempt to upset and to completely discombobulate a speaker to the extent that he is unable to continue with his remarks.

Fortunately, we had a very loud public address system, and I think I managed to be heard in spite of this relatively small group of people. But the very distinct thing that I noticed as I looked out over the crowd was that there were five or six times as many young people scattered throughout that great crowd who were interested in hearing what I had come to say and who were very embarrassed at this conduct that the others were persisting at. I attempted to say at the close of my formal remarks to those young people that no one in this country wants to stifle a difference of opinion or dissent. But this country is built on the freedoms that include a freedom to be heard and oddly enough, some of these same people who attempt to abrogate the freedom of a member of the establish-

394

ment to be heard — these are the same people who cry "repression" when someone criticizes their dissent.

I would hope that we are reaching the end of this fad of disruption of remarks of people who come to say something to people who want to hear what they have to say. Recently on the David Frost show, I had a chance to engage some young people who had completely different viewpoints than mine — and I respect their right to have different viewpoints. That experience indicates without any question that there can be courtesy and civility between people who have violently differing points of view and it shows me that there is hope for communication if we can resume the rational process of dialogue and debate to replace this senseless and very primitive visceral demonstrating that we contend with today. But the one point I want to emphasize that sticks with me out of all of these demonstrations is that I think they're on the wane and I think that the young people are becoming the worst critics of this anti-intellectual procedure.

President Nixon's recent appearance at Kansas State University and his enthusiastic reception by the students there I think were very encouraging. And what happened there should have convinced the nation that the large majority of young Americans do not approve of the rude and boisterous conduct of the few who have created this false image of their generation. When more of these concerned young people are willing to stand up against the voices of disruption as those students at Kansas State University did, I think we will be on the way toward turning the tide.

I bring you a brief message tonight from President Nixon. He needs a new Congress to carry out that mandate for change that you overwhelmingly voted him two years ago. You can start by replacing your Senatorial spendthrift and obstructionist with Laurence Burton. And you can complete the job by sending Sherman Lloyd back to the House for his fourth term and electing Dick Richard to Congressman Burton's seat.

Most Americans don't realize the degree to which the President has been hamstrung by this Ninety-First Congress. The radical–liberals who dominate the Senate have opposed nearly every more he has tried to make — in curbing inflation, in turning over the war to our South Vietnamese allies instead of abruptly pulling out and leaving them to the invader, and in seeking to restore balance to the Supreme Court.

And your junior Senator from Utah has stood steadfastly among the obstructionists, voting with these radical liberals at every turn.

He voted *against* legislation that would crack down on criminal actions during riots and campus disruptions. He voted *for* those Senate efforts to force a pullout from Vietnam that would have abandoned the South Vietnamese to the enemy.

During the Moratorium last fall, when demonstrators were demanding what would have amounted to humiliation for the United States, that Senator sent a telegram to the organizers, saying he endorsed the purpose and spirit of the Moratorium. He said, and I quote: "Your cause is just." That cause, my Utah friends, was the cause of sellout and surrender. There can be no cause more *unjust*.

And his more recent criticism of the President on Vietnam has even been quoted by North Vietnamese Communist negotiators in Paris as an effort to undermine our position.

Can such a man conceivably represent the people of Utah?

Laurence Burton, on the other hand, has acted and voted like a man from Utah throughout his eight years in Congress. It follows that his thinking is diametrically opposed to that of his opponent on almost every critical issue.

While his opponent was running up annual ratings by the Americans for Democratic Action that have ranged as high as 100 percent — the radical–liberals' Oscar — Laurence Burton was trying to keep the Congress from spending us into bankruptcy.

On economic issues last year, Congressman Burton was ranked high as a watchdog of the treasury. His opponent rated zero, sharing that big-spender accolade with only two others in the entire Senate — Ralph Yarborough, who has already heard from the outraged voters, and the junior Senator from Montana.

In the last two years your junior Senator has sponsored legislation that would have cost the taxpayers $23.5 *billion* in the first year alone, and would cost $79 *billion* by the time it was fully implemented.

Now this money that your junior Senator would have us sluice out of the United States Treasury is not *his* money, you understand. It's *your* hard-earned money and that of other taxpayers all across this land. Does such a man *really* represent Utah?

Here's the crowning touch: Now that election time has rolled around, your junior Senator is rolling around 180 degrees. Just one week ago, this leader of the big-spending fraternity told a group of accountants meeting here in Salt Lake City that — and I quote him directly — "we need to hold down federal spending to try to achieve a balanced budget."

From now to election day, you can be sure that this big spender will run away from his own record and try to palm himself off as "Frank Moss, the guardian of the federal treasury."

The fact is, your junior Senator is so highly regarded by the radical–liberal cabal that Senator McGovern designated him to receive, along with Senator Gore of Tennessee, the largest initial gifts from the radic–lib kitty raised to save their seats.

In Tennessee the other night, I referred to Senator Gore as the Southern Regional Chairman of the Eastern Liberal Establishment. To be fair, I should acknowledge that the junior Senator from Utah is the *Western* Regional Chairman of the Eastern Liberal Establishment.

I know that Utah wants to help President Nixon carry out the mandate you gave him. The surest, most effective way you can help is to elect Laurence Burton to the United States Senate and send Sherman Lloyd and Dick Richards to the House of Representatives.

And here I want to say a very special word about your splendid candidate for Laurence Burton's first district seat, and I mean, of course, Dick Richards. I have a particularly warm feeling for Dick because he was director of the Republican National Committee's political division and I know that two years ago he was your state Republican chairman. I understand that he's making a very strong and a very powerful race and I assure you that he has our complete backing and I know that you're going to elect Dick Richards to the House of Representatives.

Tonight I would like to discuss a problem of profound concern to all of us that reaches beyond partisan politics and the election of 1970.

A few nights ago in Wisconsin I discussed the general climate of permissiveness that we have fashioned for ourselves and our children since World War II. I referred to it as the "age of indulgence" and I urged that we reinstill a sense of discipline to bring some order into this chaos we have created.

Tonight in Utah, where traditional values are still cherished, I would like to speak further to this subject. For I believe our life as a nation depends on our response to the challenges now being mounted against our basic values.

I particularly would like to discuss one of these that undergirds our civilization and is today under the greatest assault — our sense of decency.

First, let me define what I mean by decency. The dictionary definition is just fine with me:

> Free of anything improper or of suggestions of the immodest, lustful or obscene; not nude, clothed with adequate modesty; indicative or suggestive of virtue or propriety; marked by a combination of goodwill, sincerity, tolerance, uprightness, generosity, or fairness; not cruel, repressive, or vindictive; decent quality, behavior, dress, or deportment.

So a sense of decency embodies moral standards that govern our conduct as civilized people — standards developed over the ages that reflect the will of the majority. It involves respect for the rights of others, a willingness to adjust to the wishes of the majority, and the self-discipline to control our impulses instead of seeking constant and instant gratification. Manners and mores, of course, do change with each generation; but this happens by will of the majority. Through the ages human beings have learned to be decent to each other and respectful of each other's rights even with changes in their social mores.

A seventeenth-century French philosopher observed:

Decency is the least of all laws, but yet it is the law that is most strictly observed.

But if the Duc de LaRouchefoucauld were writing today, about America in 1970, I believe he would have to turn it around and say:

Decency is the most important of all laws, but yet it is the law that is *least* observed.

For today decency is under assault in almost every aspect of our lives, most visibly in the posturing and shouting of obscenities by the scruffy, shaggy sons of the New Left. But it goes even beyond them. This assault now comes from almost every direction, daily, and in volume. It pervades our cultural life and is inflicted upon millions of Americans who deeply disapprove but don't know what they can do about it, since the gates were opened by public permissiveness and by courts more concerned with license of expression than with restraining indecency and vulgarity.

Consider these shabby hallmarks of modern Americana:

— Movies that once would have brought a police raid on a men's smoker are now standard fare at theaters throughout our land. Their advertisements in our paper vie for lewdness and sensuality, almost converting our daily press into pushers of pornography.

— A broadway musical that simulates a sex act and desecrates the American flag is hailed by critics, and is doing a land-office business at the box office. So much so, that it is now branching out into closed-circuit television.

— Four-letter words as old as Chaucer, once surreptitiously scrawled by the nasty-minded on the walls of public lavatories, have become the accepted jargon in some far-out circles and the chic language of those who lionize them whatever their place in society.

— Nudity is now regularly on public display at orgiastic, drug-steeped rock festivals and protest demonstrations flamboyantly staged by social misfits and dropouts to the ecstasy of the media which highlight every aberration. And if you don't see it in the daily newspaper, there is sure to be a big weekly magazine touting a photographic essay on the latest indecent revelations.

— The tabloid newspaper available on every street corner, part of the so-called underground press with a national circulation of two million, features filth in language and pictures as well as expert advice on how to shatter our society with homemade weapons.

— A national pornographic contest is sponsored by a magazine edited and published by students at one of our largest universities, and the college authorities just don't dare to interfere.

And let me digress to say that I happen to know the president of that institution. And I know that man is as strong for an American principle as any man I've ever known but he is virtually handcuffed by the faculty procedures and by a system of college administration that makes it impossible for him to take the steps that he knows he should take.

This intensifying depravity has been encouraged by court decisions, reflecting our earlier wave of permissiveness. It is capitalized on by money-grubbing publishers, movie and play producers, rock festival producers, and record makers who probably wouldn't have this muck in their own homes, but exploit our young for every dollar they're willing to pay.

This erosion of decency has been abetted by a political hedonism that permeates the philosophy of the radical–liberals. They may not openly condone indecency, but they help create the climate in which it flourishes by their inability to say no and their unwillingness to condemn.

The remedy will not be found in the kind of censorship laws which would be promptly thrown out by the courts; it will be found at the box office, the cash register, and in homes where outraged parents will exhibit the courage to say "no, we've had enough" — and will pass that moral preachment to their children. Only nationwide indignation and revulsion will be strong enough to carry the message.

Just today, the lame-duck Commission on Obscenity and Pornography weighed in with its final report. Its views do not represent the thinking of the Nixon Administration. This commission was *not* named by President Nixon. No sir, your honor, it's not our baby.

Credit, or culpability, for that commission rests with those who embrace its conclusions — and, as far as Laurence Burton, the President, and I are concerned — the radical-liberals can have it, free of charge. The only Nixon appointee on that commission submitted the kind of blistering dissent you would expect from a man concerned about decency in America.

We speak often about the quality of life in America. But that quality will only be degraded if the floodgates are further opened and more of this garbage is dumped into the mainstream of American communications. As long as Richard Nixon is President, Main Street is not going to turn into Smut Alley.

We have been told there is no proof that pornography and salacious literature have a pernicious effect on an individual. But, if a man's character is unaffected by the lurid and nasty, then he must also be impervious to any influence of works regarded as beautiful and ennobling.

We do not assume any government's right to legislate private morality. But government does have the responsibility to monitor the public morality — as laws against public indecency clearly attest. And as long as you send men to Congress who will back up the President, and the Supreme Court makes it possible — we are going to have strong laws against pornography and against obscenity. One way to guarantee that is to put into the United States Senate men like Laurence Burton who will support the President's "strict constructionist" nominees to the Supreme Court — and reject those Senators who constantly oppose such nominees, such as the junior Senator from Utah.

Pornography is a truly shabby commercial enterprise according to the New York Academy of Medicine. The reading of salacious literature, "encourages a morbid preoccupation with sex and interferes with the development of a healthy attitude and respect for the opposite sex."

I am not often moved to quote Harvard sociologists but as Professor Pitrim Sorokin has written, permissiveness toward the erotic increases immoral and antisocial behavior. He contends further, ". . . there is no example of a community which has retained its high position on the cultural scale after less rigorous sexual customs have replaced more restricting ones."

As Reo Christenson writes in a brilliant article in *The Progressive*, "The interests of the general American public are considerably more important than gratifying the erotic-esthetic yearnings of the avant-garde."

There is another area of indecency I would like to mention — one in which young people share at least an equal responsibility with adults — and I would hope they can soon be brought to realize it.

I refer to the blatant, calculated disregard for the rights of others that we now see all around us — disregard for civil rights as well as property rights.

Shout down the speaker you disagree with, goes this nihilist philosophy; don't let him finish his message. Shout every four-letter word you can think of since you don't know how to reason or argue from logic. Act like a spoiled child having a tantrum. Prevent civilized discourse; it might enlighten someone.

As for property rights — destroy the other person's property, or in today's vernacular, "liberate" it by "trashing" it.

I could never understand the motive behind this until I recently read an article in a Washington newspaper about the shoplifting that has become common among the vacant-minded fringe of today's young.

These young people, formerly from affluent homes, now live in communes and steal what they need or want from stores. By their code it is all right to steal or "liberate" this merchandise, even from small shop owners. Their rationale: It's striking a blow against the capitalist system.

It was really quite tragic in Washington during a recent demonstration. A poor man was selling hot dogs, and they just rushed in, took his stand over, threw the hot dogs up in the air and out to each other, and it was a big joke. And unfortunately all too many of the press treated it as a big joke. Well, that man was making a living within the confines of the American constitutional system and he has a right to make that living not beset and harassed and interfered with by any group of people ascribing a pseudo-political motive to what turns out to be simply immoral and criminal conduct.

As the editor of a Washington underground newspaper explains it, "[The store owners] rip off the people with their profits, so why shouldn't we rip them off?"

The police complain that when these thieves are caught, nothing happens. A girl who was caught and released by a store manager explained that just about everybody who has been caught — and as she put it "acts scared" — has been let go.

So the practice flourishes and so society continues to yawn. And in the end it all comes back, my friends, to a matter of discipline. When society itself decides to end this permissiveness, this kind of thievery is going to end with it.

And by society, I mean our young as well as our older citizens. Acceptance of indecencies against others, even when you don't participate or approve, is the only encouragement many of these novitiate degenerates need to keep going. Nothing is as important to them as the approval of their peers.

It is time, my friends, for the great silent majority of the young to make itself heard and for those of us in the older generation to listen more closely to what they are saying and back them up. This will do more than anything else to speed a return to decency in our society.

Now I mentioned just a few minutes ago peer-group approval. One of the most effective deterrents to crime is not incarceration, but the stigma that attaches to it. And if the stigma is removed by a belief that the criminal activity is simply to be justified on the basis of an act that's acceptable from a moral sense among those who are adjudging its effectiveness, then we're going to have a lot more crime. The so-called political criminal, political prisoner — you hear that phrase among some of the criminal elements in our society — is a great way to encourage the naïve to not reject the criminal on the basis that he should be thrown out of society.

What we need to do is to convince our young people that there is no such thing as a political motive for thievery and disruption and violence. These are acts that are antisocial in their own nature and should be repudiated on that basis, and those who claim some high and lofty moral cause for that are just not talking sense.

Perhaps America could learn a good lesson from Utah and its people. You dedicate your energies to making the system work. In your history, you have known lawlessness; you have known bare survival; you have known raw confrontation. You know that you can overcome oppression, persecution, and despair with productive, imaginative buildings. The fruits of success in the face of overwhelming obstacles are all around you today in every Utah community, just as they were in the colonizing struggle under the leadership of Brigham Young.

Our Declaration of Independence spoke of "a decent respect for the opinion of mankind." I believe we will earn that respect, along with a much greater self-respect, when we in America show a *new* respect for decency.

October 9, 1970, Phoenix, Arizona
Arizona Republican Dinner

I HAVE one or two things to say tonight at the dinner which I hope you won't find tedious and boring. One of the things that I've been so gratified to see as I have gone around the country — we are just about one-half through this campaign swing — we started on September 10th in Illinois and we have got another half to go — but the thing that is most encouraging to me is wherever I go I see young people, such as the ones here tonight, who come up to me and tell me how interested they are in another point of view penetrating through the prevalent opinion of the radical minority on campus that is so widely distributed via the mass media to the people of the United States.

I'm totally convinced that there is a great movement on the campus at the present time. A movement that is by the students themselves who have become disillusioned with the disruptive tactics and with the attitudes that have been widely publicized of this radical few that prevent intellectual discourse which, of course, is why we have colleges and campuses in the first place. And I see these young people beginning to say: "Well, if these people who are saying this is wrong, why do we refuse to hear them? If their opinion cannot be substantiated in logic, why should we shout them down? Why don't we just hear them and reject what they have to say?" And the young people are beginning to come to the conclusion that the opinions that can be substantiated and the opinions that can be brought to the floor in a way that they are acceptable to the broad cross-section of a free society are the things that are being said by the Establishment and not by those who would tear it apart.

So as we go along, I think we are going to see a great turnover beginning this college year and probably reaching some ascendency by the next semester that begins in February. And it's going to happen because you, in this community, have steadfastly refused to knuckle under to the forces of reaction. To be persuaded from the course of acceptable conduct by those in the community, whether they are elected officials or not, who would have you believe that there is something wrong with the American system. Because I can tell you very forthrightly and honestly, as a person who has traveled the length and breadth of this country and made two trips to Asia in the last year, that there is nothing wrong with this country. Nothing wrong that people like you speaking out won't cure very quickly.

I want to say also that the President sends you his high regards. He has a great affection for the people of Arizona. He remembers that Arizona is a state that has been good to him in the past and he knows that his programs are being wholeheartedly supported here.

It is my pleasure tonight to have with me for the first time on this particular campaign swing my wife who flew to Tulsa to join me this afternoon. Judy, would you come out and? . . .

It's just a little difficult when you are trying to raise a fourteen-year-old daughter to have your wife with you all the time. And I think it is appropriate to have her with me tonight here in Arizona where the people are so warm and hospitable. But I hope the other Republicans throughout the country will understand that the reason she is not traveling with me on every stop is because the first responsibility of a parent is to the child and that's exactly what we are trying to practice.

Thank you very much Senator Fannin, Mrs. Fannin, Governor and Mrs. Williams. Let me disgress here to express my appreciation and that of Judy for the gracious reception we have had here in Arizona, and also for the very thoughtful gifts that you have given us to make us appreciative of our honorary membership in the great Western Fraternity and Sorority.

Attorney General Gary Nelson; Candidate-to-be, Morris Herring, future Congressman; Honorable James Cameron, Candidate for the State Supreme Court; your lovely ladies;

the many distinguished representatives of Arizona public life and the very strong and supportive workers of the Republican party here, particularly those who put together such inspiring fund-raising events as this. I give you the salute of a person who has been laboring in the vineyards of political activity and is impressed with the professional competence and the enthusiasm of this great state.

Before I begin my formal remarks, I want to make this audience aware that as I sat in my very lovely suite in the hotel tonight preparing for this appearance, I was struck by the fact that there were some young people of different opinion outside who were expressing that opinion in a rather unmistakable way.

I discussed this with Senator Fannin and Governor Williams, and we decided that it may be indeed an experiment in democracy of the most meaningful type if we would invite a representative group of these youth to come into this hall this evening and to hear these remarks. And we have in fact done exactly that.

Senator Fannin, as I speak to you, is in the process of inviting and escorting representatives of some of the dissident youth, high school and college students of this area, into the hall. When I finish my remarks, I think it would be only courteous and American and democratic for us to have a few of their representatives come to this platform and make known their thoughts on the remarks I make tonight. Because, after all, this is a free nation not at all founded in any way on the seeds of repression — this is a nation founded on free expression and on the intellectual persuasiveness of individuals' remarks and their thoughts and their beliefs — and I'm sure that we will learn something from tonight and I hope that these . . .

Let me say that it's a privilege to be introduced to the people of Arizona by a man whose record of service as governor and as Senator commands the admiration of the entire nation — Senator Paul Fannin.

I am glad to be here again with my old friend and colleague, Governor Jack Williams — back in a state free of debt, free of fear, and full of faith in America.

I know the charts show that we Republicans are outnumbered here in Arizona. The fact that you nevertheless can send John Rhodes and Sam Steiger to the House of Representatives, and Barry Goldwater and Paul Fannin to the United States Senate, is a tribute to the good sense and independence of Democrats in Arizona who ignore the party label.

Paul Fannin has earned the respect of his colleagues because he is a competent, courageous, hard-working member of the United States Senate. I can tell you this administration values Paul Fannin's counsel.

The President and I are confident that the people of Arizona will reelect Paul Fannin to the United States Senate, that you will send Sam Steiger and John Rhodes back to the House, and put Morris Herring on the Arizona team in Washington.

Paul Fannin was your spokesman on the floor of the Senate when the Central Arizona Project Bill was passed, making thirty years of hopes and dreams a reality.

Paul Fannin is a worker and a doer. He has earned a seat on Senate committees crucial to the future of Arizona. He cosponsored the Environmental Policy Act of 1969, and has been a strong supporter of our antipollution efforts. And that also is why Arizona stands tall in Washington.

John Rhodes has eighteen years of seniority in the House of Representatives. He really knows his way around Washington, and that's another reason why Arizona stands tall in the nation's capital.

Sam Steiger's influence is gaining in Washington with each passing year of service, and that's another reason why Arizona stands tall in Washington, D.C.

I hope the people of Arizona will add Morris Herring to your excellent Congressional delegation. I know of his success as state treasurer, and this proves he has the qualities of fiscal responsibility so badly needed in Congress.

Here in Arizona, your governor has a magnificent record of promises made and promises kept. He has provided firm leadership and has maintained the climate of cooperation, respect and goodwill. He is able to work closely with the Legislature, and you could do nothing more constructive than to reelect Jack Williams.

Tonight I'd like to discuss with you, in a thoughtful way, a phenomenon that is much on the minds of the American people.

A new violence is spreading in America — born not of covetousness for another's property, but for another's mind.

For many decades we have exalted reason and debate as the way to examine our great social issues. When we have disagreed on the proper course for our institutions or government, we have studied, and argued, and engaged in public debate, and in recent years our vast communications network has carried the pros and cons all across the land. Then we all have participated in the decision through our votes for representatives reflecting our views, and we have accepted the results.

When we lost, as we Republicans lost in 1964, we have closed ranks, gone along with the majority, reexamined our position, and prepared to fight again.

Inherent in this process has been a common decency — a respect for the rights and opinions of others, a reciprocal courtesy allowing others to express their views as we expressed ours. Reason and logic and facts have been the cutting tools of persuasion.

But now we see in our midst little groups of intellectual bullyboys whose tools of persuasion are the threat, the blocked doorway, the broken window, the burned building, the bombed research laboratory.

What is most disturbing is that this virus of political violence is now infecting some of our youth — some of whom one day will take up the reins of responsibility and the torch of freedom. And a contemptible aspect of it all is a small group of collaborative adults who encourage the destroyers — some of their teachers, various confidants, their financiers, and other coconspirators with the violent young.

I am referring to people who have declared an intellectual moratorium. Having failed to sell the American people their program for radical change, they have taken to the streets — like the pre-Nazi brown shirts in Germany four decades ago.

They have begun with what they regard as the most vulnerable element in our society — our universities.

They began shrewdly with minor threats and small acts of violence. They counted on the universities' unfamiliarity with intimidation and violence and their deep commitment to reason.

First came demonstrations which disrupted classes and normal university activities, then the blocked doorway, then the broken window.

Some universities, with abhorrence of violence, turned away their eyes; they overlooked and excused disruptive acts as they struggled to understand how any of these young people could possibly do these things.

Then, surprised and encouraged by the feeble response, the radicals regrouped, their numbers now swollen by those who coldly noted their immunity from justice, and they escalated the violence. Then came their demand for a revolutionary change of the university and the society.

When they could not intimidate, they seized buildings. They held deans prisoners in their own offices; they burned the irreplaceable product of years of scholarly research; they fomented riots, forcing the administrators to call in the police to protect lives and property.

To America's shame, a number of great universities were forced to close their doors.

Now we begin to see the conclusion of the radicals' so-called "arguments." We see the beginning of terror. Buildings bombed. Classrooms leveled. Research laboratories ripped apart. Scholars killed.

Fellow Americans, we have tolerated too much of this. And our forebears have built the freest, most productive of all nations. We are going to preserve it.

And as our President said at Kansas State, "The time has come for us to recognize that violence and terror have no place in a free society, whatever the purported cause or whoever the perpetrators may be."

This administration has already begun.

More than six months ago the President called for legislation to curb the bombing terrorists. Finally the Congress appears to have gained a sense of urgency about the problem and now at last, thanks in part to a last minute renewed appeal from the President only this morning, we hope to get this legislation.

I wish some of these radical–liberals in Congress were as vocal about the bombings in the United States as they have been about the bombing in Southeast Asia.

Now, my friends, here let me make one explicit point about Congressional behavior. In indicting Congressional apathy, confusion, sheer cussedness in foreign policy areas, and its generally sluggish performance except when working political mischief — and I have conveyed my feelings on all this before many audiences — I have been referring to the institutional incapability and not to all Congressmen equally.

Frankly, some of these members of Congress, of both parties, are as exemplary American leaders as our country has ever known. In this crime area, for example, Senators McClellan and Hruska have been superb in their service to our country; Senator Williams of Delaware is, in my opinion, as fine a Senator as ever graced the so-called Upper Body; both Speaker McCormack and House Majority Leader Albert have extraordinary records of supporting their President in national security areas, regardless of the President's political party; and there are numerous others, too many to cite here, who have proud and responsible records that I unhesitatingly commend.

But, having said that, and while freely conceding that the House does well on national security while the Senate does well, for example, on crime legislation, I firmly insist that this Ninety-first Congress has let down America in critical respects at home and abroad; and that those who run it, and are running this year, should be held strictly to account by the American people. It is to help my countrymen do just that that I am on the campaign trail.

When disruption and violence erupt on our campuses let us not forget that the one who suffers the most is the student himself:

— It is his class that is disrupted.

— It is his laboratory that is bombed.

— It is his education that is impaired.

— It is his life that is endangered.

I believe the overwhelming majority of students want our help, and they have a right to expect it.

First, though, we must make ourselves aware of the intellectual forces that feed this violence. Have you listened closely to the rhetoric of those who try to inflame and seduce our youth? Have you read the reports of SDS rallies or of those who would free Bobby Seale? Have you read the literature of radical groups that infest the campuses? Have you read the underground press that thousands of our young people have with coffee to start their day?

Let me give one example. Last weekend, a member of my staff and his wife were shopping in Washington, D.C., and were approached by a girl about sixteen years of age. She urged them to buy an October 6 issue of something called the *Quicksilver Times*.

Now, what kind of news was this young lady selling on that quiet corner in Georgetown — news that any young man can buy for a quarter on his way to class?

Half of that newspaper — twelve detailed pages — was a revolutionary bombing manual from the Spanish Civil War of the 1930s.

This manual shows you how — with diagrams and text:

— To make a grenade out of a tin can.

— To booby-trap a telephone.

— To wire a bomb to the ignition of an automobile.

— To make an incendiary bomb.

— To make homemade dynamite.

— To make an electric time bomb that will explode when anyone touches it.

Underground papers of this ilk now have a combined circulation of some two million copies — over twice the daily circulation of the *New York Times*. And now this so-called free press movement, which started in hippie ghettos, has spread from university to the high school.

This is the fuel of political violence.

My friends, it almost defies belief that the young girl who sold this paper understands that she may be contributing to the maiming or death of other human beings. Nor can I believe that her parents are aware of her activity.

Parents and other concerned Americans simply must take time from their busy lives to find out what is happening in our streets and schools and universities.

I am convinced that an aroused public will suppress with moral condemnation and social stigma the purveyors of violence-inciting literature.

It is time to inform ourselves — to speak out in our homes, churches, places of employment, and public assemblies — against the forces of violence in our country.

And it is time for us all to speak with our votes — to reject those people in any party, in any office, who too long have double-talked or talked not at all on disruption and violence.

The attitudes of some men in public life toward political violence is revealing. Wrong in not speaking out earlier — having in effect condoned the escalation of violence — now they compound their errors.

Yes, they call upon radicals to stop their violence, but this is the reason they give, that violence will lead to repression — that our greatest danger today is not from the violent few, but from a repression which could sweep the country tomorrow.

Here is that point made by Senator Kennedy a few weeks ago: "Violence feeds in itself. It breeds reaction and repression. Invoked for the best of causes, it produces counterviolence for the worst of causes."

Political leaders who say this are doubtless well-intentioned but they dangerously err when they credit radicals with idealistic motives.

Nothing could be more naïve. Time and time again the radicals have told us that this system of ours must first be demolished before their brand of progress can be achieved. Their plan, plainly and often stated, is simply this: That their violence will lead us to repress, that our repression will then radicalize the moderates, and this in turn will bring on revolution.

Repression then is the short-term goal of our political terrorists today. Repression for them is success.

So as we move to set our house in order, let us not forget what this country stands for. Pessimists hold that terrorism can be stopped only be repression, just as they mournfully predict that the only cure for inflation is depression. Well, on both counts they are wrong.

Just as we are stopping inflation without recession, so also we will stop political violence without constricting the freedom of Americans. We must not fall into the snare of those who would destroy our country.

What is needed in America, especially in our universities, is a genuine reaffirmation of the revolutionary movement that the founding fathers began two centuries ago — a movement devoted to the elevation of mind and reason — a movement that reaffirmed moral values and rigorous intellectual inquiry.

Let me suggest two principles as part of this credo:

1. No individual has the legal or moral right to initiate physical force or the threat of force to achieve his personal political objectives in a free society.

2. Each individual has an inalienable right to his own life, his liberty and his property. He should never be regarded as simply the instrument of others to realize their goals — whether good or evil.

These two principles are not new; they were embraced in varying forms by the most constructive revolutionaries of the last two hundred years — the founders of the American Republic.

If we wish the young, moral majority, the type of young people that I've seen so many times on this campaign trail, the type of young people who have entertained us this evening, to counter intellectually and philosophically the immoral and violent minority on our campuses and elsewhere, we must join enthusiastically with them in finishing the task so well begun by our founding fathers.

Let us especially remember that the violence mongers among us are but the tiniest fraction of the youth of America. The vast majority of our youth are moral. They are deeply idealistic. They want the very best for this country. They yearn to improve America; they want to reform her where she is wrong, and preserve her where she is right.

This young moral majority want to do this peacefully. We welcome them to the task to which so many of us and so many millions before us have devoted so much of our lives.

Now in concluding, ladies and gentlemen, I have a very sad bit of information to relate to you, because I honestly had hoped that we could indeed bring to the intellectual forum for a rational discourse some of the things that divde us from our dissident youth who insist on the senseless protests, the anti-intellectual mouthings that so many of them have resorted to. The group that we invited in had agreed to have eight or ten of their representatives come and listen and speak and debate, but then the group voted down that agreement. Senator Fannin has just handed me a note that they have refused to appear. And this indeed is the tragedy of our times that there can be no confrontation on a purely intellectual basis. Let us hope that things will improve.

October 12, 1970, Amarillo, Texas
Texas Republican Dinner

I HAVE come here to talk with you about two men I like and admire — one a man from Houston, the other from Wichita Falls — both as outstanding candidates as any state can offer. I refer to your next governor — Paul Eggers; and your next United States Senator, George Bush.

George wasn't born in Texas, and some candidates who can't claim anything else make a big point about that. But George had the good sense and vision and ambition to come to Texas straight out of the Navy after World War II. He believed that the old advice — Go West, young man — was still sound, and he proved it by making not one but two successful careers — in business and in public service.

Some people — some politicians especially — like to live in the past because it relieves them of thinking about the future and acting in the present. Traditions and values die if people don't live up to them every day. George Bush stands in the great American tradition of men who have followed the sun and their dreams to the exciting West.

He's a modern pioneer and the values he lives up to every day — the values of courage, integrity, and hard work — are the fundamental values that made this nation strong and great. George Bush respects the past, but he knows that you can't retreat there. You must have what he has and what modern Texas has — the courage to change, to grow, and to make a new life.

The Texas of today, with its new cities and industries, its universities and medical centers, its abundant opportunities and rewards — this Texas grew because men like George Bush worked to make it grow. The last area of Texas life to change, the one where men of the past dug in the deepest, was in politics. Until not many years ago, it seemed that this state which had led the way into the jet and space age would by stymied in its government by men with horse-and-buggy minds, by an establishment that had no answers, no solutions, no hope and no vision — only the power to resist change at the expense of the people.

But now that establishment is breaking up and being swept away by leaders like George Bush who are in touch with the Texas of today — who are in touch with the problems and hopes of people who *want* to move with the times.

George Bush hasn't just talked about doing more for Texas. He has taken off his coat, rolled up his sleeves — just as he did in the oil fields — and gotten down to work, doing more every day for the new Texas. Unlike his opponent, he can be judged on his record and the results he has achieved.

He tackled the problems of rural development; of the political environment; of crime and campus disorder; of population control; long before these problems were in the headlines. What's more, he came up with real answers — answers that break new ground and apply tested values and fundamental principles to changing circumstances in a truly creative way.

It doesn't take any imagination to dream up ways of spending and wasting the peoples' tax money. For a generation before 1968, that was the standard "solution" for every problem — pour money on it, and maybe it will go away. That solution didn't work — in fact, it made many problems a great deal worse. But in 1968, the people told the politicians still living in the past, the big spenders, that they wanted a change — a big change.

I'm not here today to tell the people of Texas who their United States Senator should be. I am here to ask your help so that we can keep our promise to you. In 1968, we promised a big change. We promised — as George Bush says so well — to get this country back on the track. We promised to put an end to permissiveness and surrender in the face of violence. We promised to end the reign of the Fulbrights, McGoverns, Kennedys, and the rest.

We in Washington need George Bush in the United States Senate so that he can help us keep our promises to you. The big change you voted for depends on getting rid of the obstructionists in the Senate. I can testify personally to the high regard and esteem in which George Bush is held by the President and other leaders in this administration. He will be listened to — and he will be effective.

His opponent, in contrast, might as well stay back in Texas for all the influence he would have with the men who control his party — the Fulbrights, McGoverns, and Kennedys. They don't want any part of the man who beat their friend and fellow liberal, Ralph Yarborough. He would have to vote to keep these liberals in power. Let me put it this way: a vote for George Bush's opponent is a vote to keep William Fulbright chairman of the Senate Foreign Relations Committee. And I don't think that's what Texans want at all.

My friends, from time to time in this campaign I take some time out from the rough-and-tumble of political warfare to reflect on some of the underlying problems of our times. For one thing, there are important things to be talked about, whether it's campaign season or not. And there's this added enticement: it throws my journalistic critics off balance.

Tonight I would like to discuss a subject that goes beyond politics, and beyond most of what you hear from men in public life today.

I want to discuss the causes of unrest. I want to talk with you about the malaise that many Americans feel who do not join in the expression of unrest.

A couple of weeks ago, I explored with some of my friends in Wisconsin cause of unrest — the permissiveness that has permeated so much of our national life and our family lives.

I pointed out that an age of indulgence has characterized the past generation, leaving many of our young people misguided or unguided — Spock-marked, if you will. By following all those instructions about giving children their own way, many parents have given their children the impression that they don't care. As a result, we see the temper tantrums of the militant radicals, and even more important, we see the alienation of a lot of fine young people.

In politics, that same permissiveness has spilled over into our lawmaking and our court system. The result has been an encouragement of violence, a condoning of criminality, a leniency that leads to appeasement of any kind of aggressive conduct, in people as well as in nations.

That age of indulgence, now coming to an end, is one cause of unrest. But let us consider another cause tonight, one that is so obvious it is often overlooked. You may recall a story of Edgar Allan Poe called *The Purloined Letter*. A man had to hide a letter from what he knew would be an intensive search. The searchers tore the room apart and could not find the letter — because it had been left out in plain sight, the last place anyone would look.

The hidden cause of malaise in America is the success — the *success* — of the American system.

Where there is despair, no hope at all — there is no unrest. Where there is hope, there is life and unrest.

Where there is no freedom at all, there is no unrest. Where there is a breath of freedom, there is a powerful urge for more — and predictably there is unrest.

The world saw what happened in Hungary and Czechoslovakia when tyranny experimented with a taste of freedom. The people liked the taste so much, they demanded much more. And only when that little taste of freedom was ruthlessly eradicated did the expression of unrest appear to end in those countries.

In our generation in America, we have seen hope and freedom reborn for millions of Americans.

A generation ago, "one-third of a nation" was described as ill-housed, ill-clothed, ill-fed. Today, less than one-fifth of our people live in poverty. That is an enormous change unparalleled in the history of the world; tens of millions of people breaking the bonds of poverty.

When a man who has had nothing gets something, his natural impulse is not to be humbly thankful, but to want more — that's human nature. And that drive to get more is the power behind the American economic system.

Certainly that progress shakes up the status quo. Certainly it creates new strains in the social fabric when the old rigid lines between social classes become blurred.

When the percentage of people who are poor is cut almost in half in less than a generation, there is bound to be unrest — but it is the kind of unrest that is a sign of progress. Similarly, when black Americans and Spanish-speaking Americans see the gates of equal opportunity open for the first time — they are going to react by demanding their full share of freedom and their full share of economic justice. The result will be new pride, new hope, new impatience — and new unrest. That, too, is a sign of progress within the American system.

And similarly, when young people denounce what they believe to be our obsession with the material things in life, that's also a sign of progress. I say that because a hungry man is rarely an idealist. He is too occupied with the gnawing feeling in the pit of his stomach to spend much time with the still, small voice of conscience in his head.

Much of the unrest we find today among young people comes from the relatively well-to-do. Having been handed the material things on a silver platter, they think they can afford to be contemptuous of them. As Shakespeare pointed out, "He jests at scars who never felt a wound."

And, as Shakespeare also said, "There's the rub." A generation that has had to sweat to earn the good things in life is shocked to see those material benefits sneered at by some young people who take good things for granted. They are properly indignant when they see some young people treat education as a right rather than a hard-earned privilege. That indignation is a source of unrest all its own.

It is a good and healthy thing for young people to decry what they believe to be an undue emphasis on the material at the expense of the spiritual. But it would be better and healthier if they also recognized what has put them in a position of being able to make that criticism.

Some of our young people — by no means all, but some — demean the dignity of work;

407

they scoff at the values of the previous generation as they hold out their hands for the keys to the car.

Now stop and think a moment. Does this mean we were wrong to provide as well as we did? Does this mean that we were wrong to reduce the percentage of our people in poverty? Does this mean that we should never have opened the gates of opportunity and equal justice?

Of course not. It does mean, however, that we neglected to transmit something important during the time we were succeeding in offering our fellow Americans and our children new hope and new freedom.

That "something important" was this: a respect for the system itself that has produced this enormous change for the better.

Only with a renewed respect for the American system itself can all of us gain the perspective that shows the system in its true light; changing, improving, succeeding.

We will never gain that perspective, that necessary respect for the American system, from the lunatic fringe who only want to tear the system down so they can erect nothing in its place.

Nor shall we gain that perspective from the radical–liberal in office today, to whom permissiveness is second nature, and who has swallowed the line that our successful system is a failure.

Nor shall we gain perspective from men who are out of touch with the times — the big spenders of yesteryear who assuage their guilt feelings with huge expenditures of other people's tax dollars. For them the song is over; but the malady lingers on.

We shall gain an understanding between black and white, between the well-to-do and the people beginning to climb the economic ladder, between young and old, by looking to the men who see the American system as it really is — becoming more free and more just with every passing year.

These are the men who do not flinch from the growing pains of progress. These are the men who do not overlook the need to provide food for the body politic, as well as food for thought in the life of the mind.

I speak of men like George Bush, your candidate for Senator, and Paul Eggers, your candidate for governor, and Bob Price, your candidate for Congressman. These are men of balance, when men of balance have been needed as never before. These are men strong enough, experienced enough and open-minded enough to represent the Texas of today and tomorrow — at a time when each of us holds the future in his hands.

And so, my friends, when you hear people running America down; when you see people trying to tear America down — remember the story of the purloined letter. Remember that the unrest around us has largely been the product of our own progress. And I suggest the cure for that unrest is not only an end to the age of indulgence, but a speedup of that progress.

And now, my friends, before I conclude, I want to digress from my text to convey some thoughts I have had on my mind — and especially that come to mind every time I read one of the so-called in-depth pieces on how terrible the Texas gas lobby allegedly is — or how terrible the Texas oil lobby is supposed to be.

There is one particular lobby which shelled out almost four hundred thousand greenbacks in the 1968 election — a lobby you don't read much about in those Eastern liberal papers that are forever putting the screws to the Texas oil industry. I am referring to the so-called Council for a Liveable World whose idea for a liveable world — from my observation and experience — seems to be a world in which America would run around militarily naked in the global arena.

Every measure to slash America's military strength seems to have the enraptured backing of this lobby. They have been fighting against the ABM since 1964 — and their position on ABM has not changed despite the enormous changes that have taken place in both Soviet and Chinese conventional and strategic military postures.

This Council holds alarming leverage over some members of the United States Senate. Take my good friend, Senator McGovern, for example. In 1962 this lobby slipped Mr. McGovern $20,000 to spread around South Dakota in his campaign, and since Mr. McGovern came sliding home with a 600-vote wafer-thin vote margin, it can be fairly said that the Council for a Liveable World won George McGovern his seat in the Senate of the United States.

And so, my Texas friends, if you'd like to have an investment in George McGovern — why, just make out your checks to the Council for a Liveable World.

As for me, I don't think I'll be investing, because one day soon, Mr. McGovern's stock is going to drop right off the big board.

The great dollops of cash this outfit quietly drops, especially into Senate races, should be the subject of a major exposé by the press.

You know, if the American Medical Association's political arm contributed ten dollars to some conservative Senator's campaign, you could read the front page of the *New York Times* the next morning and find out whether it was by check or by cash. On the other hand, this Council for a Liveable World crowd has managed to pump hundreds of thousands of dollars into key Senate races over eight years — and has yet to be given the skeptical scrutiny of an annual, public political audit that is so essential for responsible government. Maybe what I have said here about this organization will help to move this information out of the want ads.

I most certainly hope so, in the interest of open politics in America.

Now, in conclusion, let me remind you that it is up to each and every one of us to go out and work for the victory of men who are the finest products of the American system, and who believe in that system with all their hearts — men like George Bush and Paul Eggers.

October 19, 1970, Chicago, Illinois
Illinois Republican Dinner

MY FRIENDS, before turning to my prepared remarks tonight, I want to relate two stories — stories that show how far America has traveled during the last decade.

In 1960, Lyndon Johnson, campaigning for Vice President with his most gracious lady, was rudely accosted in a Texas hotel by right-wing demonstrators. The news was instantly flashed across the country. Both the nation and the State of Texas were outraged by the insult to then Senator Johnson and his wife.

Two days ago, the President of the United States, campaigning in quiet far-off Vermont, was the target of a shower of rocks thrown by young radical thugs. Any one of those rocks could have seriously injured the President. As *Time* magazine reports, "One narrowly [missed] his head." That physical attack on the President, however, was buried in some news columns and went unmentioned in others.

From these two stories you can deduce one of the great issues of our time — the deterioration of the democratic dialogue — and one of the major goals of this campaign.

I shall say it again to night: Any public man, of any party, who has helped to create the atmosphere of permissiveness — where this kind of obscene outrageous conduct has become so commonplace that it is no longer news — that public man should go down to humiliating political defeat in the election on November 3rd.

My friends, we are advised constantly by the sophisticated media to listen to these young radicals, to ascertain the message behind their unkempt appearance and their filthy words. Well, I have certainly listened — and I'm sorry to report they have nothing to say.

The patience of the American people with these arrogant and amoral misfits should have been exhausted long ago. Henceforth let us grant these radicals, with their filthy slogans and their rock-throwing or worse, the ostracism from American society they have merited. And let us henceforth hold them in the unvarnished contempt their conduct so richly deserves.

Now, let me offer a salute. My warm thanks to the Chicago police for their friendly escort into this great city.

To them, I am sure, this was a predictably competent performance routinely repeated for many visitors. And I am sure it was less demanding than responding to a call for help, or facing sniper fire, or confronting a rock-throwing mob of obscenity-chanters.

But still it was an act of courtesy and service that deserves my thanks — which I happily extend to Chicago's sentinels in blue.

As one who is treated to this courtesy in many cities, I am grateful wherever I receive it. But it is particularly meaningful in Chicago — for here your police have taken shameful abuse. Here, two years ago, they were nationally reviled and, indeed, were insulted as "storm troopers in blue" by a man from Illinois now running for the Senate. I call him Adlai-come-lately on the issue of law and order.

I will have more to say about that. But first I want to commend your excellent Chicago Congressmen whom President Nixon and I want very much in the Ninety-Second Congress:

I refer to as outstanding a group as the Congress has — lovely Charlotte Reid, John Erlenborn, Ed Derwinski, Harold Collier, Bob McClory, and Phil Crane, as well, of course, as your wonderful host of Congressional candidates. They're all badly needed to turn back the legislative saboteurs of nearly every constructive program that President Nixon offers.

Incidentally, I find that Phil Crane and I share an appreciation of unusual words. The other day Phil sent this message: "The next time you pronounce "tomentose exhibitionists" and "troglodyctic leftists," he said, "how 'bout getting in a swing at the_____who are trying to make a shambles of this country." Phil thought that would drive the press right up the wall. I suspect he's right. I had the same reaction.

One further remark about your positively superb Congressional group. I cannot fail to especially recognize the presence here of your distinguished senior Senator, Chuck Percy. I'm delighted he's with us this evening. Chuck was with me as well when we opened up this campaign on September 10th in Springfield; flew in with me from Washington and stood up with me before a great audience. And so I very gladly and warmly recognize his presence with us tonight.

And then there's our fearless comrade in arms, the reliable, stand-up soldier, so long the beloved Leader of the House of Representatives and the dean of all House Republicans — incidentally, my very good friend and an extremely close friend of the President's — Leslie Arends. And there's none finer than Les in the entire Congress.

Nor can I fail to recognize the Republican conference chairman of the House — the articulate, dynamic John Anderson. And also that very senior House member, all along the ranking Republican on the House Interstate and Foreign Commerce Committee, Bill Springer.

Now, Bill Springer is not with us to night. I talked with him just before I left Washington. He had intended to come but, unavoidably, was unable.to accompany me on the plane. But he asked me to convey his best wishes to this magnificent Illinois audience which I do with pleasure.

I will simply say that you of Illinois are tremendously fortunate to have so eminent a Congressional delegation — a delegation, may I add, which I'm sure your delightful Margarite Church still takes great pride in.

And now, back to my basic mission — to help you elect Ralph Smith to that Senate seat that he and Ev Dirksen have so capably filled.

Ever since I opened up against the radical–liberals in Congress on September 10th, they've been after me, full cry. It took them awhile, but they finally found their theme.

The theme is a single, ugly word that they are now spreading across America. That word is "hate."

In New York, where there are three Senatorial candidates, one of the two opposition candidates — the one registered Democrat — labels me "an emissary of hate."

Here in the Land of Lincoln, Ralph Smith's opponent labels me a "peddler of hate."

And to vary the theme, Dr. Spock, for whom I have an absolute minimum of regard — the famous baby doctor whom I loved when he was on diaper rash — labels me a "racist."

And in Virginia, the Democratic candidate for the U.S. Senate says, and I quote him, "We're going to put the Baltimore Greek back on the leash."

Now, of course, these charges are not reported as demagoguery, not name-calling, not ethnic slurs, not divisiveness, not even "escalation of the rhetoric." We hear no whimpering about "polarization" from this mudslinging. And why not? Because we are led to believe that radical–liberals just never stoop to scurrility.

Traveling around the country with me is a very diligent press corps. Rightly it demands the exact source of every statement I make, and my staff always supplies it.

But it is interesting — more than that, it is meaningful — that these radical–liberals have a free throw with their charges of malevolence and racism. No quotations, no facts — only libelous mouthings, which are faithfully broadcast by the media.

Can they conceivably base these charges on my characterizing arrogant elitists and disruptive demonstrators as "impudent snobs"? Maybe they disagree that bombthrowers and obscenity-shouters should be separated from society "like rotten apples."

The fact is that their charges are spurious, and they know it. Ironically, they denounce me for what they are belatedly doing themselves. Their paragon, Senator Kennedy, has just fallen all over himself comparing campus radicals with Palestinian terrorists.

My friends, that odd sound you hear nowadays is the flip-flopping of radical–liberals on law and order.

That screech that rings in your ear is the stripping of gears as these political speedsters switch to reverse from full speed ahead on campus unrest.

Their sensitive antennae can detect an electoral tornado bearing down on them.

And as they frantically change position, those whose views they now ape are charged with being hate peddlers.

I understand their predicament. Once they were sincere. They really believed that an indulgent permissiveness would bring lawbreakers to order and peace. They believed they could accomplish that with this permissive doctrine.

Now, like addicts just off a drug, they suffer. They hurt. They plead for political salvation. They have taken the treatment in prayerful hope that they can reidentify in time with an outraged electorate.

One must sympathize with the distress of a politician as he deserts his conscience, abandons his principles, and surrenders to what he privately believes is a benighted public, poisoned with hatred and racism. And their coat-holding elitist cronies of the far left rush to their defense.

So what do these conscience-stricken people do? No wonder they charge hate-peddling. No wonder a Spock tries to spook the people by charging racism. His crowd knows they are selling out their beliefs, and they absolutely writhe over it.

So they need a release for their fear and frustration and hypocrisy. And who is the lucky outlet? He's Yours Truly — the one who has been turning the spotlight on their scurrying for political cover — their belated conversion to law and order.

So they need a political poultice, and I understand the need. One recalls the words of Franklin D. Roosevelt, in an earlier time, about a different villain: "They hate me," he said. And savoring every word, he added, "I welcome their hatred." Well, I don't solicit hatred from anyone — but there *are* a few political enemies that I'm very proud to call my own.

How ironic it is that here in Illinois I find hate-peddling by a man who bears a name long associated with ethics in politics and with personal integrity.

Recall with me a couple of decades ago. If an Illinois leader named Adlai Stevenson had then been asked, "Are you a liberal?", he would have answered quietly and proudly, "Of course I am." He would not have weaseled, or fudged, or shiftily feigned to be something else — not even at the cost of his election.

411

But a few days ago a politician who bears his name — on television, before the whole nation — went through pathetic contortions to becloud his liberalism. Why? It may cost a few votes.

A decade ago, an ambassador from the proud state of Illinois, representing our country at the United Nations, fervently joined in the search for peace. He worked wholeheartedly with America's allies, even those whose governments failed his concept of democracy, to try to win stability in a tormented world.

But today, in time of war, while President Nixon has been exercising the most delicate diplomacy to search for an end of killing, a politician who now bears that ambassador's name denounces our ally as corrupt and dictatorial.

Maybe it helps his campaign. Maybe it picks up a few dovish votes. But it injures the cause of peace, and it feeds a division that prolongs this war. Maybe it lets a hard-pressed candidate release a frustration, but it certainly is a grave disservice to the American people.

By putting vote-mongering ahead of long-held leftist convictions, by placing a yen for publicity ahead of the nation's striving for an honorable peace, by smearing others in public life — I say that Adlai the Third has demeaned his great name, and the people of Illinois will drive that home on November 3rd.

Yes, on November 3rd, Adlai Third can forget public opinion and go back to his friends in the Third World.

But I came tonight not to talk of the radical–liberal politics of hate.

Instead, I want to talk of hope, and to leave this message.

Hope abounds in our America of the 1970s, no matter how much the faint-hearts and the muddleheads proclaim that it doesn't.

There is solid basis to hope for peace in the presidency of Richard Nixon. Ours is a President who has pressed for a cease-fire in the Middle East; who returns our troops by scores of thousands from Vietnam; who endlessly strives for a cease-fire in Southeast Asia; who proves by his acts and words that he is totally devoted to achieving a generation of peace.

Yes, there is real hope for peace, but only IF —

If the Clark Clifford types would stop encouraging Hanoi to wait for more American concessions.

If radical liberals like Ralph Smith's opponent would stop undercutting our allies.

If the Bill Fulbrights in the United States Senate would stop telling North Vietnam that America is eventually going to tuck tail and run in Vietnam and abandon our ally to aggression.

Yes, if all this were suddenly to happen, our prospects for peace would amply improve.

Second, there is now clear evidence that our hopes on the economic front are being realized. The President has shown that the wild inflation brought on by years of lavish federal spending can be checked and be checked without recession, even as we move from war to peace — one of the most difficult transitions that any President has tried to make. We have cut inflation from a high of 7.5 percent to a present 2.7 percent — and now the economy is moving upward at a sustainable rate.

Yes, there is hope for economic stability IF —

If you of Illinois say no to the political profligates and elect men like Ralph Smith who will hold the fiscal line.

And finally, my friends, there is hope that the monstrous crime rate can and will be checked. Your impatience has held Congress' feet to the fire, and the President has at last gotten some — but still not all — of the tools he's requested to fight crime.

As an example, in Washington, D.C. — where the Nixon anticrime ideas have been most fully implemented — the wave of crime has finally been turned back. It *can* be done.

So at last there is hope that the criminals, the drug pushers, the bombers, the burners, and the looters will be swept from our streets.

There is this hope IF —

If you and your countrymen say no to the radical–liberals — if you join in stopping the permissiveness that has sheltered and cultivated social weeds in America — yes, there is

412

hope if you insist that we have men in the Congress who do not simply talk against crime but are tough enough to pass laws to stop it.

So, my good friends, hope does abound today. Peace, a stable dollar, respect for law and order — these are not the impossible dreams that they seemed to be only a couple of years ago.

There is hope IF —

If you give the President men like Ralph Smith and these fine Congressmen to complete the job that the people of Illinois said two years ago that they wanted done. You gave our President the mandate — now give him a Congress to go with that mandate.

Let us have not hate, but hope in our American politics. And let us turn that hope into reality.

That towering man from Illinois, Abraham Lincoln, expressed it just over a century ago. He said:

"We shall nobly save or meanly lose the last, best hope of earth."

Now the choice, my Illinois friends, rests with you. I urge you to choose to "nobly save" the hope of the world — by working for, by voting for, and by putting your friends and neighbors to work and vote for: men of good sense, men of good will, men of stalwart conviction — and that means Ralph Smith and his associates here tonight.

October 20, 1970, Baltimore, Maryland
Maryland Republican Dinner

IT'S REALLY great to be home — until, of course, the *Sun* comes out! This is the only place I know where being in the *Sun* doesn't make things a bit clearer.

But honestly, I wish the publisher would untilt those editors. The only thing that keeps them from dividing the country is limited circulation.

And, ever since I was in county government, the inflammatory alliteration those headline writers use — like Agnew Assails. I don't know how many times I have seen that alliteration. Frankly, I rather enjoy imaginative alliteration — but I had the impression that my critics felt otherwise.

Happily, there are still a few salubrious morsels on the editorial page — an occasional Yardley cartoon and letters to the editor from precocious people who concede my infallibility. With both Yardley and Ike Rehert, I share an ardent appreciation of the beauty of the Maryland countryside, the Chesapeake Bay and the magnificence of Maryland seafood.

I note that the SDS from Towson State College has made a special effort to make my homecoming memorable. They've been circularizing their flock for days to drum up a bunch of noxious nasties outside. Here — let me read their invitation to our party tonight.

There is a picture of a bomb in the middle of it and it says, "Welcome Agnew back with a blast." And a picture of a bomb and it says, "Dig it, dig it. On October 20th, Tuesday, Vice President Agnew will be at the Eastwind for $100-a-plate fund-raising dinner for J. Glenn Beall. Come for cocktails (Molotov) at 7:00. Dress optional (helmets, heavy boots, etc.). Agnew's speech will begin at approximately 9:00."

It would be helpful, now wouldn't it, if some of the ivory tower elitists, so understandably concerned about air and water pollution, would worry more about the social pollution — and worse — that their permissive prattle invites?

413

I can't tell you how many times across this country I have encountered these obscenity-chanting young dissidents. Thank God, they are a small minority of our concerned young people. But, it is embarrassing to have to face the epithets that they hurl — not for me because I have heard a few epithets in the last two years — but for the women and children who have to walk through that kind of conduct.

In my judgment, we need to find a legal, sound, enforceable way to get tough on obscenity-chanting. No individual's right of free speech should have to provide safeguards for decent women and children having to listen to that filth.

But let's get on with more important things.

For five weeks I've been crisscrossing America, quietly urging the voters to put certain Senators out to pasture.

Along the way I've had a little publicity, generated in the main by the 1970-style reactionaries — people content with the status quo in our Congress. Matter of fact, the whole liberal establishment is aggrieved by my message. They yearn to call me the Maryland Crab.

The Congressmen I've given attention to out across the country are what I generously call radical–liberals — the people who are bad on foreign policy, bad on defense, bad on spending and bad on permissiveness but who now hope the voters will themselves go permissive and will forget and forgive. You've probably noticed lately they have been desperately scrambling from the radical left toward the respectable political center in the hope that a voter memory lapse will save them on November 3rd. Then for another six years they can be carefree, independent, and irresponsibly radical–liberal again.

Well, that's not going to work. The multitude of people I have been talking with from New York to California won't buy that line. They *do* remember what these Congressmen have done, they will neither forgive nor will they forget. I can tell you one thing: They're flat out of patience with people who have arrogantly voted in Congress as if they have life tenure and no constituency but themselves. The American people are determined to hold these Congressmen accountable two weeks from today.

Marylanders know firsthand the dilettante kind of Senator I'm talking about. We have a homegrown example of our very own, and his day of reckoning is at hand. All the advice he can get from Hyannisport — or from his elitist friends in Maryland — won't bail him out.

The people know he's in tune with the times — but they also know it's only the *New York Times*.

But before we get into the campaign, how about those Orioles! How about that Billy Ray! The way they wrapped up the World Series was one of the greatest championship displays of all time. From a dyed-in-the-wool Colt fan, that's saying a lot.

This year we've got the batting order to work over the fast curve balls of the radical–liberals in Congress. Beall will ring the bell, and Blair will hit like Paul Blair did this year in the Series.

We've got some other candidates like Glenn Beall around the country who are going to help us replace the radical–liberals in Congress. When that happens, we are going to have a Congress the President could work with instead of being obstructed every time he moved creatively in foreign affairs or national defense, every time he tries to curb inflation, every time he seeks to reform the federal bureaucracy.

He will get that cooperation, fellow Marylanders, with your help and the help of other good people in the United States. That's why the President and I are on the campaign trail. We deeply believe an informed public will demand a more responsive Congress; we believe you want — no, that you *demand* — an end to the permissiveness that has undermined American institutions and undermined American beliefs. And we get that result only by electing candidates who represent that thinking, not of a self-styled elite, but of the great silent majority.

My coming home on this political mission is a welcome assignment. I've enjoyed going out among you to shake hands with so many old friends, and I apologize that I'm certain in my meandering I must have missed quite a few others. I hope that before this affair is over or certainly in the near future on other trips to Maryland for this fine campaign team, I'll have a chance to shake hands with every one of you.

But we have two candidates at this head table who lead our ticket and who are my very close friends. I have worked long and intimately with both of these men, two of the finest young men in government anywhere in the United States: Glenn Beall and Stan Blair. These men will give Maryland the kind of creative, imaginative, strong leadership in years to come that you're entitled to have.

Now first, a few thoughts about the man in whose honor we have gathered tonight. Glenn Beall is the gifted son of a talented father whose distinguished service led him from the Maryland Legislature to the House of Representatives to the United States Senate. Truly a fine man — I regret he is not able to be with us tonight — and a man whom I have deeply respected and admired during my entire political career.

At the time I came into politics, the senior Glenn Beall had already compiled a record of outstanding service. On Capitol Hill he had the reputation of being in closer touch with his constituents than probably any other man in Congress. His weekly newsletter was widely circulated, quoted, and reprinted, and was a model in Congress. He thought like his constituents thought, he voted for the direction he considered that his constitutents wanted to take, he represented his people, and he represented them faithfully and well.

But then he came up against a young opposition party politician bearing another proud Maryland name.

Now this young man did an unusual thing. He did not campaign against the senior Glenn Beall, or attack him, or question his intelligence, integrity, or service to the people of Maryland. Instead he assailed the state leaders of his own party, particularly his party's governor, Mr. Tawes. And he promised a new day in Democratic politics in Maryland. He pledged to reform his party, to bring new blood and fresh young views into the government in Annapolis. He waged such a stirring crusade that a visitor in Maryland would have thought he was running, not for the Senate, but for governor.

As U. S. Attorney, he had obtained indictments against two leading Democrats; and he had promised a total party housecleaning. The people took him at his word and trustingly put him in the Senate.

Well, as Marylanders now sadly know, Joe Tydings went to Washington, began socializing with Georgetown elitists, and forgot both his promises and the folks back home. He did not reform his political party, he did not offer new candidates for the governorship or for Congress or the legislature. And, finally, he scurried back this year to embrace the present governor — a product of the machine he so recently excoriated — he not only embraced him, but he beseeched his endorsement. He now has that endorsement.

The fact is Glenn Beall's opponent has been so busy running up a liberal voting record in Congress — so busy living it up in Manhattan, Hyannisport, and Georgetown — that he has had no time to find out how his constituents felt about the way he was representing them on the great issues of the day. And now, this being an election year, he has been desperately trying to cozy up to the people by a cleverly executed crab-walk to the political center.

My friends, his record is there for all to see. It is a classic radical–liberal record, and he cannot fox the people into thinking otherwise. The people of this State have had six years of intransigence, six years of patronizing arrogance, six years of self-representation from this young man who preaches high ethical standards but whose own standards raise questions. On November 3rd we are going to fix it so he can spend full time on his business interests.

How fortunate it is that at this moment the son of the man who so ably represented Maryland in that Senate seat is now trained and ready to enter the United States Senate. Glenn Beall stands all the way with the people of Maryland. You won't find him frustrating the President's efforts to achieve peace with honor in Asia or frustrating the President's efforts to end inflation, curb disorder, and return balance to the Supreme Court. He will stand with the people of this State on such issues, and he couldn't care less what the McGoverns, Bayhs, or Fulbrights say or think.

I've got to digress here a minute to tell about an incident that happened a couple of months ago when my golf prowess was much in the news.

The President — being a cogitating, active politician in the off-hours when he doesn't have to be running the serious efforts of the day — having a relaxing time one evening after the appointments of the day were finished, said to me:

"Why don't you play golf with Senator Fulbright?"

Now I can see a thinly veiled insult as well as the next person. But if there is anything I'm going to be, it's a loyal Vice President; and I had to tell him straight just as I would have to tell you.

I said, "Mr. President, I would like to accommodate you. There is very little that you could ask me that I wouldn't rush to do and do with enthusiasm — but to play golf with Senator Fulbright raises some serious overtones I'm not sure, Sir, that you've considered.

"First of all, you are aware of my proclivity for errant shots. And just suppose, Sir, that I hit one of my typical bad shots and it struck Senator Fulbright. Well, he would probably react to that violent, antisocial assault the same way that he acts when our enemies violently and antisocially assault the interests of the United States.

"And, Mr. President, I would hate to be kissed on both cheeks on a public golf course."

Now let me move to another fine young man who is here tonight. Before I do, let me return to our guest of honor briefly. During my two years as governor, I had the good fortune to have this experienced young legislator, Glenn Beall, as Minority Leader in the house of Delegates — he was my right arm on the floor of the Legislature.

Believe me, sometimes the going wasn't too easy. You could always depend on Glenn Beall. Not only to be staunch and steadfast in his support of the administration, but to use his beautifully persuasive powers to coax several Democrats who were amenable to reason to support our programs. He was universally respected in both political parties, and I found his counsel sound and wise.

In Annapolis he worked for legislation to control pollution, improve the environment, and strengthen local law enforcement. When the time came to take a stand, he stood up and talked out and held his ground.

Glenn Beall's voice is heard at the White House as well as in Congress. I can tell you that our President has a great admiration for him. When you elect him on November 3rd, he will bring the people of Maryland the full-time representation and close attention that has long been associated with the name of Beall in Maryland.

In Washington these past two years, he has ably represented his Maryland District in the Congress. He has been instrumental in obtaining fuller employment for industries in the state and in obtaining construction funds for the long-sought Bloomington Dam in Western Maryland. He sponsored legislation that for the first time brought House passage of a bill — as has previously been mentioned here tonight — of a bill to create a national park along the C & O Canal.

Now, another close friend of mine is running for an office that I personally know and understand — the governorship of Maryland. Stan Blair can — and I believe Stan Blair will — give Maryland the strongest leadership it has ever had from the statehouse.

That's a pretty heavy endorsement coming from a former governor, isn't that right, Governor McKeldon?

As you know, he was secretary of state and my closest advisor when I was governor — the man I depended on to do a job right and the one I entrusted with top managerial responsibilities. I could always count on Stan to stay cool under fire and offer sound recommendations. And, as you also know, I asked Stan to accompany me to Washington as my chief of staff after I became Vice President. He has accomplished wonders in effectively organizing my office. He would still be my main reliance had he not made this race for governor.

Stan Blair is making his own race for governor, and I have no doubt at all that he will show ten times the executive leadership that we now see in that office.

Despite the handicaps that he or any other Republican have in running for office in our state, the people have a clear choice two weeks from today.

If they want strong, imaginative leadership, they are going to vote for Stan Blair.

If they want innovative programs and modernization of the state government, they are going to vote for Stan Blair.

If they want a state administration that will work with the national administration in returning power to the people, they will vote for Stan Blair.

If they want a governor who will stand up to pressure groups and has the character and strength to say no when it needs to be said, they will vote for Stan Blair.

Let me digress from my text for just a moment to say that I am invariably tired of hearing from some of our enemies who seek the election of the incumbent governor, a product of a ballot of our legislature and not of our people, those people who attempt to promulgate an image of infallibility as far as his reelection is concerned.

Now you know and I know from previous experience in the State of Maryland and other states in this country, that irrespective of how interested the people are in an election, elections are won or lost in the last two weeks of the campaign. And starting tonight, this group can go forth from this great hall filled with enthusiasm for Glenn Beall and for Stan Blair and put both of these candidates across the wire on November 3rd if we really want to do it.

A final thought I want to emphasize regarding the Maryland gubernatorial race. Time and time again, both here and out of state, I have been asked whether the election of the incumbent governor will amount to a rejection of Ted Agnew by the voters of Maryland. The tactic is obvious, and the purpose is transparent. We all know that Stan Blair's race against an entrenched machine is an uphill race, but it's a winnable race. The opposition would like to discourage me from speaking out for Stan. Well, it just won't work. I am proud to stand up for one of the ablest men I have ever known.

But in the final analysis, my Maryland friends, thoughtful people know that an election is won or lost by many factors. The principal ingredient is the candidate, and the support he is able to rally around his cause. No outsider can win or lose an election.

In Stan Blair you have an outstanding candidate with the capacity to win on November 3rd. Whether he does or not depends on you, not on me.

The present state administration is the epitome of the politics-as-usual that Senator Tydings promised to change six years ago. Now he has embraced it in a desperate attempt to save his political skin.

I regarded my election to the governorship four years ago as an expression by the people that they still wanted that change. I say, let's complete this critically important job by sending to the United States Senate and the governorship Glenn Beall and Stan Blair.

Now, my friends, I want to leave you with just a few observations about the national scene. A scene that requires the intense concentration of the members of Congress, a scene that requires the assistance of dedicated young Congressmen such as your candidate for the United States Senate, J. Glenn Beall.

A new attitude prevails in Washington since Richard Nixon became President — an attitude that needs to be fortified in this election.

It is an attitude of toughness at home toward the anarchist and the criminal — on the campus as well as on the street — and a sense of compassion for their victims.

Too long we've heard too many tears shed for the criminal to make certain he had every possible safeguard and rehabilitative device one could design or encourage for his assistance. Now we need a little sympathy for the victims of that crime. We need an attitude of respect for the law — and the men who enforce the law — and a respect for America's institutions.

It is an attitude of determination to curb inflation in this Nixon Administration and restore stability to the dollar, a realization that there is a limit to what government can spend without bankrupting the nation.

It is an attitude of steadiness, sureness, and sanity in world affairs. Against vociferous opposition from the radical–liberals in the Senate, this President has renewed an attitude in foreign affairs held by five Presidents before him; and that attitude is that America should stand by her pledges around the world and help other nations help themselves in resisting naked aggression.

So there has been no tucking tail and running in Vietnam. Instead the South Vietnamese have been strengthened to defend themselves. And while this has been going on, our troops have been coming home. Our President has kept his word.

I know from my recent travels around this great land that these new attitude in Washington are shared by the majority of the American people.

In closing, let's bank one aspect of this campaign right back into the side pocket. In politics, you know, one can tell when he's getting results because the oppositions lets out a scream. I opened up on the radical–liberals in Springfield, Illinois, on September 10th; and ever since then the screams have been rising.

But they haven't bothered me. Indeed, I find them encouraging. But let's understand what these people are trying to do. This rising chorus makes my rhetoric absolutely pallid.

For example, Adlai Stevenson calls me a peddler of hate and so does the ADA. Dr. Spock gets spookier and calls me a racist. Various commentators and columnists depict my message as one of division, discord, fear, and polarization. Let's see what that really means.

What it means is that these people have been caught red-handed in the open field making off with Uncle Sam's watermelons. All I've done is to administer the buckshot you know where!

Of course, they wince; and, of course, they wail, and they will cry still more. But, my friends, let's get this straight. When a high elected official fights our President tooth and nail on a foreign policy, he's asked for it; and I gladly give it.

When a high elected official chronically undercuts the President's national defense efforts, he's asked for it; and I'll gladly give it.

When a high elected official has pampered and encouraged social misconduct, he's asked for it; and believe me, I'll give it to him in spades.

I say the most positive campaigning in this day in time is to take on those people who are dead set on blocking the President's efforts for peace at home and peace abroad. Really positive campaigning is to call their hand, and let the American people know.

Let them know loud and clear that their elected representatives are a barrier to progress, and for America's sake they have to be moved out of the way. And that's the heart of my message these past six weeks. It's a positive message. It's a crucial message. I believe deeply in the truth of it, and I'm going to continue to expound it.

My friends, I can tell you that the people are listening. I believe that you of Maryland are also listening just as your countrymen are listening all across this country. And so, on November 3rd, I believe you will elect Glenn Beall to the United States Senate; and I believe you will elect Stan Blair to the Maryland State House.

And then in his retirement, Mr. Tydings and his radical–liberal soulmates who are also destined for retirement this year, can reflect on how and when they failed the people they were supposed to represent. Thank you very much for coming tonight.

October 29, 1970, Wichita, Kansas
Kansas Republican Dinner

AS ALL OF you know, I am here on political business, but before I get into that, I would like to speak personally for just a moment.

All America grieved with you over the tragedy that befell the Wichita State football team and its coaches and followers. It was a tremendous shock not only here but throughout the country as well. I salute their teammates for going out last week, because I know it took great fortitude. They have won our admiration, and I know you are deeply proud of their courage.

I have learned since coming here that the first home game since this tragedy occurred will be played day after tomorrow. I wish I could stay and attend — but I am sure that all of you will be there to give these fine young men your full support.

Now, in the final week of the campaign, it is good to be in this heartland region. For Kansas is as typical of America as apple pie. Your great Kansas son, Dwight Eisenhower, expressed it so simply and well in his famous Guildhall Address. "I come," he said, "from the heart of America."

Indeed, you of Kansas are the heart of America — and in many ways, the heart of Republicanism. You do not, for example, send politically hybrid delegations to Washington. You have two thoroughly outstanding Republican Senators — Jim Pearson and Bob Dole. The President leans heavily on them for advice and assistance — particularly that master of verbal karate, Bob Dole. Bob enjoys nothing more than to flush out and scatter the Senate macropygia, the pigeons or cuckoo doves whose flutterings are led by Senator Fulbright.

Your House Congressional delegation is also distinguished and universally respected by their fellow House members — and count on these five able Republicans to return to the House when the Ninety-Second Congress organizes next January. Let's take a moment to recognize each of them:

Chet Mize, a top legislator going after his fourth term from the 2nd District. Incidentally, this afternoon I saw in your paper that the Democrats are using one of the oldest stunts in the trade against Chet. The governor is reported as promoting a rumor that Forbes Air Force Base in Chet's district will be closed. Well, let's spook that goblin here on the eve of Hallowe'en. I flatly and unequivocally tell you that there is not, nor has there been, any administration plan to close Forbes Air Force Base or to reduce the level of operations there. Should the Democratic-controlled Congress ordain otherwise by severe cuts in the defense budget, that's the problem of the governor's party, but our administration is out in the clear on this one.

Moving on, now, to your other Congressional races, I find Larry Winn is up for his third term from the 3rd District despite the contrary notions of a retiring lieutenant governor. The issue here, I should think, is *representation*, not a household product.

And here in your 4th District, here in Wichita, you have Garner Shriver, dean of your delegation, returning for his sixth term — a powerful man on the prestigious Appropriations Committee. You will certainly want to keep him on the job!

I refer, of course, to your attorney general for the past two years — Kansas' next governor — Kent Frizzell. He has strong statewide support, as he proved in the primary election; and he is firm and outspoken on respect for law in the street and on the campus. At the same time, he has a broad understanding of local and state government. He was president of the Wichita Board of Education for six years and served four years as a state senator before election as your attorney general in 1968. Kent Frizzell defeated four candidates and captured sixty per cent of the vote in carrying all but seven of the 105 counties of Kansas in the Republican primary for governor this year. This looks like a pretty positive endorsement to me.

There are two other major factors in his favor. First, his opponent has proven himself ineffectual in a legislature of the opposite political party. And second, ignoring history and tradition, his opponent is trying to accomplish what no other Kansas governor, except his father, ever tried — to win a third straight term.

He should go down to defeat. For he has spent state reserves of $97 million; he has increased taxes on beer and cigarettes and income; and he can claim that he has put a lid on property taxes only because the Republican-controlled legislature forced it last year. Kent Frizzell has pledged not only to restore fiscal responsibility to Kansas, but also to the governor's personal budget as well. He has pledged to reduce his personal budget ten percent across the board.

So, my friends, Kent Frizzell is my kind of man — one who favors returning power to the people. I regard that as one of the most important differences between Kent and his opponent.

419

Let me return for a moment to one of our all-time favorite Kansans. General Dwight Eisenhower, in his book, *Crusade in Europe*, recalls the night in Germany when the American forces were preparing to cross the Rhine in one of the crucial final moves in World War II. General Ike took a walk during the bombardment and fell in step with a soldier, who was silent and seemed depressed.

"How are you feeling, son?" the general asked him.

"General, I'm awful nervous," the soldier said. "I don't feel so good."

"Well, you and I are a good pair," Ike replied, "because I'm nervous too. Maybe if we just walk along together to the river we'll be good for each other."

Ladies and gentlemen, in a way that suggests how our President approaches government. He knows that we have difficult problems in this country, and he knows they concern the American people. He, too, is concerned about these problems and is not hesitant to admit it. But he believes very deeply that if we "just walk along together," the President and the people, we'll draw strength from one another — and we'll solve our problems.

So the President has proposed that we Americans do exactly that, and in a new and progressive way. He has proposed that the federal government share some of its revenue with the state governments. This program has been widely acclaimed by members of both parties. It will go far toward restoring the proper balance between the federal government and the states and will be a key factor in accenting the power of the people.

But the people of Kansas will not benefit from that program if they put their two-term governor back into office for a third term. Because Robert Docking has stated unequivocally that he opposes revenue sharing. He opposes this bold, imaginative new approach to the distribution of resources in America. He opposes returning power to the people.

Now let's visit rather seriously about this "power to the people" idea.

One night recently, at one of our rallies, I saw a sign carried by a bearded, unkempt demonstrator who thrust it arrogantly forward. The sign read: "Power to the people."

It saddened me as I thought how this slogan has been twisted into a radical rallying cry. "Power to the People" has come to symbolize tearing down representative government, and substituting mob rule for the most successful free system in all the history of mankind.

The phrase — Power to the People — has an ancient tradition and an honorable one. I say it's time we took it back.

During the last decade we lived through an era of unprecedented growth in the federal government. Since 1960, federal spending has more than doubled; the number of federal programs has ballooned to well over 1,000; and the size of the federal bureaucracy has swollen to almost three million people.

Over these years we watched with trepidation as the federal bureaucracy grew; and as it expanded, we saw it overwhelm and obliterate much of the power historically exercised by our countries and cities and states. But far too few of us were troubled enough to arouse America against the inexorable flow of power away from the people to the federal professionals in Washington. To be sure, we *did* sense the danger, though we failed to react soon enough to come to grips with it. Eleven years ago, the Gallup Poll posed this question to the American people: "Which of the following do you think will be the biggest threat to the country in the future — big business, big labor or big government?" At that time only twenty percent of those who responded picked big government as the greatest potential threat.

But the question was asked again two years ago — after almost a decade of an expanding federal presence in our society, and after almost a decade of a Congress increasingly dominated by radical–liberals.

That poll two years ago showed a sharply increased apprehension about big government. Over half — fifty-five percent — of those who responded named big government as the greatest potential threat to our country.

Well, that's not really surprising. I have seen how the arrogance of power operates. I saw it when I was governor; I see it in Washington. And the public can sense it.

You can see it in meetings where men assert that it would be somehow "dangerous" to allow state and local officials to run their own programs.

You can see it in cavalier acts and judgments on the part of men who live thousands of miles from those whose lives are directly affected by their decisions.

You can see it in the haughty demeanor of bureaucrats, some of whom are vested with immense power, yet never face the test of the ballot box.

I know at least some of you have experienced this yourselves. For example, have you, as a businessman, ever tried to appeal a bureaucratic decision that deeply affected your company?

Have you, as a local government official, ever applied for a grant-in-aid program to get back some of the dollars your community sent to Washington? Have you, as a senior citizen, ever tried to obtain benefits designed to help you in your need?

And have you, as a plain ordinary guy, ever received a cold bureaucratic rejection of a request for information — or just no answer at all?

My friends, it is time to reverse this flow of power to Washington. It is time to channel some of this excessive power back to the people.

Over the years something else of profound importance has been happening. More and more people — particularly our young people — have drifted into a sense of alienation from their society and government. Now, these sons and daughters of those who inertly watched the voracious growth of the federal government, become prey for radicals who Machiavellianly shout "Power to the People."

Well, we know that, when the radicals scream this slogan, they don't mean it as you mean it. Or as I mean it. Instead, they are thinking of ways to place that power in the hands of an elite. They want to smash the system — and they want to rule over the shattered remains.

Well, I say we must not — and we will not — let them do it.

My friends, our nation has been threatened many times before — from within and without — and we have survived. We have emerged from each of these confrontations stronger than before. And we will do it again.

There is a profound meaning — a very good and proper meaning — to the phrase, "Power to the People." That meaning is far too important to the future of this free society to allow a handful of anarchists to take over and debauch it.

Power to the People was the fundamental that guided our founding fathers as they crafted the most perfect political document ever created by man. Government, they believed, should serve the people — a free people should not serve the government. Every phrase, every paragraph of the Constitution of the United States reflects in some degree that root thought.

But a government whose ideal is responsiveness to all individuals in the society is difficult to sustain. Two essentials are: first, a basic political structure, and second, responsible officials.

Power to the People cannot survive in a society of dictatorship or mob rule.

It requires a constitutional republic — and we have such a system today.

But we still need more than the correct form of government; we need men who will act on what they believe, who will do what they know is right.

Without the vigilance of men like Senators Pearson and Dole and your fine Congressmen in Washington, Power to the People can be eroded.

Without the right men in the state capitols — men like Kent Frizzel — the states can become puppets of arrogant Federal bureaucrats.

One great issue of the 1968 campaign revolved about which philosophy of government this nation whould follow in the last third of this century. The two previous administrations had an approach that *began* with government. Richard Nixon pledged an administration that would begin with the *people.*

And we have begun.

For the first time in years, a President has sent proposals to the Congress that would return power — real power — to the people. In addition to the revenue sharing I have been discussing, he has proposed a manpower training reform to return the control of training programs to the States and metropolitan areas.

421

He has proposed reform of the federal grant-in-aid system by consolidating it and simplifying it.

He has proposed to eliminate over $2 billion worth of worthless government programs.

Such moves are part of what we describe as the New Federalism. They are beginnings of a studied policy which aims to decentralize and to reprivatize. If a government program is best managed locally, then we say local officials should run it. If a government program is not needed or can be run better in the private sector, then we say — do away with it.

But what has happened as President Nixon has tried to return Power to the People? At every turn, he has been met with obstruction from a tong of radical liberals.

The President has very earnestly tried. But where *is* the revenue-sharing legislation — where *is* the manpower training bill — where is grant-in-aid reform — where is the economy act to save the taxpayers $2 billion this year?

You know where they are: They are buried in the committees and subcommittees of a Congress whose passive resistance would put a Gandhi to shame. No wonder the prestige of Congress has ebbed to its lowest level in five years.

Yes, my friends — it's high time to return power to the people. President wants to and the people want it — and with your help, with your votes, the next Congress of the United States will make a beginning.

For doing this absolutely requires elected officials who will make this philosophy part of their everyday lives. For example:

Power to the People means that your Representatives remain responsive to the voters of your State.

It means not becoming indebted to Eastern radical–liberal slush funds like the Council for a Liveable World, or Senator McGovern's private lobby.

It means your Representatives must speak for, must support, must vote for legislative measures which would further decentralize the federal bureaucracy.

It means fighting for innovative, basic reorientations of the federal system — measures like revenue sharing and manpower training reform.

Power to the people means your Congressmen and Senators should vote to eliminate — that's right, cut out, not cut back — any program that is no longer needed or that could be run better in the private sector.

It does not mean ignoring economy proposals such as President Nixon sent to Congress this spring.

Power to the People means having Representatives who respect the skill and the knowledge of every workingman in America, who understand how hard a man has to work for what he gets — Representatives, therefore, determined to keep the workingman's taxes down.

It does not mean contempt for the working people of America as "unthinking masses" and spending their tax dollars as if they were federal property to be dispensed as federal largesse.

Finally, it means a Senator or a governor or a Congressman who practices the principles he preaches, a man who makes you proud when you tell your children you voted for him.

Four days from now, the power of the people will be felt throughout the country — not by a shout, or a threat, or blasting a building, but by pulling the most powerful lever our system has — the lever on the voting machine.

That's when you will determine whether we get on with returning Power to the People, or whether we start back along the road of increasing government interference with our lives.

That's when you will decide whether or not you want man who believe in strong state and local government, who will fight for the rights of the states and localities — men who can and will assure us effective and responsive government.

And so I take my stand with men who will return power to the people — men like Kent Frizzell in Topeka — men like Keith Sebelius, Chester Mize, Larry Winn, Garner Shriver and Joe Skubitz — men like Dick Seaton. Set out and elect them, my friends, and we will move on forward toward an even better America.

October 30, 1970, Belleville, Illinois

MY FRIENDS, we are at the close of a campaign that history will record as one of the most crucial of the postwar era. It is surely one of the most important elections in our lifetime.

For this election will give an interim response to the great question that confronts us as a people. And that question is this: will the future of the United States be guided by that small ingrown and parochial band of Eastern intellectuals who guided the social . . .

[To demonstrators:] Now wait a minute. That wasn't you. I said intellectual. I'll get to you in a little bit.

. . . Eastern intellectuals who guided the social and political policies of the determined by a new majority — the moderates, centrists, and conservatives led by the President of the United States?

Now that choice is nowhere more clear than it is right here in Illinois. No election is more crucial to that great decision than the contest between the President's candidate, Ralph Tyler Smith — and his opponent, the spokesman for Eastern Liberal Establishment.

This campaign is also going to determine the character and the operation of the United States Senate for perhaps the next decade. On Tuesday next we will give our country one of two things: Either we're going to give it a Senate that will work with your President for an early and honorable end to the war, and end to inflation, and an end to the disruption in our society, or a Senate that will go the other way and produce a deadlock in democracy — a political stalemate for America.

My friends, our country faces far too many problems at home, and far too many problems abroad, to tolerate perpetual controversy and an unproductive standoff between your President and a Senate in the grip of a band of radical–liberals.

You can break that logjam on Capitol Hill by working to defeat the radical–liberal candidate from Illinois — and by working to elect Ralph Tyler Smith to a full Senate term.

Now let me digress for a moment. I spoke up for Ralph Tyler Smith on September 10 — the first day of the campaign for me, and in your capital of Springfield. I spoke up for Ralph Tyler Smith on October 19 in the heart of Chicago.

But I am specially pleased, in these final moments of this campaign, to visit downstate in the part of Illinois that is Ralph Tyler Smith's home. Just as Ralph has fought in behalf of the great cities of this country, like Chicago, so also, Ralph Tyler Smith, as a downstate man, will fight for sometimes different interests of downstate Illinois. And Ralph, the needs and concerns of rural America, and of small-town America, need to be heard in that Senate, as you know, just as much as does the voice of metropolitan America.

Now before moving on to discuss the issues at the heart of this campaign, I would like to speak out for the entire Congressional slate in Illinois — and to single out two candidates in this immediate area. They are first of all Scott Randolph, who is waging a tough race against a long-term incumbent. Scott, you have our best wishes on November 3rd — and keep pouring on the coal. We're strongly behind you.

And the other race features a fighting lady Republican, Phyllis Schlafly, from Ralph Smith's home town of Alton. Phyllis is a dynamic woman who has the courage of her convictions; and on November 3rd, we're going to see an upset victory for this Republican leader over in the 23rd District.

Now, my friends, look for a moment at the great issues at the heart of this campaign.

First, is the war in Southeast Asia. In twenty months President Nixon has sharply reduced our involvement; . . .

423

[To demonstrators:] You fellas ought to try it over there for a while like some of the other young people. Because some people have the guts to go you don't have to.

. . .President Nixon has cut the cost of the war to American taxpayers in half; he has already scheduled the withdrawal of half of the American troops who were in Southeast Asia when he took office; he has reduced American casualties to the lowest levels in almost five years.

My friends, these are spectacular accomplishments that all the President's caterwauling critics moan about but not one of them could have brought about.

All right then, on the war in Asia — what then is the choice for Illinois? It comes down to this. Mr. Stevenson would go to Washington; throw in his lot with the radical–liberals; help keep Bill Fulbright as Chairman of the Foreign Relations Committee — and undercut the President's foreign policy on every front.

On the other hand, Ralph Tyler Smith will stand in the great bipartisan tradition that politics stops at the water's edge. He will return to Washington and stand where he has already stood — with the President of the United States for peace with honor in Asia.

If you want the foreign policy of the United States made by George McGovern and Bill Fulbright on the network news — then vote for Mr. Stevenson, because that's what he wants, too. But if you want the President whom Illinois elected to make our foreign policy — to make peace for America — then send to Washington a man who will support the President in that effort — send Ralph Tyler Smith back to the Senate for six more years.

On the question of order and justice in this society, you know where your President stands; you know where Ralph Tyler Smith stands.

Since the President has taken office, he has proposed thirteen major pieces of anticrime legislation to deal with the bombings, the terror, the violence, the disruption, and the filth that rose to flood tide in our society over the last decade. And Ralph Tyler Smith has stood with him and fought alongside the President for every one of those measures.

My friends, the only reason the President was able to get the crime measures passed in the final days of this Congress was that the public got the message through to those permissive radical–liberals in both Houses that if they didn't act, they were going down to humiliating defeat in November. And the only reason Mr. Stevenson is running around this fall talking like Wyatt Earp is that he has seen the polls — he knows that the people of Illinois are fed up with the permissiveness on the issue of law and order.

I have read about — and the people of Illinois know about — the situation that exists in the city of Cairo, Illinois, where the populace and the police are made the regular victims of urban terrorists. This administration and Senator Smith have been fighting this kind of menace in word and deed since the first day we came in to national office. We are in this fight because our greatest concerns are there — and our commitments have been there.

Now, Mr. Stevenson is also there today. But he is a recent and raw recruit to the ranks of those angered and concerned over the crisis of law and order in American society. Mr. Stevenson is there — not because his heart is in this political fight for tough anticrime legislation — but because his chief political advisors — the Gallup polls and the Harris polls — tell him that's where he darn sight better be right now, if he wants to win in November.

Now if this were two years ago, 1968, and the polls showed something else, Mr. Stevenson would be someplace else. He would be clinking glasses with his liberal friends, moaning about, quote, "police brutality," and comparing the Chicago police to Nazi Storm Troopers.

I think I can make that statement correctly — because that's exactly where Mr. Stevenson stood two years ago — and that's exactly where the people of Illinois ought to tell him where to get off — and stand with a man who doesn't change his political principles every time the political barometer registers a change — and that man is seated right here, your Senator — Ralph Tyler Smith.

Now, when I look around this room and see these courteous and concerned citizens of Illinois dominating this room and I look to the fringes and I see those fringe specimens of our society attempting to . . . [drowned out by applause] . . . it reminds me that I stood in Springfield on September 10th and I stood in Chicago later and I made known my concerns about the kind of disruption that seems to be so prevalent among the unthinking. And I said this — in Chicago, I said that people must be terribly concerned that rocks are being thrown at the President of the United States. My friends in the media rush to explain that there were only a few rocks. But yesterday in San Jose, California, and I want to read you the wire copy that came out of there this morning. It says, "President Nixon was the target of rocks, bricks, bottles, eggs, red flags and other missiles hurled by antiwar demonstrators in his native state."

It says he was attacked by an unruly mob and that's exactly what it was. The wire copy went on to say that the San Jose violence was the most serious aimed at any President in this country since the assassination of President John F. Kennedy in 1963.

Now, let me just say this about it. When a President of the United States, who is the elected representative of the majority of the people in this country, is subject to rock and other missile throwing, it's time to sweep that kind of garbage out of our society. Yes, I say separate them from a society in the same humane way that we separate the other misfits who interfere with social progress and interfere with the conduct of the business of one of the greatest nations in the world. Get them out of our hair where they do not disrupt progress.

How do we do it? We don't do it by force or rock throwing. We don't do it by bombing and violence and the most outrageous, discourteous conduct you can think of. We do it simply by going to the polls on November 3rd and with a resounding and overwhelming vote in favor of those candidates, who favor strong campus administrations and will not tolerate this kind of outrageous conduct. We elect those people and then they get the message and they go home or else their parents take them home and talk to them like they should have been talked to twenty years ago.

Now, I don't care, my friends, I don't care one whit whether the President of the United States is a Democrat or a Republican. I don't care whether his philosophy is to the left or to the right of mine. But he is the elected representative of the majority of the people in a free system; he has been given a mandate to govern for four years and no small group of self-designated elitists who don't know enough to come out of the rain in a deluge has the right to tell him how to govern this country. Let me tell you one other thing about it.

The Democratic candidates who for years have been stimulating and encouraging these people now are saying, "Oh, don't try to drape those poor people around our necks — we don't want them." They know that the American people don't want them. And, why don't they want them? Why don't those Democratic candidates want them now? Because they said they wanted them before, some of the Democratic candidates for the Senate stood with clenched fists with these people before, your own Democratic candidate for the United States Senate defended these people and their outrageous conduct against the Chicago police before, but what is he doing now?

Well, he's turned tail and he's run so fast to the center to protect himself because he knows darned well that he can't win this election by saying what he really thinks. Now, you know what he really thinks. Look at what a man says when an election is far away from him, not when its close to him. You know a man you can depend on — he's sitting right there and his name isn't the III anything. It's Ralph Tyler Smith. I think one of the most incongruous things in our society today is that they refer to these people as "intellectuals." They're about as intellectual as the Cro-Magnon man was. They are speaking for everything against academic interchange of thought. They're afraid to trade considerations with you — all they can do is shout their slogans. They're devoid of intelligence. They really don't belong on a college campus — they belong in some place where they can receive some remedial instruction.

This small segment of the young — they refer to themselves as "the young" — the young are out there listening and learning and cooperating and developing new techniques to lead America. The only difference between the antisocial elements of society now and as it used to be is that formerly these people would lie in doorways on the Bowery and places like that in New York, and today they assign themselves a high lofty motive

425

and lie anyplace they can find. I think I've made my point relatively clear and concise on these people, so I want to say another thing about the difference between Ralph Tyler Smith and his opponent — that is the issue of American security in this dangerous world.

We know from his record that, when it comes to providing the military strength to keep America secure and to enable our President to deal effectively with the Soviets at Helsinki and Vienna, Ralph Smith's vote would be for keeping America strong. His opponent, however, is from the neo-isolationist school.

[To demonstrators:] Please get in tune, will you? Please get in tune. They can't talk, they can't sing, they can't convince anybody. What are they doing here?

This neo-isolationist group I'm referring to is a group so deeply concerned about the military–industrial complex that centers around the Pentagon in Virginia that they seem to have forgotten about the enormous military–industrial complex centered around Moscow in the Soviet Union.

Contrary to what these defense critics think, we don't live in a world where weak nations can remain secure nations. We live in a world where the lion is not yet prepared to lie down with the lamb. We live in a world where great powers, with enormous military resources, still have their eyes, not on domestic improvement, but on political conquests encouraged and abetted by our friends of the ultraleft such as the ones we have here this morning.

In such a world we can be thankful that America has at her helm a President who has known war, a President who understands the nature of our adversaries, a President who has the wisdom, the patience, and the perseverance to fashion for America an honorable peace. The question you will answer in Illinois is:

Do you want the Adlai Stevensons and the Ted Kennedys, and the George McGoverns, and the Bill Fulbrights? Do you want them impairing America's defense despite your President's pleadings — or do you want the President whom Illinois supported not supported in the Senate when he strives to protect American security in a dangerous world? Do you want President Nixon to exercise the mandate that you gave him in 1968 or do you want him to turn around and follow the course that these people would like him to follow? That's the question.

If you want the defense policies and peace politics of this country weakened by the Fulbrights and McGoverns — then vote for Stevenson. But if you want these policies as proposed by the President given Congressional backing — then send to the Senate a man who will back up your President. Send Ralph Tyler Smith back to stand up for Illinois.

Throughout his Senate career, throughout this campaign, Ralph Tyler Smith has spoken out with consistency on the basis of his political principles. He has stood by his guns. And he will be found standing there, come victory or defeat, in November.

His opponent, however, is a politician of a different kind. And the whole state of Illinois knows it.

Two years ago, Mr. Stevenson, then currying favor with student militants and radicals, crudely and cruelly slandered the men of the Chicago Police Force by calling them "Storm Troopers in Blue." His elitist friends may have cheered — but the people of Illinois were appalled.

Realizing that his elitist views were not the views of the people, Mr. Stevenson did the convenient thing — unblushingly and right out in public — he changed his views 180 degrees. Now, in this campaign, instead of slandering the police, Mr. Stevenson sounds like he'd like to serve on the force.

Two years ago, Mr. Stevenson was marching proudly under the banner of ultraliberalism. But when political philosophies collided in the fall of 1970, Mr. Stevenson changed around. He began to hear the great silent majority. He didn't stand up to his banner; he deserted his flag at the first shot. But when radical–liberalism ceased to be popular, Mr. Stevenson suddenly ceased talking and acting like a radical–liberal. When the crunch came, Mr. Stevenson publicly denied his political faith and the faith of his illustrious father.

426

You know, if I were a dedicated Illinois liberal today, my friends, I'd be embarrassed for Mr. Stevenson to be my candidate.

America has too many that would rather switch than fight.

This is a time of trial in our country. We need men who will stand or fall on their political principles. We need men who under fire will fight for their political faith. We don't need any counterfeit conservatives or labile liberals like Mr. Stevenson; we need the real McCoys; we need men of courage and conviction like Ralph Smith in the Senate of the United States.

My friends, I am very proud to have visited the state of Illinois so many times during this crucial campaign. I want to leave you with one thought.

Remember that you are from the land and the state that gave this nation Abraham Lincoln, a man who stood by his principles through the best of times and through the worst of times. And consider which of these two men, the conservative or the counterfeit, Mr. Lincoln would vote for — and then cast your ballots accordingly.

Thank you and good hunting on November 3rd.

November 20, 1970, Honolulu, Hawaii
Associated Press Managing Editors Convention

I'VE REALLY looked forward to this day. Here we have America's Greatest Menace to the Free Press, in the eyes of your profession, eyeball-to-eyeball with Censorship Unlimited, according to my crowd.

The cataclysmic result of such an encounter could send tidal waves all the way to the mainland. But I surmise they will be only ripples. For when I have spoken and we've had our discussion, probably we will both find that our advertising is misleading, and we are far more compatible than we would have thought.

As your officers know, your invitation reached me months ago — well before the characteristics of a "radical–liberal" were made public — and even before there was a campaign 1970. I withheld my acceptance, however, until the campaign was nearly over and I could determine that I was going to physically survive. I must say there is serious doubt among some of your colleagues that I did, in fact, survive. But, for the record, let me say I never felt better. And let's get this straight: Any rumors that Richard Nixon will not be on the ticket with me in 1972 are totally without foundation. I don't know where reporters get that stuff. But I guess when managing editors give them a deadline, they've got to meet it — with something.

Now, when I was invited here, I puzzled over two disconcerting possibilities: One, that you hadn't bothered to read what I'd said in recent months — or worse, that you didn't give a tinker's dam about what I said.

But that didn't trouble me overlong. After a campaign involving some twoscore speeches, countless appearances before the press, and handshaking to the point that my tennis elbow footfaulted and stormed off the court — I regarded this meeting as irreproachable justification to slip out of Washington for a few days in Hawaii.

I even covertly mused that my coming was the one thing I could do that would escape the barbs of the press — for they wouldn't dare poormouth you, the eminences of their clan. And for me, my friends, anything these days that will still a newshawk's typewriter has instant appeal.

But more even than that, I was intrigued by this audience. I have visited with publishers, advertising executives, and reporters — but this is my first session with the men who actually run the papers — the managing editors. Maybe you will see fit to preside over the reconstruction of my image with the news media and at the same time will indulge a few disenchanted observations about reporting, headline writing, story positioning, and photo selection, and what survives all four editions as opposed to what makes one and then disappears.

Now, confidentially, I am reported to be a chronic whiner about all news media. That is just as untrue, just as distorted, as the repetitious accusation that I have called all students effete snobs.

First, I've never used that term. Secondly, the term that I did use was not applied to students. Let me discuss the background a minute. It offers a good case history to how words and phrases get twisted through repetition in the media and through sloppy reporting and failure to check facts.

The statement I made in New Orleans, discussing the state of society today, was as follows:

"A spirit of national masochism prevails, encouraged by an effete corps of impudent snobs who characterize themselves as intellectuals."

Now this statement says nothing about student demonstrators, peaceful or otherwise. It refers to certain public figures, columnists, editorialists, and commentators who were encouraging the antiwar movement in a very irresponsible fashion and without challenge by anyone. I called *them* — not the students — "impudent snobs who characterize themselves as intellectuals."

The next time the phrase was reported the word encouraged was dropped. Then the "impudent snobs" suddenly became leaders of the student demonstration. Then it was applied to all the demonstrators. Then it was applied to all college students everywhere. Then they became "effete snobs." The people I originally referred to were dropped out of it completely and the press had hung on me a nice antiyoung image that I still have to contend with.

Incidentally, on the night of that first Moratorium — four days before the New Orleans speech — one of the major networks, NBC, showed a documentary of the events of that day. Included in it was a spliced film clip from a speech I had made in Dallas ten days earlier. It was made to appear that I was denouncing student demonstrators. The quote from the Dallas speech was taken out of context to fit the situation.

Gentlemen, I don't make these charges lightly. I've had a few experiences with biased reporting, and I don't intend to sit back quietly and see it go uncontested. I will help you spotlight it in any way that I can.

It is true that I am denounced as the foe of all journalism by the heads of the major networks, their star commentators, various publishers and editors, and miscellaneous politicians who curry your favor by regularly harpooning the Vice President.

In what may have been the unkindest cut of all, an eminent publisher only last week referred to me as the self-appointed "Inspector General of the News Media."

Now, I haven't appointed myself anything. Vice Presidents never do! All I did was make a couple of speeches a year ago which rather candidly surveyed network news reporting and the growing concentration of power in the news business. I knew at the time that Vice Presidents are not expected to voyage into such dangerous waters, and that I was violating a political axiom — *never* challenge, never question the media.

Well, knowing that taboo, I had to give those speeches anyway, because I believed sincerely in what I said then, and I still do.

As you know, my assessments of the media got a mixed reception. Network presidents, their commentators, and some publishers and editors reacted in a manner that is most charitably described as hostile. Even now some of them accuse me of attempted intimidation and governmental censorship. This past year I doubt that there has been any meeting of media groups in which I have not been discussed — and cussed — for daring to speak my mind. But I find this very encouraging and wholesome. My highest hope was to get the industry to appraise itself critically. I believe it is now doing that.

I am aware that your APME has long had committees which have critically examined the AP report and recommended changes. It is a commendable, healthy practice which I hope will become more prevalent. If what I have done has further stimulated self-examination within the news media generally, I feel I have done your profession, not an injury, but a lasting favor. But I suggest that, if a broader look is in fact being taken, it is due to the public response to those speeches, not the speeches themselves. Many thousands of viewers and readers expressed strong support of the points I sought to make and joined in with their own criticism of the networks and some publications. I feel that this outpouring demonstrated that a bona fide basis for the criticism did in fact exist, and it came as a revelation to media officials.

Neither in those speeches — nor in any I have since made — have I advocated censorship or control by the government or anyone else. That thought is totally repugnant to me, even though interpretations of my remarks have suggested otherwise.

In referring to the television networks, I put the matter this way in a speech:

> I am not asking for government censorship or any other kind of censorhsip. I am asking whether a form of censorship already exists when the news that forty million Americans receive each night is determined by a handful of men responsible only to their corporate employers and filtered through a handful of commentators who admit to their own set of biases.

I stand by that statement. To the extent that censorship in any form exists in America, it rests solely with the media people, whether broadcast or print. You — and only you — determine what is reported and the emphasis it receives. As a public official who has been both gratified and dismayed by your news judgments, I would not have it otherwise. But I must underscore the awesome power that you hold and the trust placed in you by the public. I strongly believe you need to take a good hard dispassionate look from time to time at how your great power is being exercised.

Now let me speak with total candor about what I conceive to be the strong and weak points of our free press in America. It may surprise you to learn that I believe there are far more strengths than weaknesses.

Let me state first, very precisely, what I regard as right about your profession.

I have not the least doubt that the United States has the most self-demanding, least self-satisfied, most ingenious, least inhibited, best informed, least controlled, most professional, least subjective, most competitive, least party-line, fairest, and finest journalistic complex in the entire world.

I have found newscasters and reporters, in large majority, as fair and as objective as they are emotionally and psychologically able to be, and I have found the great preponderance of them very conscientious in their calling.

I have found most news accounts of my deeds and words adequate and factual; indeed, time and time again I have found surprisingly complimentary coverage of my viewpoints by journalists who I happen to know do not suffer from ardor for Agnew.

I have seen Niagaras of words and interpretations erupt almost overnight from your fraternity over political events, inundating the American people with astonishingly detailed information about important people and issues — and I have marveled how well you have made this the best informed nation on earth. The entire process, as well as most of its people, I admire immensely.

I regard America's press as the best and strongest in the world. It will remain so only as long as it remains free. But with that freedom goes a deep and continuing awareness of great responsibility. Since freedom of the press is constitutionally assured and not exercised directly by the individual, it imposes an extra measure of responsibility. In order to maintain the public trust and confidence the press must, in my opinion, be responsible and fair in all of its dealings with society. If it reports only one side of a controversy and discriminates against the other, it risks loss of credibility. And a credibility gap for the press would be as disastrous as it would be for government.

Now, I presume to offer a suggestion or two on how best to keep the press strong and free. Several aspects of news operations and professional group behavior seem to me to be worthy of your critical self-analysis and correction. I offer these thoughts only in a constructive spirit, and I hope you will receive them in that spirit.

First, as a public official who refuses to accept silently what he feels is excessive and unfounded criticism from segments of the news media, I wish the media would overcome their hypersensitivity to being challenged in return. It is a knee-jerk reaction that I feel ill becomes a proud profession that is guaranteed freedom by the Constitution and that ought to be eager to police itself.

A former president of this Association, Norman Isaacs, stated this last year far better than I have, in a lecture at Stanford University. He said:

> We have the arrogance of shrugging off complaints and protests about inaccuracies and slanted coverage ... the arrogance of printing hurtful half- and quarter-truths on Page One and relegating weasel-worded corrections to pages 31, 41, or 51. And worse, the arrogance of assuming to ourselves the right to criticize everything and everyone in the world, but refusing to permit the slightest criticism of newspaper journalism.

I wouldn't dare use such rhetoric! Every one of you here knows that Norman Isaacs regards Agnew as akin to asafetida. As president of the American Society of Newspaper Editors he has excoriated me for, he says, attempting to intimidate the press. But he is also a strong advocate of a responsible and self-critical press. In that he and I are in 100 percent agreement.

I noted with particular interest Mr. Isaacs' recommendation for a press council which would operate within your industry as a moral and ethical force to keep the media more responsible. As a lawyer, I subscribe to self-regulation and the setting of standards within a profession. I don't know much about this press council concept, but it apparently has done well in Great Britain, and more recently is being tried on a local basis here in Hawaii. But please don't consider this an endorsement. If it were, I would surely kill the idea. I only suggest that such proposals are worthy of your thoughtful attention and might go far toward restoring some of the eroded public confidence in your profession.

Next, I suggest that many news executives would do well to give more attention to a balanced presentation of views on controversial issues. Now I know the press is not monolithic — that it consists of many different ownerships and philosophies, and that free and independent publishers will inevitably — and should — advance pet causes and political judgments. But surely you want to — and *can* — find room for other points of view in the newspaper and surely you recognize your obligation to do so.

Of the 1,500 cities in America with daily newspapers, 1,284 — well over eighty percent — have only one paper. In 150 others there are two newspapers, one morning and one evening, publishing under the same ownership. There are only forty-five cities with two or more competing, separately owned dailies. So, for the public to be fully informed, particularly where there is no competing press, there is a pressing need for balance in reporting daily events.

Third — and this, perhaps, will be called a typical political reaction — I urge more management attention to the continuing problem of segregating factual news from opinion — to confining opinion to the editorial page or prominently labeling it as opinion if it is run elsewhere. Newspapers, I find, work harder than TV, radio, or the newsmagazines to make this critical distinction clear to readers. But still we see slanted stories, whether or not the tilt is deliberate. The stories may not be regarded as subjective by the editor, but I should think this is all the more reason to require as much objectivity as possible among reporters and deskmen and headline writers.

Now I know that objectivity is an elusive goal but I do believe that the managing editor can see it is pursued, even if it can never be captured completely. My impression is that many are now working hard at this, and I commend them for it. I do hope others will follow suit.

Incidentally, I would like to commend the observations made to this association Wednesday by Malcolm F. Mallette, Director of the American Press Institute, and Wes Gallagher, the General Manager of the Associated Press, as reported in news dispatches.

I refer specifically to Mr. Mallette's condemnation of the viewpoint of young reporters that their news stories "should take a point of view with no pretense to impartiality," and Mr. Gallaher's statement that a reporter should not decide "which side is right and then become the advocate of that side."

The fact that these two eminent professionals in the news business voice such concern justifies, in my opinion, the concern that I express to you as a government official who depends on the press to communicate his views to society.

Of course, the problem of bias in reporting is something that journalism constantly struggles against, and it seeps through in subtle ways. A heavily slanted news story is obvious. The selection of a picture and the size and content of a headline are not as obvious.

If you will pardon a personal reference, I would like to read a few comments from a young man on a large metropolitan daily. I don't want him fired, so I will not identify the paper, or even the section of the country it is in — only that it is antiadministration. I suspect the letter he sent me last spring is typical of others in your profession. He began:

> A few months ago, I was part of the "loud minority" denouncing your criticism of the liberal press. That was before I went to work at the _____. I have seen how some people are attempting to manage and distort the news.

Then he listed examples:

> When a recent national poll showed you gaining substantially in public opinion, an editor asked, "Do we have to use this damned thing about Agnew?" The story was used, but far back in the paper. When you made an errant golf shot, hitting a pro golfer on the head, the story took up nearly half of our front page. The editor, my correspondent said, insisted on "a funny-looking picture of Agnew" to go with it. "A picture of him laughing . . . we want to make him look like an ass."

The young man cited other incidents and said these were but a few among hundreds. He concluded: "As a young professional man looking forward to a happy career, I am shocked to see the ethics of my profession going down the drain."

I can't certify to this, but I have been told by people from the industry that similar things happen right along in one network's film-cutting room.

I don't know how prevalent such practices are, gentlemen, but I would like to think they are exceptions, not the rule. I am convinced that most journalists have an innate sense of fairness, whether or not they agree with one's views.

But I believe it is abundantly clear that, to the degree censorship exists in our country, it is done not by government, but by the news media.

We in government are dependent totally on you to see that news of government is carried to the public. We can issue the most detailed news release — or give the most comprehensive news briefing — but we are at your mercy after the information is released. Whether the public sees the announcement, and in what context, is entirely up to you, your reporters and deskmen.

I can give the most thoughtful speech I can compose, but how much of it is conveyed depends on the reporter. Is the reporter more interested in a catchword or phrase that he believes sensational, and perhaps will make a more appealing headline, or is he conscientiously trying to convey the message? Secondly, the handling of the story depends on what you or your deskman decide about its worth.

No matter how much I or anyone else may be accused of trying to bulldoze the press, you and I know perfectly well that you can't be intimidated. And you shouldn't be. But my appeal is that you bear constantly in mind that yours is a heavy responsibility. I urge you to exercise it thoughtfully and fairly.

For the freedom of the press that we enjoy in this country goes beyond the right of a publisher to print a newspaper or a magazine or book, or the right of a trade or professional group to give us their version of the topics of the day. More important, it is a right of the people — their right to know what is going on in their society and to have access to all pertinent information. They are entitled to that information as fully, as fairly, as impartially as you can present it. That, I believe, is what the framers of the Bill of Rights had in mind.

In the lobby of the National Press Club in Washington is a plaque bearing "The Journalist's Creed," written by Walter Williams, the first dean of the University of Missouri School of Journalism.

This statement of principles is not only applicable today, but perhaps needs greater emphasis than at some times in the past. Let me quote these excerpts:

> I believe that the public journal is a public trust; that all connected with it are, to the full measure of their responsibility, trustees for the public; that acceptance of lesser service than the public service is betrayal of this trust.
>
> I believe that clear thinking and clear statement, accuracy and fairness, are fundamental to good journalism.
>
> I believe that a journalist should write only what he holds in his heart to be true.

Gentlemen of the press: The journalist who lives by that creed serves not only himself, not only his profession, but all of society.

December 7, 1970, New York, New York
Board of Directors, Boys' Clubs of America

IT IS INDEED a privilege to be with you tonight and to receive this award from what is probably the most uncommon collection of men in America. I consider it a rare privilege and honor and I am very grateful.

When I reflect on the talent that fills this room, the success that each of you has achieved in his chosen profession, and the fact that you have gone beyond that to dedicate your energies to helping hundreds of thousands of boys become appreciative of and contributive to the greatness of America, I am doubly impressed.

Nor am I unmindful of the role that two Presidents of the United States have played in this organization — Herbert Hoover, who was your chairman for twenty-eight years and who considered that it was the most meaningful experience of his life, and Richard Nixon, who took very seriously his responsibilities as your chairman for four years preceding his inauguration as President last year.

And I'd like to say that I spent an hour with the President today, and he asked me to particularly convey to you his best wishes for your continued success and to let you know that he thinks often of the time that he spent in this work. And he's still as interested as he ever was in seeing that you continue to grow and prosper.

Here's Brooks Robinson who I've known quite some time. You saw it; I saw it — I don't believe it; I doubt if you believe it. But I know he's not only a great baseball player but a great friend and a person who I've known back in the State of Maryland from the time he joined the Orioles. I consider myself very fortunate that Brooks helped me in my campaign for governor of Maryland four years ago instead of running against me. Seriously, he's as great off the field as he is on it; he gives unstintingly of his time to numerous worthwhile religious and charitable causes. You and the 850 thousand boys' club members throughout the United States can indeed be proud that Brooks Robinson is an alumnus of one of your clubs — I believe it was Little Rock, Arkansas.

Earlier this year, I had the opportunity to learn by personal experience of the work of one of your clubs — the Silesian Boys' Club of Los Angeles. I was very impressed with the work of this club with underprivileged boys of the Spanish-speaking minority in the Los Angeles area. Through the courtesy of certain "Spiro Agnew" wristwatch manufacturers, the Silesian Boys' Club received a rather substantial check to assist in their good work. I hope that Mickey Mouse will not be offended at our effort to build up their treasury.

I can't commend too highly the work that has been done by your national organization since 1906 and by some individual clubs for more than a century. America urgently needs more of this kind of interest in our young people — more interest from the private sector — the intimate, personal leadership that inspires them to achieve and excel in our strongly competitive society. A boy, discouraged and on the ropes from initial failure, certainly needs an experienced, understanding hand to set him squarely on his feet and point him in the right direction.

One of my duties as Vice President is to serve as chairman of the President's Council on Youth Opportunity. And among its responsibilities that council has to develop state and local youth efforts — both in the summer and on a year-around basis. These coordinators who work with the governor, mayors and country officials then try to coordinate and energize public and private efforts in the area of youth opportunity — not an easy task.

These men and women must sort out and keep up with more than 200 federal programs which directly or indirectly relate to children and youth and to stimulate the flow of money from the private sector to be added to that from the federal government and state treasuries, making it possible for boys to have useful and energizing jobs, not only during the time they are out of school in the summer, but to see that they have useful employment.

It has been disturbing to me that, as the federal government has created and publicized more and more programs, people have turned increasingly to government to solve their problems. This applies to youth work as well as to other fields.

At a meeting of the youth council, just a few weeks ago, I remarked on the need to reverse this trend by using the federal money in conjunction with the state and the local money to fund increased efforts from the private sector. In other words, to use this money to fund organizations such as yours which can turn out in a doubling and even a tripling of the amount of money that is available for these programs. In too many cases, we have regarded the availability of federal money as an excuse to cease private support or to restrict the effort to that which the federal funding will finance. We have fallen into the habit of saying all to frequently that we can't do any more because "That's all the money we have from government" — particularly, "That's all Washington will give us." But many projects could be accomplished if the energy spent badgering Washington for more money would be applied to raising money for the project itself.

I do not deny that public assistance is useful. I do not deny that it's sometimes necessary. But if the federal money is to be properly utilized by local and state governments to stimulate the activity and productivity in the private sector, the return can be increased measurably.

And it's important to remember too that success depends on something more than just money. It is the involvement and dedication of men, such as yourselves who work shoulder to shoulder in a cause to which they are deeply committed. And this can overcome seemingly insurmountable obstacles. Participation is more powerful than an impersonal signature on a check. I'm not downgrading the contribution, but I am saying that the active involvement of groups such as yours is the most important ingredient in the success of the Boys' Clubs of America.

If we could use more of our federal funds to stimulate and bring about private endeavors such as yours, instead of smothering initiative in a blanket of bureaucracy and a proliferation of programs, I think America would be a stronger nation for it.

Tonight I am very honored to be in the company of men who intensely enjoy their work of serving others. But what makes your willingness to help especially important is that

433

you are successful products of our free enterprise system. You are representative of our fine institutions and of the professional freedom that is enjoyed in the United States. Every one of you, by virtue of his own intelligence, his vigor, his stamina and his fight, has attained a high peak of accomplishment in some field — be it government, labor, law, the military, sports, or some other business or profession. In short gentlemen, you are the Establishment. And because you are the Establishment — which is fashionably character- ized as cold, crass, brutal, and selfish — you are confounding the critics of the American way of life by your willingness to help others less fortunate than yourselves. To prove the critics thesis, they would prefer you to spend your time exploiting the poor, evading the law, cheating the consumer, and terrorizing all of lesser position by your arrogance and insensitivity.

In these times it is vital that you continue to stand in obvious refutation of the minority of our fellow citizens who seem to have lost their faith in American values. Your respect for our competitive system, coupled with your sincerity and compassion for the under- privileged and faltering among our youth, help to repulse the current attacks on our traditions.

I believe it is appropriate tonight to discuss the challenges to our traditional values.

In particular, the competitive, ambitious, aggressive side of our outlook is under attack: the businessman's drive for profit is labeled as money-grubbing; the politician's joust with his opponent is branded as vicious and divisive; the military commander's desire for victory is mocked as jingoistic heroics. The urge to fight one's way to the top is any undertaking is sneered at as inhumane and unworthy.

In the public mind, this attack on traditional values is believed to represent the feeling of most of our youth. And I do not think this is fair or accurate. There are many, many young people, in my opinion, the vast majority, who believe firmly in the American system and in traditional American values; while at the same time many of those who attack our values are no longer youths, but full grown adults.

Nevertheless, because of the report of the President's Commission on Campus Unrest, of which I have been both critical and commendatory, since that report has given such an excellent description of the new "anti" culture, I should like to read you a few passages. The report is speaking of what it calls the "youth culture," but I want to emphasize that I consider that label a misnomer. But here are some passages. The report says:

> This subculture took its bearings from the notion of the autonomous, self-determin- ing individual whose goal was to live with "authenticity," or in harmony with his inner penchants and instincts. It also found its identity in a rejection of the work ethic, materialism, and conventional disciplines externally imposed upon the individual, and this set it at odds with much in American society.

The Scranton Report goes on to describe this culture:

> Its aim was to liberate human consciousness and to enhance the quality of experi- ence; it sought to replace the materialism, the self-denial, and the striving for achieve- ment that characterized the existing society with a new emphasis on the expressive, the creative, the imaginative. The tools of the workaday institutional world — hier- archy, discipline, rules, self-interest, self-defense, power — it considered mad and tyrannical. It proclaimed instead the liberation of the individual to feel, to experience, to express whatever his unique humanity prompted.

So said the report.

Now in this much lionized subculture, three aspects strike me in particular. First, the avoidance of ambition and the retreat from power, struggle, and greatness. Second, the emphasis on the abandonment of discipline, on hedonism, and "doing your own thing." Third, a gradual turn to solipsism, which is the notion that there are no standards beyond oneself.

434

These three traits derive from an unwillingness to look beyond oneself or to go beyond oneself. To retreat from ambition and from the arena of great affairs, justified by the emphasis on chucking societal restraints and "doing one's thing," to me is untenable. Older standards and principles that transcend the individual, have often called him forth to something nobler than self, are rejected, and the rejection is justified by reliance upon one's individual standard of values.

I admit there is a positive side to this. After all, no less a personage than Plato once described justice as "doing one's own things." And none of us is naïve enough to believe that there are not abuses in the accumulation as well as in the exercise of power. We know that prestige is not always well earned.

But there is also a negative side. The reward of ambition is responsibility as well as power and prestige. And since power is an increment of achievement, no one will want power if achievement is considered an unworthy objective. And if there is no competition for power, it's certain to fall into the hands of those least qualified to use it constructively.

Now, there is little doubt that this new "anti" culture is opposed to what is generally considered to be the traditional American values. To use the modern jargon, they are just two different "life styles." I favor the traditional, but I firmly believe that both have the right to exist. Men can live in differing ways; they have the right to choose and tolerance demands that we try to see the good aspects of other ways of life.

I must state very emphatically that I have not given this description of the new way of life, juxtaposed to ours, simply for the purpose of criticism. Rather, I have given it in the desire simply to delineate, because I feel it is a phenomenon worthy of attention. But I believe we should also be aware of what this new outlook signifies, not so much in moral terms as in practical terms that we should know what it means for us and for our country.

Let us consider for a moment what this country stands for. It stands for freedom. It stands for equality of opportunity and for justice. I realize that these concepts in the fullest realization will always be ideals, goals; I realize that they do not exist in perfection here or anyplace else. Our principal minorities still suffer from inequality of opportunity. But we have improved greatly in the past two decades, and with the help of all fair-minded citizens we shall conquer this defect. The beauty of our system is that it dramatizes flaws rather than conceals them.

In spite of our imperfections, I believe that our country remains the bulwark of freedom in the world today. With us rests the responsibility and the capacity to see that freedom does not die. Most of you remember well the Second World War and how this country armed itself to fight one of the greatest threats to freedom the modern world has ever seen, the Nazi Reich. If we had not gone to war and hadn't fought for four long years, it is possible that freedom would have perished from this earth. The Communists had already further diminished liberty in Russia, and were on their way to doing so in China. Britain would surely have fallen, and I doubt that we in America could have remained free from invasion after the Nazis and the Communists had divided the vast Eurasian continent among themselves.

But we did go to war. Because of our decision to fight, freedom was preserved. Freedom is very precious, but it is fragile — it does not survive by itself. It must be fought for, every day, every year. Not always with arms, but always with will. Sometimes the threats to freedom are not readily apparent as threats — isolated acts of violence — an anarchist's bomb thrown in the name of peace — a policeman murdered in the name of freedom itself.

It is worth remembering that freedom is not something common in the world, nor has it always been there. Free, representative government was first developed as a political goal in Ancient Greece, and it remained for a long time a peculiarly Western response to communal needs.

We have inherited a firm belief in the correctness of an unfettered citizenry partly through the survival of great literature from Greece and Rome, and partly through the success of nations that were founded on the principle of liberty. Athens reached the attainment of her peak as a democracy. Rome grew to world power through a constitution based on self-government. But our own country is perhaps the greatest example the world has ever seen of the success that freedom brings.

But the men who founded our country did not find a ready model for their concepts of free government. Because freedom at that time was languishing. There was a king in England. There was a king in France, and an empress in Russia and an emperor in China. Self-government did not exist in any major power in the world at the end of the eighteenth century.

The men who founded this nation therefore drew their concept of freedom in large part from their reading of ancient literature, or from reading authors who were themselves influenced by reading the ancients. The example of a government by the people did not exist for them in their contemporary world, because it had been extinguished with the founding of the Roman Principate, 1,800 years before.

So we see, gentlemen, what rare a thing freedom really is and how few nations and how few people in the history of the world have been able to enjoy it. Even today, a great portion of the world's population is not free.

These facts illustrate quite vividly that freedom does not simply take root and perpetuate itself. It must be established or cultivated and guarded — conscientiously and diligently.

It is because freedom requires vigilance and effort to survive that I am really worried about this "anti" culture of today that I just described. I fear that those who espouse this way of life do not realize how quickly a massive individual rejection of responsibility and power such as this could snuff out their freedom that makes their style of life possible. They say, "Make love, not war"; and their slogan has appeal. But it misses the point because it suggests that those of us who believe that there are times when freedom must be defended would rather make war than love. This is, of course, not true. No thinking person desires war. All sane Americans want peace. But we must face the fact that there are some in this world who are not interested in peace — at least not until their dreams of conquest are fulfilled. Therefore we must retain the power and the capacity to deter them and to defend ourselves, if necessary.

It has been made clear throughout our history that we don't covet the resources of others. Certainly, all Americans want peace; all Americans want happiness; all Americans want freedom. On this we are agreed — both we who believe in traditional values and those who profess the new "anti" culture.

What sets us apart is not the ends, but the means: is freedom best preserved by striving or by resting? Are the things we value most — justice, equality and peace — best secured by effort or by ease? Perhaps there is nothing intrinsically wrong with a society of civilized withdrawal and relaxation, but in view of the terrible fragility of freedom, can such a society be preserved in today's aggressive world? That's the question.

Now, freedom is always demanding unceasing wakefulness, but most especially now, when her enemies are both powerful and aggressive. We need men in America who are strong as well as humane. We need men who understand that leadership requires effort and who are willing to make that effort — men who go beyond themselves both in joining the battle for prizes and in serving others generously.

You directors of the Boys' Clubs of America are such men. You have competed with other men. But you have also served other men. And the boys you have helped to start on a better life than they were born to, will not forget. They have noticed what sort of men you are, the sacrifices you make, the generosity you have shown, and to them you will remain an example.

Because of you they will be better able to believe in the American dream, to trust in American freedom, and to have confidence in their ability to compete and to accept responsibility. They will not need to find a cheap outlet for their desires or to lead a degrading life in a fantasy world of dangerous drugs and narcotics.

They are strong boys. I believe they represent the great majority of American youth today. I do not think that, in honesty and fairness, we can tar the bulk of our young people with the brush of this "anti" culture. In my view, our young people are too energetic, are too positive. Some of the more vocal elements in our society may disagree with my conclusions. And if you spend a great deal of your time before the television tube, you too may wonder where I get my optimism. Well, I get it from my own observations — from traveling the length and breadth of this great country — from seeing all those fresh

436

young faces at airport fences, on city streets, even at political meetings — and hearing them say in a hundred different ways spontaneously, naturally, sometimes not too articulately. But the message gets through. They believe in America. My judgment is that the youth of America is sound.

That is why I am optimistic: because we have fine young people and men like yourselves who together have accepted the responsibility of all Americans — to keep the United States strong as a guarantee of freedom in the world.

All of us want our country to be great, not just in her power, but especially in her humaneness. We want justice and equality and happiness for all our citizens. These are gentle aspirations, and it may seem strange to the advocates of the "anti" culture that there is also a tough side to happiness. But I believe that even in this sleek and prosperous age we would do well to heed the words of the great Athenian statesman, Pericles, who once said to his countrymen over 2,400 years ago, that "The secret to happiness is freedom, and the secret to freedom is courage."

January 14, 1971, Sacramento, California
County Supervisors Association of California

THANK YOU very much, President Thiel, for that endorsement, and thank you, particularly, for renewing my local credentials with this particular group.

I learned while listening to the other speakers this morning the efficacy of one immutable truth — and that is, when you're talking to people in government who are basically located in one area of government, it is unfailingly successful to propose solutions that lie in another area of government. Having resorted to that tactic on more than one occasion myself, I want to say that I understand it and that I think if you didn't, to some extent, utilize and yield to it, you'd be something less than normal.

I have a very debilitating experience in that my governmental expertise — or some would say, experience — stretches across all three levels of government. Unfortunately, before I came into government, before I undertook to run for elective office of county executive of Baltimore County, I thought I had all the solutions to what was wrong with county government. After being elected, I found out that I really didn't, and some of the things that I thought would be so easily implemented were really not quite that simple.

So then I went on to state government with the absolute conviction as county executive that there was nothing that I could not easily achieve to solve the problems of local government if I were only a governor, and I found out that was also wrong.

During both of these endeavors, I could always fall back on the idea that the federal government was the solution to all the problems, and I did frequently. But now I'm in the federal government, and I find that things don't look as good in there either as I had thought they would when I was outside. So I'm in a distressing position of having to admit very candidly to you that the answers are not easy, even though my good friend, Mr. MacDougall, says they really are. I'm sure he didn't say that in any serious sense.

I do feel very firmly that you in the state of California have a tremendous asset if I can judge by what I know of your elected officials and what I've heard them say here today. They are very avid exponents of reaching solutions, and as they continue to probe for those solutions, they are bound to make progress. This does not mean that any of us is going to be able to solve all of these problems immediately.

I know Governor Reagan personally because I had the opportunity to work with him when I was a governor. I have a profound respect, not only for his knowledge of government, but for his reasonable approach and for the energy of his efforts to grasp at potential answers and for the detailed attention to the controverting opinion that might exist to cause him to change his direction at some time. I think he's a man who is willing to admit that we learn as we go, and consequently, he's going to continue the solutions for the sake of solving the problem and not adhere to any particular view just because he may have held that view in the past. I think if we all approach government from that point of view, we're all going to be a great deal better off.

But above all, your governor has two qualities which are really very important in government today; he's articulate, and he's tough-minded. And believe me, in this business, which is a very tough business, you have to have both of those qualities if you're going to be heard above the rhetoric which seems to pervade most governmental discussions today.

Now, as you've heard, I have been designated by the President, because of my broad cross-section of experience across governmental levels, to attempt to grease the procedures through which governments at local, state, and federal level can work together.

A particularly interesting problem that I think is being overlooked very much today is one that revolves around the fact that local government is not just local government — it's city and county government. And many of the problems that we have today come about because city and county governments are really not quite working together yet. I don't think they're ever going to work together until state government brings them together in forums such as this to discuss the ways of resolving their particular problems compatibly and come to some conclusion about the amount of revenue and resources which could be dedicated to each.

Now, I listened very attentively to Mr. Carpenter's words; he is a most effective advocate for city government. I'm not in agreement with every conclusion he reached, but I can understand his partisanship because of his position and because of his long experience and the frustrations of the problems of city government.

But I do think it's wrong for cities to look totally to the federal government for solutions to their problems. One of the things the Nixon Administration is dedicated to achieving is to bring about a partnership that involves the state government in the distribution of resources from the federal government to the cities and counties. It's necessary for the state government, in the sense of creating a comprehensive plan of development, to consider the impact of city growth on county growth. You people as supervisors are completely cognizant of the fact that county lines do not stop problems, and that in a metropolitan area, which is basically a homogeneous entity separated by city–county line, the people in the city often receive the access to resources that are not available to the people in the county. I do think that the city has unique problems. I had the chance to talk to the new mayor of Newark, New Jersey, just yesterday, and he has problems that you wouldn't believe.

Now I've heard about your property tax problem. I understand your property taxes run as high as $12 a hundred in some areas, and I understand that you assess on the basis of 25 percent of market value. This means that at a hundred percent of value may mean the highest property tax in your state would be about $4 a hundred. In the city of Newark, New Jersey, the property tax right now is $8.40 a hundred, based on a hundred percent evaluation — almost double the highest property tax you have in California. I'm not advocating that kind of property tax because I know very well that what taxes are utilized to meet the burdens of government in a state depend not just on reason and logic but on tradition. I know that whether an income tax is acceptable at the state level depends on the tradition and the hostility that's been raised in the advocacy of that tax in the past. I know the same thing applies to sales tax.

Now I know something about this business of tax reform, and I know the frustrating experience that Governor Reagan has had with his effort to shift what he considers an inordinate burden from the property taxpayers into other forms of taxation. But very few people, my friends, have ever stopped to think why it is important to have a diversity of taxes. Why is it important that the property tax should not get too high based on current value? Why is it important that the income tax shouldn't get too high? Why is it important that sales taxes should be used to raise a certain part of the revenue rather than the other two? Well, it's basically for this reason: A property tax is a tax upon wealth that has already been accumulated. A property tax is a tax that relates to a home, usually, or a business or a building that has been bought in some cases and paid for, or is in the process of being paid for. An income tax is a tax on wealth as it's being accumulated. So there are two classes of potential taxpayers involved in these two taxes.

To give you an example of how — to use an extreme situation — of how you can reach across these lines to see that the impact is different: If you took a retired man, who all during his life had been paying a lot of taxes, of income taxes, but now he's retired, he's got a nice home, he doesn't have much income, maybe he's living off his retirement income — Social Security — or whatever the case may be, and he has his home which is subjected to property taxes. If the property taxes on that house keep going up at its predictable levels, that man — in spite of the fact that during his productive years he has earned the right to live in that house — is going to be forced out of it because his property taxes are going to become more than he can pay with his current income. On the other hand, look at, under the same circumstances, a young high wage earner who is making very good income. Perhaps he has in mind an ambitious move for him and for his family in the future, so he's living in a converted, very cheap residence he has made do for his children. His wife and his children are all living there. He pays very little property taxes because the home isn't worth money, and if the property tax is a source of revenue of the state, he's getting virtually a free ride. Now, if you turn that thing around and you say if you have income taxes and no property taxes, you have a situation where the man in the big residence is getting a free ride for his services, and the man who hasn't accumulated anything yet is being prohibited from doing that by an income tax that's at the confiscatory level.

So what I'm saying in regard to this — and I digress a minute to point out to you that a sales tax is a tax, of course, on what you're spending. A sales tax puts a premium on saving, but it also, unless it contains exemptions for food and medicine and necessities, can be a very regressive tax as to low-income people.

But the reason I'm pointing out the differences between these taxes is to show you that there aren't any simple answers and to show you that what you have to look for in the framework of what your people want in your state is a blend of taxes that puts no inordinate burden on any group of taxpayers and raises the tax money in an equitable manner where all productive citizens are able to produce their fair share of the revenue.

Now, coming down next to the question of why the local and state governments are in a crisis. I'm not here to tell you that I don't agree with you 100 percent that the federal government in the past has preempted too much of the tax resources of this country. The President of the United States today believes this. And that is why in his State of the Union Message next month he will propose to the Congress tax reform in the form of revenue sharing — with substantial new money, with all sorts of grant reform that will bring about, I believe, to the complete satisfaction of state and local governments, that here is a President who, for the first time, put his money where his mouth was and did something about increasing the resources that are going to be available to avert this crisis in state and local government. Now this does not mean, my California friends, that you are thereby relieved of your obligation to seek new revenue and resources and to continue the process of tax reform. Let me give you an idea about tax reform, of what you in the counties and the cities must never do, and what was done to me when I was the governor of Maryland. We put through a very, very difficult tax reform that sent a hundred million dollars in new revenues to the local governments of Maryland — Baltimore city and the counties and the other cities. What happened was this, basically. We had a difficult time trying to sell this program. The whole program raised about $120 million. The $20 million was the state's share; the rest was distributed to local government, and in addition to the distribution — because we believed as Governor Reagan did, we had to do something to hold down the property tax increases that were going out of sight — the state gave the city and county governments the right to impose a piggyback income tax in addition to the graduated income tax that this tax reform legislation proposed.

439

Some of the counties, the metropolitan areas, imposed that piggyback tax and were thereby able to shift some of the increased cost of government from the property tax to other taxes.

The thing that aroused my wrath at the time — and in retrospect, thinking of it, I'm still sore about it — is that the city of Baltimore, who came to the legislature so frequently with hat in hand asking for this relief, used the new money from the state to reduce its property tax that year because it was an election year. Now, they could have held the line on it or they could have made a minimal increase. But what they really did was to burn up the money that was there for them to make the necessary reforms and implement the new programs that the city of Baltimore was yelling for, for the political advantage of that city council and that mayor to say, "We reduced your taxes this year." Do you think they gave the state any credit for it? Not on your life.

Now that's why legislatures get pretty jumpy on things like tax reform. I think the way to stop that is for the people at the county and the city level to be a little bit appreciative of the fact that these hard political decisions that involve the imposition of taxes have a certain political, erosive quality, and that fair play dictates that one governmental official not jump on another when he's trying to help him solve his problem.

To continue with the matters of welfare. I know the federal government at the present time — and the Nixon Administration, and Governor Reagan's administration in California — do not see eye to eye on the welfare reform program that is presently being advocated by the President in Washington, at least not in the form that it has emerged from the House Ways and Means Committee. I also know that welfare is one of the most difficult areas to reform there is. While I appreciate the fact that Governor Reagan is reaching very hard for the answers to prevent the abuses that we all know are taking place in certain cities and state government throughout the country, I still believe that the answer is much more complex than will allow it to be solved simply with the idea of creating government jobs for those on welfare. I say this because I happen to be fairly well convinced that most of the welfare burden in the federal government programs today is on Aid to Dependent Children, and the number of welfare recipients who are able-bodied and able to work are not as great as one might at first suspect.

This does not mean that this idea of getting people to work shouldn't take place. But I'm not all sure that the idea of putting these people into government jobs is the best way to move them productively into the private sector of employment. It seems to me, looking back on the experience in Washington over many, many years, that when people go on the federal payroll, or any governmental payroll, they think they've found a place to light and they stop really looking for a job in private enterprise. I wouldn't want to see that happen. I suppose there are ways to prevent that from happening.

I think, too, that the focus of the welfare program that's being suggested by the President — he doesn't claim it's perfect, but he does know that the existing program is a veritable disaster, and I think you would agree with me on that — allows a way to attempt to reverse this terrible cycle of welfare recipients that goes on generation after generation.

I think, also, that there is a new cycle of people involved in welfare, from the lobbyist standpoint, that are causing grave difficulties. I'm talking about some of the caseworkers. I'm not deprecating or degrading them — one of my daughters happens to be in that line of work with the county of Baltimore, and very, very pleased with it, so I certainly am not criticizing caseworkers. But I am saying there is a tendency for caseworkers to become caseworkers in succession just as welfare recipients become welfare recipients in succession. It's probably because there's such a great inner satisfaction in working in a charitable cause and probably because reflected in the statements of that particular worker in his family later on comes a desire to do something about the frustrating experience of not being able to take care of needy people.

I know, too, though, that as I told Bill MacDougall on the way out here, there is a great problem with caseworkers forgetting what their primary purpose is — that they are custodians of the governmental position that exists at the moment, and that they are not lobbyists for welfare recipients. This is a great problem because a caseworker is a human

440

being just like you are. You put a person in a position where he has to go into a terribly depressing environment and see a child that doesn't have a pair of shoes or the proper clothing or the proper food, if he's a decent human being he's going to find out some way to get that child . . . what that child needs. But it doesn't make any difference, unfortunately, whether that child doesn't have the shoes or the food because the parent, who is taking care of that child, is wasting the money that he should be using to take care of the child. That's the difficulty with that situation.

I don't propose answers to these questions; I merely am attempting to say what Pat Moynihan said when he talked to the Cabinet not too long ago. That is; ladies and gentlemen, life is very complex. It's not as simple as you draw it when you get up in a short speech and try to tell people what you're going to do to make everything right. All we can do is move in the proper direction to keep trying to solve these problems.

I have a theory that these problems will never be subject to complete solution until somebody in public life, and probably first in the private sector, is willing to take on the hard, social judgments that very frankly no one that I know in elective office is even willing to think about tackling.

Now, what am I talking about? Simple. I'm talking about a decision in welfare. For example, if a woman has not taken care of her children properly, who is going to say to that woman, "We are going to take that child from you, the natural mother, and put that child somewhere that it will receive the proper care"? Who will take that kind of decision on without being accused of uprooting the family and destroying the mother–child relationship? And who is going to say that that's the right thing to do? But sooner or later there are going to be places where a child cannot be allowed to stay in the surroundings that some of them are being brought up in in welfare homes today. Also who is going to say to a welfare mother who has had three or four illegitimate children, who are now charges of the state, "We're very sorry but we will not be able to allow you to have any more children"? Who's going to take that one on, my friends? Until we take it on, how are we ever really going to solve this problem?

In the area of health, presently being discussed in the Congress is a health insurance plan for the entire nation. Take, for example, the problem of providing catastrophic care, which is something I think most of us feel is desirable so that any person would never have to pay more than a certain percentage of his or her income before he was termed in the throes of a health catastrophe and able to seek insurance relief provided through government. If his medical bills went over $800, at that point, perhaps, there should be some broader insurance, maybe of a governmental nature, to pick up and pay the costs over ten percent of his income. If we don't have that, I'm not sure we're going to have proper health care. But how are we going to implement that? Who's going to make the hard decision that says what is a catastrophe? Is a man who is in a terminal illness able to, by virtue of that legislation, be kept alive an extra month at a cost of $20,000 or $30,000 to the taxpayer? Who decides what care is to be continued? Who decides whether a man is to be allowed for his terminal illness to run to the end or whether he's going to be allowed to die of natural causes before that time? If you say that you're going to provide the assistance of the total spectrum, you're talking about astronomical figures — figures that I don't think any government or any nation could ever really reach.

But the point I'm making in these remarks is that we get up here at these meetings so frequently, and we talk about the superficiality of these problems, and we play with the machinery. I often accuse my coworkers back in Washington of being so infatuated with the monstrous bureaucratic federal machinery that they play with it like some gigantic Rube Goldberg device and really forget that they are seeking an answer. It's so much fun to watch everything moving through and the wheels going around and nobody knows what's supposed to come out at the end. Well, each of us has a tendency to do that. Because we shy away from the difficult — difficult decisions that perhaps would very quickly terminate our careers in government as elected representatives of the people because we would then be in a position to be victimized by the demagogues who seek office and seek always to mouth the platitudes, to say the good things.

I'm not going to stand here today and say the bad things or the good things. All I'm telling you is that life is a very, very complex matter. Intergovernmental relations is a very complex matter. There are two sides to every argument. We must, with each other, explore. . . .

January 15, 1971, Palm Springs, California
Dedication of Martin Anthony Sinatra Medical
Education Center

WE AMERICANS are among the most health-conscious people in the world. Concern about our own health, the health of our children, and of Americans who will inherit this land in years to come is becoming an increasingly powerful driving force in our society.

When you think of the many ways in which we give voice to our abiding interest in health, you cannot fail to sense the depth of our national commitment to the protection and preservation of human well-being.

Leaders in the communications media know, for example, that newspaper and television accounts of medical breakthroughs command more public attention than almost any other news. If you were to ask a sample of the American people what headline they would most like to see emblazoned across the newspapers of the country, a high percentage would answer, CURE FOR CANCER FOUND.

When the President has a medical checkup and the findings are released by the White House, that is front page news in papers all over the country.

Concern for health is the basis of our growing efforts to clean up the environment, to protect the lives and safety of workers, to revitalize decaying cities, to keep dangerous products off the market; and it is certainly one of the strongest of all reasons for eliminating poverty in this richest of all nations.

We come together here in the California desert not only to dedicate a mangificent new facility to the cause of health, but because we feel a special gratitude to the individuals who, by their selfless generosity, are helping this nation reach out toward the priceless goal of decent health care for all its citizens.

I would like to commend Frank Sinatra for the very substantial step he has taken — in this community — toward helping meet that goal. This splendid new facility, a memorial to his father, will serve the cause of medical education for many years to come. Here will be advanced the expertise of doctors, nurses and other health personnel, as well as the education and understanding of the general public. And who knows what major breakthrough in medical science may begin as a spark from some lecture or seminar or health program conducted here?

In our lifetimes we have seen astounding advances in medical science. But how pitifully slow we are as a nation in putting this care within the grasp of all of our citizens. The practicable delivery of health care is one of our most difficult problems but also one of our most exciting challenges. It is an opportunity, my friends, that the Nixon Administration welcomes.

All of us know that millions of people in this country are not getting the kind of health care they need. Our great public hospitals are crowded with young mothers who have had no prenatal attention. Their own health and that of their babies is jeopardized because they have not had the kind of health care that can spell the difference between joy and tragedy in the birth of a child.

In vast rural areas of this country and in urban slums, there simply are not enough hospitals and clinics, not enough doctors, dentists, nurses, and other health workers — not enough people and resources to deliver health services to those in need. Dr. Egeberg can tell you that there is only one physician for every four thousand people in certain sections of some of our major cities and in numerous other cities and towns all across this country.

But I didn't come here today to describe a crisis in health care. We all know what that picture looks like. And we know what it means in terms of needless illness and death for many who should have known the blessings of good health and the security of decent, quality health care.

Neither do I have to tell you that this country has a great responsibility to improve the system of health care, to make it a system that befits our greatness as a nation and the high value we place on the preservation of human health and life.

Some would say that the only way we can correct the flaws in our health care system is to replace it with some kind of nationalized health scheme that puts all responsibility and all power in the hands of the federal government. They seem to think that just because our American health enterprise is in trouble — admittedly deep trouble — we ought to put it out of its misery and trot out a radically new system.

Their arguments seem plausible on the surface. They tell us that the United States lags behind other countries in longevity and infant mortality. They point out that we spend more *per capita* on health than any other people on earth, yet we fail to provide necessary health care for all our citizens. They tell us that health care is too vital to be left to the mercies of the free enterprise system because millions of Americans simply can't afford to buy into that system.

But, admitting those facts and allegations for the sake of argument, does that mean that we have to wipe the slate clean and start over? Does it mean that this fine medical facility ought to be owned and operated by the federal government, staffed by government doctors and nurses, or told what to do and how to do it by government health officials?

I don't think so. Our patient, the health care delivery system, may indeed be in trouble, but it isn't time to concede the inevitability of his demise. He needs our help, not despair.

Without a lot of fanfare, without a panoply of promises that no one knows how to keep, this administration under President Nixon has been taking a critical look at our national health problems. We have been examining the weaknesses, as well as the strengths, of the American health system, the problems of supply and demand, the critically rising cost of health care, the delivery of health services for the poor, the financial dilemma confronting our medical schools. We have been looking at the whole range of issues and challenges that combine to produce the present crisis.

For many months we have been developing the information we need to make the right decisions. Our health advisors have consulted with the outstanding health leaders of the nation and with representatives of the public in order to get the best and most accurate understanding of what can and must be done to solve the urgent problems facing us.

Literally hundreds of options have been proposed and evaluated. When this process began many months ago, the President said that he wanted every possible viewpoint — from the most timid to the most bold — to be considered, evaluated, and allowed to rise or fall on its own merits. Many of us have been involved in this review and I can tell you from personal knowledge that the President is deeply concerned.

Here are some of the facts that we must face:

First, it is an absolute certainty that the promotion and preservation of health for all Americans depends on the continued support of biomedical research. Without a steady flow of new knowledge, our efforts to safeguard the healthy and restore the sick will dry up like a tree in the desert that is cut off from water. Biomedical research can lead to new techniques that could end or at least substantially diminish the threat of cancer, heart disease, stroke, mental illness, and the other destroyers of life and health.

Next we need more health manpower to put to use the knowledge already gained, to say nothing of that still to be acquired. We need to train health personnel better and faster. We need to develop new kinds of paramedical personnel to supplement the

443

doctors and nurses who are now having to cope with more than they can handle. We need to see to it that health workers are located in those urban and rural areas that are now desperately short of health manpower.

We need to plan and build more and better health care facilities to replace those that are becoming obsolete and to provide facilities in central city and rural poverty areas where none now exist.

And beyond all this, we need to make sure that no person goes without necessary health care because he can't afford it. A country that can spend as much as $70 billion a year on health — and that's what we are spending right now — can afford to put health care within the reach of all its citizens. Many of them, the poor and the aged, need help. We know that, and we have attempted to provide that help through Medicare and Medicaid. Neither of these programs is completely successful. They can and will be improved. Medicaid is especially in need of redirection, because it simply isn't closing the health care gap for the poor as was intended.

There are other gaps that have to be closed. We have to help lift the burden of catastrophic illness that can spell economic ruin for a family that would otherwise be financially secure.

In a few weeks, President Nixon will call on the Ninety-Second Congress to take constructive action all across the broad health field. He will submit a health plan that will build on not just the best judgments of the experts, but also the sincere hopes and ambitions of a nation that places health among the first of its high ideals.

To put good health care within the reach of every American will demand much of the people and of their government. It will require more acts of private philanthropy like that whose culmination we see here today in the new Martin Anthony Sinatra Medical Education Center. It will require renewed dedication by those men and women who devote their lives to caring for the sick and injured and protecting the health of their fellow human beings. It will require a new relationship between the public and the private sectors of the health enterprise, not as antagonists but as collaborators in a challenge that demands the best of both.

We need a sense of dedication, not unlike the spirit that brings us together today, a dedication to bring forth the best that America has to offer. We are a resourceful people. We are a people whose reach can indeed exceed our grasp. Such a people *can* survive a crisis in health and come through that crisis stronger than we entered it.

That is the health challenge we face. Government cannot meet it alone. But I am certain that together we are equal to the task.

January 21, 1971, Houston, Texas
First Annual Vince Lombardi Award Dinner

WITHIN TWENTY-FOUR hours, President Nixon will report to the nation on the State of the Union. That message will contain singularly far-reaching and explicit proposals in critical domestic problem areas. It will be light on rhetoric and heavy on substance. It will target in on difficult decision areas with rifle-shot accuracy, foregoing the emphasis on past accomplishment and shotgun promises. I have seen the program, and I can tell you that it is bold, imaginative, and statesmanlike. You will be hearing a great deal about it in the approaching months.

While it remains for the President to submit the administration's plans and priorities to the Congress — and no sane Vice President would ever upstage a President — I can tell you that one of the most important parts of the new domestic program will affect an area of special concern to this audience — the field of health care.

The Nixon Administration proposal soon to be announced offers a broad new approach to both the financing of health care and the expansion of its delivery systems. We believe that the American Cancer Society and other interested private and public organizations will be pleased with the scope of the program and will join us in a renewed national effort to prevent, treat, and cure disease, and alleviate human suffering.

We are here tonight to reflect on the challenges and achievements of another area of national life. Our purpose is to honor several outstanding young American athletes and to designate one of them as College Lineman of the Year. The winner will be presented with the Lombardi Trophy in memory of a great American teacher for all seasons.

For Vince Lombardi, as we know, was the molder of championship football teams only as part of his larger mission. First and foremost, he was a teacher. His subject matter, as students like Jerry Kramer attest, involved more than Xs and Os on a blackboard, or game plans and scouting reports in a locker room.

Vince Lombardi was a teacher of the abiding values of our society: love of God, family, and country; faith; pride; discipline; loyalty; perseverance; dedication to a cause larger than oneself. He lived by and taught a code of ethics rooted in the belief that a man's worth was accurately tested in adversity; greatly sharpened in competition; and ultimately proved in moments of supreme challenge.

Vince Lombardi possessed and taught the special grace of seeking always new heights of excellence and individual attainment. He practiced and taught a true egalitarianism, recognizing no distinction of race or creed and judging each man by his willingness to strive and his desire to prevail.

In brief, Vince Lombardi was an exemplar of a way of life vital to the molding of our nation and society. He remains an indefatigable symbol of what some latter-day social and political critics describe as the "early American ethic."

Tonight I believe it appropriate to discuss that ethic and those critics, I know of no better forum in which to consider the contention of those among our countrymen who argue, with increasing stridency in recent years, that the cultural and political values of our fathers are inapplicable to modern life; indeed, that those values are so repressive of the human spirit as to be the enemy rather than the servant of the very aspirations that brought men and women to the New World.

Thus, we are being told that, like it or not, the values exemplified and taught by Vince Lombardi are outmoded.

We are counseled and warned, in no uncertain terms, that the institutions and customs reflecting those values are due to be supplanted, in fact overthrown, in a great cultural and political revolution.

We are assured by the purveyors of a New Morality and a New Politics, that in place of the old ethic will arise original life-styles permitting a better, freer, more rewarding society for all.

Well, almost all. For I doubt that many of us here tonight would be allowed to "do our thing." I have in mind the fact that in the New Left weekly rating of the people's enemies the institution known as Football Coach ranks high in the top ten — not far behind the Joint Chiefs of Staff, General Motors, the CIA, the FBI, John Wayne, and yours truly.

In this regard, whatever your individual political persuasion, you in the football world and I in the political world are inseparably linked by more than an affinity to a game. There are those in the cadre of cultural revolution who consider us simply two peas in a common cultural pod.

Thus, in addition to routine criticism on editorial pages, I sometimes find my name, even as Woody's and Ara's and Bear's, a target of opportunity on sports pages as well. And I don't have to whack somebody with a golf ball to get there.

For example, let me cite a sports column that appeared not long ago in one of my favorite newspapers, the *Washington Post*. Reading beneath the headline, FOOTBALL PRESSED TO JOIN THE TIMES, I learned that in criticizing a speech delivered by Walter

Byers, executive director of the National Collegiate Athletic Association, the sports information director of one Eastern Establishment school could find no greater indictment than — and I quote:

He [meaning Byers] gave a Spiro Agnew-type talk. He said you can't make concessions or use appeasement.

Perhaps, after all, my message *is* getting through.

If that is the definition of a Spiro Agnew-like talk, I plead guilty as charged. However, if my accuser in this instance took time away from his study of the New Culture to familiarize himself with national history, he would learn that the American patent existed on that type of talk several centuries before I even arrived on the scene.

Conversely, if I as a political figure find my name appearing on the sports page, football and the men who earn their living according to its "early American ethic" now find themselves under attack in unaccustomed places.

Writing about the game two seasons ago, the chairman of the editorial board of one avant-garde magazine declaimed football as "the intellectuals' secret vice."

"The trouble is," he wrote, "that football seduces us by appealing to feelings that the modern intellectual has learned to scorn — and which much of the nation is now beginning to question . . . it makes respectable the most primitive feelings about violence, patriotism, manhood."

Of course, there is nothing really novel about this sort of criticism. In certain elitist circles, it is an article of faith that football — along with Spiro Agnew-type talks and other contact sports — reflect the surviving traces of cultural and political atavism. Nevertheless, my attention was particularly drawn to this critique because it encapsulates an attitude apparently held by many persons — and, editors, please note carefully my description here — *by many persons who characterize themselves as intellectuals.*

Is "patriotism" indeed a "primitive" feeling that "much of the nation is now beginning to question"? Are the age-old attributes which our society attaches to "manhood" out of fashion? Are these and other "early American" values, embraced by those who follow the example of Vince Lombardi, in process of being replaced by a "new American ethic"?

As one who has extensively traveled our country in recent years, I am prepared to answer these questions with a degree of firsthand — not theoretical — knowledge. And my reply to these self-characterized intellectuals is that they, not we here in this room, are the Americans out of touch with what's going on in our country today.

For despite the assertions of critics of American tradition, what really has come into question by most of the nation in recent years is not that which the critics patronizingly describe as " the most primitive feelings" concerning our ethic.

Rather, what is really being questioned by Americans at the grass roots is the introspection and arrogance of those critics themselves — in politics, the media and the arts — those whose judgments and opinions regarding national life are formed almost exclusively by talking and writing to and about each other's opinions and tastes, from within the cloistral compound of their own narrow and generally vicarious experience.

These are the critics — both cultural and political — described by the philosopher Eric Hoffer as "the faultfinding [men] of words" who hope "by persistent ridicule and denunciation" of existing institutions and customs, to shake "prevailing beliefs and loyalties."

To be sure, a free society encourages and thrives on the contributions made by its fault-finders. The men and women who founded and built our country were fault-finders, as were their leaders. The opportunity to effect change is, after all, what distinguishes our own society from totalitarian systems.

But in the latter-day zeal for new life-styles, morality, and politics, those who propose the overthrow of prevailing beliefs and loyalties are obliged to consider, if they mean to be responsible as well as vocal, that in a free society the desirable social and political objective is not change alone, but change for the better.

Americans are advised by their self-anointed cultural betters, for example, that the rigid disciplines of bygone eras are unrealistic and inapplicable to modern life.

Now, no one seriously contends that the Victorian code of the preindustrial age could be or should be imposed on today's society. But is it "realism" to argue, as an alternative, that American society will be the better for a cultural change which makes respectable the most primitive feelings concerning self-indulgence in indolence, in lawbreaking, in drugs, or the most prurient standards in literature and art?

Again, few would disagree that jingoism and the lust for glory in war are the sentiments of a world of cavalry charges and sabers, not the nuclear era. Yet, is the cause of individual freedom served by our ignoring the existence of ambitious competitive societies in which "the most primitive feelings about violence, patriotism, manhood" are emphasized and exalted?

And then, of course, there are the political theorists who, satisfied of consensus among their own limited circle, purport to speak for the grass roots in faulting existing institutions of American government and law as being, in their words, "unresponsive to the people."

Of this type of political criticism, the poet–philosopher Archibald MacLeish some years ago had this to say:

> Criticism in a free man's country, is made on certain assumptions, one of which is the assumption that the government belongs to the people and is at all times subject to the people's correction and criticism — correction and criticism such as a man gives and should give, those who represent him and undertake to act on his behalf. Criticism of the government made upon that basis is proper criticism, no matter how abusive.
>
> But abuse of a representative government made . . . upon the assumption that the government is one thing and the people another — that the President is one thing and the people who elected the President another — that the executive departments are one thing and people whom the departments serve another — abuse of a representative government made with the implication that the government is something outside the people, or opposed to the people, something the people should fear and hate — abuse of that kind is not "criticism" and no amount of editorial self-justification can make it sound as though it were.

Years after these lines were written, the man whose memory we honor tonight was asked by an interviewer to comment on latter-day critics of our system. And as we might have expected, Vince Lombardi, the social commentator, was no more inclined to equivocate than Vince Lombardi, the coach.

These critics of the American system raise questions, he replied — and many of the questions they raise are legitimate concerns for all thinking Americans.

However, added Lombardi the teacher, those who would criticize the system in a free society are obliged to offer constructive alternatives. The critics of America's existing institutions point to problems, yes — but they have yet to point the way to a system better equipped to solve those problems than the system they criticize.

Vince Lombardi was a man who recognized change as inevitable and essential. To men inbued and motivated by the elements of "early American ethic," change is not dreaded. It is accepted, indeed welcomed, as a challenge to the individual, to the team, and to the society.

A football team, he once wrote, never stands still. It is always in process of change. And it is either getting better, or getting worse, going forward or going backward.

Because Vince Lombardi and men like him — men of all ages, races, creeds — young Americans like Larry DiNardo, Chip Kell, Rock Perdoni, and Jim Stillwagon — are not satisfied with things as they are, they strive and succeed. Because they and the great majority of their fellow countrymen believe in America and the system which provides them opportunity to improve themselves and their society, America will not stand still. It will go forward. It will change for the better.

That is the American ethic to which Vince Lombardi dedicated his life's work as a teacher and leader of his fellowmen. It is the ethic which brought this nation together, and it is the ethic that will hold it together.

447

February 1, 1971, Washington, D.C.
Midwinter Conference of the National Association of
Attorneys General

ATTORNEY GENERAL BURCH, other distinguished attorneys general, ladies and gentlemen:

I am glad that your president and I were able to make the necessary schedule adjustments to make it possible for me to spend these few brief moments with you this morning.

Indeed it would have been most difficult for me not to have accepted this invitiation, because your president, Bill Burch, was my attorney general during the two years that I served as governor of Maryland. I consider him an old and valued friend, and our mutual trust was such that I never felt the need of what one of my colleagues once described as a "one-handed" attorney general. Let me explain.

A Midwestern governor once told me that to him the ideal attorney general would be one with only one hand, because every time he asked his attorney general for an opinion on some new program, he would receive an eight-page response. The first seven-and-one-half pages would set out all the reasons why the governor's proposal was valid, sensible, and desirable, but the last half page would tersely state: "On the other hand, the plan has substantial constitutional defects, and cannot be adopted."

So I'm grateful for having had an attorney general who used only one hand at a time when he wrote opinions. Although we were from different political parties, and were both elected on a statewide basis, I do not recall a single instance when I propounded a question to him that I received an answer tinged in any manner with partisan politics.

Of course, we were not always in 100 percent agreement on every issue. But we found a way on those few occasions when we disagreed to do so without being disagreeable. This drove the press out of their minds. For we never once engaged in the political backbiting they had so freely predicted.

I mention this because I know that many of you, the attorneys general of the states, are not of the same political party as President Nixon. Yet I am here to enlist your aid, to ask you to join with him in what he has called "A new American Revolution — a peaceful revolution" to turn the power of government back to the people.

Ten days ago in his State of the Union address, the President set out a bold new program, containing some monumental solutions to some of the problems now facing this country.

He proposed a new system of sharing federal revenues with state and local governments — a financial transfusion that can save our federal system and bring new strength to government at the grass roots level, government that you and I know is best qualified to judge and respond to the needs of people. This proposal includes $5 billion in new money the first year, with no federal restraints on its use. It would be based on a fixed percentage of the federal income tax and would increase in dollars each year as the tax base grows. The proposal also includes $11 billion in "special revenue sharing," for specific areas such as education or law enforcement but without the narrow program restrictions that have applied in the past. One billion of this $11 billion is new money. The remainder would come from converting one-third of the existing categorical grants to block grants.

The President also renewed his proposal to overhaul the archaic and unworkable welfare system, which gets worse and more destructive of human values each year. It would provide a basic income for poor families and work incentives designed to lead them out of the present perpetual welfare cycle.

He proposed a reorganization of the very framework of the federal government, to make it better able to deal with the problems of our people. Seven of the present eleven agencies would be consolidated into four new departments: Human Resources, Community Development, Natural Resources, and Economic Development, leaving only the Departments of State, Treasury, Defense, and Justice as they are now constituted.

He is offering programs to assure the preservation of land for parks and recreational areas across the breadth of America, and to provide greater assistance from the federal government in restoring clean air and clean water.

He proposes a massive assault in the war on cancer by making its cure a major governmental cause. And he will soon set forth a program to meet the urgent needs of our people for adequate health care — health care that can be achieved without bankrupting families.

He is hopeful of accomplishing all of this without an inflationary budget.

From my service at both the county and state levels of government and from my two years in the federal government, I know first hand that the preservation and restoration of America are tasks that can only be accomplished by the close interworking of government at every level. It is towards this goal that the President has committed this administration.

Within the next few weeks, the President will take his revenue sharing program to the governors of your states, seeking not only their endorsement, but also their assistance in getting the Congressional support needed to make these plans reality.

I know that your opinions will be of great persuasive value, both to your governors and to your congressmen; for few men in public life have the opportunity that is given to an attorney general to see the whole operation of government.

I do not need to tell you gentlemen how grave the problems in this country are today, nor do I need to tell you that without some redirection of governmental activity — without intensive efforts to solve our problems — the very existence of America as we know it will be seriously jeopardized.

We in this country have just concluded a decade unlike any in the history of the nation. It was a decade of great change, of controversy, and of violence. During the last decade, the entire concept of government changed and with it changed the role of almost every government official.

Certainly during these last ten years there was a material change in the role of a state attorney general. He found himself sitting in the very eye of the storm of controversy that swirled through our society. It might once have been true that an attorney general could sit in his ivory tower, far removed from the battle, and write abstract legal opinions on relatively straight forward questions of law. But if this were ever true, it is no longer.

One need look no further than at the decisions of the Supreme Court over the last ten years to see how the relationship of citizens and government has changed. Few, indeed, are the areas of governmental activity in which the Court's decisions have not had great significance, and each of those decisions affected and made more difficult the task of a state attorney general.

Our whole concept of the relationship between church and state was altered by the decision of the Court in *Murray* and in *Schemp*. Our long-established system of criminal justice and criminal prosecution was completely revised by the Court's decisions in *Mapp*, *Escobedo*, and *Miranda*. The old ground rules for dealing with obscenity and pornography were discarded in *Freedman*, *Ginzburg*, and *Jacabellis*. Indeed, the states were required to restructure the very framework of their governments by the reapportionment cases decided on June 15, 1964.

As a lawyer, I see no prospect that the problems you will face in the 1970s will be easier than those which arose in the 1960s. For our society is still undergoing a great metamorphosis, and you and I, and our children, and our children's children, will continue to feel its effects.

From all of this, I believe it is obvious why government must reexamine itself and why local governments, state governments, and the federal government must work more closely than ever before to provide one united governmental effort towards keeping America progressive and vital. We must bring about the "peaceful revolution" of which the President speaks. It is only through wide public action that we can succeed.

I believe, gentlemen, that by working together — the cities, the states, the federal government — we can effectively persuade even our severest critics that change can be accomplished in a peaceful manner.

Violence will never solve the problems of America. Acts of violence destroy not only their victims, but the perpetrators themselves.

There is presently a welcome lull in the climate of violence that was so prevalent during the past several years. Hopefully, we have seen the end of violence as a political force in our great cities and on our campuses. Hopefully, it has been replaced by reason. If so, the need for change remains no less insistent.

Even with domestic tranquillity, the years ahead will be difficult. For the problems we face in better enabling man to live at peace with his neighbor and his environment are many and great.

No responsible person would suggest that the adoption of the programs set out by the President would lead to an immediate and completely satisfactory solution to all of America's problems. But this redirection of government would provide a magnificent beginning toward the changes that must come to pass if forty years or 100 years from now we are still to be a great and prosperous nation. Perhaps by following this new course suggested by the President, it will become apparent to all men that their grievances and criticisms will not only be heard, but will be evaluated and — if meritorious — acted upon by their government. Maybe, too, this new direction in government can achieve, within our lifetime, the end of the great evil of racial discrimination and the elimination of the racial tensions that exist among us.

I believe the President's plan provides us with high hopes that we can produce an economy that will enable every man who is willing to work to support his family and to educate his children, in peace and in dignity, and that we can provide a decent standard of living for those who, despite their best efforts, are unable to support themselves.

Perhaps this new concept of which the President speaks will lead us to an America in which we can reverse the deterioration of our great cities and render them so safe that our people may walk, by day or by night, without fear of the robber, the rapist, or the killer.

I believe all of this, because I have great confidence in these United States, as you do. Together we can help translate our hopes into a stronger America.

February 3, 1971, Washington, D. C.
Hearst Senate Youth Conference

MY COMPLIMENTS to the Hearst Foundation and to you young ladies and gentlemen who have been selected from leadership positions in high schools throughout America to attend this ninth annual Senate Youth Conference. I know you are having an interesting and informative week in Washington, learning firsthand how your Senator's office operates and also something about the various departments in the executive branch. It is our hope that the knowledge and stimulation you receive here may someday interest you in positions of public leadership. And I'm sure that for many of you that will be the case.

This Senate Youth Conference, which I had the privilege of addressing two weeks after taking office as Vice President and as President of the Senate in 1969, reflects some of the best qualities of America: the eagerness of young people to prepare themselves for leadership, the willingness of busy men to assist them in attaining that goal, the generosity of a private foundation in supporting this program; and, behind all of this, the clearly expressed faith in our political system.

You have reached your present age at a particularly important time, both for youth and for America. As you know, the Supreme Court has ruled recently in favor of Congressional legislation granting eighteen-, nineteen-, and twenty-year-olds the right to vote in national elections. For some this has caused concern.

But let me assure you, as one who is often depicted as a fierce and ferocious scolder of youth, that I do not, in the least, share this concern. I believe this is a good step, a needed change, and one that is long overdue. As Vice President and, previously, as governor of Maryland, I consistently supported the enfranchisement of eighteen-year-olds. I have done so because I believe the great bulk of our young people are ready to take on adult burdens at eighteen. Now, it may surprise you but, contrary to popular opinion, that view is not an invention of our times. It is deeply rooted in history.

Why should twenty-one be the magic age for a person to become an adult? Why not twenty or nineteen or indeed eighteen? Well, I did a little research into the matter and discovered that it started back in the Middle Ages. During most of the Middle Ages, in Northern Europe, the general age of majority was fifteen, not twenty-one. Only the small knight class had a higher age, which was eventually fixed at twenty-one. Yet the reason for this was unrelated to experience or maturity. The need to bear heavy arms, to lift a lance or sword while wearing steel armor was the determining factor. As the strength and skill required for knightly pursuits were not generally acquired before twenty-one, that became for knights the age of majority.

This practice of the gentry came gradually to apply universally. The age, then, that is today so often regarded as boundary betwen maturity and immaturity derives its origin from the physical needs of medieval knights.

I need hardly note that we are no longer in the Middle Ages, even though some of my Democratic colleagues sometimes try to accuse us Republicans of thinking that we are. Furthermore, young people today are better educated and they mature physically much sooner than they did even fifty years ago. I make that observation as an experienced father of three young adults and one teen-age daughter who is fifteen going on twenty. So it's fair to conclude that Congress was acting wisely from the historical as well as the biological perspective in lowering the voting age from twenty-one to eighteen.

You young people here today, then, are really not so young. Most of you, I understand are about 16 or 17, and as juniors and seniors in high school are rapidly approaching the new voter age for national elections. Some of you probably have reached it. I urge you then to regard yourselves not as youths, but as being on the threshold of adulthood.

We hear a lot about youth these days, and the freewheeling application of that term to people from fifteen to twenty-five would astonish our most recent ancestors, to say nothing of those in the Middle Ages.

The Office of Economic Opportunity for instance, lists as eligible for its Youth Development Program "youth between the ages of fourteen and twenty-five." The National Commission on the Causes and Prevention of Violence, in its report of November 1969, spoke of "youth aged fifteen to twenty-four." Some of the most aberrational spokesmen of the wild left — now at age thirty — seem to claim eternal youth. Many sociologists and educators use the term in the same way. So do the news media.

In my opinion, young people above the ages of eighteen or twenty are too old to be classified as youth. They are young adults, and they deserve to be regarded as such. It has been so throughout history. There are numerous examples where public leadership at an early age was fully possible for those who were ready to assume the responsibilities.

When only twenty-four, William Pitt was made Prime Minister of England, at that time the most powerful nation on earth. He proved to be one of the most able leaders in modern history.

At nineteen, Caesar Augustus inherited the Roman Empire and immediately demonstrated his ability by raising an army and leading it himself against rivals who were challenging his position. His greatness is unquestioned.

At seventeen, Joan of Arc was leading a victorious army.

451

At twenty-one, Alexander Hamilton was already an important and recognized figure in the American Revolution.

At twenty-three, Alexander the Great became King of Macedon, and within seven years he had conquered a large portion of the known world.

These were not, I should stress, men or women whose accomplishments were achieved in the privacy of the home or studio or laboratory. They were *public* leaders and accepted as such by men two and three times their age.

So we can see that throughout history youthful years have seldom hindered either the assumption of normal adulthood or outstanding accomplishment by the gifted. I submit that the desire today on the part of our young men and women for recognition by society and for control over their own lives is a desire not for something new but for something old. The truly unusual development occurred long ago, when our society saw fit to place its children under tutelage for greater and greater periods of time in the interest of advancing their education. While it may appear to some that we are in the vanguard of a great youth revolt, we are in fact only returning to cultural patterns that have been found over thousands of years to be the most suited to developing the natural gifts of men.

In this sense, then, I am in sympathy with the "youth liberation" movement. But one aspect of this phenomenon distresses me. It is an aspect that affects both sides of the generation gap. Young Americans too often are represented as crying out as a class for recognition and as asking for special attentions. In response, many members of the older generation — my generation — have come to regard this cry as a class action and have chosen to shower on "youth" generally the special attentions that they thought youth wanted.

This has been, in my opinion, the wrong response. Our response to your appeal and the appeal of those a bit older than you should not be special attentions. That is not, it seems to me, what young people really want. Rather they want to be released from the bondage of youth, to be taken seriously as citizens, to compete as full members of the community. And I think they should. Our reply to the demands of young people should not be special programs, special committees, special offices, all to deal with youth. Many such things have been proposed, as you know.

On the contrary, our reply should be to accept young men and women — especially those eighteen and over — as full members of the community. Inexperienced members perhaps, but still ready to take on a great deal more in the way of responsibilities and burdens than they generally have been given today.

I am glad to note that on this point I am in full agreement with the Report of the President's Commission on Campus Unrest, better known as the Scranton Report. One of the recommendations of that report was this — and I quote from the report:

> Deal with students, and young people generally, as constituents and citizens. . . . We do not, however, recommend the creation of positions for "youth representatives" within the executive branch. Young people are politically more diverse than any other group in American life; the impossibility of finding a single "representative" young person is obvious; and it is in any case doubtful that formal recognition should be granted to groups defined merely by age.

That last statement is especially important: We should not categorize people by age. We are one nation, one people. We are all members of a single community.

I recommend to my own generation, then, that we cease thinking of people from eighteen to twenty-five as youth. We should not respond to their demands by setting them apart with special, patronizing attentions. Instead we should regard them as young adults and give them challenges and opportunities in accord with their individual abilities.

To your generation I urge this: Do not think of yourselves as "youth." Think of yourselves as individuals. Think of yourselves as being on the threshold of adulthood, one or two years away from possessing the vote. Think of yourselves not as members of a given class or group but as members of the whole of American society.

452

And to you young people in particular, you who are here, I would say: You are leaders. But do not think of yourselves as leaders of youth fighting for the rights of youth. Think of yourselves as leaders of people. Your constituency is presently very limited in age, but you will shortly be in a position to serve a much larger community, a community where your constituency will include many people older than yourselves. It will be on the basis of your ability to appreciate more than the needs of your own age group that you will be recognized as leaders.

That is why you are here. As high school leaders you are being asked to take a close look at the work of men and women who are leaders of the entire nation, not of one special group. You have not been meeting with labor leaders, or civil rights leaders, or academic leaders. You have been meeting with Senators and Representatives, secretaries of cabinet departments, and heads of agencies. These are men who represent people of all ages and all backgrounds.

Note them well. They are leaders — every last one of them. And if I can leave you with one final bit of advice as you think upon the prospect of public careers, it is this: Think of yourselves as members of society as a whole, not as representatives of some special interest group. Gain attention not as lobbyists for youth, but as individual men and women commanding the respect of all of your fellow citizens. Seek to advance not on the basis of your age, but on the basis of your ability. And remember that youth is fleeting. Not too long from now, you must adjust to middle age and eventually to old age.

If you do these things, you will be responding positively to the trust that the President, the Congress, and our highest court have so recently placed in young Americans hardly older than yourselves, a trust that I believe is well placed. I applaud your leadership thus far, and I wish each of you well in his or her future endeavors.

February 17, 1971, Richmond, Virginia
Lincoln Day Dinner

TONIGHT WE honor the first Republican President — Abraham Lincoln. My principal speech topic is not going to be about Lincoln the President, but about the federal system he struggled to preserve and the new challenges that it faces today.

Before going into that, I'd like to tell you one historical anecdote about Lincoln that's particularly appropriate at a fund-raising dinner. It said that once, when President Lincoln was making a speech, a drunk in the audience called out to him — and incidentally, fund raisers must have been a lot cheaper in those days — "Did I have to pay a dollar to see the ugliest man in the United States?" And Lincoln said, "Yes sir, I'm afraid you were charged a dollar for that privilege. But I have it for nothing."

When the founders of this republic gathered in Philadelphia 184 years ago, their principal task was to establish "a more perfect Union" without unduly weakening the states that would make up its constituent parts.

Mankind is witness that they succeeded beyond their wildest dreams and they made a lasting contribution to truly representative government.

Samuel Eliot Morison, the historian, refers to the Constitution that they created over a four-month period as "a work of genius, since it set up what every earlier political scientist had thought impossible, a sovereign union of sovereign states."

And he adds:

This reconciling of unity with diversity, this practical application of the federal principle, is undoubtedly the most original contribution of the United States to the history and technique of human liberty.

Today we still function in the federal system that our forebears created. But as we approach our 200th birthday as a nation, and seek to strengthen and preserve the system of specified and shared powers that has served us so well, we face a quite different problem from that of the founders. Their problem was to create a strong national government. Our problem is to strengthen state and local governments and to return them to full partnership in the federal system. What we are trying to restore is an essential balance.

Federalism is a delicate balance of the powers between the national government on the one hand and the state and local governments on the other. This balance has tilted dangerously to the side of the national government in recent years. It is the opinion of many that the very survival of state and local governments as effective units in the system may be at stake in how we respond to this challenge.

Correcting this present imbalance is a major aim of the Nixon Administration — a goal that the President refers to as "The New Federalism," and one to which I believe an overwhelming majority of Americans will subscribe as the national debate continues and as all the facts become known.

Let me say that this subject goes well beyond the Revenue Sharing Bill which the President recently sent to the Congress. It goes back to the very principles on which this nation was founded. And it is one which we intend to discuss with people throughout the land in the coming months. For in the end the course of the nation will depend on their judgment. When the citizen wills something strongly enough — and imparts those views to his government — government responds.

I am pleased to open in the state of Virginia tonight what I intend to be a series of speeches on the future of our federal system. Virginia's role in the making of the nation is known to all who have even a passing interest in the history of our country. I am also advised by the governor's previous remarks that this audience is bipartisan in nature even though this dinner is one sponsored by the Republican party. And this too is appropriate. Because the subject we are discussing transcends the present federal system and it transcends partisan politics. If reforms are to be made they are going to need the strongest possible support of both political parties.

Now consider with me a moment our federal system as it exists today. Consider its origin, consider its development over the years, its present condition, and then let us decide whether it is in need of revitalization and if it is how we should proceed to accomplish this.

The state government in the period immediately following the revolution was the power structure of that day. It exercised a degree of independence that present day governors could only envy. Virginia, for instance, was so independent of Congress and her sister states in the Confederation that she insisted on separately ratifying the peace treaty with Great Britain.

But the states with their separate navies — yes, they had separate navies then — separate militia, customs fees, and financial systems, felt insecure as a new nation under their loose Articles of Confederation and called for a revision of these Articles.

When their delegates got down to the task, they decided to create a new federal structure rather than strengthen the old ties and to submit this to the Congress and to the states for ratification. A new national government with executive, legislative, and judicial branches was proposed — a government that would exercise exclusively certain specified powers. These specific powers of the new national government were spelled out in the Constitution and the Bill of Rights, but the sovereignty of the State and ultimately the sovereignty of the people was protected. It was provided, and I quote, "The powers not delegated to the United States by the Constitution, nor prohibited by it to the States, are reserved to the States respectively, or to the people." Another important recognition

454

of State sovereignty, of course, was the compromise which gave each State equal representation in the Senate regardless of size and regardless of wealth. This territorial standard became another unique feature of the American federal system.

But from the start — although there was a clear separation of powers between the national and state governments — they derived their power from the same people and they cooperated in the service rendered.

Federal–state cooperation actually preceded our federal Constitution. A Congressional statute of 1785, reinforced by the Northwest Ordinance of 1787, gave grants-in-land to the states for public schools. And this was the first instance in which the national government used its resources to encourage the states to follow a national policy, an act which the political scientist and scholar Morton Grodzins called, "A first principle of American federalism."

Collaboration in fiscal affairs began with the federal government's assumption of the Revolutionary War debts of the states in 1790. In the early days of the republic there were also joint ventures between the federal, state, and local governments as partners in stock companies for various projects. Engineering as well as financial help was supplied to Virginia, North Carolina and yes, even the city of Norfolk, in their construction of a canal through the Great Dismal Swamp starting in 1816.

Throughout most of the nineteenth century, land grants remained a principal form of federal aid to the states and sometimes to government-regulated private industry, such as railroads. Cash grants to the states and localities — a source of much of today's friction and frustration in intergovernmental relations — began after the federal government started taxing income in 1913.

Yes, we didn't even have an income tax until 1913. It's hard to believe that but it's true. Also in this period the federal government moved into revenue sources previously left to the states, such as inheritance taxes, tobacco tax, alcoholic beverages, and other excises; and it has never quit these fields. Boy, once it moves in it just doesn't leave. By the same token, however, state and local governments have been extremely slow to take advantage of the income tax as a principal revenue source. There are still thirteen states that do not impose a broad-based tax on personal income.

In 1916 came the beginning of matching grants for highways. This program established the now common practice of attaching conditions to federal aid. And the shift of power to Washington actually began here with these highway grants. With the grants came federal standards, federal regulation, federal inspection and auditing.

But the biggest impact on federalism in this century, aside from the decade the Advisory Commission on Intergovernmental Relations just last year. These figures will stagger you. The Commission said:

Prior to 1930 there had been only ten grant-in-aid progams. These programs had evolved slowly from the 1880s on. They covered land grant colleges, state experiment stations, and extension services, highway construction, forestry cooperation, and vocational education and rehabilitation.

During the New Deal period fourteen additional programs were initiated covering public assistance, employment security, public and child health services, fish and wildlife, public housing, and school lunches.

During the post World War II period running through 1959, twenty new programs were established. Of these, five were extensions of already existing programs. Major new fields entered by the federal government during this period were: airports and hospital construction, mental health facilities, urban reveval, aid to "federally impacted" school districts, sewage treatment plants, and library services.

These forty-four federal aid programs in existence in 1960 — now remember, they've grown from 1880 through 1900 and they total forty-four — cost $6 billion. Of that $6 billion, $5 billion was for highways and welfare. Now, my friends, get set for the deluge.

. . . The 1960s . . . the New Frontier and the Great Society . . . a burst of federal largesse and a bypassing of state and local governments in dispensing it that has been without parallel in our history.

At the end of the decade of the sixties the number of separate federal grant-in-aid programs had proliferated from forty-four to at least 430. Approximately twenty-five were legislated during a single session of Congress, in 1965, and many programs which had been enacted earlier were expanded and broadened. Did this cost more money? Well, I'd say it did.

The federal outlay for grant-in-aid programs jumped from $6 billion in 1960 to $27 billion in 1969.

And now let me quote to you again from the bipartisan Advisory Commission on Intergovernmental Relations' Annual Report of 1970. The Commission had this to say:

> Practically all of the new grant programs (of the 1960s) were functionally oriented, with power, money and decisions flowing from program adminstrators in Washington to program specialists in regional offices to functional department heads in state and local governments — leaving cabinet officers, governors, county commissioners, and mayors less and less informed as to what was actually taking place and making effective horizontal policy control and coordination increasingly difficult at all levels of government.

And their report also noted that there was "a growing tendency to make federal assistance available to nongovernmental organizations," bypassing the local as well as the state government. This trend was most pronounced in the so-called human resources programs. It is interesting to note that twenty-three of the thirty-eight federal grant programs that completely by-passed the states were enacted after 1960.

I can tell you, as one who served as the head of a large metropolitan county government in Maryland from 1963 through 1966, and as governor of that state in 1967 and 1968, that this "Society" these programs funded was "Great" only in Washington. It was an administrative nightmare down the line. And I have a lot of company in that observation — Democrats as well as Republicans.

Not many of us who were in state office during that period can quarrel with the observation by the Advisory Commission on Intergovernmental Relations that, and I quote them again, "In no decade other than that of a century ago [and they are referring to the Civil War era] has the theory of federalism hung so much in the balance in the United States" as it did in the 1960s.

"If there is an overall theme that continues through most of this chronicle of federalism's highlights during the past decade," said the Commission, "it is the theme of imbalance, of a system getting seriously out of kilter."

That, ladies and gentlemen, is the background against which President Nixon is launching his program for a "New Federalism" in America. We seek nothing less than a return to the states — and the local governments which were created by the states and which are historically a part of them — of a measure of the power they formerly held and should hold, in the federal system.

The President has proposed that as a first step in achieving this balance, the federal government should share with state and local governments a small fixed percentage of the federal income tax — 1.3 percent of the total taxable personal income each year, which would amount to $5 billion the first year. These funds would be distributed to state and local governments with no strings attached other then they not be used in any manner that would discriminate against a person because of race, religion, or national origin. The purpose is to relieve hard-pressed state and local treasuries which are now dependent mostly on sales and real estate taxes and, in all but thirteen states, income taxes.

A second, and very vital part of this program would convert $10 billion now available

456

to states and localities in the form of narrow categorical grants into broader purpose grants that would allow the state and local governments to decide what projects this money is to be used for. This consolidation would take place in six broad program areas — education, transportation, urban community development, rural community development, manpower training, and law enforcement. Under the consolidation there would be no requirement of state and local matching funds as is now the case. But the transfer of decision-making power to the government on the scene is the important thing in this program.

At the same time, as you are well aware, the President has proposed a streamlining of the federal executive branch to promote efficiency and to make the government more viable and more responsive to today's needs.

It is our belief that this will go far toward restoring the confidence of citizens in their government at all levels — federal, state, and local. Such confidence recently has been lacking.

There have been times in the past when state and local governments have been unresponsive to the needs of their citizens — particularly those in minority groups — and I don't think there is any question that this is one of the contributing factors that brought on the glut of largely ineffectual federal aid programs and brought on the bypassing of state and even local governments that we saw in the 1960s. But I do not believe this is any longer the case. Legislatures have been reapportioned so that they more accurately reflect the distribution population; governors and legislatures have taken a greater interest in urban problems; and mayors and city councils have tried within their limited means to respond to the needs of all their citizens. But even with the best of intentions these capable and representative state and local governments cannot continue to meet the multiplying demands of their citizens without some assistance. You don't have to listen to many places to find out they are in a serious financial crunch.

The President's proposal is that the federal government release some of its superior resources, and at the same time transfer more decision-making power to state and local governments, the governments which are on the scene of action. The program faces some tough opposition in the Congress; but I assure you that the death notices — or perhaps they're death wishes — that you read and hear almost daily are exceedingly premature. The program has merit and the opinion polls show it is supported in principle by the great majority of the American people — seventy-seven percent according to the latest Gallup Poll on this question. And I am sure our distinguished Virginia Congressmen — Mr. Whitehurst, Mr. Wampler, Mr. Scott, and Mr. Robinson who are here tonight to hear these words are probably aware that the percentage of support in Virginia is somewhat higher than the national Gallup Poll.

Alternatives that would only add to the cost of present programs — whether borne solely by the federal government or shared with the states — would not put the revenue where the problem lies. They do not look to the root of the federal problem; that is, whether state and local government is to be *strengthened* in an effective lasting manner.

I read not too many days ago from many sources that some very high people in and out of the government of the United States, some in the private sector who speak for many — have said they don't think state and local governments can handle this question. I don't think that you can say that the state and local governments are unable to handle anything the people of the American nation ask them to, unless you say, at the same time, that the Americans can't handle it. Because the states are representative of the people, and the counties and the cities are representative of the people just as much as those in the federal government.

This same truth about government and the citizen applies as well to the relationship between the federal government and those at the state and local levels. To paraphrase Mr. Lincoln, the legitimate object of the federal government should be to do for the people only what they cannot do for themselves or what state and local governments cannot do or do so well.

We believe this is what the founders of our federal system had in mind when they formed our more perfect Union at Philadelphia that summer 184 years ago.

March 8, 1971, Kansas City, Missouri
National Congress of American Indians —
Conference on Indian Self-Determination

I COME BEFORE you today as the chairman of the National Council on Indian Opportunity and as a citizen who is interested in what you, as fellow Americans, are thinking and doing.

I regret that my tight schedule prohibits my being with you for the several days that you are here assembled. But I will see that several members of my staff remain behind to participate in your deliberations and to bring back to me a firsthand account of what transpired at all of your meetings. And I promise you that I will receive that information directly and will act on it as best I can.

Your purpose here is self-determination. I happen to believe that the descendants of the first Americans are entitled to that right and have earned the support of all Americans in their effort to achieve it.

I had the pleasure of meeting with many of you for the first time when I addressed the National Congress of American Indians at Albuquerque, New Mexico, in October 1969. We have come a long way since then in forging a new, productive partnership between the government in Washington and the American Indian. But we still have a long way to go. And I know that this meeting will contribute toward our progress in reaching the goal of self-determination for the American Indian.

This is a time of change in the relation of the federal government to the people. At the National Governors' Conference, held just a few days ago in Washington, a major concern was for greater opportunity for state and local governments to direct their own affairs.

And that is also, of course, why you are here today. You seek the freedom to manage your own affairs, the freedom to determine your own destiny. I intend to help you achieve that goal.

Right now, the Nixon Administration is preparing to resubmit to Congress seven bills which relate to Indian self-determination. In our preparation we are going to take very close account of the recommendations that we get from this meeting and from the other meetings you will hold and from the seventeen hearings conducted last fall throughout the country by the National Council on Indian Opportunity. So what you decide here will have a bearing on the final form of the legislation we send to the Congress. The ultimate passage of these important bills will depend largely on the support that you give them.

But let me emphasize very explicitly, just as the President did on July 8, 1970, in his Indian message to the Congress, that we are advocating self-determination and we are repudiating termination. We do not intend to shirk our responsibilities to the Indian people. And we will not.

The American government pledged long ago, in treaties and in agreements with the Indian nations of this land, to provide services to the Indian reservations. Because of those solemn obligations, we shall continue to provide those services.

We must and we will continue to oppose any doctrine of termination, no matter under what name it masquerades. Last year the President urged the Congress, in his words, "to renounce, repudiate and repeal" the policy of terminating federal aid to Indian reservations that was expressed in 1953 in House Concurrent Resolution 108. Congress did not act on the President's request but we shall not relent until it does. Although the 1953 resolution has had no practical effect we believe it should be stricken from the books as a clear Congressional abandonment of the principles of termination.

Let me say at this point how deeply grateful the President was, when — at the Conference of Tribal Leaders, which met in Billings, Montana just three weeks ago — when the Congress expressed with a formal resolution their appreciation to him for his demonstrated concern for Indians. The Indian leaders also expressed hope that the President would continue to support the Indian people and — in the words of the tribal chairmen — "alert the Congress of the United States to the needs of the Indian reservation."

*"Trail of Tears" refers to forced removal of Indians from lands in the Southeastern United States to lands in the West in 1835 and the suffering and hardships they endured. In the haste of the journey, escorting troops did not allow them to tend the sick or bury the dead. In one contingent of 12,000 one-third died enroute.

We've come a long way since the "Trail of Tears,"* if the assembled tribal leaders were willing to thank publicly the President of the United States for his recognition of the right of the Indian people to decide on their own destiny.

Ladies and gentlemen, I can assure you that the President of the United States *will* continue his support for the Indian people of this nation and he *will* alert the Congress to the needs of the reservations.

In October of 1969, when I addressed the National Congress of American Indians in Albuquerque, I made this statement, and I quote:

> This administration recognizes that the time for oratory and tokenism is past; the time for action has come. The time for studies and promises has come. . . . Let us achieve a partnership between the American Indians and their government that is productive and worthy of our highest efforts.

I believe, ladies and gentlemen, that we have achieved that partnership. As evidence, let me cite a few accomplishments of the Nixon Administration in this area before we get into a discussion of some of the unfinished business at hand.

In the area of housing, we built 4,200 units last year under a triagency agreement, and we plan to build at least 30,000 additional units over the next five years. By contrast, from 1962 through 1968 only 5,000 Indian housing unit completions were recorded. Under every project since this administration took office, the full authority to determine what housing will be erected, where it is to be erected, and by whom, has rested with the Indians themselves.

In education, we have established a subcommittee composed entirely of Indians. That subcommittee met just a few days ago in my office and I had the pleasure of meeting with them personally. The primary purposes of this subcommittee are to stimulate the transfer of the control of Indian education to Indian communities and to improve the quality of education for all Indian children. Under this administration, tribes have already begun to operate their own schools — the Navajo, for instance, at Ramah, New Mexico, and the Chippewa–Cree at Rocky Boy, Montana.

In health, we have submitted legislation that would give the Indians control over programs affecting them under the Indian Health Service, and we intend to persist in this goal. In addition, we have cooperated with Project HOPE at Ganado, on the Navajo reservation, in the knowledge that the Sage Memorial Hospital that is operated by HOPE will, within several years, be turned over entirely to the Navajo themselves.

In employment and economic development, we are seeking authority to triple the amount of money in the Revolving Loan Fund of the Bureau of Indian Affairs and, through loan guarantees and interest subsidies, to open much greater sources of private credit to Indians.

In law enforcement, I have directed the National Council on Indian Opportunity, in cooperation with the Departments of Justice and Interior, to undertake a thorough examination of the problem of reservation jurisdiction. We are well aware that on many reservations there are questions about the extent of Indian jurisdiction. We believe that Indian self-determination, as well as human justice, will be furthered considerably if these questions of jurisdiction are determined once and for all.

We have increased Indian membership on the National Council on Indian Opportunity from six to eight, giving Indians equal representation with the cabinet officers for the first time.

459

As I mentioned earlier, we have held seventeen regional meetings with Indians to discuss the President's message of last July 8th. This we have done in the belief that if Indians themselves have the opportunity to participate in the development of new programs and policies the cause of Indian self-determination will be immeasurably advanced.

And perhaps more important than all of these, the United States government, just this past year, returned to the Taos Pueblo Indians of New Mexico their ancient religious lands in the area of Blue Lake. This act directly affected only a small number of Indian people, but I believe that it was a clear demonstration to Indians everywhere that this administration is not only interested in their rights but is determined to see that those rights are protected.

Incidentally, my own fifteen-year-old daughter, Kim, had the rare privilege of visiting the Taos Pueblo Indians, and seeing their beautiful Blue Lake last summer. The thrill of that trip, and the gracious reception she received from the governor of Taos and his people are memories that she will carry with her throughout her life.

It was extremely impressive to her and I don't think she has any project, any activity that she is more taken with or more interested in than the affairs of the American Indians. And she constantly queries me on how things are going and whether we're doing as much as we should be doing in these areas. So you can see I have an incentive to keep up my interest.

As the sacred Blue Lake lands are treasured by the Taos people, so also are the lands and natural resources of all Indian tribes. I fully understand and respect the Indian's love for his land. In order to protect these treasured resources, this administration has proposed the creation of an independent Indian Trust Counsel Authority. In too many of the legal confrontations between Indian land and resource interests and those of the federal government, Indians have been treated unfairly. In those cases where the federal government is faced with an inherent conflict of interest, this independent Trust Counsel Authority must exist to properly represent and protect the interests of the Indian people.

We also have proposed establishing the post of Assistant Secretary of the Interior for Indian and Territorial Affairs and allowing federal employees transferring to tribal organizations to retain their Civil Service status.

All of these important bills failed to pass last year, but I can assure you that they will be resubmitted to the Congress after you, at this Conference, have made your recommendations or approvement of them.

I also understand your concern about the Alaskan native land claims. And I talked this morning, just before I left the office to get on the airplane, with Secretary of the Interior Morton outlining to him the disappointment over the position that has been taken by the Office of Management and Budget in this matter. It's true that some of the settlements that are being discussed by the Indians are not quite realistic. Some of them amount to as much as $100,000 per individual for the 80,000 some Indians involved. But it is also true that we must reach a fair conclusion and a fair determination if present thinking of the Bureau of the Budget is to increase the amount of land from the 2.9 they propose to something over 5 million acres, and to 40 million acres for subsistence land. I'm not sure at this moment that that's sufficient. I really don't think it is. I think we should do better than that. But I intend to enter into the discussion with Secretary of the Interior Morton and the budget people on my return after we receive from you your best estimates in these matters.

I hope you will give my staff members who will remain to deliberate on this particular, very important matter the best information you can. And I hope you will give them the most fair and the most realistic estimates that you can of what you think would be a fair settlement to these claims. They have been dragging too long.

Last year we had a Senate bill and then we had a House bill, and the two Houses of Congress were so far apart that it became utterly impossible to look to any solution. If we could just get some realistic compromise between the claims of the Alaskan natives and what the Congress can be brought to accept as reasonable, perhaps we can get this thing settled for once and for all.

So whatever help you can give my staff members here today, and the members of the

Council, will be most appreciated. And I can assure you that we will follow through with it. We need not just statements of emotion, which are natural in a case like this, we need statements of substance that will give us the arguments with which to knock down the counter arguments in the Congress, in the budget office and other places.

You might also be interested in knowing that I have asked the eight federal agencies and cabinet departments which have Indian programs to take prompt action on important issues which have been brought to my attention by the Indian members of the NCIO. When I receive their replies — from these cabinet members — you will be advised of the actions to be taken.

But these are specifics. What is really more important here is the principle of Indian self-determination.

The Indians of this country, under the leadership of elected officials like yourselves, are making significant advances. To take just one example: last year only three Indians graduated from law schools in this country, but this June there will be ten law graduates, and next year there will be twenty.

We believe that if you are given the power to direct your own affairs, there will be a much greater acceleration of progress for your people in the years ahead.

Now, this administration believes that every American can guide his own affairs better than the federal government can guide them. It believes that citizens, through their elected local governing bodies — in your case, tribal governments — can do more to solve their own problems than can Washington, if they are given the resources. We believe that resources and good local government must go together.

Now, that doesn't mean that the federal government has no purpose. And that doesn't mean that the national objectives of Congress should not be given great dignity. What that does mean is that a true reflection of the legitimate aspirations of the people are bound in the councils of government that are close to that people. In this case, that means your tribal councils. But not just for the American Indians.

In the Nixon Administration this is our policy for *all* Americans, and it has special meaning today for the American Indian. It is the heart of the New Federalism.

We believe you and your tribesmen know better than we in Washington what is right for you. We believe you know what is best for you. Because you know the people, you know the problems, and you know the land.

We in this adminstration believe in giving you control over what you have. The reservations are your lands. The lives you lead on them are your lives. The federal government has obligations to provide financial support. But you should establish the priorities, you should allocate the funds, and you should guide the projects.

In know that is how you want it. And this administration is determined to help you achieve these goals. They are right. They are just. They won't be easy. But they can be won.

March 18, 1971, Boston, Massachusetts
Middlesex Club

THERE IS no doubt that the framers of our Constitution considered the vice presidency an office suitable for men of energy. Until the ratification of the twelfth Amendment in 1804, the defeated major presidential candidate was usually elected Vice President. This created some interesting stresses. Over the years, however, the vice presidency has lost its political punch and become the most placid and uncontroversial of political positions. Indeed, as presently structured, it may be compared to an adjustable easy chair. The occupant has his choice of either reclining sleepily or sitting up alertly. The posture adopted is inconsequential, because it is virtually certain that no one will notice which attitude has been selected.

Whatever his decision, however — whether he has dozed amiably or listened attentively — it has been traditional for a Vice President to be indulged by the intellectuals and opinion makers of his time with nothing harsher than a deprecating comment or a condescending joke.

In recent years, the rules have been amended to allow Vice Presidents to talk — so long as they are careful to say absolutely nothing. This privilege was heavily exercised and refined to a high degree during the last Administration.

And in regard to vice presidential strictures, it seems appropriate to note — on the occasion of a Lincoln Day address before the oldest Republican organization in Massachusetts — that, following four years of lassitude as Abraham Lincoln's Vice President, Hannibal Hamlin suddenly found himself Collector for the Port of Boston.

In my own case, I found it an onerous choice between the ennui of easy chair existence and pointless verbosity. And so, quick Constitutional research revealing no authoritative reason why a Vice President is required to choose between catalepsy and garrulity, I forsook the comfortable code of many of my predecessors, abandoned the unwritten rules — and said something.

Well, in case you haven't heard, my unorthodoxy produced some rather sharp reverberations. It was as though an earthquake, registering eight on the Richter scale, had disturbed the foundations of the *New York Times*, or the funnel of a tornado had dipped into the editorial offices of *Time–Life*. Everywhere, big media referees were flinging down their handkerchiefs and calling foul. The *Washington Post* stepped off fifteen yards for un-Vice Presidential-like conduct. *Time* magazine waved me to the penalty box. And Eric Sevareid took two free throws at the line — both rolling around the rim and, as usual, dropping out.

Finally the tremors and tumult subsided. Whereupon my critics from all walks of life consulted among themselves and brought forth the strongest indictment they could muster.

"The Vice President," they intoned, "just doesn't seem to understand."

If true, the charge would be a serious enough reflection on the condition of the republic. But worse was yet to come. After my speech on the responsibilities of a free news media in a free society, and after the networks had been deluged with mail in support of my conclusions, a noted network newscaster enlarged the indictment by declaring that, not only the Vice President, but the American people as a whole simply don't understand.

Let me quote that spokesman directly.

"The public," said Walter Cronkite recently, "does not understand journalism. They" — that means you and me — "do not know how we work, they do not believe we can hold strong private thoughts and still be objective journalists."

And that's the way it was — or at least the way he saw it — in November 1970.

Mr. Cronkite has stated the case well. He has discerned and defined the scope of the widening credibility gap that exists between the national news media and the American people — a gap which has simply been reported, not created, by this nonunderstanding Vice President. By "national news media" I mean the powerful news outlets having not just a regional, but a national, impact.

Now, before I proceed further, let me pause to observe that, in all probability, my mere utterance of the words "national news media" has in the past few minutes again set the ideological Richter needles quivering all along the Manhattan–Washington fault line. For "national news media" is, after all, the forbidden phrase of modern American politics.

To be sure, such is the power of the national media today that of all our political, social and economic institutions, they seem to be able to cloak themselves in a special immunity to criticism. By their lights, it appears, freedom of espression is fine so long as it stops before any question is raised or criticism lodged against national media policies and practices.

Nor is the national media's refusal to abide criticism reserved for utterances of a Vice President or, as I will momentarily point out, a Congressman or a member of a presidential cabinet. Any citizen who has suffered the frustration of being rebuffed when calling or writing to complain about inaccurate or biased news reporting knows exactly what I mean.

Yet, any extremist who dignifies our adversaries and demeans our traditions is sought out and spotlighted for national attention. He is interviewed as though he were representative of a large following and is treated with the utmost deference as he unloads into millions of American living rooms his imprecations against society and disrespect for civilized law. Such attacks against American institutions are editorially lauded as healthy demonstrations of freedom of expression in a free society.

[At this point, the Vice President's remarks were interrupted momentarily by a young man who was escorted out by authorities.]

And, incidentally, ladies and gentlemen, in a graphic and personal demonstration, did you notice where the lights and cameras just went?

Again, when the president of a prestigious university assaults our nation's judiciary by declaring that certain defendants cannot receive a fair trial in an American court, he is not charged with attempting to "intimidate" the courts. On the contrary, he is praised by important segments of the national news media for contributing to what they term "the dialogue."

And, as I shall discuss in a few moments, when a major television network delivers a subtle but vicious broadside against the nation's defense establishment, accusing it of disseminating deceptive, self-serving propaganda, contrary to the country's interest, that, too, is considered a legitimate exercise of the right to free expression in the public interest.

But let no man be so bold as even to utter the words "national news media." For, as we are forewarned by the national media themselves, the merest mention of the phrase by a man in government somehow constitutes a form of "intimidation" so great as to pose a fundamental threat to the people's right to know.

And so tonight, in once again taking up matters involving an important segment of the national news media, I believe it only fitting to cite some authority within media ranks to reinforce my right to do so.

Hear now the words of Mr. Frank Stanton, president of the Columbia Broadcasting System.

"No American institution," Mr. Stanton has said, "including network news organizations, should be immune to public criticism or public discussion of its performance."

I wholeheartedly agree. Proceeding from this premise, I therefore intend to discuss the public's right to know more about the performance of Mr. Stanton's network news organization in two cases involving documentaries — instances wherein CBS itself has claimed an immunity from criticism ill-becoming one of the country's major institutional critics.

For those who would challenge a Vice President's right to discuss such matters, let me say this: I do so only to raise questions which, if answered, will shed light on an area of network news operations about which the public knows little and needs to know more. These questions do not originate with me, nor do they arise from any partisan political considerations. Others before me, including the Federal Communications Commission, a special subcommittee of the Congress and a former Democratic cabinet member, have asked Mr. Stanton similar questions, to no avail.

However, considering the serious charges leveled recently by the CBS television news organization against the public affairs activities of the Department of Defense, the matter of the network's own record in the field of documentary making can no longer be brushed under the rug of national media indifference.

Little less than a month ago, on the evening of February 23, 1971, CBS television broadcast a one-hour documentary entitled *The Selling of the Pentagon.* The substance of this documentary was that the Department of Defense is subjecting the American people to, I quote, "a propaganda barrage . . . the creation of a runaway bureaucracy that frustrates attempts to control it."

"Nothing is more essential to a democracy," read the CBS script, "than the free flow of information. Misinformation, distortion, and propaganda all interrupt that flow."

No one can disagree with the latter statement. But just as he who enters a court of equity should come with clean hands, the news organization that makes such charges should itself be free of any taint of misinformation, distortion and propaganda in its own operations. In this regard, it is the CBS television network, not the Department of Defense, that leaves much to be desired in terms of "the free flow of information."

Let me be specific. What I cite here is not simply the opinion of a single public official, but conclusions drawn by responsible investigative agencies in the government and the Congress. These conclusions are contained in reports, which in themselves would have made excellent documentary exposés, save for the fact that the national news media have given them scant attention. They concern the production and editing techniques employed by CBS personnel in the making of the documentaries *Hunger in America* and *Project Nassau.*

Many in this audience may have been watching on the evening of May 21, 1968, when the attention of millions of Americans tuned to CBS television was drawn to the onscreen image of an infant receiving emergency treatment while a narrator's offscreen voice said:

> Hunger is easy to recognize when it looks like this. This baby is dying of starvation. He was an American. Now he is dead.

This was compelling film footage and narration designed to awaken the public conscience to a serious social problem. The only thing wrong with it was that it was untrue — but wait, let the official Federal Communications Commission report tell the story. I quote from the official report:

> Our post-broadcast investigation revealed that the infant who was filmed by CBS in the nursery, and who was shown in the relevant segment of the *Hunger in America* program . . . was born prematurely . . . the previous day. . . . The infant died on October 29, 1967, the death certificate shows the cause of death as "Immediate cause: Septicemia. Due to: Meningitis and Peritonitis. Due to: Prematurity." There is no evidence to show that either the mother or father was suffering from malnutrition. . . .

Thus, although the dramatic footage which opened the documentary *Hunger in America* may have served the network's purpose of whetting viewer interest, the baby shown "dying of starvation" in fact died of other causes.

Nor, as investigation of the production revealed, was this distortion only an incidental aspect in the overall production of *Hunger in America.* Evidence was submitted that CBS personnel had, in the words of the report, "paid participants on the program to appear before its cameras and perform as per their instructions;" that the CBS crew "requested that the doors of the commodity distribution office be closed to allow a line of people to form;" that a physician was asked to make "more dramatic statements" and when he refused, the segment of the program featuring his more balanced view of the problem on malnutrition in the area was edited out for being "too technical."

In a letter to Mr. Stanton, then Secretary of Agriculture Orville Freeman cited numerous other instances of factual misrepresentation and distortion contained in the documentary. He asked for equal time to present a Department of Agriculture response to the network program. The network denied this request.

Now, having myself gained some experience in what to expect by way of negative network response to public criticism, I can fairly predict what Mr. Stanton and other CBS spokesmen are likely to say tomorrow morning concerning my recital of the case history on *Hunger in America*. They will ask why this matter should be brought up again at this time.

My answer is that I believe it both timely and in the public interest to point out that the same CBS employee who wrote the script to the 1968 documentary, *Hunger in America*, wrote the script to the 1971 documentary, *The Selling of the Pentagon*.

A second and even more startling case history of a documentary-in-the-making involves the participation of CBS personnel in an aborted effort to film a 1966 invasion of Haiti. The network's role in this effort, called *Project Nassau*, was investigated last year by the Special Subcommittee on Investigations of the House Commerce Committee. Here again, let the report of the investigative body tell the story. I quote:

> The activities preparatory to *Project Nassau* involved more than the filming of sham events, manipulation of sound tracks, and the like. Underlying the whole activity was the earnest endeavor by a group of dangerous individuals to subvert the laws of the United States. Had it been successful, the conspiracy would have produced a crisis for American foreign policy in the sensitive Caribbean area. Six men have now been convicted for their part in this conspiracy.

Continuing with the House Subcommittee report on CBS' participation in *Project Nassau*:

> CBS funds were provided for the leasing of a 67-foot schooner which was to be utilized by the invasion force; expenses were reimbursed for the transportation of weapons which were to be subsequently used by the conspirators; various payments were made to . . . the leader of the invasion conspiracy, with full knowledge of his identity and his criminal intentions. If these acts did not actually involve the network in the conspiracy to violate the U.S. Neutrality Act, they came dangerously close to doing so.

They're not my words, ladies and gentlemen. They're the words of the man of the House of Representatives charged with this investigation.

Concerning such illegal activities, the House subcommittee, in the course of its investigation, made public a CBS policy memorandum which, to quote from the views of a bipartisan group of subcommittee members, "represents a level of irresponsibility which should no longer be tolerated if the public interest is to be served."

Let me read here from that CBS policy statement to its employees and I quote:

> CBS personnel will not knowingly engage in criminal activity in gathering and reporting news, nor will they encourage or induce any person to commit a crime.

Now keep in mind, I am directly quoting the network's policy statement to its employees.

> *Obviously, there may be exceptions which ought to be made on an ad hoc basis even to so absolute a rule.*

Ladies and gentlemen, exceptions to the prohibition of CBS' employees in engaging in criminal activities, nor encouraging or inducing someone to commit a crime. That's unbelievable, but that's what this memorandum says. Small wonder that the House subcommittee termed the results of its *Project Nassau* investigation, "disquieting." The subcommittee said, quote:

> To the average viewer, unsophisticated in the intricacies of television production, a network news documentary typically represents a scrupulously objective reporting of actual events shown as they actually transpired. If *Project Nassau* is any indication, this is not always true. During the preparation of this news documentary, CBS employees and consultants intermingled and interacted with personages actively engaged in breaking the law. Large sums of money were made available to these individuals with no safeguards as to the manner in which these funds would be put to use. Events were set up and staged solely for the purpose of being filmed by the CBS camera. . . .
>
> A disturbing conclusion after the inquiry to date with respect to *Project Nassau* is that the CBS News organization, having become elated at the prospect of a sensational news first — a complete documentary of the forcible overthrow of a foreign government — proceeded in a reckless attempt to capture the hoped-for-film, and that it did so with no great regard for either accuracy or legality.

Here, again, this investigation of the making of a CBS documentary bears on the network's more recent production, *The Selling of the Pentagon*. For the executive producer of the aborted documentary, *Project Nassau*, also served as executive producer of *The Selling of the Pentagon* — a documentary, keep in mind, that sought to indict the Department of Defense for "misinformation, distortion," and the alleged staging of events.

But disquieting as are the results of these investigations by the FCC and the House subcommittee, there is an even more disturbing note to be added here concerning media treatment of the reports themselves.

Who can doubt that had the evidence uncovered and the conclusions drawn by these investigative bodies related to any other industry or institution they would long ago have become, to coin a phrase, household words? The national news media would have made them so — just as CBS even now seeks to exploit its purported "findings" regarding the Pentagon.

Yet, when the industry and institution involved is itself a part of the national news media, a strange silence and rare restraint inhibits the people's right to know. So powerful is this inhibition that neither a cabinet member, nor an executive agency, nor a Congressional committee was effective in bringing to public attention the serious matters to which I have addressed these remarks. And I have grave doubts about how much of my criticism tonight will be carried in the national media.

My purpose here, however, has not been to pillory or "intimidate" a network or any segment of the national news media in its effort to enhance the people's right to know. Rather it is, once again, to point out to those in positions of power and responsibility that this right to know belongs to the people. It does not belong to the national networks or any other agency, public or private. It belongs *to the people themselves,* and they are entitled to a fair and full accounting of the truth, and nothing but the truth, by those who exercise great influence with their consent.

The House subcommittee concluded:

> We are living through dangerous times. In these days it does not seem too strong a statement to say that the survival of the American society may depend upon the political and social judgments made during the next few years by the American electorate. Sound judgment presupposes valid information. The American public looks in great measure to the electronic news media to provide that information.

Let the people's representatives — not only in their government but in their national news media — also look, listen, and take heed.

April 1, 1971, Washington, D.C.
Veterans Administration Volunteer Service
25th Anniversary Meeting

AT A TIME when it seems fashionable to knock the military and to disparage the position of the United States in Vietnam, I count it a special privilege to meet with a group of people who are giving so much of their time to assisting our war veterans.

Your unstinting service as volunteers at our 165 veterans hospitals — which I am informed amounts to some nine million donated hours a year — deserves the gratitude of the entire nation, as well as the men you honor with your service.

I bring you the President's personal best wishes and congratulations on this 25th anniversary of the Veterans Administration Volunteer Service. Your growth from five member organizations in 1946 to twenty-eight today — with 110,000 hospital volunteers — has been of great benefit to our veterans and to the country.

Much of the strength of America, and much of the best in America, is reflected by the work of its various volunteer organizations. While others may complain and fret and wait for someone else to solve a problem, you volunteers go out and get the job done — cheerfully. It doesn't land you in the news — like protesting or burning your draft card or desecrating the flag — but you have the greater reward of knowing that you have been of service to your fellow man.

I find it interesting that your membership encompasses several generations, ranging from young people in their early teens to men and women in their eighties — all equally dedicated in their assistance to our ill and disabled war veterans.

I was impressed with the record of Mrs. Elise McCarty who has completed over 15,000 hours of service to hospitalized veterans in Iowa. She drove the twenty-five miles between her home in Oskaloosa and the VA's hospital at Knoxville, Iowa, at least 2,000 times in compiling that record. This would be remarkable for anyone. It is almost incredible when you consider that Mrs. McCarty is eighty-five years old.

And there are many other impressive examples of service from people of all ages, both men and women, in the VA files.

Your service, of course, is to the veterans of all our wars. And all are deserving of our gratitude.

But I believe an extra measure of understanding and appreciation is due the veterans of the Vietnam war.

None of their predecessors have had to fight the lonely fight of the Vietnam veterans. At least they have been made to *feel* lonely — and unappreciated.

They have been told almost daily — if they read or listen to the news from home — that they are fighting in a "worthless" and "immoral" cause, and that we ought to abandon the South Vietnamese to their enemy.

This encouragement has come to them — not from Hanoi Hannah, but from some of the leading members of the United States Senate, prestigious columnists and news commentators, academic figures, some church organizations, as well as assorted radicals, draft card burners, and street demonstrators.

Never mind that the President of the United States, the soldiers' families and close friends, *most* of the Congress of the United States and the great majority of other Americans do not share the masochistic, guilt-ridden view that they are being exploited in Southeast Asia, but feel that they have served their country honorably and well. Unfortunately, this message doesn't get through as loud and clear as does the negative one.

So the Vietnam veterans have a handicap that most of their predecessors never faced. They have fought in the first war, at least in our lifetime, that has not had the support of virtually all of the American people.

To make matters worse, the Vietnam veterans return to civilian life with the unpopularity of the war sometimes transferred to them individually. And they find hostility or indifference where there should be gratitude.

Incredibly, they may even find themselves stereotyped — and falsely stereotyped, let me emphasize — as drug addicts and cold-blooded criminals because of the negative propaganda mounted by critics of this war. Events involving a relative few have damned many. A Harvard psychiatrist suggested to a Senate subcommittee that Vietnam veterans ought, in effect, to be penned up for three or four weeks for what he called "psychosocial detoxification" before being released into the general public. Such treatment, in my judgment, is more appropriate for some elements of our civilian population.

Finally, the Vietnam veterans face an additional burden of an antimilitary attitude that is being encouraged every day in this country.

Admiral Moorer, the chairman of the Joint Chiefs of Staff, spoke of this attitude and its effect on trying to recruit a volunteer military force during an interview published in *U.S. News & World Report* this week.

"Today," said Admiral Moorer, "we have an attitude in this country against military services in general which I think is very unfortunate. The American people can't have it both ways. They can't on one hand insist on an adequate defense against this buildup of capabilities on the part of potential enemies and on the other hand demean and degrade those in uniform."

Admiral Moorer noted cases of young men being discouraged from attending the service academies and the scrapping of ROTC in some of the leading colleges. And he went on to say:

> Right now is a difficult time for the volunteer because a youngster wants to feel that when he joins an organization it's respected and that his mother and father and his friends don't say, "Well, what in the hell are you doing that for?" They ought to tell him, "Son, we're proud of you for what you're doing for your country."

So all of these things militate against the Vietnam veterans more than they have their predecessors.

Let me remind you that 7.5 million young men have served in our armed forces during the Vietnam war period — since 1964 — 2.4 million of them in the war zone itself.

The readjustment to civilian life after military service — including finding a job or resuming formal schooling — is difficult enough without having to confront an indifference or hostility in the general public.

No such feeling exists in this audience. Your record of volunteer service to hospitalized veterans automatically assures that. But it apparently is something of a problem in the country at large, according to articles on that subject published just this last week in at least two national news magazines.

It is incumbent upon all of us to go out of our way to assure our Vietnam veterans that we *do* welcome them home and *do* appreciate their service to this country; and that we will help them find jobs and get resettled. Even those who may have disagreed with United States policy in Southeast Asia owe that much to young men who answered their country's call to service. For they have carried a greater burden, piled on them by homefront snipers, than any American servicemen who ever went to war.

A grateful and understanding nation should see that they are recognized as the very special veterans that they are.

April 7, 1971, Los Angeles, California
Los Angeles Chamber of Commerce Luncheon

BACK IN the 1940s Johnny Mercer wrote a popular song hit. The words went something like this:

> You've got to ac-cent-u-ate the positive/
> E-lim-i-nate the negative/
> Latch on to the affirmative/
> Don't mess with Mister In-Between.

To achieve equal success today, Mr. Mercer would have had to modify the lyrics — make them, in the current vernacular, more relevant. I would guess they would have come out something like this:

> You've got to ac-cent-u-ate the negative/
> E-lim-i-nate the positive/
> Latch on to the disparaging/
> Or at least be Mister In-Between.

This philosophy, this attitude of "let's tell the world how rotten we are and thus expiate our sins," is being drummed into our consciousness to such an extent that it is becoming part of our national psyche.

Masochism replaces pride. Guilt becomes the new intellectual standard, the badge of neosophistication. And we bare our breast each day to a world incredulous of our naivety and beg forgiveness — for being big and powerful and successful . . . and, yes, compassionate.

I sincerely believe, ladies and gentlemen, that if we don't recognize this dangerous attitude for what it is, and overcome it, it will destroy us as a nation. That is why I would like to discuss this perplexing phenomenon with you at some length today.

The United States, long looked upon as the land of the free and the home of the brave, has become — in the characterization of our critics — the land of the oppressed and the home of the uncertain.

And who are the most rabid critics? Well, to paraphrase a well-known saying, "We have met the enemy and they are us." We are engaged in a constant battle to belittle ourselves — to deprecate our principles, to demean our leaders, to disparage our institutions, and to destroy the representative national freedom that made us a great nation.

Accentuate the negative. Here's a small, but fairly typical example, a symptom, shall we say, of the far deeper malaise.

Mr. Gallup recently took one of his periodic polls, using a question that he had used before, so that in addition to sampling the national mood he could also detect any changes in attitude.

This poll, published in most newspapers on Sunday, March 21st, showed that, among the people surveyed in nine nations, there were more in the United States who had *NO* desire to move from their homeland than in any of the other countries. In other words, the overwhelming majority of Americans like it here in spite of all our faults.

Only twelve percent of those surveyed in the United States said if they were free to do so, they would like to live in another country. This contrasted with forty-one percent in Great Britain, thirty-two percent in Uruguay, twenty-seven percent in West Germany, twenty-two percent in Greece, nineteen percent in Finland, eighteen percent in Sweden,

469

seventeen percent in Brazil, and sixteen percent in the Netherlands.

But there was one little hitch. Although eighty-eight percent of our people said they would prefer to remain here, if free to move elsewhere, Mr. Gallup found that the twelve percent who would like to move doubled the percentage so responding in a similar survey taken twelve years earlier in 1959. That's all that was needed to accentuate the negative. It was almost a reflex action.

The headline in the *New York Times* said, GALLUP FINDS 12% WANT TO QUIT U.S. It was not "88% Prefer U.S." or "U.S. Lowest in Dissatisfied Citizens." It was, I repeat, 12% WANT TO QUIT U.S. And the same negative finding was emphasized in nearly every other paper that I saw.

I should make it clear at this point that the attitude I bring to your attention is not the exclusive preserve of the news media. But they do figure prominently in reflecting — and at times helping to shape — this prevalent national malaise, and to that extent they are vitally involved in what I have to say.

The leaders in the movement to plead America guilty because they can't muster the energy to defend her, to downgrade her among the other nations, and to topple, or at least drastically alter, some of her most revered and respected institutions — all with the purest of intentions, I am sure — are to be found in positions of influence in *all* walks of American life: the government, the university, the church, business and labor, the news media, the professions. Their genuine idealism and natural tolerance are exploited to the fullest by radicals who would like to tear America down. These idealists are lulled into condoning lawbreaking — even violence — where some lofty motive is assigned as an excuse.

I for one don't intend to stand idly by and watch the destruction — wittingly or unwittingly — of the institutions that have been built in the sweat of the American free enterprise system over the last 300 years. Reform within our free and representative system — yes. Anarchy and overthrow by violence — no.

Let's look at some specific examples:

VIETNAM

Accentuating the negative, we find that as of May 1 there will be 284,000 American troops in Vietnam, ten years after our initial involvement, with no definite date set for our total disengagement. This is hammered daily at a war-weary nation, with suggestions that we should pull out completely by the end of the year regardless of the consequences and our heavy investment in American lives. In other words we should repudiate the validity of the presidential decisions that sent us to Vietnam and break our commitment to preserve self-determination for the South Vietnamese and the other presently independent people of Southeast Asia.

Eliminating the positive, there is no mention that President Nixon will have brought home 265,000 troops by next month — in a period of about two years — while drastically reducing American casualties and strengthening the South Vietnamese to defend themselves against the Communist aggressor from the North. And there is little notice that he continues to withdraw our forces at a steady clip.

It probably would be hard to find in American history a more glaring example of negative treatment of an issue than the Vietnam war. The news coverage of that war has been preponderantly negative in tone — critical of the United States and the South Vietnamese and, in that sense, helpful to North Vietnam and the Viet Cong. There are, of course, exceptions. But in the main our news media have seemed obsessed with playing up our weaknesses — real or imagined — and ignoring those of the enemy. The recent operation in Laos is an excellent case in point.

Now most knowledgeable people realize that you cannot fully assess the effect of that military operation at this time. There are exaggerated claims by both sides. We firmly *believe* the operation has been successful for the South Vietnamese and that, as in Tet and in Cambodia, the enemy has paid a heavy price and has been greatly weakened. But only the future will show for certain.

This would seem to call for restraint in judgment. But the accounts have been more lurid than ever, more emphatic than ever, and I might add, more negative than ever as concerns the United States and its program of Vietnamizing the war.

Life magazine's account last week offers a particularly interesting report for history. "An ignominious and disorderly retreat," said the headline. The account included such other well-tempered and carefully chosen descriptions as these: "The NVA drove the invading forces out of Laos with their tails between their legs."

("Invading forces" . . . you would think the North Vietnamese were defending their homeland rather than pillaging a country whose neutrality they have violated for twenty years, and where they remain despite their solemn agreement in 1962 to withdraw.)

Here are some other descriptive terms in the *Life* article for the operation: "disastrous failure," "tactical idiocy," "debacle," "palpably ill-conceived," "frantic improvisation," "escalating snafu."

"The troops spent their days and nights running and hiding," said the writer. "Like a flock of startled crows they fled in every direction," he observed at another point.

Life was so proud of the hatchet job that it took out full-page ads in the newspapers to tell us it would be coming. I could hardly wait.

Worse even than our negative attitude, in my opinion, is the feeling that we must cry out to the world that we are guilty of great transgressions. Here again Vietnam offers a good case in point. The critics of this long and difficult war would have us fall on our knees before the world, proclaim it "immoral" and recant, notwithstanding the historical facts. The most masochistic suggestion that I have seen lately comes from former U.S. Attorney General Ramsey Clark, who not only urged unilateral withdrawal by July 4th *this year* — something that is logistically impossible — but said that we must ask forgiveness and offer reparations to the Vietnamese people. "And I mean *really sacrifice*" he said. "We owe it to them, to ourselves, and we owe it to humanity." We are advised that the former attorney general received a "sustained standing ovation" when he made this statement at Yale University.

ASSAULT ON THE MILITARY

Accentuate the negative. Every day we see new assaults on the military establishment — the draft, the individual services and their potential to offer young Americans a satisfying, challenging and rewarding career. Reenlistment in all services is the lowest since 1955 with barely thirty-one percent signing up for a second tour. ROTC enrollment is at the lowest level since before Korea. A young Army major with two tours in Vietnam and a Purple Heart who reluctantly is leaving the service says, "People don't respect the man in uniform any more. The nation doesn't support its fighting men. My wife has to explain to the kids that daddy's job isn't wrong, that it isn't something to be ashamed of. That's no way to live."

And Admiral Moorer, the chairman of the Joint Chiefs of Staff, says — bluntly and appropriately — "The American people can't have it both ways. They can't on one hand insist on an adequate defense against this buildup of capabilities on the part of potential enemies and on the other hand demean and degrade those in uniform."

We also see, as part of this general assault on the military establishment, attacks in the media and in Congress on the Pentagon as a bumbling, inefficient bureaucracy which is also "caught" attempting to "spy" into private lives. The military was ordered — appropriately I think — to start surveillance during the urban riots of 1967 by President Johnson. After all, they were asked by many governors to reestablish order when cities went out of control.

Totally *eliminated* in the current critical assessment is the *positive* — the complete dedication of America's military services to the security of the country, including protection for their harshest critics to rant and rave. We are one of the few countries in the world that doesn't have to fear a military takeover of the civilian government. I wonder sometimes if our people appreciate this fact. It distinguishes us from almost all other peoples on earth.

ASSAULT ON THE FBI

Accentuate the negative. We see it again in the virulent attacks now being mounted daily against the FBI and the distinguished director of that service, who has made it one of the outstanding law enforcement agencies in the world. A presidential candidate in the Senate — one of the many in that body — even showed newsmen an *UNSIGNED* letter of complaint against J. Edgar Hoover that purported to be from ten FBI agents. When he pulled this irresponsible publicity stunt, Senator McGovern said: "The letter . . . is unsigned. The reasons are obvious. But the information it relates has been confirmed."

Accentuate the negative. Militants who would like to blow this nation apart, burglarize an FBI office in Media, Pennsylvania, pilfer unevaluated reports from files and send them to newspapers and Congressmen for public exposure. Is this felony greeted by condemnation? No, only by an escalating cry to stop all surveillance by government agencies. Wouldn't the foreign espionage agents in the United States like that!

HALT THE TECHNOLOGICAL ADVANCE

Accentuate the negative, eliminate the positive. Cut back the space budget, scrap the SST after ten years' investment. "What does it matter," intone our doomsayers, "if the country that was first to fly and first to land a man on the moon gives up its lead in technology to foreign powers? The real need is here on earth and this country hasn't been doing a proper job in meeting it. We should reorder our priorities." So goes the negative argument.

Ladies and gentlemen, there is more negativism about our effort to maintain technological superiority in the air and outer space than any area except Vietnam. It is as though America, the envy of continents, should be ashamed that she broached the unknown and put man on the moon, and that she should give no thought of going beyond to the planets. The feeling seems to be that if we hadn't done this, we could have made greater progress on the domestic scene. But I can tell you that pumping more money into programs that have been tried and have proved worthless in the ghettos of the big cities is not the way to national greatness or even to national happiness.

There has been too much productive by-product from space exploration to quash it — our whole burgeoning computer industry, communications satellites, medical advances, miniaturization. The naysayers will lose this one. Trying to blame a space program for our failures to master problems on earth is too illogical to be sustained. And the wealthiest nation on earth can do both jobs.

And what of the SST defeat? Generally, money that has been hard won and appropriated for some specific program is not easily transferred to another program that is totally unrelated. The net result is: We have invested one billion dollars over the past ten years in a plane that will never fly, we have ended direct employment for some 15,000 highly skilled workers and eliminated the potential future employment of an estimated 250,000 to 500,000 in the airframe and aviation industry. Even more important, we may have forfeited our leadership in this field.

MEETING HUMAN NEEDS

Well, what about our human needs? What are we doing to improve the well-being of our citizens? And how are our race relations progressing? Pretty well, if we accentuate the positive and put the negative in its proper perspective. In these areas, as in others, we have problems that need to be overcome. We will always have such problems, but we are working on them and we are obtaining results.

Let's look at the record — from the 1970 census.

We note first of all that poverty continues to decline. During the decade of the sixties, the ratio of poor persons to the total population declined from twenty-two percent to twelve percent. About 24.3 million persons were below the poverty level of $3,743 (for a nonfarm family of four). That's still too high, of course, but I daresay it compares favorably with most of the world's population. And it's progress.

And what about education? The illiteracy rate was cut in half. In 1959 one person in forty-five could not read and write, but in 1969, only one person in 100 was illiterate. In 1960, only 63.6 percent of people twenty years old and over had completed four years of high school or more. By 1970 the percentage had increased to 80.5 percent.

Although American blacks continue to lag behind American whites in income and in education, they have been closing the gap fast. Among all families, the ratio of Negro to white family income increased from fifty-one percent in 1959 to sixty-one percent in 1969. And among families headed by both a husband and a wife, the Negro couples increased their ratio from seventy-six percent to eighty-six percent of the income of the white couple. Among young husband–wife families outside the South — those under twenty-five years — there was *no* difference between the income of the black couple and the white couple. Not perfect yet, overall, but it's progress, and the progress continues.

In education, blacks showed even more dramatic gains — reducing from sixty percent to thirty-five percent the number of blacks who have less than four years of high school.

In almost every other area of American life, there continues to be improvement.

Consider, for example, the hunger problem that we heard so much about two years ago. Well, this administration is meeting it vigorously. The number of needy children receiving free or reduced price meals at school has increased from 3.1 million to 6.7 million. The number of poor receiving food stamps has increased from 2.8 million to 10.2 million. Even Senator McGovern, who heads the Senate Select Committee on Nutrition and Human Needs, has had rare praise for the Nixon Administration for its efforts in this field.

In spite of these gains, the Democratic National Chairman says we cannot allow "the cruel tyranny of hunger and idleness, and racism to run amok." Hunger, idleness, racism — running amok? What nonsense!

Finally, I would say that we need to accentuate the positive in an area of concern to all of you businessmen — the nation's economy.

Of course, unemployment is high. A rate of six percent nationally cannot be tolerated and will be improved. It came about for two very specific reasons — a wind-down of the war and an attack on wild inflation. These brakes caused a decline in defense and aerospace business, and curtailed unhealthy inflation-triggering expansion. Although this adjustment is painful, it is not fatal. We have weathered worse periods. We had a 6.7 percent unemployment rate in 1961 and 6.8 percent rate in 1958. And who remembers the depression? 24.9 percent of the labor force was unemployed in 1933 and the rate didn't get below fourteen percent until the defense plants were humming in World War II eight years later. We are trying to achieve coexisting peace and prosperity for the first time in our history. So let's keep our perspective. The economy responds to confidence, and confidence is not generated by poormouthing.

I would like to leave this thought with you. Self-criticism is a healthy thing. So is a good measure of skepticism — applied to our government and its leaders. This ability to examine and correct our faults and improve on our weaknesses has made us strong as a nation and as a people and — if used constructively and not for suicidal purposes — it can keep us strong.

Of course there are great urgent needs to be met, which are not yet being satisfactorily met.

Of course all of our people do not yet have the full measure of equality and economic opportunity they should have. And of course we should keep working on it until they do.

Of course our environment is precious and should be protected from our own selfish and greedy ravages, of which there have been too many.

But the fact that we have faults is no reason to flog ourselves before the world and despair of our condition. It is all the more reason to work to correct those faults and to improve on our weaknesses. It is certainly no reason to downgrade our country. Let's reinstill a little *pride* in America.

We need only to understand that in every human undertaking there is a difference between perfection and progress. We don't have to denigrate or fail to recognize the progress we've made just because we haven't achieved a state of perfection. To make progress we need only three things: a set of goals, a belief in our ability to meet them, and a determination to achieve them.

I would like to close with a quotation from one of our former Presidents who, like so many of our Presidents, had been through trials and tribulations but had complete confidence in the American people and optimism for their future.

"The only limit to our realization of tomorrow," he said, "will be our doubts of today. Let us move forward with strong and active faith."

Those words of Franklin Roosevelt were never heard by the American people, ladies and gentlemen. They were in a speech that he planned to deliver by radio broadcast on April 13, 1945. He died on April 12th.

But in them we find the real strength of America — confidence in ourselves and faith in the future. We have only to accentuate the positive.

April 14, 1971, Detroit, Michigan
National Pollution Control Conference

IT IS A great pleasure for me to be able to address this conference. As you know, the President has designated next week Earth Week, in recognition of the importance of preserving our environment. So this is a very appropriate time for a conference on pollution control.

Pollution is certainly one of today's most persistent and difficult problems, and almost everyone agrees pollution control is needed. At least to control the other guy. Many Americans have the same attitude toward pollution control that men have toward the see-through blouse: They're great — on someone else's wife.

But, seriously, ladies and gentlemen, pollution and pollution control are very important matters, and I want to commend the Jaycees for this fourth, action-oriented conference on the environment. I am grateful for the opportunity to discuss pollution with so distinguished and appropriate an audience as this one.

As a leader in business and government, each of you is very much concerned with pollution control, and with the need for cleaning up our environment in a manner that is practicable and consistent with the demands of progress and an expanding population.

You know, as well as I, that there is no simple answer to pollution. Clearly, we cannot ignore it and pretend that concern about it is just a fad or that our present efforts to combat it are sufficient. That is simply not the case. On the other hand, we cannot just stop our steel mills, our chemical and power plants, our automobiles, our oil shipments, and all the other activities that contribute to our national economic progress — and, unrestricted, also contribute to pollution.

Let me give you some examples of the problem. As you all know, the demand for electrical energy in the United States is doubling every ten years. The economic growth of this nation and the personal well-being of its citizens are to no small extent dependent on cheap and abundant electricity. At the same time, the production of power often damages the environment through discharges into the air or water.

Therefore, in policy regarding our energy requirements, we have to be judicious. We must weigh carefully the priorities and do our best to reconcile conflicting claims.

Exactly the same is true regarding the extraction of energy, as in the case of the oil pipeline in Alaska. Here, there is a conflict between the great desire to keep this last magnificent frontier unspoiled, and the very pressing need for new oil reserves to support our escalating national requirements.

Similarly, in the regulation of large industrial plants that emit solid, liquid, or gaseous wastes, we must protect against adverse effects on the environment without impairing their contribution to the national welfare.

All of this is clear to you men and women, because I know that you are sensitive to the threat against the environment, but are also well aware of economic needs, of consumer demands, and of requirements for national security.

The problems are not simple and, though pollution is widely recognized to be a real and pressing concern, the solution is hardly going to satisfy everyone. Like inflation, we all agree it's bad; but when we come to do something about it, everybody yells and nobody's happy.

Nevertheless this administration has every intention of finding a solution to these problems that will be both equitable and effective. The President feels very strongly that we must preserve our environment — so strongly that in his State of the Union Message in January of this year he identified restoration of the quality of our environment as one of the six great national goals for 1971. And he has taken concrete steps to meet the problem of pollution. Let me review them with you.

First, he has proposed legislation. In February of 1970, the President submitted to the Congress a comprehensive environmental program. It addressed itself to thirty-seven specific areas of concern. Congress did not act on every proposal, but it did appropriate for this fiscal year $1 billion for construction of waste treatment facilities. The President had requested this as part of his four-year program to improve water quality. In addition, the Congress enacted the Clean Air Amendments of 1970 — incorporating the President's proposals for national air quality standards. These include federal requirements that new industrial facilities utilize the best control technology that is available. They include federal authority to regulate the composition of automotive fuels. They include expanded federal enforcement authority.

Second, the President has utilized existing executive powers. He has made maximum use of his authority to control water pollution by ordering the implementation of a nationwide permit program under the Refuse Act of 1899, a statute having a potential for pollution control that has been only recently recognized. Implementation of this monumental program is now underway and, in the interim, the Department of Justice is actively using the Refuse Act to protect water quality. The bringing of court actions against ten dischargers of mercury is a good example.

Third, the President has recognized the executive agencies responsible for pollution control. He has established the Council on Environmental Quality and used it actively for advice, for the development of environmental policy and for the coordination of environmental programs. This council is extremely important. It developed this year's legislative program. It guides and oversees implementation of Section 102 of the National Environmental Policy Act, a section that requires all federal agencies to prepare and publish environmental impact statements in advance of any proposed major action that will affect the environment significantly. In that capacity, the council recommended terminating the project to build a Cross-Florida Barge Canal.

The President has also established the Environmental Protection Agency. This agency consolidates the programs for air and water pollution control, pesticide and radiation regulation, and solid waste management that were previously dispersed among several federal departments and consequently lacked coordination. President Nixon's consolidation has already contributed immensely to effective control of pollution of the air, the water and the land.

These are solid accomplishments. They are already improving the quality of America's environment. But it is the President's proposals for future action that deserve special attention.

First, the President has proposed strengthening substantially two pollution control programs that already exist: water quality control and pesticide control.

For water quality control, the President has asked Congress to authorize and appropriate $6 billion over the next three years as the federal share of a $12 billion municipal waste treatment program. He has requested authority to set precise standards of water quality, and asked new powers to enforce them. In addition, he proposes an extension of these standards to all navigable waters, ground waters, waters of the contiguous zone, and the high seas insofar as U.S. actions may adversely affect their purity.

For pesticide control, the President has proposed stringent federal regulation for the sale and uses of pesticides, and a streamlining of procedures for suspending or cancelling their registration.

Second, the President has proposed new laws to help fight pollution. These new laws will deal primarily with the emerging problems of toxic substances, ocean dumping, noise pollution, and mining.

The President also has proposed that our laws be supplemented by a new type of authority to control toxic substances.

To protect our oceans, the President has proposed the banning of all unregulated dumping and the strict limitation of the disposal of materials harmful to the marine environment. This is something entirely new, for at present there is virtually no effective federal or state authority to regulate ocean dumping. President Nixon has called upon other nations to follow our example and institute controls over ocean dumping.

To lessen noise pollution, the President has recommended standards to diminish some of the more offensive sounds in our cities, such as those caused by vehicles and construction equipment. In addition, he has proposed labeling certain household products to indicate their operational noise level.

Finally, the President has proposed a law that would require the states to regulate surface and underground mining activities. This would be aimed at eliminating silt and acid damage to streams and air pollution from coal waste fires.

These are all new directions in pollution control and indicate the commitment of this administration to improving our environment.

The third category of pollution control proposals submitted by the President to Congress is that of financial *disincentives*. I am referring here to taxes levied on two types of emissions: the highly dangerous sulfur oxides produced by fuel combustion and the lead produced by automobiles that burn gasoline containing lead additives. These taxes are expected to reduce the consumption of such fuels without actually prohibiting them. The money raised by the sulfur oxides tax would be used for government programs to enhance the quality of our environment.

These are the more important efforts of this administration in the area of pollution control. They involve governmental spending, the regulation of individuals and industry, and the use of tax disincentives.

These efforts will cost money — money that will be provided in part by the government, whether federal, state or local, and in part by the private sector, either industry or the consumer. In the final analysis, of course, all costs will be high. Yet if viewed in perspective, they will appear in fact not so high. First, in comparison to other well-established costs of business — such as wages and other direct production expenses — pollution control costs will be relatively small.

Second, because much of the cost of pollution control will be passed on to the consumer, we will witness a shift in consumer demand. For example, higher pollution control standards will undoubtedly increase the price of automobiles and gasoline, and this in turn can be expected to increase demand and expenditures for mass public transportation. As a result, some people may well find their transportation costs actually reduced because of new pollution control laws.

Third — and this is most important — although the costs of controlling pollution may seem high, they are as nothing compared to the tremendous costs of *not* controlling pollution. The damage caused by the air pollution from sulfur oxides alone has been estimated at more than $8 billion annually. And the total damage done by all forms of pollution to property, crops, wildlife, and human health is beyond practical estimate. Compared to these unrecorded but very real costs, the price of pollution control will be low.

But a price there will be — for direct control expenditures, for technical innovation, for research. Individual citizens as well as industries will be asked to alter their behavior to accommodate our new concern for the environment. The battle to protect our air, water, and land will not be easy.

However, despite the obstacles that confront us, I believe we have one overwhelming advantage in this battle: We are *aware* of the pollution of our environment, and we are *united* in our conviction that it *is* a problem. And, ladies and gentlemen, when Americans unite in their concern about a problem, when they unite in their resolve to find an answer, experience indicates they never fail.

Ours is no longer the challenge simply to arouse an interest in the issue: Ours is the challenge to turn that interest to constructive action.

That is in part your job, just as much as it is ours. You are leaders, and you are in a position to carry this administration's message to those who look to you for guidance.

Our program is ambitious, but, we believe, realistic. It takes account both of our ecology and of our economic progress. It makes demands of government, of industry *and* of the individual. It is a program aimed at furthering the well-being of *all* Americans, and, in that respect, I believe it merits your active support.

April 26, 1971, New Orleans, Louisiana
Southern Gas Association Convention

IN THE PAST several weeks we have witnessed a series of vitriolic attacks on one of the nation's top law enforcement agencies and particularly on the man who built it into a highly professional and efficient organization respected throughout the world.

It is not the first time that the FBI and J. Edgar Hoover have been assailed. They have withstood many assaults during their long association. The attacks generally have come from expected quarters — subversives, mobsters, extremists, and anarchists — enemies of the American system, who quite naturally detest an agency that stands between them and the accomplishment of their objectives — the perversion or destruction of our institutions.

But this time the scenario is somewhat different. While the attacks appear to be as well orchestrated as if they were being performed in concert by the professionals of disruption, this latest assault is from another direction. It gives off an unpleasant political odor — perhaps for the first time in FBI history — and it comes mainly from presidential aspirants who apparently foresee some political accretion from the radical left if they challenge the integrity of the FBI and its longtime director. These opportunists are being aided and abetted by certain of their friends in the liberal news media who automatically shout "Right on!" every time someone claims his civil liberties have been threatened, regardless of the transparency of such charges.

Now I am sure that most of these charges will fall of their own weight — or rather vaporize because of their lack of weight. Those that have an aura of credibility will be disproved in the course of thorough examination of all the evidence. But in any case, the very fact that these fractious allegations will be known by many more than ever learn of their successful refutation cannot possibly be of help, and indeed could damage an outstanding American institution. If the FBI suffers from these attacks, all law enforcement in America will suffer. And we can ill afford that, particularly at a time in our history when the FBI and the police of this nation have their hands full maintaining order and preserving our institutions of government from those who would tear down our society.

So I would like to discuss with you today this great law enforcement institution — what it means to us as citizens and what it means to our government. I also would like to examine candidly the fitness of its director, whose ouster is energetically sought by those now attacking the institution to which he has devoted his life. And in doing this we can look perhaps a little closer at some of the charges that have been brought against the FBI and Director J. Edgar Hoover.

In recognition of the nonpartisan nature of the FBI, I shall endeavor to keep politics out of this. If I succeed, I will have accomplished more than the irresponsible critics who generated this controversy.

If you took literally some of the more dramatic statements in the news accounts about the FBI controversy, you could only conclude that there is an agent behind every tree and monument in Washington, in the closet of every Congressman's office, in automobiles trailing him from work to home to parties, and in listening posts monitoring his wire-tapped conversations.

Note carefully, if you will, these words from Senator McGovern, a presidential aspirant and one of the leaders of the "Dump Hoover" movement, as reported in the *Washington Star* of April 20th:

> There is no doubt in my mind that virtually every political figure, every student activist, every leader for peace and social justice is under the surveillance of the FBI.

Now let's think about that statement for just a minute, ladies and gentlemen. I do not know how many political figures there are in Washington, to say nothing of the rest of the country. But I do know that there are 535 members of the Congress alone.

I assume that Senator McGovern is including all of these in his term "virtually every political figure," and probably would include, in addition, key members of their staffs.

Even if the FBI were to use as few as four agents per 24-hour day to keep these political figures under surveillance — and surveillance in this sense means constant, close watch — it would tie up 2,140 agents just to keep an eye on the members of Congress. Since the FBI has a total of only 8,365 agents throughout the entire nation — and the great majority of these operate outside Washington — the agency would be hard pressed indeed to keep the members of Congress under surveillance. And this doesn't even begin to consider other political figures or Senator McGovern's generous additions of "every student activist, every leader for peace and social justice." Heaven only knows how many of those there are.

As we shall see in a few minutes — when we look at some of the work that the FBI is *really* involved in and is charged by law with accomplishing — the bureau does not have the time or the manpower for the "surveillance" that it is accused of maintaining on innocent people.

But first I'd like to briefly mention two other cases that have kept the FBI controversy high in the news for several weeks.

Senator Muskie, who also is a presidential candidate, is another who has gathered considerable publicity by attacking the FBI. He shares the phobia of those who believe they are under surveillance. As proof he released publicly an FBI memorandum which was a factual report of the Earth Day activities in Washington last year, at which the Senator happened to be a speaker. Agents had been sent there primarily to watch the activities of an incendiary radical, one Rennie Davis, and a few others also better known for their subversive proclivities than for their interests in ecology.

As there was with the other principal participants in the rally, there was a brief mention of Senator Muskie in the memorandum. Here it is in full. I quote: "Shortly after 8 p.m., Senator Edmund Muskie (D) Maine, arrived and gave a short antipollution speech."

That was the report's total reference to Senator Muskie's participation, although you would not know it from the news coverage of his startling revelation that he and other innocents were spied on by the FBI.

Newsweek Magazine, for example, devoted two pages of its April 26th issue to the incidents, which it headlined, "Who Dug for Dirt on Earth Day?" Said *Newsweek:* "It is becoming plain that the Democrats sense they have a powerful public issue in the surveillance activities of the feds." It featured a photograph of Senator Muskie, a large photograph of the Earth Day crowd, and the top of the FBI document made public by the Maine Senator. The magazine account observed that one of those the FBI was interested in was Rennie Davis, convicted Chicago Seven member. *Newsweek* said Davis "spoke at the rally but was mentioned only briefly in the report." Actually, it was Senator Muskie who got only one sentence in the FBI document. In the report, Davis rated two full paragraphs summarizing his ten-minute speech. None of the news accounts that I've seen has quoted Davis. Here is what Davis had to say that apparently wasn't worth mentioning in the *Newsweek*.

"He called for tearing down the capitalistic structure," the FBI reported. After he was heckled, we are told by the FBI document, Davis proclaimed that he "opposed all pollution except [to] 'light up a joint and get stoned.'" He said "one way to fight for ecology is to go to New Haven on May 1st to stop Bobby Seale's trial." That hardly sounds like a speech on the environment, but it certainly sounds like the kind of exhortation to violence that merits FBI surveillance. How does a crowd stop a trial without violence?

Senator Muskie and his media supporters apparently feel it is terribly wrong to send the FBI to a rally where so many innocent people gather in the name of ecology, even if radicals have a prominent role in it and seek to use it as a forum.

Well, I disagree with them. I hope law enforcement officers will keep the Rennie Davises and the Abbie Hoffmans and their ilk under surveillance wherever they go to preach sedition.

Another recent well-publicized attack on the FBI was that of the well-known Congressman who claimed that his and other members' phones had been tapped and demanded the immediate resignation of J. Edgar Hoover. We have now been given what he calls his evidence — a statement that if the phone company denies your phone has been tapped, it means that the FBI did the tapping. I don't think that case deserves any further comment.

Now let's look at what the FBI is *really* up to and consider the man whose firm leadership and dedication to principle have restructured this organization from an inefficient division of the Justice Department in 1924 to the world's best-known, most professional, and scientifically efficient investigative and law enforcement agency.

The FBI has jurisdiction over some 185 federal investigative matters. These range from such longtime responsibilities as civil rights violations, bank robberies, subversion and kidnappings to aircraft hijackings, and, in the past year, broader investigative authority over syndicated gambling and bombings.

To handle its workload the bureau has a force of about 19,000 employees, of whom 8,365 are agents. It operates fifty-nine field offices in major cities throughout the United States and in the Commonwealth of Puerto Rico and maintains seventeen liaison posts in foreign countries.

One thousand agents have been added within the past year to meet new responsibilities under the Organized Crime Control Act of 1970 and to relieve a workload that had grown to the point that each agent was handling an average of thirty-one separate investigative matters at a time. The ideal load, according to Director Hoover, is eighteen cases per agent. So you can see they have had little time to do the "political sleuthing" attributed to them.

During their investigation of the burning of the ROTC building at Kent State University and the shooting of four students by National Guardsmen there last May, the FBI had a peak of 302 agents assigned to the case. They worked 6,316 hours of overtime for which they received no compensation. Their reports totaling over 8,000 pages were filed with the Department of Justice, which ordered the investigation, and with the President's Commission on Campus Unrest.

Every year the bureau brings in more money than it costs to operate. Last fiscal year, FBI investigations accounted for nearly $411 million in fines, savings, and recoveries — an average return of $1.60 for every dollar appropriated for FBI operations. Moreover, the bureau has an outstanding record of convictions. Last year, over ninety-six percent of the persons brought to trial in cases investigated by the FBI were convicted, eighty-three percent of them as a result of guilty pleas.

In addition to its work in federal law enforcement, the FBI works very closely with state and local law enforcement agencies. FBI laboratory services, provided without charge to local police departments and to other agencies, are indispensable to successful crime control. The laboratory made nearly 385,000 examinations last year, most of them relative to documents, photographs, and shoe and tire prints.

The fingerprint division started by J. Edgar Hoover in 1924, less than two months after he became director of the Bureau, now houses the fingerprint records of more than eighty-six million people — the largest collection of fingerprints in the world. These are used to identify thousands of people each year, accident victims as well as fugitives.

Adding greatly to efficient and effective law enforcement everywhere in the United States is the National Crime Information Center which the FBI established four years ago. It is the hub of a vast telecommunications network linking local, state, and federal law enforcement agencies. The computers in the FBI headquarters in Washington now store more than two and a half million record cards on crime and criminals. This information is provided in a matter of seconds to inquiring local police departments. For example, an officer in New Orleans, pursuing a car which has run a red light, can radio the license number to local police headquarters and within one minute have back from Washington information that the car was stolen four days ago in Ohio, and other pertinent information. When he pulls alongside the driver, the officer is ready to wrap up the case.

The FBI, a thoroughly professional organization since the three-year period that J. Edgar Hoover spent cleaning it out and reshaping it in the 1920s, also has been long dedicated to the full professionalization of law enforcement throughout the United States. During the last fiscal year, FBI instructors assisted in the training of more than a quarter of a million local police officers at schools throughout the country. The FBI National Academy, which can train up to 100 officers at a time in a twelve-week course that makes them better police executives, celebrated its thirty-fifth anniversary last year. The class now enrolled for graduation on June 30th, will bring to nearly 6,000 the number of graduates since it was founded. New academy facilities will be completed next year which will enable the training of 2,000 local candidates each year instead of the present 200 annually.

With all of these activities going on, there just isn't much time available for spying on Congress.

Now, if the present-day Senators who are worried about FBI surveillance had been around in the period immediately prior to Hoover's taking over the directorship, their complaints would have been justified.

In a Senate investigation of corruption at the close of the Harding era, Gaston B. Means, a former detective and patronage appointee in the Bureau of Investigation admitted to Senators that he had agents sneak into their offices, open their mail, search their files, and spy on them in an effort to find something damaging which could be used to stop their attacks on Attorney General Daugherty.

To save time, he was asked what Senators he had *not* investigated. Means replied: "Oh, there are lots of them I haven't. They are a pretty clean body. You don't find much on them, either."

The new attorney general appointed by President Coolidge, Harlan Fiske Stone, asked J. Edgar Hoover to take over the job as Director of the Bureau of Investigation. He agreed only on condition that the bureau be divorced from politics and that appointments and promotions be based strictly on merit. Stone agreed and said he wouldn't have it any other way. Incompetents were weeded out and professionalism began.

In the forty-seven years since then, Hoover has kept the bureau out of politics. The fact that he has served under ten Presidents — Republican and Democrat — and nineteen attorneys general since he joined the Justice Department as a young Master of Laws graduate in 1917 is testimony of his strictly nonpartisan and evenhanded administration of a sensitive agency. The relatively low turnover rate of agents — more than half have been with the Bureau for periods from ten to twenty-five years or more — is a further criterion of sound administration.

Yet Hoover's critics continue their drive to get rid of him. One of their principal arguments is that he is seventy-six years old — six years beyond the mandatory retirement age for federal employees. President Johnson issued an executive order exempting Mr. Hoover from that requirement and President Nixon asked the vigorous director to continue in the job. You don't judge a man's worth or his competence by his age, and that certainly holds true in Washington as well as elsewhere.

Three justices of the Supreme Court are over seventy. The senior member, Mr. Justice Black, is eighty-five years old and still going strong.

Twelve United States Senators among those who list their age in the *Congressional Directory* are over seventy, and four of them are seventy-five or over, including the eighty-year-old chairman of the Senate Appropriations Committee. I haven't heard any Hoover critics in the Senate calling on their colleagues to resign.

At least fourteen members of the House of Representatives among those who list their age are over seventy, including the eighty-two-year-old chairman of the House Judiciary Committee and four other committee chairmen. And I don't hear any Hoover critics in the House calling on them to resign.

And outside the government we find many men in their seventies and eighties active and vigorous, including such spokesmen for the left as Cyrus Eaton, eighty-seven; Averell Harriman, seventy-nine; Herbert Marcuse, seventy-two; Robert Hutchins, seventy-two; and Linus Pauling, seventy.

Dr. Benjamin Spock, almost sixty-eight, does not qualify but is moving up fast. However, he really doesn't seem to improve with age, so we have little to look forward to.

Walter Lippmann at eighty-one still finds the opportunity to write a stinging essay now and then.

We don't hear these men put down for their age by Hoover critics. To the contrary, they enjoy among their followers wide respect for their experience, as well they should.

But still we find those, particularly among the news media, who try to make some issue of Mr. Hoover's age. Most news stories out of Washington about the current controversy carry the director's age, whether or not it is pertinent to that day's developments. And just the other night, the commentator, Eric Sevareid, in a mild disparagement described the FBI director as "surrounded by old cronies." One would assume that Mr. Sevareid isn't surrounded by old cronies. Yet, with silver hair and silken voice, he has appeared before us nightly for years in tandem with the familiar countenance of Walter Cronkite.

No, I think it is something more than age that is the real issue in the effort to drive J. Edgar Hoover out of office. A more likely explanation is the fact that he is anathema to the New Left and extremists of every stripe, and he doesn't mince words in calling attention to them as dangerous to the country. Not surprisingly, this firm stand is a constant irritation to those who would have us believe that there is more to be feared from effective law enforcement than from the radicals and fledgling anarchists who daily call for the destruction of our institutions.

The FBI has frequently been called a Gestapo or secret police by its critics, and is again being called that today. But the bureau's director has resisted every effort to make the FBI a national police force and has succeeded in keeping it a fact-finding agency within the Justice Department throughout the past forty-seven years.

J. Edgar Hoover prepared the Justice Department's first brief on the newly formed Communist party in the fall of 1919, and he has watched the party with an expert's eye ever since. He has authored three best-selling books on the menace of communism to the United States. He understands perhaps better than anyone in this nation the nature and danger of subversion.

Listen to his own thoughts on this subject, expressed in his foreword to the book, *The FBI Story*, in 1956:

> The acts of the subversive, particularly the "dyed-in-the-wool" Communist, call for increased vigilance. The security of our country has suffered because too many of our people were "hoodwinked" by the propaganda which claimed that the Communist party was a political party like the Democratic or Republican party. Likewise, too many of our people have fallen for the line that spies, subversives, agents of foreign governments and Communists who have been convicted and sent to prison are "political prisoners." "Political prisoners" do not exist in the United States. Those who are prisoners violated the laws of the United States, were indicted by federal grand juries

and convicted in federal courts. I do not think they deserve the special treatment, with special rights and privileges, which is sought for them by their sympathizers.

In the United States, the subversive is a lawbreaker when he violates the law of the land, not because he disagrees with the party in power. And anyone who violates the law commits a criminal act even if the motives of the lawbreaker are self-servingly claimed to be political. If we ever permit political motives to justify lawbreaking, we shall develop political tyrannies in this country as similar instances have developed tyrannies in other countries.

In 1936, on direct orders from President Roosevelt, Mr. Hoover and the FBI began gathering information on Communist and Fascist groups in this country. In 1939 President Roosevelt issued a proclamation announcing the FBI's broadened responsibility for national security.

Later, when the FBI arrested a dozen Communists and sympathizers who had been indicted for conspiring to recruit volunteers for the Spanish Loyalist Army, a barrage of protests broke around Hoover and the FBI. He was accused of running a Gestapo and trying to persecute people who held political views contrary to his own. He was attacked in Congress, but backed up by the Democratic President and attorney general and eventually weathered the storm.

In his 1956 foreword to *The FBI Story*, recalling some of the earlier battles, Mr. Hoover wrote:

> In recent years a campaign of falsehood and vilification has been directed against the FBI by some ignorant and some subversive elements. In the worldwide struggle of free peoples, the truth is still one of our most potent weapons. And the record of the FBI speaks for itself. It is the best answer to the falsehoods, half-truths and rumors. . . .

With a little dusting off and the change of a word or two, he could use the same statement again today.

Personally I have complete confidence in this dedicated, steel-willed public servant with the 20–20 vision into our national security and crime control problems and the institution that he has made the beacon of law enforcement in America. I am sure they will again triumph over their critics, and the American people will be the winners.

May 8, 1971, Hot Springs, Virginia
Business Council Dinner

DURING THE past two days you have heard from several spokesmen for the administration about various aspects of the nation's economy. As they have told you, we in government are encouraged by the recent positive evidence of economic recovery, the *Washington Post* aside, I feel confident that these trends will continue and that 1971, as the President has predicted, will be a very good year.

The fulfillment of that prediction will not have resulted from accident. It will have come from a willingness to make the tough decisions leading to a long-term cure rather than to yield to pressures to patch over the problem for temporary relief. It will have come from a conscious effort to keep the government out of business — or at least in the position of junior partner — rather than to involve it more deeply than it already is. It will have come from more confidence that our remarkable free enterprise system can regenerate its own strength than a false hope that the government can ever completely manage the economy.

One of the most enlightening experiences I have had in Washington has been to examine, in all of its complexities, an economic problem that might appear on the surface to be very easy of solution; to see how easily one course of action produces an interaction of a quite different nature; to become aware that an effort that benefits one segment of our population may necessarily handicap or even work hardship on another segment.

The Cabinet Committee on Economic Policy, which I chair by designation of the President, deals with such problems on a regular basis.

This committee was created by executive order four days after this administration took office. Its purpose is to bring around one table cabinet level officers who can focus on a wide range of views simultaneously on a single economic problem, who can coordinate efforts to solve it and make recommendations to the President and to the various departments involved.

Members of this committee include the secretaries of the Treasury, Agriculture, Commerce, Labor, and Housing and Urban Development. Included also are the Director of the Office of Budget and Management, the Chairman of the Council of Economic Advisers and the deputy undersecretary of State for Economic Affairs. Other agencies are represented when there is some specific matter of interest to them on the agenda.

Our discussions and task force studies have involved such various subjects as interest rate ceilings on deposits and shares of savings institutions, requirements for federal housing, post-Vietnam planning, federal lending policies, softwood lumber and plywood, steel, copper, agricultural trade, and transportation.

I would like to take just a couple of these subjects — lumber and steel — and illustrate to you the built-in conflicts that we encounter, the natural interest of the government in their solution, and the efforts to bring about more governmental involvement. As businessmen, I am sure you will appreciate the complexities and the intricacies of the problems they present.

The United States, as most of you realize, is deeply involved in the lumber situation. For one thing, the federal government is one of the biggest producers of timber. We've harvested more than twenty-five percent of the national total. And the federal government is also a very large user of lumber. Beyond that the government has a strong interest in the housing market, particularly in seeing that sufficient low and moderate income housing is constructed to meet the needs of our citizens. The more than 470,000 federally subsidized housing starts last year were twice the number of the previous year, and this year there will be approximately a half million. Finally, as a grower, buyer, and regulator, the federal government becomes directly involved in the struggle between those who don't want any trees cut and those who would endanger our future supply of timber by overcutting.

The challenges to timber sales from federal lands by conservation groups have now tied up almost two billion feet of timber — fourteen percent of a year's harvest of the U.S. Forest Service. And the figure may increase because of contests involving expected additional sales this spring.

One of the ironies of this situation is that some of the people who complain loudest that low and moderate income housing is not being constructed fast enough are among those who oppose the cutting of timber. It is their opposition which may well trigger the shortages, cause the higher prices and lessening of ability to provide this needed housing. That's the trouble, I guess, with being an idealist these days. You can't have it both ways. There must be some striking of balances.

In view of our current critical housing needs, it is vital that we get as much from our national forests as we can without impairing an adequate supply to our future generations. At the same time we must follow sound conservation practices. Our national forests have long been managed under the multiple-use concept, which provides not only for the cutting of timber at a rate justifiable by continued forest growth but also for recreation, watershed protection, forage production, and wildlife management.

One of the practices complained of by the environmentalists is called "clear-cutting." This involves the cutting of all trees in a harvest area. It does leave a visible mark on the landscape. On the other hand, young Douglas fir trees — which are the principal species used for lumber — are intolerant of shade, so that it would be difficult if not impossible to replant harvested areas with this fast-growing species without clear-cutting.

The President is expected to announce soon the appointment of a distinguished citizens committee to look into this problem. Its members will represent many different viewpoints, running the gamut from those anxious to help this nation's pressing housing needs, to those dedicated to protecting and preserving the environment. Both are worthy goals, and a proper balance must be struck. A solution can be found — but not without some frank and forthright discussion, and perhaps some real eyeball-to-eyeball confrontation among the committee members.

Our lumber problems, unfortunately, do not end there. We also have other conflicts and pressures to consider — in international trade, in logs, lumber, and plywood, in contract procedures for cutting portions of national forests, and in domestic transportation.

The problem of steel is an altogether different one, although it too is a basic industry and is of basic concern to the government. Our steel industry used to be one of the strongest, having a more than average profitability and making a sizable contribution to our foreign trade surplus. In the last fifteen years, however, the situation has changed drastically. The American steel industry is today having great difficulty competing with a rising volume of imports, especially from Japan and from the European Economic Community. To give you an idea of the magnitude of the problem, in 1950 the United States share of world steel production was forty-seven percent. Today it is twenty-two percent.

Recognizing these problems, the industry has made considerable investments in new equipment, but these have so far not shown up in the increased productivity that would be necessary to overcome the much higher wage rates prevailing in the United States. In order to give our steel industry some protection the previous administration negotiated a voluntary restraint arrangement with the steel producers of Japan and the EEC. While this arrangement has given the industry some relief, 1970 was nevertheless one of the worst years in its history. The voluntary arrangement will expire at the end of 1971 unless an extension is negotiated with overseas producers.

Given the importance of the steel industry to our economy we have had to consider its future over the longer run. This is currently being done by a task force under the Cabinet Committee on Economic Policy. We have to know exactly why our steel industry got into this predicament, and what can be done to raise its productivity to restore its international competitive position. We are, of course, concerned about the welfare of this basic industry and its many employees, but we must also be concerned about inflation. One of the best defenses against inflation is higher productivity, and that is just what the steel industry has been unable to achieve in the past few years. Another defense is active competition. These two factors actually go hand in hand. Unless the industry relies more on price competition, cutting prices when demand is low, its output will tend to fluctuate greatly. The industry will continue to work at less than full capacity for much of the time, which will raise its costs. The current situation, which is dominated by strike hedging, is, of course, exceptional.

The upcoming wage negotiations are of particular interest in this respect. Our steel industry is already at a serious disadvantage because the wages it pays are much higher than those paid by its competitors abroad while its productivity is not much greater. A further increase in unit labor costs would therefore be very hard to bear, unless prices are raised further, which would have adverse consequences for steel users and for the economy generally.

We can find just as many built-in conflicts in other problem areas that I have mentioned only in passing — in agricultural trade, in housing, transportation. One that comes to mind, and would be discussed by Secretary Connally if he could be here, relates to the international financial situation. I have discussed this matter with the secretary, and would like to make a few comments about it.

Surely we are concerned about the situation. We regret it. Anything that causes foreign exchange markets to close in Europe has implications for all of us.

But it is important to recognize that the recent large dollar flows to Europe reflect, first, transitory differentials in short-term interest rates — ours are relatively low, theirs higher — and, second, speculation that the par values of one or more European currencies would be increased.

Although we have problems — after all, we are just now beginning to emerge from the inflation brought on by the spending excesses of the 1960s — our basic balance of payments position surely should improve as we move back towards wage–price stability. As a matter of fact, cost performance in this country, as unsatisfactory as it has been, is markedly better than among most of our industrial competitors abroad. This holds promise for the rebuilding of our once strong trade surplus — surely the fundamental strength of any nation competing in the international market.

I should add a strong qualifier here — we can generate the trade surplus we need and deserve *only* if we are treated fairly by our trading partners abroad. To be blunt, we are not in my judgment being treated fairly today.

The lessons seem to me obvious. First, we should continue our strong efforts to dampen inflation — and, quite frankly, we could use more business, financial, and labor statesmanship in this effort. I pledge to you that the government will do its part.

Second, we cannot allow transitory flare-ups in the international monetary situation to drive us into actions which are against the long-run interests of both this nation and its friends abroad.

Third, we must redouble our efforts to reduce barriers against U.S. goods abroad — to create truly equitable and progressive systems of international trade. The disproportionate responsibilities that we bear — and you gentlemen know how true that is — we have borne them for so many years — constrain our trading partners to work with us, cooperatively and constructively, toward this goal.

We shall continue to watch and study. We shall continue to cooperate. We shall continue to take appropriate actions to reduce the temporary glut of dollars abroad. But what we will not do is put the U.S. economy through the wringer in order to deal with a temporary situation.

This is not to say that restoration of balance in our international financial transactions is unimportant. It has been and continues to be in the highest order of our national priorities. But we can serve this vital end while also dealing fully with domestic problems.

This is our goal. This is our pledge.

All of these things I have discussed are complex matters, which deal with many diverse interests, not the least of which is the public's interest. Because the government has a historic role as a protector of the public interest, some degree of governmental involvement in the private sector is inevitable. What we have to guard against is the sort of heavy-handed involvement that stifles rather than encourages competition.

We must weigh carefully the cries of business for protection. We have seen in the case of lumber how an effort to protect shipping interests causes higher prices for home builders and buyers in the heavily populated northeast. It is against the background of our housing needs that we must also evaluate the demands of some environmentalists for tighter restrictions on lumber cutting. Some of these demands are valid and in the public interest; others are unreasonable and against the public interest.

We must bear in mind that for every government action there must be a reaction. The ripples spread across the pond. Regulation brings demands for more regulations, controls for more controls, actions for more actions. Government's role is to strike a necessary balance, to let our huge engine of free enterprise operate under the restraints of the marketplace rather than the government insofar as that is possible.

And above all else, we must not forsake the long-range solution for the quicker, more tempting action that may be popular at the moment but temporary in its effect and inimical to our lasting interests.

President Nixon has demonstrated, in his deescalation of crises in both Vietnam and in the nation's economy, that he will not be stampeded into pressure to sacrifice the country's long-term interest for simplistic answers and political expedience.

He appreciates your patience and your understanding, as businessmen who must deal daily with complex problems, and I think we would agree that it's better to painstakingly unravel the knot than to impulsively sever the cord.

Now these matters we would all admit are terribly complex. They involve varied points of view and the men in this room, many of whom I know personally, I think are fair-minded and equitable enough to consider that they are biased to some extent by the needs of their individual enterprises. Similarly, the government is biased to some extent by the political realities of its position. I want you to know that as a person who has been privileged to serve in the Vice Presidency and been close to presidential decisions in the highest councils of government over the last three years, I feel I can stand before you as a fair-minded, free, and a relatively unbiased individual, a person who has little in the way of ambition or aspiration of a personal nature, can say to you that I think your President, in the time that I have had to observe him personally and to work with him, has attempted to be as fair and forthcoming as any man I've ever dealt with, in or out of government. Sometimes his decisions are not reaching you in the clarity and the purtiy with which you should be able to deal with them, principally because the President's statements are subject to evaluation and interpretation through the pundits in the media and other places which sometime distort the true meaning.

But no group of individuals in our country bears a greater responsibility than you ladies and gentlemen; you are the elite of the free enterprise system. To some extent it depends on you whether that system continues as we know it, and I think you have a profound obligation to — not simply accept the secondhand impressions that reach you through your normal media of communications every day, but to utilize the superior ability that you have to reach for the truth in what your government is trying to do in representing the interests of the system that made you what you are today and hopefully will continue this country in the manner that it has been operated over the years. I sense we are in a terribly distressing time of potential change. A change that's not necessarily of an advantageous nature. I think that change will not come, and I don't think it should come. If you who are the custodians of a system that allowed the best that America has produced to rise to the surface, will continue your vigilance and your interest and will not simply disengage on the basis of what you might say parochial interest of your particular business; if you will look at the welfare of the country and look at the work of your cooperation as it affects that welfare, I believe we can still bail out what seems to me to be a downhill slide in the past five years. I hope that you'll consider that carefully. I have every confidence that you'll react in the proper way.

May 14, 1971, Fort Knox, Kentucky
Armor and American Ordnance Association

I MUST TELL the members of the Armor Association that I am really overwhelmed with the reception I've had on my first return to Fort Knox after an absence of almost thirty years. But I must say to you also that the honors were extremely impressive, and the feeling of nostalgia that overwhelmed me when I had the opportunity to participate in a retreat ceremony involving the 54th Infantry, which I understand retains some remnants of identification with the 54th Armored Infantry Battalion that I served with.

The thing that impressed me most tonight was my chance to speak informally with a group of very dedicated captains who are attending the advanced school here, and who had a chance to discuss with me some of the things that they are attempting to bring to the attention of the American public and particularly to the establishment of the Army with regard to the fundamental requisites of leadership, be it military or civilian today. I'm very sincere when I say to you I've never talked with a group of young people who charged my batteries any more than this group. And I pledged to them, because of my intense interest in their remarks and in their demeanor and in their conviction — and let me say this — that I'm certain they don't agree with everything I say, nor with everything that most of the senior officers here believe, but I'm convinced that they seek the solutions within our establishment's system, because after all, they are convinced that they must someday become the Establishment. And I want to tell them in a very personal way in this response that they have done much for my morale, and I look forward to continuing our dialogue, and to having the opportunity perhaps to give the American people in a more wide forum the opportunity of hearing from them.

Now this is the largest group of military officers I've ever addressed. I haven't seen this much brass since George McGovern declared for the Presidency.

General Westmoreland would have been here tonight, but he had to stop by the jewelers to have his uniform appraised.

I particularly want to welcome the gentlemen from private industry that supply so much of America's military hardware. I trust you've had a pleasant flight from Japan and that you'll enjoy your visit here.

Well, you know, being part of the military industrial establishment isn't easy these days. Some members of the press have even accused Mel Laird of hiding inside the Pentagon and making himself inaccessible, but I think they're being kind of unreasonable. It's not Mr. Laird's fault that Roger Mudd slipped off the drawbridge and fell into the moat.

And the waitresses who serve cocktails outside have all asked me to commend you for your generosity. The dinner isn't even completed and already they've collected $20.00 in tips, 112 Hershey bars, and seven pairs of nylons.

And I confess that I find conditions at Fort Knox just a little bit different than they were when I was here some twenty-nine years ago. I had a chance to go back to the old OCS barracks which have since been converted to more esoteric purposes, and maybe more constructive. And I find that one of the most singular changes of all lies in the fact that the old dust bowl where we used to take calisthenics at five o'clock or so in the morning across from the barracks is now a beautiful lawn suitable for chipping or any other purpose. And there are some buildings on it.

But they're not the only changes — the changes that have happened to Fort Knox are not the only changes that have taken place. Even the attitude among the new GIs toward the Army menus has changed. I overheard a private in the chow line actually refer to creamed chipped beef on toast as "creamed chipped beef on toast."

But opinions are changing, I said to Bill Desobry — and let me say this — it's really an unusually wonderful occasion to be able to come back to Fort Knox and find out that the commander of the post is a man who served in the same battalion as you did during the war, and a very distinguished member of that outfit who has made it big, and not only made it big, but made it permanent. I'm a very temporary officer, you know.

But things have changed in veterans' attitudes. The veterans who showed up in Washington last month to demonstrate against the war didn't resemble the majority of veterans that you and I have known and seen. I don't know how to describe them, but I heard one of them say to the other: "If you're captured by the enemy, give only your name, age, and the telephone number of your hairdresser."

Well, there's a very difficult problem involved with speech-giving, and that's when whoever your aide is loses page one somewhere. But I found it. I wish I'd lost it.

Although I vividly recall the weight of responsibility shouldered by the military in those World War II days, even though I was not in a position of high responsibility, those in positions of high command had a distinct advantage over their counterparts today, and that lay in the fact that their detractors were all overseas.

The challenge to military professionalism has never been greater than today. The armed forces are being subjected to an antiwar and antimilitary movement, perhaps even more vitriolic this time than in any time in our history. For today the unpopularity of a war is compounded by the fact that our country is experiencing very intense social pressures which result from vast scientific, technological and cultural changes. And in an international sense, while we are still engaged in the crucial, final stages of our Vietnam involvement, the overriding requirement of an effective nuclear deterrent is being made more difficult by accelerated efforts on the part of the Soviets in strategic weapons development.

Except for World War II, when Pearl Harbor peremptorily silenced the pacifist–isolationist movement of the twenties and thirties, a substantial antimilitary sentiment has existed in our country, even in the ranks of its citizen–soldiers. Furthermore, deeply ingrained in the American tradition is the belief that, once the battle is over and once the mission has been accomplished, the armed forces should be brought home and disbanded without delay.

Going back beyond the experiences of World Wars I and II, which are more familiar to most of us, the Civil War is a good example of the two traits I've just described. During that war there were large draft riots in New York that had to be quelled by armed force. And after the war, the Union Army, of over a million men in 1865, was reduced to one-tenth its size in just one year. In 1880 our Army had leveled off at a strength of approximately 25,000. These forces had to be expanded to over 200,000 during the Spanish–American War, but they were drastically reduced thereafter despite the requirements of the Philippine Insurrection.

Commitment of U.S. forces in the Philippines really did cause widespread domestic dissent. A motion was even passed in one of our state legislatures — get this — "extending sympathy to the people in the Philippines in their heroic struggle" against the U.S. forces. Also, the Army's control of the transoceanic cable from Manila back to the United States led to expressions of outrage in the press over "news management." Does that sound familiar? Well, that was the same newspaper that I complain about sometimes today.

Between World War I and World War II, the Army, and in particular its ROTC program, came under attack by pacifists and other critics. Once again reduced to a small force, averaging between 150,000 and 200,000, the Army grew more isolated from society. But with remarkable dedication, the Army directed its energies inward — to improvement through greater professionalism.

And thus I urge you to reflect and take courage in the realization that, as far as dissent and domestic antimilitary sentiment go, you are traveling a familiar and well-worn path.

Today the armed forces face a domestic situation similar in many respects to that prevailing after the Korean War. In that conflict, enthusiastic early support for the war later turned to frustration and an unwillingness to accept the costs in human lives and fiscal expenditures to achieve the limited goal of a battlefield stalemate. Yet, as we all know, the stalemated war in Korea stopped the Communist aggression and provided for the South Korean people the opportunity to establish a stable, democratic government.

As a person who's recently visited South Korea and had the opportunity to inspect their troops and talk with their leaders, I want to assure you that the work that many of you in this room did to assist in achieving stability for that fine country, that is making such dramatic economic progress, and doing so much toward the establishment of freedom and stabilization, is formidable and can never be forgotten by the Korean or the American people.

One puzzling aspect about current dissent is the frequency with which the word "defeat" is used to characterize our Vietnam experience. I challenge anyone to justify that conclusion. The mission of the armed forces has essentially been twofold: first, to prevent the military domination of South Vietnam through unchecked Communist aggression; and, second, to advise and train the armed forces of the South Vietnamese. The first goal has been achieved. Communist troops have been unable to take over the South by military force. Moreover, the heavy casualties inflicted on the enemy have proven, time and again, the inability of the invaders to mass significant forces without being subjected to punishing firepower of Allied ground and air forces. We have made dramatic progress in our advisory and training efforts, particularly in the past two years. The South Vietnamese have now assumed responsibility for almost all naval operations. They are conducting airmobile operations with their own helicopters and taking over an extended share of the close air support mission. The South Vietnamese are continuing an impressive effort to upgrade the regular as well as provincial ground forces into competent, professional military units. No one has had more experience, personal observation of the progress that South Vietnamese have made in this respect, than your post commander, General Desobry, who is a man with long experience in the early days of Vietnam. Clearly the struggle has not ended and American casualties, although reduced, still exact a painful cost. But to characterize this performance as a "defeat" and to demand that we precipitately abandon it is ludicrous — and an undeserved injustice to those valiant men who have borne this burden.

Now, looking ahead, what can we expect to happen to the military? Have we really learned anything from history? I believe we have.

The United States cannot afford, nor does it intend, to decimate its general purpose forces as our involvement in Vietnam is brought to a conclusion.

The President has made it clear on many occasions that international realities and imperatives of national security require strong military forces. I can assure you that, unlike some periods in the past, our military leaders, in planning for the future, have ready access to the highest civilian policy makers in the government. Military counsel is considered indispensable in the consideration of basic issues affecting national security.

The "massive retaliation" strategy of the 1950s, which relied on our strategic nuclear superiority, is inappropriate to our present needs. The requirement for credible conventional forces — a basic ingredient of the "flexible response," which is the strategy of the 1960s — is essential to our strategy of "realistic deterrence" — a strategy designed to discourage both nuclear and conventional conflicts.

This strategy acknowledges the realities of the contemporary world in which the United States must exist. Domestic considerations — fiscal, political, and humanitarian — cannot be ignored. But they cannot be even relevant unless we effectively deal with the overriding strategic realities which face us today. For we live at a time in history when the consequences of instability and disorder in the world are more menacing than ever before.

The conditions of near nuclear parity with the Soviets and their momentum in the strategic field give us great cause for concern. The inability of either the Soviet Union or the United States to dictate events in their respective areas of special interest around the world, and the increasing need for reaching some agreement on strategic arms limitations have shaped our strategy for the post-Vietnam period. This strategy is designed to implement a foreign policy based on the principles of partnership, strength, and a willingness to negotiate.

We are a world power and we intend to remain one. Although the Nixon Doctrine seeks a clearer definition of our interests in specific areas, it assumes that a world order of stability and peace is linked to United States' interests and security. Thus the doctrine does not suggest that our interests and/or our responsibilities can ever be confined to United States territory and surrounding waters, nor that our security can be assured from within a "Fortress America." While it announces, as policy, a reduction in the United States presence overseas and an expectation, hopefully, that our Allies will contribute more fully to the collective security, the Nixon Doctrine is a policy which reaffirms the treaty commitments which now exist — commitments that are all too frequently forgotten in discussion in the higher councils of our government. These commitments, adequately supported, represent the best hope for the strategy of peace set forth by the President.

Gentlemen, the concept of partnership to serve as an effective component of a strategy of realistic deterrence must be based on strength. It is also essential that we establish evidence of a shared mission with our allies. Such evidence may vary from region to region, but the basic principles that should apply in all cases are these:

— A common interest in a forward defense.

— Second, a capability to assist or support our Allies with a wide range of options.

— And third, a guarantee of U.S. involvement that is relevant to the Ally concerned and proportionate to our national interest in the area.

We've demonstrated our commitment to the security of Western Europe for more than two decades. Our forces stationed there provide the most visible and viable indication of this commitment. They are committed to the deterrence of aggression at any conflict level, and, should deterrence fail, they are capable of applying whatever force may be required to counter that aggression.

The commitment in our armed forces, in Vietnam as in Korea, has demonstrated our determination to make good our pledges to assist our Allies. In Vietnam the Army has had the principal role . . . and has performed in an outstanding manner, despite the unprecedented difficulties encountered in fighting that war. The fruits of your efforts have been long in coming. But as the South Vietnamese become increasingly able to take care of their own defense, the goals we seek become nearer at hand. The military's achievements, both in combat in Asia and in carrying out our military assistance programs there, have provided the necessary framework for peace and security in that part of the world.

Because the Soviet Union and others may view domestic dissent against the war and the military as a picture of apparent American exhaustion of the American will, it is essential that the strategy we adopt be supported by a visible capability. Strength, then, is the central pillar of the Nixon Doctrine. Although our strategic nuclear power remains the essential backdrop to our total deterrent, shifting strategic realities could cause a potential foe, perhaps, to test our will by the threat or use of force below the level of general nuclear war. Thus, as the President has stated, our conventional forces play a vital role in deterring war as well as providing the appropriate and responsive capacity to defeat conventional aggression. The President has therefore pledged to "maintain the required ground and supporting tactical air forces in Europe and Asia, together with naval forces." The presence of U.S. ground forces, standing guard on our Allies' soil, is the ultimate demonstration to any potential aggressor that we will honor our national commitments. Tactical airpower provides a swift and flexible military instrument which forms, with the Army, a natural land-based team. Naval forces guarantee the extension of U.S. conventional forces overseas by maintaining essential sealines of communication and augmenting our conventional capabilities by performing special operations in conjunction with Marine Corps and Army forces. These resources must be backed by a ready reinforcing capability, and, ultimately, the vast mobilization potential of the United States, which has been so important in our history.

The challenge to today's military professionals is clear. Responsive to the Nixon Doctrine, and our strategy of realistic deterrence, you must maintain the military skills, you must provide the proper organizations, and you must determine the required weapons and equipment to insure this nation's preparedness to defend itself and to meet its commitments. Your tasks will require:

— First, constant evaluation and evolution of doctrine to include adaptation of lessons learned in Vietnam, as well as other areas of the world.

— Second, first class research and development, test and evaluation programs to ensure that we capitalize on technological advances which may impact heavily on military tactics and national strategy.

— Third, military assistance to allies, a key ingredient of the Nixon Doctrine, that is perceptive, imaginative, and well managed, if we are to make the most of our limited funds.

— Fourth, intelligently fashioned decisions concerning the allocation of funds between the competing requirements of strategic and conventional forces, and between the demands for modernization, readiness, research, and manpower requirements.

— Fifth, reserve components maintained at an unprecedented level of readiness.

The smaller Army of the 1970s must be a better one . . . with greater skill, flexibility, mobility, and firepower. And, in the face of public criticism, the Army — like all the armed forces — must maintain the discipline, the esprit, and the morale of its men and women despite the considerable problems of drug abuse, dissent, and racial discord.

And as I said in the beginning of these remarks, one of the reasons that I feel so encouraged is my informal conversation with those captains, who have addressed themselves to these difficult and provocative subjects. I believe that we have within our military establishment, not necessarily the finest young men who have ever served the United States, because I reject the premise that any generation on the average has produced finer people than the one before — I reject that premise in comparing my generation with my father's or my grandfather's. But I do believe after looking at these young people that they certainly are of equal caliber with the finest that this country's ever produced.

The challenge to military professionalism in the 1970s will be great indeed. The accomplishment of the tasks I have enumerated will require leadership and dedication of the highest order. You're going to have to accept virulent criticism from some sectors of the public, and you're going to have to do it without becoming embittered. Your responsibilities — to achieve preparedness, to be effective in war, and to offer sound guidance on national matters involving security — will require an extraordinary effort.

Although the challenge is great, I am convinced that you can and will meet it. And I'm delighted that after twenty-nine years away from the post of Fort Knox, I can return on such an auspicious occasion and find that things are better than they were when I left, and that the feeling of pride and patriotism that runs through Fort Knox, Kentucky is augmented since I last came.

May 17, 1971, Washington, D.C.
American Red Cross Convention

LADIES AND GENTLEMEN of the American Red Cross:

It's a pleasure to be with you for the opening of your National Convention and to bring you personal greetings and best wishes from your honorary chairman, the President of the United States.

Throughout America and throughout most of the world, the symbol of your organization has come to stand for care and devotion — concern for humanity, dedication to the relief of human suffering and misery wherever it may exist, and service to people of all races, creeds and nationalities, in war and in peace.

When disaster strikes, the Red Cross is among the first units on the scene. I saw your volunteers in action in the Mississippi Gulf Coast region in the wake of destructive Hurricane Camille. When I flew into Los Angeles following the earthquake earlier this year, your volunteers had been at work for many hours.

Your training programs in first aid, small craft and water safety, and your services to members of the armed forces, to veterans, and to their families have become a familiar part of the American scene.

Now that you have made drug abuse one of your primary national concerns, I am sure we can look to greater progress in this area than we have ever had before. The driving spirit that developed blood banks and that has led to other life-giving and lifesaving practices has never been more needed in our society than it is today to help us curb the drug menace. I congratulate you and wish you every success in this undertaking.

As the husband of one of your 2,310,000 volunteers, I may have a broader appreciation for the work of the Red Cross than do some others. My wife serves as President of the Ladies of the Senate Red Cross Unit. And I'll let you in on a family secret — she enjoys that more than any other role in her official duties as wife of the Vice President. She has already earned her third stripe for volunteer service in the little over two years that we've been here. These ladies get together every Tuesday at the Senate Office Building, prepare dressings for your mobile units and perform other services for the Red Cross. In contrast to their husbands, the members of the Senate, they don't argue and contend with each other, but are completely united in their services. And they accomplish quite a bit. Come to think of it, maybe that says something for *their* leadership that is missing on our side.

The Red Cross functions that I have mentioned thus far are familiar to all Americans, things we have come to take for granted as part of our everyday life.

But I would like to devote the rest of these remarks to an area of your activity that is not quite as familiar to the American people — a role of service, to your nation and your fellowman, that you have pursued with customary zeal and dedication. I refer to your very valuable assistance in our painstaking, frustrating efforts to free — or at least obtain decent care for — our American prisoners of war and missing in action in Southeast Asia. No aspect of the work of the Red Cross is of greater personal interest to me and to this administration than your efforts on behalf of these courageous men and their families.

All of you are generally aware of the problem, but let me recount the bleak facts:

Some 1,650 American military personnel are missing or captured in Indochina. We know that at least 450 of these are captured. The total is probably higher, but how much higher, and which men are captured, is not known because of the other side's refusal to identify all prisoners. They have furnished a list of 339 men held in North Vietnam, but they have provided no information whatever on men missing or captured in South Vietnam, Laos, and Cambodia.

Some fifty American civilians also are missing or have been captured in South Vietnam, and two of our pilots are known to be prisoners in China.

Not one of these prisoners has ever been visited nor have their places of detention been inspected by a neutral, impartial authority such as the International Committee of the Red Cross. Mail is restricted and comes through irregular channels. We are concerned that many of our men are held under grim conditions of detention, enduring long periods of solitary confinement, and experiencing other forms of grave mistreatment.

Rules for treatment of prisoners of war are stated in the Geneva Prisoner of War Convention of 1949, which North Vietnam signed in 1957. The Geneva Conventions express the conviction of the world community that prisoners of war and other war victims are entitled to humane and decent treatment. It is not by accident that these conventions are often referred to as the "Red Cross Conventions," for it was the Red Cross that took the lead in their formulation; and it is the Red Cross to this day that takes the lead in seeking their universal observance and application.

The International Conference of the Red Cross, meeting at Istanbul in the fall of 1969, gave forceful voice to the concern felt by people everywhere about violations of the Geneva Prisoner of War Convention. In a resolution adopted without dissent, the Red Cross Conference stated "the International community has consistently demanded humane treatment for prisoners of war."

The International Committee of the Red Cross has continued its efforts, year after year, to bring about compliance with the Geneva Convention. What the Convention requires is not complex nor does it place excessive demands on the detaining power. It does not seek a life of privilege for a prisoner of war. What it does do is set forth clear standards for the protection of prisoners from the abuses that all too frequently occur in war time.

It states that prisoners must at all times be protected from insults and public curiosity. We have seen how Hanoi uses our men for propaganda films and humiliates them by forced marches through the streets of Hanoi.

The Convention provides for regular communication between the prisoners and their families. Many of our men held in Indochina have never been heard from by their families.

The Convention provides for adequate diet, recreation, and medical care. We have seen from the evidence of films released by North Vietnam that our prisoners suffer from inadquate diet and that they have unhealed wounds years after their capture.

The Geneva Convention also requires impartial inspection. This is a subject which must concern all Americans and all nations for it is crucial to the assurance that prisoners in any conflict are being treated in accordance with accepted international standards. Men who have escaped from Communist prisons in Indochina, or who have — in a few instances — been released have told us about their mistreatment and that of others. Men have been held in solitary confinement, manhandled, and subjected to torture and other forms of pressure. We do not know whether this is still happening, but we know that it has occurred.

The Communists deny these stories. They assure the world that they are treating our men in a humane way.

They even invite photographers to visit a showplace camp to demonstrate that our men are properly treated.

We welcome these assurances, but they are not enough. If the Communists are treating our men properly, they should not refuse impartial inspection, for their refusal creates concern. If they are complying with the conditions of the Geneva Convention, they should not be ashamed to let people in to see what they are doing. They should welcome and invite inspection, as the South Vietnamese have done.

The American Red Cross has played an important role in trying to improve the lot of our prisoners. Your efforts to forward packages and mail to them have earned the gratitude of all of us. You also have helped immeasurably to call public attention to the plight of our men in Communist prisons and to North Vietnam's intransigent attitude. Your "Write Hanoi" campaign has done much to bring this subject to world attention, in a way that we hope helps tell Hanoi and its Communist allies that their treatment of our men does not pass muster in the community of nations. I hope you continue and enlarge your efforts in this field. We cannot rest until all our men are released and the fullest possible accounting is obtained of the missing.

There is only one plausible explanation for Hanoi's attitude, and that is that they are using our men as political hostages to bargain for concessions, the very concessions that encompass their war aims in Vietnam. North Vietnam thinks that, by holding our men hostages, they can compel the President to cave in to their demands — demands for a United States pullout, abandonment of the present elected government of South Vietnam, an end to all U.S. military activity — in effect to the turning over of South Vietnam to the aggressors.

They are pressing now for the President to announce a withdrawal date, saying that "discussions" of prisoner release could follow such a declaration. We cannot help but recall that similar promises of "negotiations" were made contingent on a halt of United States bombing of North Vietnam. The bombing stopped November 1, 1968; but the discussions that ensued have been unproductive due to the other side's listing of additional preconditions for serious negotiations. To this day they have refused to negotiate on any subject.

In recent weeks North Vietnamese spokesmen have been reported as hinting that their demands were more flexible, and that prisoner release would in fact result from a United States withdrawal commitment. Ambassador Bruce probed their position on this in the Paris meetings May 6 in an effort to find out if there had been any softening of the other side's position. He offered to discuss these questions in any forum where discussions might be conducted fruitfully. The other side's answer left no room for doubt. Their position represents the same hard line they set forth in their so-called "Eight Points" of September 1970 and the earlier "Ten Points" of May 1969.

North Vietnam's statements in Paris, plus their steadfast refusal to give any commitment to do more than "discuss" the prisoner of war question in return for a U.S. withdrawal declaration, indicate that announcement of such a date on our part would be met with demands for further concessions, rather than by the release of our men.

This somber conclusion about the enemy's attitude toward our prisoners does not mean that we have given up our efforts to reach an agreement for the release of our men. In recent weeks our government and the Republic of Vietnam have made a series of far-reaching proposals that could bring about swift and humane resolution of the problem.

Building on President Nixon's proposal of last October for the immediate exchange of all prisoners of war, without awaiting agreement on other matters, we have proposed, as a first step, the repatriation of all sick and wounded POWs. This is a specific requirement of the Geneva Convention. The Republic of Vietnam on April 29 specifically offered to repatriate 570 sick and wounded North Vietnamese prisoners of war. This offer was endorsed by President Nixon at his news conference the same evening. Repatriation of small groups of North Vietnamese captives had taken place in the past, despite Hanoi's refusal to cooperate in orderly arrangements. But this was the largest offer by far.

Just three days ago Hanoi broadcast its acceptance of this offer, stating that the prisoners should be brought by unarmed ship to a point just off the coast of North Vietnam. The ship is to be marked with a red cross, and a North Vietnamese ship similarly marked is to come out to receive the POWs. We and the Republic of Vietnam are now working out the final arrangements for this repatriation, in consultation with the International Committee of the Red Cross.

Needless to say, our fervent hope is that this action by our side will lead promptly to the release of American and allied POWs held by the other side.

In a further initiative our side proposed that long-held prisoners of war, as well as sick and wounded, be interned in a neutral country. This also is provided for in the Geneva Convention. In a statement April 14 endorsing this proposal, President Nixon said:

> Although short of the release of prisoners of war which is our goal, neutral internment would be a reasonable and responsible way to alleviate the plight of prisoners of war on both sides. I hope the other side will respond positively to this initiative. There can be no constructive purpose to the continued long detention of prisoners of war. They and their families have suffered too much already.

I would note that over 400 of our men have now been missing or captured in Indochina for four years or more, far longer than any prisoners of war ever before in our history. Some of these are known to be in their seventh year of captivity.

A few weeks ago Sweden publicly indicated its readiness to accept prisoners of war for internment provided the two sides agreed. In a statement following the Swedish offer, President Nixon expressed his "great satisfaction" and stated his "hope that Hanoi will move promptly to negotiate an agreement on this issue to take advantage of this humanitarian offer on the part of the Swedish government."

North Vietnam and its Communist allies have dismissed these initiatives, describing them as "maneuvers." The President has made clear that we will press forward with these efforts — for repatriation, for neutral internment, and for impartial inspection.

Let there be no doubt that this administration is committed in the fullest sense of that word to taking every action, exploring every avenue, and proposing every possibility that can alleviate the plight of our men.

We will not rest until all are released and reunited with their families.

As the President has said repeatedly, we will continue to have forces in Vietnam as long as the enemy continues to hold our prisoners.

And I know that these men and their families can continue to count on the strong support and dedication of all Americans in and out of government until they are reunited.

May 18, 1971, Jackson, Mississippi
Mississippi State Republican Dinner

LADIES AND GENTLEMEN:

It's good to be back in Jackson, even at the risk of being accused of pursuing the Nixon Administration's "Southern Strategy." We all know what "Southern Strategy" really is, of course. It is a political phenomenon that is born in the suspicious minds of the liberal pundits and flung at an unsuspecting public via tons of newsprint and network rhetoric whenever a national administration attempts to treat the South on equal terms with other regions of this country.

Little more than thirty months ago the American people elected just such an administration — one pledged to equal treatment under the law — not only for every citizen but for every region, regardless of previous condition of political servitude.

Now, an audience such as this, residing as do most of you outside the first strike capability of the *Washington Post* and the *New York Times*, might actually be deluded into believing that a policy of equal-treatment-for-all-regions is an effort on the part of this national administration to unify the country.

However, those of us residing in the Northeastern zone of revealed truth, blessed as we are each morning with the editorial guidance of our intellectual betters, are counseled to know better.

We are advised to recognize the Nixon Administration's equal treatment doctrine for what it is — or rather what Tom Wicker says it is — an obvious effort to divide the country.

Nor is that all that the inhabitants of the seaboard media impact zone are given to understand.

For example, thanks to our immediate proximity to Mr. Wicker and other pundits and commentators of national scope, we have been instructed that when 10,000 persons rage through the streets and neighborhoods of our nation's capital, defacing buildings with their favorite obscenity or Maoist slogan of the moment, disabling automobiles, burning public park benches, strewing garbage, and otherwise depriving other citizens of their right of unhindered movement in a free community, the perpetrators of such actions are engaging in nonviolent dissent.

From the vantage point of Jackson, these people may look like hoodlums and lawbreakers, to be sure. But given the editorial insight of the *Times*, the *Post*, and some national magazines, they undergo a metamorphosis — or should I say, "mediamorphosis." And they emerge simply as "kids" who are "trying to tell us something, if we would only listen."

On the other hand, if by chance some outspoken public official who has totally lost patience with such fatuous nonsense — let's say, for purposes of argument, a Vice President who simply doesn't understand — if such an official were so insensitive as to disagree publicly with this media assessment — he isn't just exercising his right to dissent. Far from it. He's being "repressive." He's trying to "intimidate" the national news media.

Or if such a public spokesman were to argue that simply because a demonstration is nonviolent doesn't make it right; or that however "nonviolent" a demonstration may be, the physical obstruction by one group of citizens of other citizens' freedom of movement is itself a form of repression of constitutional rights — you may be sure that the sages of the liberal establishment would undertake to lecture that official on the Neanderthal error of his ways.

Unless, of course, some dissident group should one day engage in the "nonviolent" obstruction of access to the *Times* offices or the CBS studios. Then, I feel safe in predicting that we insensitive simpletons who condemn such actions will gain some new allies — at least until the incident is forgotten.

There are numerous other examples I could cite of this kind of editorial doublethink. One recent instance comes to mind:

When an ecstatic reporter visiting the Communist mainland came upon an entire family living in a single room only fifteen feet square, what impression did he leave with his readers here at home? That the Chinese family was suffering from conditions of poverty and oppression? Certainly not. Undoubtedly that would have been the resulting impression had the same reporter come upon an American family living under such conditions. But viewed in the land of "Big Brother," what would have been described as poverty and oppression in America was instantly "mediamorphosed" into a marvelous demonstration of Communist Chinese austerity and discipline.

Indeed I could go on. But the examples of this double-think abound in such quantity that anyone from Jackson or points west of the Manhattan–Washington media–academic complex who visited our nation's capital in recent weeks might well have concluded that George Orwell's frightening projection of *1984* and its reverse language of "Newspeak" had come to pass. For that person would have witnessed, as I did, the sickening spectacle of enemy flags and the visage of "Big Brother" being paraded down the streets under banners proclaiming the cause of "Peace" and "Freedom" and "Justice."

Yet while this travesty of free expression and reason was taking place, there were those establishment apologists — not only some members of the national media but prominent leaders of academe and politicians ambitious to hold higher office — who chose not to condemn but to pander to the totalitarian instincts of the New Left mob.

The sympathy and support of these leaders and would-be opinion molders provide an undeserved respectability to the radicals of the New Left, who are bent on destroying our free society. When members of Congress participate with Trotskyites and Marxists in a demonstration geared to the ultimate aim of destroying an elected government's ability to govern — when members of Congress share a speaker's platform with raving radicals convicted by a federal court of inciting to riot — a new and frightening degree of demagogy is upon us. And when the intellectual community and the national media, with few exceptions, are blind to faults and failures of our enemies but ultracritical of the slightest error of our free society, the preservation of our national heritage is in grave danger.

We have already witnessed the impact of this new demagogy on some elements of the national Democratic party. The irresponsible and unfounded charges made against the director of the Federal Bureau of Investigation by influential national Democrats may have endeared these leaders to the shock troops of the New Left. But they have ill-served the nation at a time when the American people have a right to expect responsible, not hysterical, opposition leadership.

Nor can it be said to be in the tradition of constructive opposition when well-motivated but naïve members of Congress send emissaries or go themselves to Paris to engage representatives of North Vietnam in ad hoc diplomatic dialogue.

In this regard, a few days ago Senators Fulbright and Javits declared that I had impugned the patriotism of Senators who disagree with the administration's Vietnam policies. Specifically the charge was made that I had accused opponents of these policies of being "unpatriotic or worse."

Senator Javits said that I had "intimated" as much, whatever that means or is intended to mean. Let me say this: Senator Javits, as might be his political habit, may "intimate" what he will. But I think that those who have followed my career know by now that when I hold an opinion or have something to say, I don't "intimate" it. I come right out and say it.

Senator Fulbright, rushing into the verbal breach created by his colleague from New York, alleged that I had in fact *said* that opponents of the administration's Vietnam policies were "unpatriotic or worse."

I felt it necessary to answer Senator Fulbright and I did. The answer is as true tonight as it was when I first stated it. He lies in his teeth.

The truth of the matter is that on many occasions I have said just the opposite of what Senator Javits "intimates" and Senator Fulbright charges. I have said that the doves of the Senate and House are patriotic and well-motivated. However, good motivations and intentions do not keep these Congressional doves from being absolutely wrong in the policies which they urge upon the nation.

Who doubts, for example, that in the late 1930s Neville Chamberlain was every bit as patriotic and concerned with the future of his country as was Winston Churchill? No one questions Chamberlain's love of country or his good intentions. But in his judgment of events — of what was right for England and right for the cause of lasting peace in the world — Chamberlain was wrong.

Now, Senator Fulbright, as we know, prides himself on his gift for the English language. Surely he knows that the meaning of the word "patriotism" is "love for or devotion to one's country." And now, several days having elapsed since his intemperate outburst, he knows, too, that while I have questioned the judgment of the Congressional doves, I have never impugned their love for or devotion to this country.

Thus, in his most recent statement on the subject, Senator Fulbright appears to be adopting Senator Javits' obfuscatory language. It was, says Senator Fulbright, the "thrust and implication" of many of my remarks to impugn the patriotism of members of Congress.

But I'm not going to let the junior Senator from Arkansas off the hook that easily. He made his charge. I challenged him to prove it. Tonight, here in Mississippi, I repeat that challenge.

In these reckless accusations, we see the double standard at work. For what Senator Fulbright and Senator Javits are engaged in is precisely what they attribute to me. They are using the tactics of verbal smear in order to discredit and intimidate those who disagree with their viewpoint.

I have no intention of being intimidated or silenced by such tactics.

Let me repeat: No matter how good their intentions, when members of Congress engage in ad hoc diplomatic dialogue with representatives of North Vietnam, as occurred recently, they are misguided and wrong in believing they are serving the cause of peace. I do not doubt their love of country or of peace. But I seriously doubt their judgment that these tactics are serving the best foreign policy interests of their country or the cause of peace. Certainly these self-designated fledgling diplomats are not properly briefed on the administration's foreign policy position, and it is the administration which bears the responsibility for conducting foreign policy.

Not long ago such irresponsibility on the part of a public official would have been unthinkable. Who can doubt that, had a Republican Senator or Congressman indulged in private diplomacy with an enemy nation during the administration of John F. Kennedy, a deafening outcry would have been forthcoming from national editorialists and commentators, as well as their ideological allies in the academic world?

But this is 1971, and the President is Richard Nixon — a chief executive who must cope each day not only with the crises inherited as a result of the foreign and domestic policy errors of his predecessors — but must also cope with the politically oriented criticism and carping of many of the very men who urged the decisions that created those crises.

For the Nixon Administration, lest the national Democrats and their media–academic allies make us forget, entered office following almost a decade of escalating war and inflation; a period of so-called political "style" and liberal rhetoric long on raising popular hopes but woefully short on fulfilling those hopes; eight years of domestic discord and disruption exacerbated by promises — and failure to perform.

Thus did this administration enter office pledged and determined to heal the wounds inflicted upon the national spirit during the first eight years of the decade of the sixties. Let us, said President Nixon at the outset of his term — much as the first President of his party had said more than a century before — let us seek a resolution of our differences not through conflict but through reconciliation.

Nevertheless, in the 1970s as in the 1860s, an American President has been confronted every step of the way by an opposition that views his defeat and the defeat of his policies as its prime order of national business — second to none.

Now I realize full well that heated arguments concerning the efficacy of many of the policies of the first Republican President carry over to the present day. Indeed, there are those who might make the argument that even today, 106 years after his death, to invoke Lincoln's memory in Jackson, Mississippi, is not politically sagacious.

I disagree. For though I am a native and former governor of a state that served as the battleground for many of the bloodiest engagements of the Civil War, I find it hard to dispute the fact that in his effort to preserve the American Union — to bring together and make whole again the world's greatest representative government — Lincoln was right and the critics of his day were wrong.

Indeed the ultimate vindication of his policy of reconciliation is borne out by the fact that, despite the violence and bitterness that divided our country during Lincoln's time, a Republican Vice President stands here tonight, in the heartland of the old Confederacy, and speaks — as one American who loves and would preserve our country's free institutions — to his fellow Americans who love and would preserve our country's free institutions.

And so I have come here tonight not simply on behalf of a party, but of a President who more than ever needs the aid and support of his countrymen in carrying out the mandate he was given thirty months ago:

— A mandate to reconcile the differences and antagonisms that had grown among Americans during the eight years that had passed since Dwight Eisenhower presided over a nation at peace, both overseas and here at home;

— A mandate to maintain the security of our country against its foreign enemies in a time of great international tension;

— A mandate to end the war in Southeast Asia on terms which would establish a just, honorable and lasting peace;

— A mandate to uphold America's position of world leadership and to restore our people's confidence in their government and its institutions;

— A mandate to expand the boundaries of opportunity for all Americans, regardless of race, sex, creed, or age, and to assure for this and future generations a nation in which every individual may fulfill his or her God-given potential.

In doing my part to help carry out that mandate, I have been accused in some quarters of being divisive — of hurting the cause of reconciliation of the American people. It is said by some that my rhetoric is too strong — that I am insensitive and blunt.

To be a public man is not always easy. But to be a public man who is loyal to one's principles and benign in all of one's pronouncements is wholly impossible. Politics is the arena. Ours is an adversary system. The options are simple — fight for your principles or abandon them. Weasel or take the flack. Give in or fight.

I try to make my positions clear. I know they are consistent. They represent what I honestly believe. I shall continue to state them in such a way that I will not be misunderstood.

My fellow Americans, if I leave no other impression tonight, let me impart this thought:

As your Vice President, I have been privileged to witness, firsthand, the unsparing effort which your President has made to fulfill the mandate for peace, prosperity, and national unity.

I know the deep sense of responsibility which your President feels toward the people who, thirty months ago, placed their confidence in him to guide our country through difficult times, overseas and here at home.

And I know, first-hand, too, the toll taken by the partisan obstructionism and sniping which have characterized the opposition's efforts to defeat this administration's program for the nation.

Nevertheless, despite the opportunism of the new demagogues and the actions of the New Left street gangs, this administration is not going to be intimidated.

We will not be intimidated — we will not be coerced — and the policies and programs which this administration was elected to implement will prevail.

We will prevail not because of demagogic appeals to Americans as members of genera-

498

tional, racial, or economic blocs — as do our opponents in their banal invocation of the phrase "the young, the black, and the poor" — but by appealing to and performing on behalf of every American as an individual, with *individual* rights, *individual* responsibilities, *individual* aspirations, and *individual* potential to fulfill those aspirations as a member of our national community.

We will prevail not because of appeals to mass emotions based on simplistic slogans, as do the new demagogues — but by appealing to and performing on behalf of the thoughtful majority of Americans who seek solutions to our problems based on reason.

But make no mistake: More than ever, this administration needs your help — the support and aid of the great majority of thoughtful Americans — South, North, East, and West — Republican, Democrat, and Independent — who love their country and are unwilling to see its institutions and freedoms denigrated and destroyed by a willful minority of political opportunists in the vanguard of a New Left rabble.

My fellow Americans — your President needs your help — to restore confidence in our nation as the bulwark of freedom in a troubled world — and to restore the confidence needed here at home to safeguard and strengthen the free institutions that have made, sustained — and must continue to sustain — America as one nation, under God, indivisible, with liberty and justice for all.

June 1, 1971, Nassau, Bahamas
Mutual Broadcasting System Affiliates Meeting

IT'S A PLEASURE to get away from Washington for a day and to join you on this lovely island. I even find it worth making another speech on the news media to come here.

By way of explanation, let me say that I do intend to discuss the media with you. Who could pass up an audience like this one that can really do something about the things I've been complaining about?

But I hope you will hear me out before further crystallizing those opinions that I'm sure you have already formed from news reports or commentaries on what I may have said or done or "threatened."

My staff, which is composed largely of sadists, sees that I am fully informed each day on the news of the world. In addition to the daily news summary that goes to the President, they place before me every article or report of a broadcast they can find that has been critical of me personally or that deals with some subject in which I have expressed a particular intrest. They figure the critical cartoons and articles will toughen my hide and might prevent some future memoir by a press secretary saying I have been kept isolated from adverse opinion. Let me observe here that if Herblock won't toughen you, nothing will.

Last week, in one day's news report, there was a clutch of articles responding to what were portrayed as the latest "threats" to the news media from the government.

In Milwaukee a television network news executive responded to what UPI called "recent administration criticism of broadcast reporting." The story never did explain exactly what the criticism was, but it quoted the executive, as saying the criticism posed — and I quote — "a 'most formidable challenge' to the freedom of the press."

From San Diego, AP reported that the President of Sigma Delta Chi, the national journalism fraternity, said "the news media welcome criticism from Nixon Administration officials but not threats." He does not bother to specify what "threats" he's referring to.

I know we have made no threats. The article went on to quote the official as saying, "I object to Agnew telling us our job is to tell it his way or else, and I object to the same reaction from campus radicals or chamber of commerce presidents."

(For your information, gentlemen, I have never said "tell it my way or else." I have only said to the news profession, "Why don't you tell it like it is?" — not my way, or the chamber of commerce's way, or the radicals' way, or even the way you think it should be, but *like it is.* I thought that was the historic role of news reporting in our society. I'm a little surprised that the head of Sigma Delta Chi might feel differently.)

And next, from Washington, came a report on a speech by Senator Frank Moss with references to what he called an "administration-fired inquisition into the journalistic process" and "thought" control by an administration paranoid with fear, suspicion, and loathing of a free and undomesticated press."

That's inflated rhetoric but it received serious attention and it probably helped the Senator ingratiate himself with the broadcast media, by whom, he complained, he was — these are his words — "bitterly unloved."

But I would say that these stories — and the hundreds of others like them that have appeared regularly ever since I criticized the excessive bias and slant of television network news operations in a speech some eighteen months ago — indicate that if anyone is "paranoid with fear, suspicion, and loathing" it is not the administration, but rather those who keep voicing fear, suspicion and loathing.

This frenzy about intimidation and repression is not confined to the news media, or even to those in Congress who would like to curry favor with the news media. It is helped along by an occasional voice from academe.

Consider with me for a moment a statement, reported in the *New York Times* recently, by a professor described as an expert in constitutional law. This professor is preparing the United States' contribution to a worldwide survey of freedom of information. According to the *Times* he — quote — "has surveyed the development in this country of freedom of information since colonial times and has concluded that this basic freedom is now undergoing its most formidable challenge."

Let me repeat that conclusion — *"most formidable challenge."* And that's in all of our history of disputes between Presidents and the press, disputes that from the time of Washington and Jefferson have often bordered on open warfare.

This professor believes that my criticism of the media is part of the problem and that an even more serious threat comes from what he describes as the President's use of the media to bring about the defeat of political opponents. (Wouldn't that leave some of our former Presidents chuckling!)

But listen to it in his words, as reported in the *Times:*

"Mr. Agnew's tirades do tend to inhibit weak-kneed and weak-bellied individuals involved in the flow of information." (You can see he is quite complimentary about you, gentlemen).

"But Mr. Agnew can't win. The administration, to stay in power, must get itself reelected. If the media let the people know about this effort to inhibit if not intimidate them, public resentment at the effort to make the people 'know-nothings' could cost the administration the election." (Now, he's starting to campaign against us and he wants you to join him.)

"So it is the information media," he continues, "by how it fights back, that will decide whether the public's right to know is abridged."

While he urges you to "fight back," this constitutional scholar would deny that privilege to a public official, particularly to any President.

"The power of the office," he says, "is such that a democracy cannot tolerate its abuse of the media for partisan ends."

The abuse he is talking about, according to the *Times,* is the President's right to use the media "to bring about the defeat of certain Senators who disagreed with him."

Presumably the constitutional scholar would restrict the President to the use of a megaphone and a mimeograph machine to get his views to the people who elected him to head their government.

There's no question we have a wave of paranoia today. The question is which direction it's coming from. And the comments that I have cited to you, including those of a scholar, leave no doubt in my mind about the direction.

Now, I realize that you are not news executives as such but rather individual station owners and managers who make up a national advisory board to the Mutual Broadcasting Company. Therefore, you are the men to whom news executives are either directly responsible, in the case of your own stations, or to whom they feel a sense of responsibility, as in the case of this vast radio network of some 550 stations.

So I welcome this opportunity to discuss with you, in some detail and on a national basis, what we have and have not said about the news media and their relations with government and the actions that are imputed to us that have neither been threatened nor taken.

First, let it clearly be understood by one and all that this is not a partisan or an administration issue. Criticizing the news media predates the Nixon Administration. Sincere individuals in the past and in the present, in both political parties and in the news profession itself, have expressed grave concern about excessive bias and distortion in the news media.

Today, despite broadside charges that a monolithic administration "conspiracy" is at work, it is significant that it is not the administration but a Democrat-controlled Congressional subcommittee that is pursuing the matter of editing techniques used in the final production of a recent television documentary. Yet, from some of the news accounts on this controversy, you would think the administration was sponsoring it.

Secondly, *never* has this administration or anyone in it advocated censorship of the press in any form. It might surprise some of you, but you would find me among your staunchest defenders if anyone tried to impose any measure of censorship on the free flow of information to the public, or on your right to criticize those of us in government. And you would find that the Attorney General and Senator Robert Dole — who are often portrayed as the other partners in an administration "conspiracy" against the news media — feel the same way.

What we *have* done — and we have done it regularly, consistently, and with deep conviction — is to call on the free press of this country to exercise *responsibility* commensurate with its freedom and to police itself against excesses that on occasion have been so blatant they have undermined the confidence of the public in the credibility of the news media as well as the credibility of the government.

We in government are wholly dependent on you who run the news media in this country to get our message to the people — in a straightforward and accurate manner, as undiluted as possible. Unlike most governments, this government has no newspaper or radio or television network to publish or broadcast its message, or to respond to what it considers to be bias or distortion in the presentation of its message. There is no Pravda or Izvestia or Radio Moscow, Radio Peking, Radio Hanoi, or Radio Havana in the United States of America. There's not even a BBC. But as tempting as it would be to me to have such an outlet to vent my ire some mornings, I'm glad we're dependent on a free and independent and honestly skeptical press to relay our message and to report to the people on our stewardship. It is one of the great strengths of our society. That's because there are a great many more honest, dedicated newsmen than there are unprincipled prima donnas in your profession.

But I cannot overemphasize that you are effective as a news medium only so long as you can be believed. Like government, you will fail if you don't have the confidence of the people. You should, therefore, guard that credibility with the same zeal that you would nail a politician who lies or exaggerates or distorts. I fear there are still too many in the news profession who do not give enough serious thought to that subject and who think that the shoe is always pinching the other person's foot.

The television industry took out a full-page ad in the newspapers last week. The ad boasted that more people depended on television than any other medium for news. And it said that when there was a conflict in news accounts most people believed the version they saw on television to the one they heard on radio or read in newspapers or magazines. There was a chart showing that fifty percent of the public had this superior faith in what they saw with their own eyes. I don't believe I'd brag about that fifty percent figure, even though radio and newspapers and news magazines were less. With the naturally convincing power of live photography, the credibility rating of television *ought* to be higher.

501

This same advertisement emphasized that sixty-nine percent of the people contacted in the hired survey felt that television presented a fair balance of opinion. I could certainly debate them on *that* one for a few days.

And, finally, the poll got around to the point of the paranoia game. It said, "there has been some talk recently about the government investigating news programs on television. Some people are in favor of this as a way of insuring that television news programs would be fair, complete, and impartial." Then it asked the question, "Do you think the government should or should not have control over TV news?" Eighty percent voted against control. Well, so what? What American who understands the principle of the First Amendment wouldn't answer such a question in the negative?

Now I believe that all of us know that polls can be helpful in finding out how the public thinks. But you and I know perfectly well that the result often depends on what is asked and how it is asked. The attitude of the polltaker in asking the question can even help shape the answer. And I have seen no more blatant attempt to influence an answer than the one I've just read you. The poll subtly suggests to the person that there is indeed considerable concern about the government trying to control the news industry and it says, you don't want that, do you?

Gentlemen, I believe that this recent wave of attempts to portray the government as anxious to control or suppress the news media in the United States can only backfire on those who foster such moves. Over the long haul they will add to the credibility problem that the industry ought to concern itself with correcting.

Yet, instead of responding to constructive criticism about specific distortions or inaccuracies in the news media, the tendency is to yell "intimidation" instead of examining the facts of the matter. When a television network is criticized for pasting together film to present a distorted impression, and this charge is publicly documented, the reaction in the profession is not to condemn but to defend the practice as normal and even desirable. In the case of the flagrantly inaccurate documentary that I recently denounced, the industry rallied around and voted its highest honor to that program whose principal merit, by the standard of many in the profession, was that it had been criticized by government officials.

If the judges honestly thought that program merited an Emmy — and didn't award it out of spite — then I'm surprised they didn't vote an Emmy for costume design to the producers of *Oh Calcutta!* It would make about as much sense.

Certainly heaping honor and hasty acclaim on a questionable product does nothing to enhance the credibility of the news profession of the medium itself. It will not wash away the problem. But you who are in the profession can do something about it. You can regulate yourselves. I have said time and time again that the responsibility is yours. Certainly it is not the government's.

Whatever the television industry may claim through its commissioning of polls, you in radio are responsible for one of the country's great news outlets. You reach millions of commuters every day, for example, through car radios — a facility the other news media do not have. I notice your studies have also shown a larger daytime audience at home than any other medium has.

I believe that on balance you do a good job of reporting the news. In my own relations with the news media, my only complaint with radio as a medium has been the superficiality of the coverage that you often give events — not taking full enough advantage of that unique ability you have to get the word out faster and more often than can television or newspapers. A radio reporter often can get his story on the air as soon as he can get to a telephone. But what he has to say is too often covered in less than a minute and in the barest detail. I would like to see you go much more in depth on subjects that perhaps could be made more interesting to listeners. I'm aware that there has been a recent trend in this direction, and I commend you for it. Government and the public certainly benefit from more in-depth coverage of the issues.

In one of the news items that I mentioned at the outset of this speech, the news executive said — and I quote from the UPI account — "We are not a small group of decision makers, kingmakers, policy-benders. We are journalists."

That's going to come as crushing news to some of the eminences in the news business . . . those who seem to believe that one of their primary missions is decision making and policy bending. That has been one of my principal complaints against the news media — namely, that there is a relatively small but prestigious group of men in the news business who spend more time trying to run the country — without the inconvenience of getting elected — than they do in telling the people what is going on.

Again, let me quote from the news story regarding that network executive. It said that he "also questioned the theory that the public can easily be led astray by slanted reports" and it quoted him as follows: "I honestly believe," he said, "that critics of the media — those so frightened of what television might do in leading unsuspecting viewers down the garden path of misinformation — truly underestimate the sophistication of the American viewer.

"We know the viewer can sort through the subterfuge. We know he is after — and will get — the fact of the matter."

End of quote, end of news story.

Gentlemen, my point is that the viewer should not *have* to sort through a subterfuge to get his information from a newscast. The subterfuge should not be there, nor should the public be expected to sort its way through it.

If we were to apply this man's philosophy to everything, we would have absolutely no need for consumer protection laws.

Now, lest it appear that I am picking on one network news executive — who really was speaking for the whole industry — let me quote something from one at a rival network. According to *Broadcasting* magazine this executive recently told an audience at the University of Missouri School of Journalism "that television news executives and personnel 'have had enough' of the severe criticism from high government officials and are fighting back."

Fighting back? I didn't know they had ever stopped attacking.

The *Broadcasting* account continues: "He said the television news medium has 'been pushed and prodded, palpated and probed like a fish-market mackerel on a Friday morning. . . .'"

Indeed this executive would do well to himself probe and palpate some of the shining mackerel in his network news aquarium. For example, after the recent protest demonstrations in Washington, that network's foreign news editor was asked whether they had carried anything on Communist coverage of these demonstrations. He said no, and added that he considered it "irrelevant" whether or not the demonstrations gave aid or comfort to the enemy. He ventured the further personal opinion that what the United States is doing in Vietnam "is the same thing the Nazis did in Germany." The difference, he said, "is numbers."

I found it rather shocking that this man's attitude might have a bearing on what kind of news we are shown on that network each night from Vietnam — the "living room" war that TV news has influenced to such a large extent.

I would also like to observe to this first media audience that I have addressed in some time, that I believe journalism fell short as an investigative and reporting profession during the recent demonstrations in Washington by veterans opposed to the Vietnam war. Nowhere did I see any *real* effort to ascertain or disclose how many, or what percentage, of the demonstrators were bona fide veterans, although there were broad indications that a sizable portion of their number were nonveteran interlopers from college campuses and high schools.

There also was very scant publicity given the belated discovery that one of the leaders who passed himself off on national television as a former Air Force captain and combat pilot was in reality a former flight sergeant and non-Vietnam veteran. The sergeant-cum-captain admitted later to a newsman that he had assumed the phony status because he thought it was more impressive for the cause he represented. And his coleader, who drew rave notices in the media for his eloquent testimony before Congress, was later revealed to have been using material ghosted for him by a former Kennedy speechwriter and to have spent most of his nights in posh surroundings in Georgetown rather than on the Mall with his buddies. This was reported by Jerry ter Horst, a columnist for the *Detroit News*, but generally it was ignored in the rest of the media.

The national commander of the Veterans of Foreign Wars told a Senate committee last Friday that the demonstrating veterans comprised "a very confused minority" of the men who had served in Vietnam. He added: "Neither their alleged experiences or opinions represent the average veteran."

The VFW membership includes over 400,000 men who have served in Vietnam. The national commander, H.R. Rainwater, told the Senate Committee he tried in vain to get his members equal time for the 120 minutes the networks had given the demonstrators.

He is quoted as follows in the *Washington Post:* "I told them I would bring 1,000 vets to the Mall, we would demonstrate peacefully, we would march with the American flag — right side up.

"We would lay a wreath at Arlington cemetery, we would show atrocity films from North Vietnam, we would call on you, Mr. Chairman, not to throw red paint all over your office, but to demonstrate our concern.

"It might interest you to know that the media turned me down cold — saying they would not guarantee me thirty seconds."

So stated the commander of the Veterans of Foreign Wars last Friday.

Gentlemen, if the representatives of the news media are sincere about their claims that they provide balanced news coverage why didn't they give Mr. Rainwater's large, established veterans' organization equal time with the dissidents and protesters? Why? One can reasonably conclude they didn't *want* the coverage to be balanced.

But enough of criticism . . . for the moment and for this speech.

In the constant exchange that I seem to have been involved in with certain prominent personalities and publications in the news business over the past two years, it is easy to acquire an unwanted image of being completely "antimedia."

However, let me say again — as I have said before — that I recognize the contribution made by the vast majority of men and women in the news business who do a thorough, professional job day in and day out of keeping the American people well informed — not only about their government, but about their community and the essential things they must know to operate their businesses and run their everyday lives. This kind of competence is practiced daily at your radio stations, at the stations affiliated with television networks, in the network news rooms themselves and in newspaper offices and bureaus throughout the country and around the world — including some of those that I find much fault with.

So I would like to leave with you the very clear impression that I value the free press of this country as an indispensable bulwark of our democracy. It is the best, most professional news fraternity in the world. I want to see it stay strong and free. I believe it can best guarantee that strength by occasionally turning its own critical powers inward and looking hard at the way it is doing its job, rather than screaming "intimidation" every time it is criticized by a public official.

As I have said earlier here, the dedicated, honest, hardworking men and women in the news profession far outnumber the prima donnas. What our country needs today is for these responsible professionals to assert themselves and their principles — not for themselves, not for those in government, but for the millions of Americans who depend upon them for knowledge and understanding of what is going on.

June 9, 1971, Colorado Springs, Colorado
Air Force Academy Commencement

IT HAS BEEN twelve years since the first graduates of the United States Air Force Academy were awarded their diplomas and commissions.

Since that June day, almost 6,000 young men like you who will graduate today have left the shadow of Pikes Peak to serve their country in other places.

Some of them have flown to the dark edge of space, testing the latest aircraft. Others have fought bravely in Southeast Asia. Some have served with great effectiveness in support assignments, in laboratories, and on planning staffs.

In twelve short years they have compiled a proud record of service and set a high standard for those who follow.

One has been nominated for the Medal of Honor, six have been awarded the Air Force Cross, and 126 have received the Silver Star. One, Captain Richard Arnold, has been awarded the Silver Star four times since leaving here in 1963.

This is eloquent testimony to bravery and valor.

More than fifty of your alumni have paid the supreme price — they have given their lives in combat. Sixty-four others are either prisoners of war or missing in action in Southeast Asia.

There can be no greater devotion to duty and country than these graduates have displayed.

Within the brief span of twelve years this academy has also established sound educational credentials. It has produced forty-seven doctors of philosophy, fourteen Rhodes scholars and two White House fellows. Four other Air Force Academy graduates have been awarded the Legion of Merit for outstanding staff work.

So your alumni have acquitted themselves well. Theirs has been a pursuit of excellence which has shown them unwilling to offer any effort but their best or to accept any result but the exemplary.

All have had a great common bond, a common denominator of professionalism, which has its roots right here in the classrooms and on the parade fields which each of you has come to know so well.

As you leave the Air Force Academy today and move away from the rigorous study and discipline, the creative competition of sports and studies, and the warm fellowship of classmates, you will find the experiences which you have enjoyed and shared during the past four years will carry you through times of trial and times of testing. And you will certainly face great tests, tests of yourselves and the nation.

I am sure that you will continue to build on the individual foundations which each one of you has laid. You will continue to study, whenever time and duty permit, those subjects which will improve your military proficiency. You will apply with vigor, dedication, and skill the knowledge and experience which you have acquired.

To couple the lessons of history with creative inquisitiveness, and then astutely and relentlessly apply the result to a particular problem is what characterizes professionalism. It is the hallmark of the Air Force Academy graduate and of the professional military man.

Professionalism is a philosophy which has sustained members of the military services for centuries, and it sustains them today. It is a philosophy that permits men to think the unthinkable and to endure the unendurable.

Professionalism equips each of you who will graduate today to stand up for freedom even in the face of conflict and even in times when it is not popular to be a member of the armed services.

Fighting and violence, death and destruction, the inevitable products of war, are abhorrent to civilized men. For some, the avoidance of war and its carnage is worth any price — so long as that price need not be paid immediately. Even the sacrifice of the power to defend freedom, liberty and justice is an acceptable price to some. The best among them rationalize that the bill will never come due; the worst, that it will be paid by someone else.

For the military professional like the Air Force Academy graduate, war is dreadful, but the loss of freedom is the ultimate catastrophe.

The great philosopher John Stuart Mill, writing during the time of the American Civil War, said:

War is an ugly thing, but not the ugliest of things. The decayed and degraded state of moral and patriotic feeling which thinks that nothing is worth fighting for is much worse. A man who has nothing for which he is willing to fight, nothing he cares about more than his own personal safety, is a miserable creature who has no chance of being free, unless made and kept so by the exertions of better men than himself.

This, then, is your calling. And I come before you today to commend you for accepting it and to share your pride in it.

I am sure you will remain proud, and you will remain dedicated. You will help keep America free — a challenge of ever-growing magnitude for today's world but an absolute necessity if our civilization, as we know it, is to survive.

America still offers the single best hope for advancement of the human race. The vast majority of Americans know that, even if some of our more nihilistic fellow citizens, the professional deplorers, do not. You would do well to remember it.

We live in a world where much has been accomplished to remove mankind's ancient crosses, but where there are still grave dangers — from overpopulation, from pollution, from war.

Some nations are doubling in size with each generation, and our own population is expanding at a phenomenal rate. Our ingenuity will be challenged to feed, clothe, and house our own people, to say nothing of assisting others. But our great system of free enterprise and our industrial society are up to meeting that challenge if we keep them strong and free.

Pollution is another problem of our age. The destruction of our environment has finally aroused our attention as a nation. We have the technological ability to halt it, and it will be halted. But there is an even more insidious form of pollution which threatens us as a people — pollution of the mind and spirit. This is a pollution that can destroy civilization just as surely as choking off the air or contaminating the water. While we may be far from perfect as a people, ours is still a land that offers the refreshing freedom, compassion, and personal liberty which sets mind and spirit free.

We have had difficulties — and magnified them to the world — in bringing about a genuine equality of opportunity among men, particularly for minority races. But it is extremely important to give ourselves credit for having recognized these shortcomings and made efforts to correct them. High-minded idealism led to the great breakthroughs in civil rights achieved during recent decades. Idealism — not disruptive demonstrations — accounted for the far-ranging improvements in human opportunity which we have seen and which we will continue to see. And never forget, in these days when it is popular to disparage the military, that the military services led the rest of the country in making equal rights a reality.

Yes, we have many blessings in America. Here a child is free to grow up and make of himself what his talents, character, and heart will allow.

In some countries a child is forced into one or another occupational pathway by the time he reaches his teens. Only those who demonstrate a bright intellect at a very early age will ever be given the chance to become professional men, teachers, businessmen, artists, or leaders.

In some countries minority races will be given no opportunity for improvement. Girl children are no more than chattels. And in the Communist countries, where those few belonging to the party reign supreme, small indeed is the number who have a say in how their nations conduct their business or shape their societies.

Pollution of the mind and spirit is a problem which plagues some other lands more than it does ours, but it can be a threat to us too if we ever relax our ideals or abandon our sense of values.

As I see it, ours is a land where maximum personal liberty prevails; where a free enterprise system has built the base upon which our overpopulated world might yet thrive; and where problems of discrimination, inequity, and injustice are dealt with by the inexorable force of the public conscience in a truly representative society. Sometimes this process is painfully slow, but it is secure and the progress is permanent.

So, because American ingenuity and American idealism offer hope to the world, they must be preserved. That is where you, the Class of 1971, United States Air Force Academy, come in.

The truths of history cannot be denied. Unless a nation has been prepared to fight to defend its rights and resources, it has usually been forced to surrender them.

We have seen in this century what truly awful events will occur when a nation in the hands of a few aggressive men bent on conquest is offered appeasement instead of the sword. The Second World War, replete with destruction, savagery, and killing unprecedented in the history of the world, might have been avoided. A third world war *must* be avoided.

Adolf Hitler was tormented by almost overwhelming doubt and fear when he first set his forces into motion. Had France, England, or any other world power unsheathed the sword, Hitler's increasingly bold marches into the Rhineland, Austria, and Czechoslovakia might never have occurred.

When France and England did try to call a halt, it was too late. Contempt for weak and vacillating opponents and growing confidence in their own infallibility led Hitler and his henchmen to inflame the world.

Only after sustaining millions of casualties, and an irreplaceable loss of talent, vigor, and future leadership, did the nations of the world find peace.

Although intervention in the Rhineland, Austria, or Czechoslovakia might have meant sending French, British, or even American youth to fight a small, dirty war removed from their own borders, the cost would have been incomparably smaller in the long run.

A primary cause of Allied indecision and appeasement of Hitler was a lack of military preparedness. Not knowing how timorous Hitler was in the early stages of his adventures, but knowing themselves to be militarily bankrupt, the free world hesitated.

With a major war in Europe a certainty and the grave likelihood of America's being drawn into it, we had in 1939 only 174,000 men in uniform and our Air Force existed for the most part in the minds of men like Hap Arnold.

Fortunately, by the time of Pearl Harbor, we had begun to mobilize and train an Army and develop the industrial might to support it. In this nuclear age, we will never again have that much time to act.

After World War II, we vowed we would not be caught napping again. The old cycle of war, disarmament, rearmament, and war would be replaced by a continual state of military readiness. Aggression anywhere would be struck hard very early in the game. Unfortunately, this idea of our military planners did not prevail and America disarmed. The Soviet Union did not.

The Red Army seized all Eastern Europe and halted only when the West stood firm in Greece and Iran and against a cruel blockade of the battered people of Berlin.

The attack on the Republic of Korea by a well-equipped Communist army and the spread of atomic weapons to the Soviet Union led to large-scale American rearmament.

Since that time, America has steadfastly tried to stamp out the fires of war before they could spread into an all-consuming nuclear inferno. At times, as in Southeast Asia, we have met an aggressive enemy on the field of battle. But we have met him with courage instead of cowardice, and with the intent of containing conflict rather than of waging wider war.

The decisions of four Presidents to pursue this course are now being derided by a highly vocal minority of Americans.

We are told that there is no threat to the United States in Southeast Asia, that there is no threat of a wider war developing from the small aggression waged by North Vietnam and supported by other Communist nations.

We are told that if the President will set a date for withdrawal of all of our forces from Vietnam, without any reciprocal action by the other side, there will be peace in our time.

We are told that the Soviet Union has no expansionist tendencies and is a greatly mellowed member of the community of nations.

We are being asked once again to put faith in our adversaries basic humanity and to ignore our own common sense. If we will but believe, we are told, we can get on with disarmament and the dissolution of the military–industrial complex.

The drive to disarm America — unilaterally — has given birth to many of the outrageous assaults and ridiculous charges with which our great institutions are being bombarded today.

It is reminiscent in some ways of the period of my youth, the 1930s, when an antimilitary spirit also prevailed, not just here but abroad. Winston Churchill, writing after World War II, noted the potential impact of an incident on a prestigious campus in England in 1933. The Oxford Union passed a resolution stating "this house refuses to fight for King and country."

Said Sir Winston:

> It was easy to laugh off such an episode in England, but in Germany, in Russia, in Italy, in Japan, the idea of a decadent, degenerate Britain took deep root and swayed many calculations. Little did the foolish boys who passed the resolution dream that they were destined quite soon to conquer or fall gloriously in the ensuing war, and prove themselves the finest generation ever bred in Britain.

My friends, graduates of the Air Force Academy and your guests here today, we ignore such lessons of history only at our peril.

As you complete your years here, you are facing a world where your efforts, your patriotism, your sacrifice will probably be denigrated. Some of you will even be tempted to lay aside your blue suits.

But others of you will never lose sight of the fact that our nation, offering the single greatest hope for today's world, faces formidable enemies; that aggression historically has been halted only by the sword, or a convincing willingness to use it; that there will be no time for leisurely rearmament in the future; and that the consequence of nuclear war is death.

There are two great factors which will continue to strengthen the characters of those of you who continue to serve.

First, you will be bolstered by membership in a growing body of men who are developing a great tradition — the graduates of the United States Air Force Academy.

Second, you will gain strength from the moral decision that what you are doing is right. Your faith in the inherent goodness of your country will be too strong to be shaken.

As you rise in responsibility you will never hesitate to warn of enemy capabilities and what they could mean; you will never cease to let your superiors and Congress know what weapons and what forces you will need; and you will never be cowed — either by malicious lies or well-intentioned criticism at home or by enemy attack from abroad.

Never will it be said of you: He stood for nothing and fell for anything.

It *will* be said of you: He stood for his country and the world was a better place for it.

June 19, 1971, Louisville, Kentucky
Kentucky Republican Rally

THANK YOU very much for that typical warm Kentucky welcome.

Ladies and gentlemen: On April 5th I had the privilege of meeting with the Kentucky Legislature in Frankfort to discuss the President's proposals for federal revenue sharing with the states, which I believe is one of the most important domestic issues of our time.

On May 14th I returned for a meeting at Fort Knox with the Armor Association and a renewal of some memories of my days as an officer candidate there.

One week after that, on May 20th and 21st, my wife, Judy, had a pleasant visit in this state as a guest of Governor and Mrs. Nunn.

And today, less than a month later, here I am back again for this very important occasion.

I guess that should qualify me for the right to lead the first two stanzas of "My Old Kentucky Home." But I will not inflict that on you today.

Being in this ball park reminds me that a couple of years ago Governor Nunn invited me down to a Kentucky Colonels game. I was scheduled to throw out the first ball. Unfortunately, the game was postponed on account of fear. If there is one thing I can't stand it's a catcher who whimpers.

Governor Nunn thought it would be fun if I would stage a little pitching exhibition today and try out my screwball on the Colonels' leading hitter, Jose Calero. The governor suggested this earlier today to Jose and he was fairly enthusiastic. Let's see, he should just about be landing in Cuba in two or three minutes.

America looks to the Kentuckian with pride for his contribution to the pleasures of life: tobacco, whiskey, and horse racing. Well, that's not bad, three out of four.

Seriously, my Kentucky friends — and friends and supporters of the Nixon and Nunn Administrations — it is an honor to be asked to help launch what I am sure will be the successful campaign of Tom Emberton for governor and Jim Host for lieutenant governor.

These two young men, both of them seasoned in the able state administration of Louie Nunn, are going to give Kentucky four more years of outstanding, innovative leadership. I'm here to officially wish them well and to urge you to give our national administration a goal to emulate in 1972 with a smashing victory for this year's Republican team in Kentucky. Your pioneer state was a trailblazer for the national ticket in 1967, and I'm sure you're going to do exactly that same thing again.

And I can assure you that we in Washington who have worked so closely with Louie Nunn, at the White House and throughout the executive branch these past 2½ years, welcome the opportunity to continue that relationship with Tom Emberton.

Tom has shown that he intends to build on the fine record that Governor Nunn has established these past four years in education, transportation, recreation, and the participation of young people in government. It is a solid foundation on which to build.

And speaking of young people, I am not unmindful that Kentucky was a pioneer in extending the vote to eighteen-year-olds. The young people of this state have had the franchise since 1955. Those who claim that its extension nationally will hurt the GOP should examine the party credentials of your governor and your two fine United States Senators.

The issue in this election, my friends, as it will be throughout the nation next year, is one of leadership — *responsible* leadership. Not promises, not pie-in-the-sky schemes to make headlines or to raise false hopes, but realistic, solidly based, workable programs.

In Tom Emberton and Jim Host, you will have strong, responsible leadership at the State level, just as you've had with Louie Nunn. Althouth this rally is billed as the kickoff of the gubernatorial campaign, I am impressed by the fact that Tom Emberton has already been getting around the state, taking his case to the people. And I am impressed by the fact that he has already announced a fifteen-point program to provide 200,000 new jobs for Kentuckians, and we know nothing is more important than jobs. I am sure you will be hearing other practical proposals as the campaign progresses, and the people of Kentucky will know that they have an action candidate for governor who will really deliver — a worthy successor to Louie Nunn.

Let me digress here a moment to tell you how fortunate I think you in this great state are to have the kind of leadership at the helm that you have in Louie Nunn. I have known Governor Nunn, as he indicated during his remarks introducing me, for some time. We were fellow governors together. He was respected as a governor from the moment he walked into the Governors' Conferences, and I'm not just talking about the Republican Governors' Conferences of which he is presently chairman, but the National Governors' Conference where the Democratic governors as well as the Republican governors respected, admired, and trusted, above all trusted, Louie Nunn. Not just trusted him because he's honest, but trusted him because of the reasoning capacity he has and the fact that his decisions are always moderate and always considerate of the opposition point of view and yet notwithstanding this moderation, this consideration, this desire to ameliorate his decisions, Governor Nunn is a governor who has real fortitude, one who will stand up for a point of view he is convinced is right for his citizens even in the face of what might appear at the moment to be a preponderant criticism. He has my profound respect and I know he has yours.

And I am proud to say that at the national level we have also had solid responsible leadership in our great President, Richard Nixon — President Nixon's leadership that has been imaginative and progressive, and yet always conscious of cost restrictions. The President has carefully constructed, plank by plank, an administrative and legislative program on which Republicans can stand solidly in 1972, no matter how hard the obstructionists in Congress try to dismember it.

One by one, the President has met the nation's problems head-on, and after careful study has come up with proposals for action — workable proposals that the nation can afford without spending ourselves into bankruptcy.

And I want to remind you, my friends, that it wasn't more than two or three months after President Nixon assumed the reins than the Democrats began clobbering him over the fact that he had not sent fully defined programs to the Congress for action. Surely we went through a period of intense preparation, but no President in our history has sent more carefully defined and carefully thought out legislation affecting a myriad of problems in our country to the Congress than has Richard Nixon. And you don't hear that cry anymore.

One by one, the President has met the nation's problems headon. And you have just seen the latest example — a bold frontal assault on the nation's drug problem. If Congress will act on it with dispatch, you will see some results — not just token results but the start of a long-range solution to what will obviously become our biggest domestic nightmare if we allow it to persist.

For those of you who may not be familiar with this program, which was sent to Congress just Thursday, let me briefly review the major points.

The President proposes the creation of a single office — a Special Action Office — to coordinate all federal efforts to curb drug abuse and to treat and rehabilitate addicts. This new program is especially geared to cope with the drug addiction problem among members of the armed forces. The office will be headed by an experienced director and will be located in the executive office of the President. It will bring into single focus for the first time the federal government's broadly scattered efforts in this field.

The President has requested that Congress appropriate $155 million above the amount already being spent to mount this fullscale offensive. This will increase by seventy-two percent the amount presently budgeted for the control of drug abuse. These funds will finance intensified research, treatment, and rehabilitation programs, and will vastly increase inspection and enforcement efforts to curb the flow of dangerous drugs in this country.

The President is also initiating a major effort to get other nations to join in eliminating the sources of heroin, the major drug menace and the breeder of so much of the crime in America today.

The President said in his message to Congress Thursday that America has the largest number of heroin addicts of any nation in the world. And yet, America does not grow opium — of which heroin is a derivative — nor does it manufacture heroin, which requires a laboratory process and is carried out abroad. This deadly poison in the American lifestream is, in other words, a foreign import.

But the major thrust of this intensified new effort is in research into the causes and cures of drug addiction, in the treatment and in the rehabilitation of persons who have been victimized by this damnable habit and, through broad public education, in the prevention of addiction in millions of *potential* victims.

The President's interest in this problem has been deep and continuing. Five months after taking office, in July 1969, he sent to Congress legislation for a comprehensive reform of federal drug enforcement laws. But it was not until fifteen months later, in the heat of the Congressional elections of 1970, that Congress saw fit to pass that legislation. Although valuable time was lost, fortunately, excellent results are now being achieved.

Also, early in the administration, the President met with the nation's governors to enlist their support in a broad attack on the drug problem at state and local levels. The efforts of Governor Nunn and your own state of Kentucky in this regard have been noteworthy and are highly commendable.

The President has also developed and sent to the Congress carefully planned programs to meet other critical needs, such as reform of the welfare system and a proposal to put health care within the reach of all citizens . . . with due regard for the price tag, I might add.

The most dramatic and meaningful new initiatives of the many that were brought forth by this administration, in my opinion, have been the proposals for the reform of government itself. These go to the very heart of our federal system and, in the end, may well prove to be its salvation. The President has suggested a restructuring of the executive branch of the federal government to make it more efficient and responsive to the needs of the people, and he has asked that state and local governments be given control over many of the decisions that are now being mishandled at the national level. To help accomplish this return of power to states and localities and to provide revenue resources, he has proposed revenue sharing — that states and localities be given a fixed annual share of the federal income tax. These proposals have alarmed the advocates of the status quo in Washington, and we have seen strong opposition to them from powerful men in Congress.

I have been around the country from East to West discussing these proposals and people are interested and are concerned about the constant flow of power to Washington. And I am convinced that in the end, the very logic of revenue sharing and reorganization, and the strong support they have won at the grass roots will guarantee their enactment.

We are talking about leadership, my friends — we are talking about meeting problems forthrightly, analyzing them, offering workable, practicable solutions with a proper regard to cost.

Now, responsible leadership also entails making hard decisions. This administration took office with a war raging in Southeast Asia and inflation raging at home. President Nixon has banked the fires of both and dampened them down. The economy is still not fully recovered from the spending binge that preceded this administration, but the fever has subsided and I am pleased to report that the patient is recovering. Those same people who criticize the President over the gradual nature of the recovery irresponsibly try to boost the cost of every idea he sends to Capitol Hill. There is one exception, of course. They want to cut the spending that's necessary to the defense of the country. But generally, their antidote for inflation is a simple one: Spend us into a relapse. But the President will continue to resist their quick remedies for quick relief in favor of a more disciplined, long-term cure.

The Vietnam war has been an even stronger test of patient, responsible leadership. The President chose the tougher course in the long-range interests of the United States. He has resisted the politically expedient pleas for abrupt withdrawal in favor of a gradual but steady termination of our involvement. And this has allowed the South Vietnamese to strengthen themselves and to take over their own defense against a Communist invader from the North, one who otherwise would have overrun the country. The unmistakable fact remains: American troops, streaming into Vietnam when President Nixon took office, are now streaming home. Our combat role there has virtually ended. And South Vietnam still stands.

The test of leadership, my friends — as Governor Nunn has so aptly demonstrated during the past three-and-a-half years and as Tom Emberton well knows from his inside view — is not how fast you do a job, is not how pretentious you make it look, but what you've accomplished after the activity is completed.

The Republican party is alive and well — in Frankfort and in Washington. And it intends to remain that way.

June 21, 1971, White Sulphur Springs, West Virginia Grocery Manufacturers of America, Inc. Annual Meeting

I WELCOME the opportunity to keynote this gathering of the executive leadership of the Grocery Manufacturers of America.

Not only as a member of the Nixon Administration but as a citizen deeply concerned about the future of our free enterprise system, I commend the selection of the subject, "Corporate Responsibility in modern American society" as the key idea for your meetings.

In considering this theme, I referred back to a recent article by Professor Milton Friedman on the subject of the social responsibilities of business in our free and competitive society.

Professor Friedman makes the point that much of the current rhetoric we hear and read regarding the "social responsibilities" of business is characterized by analytical looseness.

In brief, as I understand Professor Friedman's thesis, the free enterprise factor is integral to our social and political progress. Businessmen, therefore, need not feel that they are somehow acting in a socially irresponsible manner because they are daily engaged in making a profit for their company and stockholders.

Attacking or questioning the morality of the profit motive is, of course, an ideological touchstone for all opponents of the free enterprise system.

There is, for example, an apocryphal Lenin quotation to the effect that when the enemies of capitalism prepare to hang the system, the capitalists themselves will bid for the rope concession.

We may speculate whether this quotation attributed to the founder of the world's first modern Communist state was intended to reflect on the venality of free enterprise businessmen, or their shortsightedness.

In any case, neither in Lenin's time nor in that of his successors have Communist predictions concerning the demise of capitalism proved accurate. On the contrary, Marxist–Leninist projections that doomed the free enterprise system to economic failure appear absurd in the light of post–World War II history.

As the economic bulwark of postwar Western society, the American economic system has not only outstripped every nation throughout history in raising the living standards of our own people, but has also exported a dynamic technology and expertise to revolutionize and elevate living standards for people the world over.

Indeed, even Lenin's Soviet successors have in recent years found it expedient to borrow and adopt many of the techniques of America's free enterprise marketing system in order to meet the needs of their own consuming public.

Thus in a period of our history saturated with negativism and induced self-doubt regarding our nation's political, social, and economic institutions, let us recognize this paramount truth: For all the television news time and newspaper attention given the professional critics of our free enterprise system, it remains the greatest in the world, bringing more benefit to more people than any economic mechanism since the beginning of time.

Admittedly it isn't perfect. But to paraphrase Winston Churchill's description of democracy: The free enterprise system is the worst of all economic systems — except for all those other forms that have been tried from time to time.

Marx and Lenin were wrong in their economic predictions regarding the failure of capitalism. But in recent years the Hegelian theory that our system carries within it the seeds of its own destruction has taken on unique implications.

Ironically, the very success of the American system has created vast new problems in terms of consumer needs and expectations. And now, as always, there are those social and economic critics who would exploit these problems as a means of reordering society in accordance with their own arbitrary theories and methods.

Several weeks ago I addressed an audience on the subject of the new demagogy that has infected our nation's body politic.

The critics to whom I refer today are modern America's new demagogues of economic thought and activity. '

These new demagogues may address us in modulated tones and under the protective cover of scholarship; but their scholarship, on close examination, is not creative scholarship. It is instead the strictured scholarship of the narrow ideologue bent on shaping selected facts and statistics into propaganda weapons.

Such ignoble scholars do not seek truth. They seek issues to further their own ambitions and designs for a new economic order.

Needless to say, since sensational negativism is the stock-in-trade of the new demagogues, their every utterance, report and declamation directed against American economic institutions is faithfully given front page space and prime time attention by the news media.

From time to time even the editorial allies of these professional critics concede that they are often guilty of rhetorical exaggeration or irresponsible accusation against certain institutions, industries, or individuals.

Nevertheless, their editorial defenders would have us excuse such questionable means on the grounds that the ends sought are necessary and desirable for the good of society. After all, we are told, these attacks aim at not the destruction but the reformation of our free enterprise system. All, of course, in the general public interest.

Speaking, however, as one American who has studied the charges and the modus operandi of these disseminators of discontent, I would submit the following observation: Whatever the ostensibly noble purpose such professional critics claim to serve, their real goal is ego feeding and self-promotion.

What then is the ideological essence of this new demagogy? It is the concept of perfectibility carried to an illogical, impractical conclusion.

In brief, because the system is not perfect — even if it were to be, to borrow the phrase of one of your member companies, 99 and 44/100th percent pure — the new demagogues prefer, for their own purposes, to pinpoint and exploit whatever areas of imperfection exist.

In some cases, such attacks may actually stimulate demands for the needed improvement. But the public should not assume that appropriate reform is the end the new demagogues truly seek. Their game is bigger. They desire nothing less, according to one of their number, than "the assumption of power in a postindustrial society."

In the guise of economic reform, the new demagogues urge as an alternative system a thinly veiled version of statism.

Far from being concerned with the protection and enhancement of individual rights against bureaucratic encroachment, the new demagogues are indeed confirmed statists, who believe that the ultimate solution depends upon placing the authority to regulate economic life in the hands of a select bureaucratic elite.

Occasionally, a practitioner or advocate of this new demagogy is bold enough to declare publicly what he and his colleagues have in mind for the future of the American economy.

One example of such candor was an editorial that appeared some two and a half years ago in the publication, *Hard Times*. Here, in part, is what that editorial, written by one James Ridgeway, said about the need to protect consumer interests:

> On the simplest level, it is not necessary to buy a car every year, to eat plastic food, to have clean smelling breath. . . . Babies need not be fed food that is made to taste pleasant for their mother's benefit. Stores don't have to buy colored oranges, and so on. As war is the method of extending empire abroad, mindless consumption is the method of colonizing us at home.

513

This, of course, is the doctrine of "Big Brother knows best" in its most unadulterated form. Here we see the philosophy that the "mindless" individual American, on his own, doesn't know what's good for him or his society. He needs not simply protection, but direction — for his own good — whether he wants it or not.

Such rhetoric should not be discounted or ignored. For the sentiments expressed in this editorial encapsulate the battle plan of a dedicated and articulate cadre of socioeconomic activists. Indeed, what makes this particular editorial especially significant is the fact that, at the time it appeared, the foremost professional consumer advocate of our day served the publication as consulting editor.

Obviously we ignore the true thrust of these professional critics at the peril of all that distinguishes the American economic system from that of totalitarian societies. Nor can we dismiss the need to respond to such attacks on our system in positive ways.

Toward this end, the Nixon Administration has advanced a comprehensive program to safeguard the American consuming public in today's changing, increasingly complex marketplace. It is a program aimed at providing solutions to the problems of the modern marketplace *within* the framework of our free enterprise institutions.

In socioeconomics as in the political sphere, the best answer to the appeal of the demagogue is responsible leadership. The Nixon Administration is providing such leadership in the nation's capital. But if we are to succeed in our efforts, leaders of private industry like yourselves, along with all others who value our free enterprise system, must meet their own organizational and individual responsibilities.

The food and grocery industry, for example, comprising more than ten percent of the country's gross national product, constitutes a vital segment of our American consumer economy. The corporate policies which members of this audience establish bear directly upon the lives of millions of Americans each day.

In this sense you represent not simply the executive leadership of individual companies or an industry. You occupy positions of leadership in the society as well. Your executive decisions affect and influence the quality of American life as much, and in some areas more, than the decisions made by those in government.

In defending your industry against the assaults of the new demagogues you are defending the free enterprise system as a whole. By implementing such corrective action within your own ranks as is necessary to safeguard the interests of the consumers of your products and services, you are helping to disarm the new demagogues of their heaviest rhetorical artillery.

But beyond these points, I would also urge that members of this audience, along with other leaders of business and industry, reexamine their policies and practices in the light of Lenin's cynical prophecy regarding free enterprise capitalism.

In brief, America's free society and economy cannot survive the assault of the new demagogues if the executive echelon of business washes its hands of any responsibility to defend the system against attack; or if you fail to recognize the imperative need to begin mustering, in the media and in the nation's educational institutions, the necessary resources to counter the propaganda supremacy now held by the adversaries of our free enterprise system — a supremacy, I regret to say, all too often sponsored and subsidized by the very industries and companies that are under attack.

Four decades ago, during the Great Depression, Will Rogers commented that the American people might be the first in history to travel to the poor house in a limousine. To paraphrase and update that observation: If, having survived the Depression and grown to hitherto undreamed heights of prosperity and plenty, our economic system were to be dismantled, we would be remembered in history as a nation that traded in its free enterprise limousine for a collectivist horse and buggy.

The first priority of corporate responsibility for American businessmen today is to see to it that this trade-down does not occur.

It is your responsibility, not that of government. It is an obligation that carries with it much more than the future of your company, your industry, or even industry as a whole. For the competitive free enterprise system lies at the very foundation of all our freedoms. You are on the front lines in the war being waged by the new demagogues against

America's institutions and heritage. As your battle goes, so will go the nation's fight to preserve our free society.

June 25, 1971, Phoenix, Arizona
Young Republicans National Convention

WERE THEODORE ROOSEVELT in the nation's capital addressing those thousands who recently marched on Washington, he might have reminded his audience that:

> Probably no other great nation in the world is so anxious for peace as we are. There is not a single civilized power which has anything whatever to fear from aggressiveness on our part.

He might have added:

> All we want is peace; and to this end we wish to be able to secure the same respect for our rights in return, . . . and to guarantee the safety of the American people.

Those words, which Roosevelt spoke in 1901, are every bit as relevant today as they were then. All President Nixon wants is peace. And he works constantly for the cause of peace.

Yet throughout the country the din grows, amplified night after night by our television networks and day after day in powerful liberal newspapers and journals. The dominant message they seek to convey is this:

That President Nixon is not concerned about peace. That he is a war hawk perpetuating the war in Vietnam. That he has not been honest. That he has no plan to end the war. And why stay involved in a war thousands of miles away? Why not admit we have lost an immoral war and just go home?

On and on that message goes. War-weary Americans cannot escape being bombarded with this tired refrain.

So tonight, I intend to exercise *my* right of dissent. We are going to look at the record. And it will leave no doubt, because it supports the policy of the President of the United States. He not only deserves your support; he has *earned* your support — and the support of every American who is willing to see the facts as they are, not as they are mangled on the twenty-four-inch screen.

Briefly, let's review the record of Richard Nixon.

He is the first President to *reduce* American involvement in Vietnam. The day he was inaugurated there were 542,000 American troops in South Vietnam; today there are approximately 240,000. He has met every withdrawal commitment, and by December 1st he will have brought a total of 365,000 men home, with more slated to follow.

When President Nixon came into office, casualties averaged 281 per week. Today, they stand at less than one-seventh of that. On January 20, 1969, our government had no plan to end this war, but President Nixon had devised a plan and it is now being implemented.

In short, that is a record of performance. We are on our way out, and we are on our way out honorably, leaving behind a nation better prepared to defend itself from a ruthless aggressor.

515

Even this exemplary record does not quiet the keening of the President's prominent critics. They are now heard to say: Well, yes, we supported the war back in the sixties. We gave speeches in favor of America's Vietnam policy. We thought it was a wise policy. But we were deceived. We have now changed our minds. Secretly we always had doubts about the war but we never made our views public.

This type of hypocritical, self-serving rhetoric is hardly admirable. This great reawakening of the critics' conscience is amazing to say the least. Are these same people who marched lockstep with previous administrations into war, now to be allowed to get away with saying that they really didn't mean it? Are these former apologists for our involvement now to be believed when they say there is no partisan purpose for their attacks on President Nixon?

Of great concern to me and I think to millions of Americans is the monumental arrogance of these armchair commanders-in-chief who insist that they alone stand for peace; that they alone have the answers; that they alone are sincere people who wish to end this war. They won't say it explicitly, but their message is nevertheless clear: "We are antiwar, and President Nixon is prowar."

Let me submit to you, my friends, that the greatest enemy of war today sits in the oval office of the White House. Yes, irrespective of posturing, the greatest antiwar leader is the President of the United States. The man who can do the most, the man who has done the most, for peace is President Nixon.

What the President has done is to bring about the conditions which will promote a responsible peace — a peace which has a chance. He has done this even though he has been the subject of persistent and vitriolic attacks. It is no small feat that, in the face of the best organized and most debilitating protests in our recent history, the President has accomplished progress that would have been unthinkable a little over two years ago.

It is interesting that the critics have been so changeable over the years. We know, of course, that today they clamor for a "withdrawal date," which they insist will be the magic wand to end the war. This crude effort to play on the fears and emotions of the America public is all too familiar to us. Listen to their track record on actions which would supposedly end the war.

In 1968 we read the outrage on the editorial pages. Why not stop the bombing? This will indicate to the enemy that we are willing to negotiate, and the war's end will quickly result. On March 31, 1968, President Johnson did just that, stopping all bombing raids north of the 19th parallel in North Vietnam. When the enemy answered with mortar shells instead of olive branches, the critics were undismayed.

No, they said, a partial bombing halt is not enough. If only you would stop *all* the bombing, there will be peace. President Johnson stopped all the bombing in the north. The attacks and the invective continued.

Were the critics taken aback? Of course not. They then said, we must agree to negotiate with the National Liberation Front. All parties to the fighting should be represented at the peace table. When we do this, there will be peace. So we did that. We invited the NLF to the negotiating table — to participate fully in the Paris talks. What happened? You guessed it. We didn't get peace — only an agreement about the seating arrangements at the table — a major tribute to the negotiating capabilities of Averell Harriman — the same Mr. Harriman who now urges further fruitless concessions upon us.

Well, that's still not enough, said the critics. If only we start withdrawing troops, the enemy will negotiate, and there will be peace. American withdrawal began and is being continued, and now, after we have reduced our forces by nearly 300,000 men, Hanoi and the Viet Cong still refuse to negotiate meaningfully.

Let me say it straightforwardly and frankly. Every single step which the critics proposed has been taken, and on every occasion we had their assurances that peace would follow. After all these "if onlys," Hanoi still has not heeded mankind's concern for peace. So let me add my "if only": *If only* the proponents of "peace now" and "out now" would let President Nixon conduct the foreign policy of our country; *if only* they would still their strident voices; *if only* they would cease attempting to undercut realistic policy decisions, *then* peace would have a chance in Vietnam. Then at least, Hanoi would cease to hold out for the bargain rates they hope to get from the supersalesmen of retreat.

But I am not sanguine that the superdoves have sense enough to quiet their shouting. No, instead they have come up with one more "if only." If only the President would set a withdrawal date, our prisoners could be released and American fighting men could come home. Not only does the doves' track record indicate their error, but this latest proposition is no less than a cruel hoax played on the hopes of all Americans.

Let's look at the withdrawal date proposition — a proposition, by the way, which the Democrats have turned into a partisan issue, first by a vote in their Congressional caucus and second, by the unprecedented Democratic National Committee television appearance which was used to tell the world that there is a different foreign policy for Democrats than there is for America.

I will put it starkly: If the President followed the doves' advice and set a date for a unilateral, final, and total withdrawal of all American forces from South Vietnam, it would undercut the Allied effort to negotiate a just peace and would end any incentive whatsoever for Hanoi's leaders to negotiate seriously. It would deliver to the Communists a victory they have no hopes of achieving on the battlefield and which they have never dared to seek via a test of verifiably free political competition. It would also indicate to Hanoi that we are preparing to reward its intransigence by making more and more concessions whenever it creates a deadlock. This will make the Communists decide that it pays not to negotiate but simply to reiterate their own demands until we yield.

In their grand tradition of overstatement and misstatement, the President's critics say that setting a date for total withdrawal will solve all our problems including the release of American prisoners of war and those missing in action. What self-serving distortion! While you listen to their promises of prisoner release, consider this one salient point: The other side has never — not once — promised that setting an American withdrawal date would result in the release of our prisoners of war. They have made no reliable statement on which any such claim of release can be based.

Indeed, our setting a date without reciprocal concessions would be a coup for the enemy. They will have had their cake and eaten it too. Because when we perform unilaterally on our promise, American prisoners will still be languishing in their barbaric prison camps. With that ace up the enemy's sleeve they will continue to be in a position to barter human beings for political concessions that they cannot legitimately justify.

Assuming that Hanoi said tomorrow: Yes, you withdraw your troops, and we will give you back your prisoners. What, in the history of this war, has Hanoi done to assure us that it can keep a promise? Let's take a look at Hanoi's record.

On October 7, 1970, President Nixon proposed the following generous five-point program: Incidentally, this program is overlooked from time to time. Nobody seems to mention it anymore and I think it is very important I emphasize it at this point. This was October 1970 when this offer was made, and it's still lying open on the peace table in Paris.

— an internationally supervised cease-fire in place throughout Indochina;

— the establishment of an Indochina Peace Conference;

— negotiation of an agreed timetable for the complete withdrawal of all U. S. forces from Vietnam on the basis of North Vietnamese reciprocity and international verification;

— a fair political settlement reflecting the will of the South Vietnamese people and of all the political forces in South Vietnam;

— the immediate and unconditional release of all prisoners of war by all sides.

In addition, South Vietnam and the United States have called for free elections in which all people and parties of South Vietnam, including the National Liberation Front, can participate, and for a mixed electoral commission on which all parties including the NLF can be represented to work out the modalities and verification procedures for such elections.

What have been the Communists' answers? Hanoi and the Viet Cong, which have claimed to be fighting to give the South Vietnamese people freedom from a repressive government and the right of self-determination, have rejected these and all other proposals and all other steps for peace. They refuse even to consider the Allied proposals as agenda items for the Paris talks. They have continued to reject all notions of reciprocity, verifiably open elections or international verification. Despite their promises, they refuse to negotiate with the government of Vietnam. They demand that the United States commit itself unilaterally and unconditionally to total withdrawal of all troops and war materiel and the overthrow of the leaders of the government of Vietnam.

In exchange for such a total unilateral commitment by the United States, Hanoi and the NLF have generously pledged — absolutely nothing! The best they have done is say that they will "discuss" — discuss, not release — our prisoners of war.

Also in the firm Communist tradition of candor, Hanoi continues to this day to deny that there is a single North Vietnamese soldier outside of North Vietnam — imagine that — despite the presence of 100,000 North Vietnamese soldiers in South Vietnam, 90,000 in Laos, and 50,000 in Cambodia — all waging wars of aggression on their neighbors.

Finally, having looked at Hanoi's freedom-loving record, let us politically assess its intransigence.

First, the Politburo of Hanoi's Lao Dong (Communist) Party has massively violated the solemn international agreements it has signed concerning South Vietnam, Laos, and Cambodia, all the while denying that it has a single soldier outside its borders.

Second, Hanoi's self-proclaimed Marxist–Leninist "people's dictatorship" has never dared risk the revealing political litmus test of tolerating the slightest diversity, political competition or international inspection in areas under its control. The Hanoi regime is built on the liquidation of all earlier non-Communist "coalition" and "Front" partners and on total monopoly of all political, economic, cultural, as well as military affairs.

Third, the so-called National Liberation Front is committed, as it demonstrated by systematic political assassinations in the city of Hue during the 1968 Tet offensive, to imposing a rigid Communist "peoples' dictatorship" on the South Vietnamese.

Fourth, far from involving a small independent group of nationalists in a "civil war" in South Vietnam, tens of thousands of Communist Hanoi's regular army troops have for years carried on assassination and warfare against the South.

The issue of setting a withdrawal date, seen in context, is a false issue raised by false prophets to encourage false hopes. It is a sham and a delusion. It offers nothing of substance but rather more heartache for Americans and their allies. There is not a scintilla of evidence in the record to suggest that Hanoi will be more reasonable if we set a withdrawal date. In sum, those who advocate a set withdrawal date without reciprocal and enforceable concessions by the enemy have been misled and are in turn tragically misleading Americans.

With this look at Hanoi's credibility, let's take up the question of President Nixon's credibility. No one has been more forthright or honest than President Nixon about the American presence in Vietnam. I don't ask you to take that on assumption, but rather I submit that the point is proved by the record.

Every pledge has been kept. The American people have not been deceived. The difficulty of our task has not been underestimated, and American expectations have not been unfairly raised.

On the contrary, it is the President's critics who must answer for their lack of credibility. I have in mind last year's operations in Cambodia. What did the critics say?

They said it was an expansion of the war. They said Cambodia would fall within months. Americans would be mired in another war on another front. Week after week we were lectured that the President was wrong. Well, if words could really be eaten, I'd be very pleased to ring the dinner bell.

The President said we would be out of Cambodia by June 30th, and we were out. He said that casualties would be lowered as a result, and indeed American casualties have been dramatically cut since Cambodia. The President said the operation would enable him to speed up troop withdrawals, and withdrawals have been stepped up since the incursion. The President said that the enemy's capability to launch a major offensive would be reduced, and indeed the enemy has been unable to launch any substantial offensive in the III and IV Corps Areas of South Vietnam, where over half the population resides.

Where are the critics now? They have engaged in newspeak. Since the actual result of Cambodia does not support their thesis, they have expunged it from their recollection.

And Laos? The story was very familiar, was it not? Far be it from the critics, the networks, and liberal print media to admit that progress shown by the Laotian operations really existed.

The North Vietnamese paid a very high price for massing their forces against ARVN ground troops and American air support in Laos. Conservative estimates place the losses at over 13,000 killed and many more wounded, with the equivalent of thirteen of the enemy's best combat battalions — the same elite divisions which during the Tet offensive seized Hue, entered the Danang defenses and attacked the coastal population in that time — those outfits were rendered totally ineffective.

Most importantly, South Vietnamese forces physically blocked various branches of the Ho Chi Minh Trail at the height of the dry season. ARVN forces and U. S. air power destroyed or captured nearly 5,000 individual weapons, 2,000 crew-served weapons, 100 tanks, 4,600 trucks, many artillery pieces, and thousands of tons of ammunition and other materiel. An estimated 3,500 trained enemy rear service personnel vital to the Trail logistical operation were killed.

Now, if some of this information surprises you, I can understand it. Americans have been hearing a very different and distorted story from their prime sources of news that it is bewildering that the Communists haven't even been parading in their streets about this thing. I don't understand why they're not out celebrating their great victory.

Well, these same people who are putting this most distorted viewpoint of American participation of the Vietnamese war before the American people — the same people who rushed to expose those portions of secret documents that support their point of view, even though they may just be contingency plans that were drawn up to take care of events that never happened — are the same people who are presently controlling American opinion through a biased and a slanted, and an oversighted viewpoint of what's taking place around the world.

And if you read the papers that have made these exposés and the commentary on some of the networks in support of those revelations you'll get the opinion right off the bat that the American people are solidly behind this thing they call "freedom of the press." I call it a common, cheap fencing operation.

Let me read you the results of a little poll taken June 21st by Opinion Research. The questions: "Do you think the press should publish top secret government material once it comes into their hands, or should it be withheld until the government decides publication will not harm national security?" "Should publish" — fourteen percent; "should be withheld" — seventy-six percent; "no opinion" — ten percent.

Second question: "Do you think freedom of the press includes the freedom of the paper to print stolen, top-secret government documents or not?" "Yes" — fifteen percent; "No" — seventy-four percent; "no opinion" — eleven percent.

Well, I'm not surprised. I don't want to overlook some points which I believe to be more gratifying than that sad tale told by the purveyors of doom. These are points which probably should be emphasized, but most people in America have never heard these points. The untold story of a small nation building itself in the midst of a war.

Let us remember that this beleaguered victim of Communist aggression has made remarkable progress. These courageous people have written a constitution; held national elections in which more than seventy-five percent of the vote was recorded; developed a lively multiparty system, a national assembly, and an independent judiciary. They elected a President and their local leaders in over 2,000 of the 2,300 villages in the country. This constitutional process will continue with the next round of national elections scheduled to be held late this summer and in the fall.

The government of Vietnam's Land-to-the-Tiller program is transforming the countryside from a battleground to a prosperous, lively community of small landowners. As the war subsides, the government of Vietnam has been able to turn more attention to constructive tasks necessary to develop a country. Three million young people are enrolled in South Vietnam's schools today compared with less than a half million enrollment in 1955. This figure does not include the millions of Vietnamese who are receiving job training under the Vietnamization program.

We frequently hear that the South Vietnamese government is corrupt; it is not democratic, they say, as we might want it to be. Such criticism surely overlooks the great progress made in time of war for a nation which has not long known real democracy. But what is most disconcerting to me is the curious double standard applied to the government of South Vietnam.

Let us ask: Who pursues a policy of deliberate terror and assassination? Who stridently asserts a claim to total victory? Who rejects compromise? Who refuses to permit free elections, a free press, and any freedom of expression? Is it not the government of North Vietnam, rather than the government of South Vietnam? Is it not the government of North Vietnam which our critics hold up to us as a model of virtue and justice that commits these intolerable, repressive tactics on their people?

I suggest we cease using this unique form of double bookkeeping and recognize that the totalitarian enemy is a totalitarian enemy. When moral yardsticks are bandied about so loosely in some quarters, I heartily recommend that the same standards of morality be applied to the North as well as the South.

Rather than being ashamed of our ally, we ought to take pride in how we have helped him and in how he is helping himself. For every acre of wasteland the photographs show, there are dozens of acres of prosperous communities and fertile farms.

What greater tribute can be paid to America than that it helped a small nation to stay free? What greater example of our nation's generosity than that we believe enough in freedom to sustain it with actions and not just words? I am not embarrassed for America, for we can look back in pride for taking up a just cause that much of the world had abandoned in these troubled times.

Still, I am bothered. I am bothered because those who disagree with what we do mock the American character. The 180-degree revisionists whose voices are steeped in self-pity and self-doubt in a masochistic frenzy have lost the capacity in time of trial, either to speak for or to lead a great nation. I happen to believe that America is made of sterner stuff. And I happen to believe that the young people of America are made of the same stuff that all Americans historically have been made of. In this period of stress, America can be thankful that it has a President to match the strength of its people. I can tell you with conviction that America is in strong and good hands.

President Nixon does not want war. Our military, so maligned and battered, is today, and always has been, the strongest opponent of war. Douglas MacArthur, a military man all his life, but more than that, a man of peace, was in 1962 awarded the Thayer Medal, the highest honor of the United States Military Academy. In accepting that award, he responded:

> . . . the soldier, above all other people, prays for peace, for he must suffer and bear the deepest wounds and scars of war. But always in our ears ring the ominous words of Plato, that wisest of all philosophers, "Only the dead have seen the end of war."

More than anyone, General MacArthur would have yearned to have proved the great philosopher wrong, and more than anyone, President Nixon is striving with all his energy and with all his skill to do just that.

As our nation struggles internally with the forces of self-deprecation, let us remember this: If we don't believe in ourselves, who can believe *us?* If we cannot act responsibly, who will see us as responsible? If we find fault in all that we do, who will fail to fault us? If the American philosophy has not faithfully fulfilled its promise of freedom, where will the world turn for liberty's promise? If we falter now, who will shoulder mankind's burden?

Index

521

522

BA273C

Coyne.

The impudent snobs.

June 1972